EIGHTH EDITION

LANGUAGE AWARENESS

Readings for College Writers

Paul Eschholz

Alfred Rosa

Virginia Clark

UNIVERSITY OF VERMONT

BEDFORD/ST. MARTIN'S   Boston • New York

For Bedford/St. Martin's
DEVELOPMENT EDITOR: Aron Keesbury
EDITORIAL ASSISTANT: Amy Thomas
SENIOR PRODUCTION SUPERVISOR: Joe Ford
MARKETING MANAGER: Brian Wheel
TEXT DESIGN: Anna George
PROJECT MANAGEMENT: Books By Design, Inc.
COVER DESIGN: Donna Lee Dennison
COVER AND SPINE DETAIL: Robert Cottingham, *Barrera-Rosa's*, 1985.
    Oil on canvas, Forum Gallery, New York. © Robert Cottingham, 1999.
COMPOSITION: Pine Tree Composition
PRINTING AND BINDING: Haddon Craftsmen, an R. R. Donnelley Company

PRESIDENT: Charles H. Christensen
EDITORIAL DIRECTOR: Joan E. Feinberg
EDITOR IN CHIEF: Karen S. Henry
DIRECTOR OF MARKETING: Karen R. Melton
DIRECTOR OF EDITING, DESIGN, AND PRODUCTION: Marcia Cohen
MANAGER, PUBLISHING SERVICES: Emily Berleth

Library of Congress Catalog Card Number: 99-66286

Manufactured in the United States of America.

5 4 3 2 1
f e d

For information, write:

Bedford/St. Martin's, 75 Arlington Street
Boston, MA 02116   (617-399-4000)

ISBN: 0-312-19768-3

Acknowledgments

Gordon Allport, "The Language of Prejudice." From *The Nature of Prejudice* by Gordon Allport. Copyright © 1979, 1985, 1954 by Addison-Wesley Publishing Company, Inc. Reprinted by permission of Perseus Books Publishers, a member of Perseus Books, L.L.C.

PREFACE

Since the first edition of *Language Awareness* appeared in 1974, its purpose has been twofold: to foster an appreciation of the richness, flexibility, and vitality of the English language and to encourage and help students to use their language more responsibly and effectively in speech and particularly in writing. Because of these purposes, *Language Awareness* has been used successfully in a variety of courses over the years. Its primary use, however, has been and continues to be in college composition courses. Clearly, many instructors believe as we do that the study of language and the study of writing go hand in hand.

Because the study of language is so multifaceted, we cover a broad spectrum of topics, including the history of English, the relationship between language and culture, and the power of language in influencing advertising, politics, the media, and gender roles. Opening students' eyes to the power of language — its ability to shape and manipulate perceptions and cultural attitudes — is, we believe, one of the worthiest goals a writing class can pursue.

NEW TO THIS EDITION

As in previous editions, we have emphasized selections that are written in nontechnical language on topics of current interest. Our questions and introductory material help students to understand those topics, providing clearly defined opportunities for thoughtful writing. Guided by comments and advice from hundreds of colleagues and students across the country who have used the previous editions, we have made some dramatic improvements in this eighth edition, especially strengthening the language-writing connection.

Four New Introductory Chapters on Writing with Three New Student Papers

To supplement the study of language with instruction in writing itself, we have added four new chapters. Based on years of classroom experience, these four chapters provide students with sixty pages on the essentials of college writing. Chapter 1 introduces students to the writing process, and Chapters 2–4 discuss the three types of writing students will encounter throughout the text. Chapter 2, "Writing from Experience," gives practical advice on how to use experimental writing for a purpose. Chapter 3, "Writing from Reading," shows students how to read carefully and analytically; it includes hints on annotating and an annotated essay. Chapter 4, "Writing from Research," offers a thorough discussion of the research process and includes MLA-style models for preparing in-text citations and a list of works cited. To further aid student understanding, the writing principles in Chapters 2–4 are modeled in three sample student papers—one in each chapter, and two new to this edition. Although these four introductory chapters can be used sequentially—each building on the last—we have tried to keep the structure flexible enough to allow instructors to teach the chapters in any order. No other language reader offers students this much help with writing.

New Selections

Over half of the seventy-four selections in *Language Awareness* are new to this edition. However, we have retained many of the accessible, informative, well-written, class-tested, and very often entertaining essays from earlier editions, such as William Lutz's "The World of Doublespeak," George Orwell's "Politics and the English Language," Dorothy Z. Seymour's "Black Children, Black Speech," and Richard Lederer's, "The Case for Short Words."

The thirty-eight new selections, chosen for their insight and clear, graceful writing, include Leslie Savan's discussion of the language of sitcoms, Kurt Vonnegut Jr.'s advice on style, Gordon Allport's classic analysis of the language of prejudice, Nathan Cobb's investigation of gendered language in cyberspace, Caryl Rivers's analysis of persistent myths about women, and Ethan Bronner's investigation of political correctness on American college campuses. We believe these new selections will spark student interest and bring currency to the otherwise class-proven essays retained from earlier editions.

New Thematic Chapters

Students and teachers, pleased with the relevancy of the thematic chapters in past editions of *Language Awareness,* have asked us to add new material on the media. In addition to the chapters "Coming to

Terms with Language," "Writers on Writing," "Names and Naming," "Prejudice, Stereotypes, and Language," "The Language of Persuasion: Politics and Advertising," and "Doublespeak, Euphemism, and Jargon," we have included a new chapter titled "Language and the Media," made up of essays that discuss the importance of language in news reporting and entertainment. Another new chapter, also created in response to reader demand, is Chapter 9, "Language and Culture," with essays that examine how language transmits culture and is at the very heart of the issues surrounding diversity and multiculturalism.

New Chapter Structure

To better organize broad language issues, we have divided each chapter into two or three bite-sized subchapters, each containing three to five essays. For example, Chapter 10, "Language and the Media," has two subchapters: "Finding the Truth in the News" and "The Language of Entertainment." Similarly, the popular Chapter 6, "Writers on Writing," is divided into the subchapters "Writing: The Transaction," and "Revising and Editing." These subchapters not only provide students with a structure for understanding interrelated subjects, but they are designed to be just the right size to encourage papers requiring the synthesis of several sources on a single topic.

New Language-in-Action Activities

To bring a bit of the outside world into *Language Awareness* and to give students a chance to analyze real examples of the language issues discussed by the essayists, exciting new Language-in-Action activities now accompany every selection in the text. These activities—designed to be completed in about twenty minutes—ask students to take a hands-on approach to what they are learning from the essays, and to demonstrate their growing language aptitude. The activities include poems, cartoons, movie reviews, parodies, advertisements, photographs, essay excerpts, letters to the editor, syndicated columns, and more. We believe they will challenge students to apply what they have learned to the world around them.

New and Innovative Casebooks

Each chapter concludes with a casebook that encourages both in-depth comparative analysis and writing. Thought-provoking Writing Suggestions, called Making Connections, appear at the end of the casebooks, which are of two types:

- **LANGUAGE-IN-USE CASEBOOKS.**   These casebooks, which occur in five chapters, present clusters of related documents for analysis, including groups of short stories, speeches, parodies of manipulative language, political documents, and a portfolio of magazine advertisements.
- **CASE-IN-POINT CASEBOOKS.**   Appearing in three chapters, these casebooks, present two or three different perspectives on narrowly focused and hotly debated language issues, such as the English-only movement, what constitutes correct usage, and names and naming in the business world.

New End-of-Selection Questions

The format for the questions at the end of each selection has been improved significantly to emphasize content and writing issues. The new format includes two types of questions:

- **FOCUSING ON CONTENT.**   These questions help students to understand the content of the selection (and thus to understand an aspect of language) and to connect the information and ideas in the selection to their own experiences.
- **FOCUSING ON WRITING.**   The questions in this section take a number of directions. They may, for example, take a language principle presented in the selection, ask students to explore it, directing students to comment on writing applications they can envision for that principle. Other Focusing on Writing questions may highlight such techniques as the use of strong verbs, the active voice, tone, punctuation, or sentence structure not explicitly discussed in the selection but exhibited therein, and ask students to discuss them.

New End-of-Selection Writing Assignments

To give students more opportunities to practice thinking and writing, we provide several Writing Suggestions at the end of every selection, each of which is designed to elicit a three-to-five-page paper. The Writing from Experience assignments ask students to use their journal entries as springboards for an extended essay; in Writing from Reading, students use their analytical skills to play one article off against another; and the Writing from Research assignments ask students to do—and write about—some library or community-based research. Students may, for example, examine the language used in local public documents, the language used in law offices, or campus slang. All of these assignments reinforce the coverage of writing in the new Chapters 1–4.

RETAINED FROM THE SEVENTH EDITION

Tested Areas of Language Study

Although new essays have been added to each of them, six chapters in this new edition are carryovers from the seventh edition. Instructors have told us that the chapters on "Coming to Terms with Language," "Writers on Writing," "Names and Naming," "Prejudice, Stereotypes, and Language," "Doublespeak, Euphemism, and Jargon," and "The Language of Persuasion: Politics and Advertising" are indispensable in the writing courses they teach. Not only are these topics legitimate areas of language study, but they also teach students useful ways to look at and write about the world around them. Each of these chapters has been updated to reflect recent trends, but they still retain the spirit and purpose of their predecessors.

Writing to Discover

Each selection begins with a journal prompt designed to get students writing—before they start reading—about their own experiences with the language issues discussed in the selection. Students are then more likely to approach the selection with a critical eye. From time to time, class activities or writing assignments ask students to return to these journal writings and to reflect on them before proceeding with more formal writing tasks.

Informative Headnotes

Headnotes preceding each selection discuss the content of the essay and emphasize the key language principles involved. Pertinent information about the author and where and when the selection was first published is also included.

Rhetorical Contents

At the end of the text, an alternate table of contents classifies the selections in *Language Awareness* according to the rhetorical strategies they exemplify, making it easier for instructors to assign readings that parallel the types of writing their students are doing.

Glossary of Rhetorical and Linguistic Terms

The Glossary of Rhetorical and Linguistic Terms includes definitions of key language terms and concepts as well as the standard terminology of rhetoric. Having all of these definitions in the book itself makes it easy for students to look up unfamiliar terms as they read.

Instructor's Manual

Packed with teaching tips and suggested answers to end-of-selection questions, the new *Instructor's Manual* reflects all the changes in the apparatus that accompanies each selection. It also offers advice on how to approach the four new introductory chapters on writing, each of the Language-in-Action activities, and each chapter-ending casebook.

ACKNOWLEDGMENTS

We are grateful to the following respondents to a user survey, whose comments helped us shape this edition: Michael Bowler, Saint Mary's University of Minnesota; John W. Brooks, Okaloosa–Walton Community College; Linda Burgess, Victor Valley College; Ralph S. Carlson, Azusa Pacific University; Dennis Ciesielski, University of Wisconsin at Platteville; Paula Coomer, University of Idaho; Patti Hanlon, University of Nevada at Reno; James L. Hedges, Azusa Pacific University; Gary C. LaPointe, Elmira College; Bill Mangan, Saint Mary's University of Minnesota; Patricia R. McClure, West Virginia State College; Julie Nichols, Okaloosa–Walton Community College; Linda Parks, Miami University of Ohio; Carol Rossi, Santa Clara University; Gregory J. Stratman, University of Missouri; Patricia Wangler, Cypress College.

We would like to express our appreciation to the staff at Bedford/St. Martin's, especially Aron Keesbury for supporting us in our efforts to design innovative and engaging Language-in-Action activities that provide strong links between language study and writing in this new edition. His assistant, Amy Thomas, handled a number of important tasks and oversaw the *Instructor's Manual* throughout its development. Thanks go to Herb Nolan of Books By Design, our production editor; to our old friend Judy Green Voss, our superlative copyeditor; to Nicole Simonsen for clearing permissions; and to Mark Wanner and Betsy Eschholz for their cheerful and prompt editorial and research assistance. We are also proud of Jake Jamieson and Sara Daniels, students in our "Language Awareness" course, for the energy and enthusiasm they brought to their essays on the English-only movement and cynical speech in television sitcoms. Thanks also go to Betsy Eschholz for writing the *Instructor's Manual* that accompanies this edition. Finally, we are grateful to all our students at the University of Vermont for their enthusiasm for language study and writing and their invaluable responses to the new materials included in this book. They teach us something new every day.

PAUL ESCHHOLZ
ALFRED ROSA
VIRGINIA CLARK

CONTENTS

> "I saw that the best thing I could do was get a hold of a dictionary—to study, to learn some words."

6 WRITERS ON WRITING   *131*

8 PREJUDICE, STEREOTYPES, AND LANGUAGE   *243*

THE NATURE OF PREJUDICIAL LANGUAGE

LANGUAGE, RACE, AND GENDER

9 LANGUAGE AND CULTURE   309

THE LANGUAGE-CULTURE CONNECTION

12 THE LANGUAGE OF PERSUASION: POLITICS AND ADVERTISING *525*

1
THE WRITING PROCESS

Have you ever thought about what you do when you write, the process that you follow in writing a composition? Do you try to write a finished essay in one draft, or do you revise a number of times? Do you start to write as soon as you have a general subject, or do you gather information and ideas first? Do you worry about grammar and punctuation at every stage of the writing, especially if you are writing for your English instructor? It is helpful to think about the way you write and learn how others go about it because you may find ways to refine or improve the steps in your own writing process. You may even learn a new approach to writing.

Although each writer approaches a writing task somewhat differently, most experienced writers follow similar steps. For example, they usually decide on a specific topic and collect information about it before proceeding with drafting, revising, and editing. This chapter describes the various activities in each step of the typical writing process. The following description briefly summarizes these steps and provides a general overview.

PREWRITING

Collecting Information: Information lies at the heart of good writing. Experienced writers realize that effective writing draws from an abundance of specific, accurate information. You can acquire information in a variety of ways, by reading, interviewing people, doing online research, plumbing your memory, observing events and processes, and jotting down what your five senses tell you. The discovery techniques discussed later in this chapter, such as journal writing and brainstorming, will help you keep track of your information and ideas and begin to see the connections among them.

Connecting Information, Linking Ideas, and Planning: It is also important to connect or see relationships in the information and ideas that you gather. By studying what you have collected and by thinking about it, you will begin to see patterns of meaning, linkages on which to build your writing. With these connections in mind, you can begin to plan your first draft's thesis and organization.

WRITING

Drafting the Paper: A first draft, which is usually written fairly quickly, helps you discover what you know and what you still need to find out, what works and what doesn't. Discovering what works is especially important because you can best build your writing on a strong foundation.

REVISING

Developing the Draft: The next step is to analyze your draft to see if each point you make is thoroughly developed. You may need to add definitions, descriptions, stories, statistics, or other types of support to your draft to deepen and extend its meaning. You will also want to pay attention to how the draft holds together, making sure that all your ideas progress logically.

Clarifying Meaning: At this point, you should try to read your writing as your audience might, asking the questions that your readers might ask. Then try to answer those questions by building explanations into your draft. Your writing should answer most, if not all, of the questions that it raises.

EDITING AND PROOFREADING

Editing and Proofreading Your Draft: At this final stage, you need to make sure that your writing flows smoothly from sentence to sentence and from paragraph to paragraph. You also need to check your composition for accurate spelling, grammar, and punctuation. Reading aloud, line by line, is a good way to assess the smoothness of the writing and to test for appropriate word choice and correct grammar and punctuation.

Now that you have a general idea of the typical writing process, let's look at each step in that process in more detail.

PREWRITING

Understand Your Writing Assignment

When you first receive an assignment, read it over several times and pay attention to the main verbs. For example, consider what you are being asked to do in each of the following assignments:

Tell about an experience you have had that dramatically revealed to you the importance of being accurate and precise in your use of language.

Many languages are lost over time because the speakers of those languages die. When a language is lost, the particular culture embodied in the language is also lost. Using an extinct culture and language as an example, explain how a language embodies a culture and exactly what is lost when a language becomes extinct.

Advocates of the English-only movement want to see English adopted as our country's official language. Argue against the philosophy behind this movement.

The first assignment asks you to write about a personal experience that gave you some insight into the power of language in general and more specifically into the importance of using accurate and precise language. Have you ever been seriously inconvenienced or denied an opportunity because the directions or explanations you were following were unclear? Have you ever been unclear in your own statements to someone, causing that person to fail? To gain an advantage? The verb *tell* is important in this assignment because it alerts you to the fact that you must share the details of the experience so that your readers can appreciate it firsthand.

The verb *explain* is the key to the second assignment. The assignment asks for clearly illustrated insights into the subject of dying languages, a subject not understood by the general public. How many languages have become extinct? How many are threatened with extinction today? In what specific ways is culture carried within a language? Should the loss of languages concern us? Why?

The third assignment asks you to *argue* for a particular position — to persuade readers to see things your way. To do so you need to understand all sides in the English-only controversy. Why do some people think our country needs an official language? What problems are created when a nation's people speak a wide variety of languages? What are the advantages of a multilingual people? What problems might result if English were declared the official language of the United States?

After reading an assignment several times, check with your instructor if you are still unsure about what is being asked of you. He or she will be glad to clear up any possible confusion before you start writing. Be sure, as well, that you understand any additional requirements of the assignment, such as length or format.

Determine Your Purpose

All effective writing is done with a purpose. While good writing may be written for many specific reasons, it generally has one of three purposes: to express thoughts and feelings and lessons learned from life experiences, to inform readers by explaining something about the world around them, or to persuade readers to accept some belief or take some action.

EXPRESSION.   In *expressive writing,* most commonly written from experience, writers put their thoughts and feelings before all other concerns.
You will encounter several examples of expressive writing in later chapters.
In Chapter 5, for example, Edite Cunha shares with us her anxiety about
having to translate her father's Portuguese into English, and Julia Alvarez
bases her short story "Snow" on childhood experiences she had during the
nuclear-war threat of the 1950's; in Chapter 8, Sojourner Truth, the great
traveling preacher and abolitionist, tells us in a very personal way what a
woman can do and what it means to be a woman. Each of these writers clar-
ifies an important life experience and conveys what she has learned from it.

EXPLANATION.   *Informative writing* provides information to the
reader about the outside world. Informative writing reports, explains, analyzes, defines, classifies, compares, describes a process, or examines causes
and effects. When Paul Roberts explains what language is (in Chapter 5),
when Kurt Vonnegut Jr. offers advice on how to write with style (in Chapter 6), and when J. N. Hook explains where many of our nation's surnames
came from (in Chapter 7), each is writing to inform.

PERSUASION.   *Persuasive writing,* or *argument,* seeks to influence
readers' thinking and attitudes toward a subject or issue and, in some cases,
to move them to a particular course of action. Persuasive writing often uses
logical reasoning, authoritative evidence, and testimony, and it sometimes
includes emotionally charged language and examples. Richard Lederer
(in Chapter 6) uses numerous examples to persuade us of the power of
short words, S. I. Hayakawa (in Chapter 9) argues for the English-only
movement, and George Orwell (in Chapter 12) argues against doublespeak and for truth in the language of politics.

Know Your Audience

The best writers keep their audience in mind as they write. They try
to empathize with their readers, address their difficulties and concerns,
and appeal to their rational and emotional faculties. To identify the audience for whom you are writing and to therefore direct your essay, ask
yourself the following questions:

- Who are my readers?
- Are they a specialized or a general group?
- What do I know about my audience's age, gender, education, reli-
  gious affiliation, economic status, and political attitudes?
- What does my audience know about my subject? Are they experts or
  novices?
- What does my audience need to know from me?

- Do I need to explain any specialized language so that my audience can understand my subject? Is there any language that I should avoid?
- What do I want my audience to think or do as a result of reading my writing?

Find a Subject and Topic

Although your instructor will usually give you specific writing assignments, sometimes you may be asked to choose your own subject and topic. When this is the case, first select a broad subject within the area of language studies. Try to find a subject that interests you and that you think you may enjoy writing about—a general subject like professional jargon, dialects, political speeches, advertising language, or propaganda. A language issue that you have experienced firsthand or something you've read, such as an essay in *Language Awareness,* may bring particular subjects to mind. You might also consider a language-related issue that involves your career ambitions, such as the areas of business, law, nursing, journalism, medicine, architecture, or computer programming. Another option is to list some subjects you enjoy discussing with friends and that you can approach from a language perspective: music, food, television, dating, roommates.

Next, try to narrow your general subject by coming up with topics or issues that are more specific. The process of narrowing your subject is an important one because it is too difficult to tackle an entire general subject in a brief essay. Finally, narrow your topic further until you arrive at one that will be interesting to your readers and appropriate for the length of your paper. The following chart shows how the general areas of jargon, journalism, and television commercials might be narrowed to a specific essay topic. Some of the discovery techniques discussed in the next section may help you think of general subjects and develop specific topics as well.

General Subject Area	Narrowed Topic	Specific Essay Topic
Jargon	Medical jargon	Medical jargon used between doctors and terminally ill patients
Journalism	Slanted language in newswriting	Slanted language in newspapers' coverage of international events
Television commercials	Hidden messages in television commercials	Hidden messages in television commercials on children's Saturday morning programs

Use Discovery Techniques

Most writers use one or more discovery techniques to help them gather information, zero-in on a specific topic, or find connections among ideas. Some of the most common techniques are discussed in the following section.

KEEPING A JOURNAL.   Many writers use a journal to record thoughts and observations that might be mined for future writing projects. They have learned not to rely on their memories to retain ideas, facts, and statistics they have heard or read about. Writers also use journals to keep all kinds of lists: lists of questions they would like answers to; lists of issues that concern them; lists of topics they would like to write about someday.

To aid your journal writing as you use this text, each reading selection in *Language Awareness* begins with a journal prompt called "Writing to Discover." The purpose of each prompt is to get you thinking and writing about your own experiences with the language issues discussed in the selection before you start reading. You thus have the opportunity to discover what you already know about a particular topic and to explore your observations, feelings, and opinions about it. The writing you do at this point is something you can always return to after reading each piece.

FREEWRITING.   Journals are also useful if you want to freewrite. *Freewriting* is simply writing for a brief uninterrupted period of time — say, ten or fifteen minutes — on anything that comes to your mind. It is a way to get your mind working and to ease into a writing task. Start with a blank sheet of paper or computer screen and write about the general subject you are considering. Write as quickly as you can, don't stop for any reason, and don't worry about punctuation, grammar, or spelling. Write as though you were talking to your best friend, and let your writing take you in any direction. If you run out of ideas, don't stop; just repeat the last few things you wrote over and over again, and you'll be surprised — more ideas will begin to emerge. Once you become comfortable with open-ended freewriting, you can move to more focused freewriting, in which you write about a specific aspect of your subject. For example, if your original freewriting was on the subject of occupational jargon, your more focused freewriting might be limited to the topic of lawyers' language. Just as regular exercise gets you in shape, regular freewriting will help you feel more natural and comfortable when writing.

BRAINSTORMING.   Another good way to generate ideas and information about a topic is to *brainstorm* — to list everything you know about a topic, freely associating one idea with another. Don't worry about order or level of importance. Try to capture everything that comes to mind because you never know what might prove valuable later on. Write quickly, but if you get stalled, reread what you have written; doing so will help you move in new directions. Keep your list handy so that you can add to it over the course of several days. Here, for example, is a student's brainstorming list on why Martin Luther King Jr.'s speech, "I Have a Dream," has endured:

Why "I Have a Dream" Is Memorable

civil rights demonstration in Washington, DC, delivered on steps of Lincoln Memorial

repetition of "I have a dream"

references to the Bible, spirituals

"bad check" metaphor

other memorable figures of speech

200,000 people

reminds me of other great American documents and speeches — Declaration of Independence and Gettysburg Address

refers to various parts of the country

embraces all races and religions

sermon format

displays energy and passion

ASKING QUESTIONS. Asking questions about a particular topic or experience may help you generate information before you start to write. If you are writing about a personal experience, for example, asking questions may refresh your memory about the details and circumstances of the incident or help you discover why the experience is still so memorable. The newspaper reporter's five Ws and an H — *Who? What? Where? When? Why?* and *How?*—are excellent questions to start with. One student, for example, developed the following questions to help her explore an experience of verbal abuse:

1. Who was involved in the abusive situation?
2. What specific language was used?
3. Where did the abuse most often take place?
4. When did the verbal abuse first occur?
5. Why did the abusive situation get started? Why did it continue?
6. How did I feel about the abuse as it was happening? How do I feel about it now?

As the student jotted down answers to these questions, other questions came to mind, such as, What did I try to do after the verbal abuse occurred? Did I seek help from anyone else? How can I help others who are being verbally abused? Before long, the student had recalled enough information for a rough draft about her experience.

CLUSTERING.   Another strategy for generating ideas and gathering information is *clustering*. Put your topic, or a key word or phrase about your topic, in the center of a sheet of paper and draw a circle around it. (The student example below shows the topic "hospital jargon at summer job" in the center.) Draw three or more lines out from this circle, and jot down main ideas about your topic, drawing a circle around each one. Repeat the process by drawing lines from the main-idea circles and adding examples, details, or questions you have. You may wind up pursuing one line of thought through many add-on circles before beginning a new cluster.

One advantage of clustering is that it allows you to sort your ideas and information into meaningful groups right from the start. As you carefully sort your ideas and information, you may begin to see an organizational plan for your writing. In the following example, the student's clustering is based on the experiences he had while working one summer in a hospital emergency room. Does the clustering provide any clues to how he might organize his essay?

Formulate a Thesis Statement

Once you have chosen a subject and topic and generated sufficient ideas and information, you are ready to organize your material and write a thesis statement. The *thesis* of an essay is its main idea, the point the essay tries to make. The thesis is often expressed in one or two sentences called a *thesis statement,* such as the following example:

> There is no better place to see language change take place than in the area of student slang.

The thesis statement should not be confused with a *purpose statement.* While a thesis statement makes an assertion about your topic, a purpose statement specifically addresses what you are trying to do in the paper. For example,

> I plan to distribute a questionnaire to the students on our campus to learn how much slang is used on campus and in what areas of student life slang is the most prevalent.

A thesis statement should be

  a. the most important point you make about your topic
  b. more general than the ideas and facts used to support it
  c. focused enough to be covered in the space allotted

A thesis statement should not be a question but an assertion. If you find yourself writing a question for a thesis statement, answer the question first and then write your statement.

An effective strategy for developing a thesis statement is to begin by writing *What I want to say is that . . . ,* as in this example:

> *What I want to say is that* unless language barriers between patients and health-care providers are bridged, many patients' lives will be endangered.

Later, you can delete the formulaic opening, and you will be left with the thesis statement.

> Unless language barriers between patients and health-care providers are bridged, many patients' lives will be endangered.

The thesis statement is usually set forth near the beginning of an essay, after a few writers offer several sentences that establish a context for the piece. One common strategy is to position the thesis statement as the final sentence of the first paragraph. Occasionally, the thesis is stated elsewhere in an essay, sometimes at the very end.

Use One or More Strategies of Development

After you have done enough discovery work and have a tentative thesis in mind, it is time to put your ideas and information together more carefully. Think again about your purpose and ask yourself, "What is the best way to guide readers through my essay so that they understand my main point?" Before writers begin writing, they have usually thought about one or more strategies that will help them develop their essay. These strategies, such as description, narration, or definition, are basic ways of thinking about a topic and aiding readers in understanding it.

As you plan your essay, you may decide to focus on one strategy of development throughout. For example, if you were writing an essay to inform readers about two extinct languages, you might use the strategy of *comparison and contrast,* discussing the similarities and differences between the two languages.

Usually, though, you will want to use several strategies within a single essay. At some point, for example, you may want to *describe* a person or object to your readers so that they get a clear sense of its details. Or you may want to *narrate* a story at the outset of your essay to get your readers' attention. With another strategy, *process analysis,* you explain to readers how a particular process works, sometimes even showing them how to do something themselves in step-by-step fashion. Often, *dividing* your subject into smaller parts and putting each part into a *classification* also helps readers because you are presenting your subject in more easily digestible parts. And in almost every essay, you will want to *define* difficult words or concepts and provide *examples* to support your ideas.

Suppose, for instance, that you want to write an essay about the college slang you hear on campus. For this kind of essay, you might find it helpful to use a variety of strategies:

Definition: to explain what slang is

Exemplification: to give examples of slang

Comparison and Contrast: to differentiate slang from other types of speech, such as idioms or technical language

Division and Classification: to categorize different types of slang or different topics that slang terms are used for—courses, students, food, grades

As you try different strategies and combine them in different ways, you will become a more skillful writer. You will learn how to move naturally from one approach to another, and you will come to know almost intuitively when it is best, for example, to compare or define rather than to narrate or classify.

Determine Your Organization

Once you have thought about the strategies of development you will use, your next task is to determine an organizational pattern, or order, that seems both natural and logical to you. There are several organizational patterns you might follow. You are already familiar with the most common one — *chronological order.* In this pattern, which is often used when you narrate a story, explain a process, or relate a series of events, you start with the earliest occurrence and move forward in time.

In a comparison-and-contrast essay, you might follow a *block* pattern or a *point-by-point* organization. In a block pattern, a writer provides all the information about one subject, followed by a block of comparable information about the other subject. In a point-by-point comparison, on the other hand, the writer starts by comparing both subjects in terms of a particular point, then compares both on a second point, and so on. In an essay about two dialect languages, you could follow the block pattern, covering all the characteristics of one dialect and then all the characteristics of the other. Or, you could cover several major characteristics of (points about) the two dialects, comparing both point by point.

Other patterns of organization include moving from the *general to the specific,* from *smallest to largest,* from *least important to most important,* or from the *usual to the unusual.* In an essay about an extinct language, for instance, you might cover its general characteristics first and then move to specifics, or you might begin with what is most usual about the language and then discuss what is unusual about it. Whatever order you choose, keep in mind that what you present first and last will probably stay in the reader's mind the longest.

After you choose an organizational pattern, jot down the main ideas in your essay. In other words, make a scratch outline. As you add more information and ideas to your scratch outline, you may want to develop a formal and more detailed outline of your paper. In writing a formal outline, follow these rules:

1. Include the title of your essay, a statement of purpose, and the thesis statement.
2. Write in complete sentences unless your meaning is immediately clear from a phrase.
3. If you divide any category, make sure there are at least two subcategories. The reason for this is simple: You cannot divide something into fewer than two parts.

4. Observe the traditional conventions of formal outlining. Notice how each new level of specificity is given a new letter or number designation.

Title:
Purpose:
Thesis:

I.
  A.
  B.
    1.
    2.
      a.
      b.
      c.
II.

WRITING YOUR FIRST DRAFT

Sometimes we are so eager to get on with the writing of a first draft that we begin before we are ready, and the results are disappointing. Before beginning to write, therefore, ask yourself, "Have I done enough prewriting? Is there a point to what I want to say?" If you have done a thorough job of gathering ideas and information, if you think you can accomplish the purpose of your paper, and if you are comfortable with your organizational plan, your answer will be "yes."

If, however, you feel uneasy, review the various prewriting steps to try to resolve the problem. Do you need to gather more information? Sharpen your thesis? Rethink your purpose? Refine your organization? Now is the time to think about these issues, to evaluate and clarify your writing plan. Time spent at this juncture is time well spent because it will not only improve your paper but will save you time and effort later on.

As you write, don't be discouraged if you do not find the most appropriate language for your ideas or if your ideas do not flow easily. Push ahead with the writing, realizing that you will be able to revise the material later, adding information and clarifications wherever necessary. Be sure to keep your audience in mind as you write, so that your diction and coverage stay at the appropriate level. Remember also to bridge all the logical and emotional leaps for your audience. Rereading what you have already written as you go along will help you to further develop your ideas and tie them together. Once completed, a first draft will give you a sense of accomplishment. You will see that you now have something to work with, something to build on and improve during the revision process.

REVISING

After you complete your first draft, you will need to revise it. During the revision stage of the writing process, you will focus on the large issues of thesis, purpose, evidence, organization, and paragraph structure to make sure that your writing says what you want it to say. First, though, it is crucial that you set your draft aside for awhile. Then you can come back to it with a fresh look and some objectivity. When you do, resist the temptation to plunge immediately into a second draft: Scattered changes will not necessarily improve the piece. Instead, try to look at your writing as a whole and to tackle your writing problems systematically. Use the following guidelines:

- Make revisions on a hard copy of your paper. (Triple-space your draft so that you can make changes more easily.)
- Read your paper aloud, listening for parts that do not make sense.
- Ask a fellow student to read your essay and critique it.

One way to begin the revision process is to compare the earlier outline of your first draft to an outline of how it actually came out. This will help you see, in abbreviated form, the organization and flow of the essential components of your essay and perhaps detect flaws in reasoning.

Another method you can use in revising is to start with large-scale issues, such as your overall structure, and then concentrate on finer and finer points. As you examine your essay, ask yourself about what you have written. The following questions address the large elements of an essay: thesis, purpose, organization, paragraphs, and evidence.

- Is my topic specific enough?
- Does my thesis statement identify my topic and make an assertion about it?
- Is my essay organized the best way, given my purpose?
- Are my paragraphs adequately developed, and does each support my thesis?
- Have I accomplished my purpose?
- How effective is my beginning? My ending?
- Is my title effective?

Once you have addressed the major problems in your essay by writing a second draft, you should be ready to turn your attention to the finer elements of sentence structure, word choice, and usage. The following questions focus on these concerns:

- Do my sentences convey my thoughts clearly, and do they emphasize the most important parts of my thinking?
- Are my sentences stylistically varied?

- Is my choice of words fresh and forceful, or is my writing weighed down by clichés and unnecessary wordiness?
- Have I made any errors of usage?

Finally, if you find yourself dissatisfied with specific elements of your draft, look at several essays in *Language Awareness* to see how other writers have dealt with the particular situation you are confronting. For example, if you don't like the way the essay starts, find some beginnings you think are particularly effective; if your paragraphs don't seem to flow into one another, examine how various writers use transitions; if an example seems unconvincing, examine the way other writers include details, anecdotes, and facts and statistics to strengthen their illustrations. Remember that the readings in the text are there as a resource for you as you write.

EDITING AND PROOFREADING

Now that you have revised in order to make your essay "right," it is time to think about making it "correct." During the editing stage of the writing process, check your writing for errors in grammar, punctuation, capitalization, spelling, and manuscript format. The following list of questions will guide you in the editing of your essay:

- Do my verbs agree in number with their subjects?
- Do my pronouns have clear antecedents—that is, do they clearly refer to specific nouns earlier in my sentences?
- Are any of my sentences fragments, comma splices, or run-ons?
- Have I made any unnecessary shifts in person, tense, and number?
- Have I used the comma properly in all instances?
- Have I checked for misspellings, mistakes in capitalization, and typos?
- Have I inadvertently confused words such as *their, they're,* and *there,* or *it's* and *its?*
- Have I followed the prescribed guidelines for formatting my manuscript?

Both your dictionary and your college handbook will help you answer specific editing questions about your paper.

Having revised and edited your essay, you are ready to print your final copy. Be sure to proofread your work before submitting it to your instructor. Even though you may have used your computer's spell-check, you might find that you have typed *worm* instead of *word,* or *form* instead of *from.* Also check to see that your essay is properly line-spaced and that the text is legible.

2

WRITING FROM EXPERIENCE

Writing that grows out of personal experience is often powerful; it grabs our attention. Reading about a personal experience enables us to live the experience along with the writer and feel the emotions the writer had at the time. And our responses to such writing provide insights into who we are.

Consider the following passage from Anna Quindlen's essay "The Name Is Mine," which originally appeared in the *New York Times* on March 4, 1987. Here a call from an emergency room elicits a surprising response.

> I am on the telephone to the emergency room of the local hospital. My elder son is getting stitches in his palm, and I have called to make myself feel better, because I am at home, waiting, and my husband is there, holding him. I am 34 years old, and I am crying like a child, making a slippery mess of my face. "Mrs. Krovatin?" says the nurse, and for the first time in my life I answer "Yes."
>
> This is a story about a name. The name is mine. I was given it at birth, and I have never changed it, although I married. I could come up with lots of reasons why. It was a political decision, a simple statement that I was somebody and not an adjunct of anybody, especially a husband. As a friend of mine told her horrified mother, "He didn't adopt me, he married me."
>
> It was a professional and personal decision, too. I grew up with an ugly dog of a name, one I came to love because I thought it was weird and unlovable. Amid the Debbies and Kathys of my childhood, I had a first name only my grandmothers had and a last name that began with a strange letter.

What is your reaction to this passage? What, for you, is most significant about Quindlen's telling of this experience? Suppose Quindlen had not chosen to approach her topic through the emergency room episode. Instead, she might have addressed the topic of adopting her husband's

surname through an objective discussion of what contemporary professional women are doing. This kind of essay would, of course, be very different from the passage you just read because you would not learn about
the feelings and emotions that were at the heart of Quindlen's decision.

When you write from experience, you put your firsthand knowledge
before all other concerns. When you describe the excitement your niece
felt when she uttered her first words, narrate a travel experience about a
time when you didn't speak the language of the country, discuss the jargon of construction workers on your summer job, or explore your fascination with the language on your favorite television program, you are
writing from experience. To write from experience, then, you need to
clarify personal events and emotions and to understand why they are both
important and memorable. You also need to communicate what you
learn to someone else. In the United States, experiential writing is extremely popular because it appeals to the human side of readers. The reflections of a thoughtful and sensitive writer help readers understand
their own feelings and ideas.

GENERATING IDEAS FROM EXPERIENCE

Not surprisingly, many people feel anxious or insecure when they
first try to write from experience. Such thoughts as "I've never done anything exciting" or "Nobody's going to be interested in reading about
this" may immobilize us and make it difficult to get started. However,
once we get over the notion that experiences have to be major events or
something totally out of the ordinary, these feelings of inadequacy should
start to disappear. After all, it is often the seemingly insignificant events in
our lives that turn out to be ones of great consequence. Most of us just
haven't taken the time to stop and think about the smallest things that
have happened, to reflect about our experiences as possible material for
writing. And rarely do we consider how some of these experiences have
been significant turning points.

Ideas and information lie at the heart of all good prose. Ideas grow
from information, and information supports ideas. To inform and intellectually stimulate your readers, then, you'll need to gather as many ideas
and as much specific information as you can. If you try to write before
doing so, you run the risk of producing a shallow, uninteresting draft that
is usually much shorter than your subject warrants.

When you write from experience, your information and ideas come
from your memory, not from outside research. Thus, before you start
to write it is especially important to use some discovery techniques, such
as brainstorming, clustering, journal writing, or freewriting (see pp. 6–8).
These techniques help you to work in a productive way and find experiences that might be developed into a piece of writing. They jog your

memory about the details of various experiences and get you thinking about their significance. Last but not least, discovery techniques help you make connections between the pieces of information you accumulate.

USING EXPERIENCE WITH A PURPOSE

Each time you draw on a personal experience you need to determine how you plan to use that experience. While the reasons for writing are as varied as the writers themselves, most often the purpose for writing will fall into one of three broad categories: to express feelings or ideas, to inform readers about something, or to persuade them. Start by asking yourself, "What am I trying to accomplish in this piece of writing?" Perhaps your purpose will be expressive, to tell a story so that you can share a lesson you have learned from an experience. Or you may want to inform readers or instruct them in how to do something based on your firsthand knowledge. A third possibility is to argue a position or persuade readers to take a particular action based on an experience that you've had. Being clear about your purpose at the outset is important; it helps you choose the best supporting details and arrange them in the most effective order.

Use Personal Experience to Express Feelings or Ideas

A good story may entertain readers or move them to tears, but it also provides a meaningful account of some significant event. Readers want to know what has happened to other people so that they can gain insights into their own lives. A good narrative may have a straight-forward moral or make a more subtle point about people and the world we live in. In the following passage from "Coming to an Awareness of Language" (pp. 63–66), Malcolm X tells how he discovered the power of the written and spoken word while in prison.

> I saw that the best thing I could do was get hold of a dictionary—to study, to learn some words. I was lucky enough to reason also that I should try to improve my penmanship. It was sad. I couldn't even write in a straight line. It was both ideas together that moved me to request a dictionary along with some tablets and pencils from the Norfolk Prison Colony school.
>
> I spent two days just riffling uncertainly through the dictionary's pages. I'd never realized so many words existed! I didn't know *which* words I needed to learn. Finally, just to start some kind of action, I began copying.
>
> In my slow, painstaking, ragged handwriting, I copied into my tablet everything printed on that first page, down to the punctuation marks.

I believe it took me a day. Then, aloud, I read back, to myself, everything I'd written on the tablet. Over and over, aloud, to myself, I read my own handwriting.

I woke up the next morning, thinking about those words—immensely proud to realize that not only had I written so much at one time, but I'd written words that I never knew were in the world.

Malcolm X concludes his essay by reflecting on how his discovery of language changed him as a person and liberated his spirit even though he was still in prison.

Use Personal Experience to Inform Your Readers

On occasion, personal experience provides an example that helps a writer inform readers about a particular concept or activity. In the following passage from the essay "Words with Built-in Judgments" (pp. 255–60), S. I. Hayakawa uses personal experience to show how the meanings of words can change. He brings a new dimension to the word *experience* by using stories that two friends had told him. In effect, their experiences become part of his experience.

The meaning of words also changes from speaker to speaker, from hearer to hearer, and from decade to decade. An elderly Japanese woman of my acquaintance used to squirm at the mention of the word "Jap." "Whenever I hear that word," she used to say, "I feel dirty all over." She was reacting to the negative connotations as it was used during the Second World War and earlier. More recently, "JAP" is an acronym for "Jewish American princess," heard as an insult by an entirely different ethnic group.

A black friend of mine recalls hitchhiking as a young man in the 1930s through an area of the country where very few blacks lived. He was given a ride by a white couple, who fed him and gave him a place to sleep in their home. However, they kept referring to him as "little nigger," which upset him profoundly. He finally asked them not to call him by that "insulting term," a request they had difficulty understanding, as they had not meant to offend him. One way my friend might have explained his point further would have been to say, "Excuse me, but in the part of the country I come from, white people who wish to show contempt for my race call us 'niggers.' I assume this is not your intention."

In recent times, the negative connotations of the word "nigger" are more widely understood.

Hayakawa uses these two examples to help readers understand his generalization in the opening sentence about the meaning of words.

Use Personal Experience to Persuade Your Readers

Writers often use personal experience to add a sense of reality and immediacy to an issue and to speak authoritatively when arguing for a particular position. In the following passage from the essay "What's Natural about Our Natural Products?" (pp. 597–600) Sarah Federman tells readers about a shopping trip to her local grocery store, an experience most of us can readily identify with. She reveals her predilection for "natural" products and her surprise when she takes the time to carefully read product labels.

> Nowhere is the buzzword "natural" more prevalent than at the local grocery store where Fantastic Soups, Enrico's Pizza Sauce, Health Valley Cereals, and Celestial Seasonings tea, among others, brag unabashedly about the "naturalness" of their products. I often find myself seduced by the lure of the "Natural" label on goods. I throw Tom's Natural Toothpaste, Pop-Secret Natural Flavored Popcorn, and Grape-Nuts Natural Wheat and Barley Cereal into my shopping cart with the utmost confidence that these natural varieties prove far superior to their "unnatural" or "less natural" counterparts. Recently, I took a closer look at the labels of my revered products only to discover the widespread abuse of the word "natural." The word "natural" has become more a marketing ploy than a way to communicate meaningful information about a product.

Federman uses her brief shopping experience to establish the thesis of her persuasive essay: "The word 'natural' has become more a marketing ploy than a way to communicate meaningful information about a product." She argues this position throughout the remainder of her essay, using other personal experiences as well as researched information for support.

WRITING FROM EXPERIENCE: A SAMPLE STUDENT ESSAY

The following essay was written by Rebekah Sandlin while she was a student at Miami University in Oxford, Ohio. After Rebekah read the essays in the chapter on prejudice, stereotypes, and language, her instructor, Linda Parks, asked her to write about a personal experience with biased language and how that language affected her. Rebekah vividly remembered an experience she had in the third grade, when she used the phrase "just like a nigger" to mock a classmate. Using that experience as the starting point of her essay, she then traces a series of subsequent encounters she had with the word *nigger* and recounts her resulting personal growth. By the end of her essay, Rebekah makes it clear to her readers why she felt compelled to tell her story.

Rebekah Sandlin
English 111 sec. BD
October 23, 1997
Paper #3

The "Negro Revolt" in Me

She said "seven" when the answer was clearly "ten." We were in
the third grade and had been studying multiplication for a few weeks.
Our teacher, Mrs. Jones, reminded Monica that, "we are multiplying now,
not adding. Five times two will always be ten." I laughed at Monica. How
did she not know the answer to five times two? We had been over it and
practiced it so many times. My laughter encouraged the other kids in the
class to join in with me. Within seconds the laughing had escalated into
pointing fingers and calling her stupid. That's when "it" happened. That's
when I said what I will always regret for the rest of my life. I said, "just
like a nigger." Playing on her weaknesses in math, laughing at her, encouraging the rest of the class to point at her, and calling her the most
degrading word in history still eats at my insides. The class stopped
laughing. Monica cried. Mrs. Jones gasped and yanked me into the hall-
way where she scolded me for a good half an hour. That is how I learned
that language could be used as a dangerous tool. That's when I learned
about prejudice and its effects on people. That's how it happened. This is
how it has affected my life.

Mrs. Jones sent me home with a note explaining my "behavior" in
class. I remember being terribly afraid to give that note to my mom. I felt
guilty, confused, and embarrassed, but I wasn't sure why I felt that way.
No one had taken the time to explain to me why the word had such a negative connotation. No one told me that blacks were once treated terribly
wrong or that they were used as slaves. No one told me about the interra-
cial rapes that occurred on plantations or about the children being taken
and sold to rich white landowners. No one told me about them being denied
an education and proper shelter. No one told me. I was just a small white
girl living in a predominately white city and going to a predominately white
school. I knew nothing about diversity and equal rights for everyone. I
knew nothing.

My mom sat me down at the kitchen table and asked me how I could
have said such a terrible thing. "Where did you learn that word?" she
asked. She sounded furious and embarrassed. She kept asking me where I
had heard the word and who taught it to me. Before I had a chance to respond she knew the answer. My dad was on the phone in the next room
talking to his father. He was laughing and he said, "just like a nigger." My
mom lowered her head and whispered, "go to your room." I quietly got up
and obeyed her command. I'm not sure what she said to him, but I could

hear their mumbled fighting through the vents. I pressed my ear to the vent on the floor to try and make sense of my mother's cries. It was no use. Two hours later they came upstairs to give me one of their "you did something wrong" speeches. Except this speech was different from most. It began with an apology and an attempt to justify my father's words.

It started with a story. My dad grew up on a tobacco farm in southern Georgia. His family hired blacks to work out in the fields. "No," he reassured, "they weren't slaves. We paid them." His family was prejudiced toward blacks. Their language and actions rubbed off onto my dad. The only difference was that my dad learned that what he said and how he treated blacks was wrong. Through growing up and living in integrated working environments, he learned how "not to act" in the presence of a black person. However, when he talked to his father he still acted and talked like he was prejudiced. He said that he didn't understand why he did it other than he desperately wanted to be accepted by his own father. He admitted that he was wrong and told me that I was lucky because I was going to learn the "real way" to treat people. He promised to never use the word again as long as I promised to do the same thing. I agreed.

I was in the fifth grade the next time I heard the word used. Ironically, I was in a math class again. Except this time I didn't say it, someone else did. Unlike Monica, this girl didn't cry. Instead, she gave an evil glare. I was the one that stood up to say something in her defense. I yelled at Dan and told him that what he had said was rude and degrading. "How would you like it if someone called you honky?" I screamed. He hauled off and hit me right in the arm! He called me a "nigger-lover." The teacher broke it up, and we were sent to the principal's office. I was suspended for using vulgar language. I had used the word "honky." Dan was given a warning and sent back to class. I had plenty of time to think about what I had done wrong while I waited in the office for my mom to come and pick me up. No matter how hard I tried, I couldn't see what I had done wrong. That girl did not want to be called a nigger. I was just trying to show him what it would feel like if someone had said something like that to him. My mom did not agree with me. I learned an important lesson that day. Using bad words to stop other bad words is like using violence to stop violence—it doesn't work. My mom was supportive and said that she respected what I was trying to do but next time I should use better sense. I didn't want there to be a next time.

Unfortunately, there was a next time. I was in the seventh grade. It was the week of April 26th, 1992. Riots based on the Rodney King verdict "broke-out" through our public school system. Blacks attacked whites. Whites attacked blacks. Racism. Hatred. Anger. Stupidity. I was confused and feared for my personal safety within the hallways of my school. There was a black eighth grader running down the hallways pushing and hitting every white kid that he saw. He was screaming, "down with whitey." He was approaching me fast. I'll never forget his anger or the sound of his voice. I was terrified. As he ran past he slammed my locker door shut on my hand. Frustration. Pain. We both felt it. I yelled directly at him. "Don't you understand that I'm on your side. I know," I said, "it's not fair. But, we aren't all the same. I'm on your side. I'm on your . . . " He hovered over the top of me. He had heard my words, and I was terrified that he was going to hurt me. That wasn't at all what he wanted to do. Instead, he just stared at me. His mouth was half open as if he was shocked by my comment. I wasn't sure if he was going to hurt me or hug me.

"How's your hand?" he asked.

"It will be okay, I guess."

"You have guts. Most people wouldn't have said what you said."

"Violence doesn't solve anything. I wish everyone could see that."

"You should put your ideas to use. Who knows, someone might actually like to hear what you have to say."

He shrugged his shoulders and walked away. Halfway down the hall he turned to look back at me and gave a subtle wink. Even though my hand "hurt like hell," I was a lucky girl. I could have been seriously hurt. That afternoon I went to my counselor's office and asked him what *I* could do to stop the riots in our school. He chuckled and said, "not much." He told me about a meeting that would be held in the auditorium the next morning. The principal was going to give a speech to the student body. It seemed to be the counselor's opinion that the principal was going to deal with the situation by telling us how stupid we were being. That wasn't the solution that I was hoping for.

So, I went to see the principal. I begged for his attention on this serious matter. I told him that none of us wanted to be put down and talked to like we were stupid. Abuse doesn't stop abuse. "Please," I begged, "talk to us like we are adults. Treat us like you would want to be treated. This is a touchy, painful subject for many people. Please don't make things worse than what they already are." I left his office feeling conquered and as though I was fighting for the equality that everyone wanted but no one expected to get. I prayed that night. I prayed that God would give our principal the strength, knowledge, and patience to deal with our problem. I'm not sure if God answered my prayer or if what I said triggered something in our principal, but his speech was incredible. It was the only time that I saw the entire seventh and eighth grade class sit quietly and respectfully during an auditorium gathering.

Throughout high school I joined many clubs and groups that promoted integration between blacks and whites. Sometimes I gained respect from my peers and other times I was called a "nigger-lover." These experiences were difficult and frustrating, but they turned out to be some of the best experiences that I ever had during high school. Now I am a freshman here at

Miami University. Once again I am a small white girl in a predominately white town and in a predominately white school. The only difference between this time and the time before is that I've learned from my mistakes. I only hope that the same is true about the people that I sit next to in my classes. I was never able to express how sorry I was for what I said to Monica. I wonder how my comment has affected her life. Maybe she is writing a similar paper right now. I learned a lesson on that cool autumn day in the third grade that will stick with me for the rest of my life. My fear is that Monica also learned something that will stick with her for the rest of her life.

3

WRITING FROM
READING

The readings in *Language Awareness* emphasize the crucial role language plays in virtually every aspect of our lives and reveal the essential elements of the writer's craft. As you read and study the selections in this text, you will become more sensitive to your own language use and to how the language of others affects you. You will also become more familiar with different types of writing and learn how good writers make decisions about their writing. All of the insights that you gain will help you become a better reader and, equally important, a better writer.

READING ACTIVELY

Reading is most rewarding when you do it actively, in a thoughtful spirit and with an alert, inquiring mind. To read actively, you need to learn how to analyze what you read. You must be able to discover what is going on in an essay, to figure out the writer's reasons for shaping the essay in a particular way, to decide whether the result works well or poorly—and why. At first, such analysis may seem odd because active reading, like writing itself, is a skill that takes time to acquire. It is a skill you need, however, if you are truly to understand a piece of writing.

Active reading is not simply an end in itself; it is also a means to help you become a better writer. At one level, reading stimulates your thinking by providing you with information and ideas to enliven your writing as well as subjects to write about. You might, for example, take up your pen to describe your own experiences with a writer's topic or to elaborate on what another has written, to agree with the examples of others or to generate better ones of your own, to qualify what you have read or simply to oppose its wrongheadedness. These are just a few of the ways in which your reading can stimulate and enrich your writing.

In a more subtle way, active reading can increase your awareness of how others' writing affects you, thus making you more sensitive to how your own writing will affect your readers. For example, if you've ever been impressed by an author who uses convincing evidence to support each of her claims, you might be more likely to back up your own claims carefully. If you've been impressed by an apt turn of phrase or absorbed by a writer's new idea, you may be less inclined to feed your readers clichés and platitudes. Gradually, active reading will help you become a more perceptive writer.

More to the point, however, the active reading you'll be encouraged to do in this text will help you to practice and master important strategies of thinking and writing. In conference with your instructor, for instance, you may discover a faulty beginning or ending, realize that your tone is inappropriate, decide that the various parts of your essay are not quite connected, or notice that you are overusing certain words and phrases. Active reading can help you solve such problems at every stage of the writing process: prewriting, writing a draft, revising, and editing.

GETTING THE MOST OUT OF YOUR READING

Active reading requires, first of all, that you commit time and effort. Second, try to take a positive interest in what you are reading, even if the subject matter is not immediately appealing. Remember, you are reading not for content alone but also to understand a writer's methods—to see firsthand the kinds of choices writers make while they write.

Here are some tips to help you get the most out of your reading.

Read and Reread

Allow yourself time to read a selection at least twice. A first reading gives you the chance to get acquainted with the essay and form an initial impression of it. You may learn new information or new ideas and arguments—and you may be surprised by some of what you read. During a first reading, you will also start to understand the writer's purpose and the essay's organizational pattern.

Your second reading should be quite different from the first. Since you already know what the essay is about, where it is going, and how it gets there, you can begin to analyze the essay more closely. Use your second reading to test your first impressions against a more critical evaluation. Pay special attention to the writer's purpose, tone, and use of evidence. Look for features of organization and style that you can learn from and adapt to your own work.

Ask Yourself Questions

As you probe the essay, pay careful attention not only to what the writer says but also to the way the writer has put the essay together. To see how a writer has crafted an essay, ask yourself some basic questions about its content and form:

1. What does the writer say about language? What is the essay's main point or thesis?
2. What is the writer's general purpose? Is it to *express* an idea or feelings? To *inform* you about a particular concept or activity? To *persuade* you to accept a point of view or take a certain action? Does the writer state his or her purpose directly? If not, how do you know what the purpose is?
3. How is the essay organized and developed? Does the writer use chronological order, go from the most important point to the least important, use spatial order, or follow some other pattern of organization? What strategies of development are used? Narration? Exemplification? Comparison and Contrast? Description? Others?
4. What is the writer's attitude toward the subject of the essay—positive, critical, objective, ironic, hostile?
5. To whom is the essay addressed? To a general audience with no background knowledge of the subject? To a specialized group familiar with the topic? To those who are likely to disagree with the argument? How can you tell what audience the writer is addressing?
6. Does the writer supply enough information to support the essay's ideas? Are there sufficient examples, descriptions, expert opinions, or other kinds of support? Is all of the supporting information relevant and, as far as you can tell, accurate?
7. Overall, how effective is the essay? Has the writer accomplished his or her purpose?

You might use these questions when you reread a selection or prepare for a class discussion. If you keep a reading journal, these questions can be starting points for your responses. They will undoubtedly help you answer the more specific questions that follow each selection in *Language Awareness*. And by all means ask these seven questions of your own essays as you write and revise.

Annotate the Text

As you read and ask questions, write down your thoughts in the margins (or in a journal or on a separate piece of paper). Mark the selection's main point when you find it stated directly. Look for the strategy or strategies the writer uses to develop that point, and jot down the information. If you disagree with a statement or a conclusion, write "No!" in the margin. If you feel skeptical, write "Why?" or "Explain." If you are impressed by an argument or turn of phrase, you might compliment the author by saying "Good point" or "Nicely stated." Place vertical lines or stars in the margin to indicate the essay's important points. Make other marginal notes as well about whatever seems significant to you. These quick, brief responses will help you remember what you have read and answer more specific and analytical questions later on.

When annotating a text, don't be timid. Mark up your book as much as you like, and make additional notes in your journal. Keep in mind, though, that annotating should be an aid, not a chore; a word or phrase is usually as good as a sentence. You may, in fact, want to delay much of your annotating until a second reading, so that you can move rapidly during your first reading and concentrate on larger issues. If done in the right spirit, annotating encourages active engagement with a text and in time helps you understand the text much more fully.

Actively Read an Essay: Leslie Savan's "Yadda, Yadda, Yadda"

Now that you've learned some tips for active reading, it's time to apply those tips to an actual essay, Leslie Savan's "Yadda, Yadda, Yadda." A native of St. Louis, Missouri, Leslie Savan earned a degree in psychology from New York University in the mid-1970s. Today she is a columnist for the *Village Voice* and the author of *The Sponsored Life: Ads, TV, & American Culture* (1994), a critical commentary on advertising in America. She frequently writes about the world of movie and television entertainment. "Yadda, Yadda, Yadda," a brief essay whose title echoes a line from the popular *Seinfeld* television show, first appeared in *Time* magazine on December 16, 1996.

As you read this essay for the first time, try not to stop—take it all in as if in one breath. The second time, however, pause to annotate the text as often as you like, keeping in mind the seven basic questions listed earlier. Here those questions are applied specifically to Savan's essay.

1. What does Savan say about the language of television and movies? What is her main point or thesis?
2. What is Savan's purpose in this essay? Is her purpose stated directly or implied?
3. How is Savan's essay organized and developed? What kind of order does she follow? What strategies of development does she use?
4. What is Savan's attitude toward the language of television and movies?
5. To whom does Savan address her essay? How can you tell?
6. Does Savan supply enough information to support the ideas in her essay? Is her information relevant and accurate?
7. Overall, how effective is the essay? Has Savan accomplished her purpose?

Yadda, Yadda, Yadda

LESLIE SAVAN

During the fall [1996] campaign, Bob Dole said on TV that General Motors has been replaced as the nation's largest employer by a temp agency, and he asked, "That's a good economy? I don't *think* so." You don't have to be running for President to be fond of tossing off that pat rejoinder. The police in Madison, Wisconsin, for example, reported that when they ordered a young scofflaw to approach their squad car, he replied, "I don't *think* so," and tried to run. (The cops caught him by his fanny pack.)

If pols and petty criminals use the same buzzphrases these days, they probably get them from TV, like everyone else. One week on *Friends,* when David Schwimmer's all-thumbs buddies offered to baby-sit his infant son, he said, "I don't *think* so"; an hour later, Jerry Seinfeld told an unctuous magician who asked to borrow him for a trick, "I don't *think* so."

Oh, pulleeze. Don't even think about telling me. I hate when that happens. Get over it. These phrases from hell are history. I'll be their worst nightmare. Yeah, right. As if. Hel-lo-oh!

Every day, Americans are belting out more of these ready-made, media-marinated catchphrases, usually of the in-your-face (to use another) variety. Conversations, movies, E-mail, ads, lovers' quarrels, punditry, and stand-up comedy can barely be conducted without resort to an annoyingly popular riposte. A random gleaning, from just one *Cybill* episode on CBS, produced: *Hel-lo-oh; Oh, pulleeze; Get a life; Yadda yadda; Yesss!;* and *Haven't we had enough fun yet?*

These pop phrases are not just clichés. They're more like a bad case 5 of televisionary Tourette's — snappy, canned punch lines that bring the rhythms of sitcom patter into everyday experience. Whether originating from Valley Girls, drag queens, or CEOs, these phrases, once they're disseminated by the media, become part of our shared response to the little frustrations of modern life. More and more, that response tends to be a dismissive pique, as these buzzbarbs — expressed with just the right inflections — verbally roll up the window on any nuisance that might come tapping at the tinted glass.

TV and movies have catapulted catchphrases before — *Get Smart* launched *Would you believe . . . ?* and *Sorry about that* into nationwide use in the 1970s — but this newer slang is different. It is supposed to confer upon its users an edge, sometimes a comedic but always a faintly combative edge. The era of *Saturday Night Live* that dished out Dennis Miller's "I'm outta here" and Dana Carvey's "Isn't that special?" fed a hunger for a renewable supply of ironic put-downs. But what may have started as a boomer/Xer shtick has now become a reflex common to all ages, from Bob Dole to Macaulay Culkin (who gave *I don't think so* its big push by uttering it twice in the top box-office hit of 1990, *Home Alone*). The militia code name for a possible counterattack on the feds? "Project Worst Nightmare." The would-be zinger in the G.O.P.'s last-minute ads warning against Democratic control of both Congress and the White House? "Been there, done that."

A whole nation barking Hollywood retorts—creepy but all too useful. In the daily battlefield of misunderstandings and impatient busyness, such locutions as *Don't go there, In your dreams,* and *What part of no don't you understand?* are Nerf-like weaponry: When you're blind with anger or exasperation, you grab the nearest item of modular meanness. Of course, not all coolster coinages are overtly fightin' words. Indeed, some affect affectlessness: *Same old, same old; Blah blah blah; Yadda yadda yadda.* But given the right nuances, indifference can pack a wallop: *Yadda* will outsnide *blah,* for instance, but wither before the passive-aggressive champ (and Bob Dole favorite), *Whatever.*

Even if these phrases were the nastiest bomb mots on earth, who'd want a civilization without frequent hits of wicked wit? The real reason modular meanness grates isn't the meanness—it's the modularness.

Whether biting or benign, what these supposedly trenchant comebacks have in common is the roar of a phantom crowd; they always speak of other people having spoken them. It's as if they come with a built-in laugh track. And keeping us on track, they provide in us click responses, the sort of electronic-entertainment reaction we twitch and jerk to more often lately. We hear *Not even close, He's history* or *What's wrong with this picture?,* and we immediately sense the power structure of the moment. In fact, we may subconsciously applaud such speakers because they've hypertexted our little lives right into *Friends, Seinfeld* or the "I love you, man" ads, and for a moment, at least, we know perfectly how to relate to people, deal with conflict, and banish discomfort. Not being in control— that's our real worst nightmare.

Think about it. For all the references to thinking—*I don't* think *so,*   10 *no-brainer, clueless,* all the brain surgeons and rocket scientists you don't have to be, and the injunction on some New York City street signs, "Don't even think of parking here"—isn't the real message of these phrases simply, Don't even think?

Duh.

———

Once you have read and reread Savan's essay, write your own answers to the seven basic questions listed before the essay. Then compare your answers to those that follow.

1. *What does Savan say about the language of television and movies? What is her main point or thesis?*

Savan wants to call attention to the buzzphrases, generated by popular movies and television shows, that Americans use in their conversations. Savan argues that today's catchphrases, unlike those of a generation ago, are "combative" and "usually of the in-your-face variety." She also believes that the real message of today's slang is not to think at all. This is her main point, which she states at the end of her essay.

2. *What is Savan's purpose in this essay? Is her purpose stated directly or implied?*

    Savan's purpose is twofold: She wants to make her readers aware of just how widespread movie and television-show catchphrases have become in everyday life, and she wants her readers to consider the effects of such phrases on their thinking and relationships. She implies that we should take control of our language so that we don't use such phrases mindlessly.

3. *How is Savan's essay organized and developed? What kind of order does she follow? What strategies of development does she use?*

    Overall, the essay is an argument, in which Savan follows a specific-to-general organizational pattern. She moves from a discussion of particular catchphrases to a general conclusion about most, if not all, such phrases. She is careful to support her argument with the strategy of exemplification. Her numerous examples serve to convince readers that catchphrases are very widespread, that they convey a put-down attitude, and that they encourage a certain don't-even-think mentality. Savan's examples also act as a catalyst, helping readers recall other catchphrases they may have heard.

4. *What is Savan's attitude toward the language of television and movies?*

    Savan is openly critical of the catchphrases generated by many of today's movies and television shows. Her diction— *riposte, buzzbarbs, put-downs, reflex, modular meanness*—clearly indicates her contempt for popular coinages. Savan's concluding paragraph, "Duh"—a catchphrase itself—stops us in our tracks and shows us how utterly mindless she thinks these phrases are.

5. *To whom does Savan address her essay? How can you tell?*

    Savan directs her essay, which first appeared in *Time* magazine, to an educated, general readership. Her many references to movies and television shows make it clear that she is talking to regular movie-goers or television viewers. Her reference, in paragraph 5, to Tourette's syndrome (a disease involving uncontrollable movement and language) also indicates that she is writing for an educated audience.

6. *Does Savan supply enough information to support the ideas in her essay? Is her information relevant and accurate?*

    Savan supports her criticisms of catchphrases with numerous references to movies and shows (*Home Alone, Friends, Cybill, Get Smart,*

Saturday Night Live, Seinfeld) and examples of buzzphrases ("I don't *think* so," "Oh, pulleeze," "Get over it," "Get a life," "Hel-lo-oh," "Yeah, right," "What part of no don't you understand?") The number of examples clearly shows the prevalence of catchphrases and that they are nasty and combative. Moreover, her information seems to be accurate, and her conclusions provide a relevant commentary on contemporary entertainment and behavior.

7. *Overall, how effective is the essay? Has Savan accomplished her purpose?*

Savan's essay is effective because she helps her readers understand how catchphrases operate and the effect these phrases have on social relationships. Because her examples are to the point and easy to follow, her conclusion is both thought provoking and convincing.

WRITING FROM READING:
A SAMPLE STUDENT ESSAY

Sara Daniels wrote the following paper while she was a student at the University of Vermont. Her paper grew out of her interest in the language of television and movies. She knew from past experience that in order to write a good essay she would have to write on a topic she cared about. After some thought, she decided to work with Leslie Savan's "Yadda, Yadda, Yadda." Savan's indictment of movie and television catchphrases intrigued Sara because today's catchphrases seemed so different from the ones she remembered hearing in the movies and television shows she watched as a child. Sara wanted to discover what had changed in America since the late 1980s and why Americans had started to use cynical, in-your-face catchphrases.

Sara began by brainstorming about the topic. She made an extensive list of the movie and television catchphrases she remembered using or hearing while growing up and another list of ideas, facts, and issues that might help her account for the disturbing shift in tone and attitude that both she and Savan had noticed. Once she was confident that she had enough information to begin writing, she made a rough outline, following an organization she thought would work well for her. Keeping this plan in mind, Sara wrote a first draft of her essay and then went back and examined it carefully, assessing how it could be improved.

Sara was writing this particular essay toward the end of the semester, after she had read a number of professional essays and written several of her own. She knew the importance of having a strong thesis and purpose, good paragraphing, informative examples, unity, and transitions. In rereading her first draft, she realized that her essay's organization could be improved if she adopted a chronological ordering instead of jumping back and forth between the late 1980s and the late 1990s. As she repositioned some of her paragraphs, she realized that some material could be eliminated. She tightened up a number of sentences, added several key transitions, and carefully edited her diction to better convey what she wanted to say.

The final draft of Sara's paper, which follows, illustrates that she has learned how the parts of a well-written essay fit together and how to make revisions. Clearly, she has learned many writing techniques by reading and studying the essays in *Language Awareness.* The page numbers in Sara's in-text citations refer to the pages on which the Savan essay appears in this book.

Daniels 1

Sara Daniels
Professor P. Eschholz
English 104, Language Awareness
May 4, 1999

Catching the Wave of the '90s: Cynical Speech

Catchphrases from television shows and movies pepper our everyday conversations. "Oh, pulleeze" and "Whatever" don't exactly promote pleasant conversations between people, but we still use them. Catchphrases are not new to our pop-culture scene. Every generation has had its sayings or pet phrases. The late '80s, for example, brought us catchphrases that were on the humorous and comical side: "Cowabunga Dude!" and "You look marvelous" made us laugh and smile. The phrases caught on for their inherent humor. Phrases from '90s culture have a different feeling. Phrases such as "Loser" and "Respect my authority" are sarcastic and instill anger and confusion. It is the tone and attitude of these catchphrases that seems to have been transformed from what was once fun humor to what is now harsh cynicism. The inherent humor of these phrases seems to have changed in a decade's time, bringing us more of what Leslie Savan in her article "Yadda, Yadda, Yadda" calls "in-your-face" catchphrases (29).

What is it that has caused such drastic changes in the humor of America in just under a decade's time? Most noteworthy is the shift in the types of television shows and movies that have been produced in the nineties. The "family prime-time hour" and "feel-good movies" of the '80s have been replaced with violent action movies and cynical low-brow sitcoms.

The popular late '80s television show Family Matters introduced us to Steven Urkel. Each time Steve broke something or ruined someone's plans he said, in his nasally voice, "Did I do that?" Audiences anxiously waited for the line to come up during each show. In the real world people used this same line each time they knocked something down or made a mistake. This catchphrase took the pressure out of a potentially embarrassing situation and put a comical spin on the incident. Phrases like "Did I do that?" gave the user control of the situation at hand. The '90s phrases seem to take a different sort of edge. The comical control that people once looked for when using these phrases has changed to cynical power over a situation, a sort of "combative edge" as Savan puts it (29).

The '80s feel-good movies such as Field of Dreams and When Harry Met Sally, gave us feel-good catchphrases as well. "If you build it, they will come," and "I'll have what she's having" are enduring phrases that continue to remind people of these heartwarming movies. The '90s have brought us an age of action movies and a rise in horror flicks. The feel-good movies are in decline. This decline of the feel-good genre and rise in harsh films reflects a pattern in society. As people seem to lose control of situations, they tend to rely on the harsher catchphrases, as Savan says, to conquer what she calls our worst nightmare—not being in control.

The feel-good movies showed us love, vulnerability, and risk-taking. Vulnerability promotes a sense of community—we have to depend on each other. Cynicism does the reverse. It makes us not want to be vulnerable. We are losing our sense of community through the phrases of the '90s. Society is looking for power and the domination of situations. Our lack of control in society makes us feel powerless and alone. By taking control we solidify our solitude through these cynical statements.

Late '80s television shows such as the Saturday Night Live comedy sketch "The Church Lady" had viewers repeating the catchphrase, "Isn't that special!" Each time the Church Lady said it to one of the guests, the guest showed an expression of dismay and defeat. This catchphrase was one of the first in the '80s to use cynicism to control another person. If it wasn't Saturday Night Live that changed the catchphrases of comedy to catchphrases of cynicism, then it may have been Bart Simpson's phrase, "Eat my shorts." The Simpson's television show began in the late '80s but didn't have a strong following until the early '90s. By 1992, Simpson's television-show merchandise skyrocketed, and children all over the nation had Bart dolls that would say, "Don't have a cow man!" and posters of Bart saying, "Eat my shorts!"

Television producers saw the response to such cynical phrases of the late '80s and began to transform the nature of television comedy to meet the demands of the consumers—American culture was changing. The population of the nineties is angry, confused, and feels out of control. Violent shows and cynicism show how to take control in socially acceptable ways. The in-your-face catchphrases are a way to verbally annihilate the person that you are talking to. The sayings are designed to shut a person up rather than promote conversation.

Savan contends that television's popular phrases have given us a "bad case of televisionary Tourette's" (29). Much like those who suffer from real

Tourette's syndrome, society is not considering the things that they say or the implications of their cynicism. People are venting whatever is on their mind. These responses tend to be of the "dismissive pique" and "verbally roll up the window on any nuisance that might come tapping" (29). Savan's examples of "Yadda yadda yadda," "In your dreams," and "What part of no don't you understand?" are conversation-stopping phrases that cause some-one to feel alone and emotionally hurt.

The '90s phrase that best fits this genre is "Whatever." This catch-phrase from the movie Clueless can be used to express disregard or apathy to any subject. It is like giving someone "the bird" without even expending the effort to raise the middle finger. Such a phrase encompasses a genera-tion of disregard and slackers. It closes the door to any further conversa-tion with a three syllable blow-off.

American society has lost interest in comical catchphrases from '80s television shows. The enthusiastic greeting "Cowabunga Dude" from the '80s movie Teenage Mutant Ninja Turtles has faded into the slacker generation of "What's Up." The range of catchphrases has narrowed as television pro-ducers incorporate more and more cynicism into their television shows.

The '90s television show Seinfeld was a show about nothing. It was the ultimate display of cynicism as producers worked hard to create a show that viewers would respond to and had no plot. The irony that such a show would be so popular and enduring allowed producers to continually promote memorable sayings that incorporated a feeling of power through cynicism. The example that Savan uses that best fits this description is "Yadda yadda yadda." Characters used this phrase instead of "Blah blah blah" to show their indifference to telling the whole story — a sort of You're not impor-tant enough to tell the whole story to anyway. Other phrases from this show, such as "Who asked you anyways!" show how upfront and in your face the characters were.

The decline of feel-good catchphrases and the rise in cynicism shapes society's conversations and interactions among people. Such a shift has the potential to change once media see the need to incorporate more upbeat comedy into the television genres.

Feel-good movies and upbeat family shows of the late '80s have been hidden under the carpet of cynical comedy and action shows of the '90s. Once upbeat shows reemerge, the tone of the catchphrases will change as well. A very recent trend in movies proves that there is a push to have feel-good movies return. The comedy/drama Patch Adams presents a story of a doctor who uses laughter as medicine — not cynicism. Life is Beautiful and Shake-speare in Love carry story lines of hope and love. These movies may not be selling out as fast as action movies such as Star War's The Phantom Menace, but they do prove a change in the trend. These movies received several Acad-emy Awards but continue to have empty seats in the theaters. There is hope that cynicism can be replaced with hope and love once again.

4

WRITING FROM RESEARCH

The research paper is an important part of a college education and for good reason. In writing such a paper, you acquire a number of indispensable research skills that you can adapt to other college assignments and to situations after graduation.

The real value of writing a research paper, however, goes beyond acquiring basic skills; it is a unique hands-on learning experience. The purpose of a research paper is not to present a collection of quotations that show you can report what others have said about your topic. Rather, your goal is to analyze, evaluate, and synthesize the materials you research—and thereby learn how to do so with any topic. You learn how to view the results of research from your own perspective and arrive at an informed opinion of a topic.

Writing a researched essay is not very different from the other writing you will be doing in your college writing course. You will find yourself drawing heavily on what you have learned in Chapter 1, "The Writing Process." First you determine what you want to write about. Then you decide on a purpose, consider your audience, develop a thesis, collect your evidence, write a first draft, revise and edit, and prepare a final copy. What differentiates the researched paper from other kinds of papers is your use of outside sources and how you acknowledge them.

In this chapter you will learn how to locate and use print and Internet sources; how to evaluate these sources; how to take useful notes; how to summarize, paraphrase, and quote your sources; how to integrate your notes into your paper; how to acknowledge your sources; and how to avoid plagiarism. You will also find extensive guidelines for documenting your essay in MLA (Modern Language Association) style. MLA guidelines are widely accepted by English and foreign-language scholars and teachers, and we encourage their use. Before you begin work on your research paper, your instructor will let you know which style you should follow.

Your library research will involve working with print as well as electronic sources. In both cases, however, the process is essentially the same: Your aim is to select the most appropriate sources for your research from the many that are available on your topic.

USING PRINT SOURCES

In most cases you should use print sources (books, newspapers, journals, periodicals, encyclopedias, pamphlets, brochures, and government publications) as your primary tools for research. Print sources, unlike many Internet sources, are often reviewed by experts in the field before they are published, are generally overseen by a reputable publishing company or organization, and are examined by editors and fact checkers for accuracy and reliability. Unless you are instructed otherwise, you should try to use print sources in your research.

To find print sources, search through your library's reference works, card catalog, periodical indexes, and other databases to generate a preliminary listing of books, magazine and newspaper articles, public documents and reports, and other sources that may be helpful in exploring your topic. At this early stage, it is better to err on the side of listing too many sources. Then, later on, you will not have to relocate sources you discarded too hastily.

Preview Print Sources

Although you want to be thorough in your research, you will soon realize that you do not have enough time to read every source you encounter. Rather, you must preview your sources to decide what you will read, what you will skim, and what you will simply eliminate.

QUESTIONS FOR PREVIEWING PRINT SOURCES
1. Is the book or article directly related to your research topic?
2. Is the book or article obviously outdated (for example, a source on language-related brain research that is from the 1970s)?
3. Have you checked tables of contents and indexes in books to locate material that may be important and relevant to your topic?
4. If an article appears to be what you are looking for, have you read the abstract (a summary of the main points of the article, which appears in some journals) or the opening and concluding paragraphs?
5. Is it necessary to quickly read the entire article to be sure that it is relevant?

Develop a Working Bibliography

It is important to develop a working bibliography of the books, articles, and other materials that you think are relevant to your topic. Compiling such a bibliography lets you know at a glance which works you have consulted and the shape your research is taking. A working bibliography also guides you to other materials you may wish to consider. Naturally, you will want to capture early on all the information you need for each work so that you do not have to return to the library at a later time to retrieve publication data for your final bibliography or list of works cited. Accuracy and completeness are, of course, essential at this final stage of the research.

For each work that you think might be helpful, make a separate bibliography card, using a 4 x 6-inch index card. As your collection of cards grows, alphabetize them by the authors' last names. By using a separate card for each book or article, you can continually edit your working bibliography, dropping sources that are not helpful for one reason or another and adding new ones. You will also use the cards to compile your final list of works cited.

For books, record the following information:

- All authors; any editors or translators
- Title and subtitle
- Edition (if not the first)
- Publication data: city, publishing company, and date
- Call number

For periodical articles, record the following information:

- All authors
- Title and subtitle
- Title of journal, magazine, or newspaper
- Volume and issue numbers
- Date and page numbers

Using correct bibliographic form ensures that your entries are complete, reduces the chance of introducing careless errors, and saves time when you are ready to prepare your final list of works cited. You will find MLA style guidelines for the List of Works Cited on pages 50–54.

Evaluate Print Sources

Before beginning to take notes, you should read your sources and evaluate them for their relevance and reliability in helping you explore your topic. Examine your sources for the writer's main ideas. Pay particular attention to abstracts or introductions, tables of contents, section headings, and indexes. Also, look for information about the authors themselves—information that will help you determine their authority and perspective on the issues.

QUESTIONS FOR EVALUATING PRINT SOURCES

1. Is your source focused on your particular research topic?
2. Is your source too abstract, too general, or too technical for your needs?
3. Does your source build on current thinking and existing research in the field?
4. Does your source promote a particular view or is it meant to provide balanced coverage of the topic? What biases, if any, does your source exhibit?
5. Is the author of your source an authority on the topic? Do other writers mention the author of your source in their work?

USING INTERNET SOURCES

You will find that Internet sources can be informative and valuable additions to your research. The Internet is especially useful in providing recent data, stories, and reports. For example, you might find a just-published article from a university laboratory or a news story in your local newspaper's online archives. Generally, however, Internet sources should be used along with print sources and not as a replacement for them. Whereas print sources are generally published under the guidance of a publisher or an organization, practically anyone with access to a computer and a modem can put text and pictures onto the Internet; there is often no governing body that checks for content or accuracy. The Internet offers a vast number of useful and carefully maintained resources, but it also contains many bogus facts and much unreliable information. It is your responsibility to evaluate whether or not a given Internet source should be trusted.

Your Internet research will probably produce many more sources than you can reasonably use. By carefully previewing Web sites and other Internet sources, developing a working bibliography of potentially useful ones, and evaluating them for their reliability, you will ensure that you are making the best use of Internet sources in researching your topic.

If you do not know how to access the Internet, or if you need more instruction on conducting Internet searches, you should go to your on-campus computer center for more information or consult one of the many books written for Internet beginners. You can also access the links to Internet information offered by Bedford/St. Martin's at <http://www.bedfordstmartins.com/hacker/resdoc>.

Preview Internet Sources

The key to successful Internet research is being able to identify those sites that will help you the most. Answering the following questions will help you weed out sources that hold no promise.

QUESTIONS FOR PREVIEWING INTERNET SOURCES

1. Scan the Web site. Do the contents and links appear to be related to your research topic?
2. Can you identify the author of the site? Are the author's credentials available, and are they appropriate to the content of the site?
3. Has the site been updated within the last six months? It is not always necessary to use updated information, especially if your topic is not a current one and the information about it is fairly stable. Information about the most recent update is usually provided at the bottom of the homepage of the Web site.

If you answer "no" to any of these questions, you should consider eliminating the source from further consideration.

Develop a Working Bibliography

Just as for print sources, you must maintain accurate records for the Internet sources you use. Here is what you need for each source:

- All authors or sponsoring agents
- Title and subtitle of the document
- Title of complete work (if applicable)
- Document date (or date "last modified")
- Date you accessed the site
- Publishing data for print version (if available)
- Address of the site, uniform resource locator (URL), or network path

Evaluate Internet Sources

Because the quality of sources on the Internet varies tremendously, it is important to evaluate the information you find there. Answering the following questions will help you evaluate the sites you have included in your working bibliography.

QUESTIONS FOR EVALUATING WEB SITES

1. *What type of Web site is it?*

   Who sponsors the site? A corporation? An individual? The URL indicates the sponsor of the site. Some common domain names are:

   .com Business/Commercial

   .edu Educational institution

   .gov Government sponsored

   .mil Military

   .net Various types of networks

   .org Nonprofit organization

2. *Who is the authority or author?*

> What individual or company is responsible for the site?
>
> Can you verify if the site is official, actually sanctioned by an organization or company?
>
> What are the author's or company's qualifications for writing on this subject?
>
> Is there a way to verify the legitimacy of this individual or company? Are there links to a homepage or résumé?

3. *What is the site's purpose and audience?*

> What appears to be the author's or sponsor's purpose or motivation?
>
> Who is the intended audience?

4. *Is the site objective?*

> Are advertising, opinion, and factual information clearly distinguished?
>
> What biases, if any, can you detect?

5. *How accurate is the site?*

> Is important information documented through links so that it can be verified or corroborated by other sources?
>
> Is the text well written and free of careless errors in spelling and grammar?

6. *Is the coverage thorough and current?*

> Is there any indication that the site is still under construction?
>
> For sources with print equivalents, is the Web version more or less extensive than the print version?
>
> How detailed is the site's treatment of its subject matter?
>
> Is there any indication of the currency of the information (the date of the last update or a statement regarding frequency of updates)?

7. *Is the site easy to use?*

> Is the design and navigation of the site user-friendly?
>
> Do all links work, and do they take you to relevant information?
>
> Can you return to the homepage easily?
>
> Are the graphics helpful, or are they simply window dressing?

You can also find sources on the Internet itself that offer useful guidelines for evaluating electronic sources. One excellent set of guidelines has been created by reference librarians at the Wolfgram Memorial Library at Widener University; see <http://www2.widener.edu/Wolfgram-Memorial-Library/webeval.htm>.

TAKING NOTES

As you gather and sort your source materials, you'll want to record the information that you consider most pertinent to your topic. As you read, take notes. You're looking for ideas, facts, opinions, statistics, examples, and other evidence that you think will be useful in writing your paper. As you work through books and articles, look for recurring themes and notice where writers are in agreement and where they differ. Try to remember that the effectiveness of your paper is largely determined by the quality—not necessarily the quantity—of your notes. You will want to analyze, evaluate, and synthesize the information you collect to use it for your own purpose.

Now for some practical advice on taking notes: First, be systematic in your note-taking. As a rule, write one note on a card and include the author's full name, the complete title of the source, and a page number indicating the origin of the note. Use cards of uniform size, preferably 4 x 6-inch cards because they are large enough to accommodate even a long note on a single card and yet small enough to be easily handled and conveniently carried. Following this system will also help you when you get to the planning and writing stage because you will be able to sequence your notes according to the plan you have envisioned for your paper. Furthermore, should you decide to alter your organizational plan, you can easily reorder your cards to reflect your revisions. You can, of course, do note-taking on your computer as well, which makes it easy for you to reorder your notes. An added advantage of the computer is that the Copy and Paste feature lets you move notes and their citations directly into your essay.

Second, try not to take too many notes. One good way to control your note-taking is to ask yourself, "How exactly does this material help prove or disprove my thesis?" Try to envision where in your paper you could use the information. If it does not seem relevant to your thesis, don't bother to take a note. Once you decide to take a note, you must decide whether to summarize, paraphrase, or quote directly. The approach you take should be determined by the content of the passage and the way you plan to use it in your paper.

Summary

When you *summarize* material from one of your sources, you capture in condensed form the essential idea of a passage, article, or entire chapter. Summaries are particularly useful when you are working with lengthy, detailed arguments or long passages of narrative or descriptive background information in which the details are not germane to the overall thrust of your paper. You simply want to capture the essence of the passage because you are confident that your readers will readily understand the point being made or do not need to be convinced about its validity. Because you are distilling information, a summary is always shorter than the original; often a chapter or more can be reduced to a paragraph, or several paragraphs to a sentence or two. Remember, in writing a summary you should use your own words.

Consider the following passage from Rosalie Maggio's 1991 book, *The Dictionary of Bias-Free Usage; A Guide to Nondiscriminatory Language*, page 5.

> The greatest objection to bias-free language is that it will lead us to absurdities. Critics have posited something utterly ridiculous, cleverly demonstrated how silly it is, and then accounted themselves victorious in the battle against linguistic massacre. For example: "So I suppose now we're going to say: He/she ain't heavy, Father/Sister; he/she's my brother/sister." "I suppose next it will be 'ottoperson.'" Cases have been built up against the mythic "woperson," "personipulate," and "personhole cover" (none of which has ever been advocated by any reputable sociolinguist). No grist appears too ridiculous for these mills. And, yes, they grind exceedingly small. Using a particular to condemn a universal is a fault in logic. But then ridicule, it is said, is the first and last argument of fools.

A student wishing to capture the gist of Maggio's point without repeating her detailed account wrote the following summary:

SUMMARY NOTE CARD

Critics of bias-free language undermine their credibility by using ridicule — and ridiculous examples — to argue their case.

Rosalie Maggio, The Dictionary of Bias-Free Usage, (5)

Paraphrase

When you *paraphrase* material from a source, you restate the information in your own words instead of quoting directly. Unlike a summary, which gives a brief overview of the essential information in the original, a paraphrase seeks to maintain the same level of detail as the original to aid readers in understanding or believing the information presented. A paraphrase presents the original information in approximately the same number of words, but in your own wording. To put it another way, your paraphrase should closely parallel the presentation of ideas in the original, but it should not use the same words or sentence structure as the original. Even though you are using your own words in a paraphrase, it's important to remember that you are borrowing ideas and therefore must acknowledge the source of these ideas with a citation.

How would you paraphrase the following passage from "Selection, Slanting, and Charged Language" by Newman P. and Genevieve B. Birk, which appears on pages 397–408 of this text?

> When we put our knowledge into words, a second process of selection, the process of slanting, takes place. Just as there is something, a rather mysterious principle of selection, which chooses for us what we will notice, and what will then become our knowledge, there is also a principle which operates, with or without our awareness, to select certain facts and feelings from our store of knowledge, and to choose the words and the emphasis that we shall use to communicate our meaning.

The following note card illustrates how a student paraphrased the passage:

PARAPHRASE NOTE CARD

> *Every time we communicate information and ideas, we engage in a secondary process known as slanting. An even earlier selection process, that of acquiring knowledge, remains something of a mystery because who can say why we notice what we do and why it becomes a part of what we know. Slanting, a conscious or subconscious process, further selects the facts and emotions we convey; it finds not only the words we use but also the way we emphasize them when we communicate.*
>
> *Newman P. Birk, Genevieve B. Birk, "Selection, Slanting and Charged Language," 399*

It is important to note how carefully the student captures the essence of the Birks' ideas in her own words as well as her own sentence structure.

In most cases it is better to summarize or paraphrase material—which by definition means using your own words—instead of quoting verbatim (word for word). Capturing an idea in your own words ensures that you have thought about and understood what your source is saying. (Note that for passages from essays in *Language Awareness,* page numbers refer to this text.)

Direct Quotation

To quote a source directly, copy onto your note card the exact words of your source, putting all quoted material in quotation marks. When you make a quotation note card, check the passage carefully for accuracy, including punctuation and capitalization. Be selective about what you choose to quote; reserve direct quotation for important ideas stated memorably, for especially clear explanations by authorities, and for arguments by proponents of a particular position in their own words.

Consider, for example, the following passage from William Zinsser's "Simplicity," on page 155 included in this text, emphasizing the importance—and current rarity—of clear, concise writing:

QUOTATION NOTE CARD

> "Clutter is the disease of American writing. We are a society strangling in unnecessary words, circular constructions, pompous frills, and meaningless jargon."
>
> William Zinsser, "Simplicity," 155

On occasion you'll find a useful passage with some memorable wording in it. Avoid the temptation to quote the whole passage; instead, try combining summary or paraphrase with direct quotation.

Consider the following paragraph from Martin Luther King Jr.'s "I Have a Dream" speech, which appears on pages 302–06 of this text.

Five score years ago, a great American, in whose symbolic shadow we stand today, signed the Emancipation Proclamation. This momentous decree came as a great beacon light of hope to millions of Negro slaves who had been seared in the flames of withering injustice. It came as a joyous daybreak to end the long night of their captivity. But one hundred years later, the Negro still is not free. One hundred years later, the life of the Negro is still sadly crippled by the manacles of segregation and the chains of discrimination. One hundred years later, the Negro lives on a lonely island of poverty in the midst of a vast ocean of material prosperity. One hundred years later, the Negro is still anguished in the corners of American society and finds himself in exile in his own land. And so we have come here today to dramatize a shameful condition.

Notice how the student in taking the following note was careful to put quotation marks around all the words that were borrowed directly.

QUOTATION AND SUMMARY CARD

According to MLK, the promise of the Emancipation Proclamation has not been fulfilled. "One hundred years later, the Negro is still anguished in the corners of American society and finds himself in exile in his own land."

Martin Luther King Jr., "I Have a Dream," 303

Notes from Internet Sources

Working from the computer screen or from a printout, you can take notes just as you would from print sources. You will need to decide whether to summarize, paraphrase, or quote directly the information you wish to borrow. Use the same 4 x 6-inch index-card system that you use with print sources. The medium of the Internet, however, has an added advantage. An easy and accurate technique for capturing passages of text from the Internet is to copy the material into a separate computer file on your hard drive or diskette. In Netscape, for example, you can use your mouse to highlight the portion of the text you want to save and then use the Copy and Paste features to add it to your file of research notes. You can also use the same commands to capture the bibliographic information you will need later.

INTEGRATING BORROWED MATERIAL INTO YOUR TEXT

Being familiar with the material in your notes will help you decide how to integrate it into your drafts. Though it is not necessary to use all of your notes, nor to use them all at once in your first draft, you do need to know which ones support your thesis, extend your ideas, offer better wording of your ideas, and reveal the opinions of noted authorities. Occasionally you will want to use notes that include ideas contrary to your own so that you can rebut them in your own argument. Once you have analyzed all of your notes, you may even alter your thesis slightly in light of the information and ideas you have found.

Whenever you want to use borrowed material, be it a summary, paraphrase, or quotation, it's best to introduce the material with a *signal
phrase* —a phrase that alerts the reader that borrowed information is to
follow. A signal phrase usually consists of the author's name and a verb.
Well-chosen signal phrases help you integrate quotations, paraphrases,
and summaries into the flow of your paper. Besides, signal phrases let
your reader know who is speaking and, in the case of summaries and
paraphrases, exactly where your ideas end and someone else's begin.
Never confuse your reader with a quotation that appears suddenly without introduction. Unannounced quotations leave your reader wondering
how the quoted material relates to the point you are trying to make.
Look at the following example. The quotation is from William Bennett's
essay, "Should Drugs Be Legalized?" which first appeared in the March
1990 issue of *Reader's Digest*.

UNANNOUNCED QUOTATION

Many Americans believe that our war on drugs is a losing battle and that
we would be far better off to make drugs legal. "The legalizers want
peace at any price, even though it means the inevitable proliferation of a
practice that degrades, impoverishes, and kills." (Bennett 137)

In the following rewrite, the writer has integrated the quotation into
the text not only by means of a signal phrase but in a number of other
ways as well. By giving the name of the speaker, referring to the speaker's
credentials, and noting that the speaker "sees the issue differently," the
writer provides more context so that the reader can better understand
how the quotation fits into the discussion.

INTEGRATED QUOTATION

Many Americans believe that our war on drugs is a losing battle and that
we would be far better off to make drugs legal. William Bennett, former
United States drug czar, sees the issue differently, however; he believes
that "the legalizers want peace at any price, even though it means the
inevitable proliferation of a practice that degrades, impoverishes, and
kills." (137)

How well you integrate a quote, paraphrase, or summary into your
paper depends partly on varying your signal phrases and, in particular,
choosing a verb for the signal phrase that accurately conveys the tone and
intent of the writer you are citing. If a writer is arguing, use the verb *argues* (or *asserts, claims,* or *contends*); if a writer is contesting a particular
position or fact, use the verb *contests* (or *denies, disputes, refutes,* or *rejects*). In using verbs that are specific to the situation in your paper, you
bring your readers into the intellectual debate and avoid the monotony of
such all-purpose verbs as *says* or *writes*. Following are just a few examples
of how you can vary signal phrases to add precision to your paper:

Malcolm X confesses that . . .
To summarize Deborah Tannen's observations, . . .
Louise Erdrich, popular fiction writer, emphasizes . . .
George Orwell rejects the widely held belief that . . .

Other verbs that you should keep in mind when constructing signal phrases include the following:

acknowledges	declares	points out
adds	endorses	reasons
admits	grants	reports
believes	implies	responds
compares	insists	suggests
confirms		

DOCUMENTING SOURCES

Whenever you summarize, paraphrase, or quote a person's thoughts and ideas, and when you use facts or statistics that are not commonly known or believed, you must properly acknowledge the source of your information. If you do not properly acknowledge ideas and information created by someone else, you are guilty of *plagiarism,* of using someone else's material but making it look as if it were your own. You must document the source of your information whenever you do the following:

- quote a source word-for-word
- refer to information and ideas from another source that you present in your own words as either a paraphrase or a summary
- cite statistics, tables, charts, or graphs

You do not need to document these types of information:

- your own observations, experiences, and ideas
- factual information available in a number of reference works (known as "common knowledge")
- proverbs, sayings, and familiar quotations

A reference to the source of your borrowed information is called a *citation.* There are many systems for making citations, and your citations must consistently follow one of these systems. As noted earlier, the documentation style recommended by the Modern Language Association (MLA) is commonly used in English and the humanities and is the style used throughout this book. Another common system is the American Psychological Association (APA) style, which is generally used in the social sciences. Your instructor will usually tell you which style to use. For more information on documentation styles, consult the appropriate manual or handbook. For MLA style, consult the *MLA Handbook for Writers of Research Papers,* 5th ed. (New York: MLA, 1999). You may also check MLA guidelines on the Internet at <http://www.mla.org>.

There are two components of documentation: *in-text citations* are placed in the body of your paper; the *list of works cited* provides complete publication data for your in-text citations and is placed at the end of your paper. Both are necessary for complete documentation.

In-Text Citations

In-text citations, also known as parenthetical citations, give the reader citation information immediately, at the point at which it is most meaningful. Rather than having to turn to a footnote or an endnote, the reader sees the citation as a part of the writer's text.

Most in-text citations consist of only the author's last name and a page reference. Usually the author's name is given in an introductory or signal phrase at the beginning of the borrowed material and the page reference is given in parentheses at the end. If the author's name is not given at the beginning, put it in parentheses along with the page reference. The parenthetical reference signals the end of the borrowed material and directs your readers to the list of works cited should they want to pursue a particular source. Treat electronic sources as you do print sources, keeping in mind that some electronic sources use paragraph numbers instead of page numbers. Consider the following examples of in-text citations, which are from a student paper.

IN-TEXT CITATION (MLA STYLE)

Americans are obsessed with thinness, even at the risk of dying. They have used hormone injections, amphetamines, and liquid protein, all in the name of looking good and feeling healthy. But, as Sallie Tisdale reveals, diet pills are not the answer: "They made me feel strange, half-crazed, vaguely nauseated. [. . .] [W]ith every passing week I also grew more depressed and irritable" (50). The obsession has also taken on a moral dimension. As another social commentator has noted, "[T]here's a difference between health and health<u>ism</u>, between health as a reasonable goal and health as a transcendent value" (Ehrenreich 101).

Citation with author's name in the signal phrase

Citation with author's name in parentheses

What follows are the ways in which the preceding in-text citations should appear in the list of works cited at the end of the essay.

LIST OF WORKS CITED ENTRIES (MLA STYLE)

Ehrenreich, Barbara. "The Naked Truth about Fitness." <u>The Snarling</u>

<u>Citizen</u>. New York: Farrar, 1995.

Tisdale, Sallie. "A Weight That Women Carry." <u>Harper's</u> Mar. 1993: 49–55.

List of Works Cited

In this section you will find general MLA guidelines for creating a works cited list followed by sample entries that cover the citation situations you will encounter most often. Make sure that you follow the formats as they appear on the following pages.

GENERAL GUIDELINES

- Begin the list on a new page following the last page of text.
- Organize the list alphabetically by author's last name. If the entry has no author name, alphabetize the first major word of the title.
- Double-space within and between entries.
- Begin each entry at the left margin. If the entry is longer than one line, indent the second and subsequent lines five spaces or one-half inch.
- Do not number entries.

Books

BOOKS BY ONE AUTHOR

List the author's last name first, followed by a comma and first name. Underline the title. Follow with the city of publication and a shortened version of publisher's name—for example, *Houghton* for *Houghton Mifflin,* or *Cambridge UP* for *Cambridge University Press.* End with the date of publication.

Pinker, Steven. <u>The Language Instinct: How the Mind Creates Language</u>.
  New York: Morrow, 1994.

BOOKS BY TWO OR THREE AUTHORS

List the first author (following order on title page) in the same way as for a single-author book; list subsequent authors first name first in the order they appear on the title page.

Young Bear, Severt, and R. D. Theisz. <u>Standing in the Light: A Lokata</u>
  <u>Way of Seeing</u>. Lincoln: U of Nebraska P, 1994.

BOOKS BY FOUR OR MORE AUTHORS

List the first author in the same way as for a single-author book, followed by a comma and the abbreviation *et al.* ("and others").

Morris, Desmond, et al. <u>Gesture Maps</u>. London: Cape, 1978.

TWO OR MORE BOOKS BY THE SAME AUTHOR

List two or more books by the same author in alphabetical order by title. List the first book by the author's name. After the first book, in place of the author's name substitute three unspaced hyphens followed by a period.

Lederer, Richard. Anguished English. Charleston: Wyrick, 1987.

---.Crazy English: New York: Pocket Books, 1990.

REVISED EDITION

Hassan, Ihab. The Dismemberment of Orpheus: Toward a Postmodern

Literature. 2nd ed. Madison: U of Wisconsin P, 1982.

EDITED BOOK

Douglass, Frederick. Narrative of the Life of Frederick Douglass, an

American Slave, Written by Himself. Ed. Benjamin Quarles.

Cambridge: Belknap, 1960.

TRANSLATION

Ueda, Akinari. Tales of Moonlight and Rain: Japanese Gothic Tales. Trans.

Kengi Hamada. New York: Columbia UP, 1972.

ANTHOLOGY

Rosa, Alfred, and Paul Eschholz, eds. Language: Readings in Culture and

Language. 5th ed. New York: St. Martin's, 1998.

WORK IN AN ANTHOLOGY

Lutz, William. "Types of Doublespeak." Subjects/Strategies. Ed. Paul

Eschholz and Alfred Rosa. 8th ed. Boston: Bedford, 1999. 366–70.

SECTION OR CHAPTER IN A BOOK

Carver, Raymond. "Why Don't You Dance?" What We Talk about when We

Talk about Love. New York: Knopf, 1981.

Periodicals

ARTICLE IN A JOURNAL WITH CONTINUOUS PAGINATION THROUGHOUT AN ANNUAL VOLUME

Some journals paginate issues continuously, by volume; that is, the page numbers in one issue pick up where the previous issue left off. For these journals, follow the volume number by the date of publication in parentheses.

Gazzaniga, Michael S. "Right Hemisphere Language Following Brain

Bisection: A Twenty-Year Perspective." American Psychologist 38

(1983): 528–49.

ARTICLE IN A JOURNAL WITH SEPARATE PAGINATION IN EACH ISSUE

Some journals paginate by issue; each issue begins with page 1. For these journals, follow the volume number with a period and the issue number. Then give the date of publication in parentheses.

Douglas, Ann. "The Failure of the New York Intellectuals." Raritan 17.4

(1998): 1–23.

ARTICLE IN A WEEKLY OR BIWEEKLY MAGAZINE

Delbanco, Andrew. "On Alfred Kazin (1915–1998)." New York Review of

Books 16 July 1998: 22.

ARTICLE IN A NEWSPAPER

If an article in a newspaper or magazine appears discontinuously — that is, if it starts on one page and skips one or more pages before continuing — include only the first page followed by a plus sign.

Faison, Seth. "President Arrives in Shanghai; Focuses on Talk with

Citizens." New York Times 30 June 1998, late ed.: A1+.

EDITORIAL OR LETTER TO THE EDITOR

"The Court Vetoes Line Item." Editorial. New York Times 26 June 1998,

late ed.: A32.

Gitter, Elizabeth. Letter. New York Times 28 June 1998, late ed., sec. 4: 16.

Internet Sources

When listing sources from the Internet or the World Wide Web, give the title of the project or database and underline it. Also include the editor, if available. Give the date of publication or date of latest update, if available, the name of any sponsoring institution, and the date you

accessed the source. The Universal Resource Locator, or URL, which is
the address of the source, appears in angle brackets at the end of the
entry.

SCHOLARLY PROJECT

Project Gutenberg. Ed. Michael Hart. 1998. 15 June 1999
     <http://promo.net/pg>.

PROFESSIONAL SITE

MLA on the Web. Modern Language Association. 6 May 1998. 15 July 1999
     <http://www.mla.org>.

PERSONAL SITE

Rosa, Alfred. English 104: Language Awareness. 15 July 1999
     <http://www.uvm.edu/~arosa/1041a.htm>.

BOOK

Whitman, Walt. Leaves of Grass. 1900. Project Bartleby. Ed. Steven van
     Leeuwen. Feb. 1994. Columbia U. 30 Jan. 1998
     <http://www.columbia.edu/acis/bartleby/whitman>.

POEM

Blake, William. "London." The William Blake Page. Ed. Richard Record. 25
     Feb. 1998 <http://members.aa.net/~urizen/experience/soe.html>.

ARTICLE IN A JOURNAL

Kallen, Evelyn. "Hate on the Net: A Question of Rights/A Question of
     Power." Electronic Journal of Sociology 3.2 (1997). 1 July 1999
     <http://www.sociology.org/vol003.002/kallen.article.1997.html>.

ARTICLE IN A NEWSPAPER

Broder, David S. "Quayle to Pull Out of GOP Race." Washington Post 27
     Sept. 1999. 27 Sept. 1999 <http://washington.com/wp-srv/
     politics/campaign/wh2000/stories/quayle/092799.html>.

Other Sources

TELEVISION OR RADIO PROGRAM

The American Experience: Chicago 1968. Writ. Chana Gazit. Narr. W. S.

Merwin. PBS. WNET, New York, 13 Nov. 1997.

MOVIE, VIDEOTAPE, RECORD, OR SLIDE PROGRAM

The X Files. Dir. Rob Bowman. Perf. David Duchovny, Gillian Anderson,

Martin Landau, Blythe Danner, and Armin Mueller-Stahl. Twentieth

Century Fox, 1998.

PERSONAL INTERVIEW

Alameno, Joseph. Personal interview. 15 Apr. 1998.

LECTURE

Losambe, Lokangaka. Lecture. English 104. U of Vermont Department of

English, Burlington, 8 Apr. 1998.

A NOTE ON PLAGIARISM

The importance of honesty and accuracy in doing research can't be stressed enough. Any material borrowed word-for-word must be placed within quotation marks and be properly cited; any idea, explanation, or argument you have paraphrased or summarized must be documented, and it must be clear where the borrowed material begins and ends. In short, to use someone else's ideas, whether in their original form or in an altered form, without proper acknowledgment is to be guilty of plagiarism. And plagiarism is plagiarism even if it is accidental. A little attention and effort at the note-taking stage can help you eliminate the possibility of inadvertent plagiarism. Check all direct quotations against the wording of the original, and double-check your paraphrases to be sure that you have not used the writer's wording or sentence structure. It is easy to forget to put quotation marks around material taken verbatim or to use a writer's sentence structure and most of his or her words—and record it as a paraphrase. In working closely with the ideas and words of others, intellectual honesty demands that you distinguish between what you borrow—and therefore acknowledge in a citation—and what is your own.

WRITING FROM RESEARCH:
AN ANNOTATED STUDENT ESSAY

Each semester in our "Language Awareness" course at the University of Vermont, we ask students to write papers in which they take a position on a language issue. One student, Jake Jamieson, decided to write on the English-only movement, and what follows is his essay. To help you get more out of Jake's essay, we have provided Jake's comments about his writing process and our annotations pointing out the composition strategies he used.

Why did I choose this topic? I chose this topic on which to do my paper because it is an aspect of speech that I had not previously explored, and my interest was piqued when I heard Professor Rosa speak of it during class. I have done research before on aspects of free speech and people who are attempting to restrict it, but I had never really looked into this issue. After doing some reading on the subject, I realized that it absolutely intrigued me, from the prospect of banning languages other than English right down to the question of funding for bilingualism. It is hard for me to believe that this type of legislation can be construed as helpful and inclusive, when it is merely showcasing ignorance and fear of what is different. It is an outright lie to say that this kind of legislation is intended to include immigrants. In actuality, all it is doing is driving a wedge between immigrants and "mainstream" society, forcing the immigrants to choose between their heritage and their newfound home.

The English-Only Movement: Can America
Proscribe Language with a Clean Conscience?

Jake Jamieson

Melting pot
debate
announced

A common conception among many people in this country is that the United States is a giant cultural "melting pot." For these people, the melting pot is a place where people from other places come together and bathe in the warm waters of assimilation. For many others, however, the melting pot analogy doesn't work. They see the melting pot as a giant cauldron into which immigrants are placed; here their cultures, values, and backgrounds are boiled away in the scalding waters of discrimination.

Asks question to
be answered in
paper

One major point of contention in this debate is language: Should immigrants be pushed toward learning English or encouraged to retain their native tongues?

I chose the melting pot analogy in this paragraph because I liked the way in which I was able to turn its normal, comfortable meaning on its head. The connotation was changed from something that was acceptable and even desirable to something that was frightening and even oppressive, which is how I see the melting pot.

Those who argue that the melting pot analogy is valid believe that people who come to America do so willingly and should be expected to become a part of its culture instead of hanging on to their past. For them, the expectation that people who come to this country celebrate this country's holidays, dress as we do, embrace our values, and most importantly speak our language is not unreasonable. They believe that assimilation offers the only way for everyone in this country to live together in harmony and the only way to dissipate the tensions that inevitably arise when cultures clash. A major problem with this argument, however, is that no one seems to be able to agree on what exactly constitutes "our way" of doing things.

I definitely chose a side in this paragraph, but I tried to do so fairly subtly. Even though I was trying to be persuasive in this paper, I did not just come out and say "English-only legislation is stupid." Instead, what I did was describe the opinion to which I am opposed, and then pulled the rug out from under it a bit by stating that there was no objective way to decide what "our way" of living is.

Defines English as the official language

Not everyone in America is of the same religious persuasion or has the exact same set of values, and different people affect vastly different styles of dress. There are so many sets of variables that it would be hard to defend the argument that there is only one culture in the United States. What seems to be the most widespread constant in our country is that much of the population speaks English, and a major movement is being staged in favor of making English the official language. Making English America's official language would, according to William F. Buckley, involve making it the only language in which government business can be conducted on any level, from federal dealings right down to the local level (16). Many reasons are given to support the notion that making English the official language is a good idea and that it is exactly what this country needs, especially in the face of growing multilingualism. Indeed, one Los Angeles school recently documented sixty different languages spoken in the homes of its students (National Education Association, par. 4).

Use of in-text MLA citation format which includes introductory signal phrase and parenthetical page number

There were many reasons given for supporting official English, and I state some of them in the next paragraph. It was hard to choose only a few of these reasons. I paged through my research notes and the articles I had and noted those that made me raise an eyebrow or throw up my hands in frustration. These, I decided, were the examples I would use.

Introduces
English-only
position   Supporters of English-only contend that all government communication must be in English. Because communication is absolutely necessary for a democracy to
survive, they believe that the only way to insure the existence of our nation is to make sure a common language exists. Making English official would insure that
all government business from ballots to official forms to
judicial hearings would have to be conducted in English.
According to former senator and presidential candidate
Bob Dole, "Promoting English as our national language is
not an act of hostility but a welcoming act of inclusion."
He goes on to state that while immigrants are encouraged to continue speaking their native languages, "thousands of children [are] failing to learn the language,
English, that is the ticket to the 'American Dream.'"
(qtd. In Donegan 52).

I found Mr. Dole's comment in an article I read during my research. It seemed to exemplify the exact opinion that I was railing against. His name recognition helps to emphasize the pervasiveness of such thinking.

Introduces
anti-English-
only position   For those who do not subscribe to this way of thinking, however, this type of legislation is anything but the
"welcoming act of inclusion" that it is described to be. For
them, anyone attempting to regulate language is treading
dangerously close to the First Amendment and must have
a hidden agenda of some type. Why, it is asked, make a
language official when it is already firmly entrenched
and widely used in this country and, according to GAO
statistics, 99.96 percent of all federal documents are
already in English without legislation to mandate it
(Underwood, par. 2)? According to author James
Crawford, the answer is quite plain: discrimination.
He states that "it is certainly more respectable to discriminate by language than by race." He points out that
"most people are not sensitive to language discrimination
in this nation, so it is easy to argue that you're doing
someone a favor by making them speak English" (51).
English-only legislation has been described as bigoted,
anti-immigrant, mean-spirited, and steeped in nativism
by those who oppose it, and some go so far as to say that
this type of legislation will not foster better communication as is the claim, but will instead encourage a "fear of
being subsumed by a growing 'foreignness' in our midst"
(Mujica and Underwood 65).

The main reason that I waited before introducing the viewpoint with which I obviously agree is simple: I'm bloodthirsty. I like to set up the opposition, examine it for a moment, and then cut it off at the knees. I have found that this technique has worked for me in many situations in which I was trying to write subjectively or persuasively. I then explain the opinion I endorse, discuss it, and then bring in facts that support it much more strongly and try to win over the reader. I have found it to be a more effective technique than coming on strong with my own opinion from the outset.

Uses example to question English-only position that speaking Spanish in the home is abusive

For example, when a judge in Texas ruled that a mother was abusing her five-year-old girl by speaking to her only in Spanish, an uproar ensued. This ruling was accompanied by the statement that by talking to her in a language other than English, she was "abusing that child and [. . .] relegating her to the position of house maid." This statement was condemned by the National Association for Bilingual Education (NABE) for "labeling the Spanish language as abuse." The judge, Samuel C. Kiser, subsequently apologized to the housekeepers of the nation, adding that he held them "in the highest esteem," but stood firm on his ruling (Donegan 51). One might notice that he went out of his way to apologize to the housekeepers he might have offended but saw no need to apologize to the hundreds of thousands of Spanish speakers whose language had just been belittled in a nationally publicized case.

Every time I mentioned this case to someone, they would roll their eyes and groan. Even people who do not agree with my stand on this topic agree with the fact that this judge was out of line.

Argues against the English-only idea of multilingualism as irrational

This tendency of official-English proponents to put down other languages is one that shows up again and again, even though it is maintained that they have nothing against other languages or the people who speak them. If there is no malice toward other languages, why is the use of any language other than English tantamount to lunacy according to an almost constant barrage of literature and editorial opinions? In a recent publication of the "New Year's Resolutions" of various conservative organizations, a group called U.S. English, Inc. stated that the U.S. government was not doing its job of convincing immigrants that they "must learn English to succeed in this country." Instead, according to this publication, "in a bewildering display of irrationality, the U.S. government makes it possible to vote, file a tax return, get married, obtain a driver's license, and become a U.S. citizen in many languages." (Moore 46)

As I stated earlier, I choose my examples based on the reactions they bring up in myself and the people I share them with. This quote by U.S. English actually made my stomach churn because the connotation is that those who speak other languages are undeserving of such things as being able to vote or get a driver's license, or even stay in this country.

Asks rhetorical
questions

　　Now, according to this mindset, not only is speaking any language other than English abusive, but it is also irrational and bewildering. What is this world coming to when people want to speak and make transactions in their native language? Why do they refuse to change and become more like us? Why can immigrants not see that speaking English is right and anything else is wrong? These and many other questions are implied by official-English proponents as they discuss the issue.

I have always enjoyed using these kinds of rhetorical questions, and I was excited when I got a chance to sneak them into this paper, lampooning the air of superiority and unwillingness to accept difference that seem to fill the English-only viewpoint.

Points to
growing
popularity of
English-only
position

　　Conservative attorney David Price wrote that official-English legislation is a good idea because many English-speaking Americans prefer "out of pride and convenience to speak their native language on the job" (13). Not only does this statement imply that the pride and convenience of non-English-speaking Americans is unimportant, but that their native tongues are not as important as English. The scariest prospect of all is that this opinion is quickly gaining popularity all around the country.

In this paragraph, I wanted to show the only convenience on the minds of English-only proponents was their own and that of people like them. The fact that this opinion can be couched in terms that make it seem like a favor is being done for non-English speakers blows my mind.

Presents status
report of
English-only
legislation

　　As of early 1996, six official-English bills and one amendment to the Constitution have been proposed in the House and Senate. There are twenty-two states, including Alabama, California, and Arizona, that have made English their official language, and more are debating it every day (Donegan 92). An especially disturbing fact about this debate is that official-English laws always seem to be linked to other anti-immigrant legislation, such as proposals to "limit immigration and restrict government benefits to immigrants" ("English-Only Law Faces Test" 1).

As I was writing this paper, it seemed that this topic showed up everywhere I turned. It came up in many of my classes. There were endless stories about it on the evening news. I have found that the best way to research for something like this is not just to pore over books and articles, but also watch the news and have discussions with people, and see what can be found out about it in other ways. This paragraph was the only place that I used facts and figures to state exactly what was happening around the country instead of just speaking of the entire issue on more general terms. I actually wish that I had spent more time with this information because I think that it might have made this part of the paper more convincing.

Concludes that
English-only
legislation is
not in our
best interest

Although official-English proponents maintain that their bid for language legislation is in the best interest of immigrants, the facts tend to show otherwise. A decision has to be made in this country about what kind of message we will send to the rest of the world. Do we plan to allow everyone in this country the freedom of speech that we profess to cherish, or will we decide to reserve it only for those who speak the same language as we do? Will we hold firm to our belief that everyone is deserving of life, liberty, and the pursuit of happiness in this country? Or will we show the world that we believe in these things only when they pertain to ourselves and people like us?

This may seem self-evident, but I have always felt that the two most important things about a paper are the opening and closing paragraphs. The other stuff in the middle is important as well, of course, but I think that the opening paragraph is necessary to draw readers in, and the closing paragraph is needed to give the reader a sense of closure. I like my closing paragraph, and I hope that it brought my closing point across effectively.

Works Cited

Follows MLA
citation
guidelines

Buckley, William F. "Se Hable Ingles: English as the Offi-
        cial American Language." National Review 9 Oct.
        1995: 70–71.

Donegan, Craig. "Debate over Bilingualism: Should English
        Be the Nation's Official Language?" CQ Researcher
        19 Jan. 1996: 51–71.

"English-Only Law Faces Test." Burlington Free Press 26
        Mar. 1996: 1.

Moore, Stephen, et al. "New Year's Resolutions." National
        Review 29 Jan. 1996: 46–48.

Mujica, Mauro, and Robert Underwood. "Should English Be the Official Language of the United States?" CQ Researcher 19 Jan. 1996: 65.

National Education Association. "NEA Statement on the Debate over English Only." Teacher's College, U. of Nebraska, Lincoln. 27 Sept. 1999 <http://www.tc.unl .edu/enemeth/biling/engonly.html>.

Price, David. "English-Only Rules: EEOC Has Gone Too Far." USA Today 28 Mar. 1996, final ed.: A13.

Underwood, Robert A. "English-Only Legislation." U.S. House of Representatives, Washington, D.C., 28 Nov. 1995. 26 Sept. 1999 <http://www.house.gov/ underwood/speeches/english.htm>.

5

COMING TO TERMS
WITH LANGUAGE

Coming to an Awareness of Language

MALCOLM X

On February 21, 1965, Malcolm X, the Black Muslim leader, was shot to death as he addressed an afternoon rally in Harlem. He was thirty-nine years old. In the course of his brief life, he had risen from a world of thieving, pimping, and drug pushing to become one of the most articulate and powerful African Americans in the United States during the early 1960s. In 1992 his life was reexamined in Spike Lee's film Malcolm X. *With the assistance of the late Alex Haley, the author of* Roots, *Malcolm X told his story in* The Autobiography of Malcolm X *(1964), a moving account of his search for fulfillment. This selection is taken from the* Autobiography.*

All of us have been in situations in which we have felt somehow betrayed by our language, unable to find just the right words to express ourselves. "Words," as lexicographer Bergen Evans has said, "are the tools for the job of saying what you want to say." As our repertoire of words expands so does our ability to express ourselves—to articulate clearly our thoughts, feelings, hopes, fears, likes, and dislikes. Frustration at not being able to express himself in the letters he wrote drove Malcolm X to the dictionary, where he discovered the power of words.

WRITING TO DISCOVER: *Write about a time when someone told you that it is important to have a good vocabulary. What did you think when you heard this advice? Why do you think people believe that vocabulary is important? How would you assess your own vocabulary?*

I've never been one for inaction. Everything I've ever felt strongly about, I've done something about. I guess that's why, unable to do anything else, I soon began writing to people I had known in the hustling world, such as Sammy the Pimp, John Hughes, the gambling house owner, the thief Jumpsteady, and several dope peddlers. I wrote them all about Allah and Islam and Mr. Elijah Muhammad. I had no idea where most of them lived. I addressed their letters in care of the Harlem or Roxbury bars and clubs where I'd known them.

I never got a single reply. The average hustler and criminal was too uneducated to write a letter. I have known many slick sharp-looking hustlers, who would have you think they had an interest in Wall Street; privately, they would get someone else to read a letter if they received one. Besides, neither would I have replied to anyone writing me something as wild as "the white man is the devil."

What certainly went on the Harlem and Roxbury wires was that Detroit Red was going crazy in stir,* or else he was trying some hype to shake up the warden's office.

During the years that I stayed in the Norfolk Prison Colony, never did any official directly say anything to me about those letters, although, of course, they all passed through the prison censorship. I'm sure, however, they monitored what I wrote to add to the files which every state and federal prison keeps on the conversion of Negro inmates by the teachings of Mr. Elijah Muhammad.

But at that time, I felt that the real reason was that the white man   5
knew that he was the devil.

Later on, I even wrote to the Mayor of Boston, to the Governor of Massachusetts, and to Harry S. Truman. They never answered; they probably never even saw my letters. I handscratched to them how the white man's society was responsible for the black man's condition in this wilderness of North America.

It was because of my letters that I happened to stumble upon starting to acquire some kind of homemade education.

I became increasingly frustrated at not being able to express what I wanted to convey in letters that I wrote, especially those to Mr. Elijah Muhammad. In the street, I had been the most articulate hustler out there — I had commanded attention when I said something. But now, trying to write simple English, I not only wasn't articulate, I wasn't even functional. How would I sound writing in slang, the way I would *say* it, something such as, "Look daddy, let me pull your coat about a cat. Elijah Muhammad — "

Many who today hear me somewhere in person, or on television, or those who read something I've said, will think I went to school far beyond the eighth grade. This impression is due entirely to my prison studies.

---

*Slang for being in jail.

It had really begun back in the Charlestown Prison, when Bimbi first   10
made me feel envy of his stock of knowledge. Bimbi had always taken
charge of any conversation he was in, and I had tried to emulate him. But
every book I picked up had few sentences which didn't contain anywhere
from one to nearly all of the words that might as well have been in Chinese.
When I just skipped those words, of course, I really ended up with little idea
of what the book said. So I had come to the Norfolk Prison Colony still
going through only book-reading motions. Pretty soon, I would have quit
even these motions, unless I had received the motivation that I did.

I saw that the best thing I could do was get hold of a dictionary — to
study, to learn some words. I was lucky enough to reason also that I should
try to improve my penmanship. It was sad. I couldn't even write in a straight
line. It was both ideas together that moved me to request a dictionary along
with some tablets and pencils from the Norfolk Prison Colony school.

I spent two days just riffling uncertainly through the dictionary's
pages. I'd never realized so many words existed! I didn't know *which*
words I needed to learn. Finally, just to start some kind of action, I began
copying.

In my slow, painstaking, ragged handwriting, I copied into my tablet
everything printed on that first page, down to the punctuation marks.

I believe it took me a day. Then, aloud, I read back, to myself, everything I'd written on the tablet. Over and over, aloud, to myself, I read
my own handwriting.

I woke up the next morning, thinking about those words — im-   15
mensely proud to realize that not only had I written so much at one time,
but I'd written words that I never knew were in the world. Moreover,
with a little effort, I also could remember what many of these words
meant. I reviewed the words whose meanings I didn't remember. Funny
thing, from the dictionary's first page right now, that "aardvark" springs
to my mind. The dictionary had a picture of it, a long-tailed, long-eared,
burrowing African mammal, which lives off termites caught by sticking
out its tongue as an anteater does for ants.

I was so fascinated that I went on — I copied the dictionary's next page.
And the same experience came when I studied that. With every succeeding
page, I also learned of people and places and events from history. Actually
the dictionary is like a miniature encyclopedia. Finally the dictionary's A
section had filled a whole tablet — and I went on into the B's. That was the
way I started copying what eventually became the entire dictionary. It went
a lot faster after so much practice helped me pick up handwriting speed. Between what I wrote in my tablet, and writing letters, during the rest of my
time in prison I would guess I wrote a million words.

I suppose it was inevitable that as my word-base broadened, I could
for the first time pick up a book and read and now begin to understand
what the book was saying. Anyone who has read a great deal can imagine
the new world that opened. Let me tell you something: from then until I

left that prison, in every free moment I had, if I was not reading in the library, I was reading on my bunk. You couldn't have gotten me out of books with a wedge. Between Mr. Muhammad's teachings, my correspondence, my visitors . . . and my reading of books, months passed without my even thinking about being imprisoned. In fact, up to then, I never had been so truly free in my life.

FOCUSING ON CONTENT

1. What motivated Malcolm X "to acquire some kind of homemade education" (7)?

2. For many, *vocabulary building* means learning strange, multisyllabic, difficult-to-spell words. But acquiring an effective vocabulary does not need to be any of these things. What, for you, constitutes an effective vocabulary? How would you characterize Malcolm X's vocabulary in this passage? Do you find his word choice appropriate for his purpose? (Glossary: *Purpose*) Explain.

3. What is the nature of the freedom that Malcolm X refers to in the final sentence? In what sense is language liberating? Is it possible for people to be "prisoners" of their own language? Explain.

FOCUSING ON WRITING

1. In paragraph 8, Malcolm X remembers thinking how he would "sound writing in slang" and feeling inadequate because he recognized how slang or street talk limited his options. (Glossary: *Slang*) In what kinds of situations is slang useful and appropriate? When is Standard English more appropriate? (Glossary: *Standard English*)

2. In paragraph 8, Malcolm X describes himself as having been "the most articulate hustler out there" but in writing he says he "wasn't even functional." What differences between speaking and writing could account for such a discrepancy? How does the tone of this essay help you understand Malcolm X's dilemma? (Glossary: *Tone*)

3. Malcolm X narrates his experience as a prisoner using the first-person pronoun *I*. Why is the first person particularly appropriate? What would be lost or gained had he told his story using the third-person pronoun *he*? (Glossary: *Point of View*)

LANGUAGE IN ACTION

Many newspapers carry regular vocabulary-building columns, and the *Reader's Digest* has for many years included a section called "It Pays to Enrich Your Word Power." You might enjoy taking the following quiz, which is excerpted from the April 1999 issue of *Reader's Digest*.

IT PAYS TO ENRICH YOUR
WORD POWER

Zeus and his thunderbolts, Thor and his hammer, Medusa and her power to turn flesh into stone: these are all fascinating figures in mythology and folklore. Associated with such legends are words we use today, including the 10 selected below.

1. **panic** *n.*—A: pain. B: relief. C: mess. D: fear.

2. **bacchanal** *(BAK ih NAL) n.*— A: drunken party. B: graduation ceremony. C: backache remedy. D: victory parade.

3. **puckish** *adj.*—A: wrinkly. B: quirky. C: quarrelsome. D: mischievous.

4. **cyclopean** *(SIGH klo PEA en) adj.*—A: wise. B: gigantic. C: wealthy. D: repetitious.

5. **hector** *v.*—A: to curse. B: bully. C: disown. D: injure.

6. **cupidity** *(kyoo PID ih tee) n.*— A: thankfulness. B: ignorance. C: abundance. D: desire.

7. **mnemonic** *(knee MON ik) adj.*— pertaining to A: memory. B: speech. C: hearing. D: sight.

8. **stygian** *(STIJ ee an) adj.*—A: stingy. B: hellish. C: uncompromising. D: dirty.

9. **narcissistic** *adj.*—A: indecisive. B: very sleepy. C: very vain. D: just.

10. **zephyr** *(ZEF er) n.*—A: breeze. B: dog. C: horse. D: tornado.

ANSWERS:

1. **panic**— *[D]* Fear; widespread terror; as, An outbreak of Ebola led to *panic* in the small village. *Pan,* frightening Greek god of nature.

2. **bacchanal**— *[A]* Drunken party; orgy; as, Complaints to the police broke up the *bacchanal. Bacchus,* Roman god of wine.

3. **puckish**— *[D]* Mischievous; prankish. *Puck,* a trick-loving sprite or fairy.

4. **cyclopean**— *[B]* Gigantic; huge; as, the *cyclopean* home runs of Mark McGwire. *Cyclopes,* a race of fierce, one-eyed giants.

5. **hector**— *[B]* To bully; threaten. *Hector,* Trojan leader slain by Achilles and portrayed as a bragging menace in some dramas.

6. **cupidity**— *[D]* Strong desire. *Cupid,* Roman god of love.

7. **mnemonic**— *[A]* Pertaining to memory; as "Spring forward and fall back" is a *mnemonic* spur to change time twice a year. *Mnemosyne,* Greek goddess of memory.

8. **stygian**— *[B]* Hellish; dark and gloomy. *Styx,* a river in Hades.

9. **narcissistic**— *[C]* Very vain; self-loving; as, The *narcissistic* actress preened for the photographers. *Narcissus,* a youth who fell in love with his own reflection.

10. **zephyr**— *[A]* Soft breeze; as, The storm tapered off to a *zephyr. Zephyrus,* gentle Greek god of the west wind.

Are you familiar with most of the words on the quiz? Did some of the answers surprise you? In your opinion, is the level of difficulty appropriate for the *Reader's Digest* audience? What does the continuing popularity of vocabulary-building features suggest about the attitudes of many Americans toward language?

WRITING SUGGESTIONS

1. (*Writing from Experience*) All of us have been in situations in which our ability to use language seemed inadequate—for example, when taking an exam; being interviewed for a job; giving directions; or expressing sympathy, anger, or grief. Write a brief essay in which you recount one such frustrating incident in your life. Before beginning to write, review your reactions to Malcolm X's frustrations with his limited vocabulary. Share your experiences with your classmates.

2. (*Writing from Reading*) What do you usually do when you encounter a new word in your reading? Do you skip those words as Malcolm X once did, or do you take the time to look them up in a dictionary or try to figure out the meaning from the context? Carefully read the following passage from Lincoln's "Gettysburg Address," paying particular attention to his use of the words *dedicate, consecrate,* and *hallow.*

   > But, in a larger sense, we can not dedicate—we can not consecrate—we cannot hallow—this ground. The brave men, living and dead, who struggled here, have consecrated it, far above our poor power to add or detract. This world will little note, nor long remember what we say here, but it can never forget what they did here.

   Can you determine the meanings of *dedicate, consecrate,* and *hallow* from their context in the passage? For which word(s) will you need to consult a dictionary? Using your own words, write a clear definition of each one. What part of Lincoln's message would you miss if you didn't understand the precise meaning of each of these words?

3. (*Writing from Research*) Malcolm X solved the problem of his own illiteracy by carefully studying the dictionary. Would this be a viable solution to the national problem of illiteracy? Are there more practical alternatives to Malcolm X's approach? What, for example, is being done in your community to combat illiteracy? What are some of the more successful approaches being used in other parts of the country? Write a brief essay about the problem of illiteracy. In addition to using your library for research, you may want to check out the Internet to see what it has to offer.

The Day Language Came into My Life

HELEN KELLER

Helen Keller (1880–1968) became blind and deaf at the age of eighteen months as a result of a disease. As a child, then, Keller be- came accustomed to her limited world for it was all that she knew. She experienced only certain fundamental sensations, such as the warmth of the sun on her face, and few emotions, such as anger and bitterness. It wasn't until she was almost seven years old that her family hired Anne Sullivan, a young woman who would turn out to be an extraordinary teacher, to help her. As Keller learned to communicate and think, the world opened up to her. She recorded her experiences in an autobiography, The Story of My Life *(1903), from which the following selection is taken.*

Helen Keller is in a unique position to remind us of what it is like to pass from the "fog" of prethought into the world where "everything has a name, and each name gave birth to a new thought." Her experiences as a deaf and blind child also raise a number of questions about the relationship between language and thought, emotions, ideas, and memory. Over time, Keller's acquisi- tion of language allowed her to assume all the advantages of her birthright. Her rapid intellectual and emotional growth as a result of language suggests that we, too, have the potential to achieve a greater measure of our humanity by further refining our language abilities.

WRITING TO DISCOVER: *Consider what your life would be like today if you had been born without the ability to understand lan- guage or speak or if you had suddenly lost the ability to use lan- guage later in life. Write about those aspects of your life that you think would be affected most severely.*

The most important day I remember in all my life is the one on which my teacher, Anne Mansfield Sullivan, came to me. I am filled with wonder when I consider the immeasurable contrast between the two lives which it connects. It was the third of March 1887, three months before I was seven years old.

On the afternoon of that eventful day, I stood on the porch, dumb, expectant. I guessed vaguely from my mother's signs and from the hurry- ing to and fro in the house that something unusual was about to happen, so I went to the door and waited on the steps. The afternoon sun pene- trated the mass of honeysuckle that covered the porch and fell on my up- turned face. My fingers lingered almost unconsciously on the familiar leaves and blossoms which had just come forth to greet the sweet

southern spring. I did not know what the future held of marvel or surprise for me. Anger and bitterness had preyed upon me continually for
weeks and a deep languor had succeeded this passionate struggle.

Have you ever been at sea in a dense fog, when it seemed as if a tangi-
ble white darkness shut you in, and the great ship, tense and anxious,
groped her way toward the shore with plummet and sounding-line, and
you waited with beating heart for something to happen? I was like that
ship before my education began, only I was without compass or sounding-
line and had no way of knowing how near the harbor was. "Light! give
me light!" was the wordless cry of my soul, and the light of love shone on
me in that very hour.

I felt approaching footsteps. I stretched out my hand as I supposed
to my mother. Someone took it, and I was caught up and held close in
the arms of her who had come to reveal all things to me, and, more than
all things else, to love me.

The morning after my teacher came she led me into her room and   5
gave me a doll. The little blind children at the Perkins Institution had
sent it and Laura Bridgman had dressed it; but I did not know this until
afterward. When I had played with it a little while, Miss Sullivan slowly
spelled into my hand the word "d-o-l-l." I was at once interested in this
finger play and tried to imitate it. When I finally succeeded in making the
letters correctly I was flushed with childhood pleasure and pride. Running downstairs to my mother I held up my hand and made the letters
for doll. I did not know that I was spelling a word or even that words existed; I was simply making my fingers go in monkeylike imitation. In the
days that followed I learned to spell in this uncomprehending way a great
many words, among them *pin, hat, cup* and a few verbs like *sit, stand* and
walk. But my teacher had been with me several weeks before I understood that everything has a name.

One day, while I was playing with my new doll, Miss Sullivan put my
big rag doll into my lap also, spelled "d-o-l-l" and tried to make me understand that "d-o-l-l" applied to both. Earlier in the day we had had a
tussle over the words "m-u-g" and "w-a-t-e-r." Miss Sullivan had tried to
impress it upon me that "m-u-g" is *mug* and that "w-a-t-e-r" is *water*,
but I persisted in confounding the two. In despair she had dropped the
subject for the time, only to renew it at the first opportunity. I became
impatient at her repeated attempts and, seizing the new doll, I dashed it
upon the floor. I was keenly delighted when I felt the fragments of the
broken doll at my feet. Neither sorrow nor regret followed my passionate
outburst. I had not loved the doll. In the still, dark world in which I lived
there was no strong sentiment or tenderness. I felt my teacher sweep the
fragments to one side of the hearth, and I had a sense of satisfaction that
the cause of my discomfort was removed. She brought me my hat, and I
knew I was going out into the warm sunshine. This thought, if a wordless
sensation may be called a thought, made me hop and skip with pleasure.

We walked down the path to the well-house, attracted by the fragrance of the honeysuckle with which it was covered. Some one was drawing water and my teacher placed my hand under the spout. As the cool stream gushed over one hand she spelled into the other the word *water*, first slowly, then rapidly. I stood still, my whole attention fixed upon the motions of her fingers. Suddenly I felt a misty consciousness as of something forgotten—a thrill of returning thought; and somehow the mystery of language was revealed to me. I knew then that "w-a-t-e-r" meant the wonderful cool something that was flowing over my hand. The living word awakened my soul, gave it light, hope, joy, set it free! There were barriers still, it is true, but barriers that could in time be swept away.

I left the well-house eager to learn. Everything had a name, and each name gave birth to a new thought. As we returned to the house every object which I touched seemed to quiver with life. That was because I saw everything with the strange, new sight that had come to me. On entering the door I remembered the doll I had broken. I felt my way to the hearth and picked up the pieces. I tried vainly to put them together. Then my eyes filled with tears; for I realized what I had done, and for the first time I felt repentance and sorrow.

I learned a great many new words that day. I do not remember what they all were; but I do know that *mother, father, sister, teacher* were among them—words that were to make the world blossom for me, "like Aaron's rod, with flowers." It would have been difficult to find a happier child than I was as I lay in my crib at the close of that eventful day and lived over the joys it had brought me, and for the first time longed for a new day to come.

FOCUSING ON CONTENT

1. In paragraph 6, Keller writes, "One day, while I was playing with my new doll, Miss Sullivan put my big rag doll into my lap also, spelled 'd-o-l-l' and tried to make me understand that 'd-o-l-l' applied to both." Why do you think Miss Sullivan placed a different doll in her lap? What essential fact about language did the action demonstrate to Keller?

2. In paragraph 6, Keller also tells us that in trying to learn the difference between "m-u-g" and "w-a-t-e-r" she "persisted in confounding the two" terms. In a letter to her home institution, Sullivan elaborated on this confusion, revealing that it was caused by Keller thinking that both words meant "drink." How in paragraph 7 does Keller finally come to understand these words? What does she come to understand about the relationship between them?

3. In paragraph 8, after the experience at the well, Keller comes to believe that "Everything had a name and each name gave birth to a new thought." Reflect on that statement. Does she mean that the process of naming leads to thinking?

FOCUSING ON WRITING

1. Keller realized that over time words would make her world open up for her. Identify the parts of speech of her first words. In what ways do these parts of speech open up one's world? Explain how these words or parts of speech provide insights into the nature of writing. How does Keller's early language use compare to her use of English in her essay?

2. While it is fairly easy to see how Keller could learn the names of concrete items, it may be more difficult for us to understand how she learned about her emotions. What does her difficulty in coming to terms with abstractions — such as love, bitterness, frustration, repentance, sorrow — tell us as writers about the strategies we need to use to effectively convey emotions and feelings to our readers? In considering your answer, examine the diction Keller uses in her essay. (Glossary: *Diction*)

3. In paragraph 3, Keller uses the metaphor of being lost in a fog to explain her feeling of helplessness and her frustration at not being able to communicate. Perhaps you have had a similar feeling about an inability to communicate with parents or teachers or of not being able to realize some other longed-for goal. Try using a fresh metaphor to describe feelings you might have had that are similar to Keller's. (Glossary: *Figures of Speech*) Before beginning, however, think about why the fog metaphor works so well.

LANGUAGE IN ACTION

A recent series of books by Rich Hall "and friends" gives lists of so-called *sniglets,* words for things without names. Notice that *sniglet* is itself a made-up word. Do you know of a person, place, thought, or action that is without a word but needs one? What word would you give it? What does the experience of "naming the unnamed" reveal about the desirability of an extensive vocabulary? What does it reveal about the possibilities and limitations of language? What do the following sniglets reveal about the authors' understanding of the world?

---

elbonics (*el bon′ iks*) n. The actions of two people maneuvering for one armrest in a movie theater.

glackett (*glak′ it*) n. The noisy ball inside a spray-paint can.

gription (*grip′ shun*) n. The sound of sneakers squeaking against the floor during basketball games.

hangle (*han′ gul*) n. A cluster of coat hangers.

lactomangulation (*lak′ to man gyu lay′ shun*) n. Manhandling the "open here" spout on a milk carton so badly that one has to resort to using the "illegal" side.

motspur (*mot′ sper*) n. The pesky fourth wheel on a shopping cart that refuses to cooperate with the other three.

napjerk (*nap′ jurk*) n. The sudden convulsion of the body just as one is about to doze off.

optortionist (*op tor' shun ist*) n. The kid in school who can turn his eyelids inside out.

psychophobia (*sy ko fo' be uh*) n. The compulsion, when using a host's bathroom, to peer behind the shower curtain and make sure no one is waiting for you.

xiidigitation (*ksi dij I tay' shun*) n. The practice of trying to determine the year a movie was made by deciphering the roman numerals at the end of the credits.

WRITING SUGGESTIONS

1. (*Writing from Experience*) It could be said that we process our world in terms of our language. Using a variety of examples from your own experience, write an essay illustrating the validity of this observation. For example, aside from the photographs you took on your last vacation, your trip exists only in the words you use to describe it, whether in conversations or in writing.

2. (*Writing from Reading*) Helen Keller explains that she felt no remorse when she shattered her doll. "In the still, dark world in which I lived there was no strong sentiment or tenderness" (6) she recalls. However, once she understood that things had names, Keller was able to feel repentance and sorrow. In your own words, try to describe why you think her feelings changed. Before you begin to write, you may want to reread your Writing to Discover entry for the Keller article. You may also want to discuss this issue with classmates or your instructor and do some research of your own into the ways language alters perception among people who are blind or deaf.

3. (*Writing from Research*) There has evolved in recent years considerable controversy in the deaf community at large. Some believe that if deafness could be cured, by medical or technological advances, then deaf people would become, in effect, no different from anyone else. Others, however, believe that a distinct deaf culture has evolved and that the culture has notable attributes apart from whether one can hear or not. Do some research into this controversy and write a paper with a thesis supporting one side or the other or a compromise view. (Glossary: *Thesis*)

Talking in the New Land

EDITE CUNHA

A native of Portugal, Edite Cunha moved with her family to Peabody, Massachusetts, when she was seven years old. In 1991 Cunha graduated from Smith College, where she was an Ada Comstock scholar. Later, she went on to earn an MFA degree in literature and creative writing at Warren Wilson College, and she now has her own business. Despite this success, her experiences in the United States were not always easy ones. Shortly after moving to Massachusetts, Cunha's first and middle names were changed by her elementary school teacher. Although her teacher may have viewed this as a helpful gesture, which would allow Cunha to fit into a new culture, the name change left the young girl feeling deprived of her personal identity. It also added to her difficulties in learning a new language.

Because of the challenges of a bilingual world, Cunha became her family's translator; being her father's "voice" was a responsibility she dreaded. As a consequence of her unusual childhood chore, Cunha learned far more about the conflict between cultures—and conflict in general—than she wanted to at an early age. In the following essay, which first appeared in the New England Monthly *in August 1990, Cunha recounts some of her early experiences in America.*

WRITING TO DISCOVER: *Imagine that you moved to a new country and had to adopt new first and middle names when you reached your destination. Write about what you would lose if you lost your name. What might you gain? How strongly do you identify with your name? Why?*

Before I started school in America I was Edite. Maria Edite dos Anjos Cunha. Maria, in honor of the Virigin Mary. In Portugal it was customary to use Maria as a religious and legal prefix to every girl's name. Virtually every girl was so named. It had something to do with the apparition of the Virgin to three shepherd children at Fatima. In naming their daughters Maria, my people were expressing their love and reverence for their Lady of Fatima.

Edite came from my godmother, Dona Edite Baetas Ruivo. The parish priest argued that I could not be named Edite because in Portugal the name was not considered Christian. But Dona Edite defended my right to bear her name. No one had argued with her family when they had christened her Edite. Her family had power and wealth. The priest considered privileges endangered by his stand, and I became Maria Edite.

The dos Anjos was for my mother's side of the family. Like her mother before her, she had been named Mario dos Anjos. And Cunha was for my father's side. Carlos dos Santos Cunha, son of Abilio dos Santos Cunha, the tailor from Saíl.

I loved my name. "Maria Edite dos Anjos Cunha," I'd recite at the least provocation. It was melodious and beautiful. And through it I knew exactly who I was.

At the age of seven I was taken from our little house in Sobreira, São   5
Martinho da Cortiça, Portugal, and brought to Peabody, Massachusetts. We moved into the house of Senhor João, who was our sponsor in the big land. I was in America for about a week when someone took me to school one morning and handed me over to the teacher, Mrs. Donahue.

Mrs. Donahue spoke Portuguese, a wondrous thing for a woman with a funny, unpronounceable name.

"Como é que te chamas?" she asked as she led me to a desk by big windows.

"Maria Edite dos Anjos Cunha," I recited, all the while scanning Mrs. Donahue for clues. How could a woman with such a name speak my language?

In fact, Mrs. Donahue was Portuguese. She was a Silva. But she had married an Irishman and changed her name. She changed my name, too, on the first day of school.

"Your name will be Mary Edith Cunha," she declared. "In America   10
you only need two or three names. Mary Edith is a lovely name. And it will be easier to pronounce."

My name was Edite. Maria Edite. Maria Edite dos Anjos Cunha. I had no trouble pronouncing it.

"Mary Edith, Edithhh, Mary Edithhh," Mrs. Donahue exaggerated it. She wrinkled up her nose and raised her upper lip to show me the proper positioning of the tongue for the *th* sound. She looked hideous. There was a big pain in my head. I wanted to scream out my name. But you could never argue with a teacher.

At home I cried and cried. *Mãe* and *Pai* wanted to know about the day. I couldn't pronounce the new name for them. Senhor João's red face wrinkled in laughter.

Day after day Mrs. Donahue made me practice pronouncing that name that wasn't mine. Mary Edithhhhh. Mary Edithhh. Mary Edithhh. But weeks later I still wouldn't respond when she called it out in class. Mrs. Donahue became cross when I didn't answer. Later my other teachers shortened it to Mary. And I never knew quite who I was. . . .

Mrs. Donahue was a small woman, not much bigger than my seven-   15
year-old self. Her graying hair was cut into a neat, curly bob. There was a smile that she wore almost every day. Not broad. Barely perceptible. But it was there, in her eyes, and at the corners of her mouth. She often wore

gray suits with jackets neatly fitted about the waist. On her feet she wore matching black leather shoes, tightly laced. Matching, but not identical. One of them had an extra-thick sole, because like all of her pupils, Mrs. Donahue had an oddity. We, the children, were odd because we were of different colors and sizes, and did not speak the accepted tongue. Mrs. Donahue was odd because she had legs of different lengths.

I grew to love Mrs. Donahue. She danced with us. She was the only teacher in all of Carroll School who thought it was important to dance. Every day after recess she took us all to the big open space at the back of the room. We stood in a circle and joined hands. Mrs. Donahue would blow a quivering note from the little round pitch pipe she kept in her pocket, and we became a twirling, singing wheel. Mrs. Donahue hobbled on her short leg and sang in a high trembly voice, "Here we go, loop-de-loop." We took three steps, then a pause. Her last "loop" was always very high. It seemed to squeak above our heads, bouncing on the ceiling. "Here we go, loop-de-lie." Three more steps, another pause, and on we whirled. "Here we go, loop-de-loop." Pause. "All on a Saturday night." To anyone looking in from the corridor we were surely an irregular sight, a circle of children of odd sizes and colors singing and twirling with our tiny hobbling teacher.

I'd been in Room Three with Mrs. Donahue for over a year when she decided that I could join the children in the regular elementary classes at Thomas Carroll School. I embraced the news with some ambivalence. By then the oddity of Mrs. Donahue's classroom had draped itself over me like a warm safe cloak. Now I was to join the second-grade class of Miss Laitinen. In preparation, Mrs. Donahue began a phase of relentless drilling. She talked to me about what I could expect in second grade. Miss Laitinen's class was well on its way with cursive writing, so we practiced that every day. We intensified our efforts with multiplication. And we practiced pronouncing the new teacher's name.

"Lay-te-nun." Mrs. Donahue spewed the *t* out with excessive force to demonstrate its importance. I had a tendency to forget it.

"Lay-nun."

"Mary Edith, don't be lazy. Use that tongue. It's Lay-te"—she   20
bared her teeth for the *t* part—"nun."

One morning with no warning, Mrs. Donahue walked me to the end of the hall and knocked on the door to Room Six. Miss Laitinen opened the door. She looked severe, carrying a long rubber-tipped pointer which she held horizontally before her with both hands. Miss Laitinen was a big, masculine woman. Her light, course hair was straight and cut short. She wore dark cardigans and very long, pleated plaid kilts that looked big enough to cover my bed.

"This is Mary Edith," Mrs. Donahue said. Meanwhile I looked at their shoes. Miss Laitinen wore flat, brown leather shoes that laced up and squeaked on the wooden floor when she walked. They matched each other perfectly, but they were twice as big as Mrs. Donahue's.

"Mary Edith, say hello to Miss Laitinen." Mrs. Donahue stressed the
t—a last-minute reminder.

"Hello, Miss Lay-te-nun," I said, leaning my head back to see her
face. Miss Laitinen was tall. Mrs. Donahue's head came just to her chest.
They both nodded approvingly before I was led to my seat.

Peabody, Massachusetts. "The Leather City." It is stamped on the   25
city seal, along with the image of a tanned animal hide. And Peabody, an
industrial city of less than fifty thousand people, has the smokestacks to
prove it. They rise up all over town from sprawling, dilapidated factories.
Ugly, leaning, wooden buildings that often stretch over a city block.
Strauss Tanning Co. A. C. Lawrence Leather Co. Gnecco & Grilk Tanning Corp. In the early sixties, the tanneries were in full swing. The jobs
were arduous and health-threatening, but it was the best-paying work
around for unskilled laborers who spoke no English. The huge, firetrap
factories were filled with men and women from Greece, Portugal, Ireland, and Poland.

In one of these factories, João Nunes, who lived on the floor above
us, fed animal skins into a ravenous metal monster all day, every day. The
pace was fast. One day the monster got his right arm and wouldn't let go.
When the machine was turned off João had a little bit of arm left below
his elbow. His daughter Teresa and I were friends. She didn't come out
of her house for many days. When she returned to school, she was very
quiet and cried a lot.

"Rosa Veludo's been hurt." News of such tragedies spread through the
community fast and often. People would tell what they had seen, or what
they had heard from those who had seen. *"She was taken to the hospital by
ambulance. Someone wrapped her fingers in a paper bag. The doctors may
be able to sew them back on."*

A few days after our arrival in the United States, my father went to
work at the Gnecco & Grilk leather tannery, on the corner of Howley
and Walnut streets. Senhor João had worked there for many years. He
helped *Pai* get the job. Gnecco & Grilk was a long, rambling, four-story
factory that stretched from the corner halfway down the street to the railroad tracks. The roof was flat and slouched in the middle like the back of
an old workhorse. There were hundreds of windows. The ones on the
ground were covered with a thick wire mesh.

Pai worked there for many months. He was stationed on the ground
floor, where workers often had to stand ankle-deep in water laden with
chemicals. One day he had a disagreement with his foreman. He left his
machine and went home vowing never to return. . . .

Pai and I stood on a sidewalk in Salem facing a clear glass doorway.   30
The words on the door were big. DIVISION OF EMPLOYMENT SECURITY.
There was a growing coldness deep inside me. At Thomas Carroll School,

Miss Laitinen was probably standing at the side blackboard, writing perfect alphabet letters on straight chalk lines. My seat was empty. I was on a sidewalk with *Pai* trying to understand a baffling string of words. DIVISION had something to do with math, which I didn't particularly like. EMPLOYMENT I had never seen or heard before. SECURITY I knew. But not at that moment.

Pai reached for the door. It swung open into a little square of tiled floor. We stepped in to be confronted by the highest, steepest staircase I had ever seen. At the top, we emerged into a huge, fluorescently lit room. It was too bright and open after the dim, narrow stairs. *Pai* took off his hat. We stood together in a vast empty space. The light, polished tiles reflected the fluorescent glow. There were no windows.

Far across the room, a row of metal desks lined the wall. Each had a green vinyl-covered chair beside it. Off to our left, facing the empty space before us, was a very high green metal desk. It was easily twice as high as a normal-size desk. Its odd size and placement in the middle of the room gave it the appearance of a kind of altar that divided the room in half. There were many people working at desks or walking about, but the room was so big that it still seemed empty.

The head and shoulders of a white-haired woman appeared to rest on the big desk like a sculptured bust. She sat very still. Above her head the word CLAIMS dangled from two pieces of chain attached to the ceiling. As I watched the woman she beckoned to us. *Pai* and I walked over toward her.

The desk was so high that *Pai's* shoulders barely cleared the top. Even when I stood on tiptoe I couldn't see over it. I had to stretch and lean my head way back to see the woman's round face. I thought that she must have very long legs to need a desk that high. The coldness in me grew. My neck hurt.

"My father can't speak English. He has no work and we need money."   35

She reached for some papers from a wire basket. One of her fingers was encased in a piece of orange rubber.

"Come around over here so I can see you." She motioned to the side of the desk. I went reluctantly. Rounding the desk I saw with relief that she was a small woman perched on a stool so high it seemed she would need a ladder to get up there.

"How old are you?" She leaned down toward me.

"Eight."

"My, aren't you a brave girl. Only eight years old and helping daddy   40
like that. And what lovely earrings you have."

She like my earrings. I went a little closer to let her touch them. Maybe she would give us money.

"What language does your father speak?" She was straightening up, reaching for a pencil.

"Portuguese."

"What is she saying?" Pai wanted to know.

"Wait," I told him. The lady hadn't yet said anything about money.   45
"Why isn't your father working?"
"His factory burned down."
"What is she saying?" Pai repeated.
"She wants to know why you aren't working."
"Tell her the factory burned down."   50
"I know. I did." The lady was looking at me. I hoped she wouldn't ask me what my father had just said.
"What's your father's name?"
"Carlos S. Cunha. C-u-n-h-a." No one could ever spell *Cunha. Pai* nodded at the woman when he heard his name.
"Where do you live?"
"Thirty-three Tracey Street, Peabody, Massachusetts." *Pai* nodded   55
again when he heard the address.
"When was your father born?"
"Quando é que tu naçestes?"
"When was the last day your father worked?"
"Qual foi o último dia que trabalhastes?"
"What was the name of the factory?"   60
"Qual éra o nome de fábrica?"
"How long did he work there?"
"Quanto tempo trabalhastes lá?"
"What is his Social Security number?"
I looked at her blankly, not knowing what to say. What was a Social   65
Security number?
"What did she say?" Pai prompted me out of silence.
"I don't know. She wants a kind of number." I was feeling very tired and worried. But *Pai* took a small card from his wallet and gave it to the lady. She copied something from it onto her papers and returned it to him. I felt a great sense of relief. She wrote silently for a while as we stood and waited. Then she handed some paper to *Pai* and looked at me.
"Tell your father that he must have these forms filled out by his employer before he can receive unemployment benefits."
I stared at her. What was she saying? Employer? Unemployment benefits? I was afraid she was saying we couldn't have any money. Maybe not, though. Maybe we could have money if I could understand her words.
"What did she say? Can we have some money?"   70
"I don't know. I can't understand her words."
"Ask her again if we can have money," Pai insisted. *"Tell her we have to pay the rent."*
"We need money for the rent," I told the lady, trying to hold back tears.
"You can't have money today. You must take these forms to your father's employer and bring them back completed next week. Then your

father must sign another form which we will keep here to process his claim. When he comes back in two weeks there may be a check for him." The cold in me was so big now, I was trying not to shiver.

"Do you understand?" The lady was looking at me.   75

I wanted to say, "No, I don't," but I was afraid we would never get money and *Pai* would be angry.

"Tell your father to take the papers to his boss and come back next week."

Boss. I could understand boss.

"She said you have to take these papers to your 'bossa' and come back next week."

"We can't have money today?"   80

"No. She said maybe we can have money in two weeks."

"Did you tell her we have to pay the rent?"

"Yes, but she said we can't have money yet."

The lady was saying good-bye and beckoning the next person from the line that had formed behind us.

I was relieved to move on, but I think *Pai* wanted to stay and argue   85
with her. I knew that if he could speak English, he would have. I knew that he thought it was my fault we couldn't have money. And I myself wasn't so sure that wasn't true.

That night I sat at the kitchen table with a fat pencil and a piece of paper. In my second-grade scrawl I wrote: Dear Miss Laitinen, Mary Edith was sick.

I gave the paper to *Pai* and told him to sign his name.

"What does it say?"

"It says that I was sick today. I need to give it to my teacher."

"You weren't sick today."   90

"Ya, but it would take too many words to tell her the truth."

Pai signed the paper. The next morning in school, Miss Laitinen read it and said that she hoped I was feeling better.

When I was nine, *Pai* went to an auction and bought a big house on Tremont Street. We moved in the spring. The yard at the side of the house dipped downward in a gentle slope that was covered with a dense row of tall lilac bushes. I soon discovered that I could crawl in among the twisted trunks to hide from my brothers in the fragrant shade. It was paradise. . . .

I was mostly wild and joyful on Tremont Street. But there was a shadow that fell across my days now and again.

"Ó Ediiiite." *Pai* would call me without the least bit of warning, to   95
be his voice. He expected me to drop whatever I was doing to attend him. Of late, I'd had to struggle on the telephone with the voice of a woman who wanted some old dishes. The dishes, along with lots of old

furniture and junk, had been in the house when we moved in. They were in the cellar, stacked in cardboard boxes and covered with dust. The woman called many times wanting to speak with *Pai.*

"My father can't speak English," I would say. "He says to tell you that the dishes are in our house and they belong to us." But she did not seem to understand. Every few days she would call.

"*Ó Ediiiite.*" *Pai's* voice echoed through the empty rooms. Hearing it brought on a chill. It had that tone. As always, my first impulse was to pretend I had not heard, but there was no escape. I couldn't disappear into thin air as I wished to do at such calls. We were up in the third-floor apartment of our new house. *Pai* was working in the kitchen. Carlos and I had made a cavern of old cushions and were sitting together deep in its bowels when he called. It was so dark and comfortable there I decided not to answer until the third call, though that risked *Pai's* wrath.

"*Ó Ediiite.*" Yes, that tone was certainly there. *Pai* was calling me to do something only I could do. Something that always awakened a cold beast deep in my gut. He wanted me to be his bridge. What was it now? Did he have to talk to someone at City Hall again? Or was it the insurance company? They were always using words I couldn't understand: liability, and premium, and dividend. It made me frustrated and scared.

"You wait. My dotta come." *Pai* was talking to someone. Who could it be? That was some relief. At least I didn't have to call someone on the phone. It was always harder to understand when I couldn't see people's mouths.

"*Ó Ediiiite.*" I hated Carlos. *Pai* never called his name like that. He never had to do anything but play.   100

"*Que ééé?*"

"*Come over here and talk to this lady.*"

Reluctantly I crawled out from the soft darkness and walked through the empty rooms toward the kitchen. Through the kitchen door I could see a slim lady dressed in brown standing at the top of the stairs in the windowed porch. She had on very skinny high-heeled shoes and a brown purse to match. As soon as *Pai* saw me he said to the lady, "Dis my dotta." To me he said, *"See what she wants."*

The lady had dark hair that was very smooth and puffed away from her head. The ends of it flipped up in a way that I liked.

"Hello. I'm the lady who called about the dishes."   105

I stared at her without a word. My stomach lurched.

"*What did she say?*" *Pai* wanted to know.

"*She says she's the lady who wants the dishes.*"

Pai's face hardened some.

"*Tell her she's wasting her time. We're not giving them to her. Didn't*   110
you already tell her that on the telephone?"

I nodded, standing helplessly between them.

"*Well, tell her again.*" *Pai* was getting angry. I wanted to disappear.

"My father says he can't give you the dishes," I said to the lady. She clutched her purse and leaned a little forward.

"Yes, you told me that on the phone. But I wanted to come in person and speak with your father because it's very important to me that—"

"My father can't speak English," I interrupted her. Why didn't she just go away? She was still standing in the doorway with her back to the stairwell. I wanted to push her down.   115

"Yes, I understand that. But I wanted to see him." She looked at *Pai*, who was standing in the doorway to the kitchen holding his hammer. The kitchen was up one step from the porch. *Pai* was a small man, but he looked kind of scary staring down at us like that.

"What is she saying?"

"She says she wanted to talk to you about getting her dishes."

"Tell her the dishes are ours. They were in the house. We bought the house and everything in it. Tell her the lawyer said so."

The brown lady was looking at me expectantly.   120

"My father says the dishes are ours because we bought the house and the lawyer said everything in the house is ours now."

"Yes, I know that, but I was away when the house was being sold. I didn't know . . ."

"Eeii." There were footsteps on the stairs behind her. It was *Mãe* coming up from the second floor to find out what was going on. The lady moved away from the door to let *Mãe* in.

"Dis my wife," *Pai* said to the lady. The lady said hello to *Mãe*, who smiled and nodded her head. She looked at me, then at *Pai* in a questioning way.

"It's the lady who wants our dishes," *Pai* explained.   125

"Ó." *Mãe* looked at her again and smiled, but I could tell she was a little worried.

We stood there in kind of a funny circle; the lady looked at each of us in turn and took a deep breath.

"I didn't know," she continued, "that the dishes were in the house. I was away. They are very important to me. They belonged to my grandmother. I'd really like to get them back." She spoke this while looking back and forth between *Mãe* and *Pai*. Then she looked down at me, leaning forward again. "Will you please tell your parents, please?"

The cold beast inside me had begun to rise up toward my throat as the lady spoke. I knew that soon it would try to choke out my words. I spoke in a hurry to get them out.

"She said she didn't know the dishes were in the house she was away they were her grandmother's dishes she wants them back." I felt a deep sadness at the thought of the lady returning home to find her grandmother's dishes sold.   130

"We don't need all those dishes. Let's give them to her," Mãe said in her calm way. I felt relieved. We could give the lady the dishes and she would go away. But *Pai* got angry.

"I already said what I had to say. The dishes are ours. That is all."

"Pai, she said she didn't know. They were her grandmother's dishes. She needs to have them." I was speaking wildly and loud now. The lady looked at me questioningly, but I didn't want to speak to her again.

"She's only saying that to trick us. If she wanted those dishes she should have taken them out before the house was sold. Tell her we are not fools. Tell her to forget it. She can go away. Tell her not to call or come here again."

"What is he saying?" The lady was looking at me again.   135

I ignored her. I felt sorry for *Pai* for always feeling that people were trying to trick him. I wanted him to trust people. I wanted the lady to have her grandmother's dishes. I closed my eyes and willed myself away.

"Tell her what I said!" Pai yelled.

"Pai, just give her the dishes! They were her grandmother's dishes!" My voice cracked as I yelled back at him. Tears were rising.

I hated *Pai* for being so stubborn. I hated the lady for not taking the dishes before the house was sold. I hated myself for having learned to speak English.

FOCUSING ON CONTENT

1. Explain the importance of Cunha's given name. How does she describe it? In what way does it give her identity?

2. Why is it important for Cunha to describe Mrs. Donahue? What ironic information do we get from that description? (Glossary: *Irony*)

3. Why does Mrs. Donahue change Cunha's name? Do you think Mrs. Donahue's own ethnic heritage is part of her motivation? Why or why not?

4. Why does Cunha say she hated her brother?

FOCUSING ON WRITING

1. Cunha refers to a "coldness" (34) or "cold" (74) or "the cold beast (129) that comes over her. What does she mean by these references to coldness? What brings about the feeling?

2. Why does Cunha re-create the scene in which she and her father visit the Division of Employment Security in such detail? How does the scene help her achieve her purpose in writing the essay? (Glossary: *Purpose*)

3. Cunha ends her essay with the sentence "I hated myself for having learned to speak English." Why does she say this? Do you find the ending effective? Why or why not? (Glossary: *Beginnings and Endings*)

4. Cunha does not explicitly describe her relationship with the members of her family, but she provides many clues. What impressions does the essay give you regarding Cunha's relationship with her brothers, her mother, and her father? Use passages from the essay to support your answer. Would it have been better for her to be more explicit? Why or why not?

LANGUAGE IN ACTION

The following passage is from Mari Tomasi's *Like Lesser Gods* (1949), an immigration novel about Italian stone carvers living in Vermont. In this excerpt, the protagonist Mr. Tiff is met at the train station by Petra, his friend's daughter, and Tiff explains how he came to acquire his name. Read the passage in light of Cunha's comments about the significance of her name and the change that was made to it. Is Mr. Tiff's situation similar to Edite Cunha's? Why or why not?

"Look," she bargained. "I'll teach you English after I do my lessons every night, if you teach me to read Italian. I'll—gee, I don't even know your name—"

"I have a name, and to spare," he assured her gravely. *"Maestro* Michele Pio Vittorio Giuseppe Tiffone."

"Gee—"

He counted them off on his fingers. "Michele for the great Archangel—this one." He indicated the silver San' Michele figurine on the dresser. "Pio for the pope who reigned when I was born and whom you may some day call *Santo Pio;* Vittorio, who is king and whose birthday is November 11—the same as mine; and Giuseppe for my father, who humbled his name into obscurity by tacking it at the end."

Tiffone. She frowned. *Maestro* Michele Pio. . . . A happy thought smoothed the wrinkles from her brow. "I'll call you Mister Tiff. I'm glad, glad I saw you first—I mean at the station."

WRITING SUGGESTIONS

1. (*Writing from Experience*) Write an essay in which you discuss what your name means to you. You might consider addressing some of the following questions: Who named you? How did that person or persons decide on your name? Does your surname carry any ethnic identification? How do you like your name? What does your name mean? How do others respond to your name? Do you have any nicknames? How do people react to your nickname?

2. (*Writing from Reading*) Write an essay in which you put yourself in Cunha's shoes as the only speaker of a new language in your family. How would your reactions and those of your family differ from those of Cunha and her family? What difficulties would you have if you had to translate everything for your parents? How do you think the job of "translator" would affect your relationships with the rest of your family? How would it feel to have your parents dependent on you for communication?

3. (*Writing from Research*) It is not always possible to know a person's cultural background from a surname. Edite Cunha was surprised to learn that Mrs. Donahue was, in fact, Portuguese. A woman who marries a man from a cultural background different from her own and takes her husband's name may be surprised to find that she is regarded differently because of her surname. Either find someone for whom this is true and interview her about her change of name, or search through newspaper and magazine databases for articles about women who have married into a different culture. Did the women find that they had a new identity? Were they regarded differently? What revealing stories, if any, can they tell? Write an essay discussing what you learned from your research that you think might be interesting for your readers.

What Is Language?

VICTORIA FROMKIN AND ROBERT RODMAN

The prominent author and linguist Victoria Fromkin was born in Passaic, New Jersey. She completed her undergraduate studies at the University of California at Berkeley with a degree in economics, and many years later, she entered the graduate program in linguistics at UCLA, earning her Ph.D. in 1965. During her years as a professor of linguistics at UCLA, she has served as chair of the Department of Linguistics and as dean of the Graduate Division/vice chancellor—Graduate Programs. She has also served as president of the Linguistic Society of America (LSA) and is currently chair of Section Z—Linguistics and the Language Sciences—of the American Association for the Advancement of Science. Her books include Tone *(1978) and* Phonetic Linguistics *(1985). Professor Fromkin died in January 2000.*

Robert Rodman was born in Boston, Massachusetts, and grew up in North Hollywood, California. He received his B.A. in mathematics from UCLA in 1961 and then went on to receive advanced degrees in both mathematics and linguistics at UCLA, finishing with a Ph.D. in linguistics in 1973. He entered the teaching profession as a linguistics professor at the University of North Carolina and then moved to North Carolina State in 1978 to teach computer science, where he remains as an associate professor. Rodman is currently working in the field of computer speech technology and voice recognition.

Language is something that most of us take for granted because we use it—almost without thinking—to communicate with the people in our lives. But what does it mean to know a language? In the following selection from An Introduction to Language, *(1978) Fromkin and Rodman discuss exactly what each of us does know when we use a language.*

WRITING TO DISCOVER: *Think about what language is, and try to write a brief definition of it. Do you believe that animals have languages of their own? If so, how did you arrive at this belief? Were you influenced by children's books, cartoons, research accounts, friends and teachers, your own personal experiences with animals? Briefly characterize the language of a particular animal. If you do not believe that animals have language, explain the basis of your belief.*

Whatever else people do when they come together—whether they play, fight, make love, or make automobiles—they talk. We live in a world of language. We talk to our friends, our associates, our wives and husbands, our lovers, our teachers, our parents and in-laws. We talk to bus drivers and total strangers. We talk face to face and over the telephone, and everyone responds with more talk. Television and radio further swell this torrent of words. Hardly a moment of our waking lives is free from words, and even in our dreams we talk and are talked to. We also talk when there is no one to answer. Some of us talk aloud in our sleep. We talk to our pets and sometimes to ourselves.

The possession of language, perhaps more than any other attribute, distinguishes humans from other animals. To understand our humanity one must understand the nature of language that makes us human. According to the philosophy expressed in the myths and religions of many peoples, it is language that is the source of human life and power. To some people of Africa, a newborn child is a kuntu, a "thing," not yet a muntu, a "person." Only by the act of learning does the child become a human being. Thus, according to this tradition, we all become "human" because we all know at least one language. But what does it mean to "know" a language?

LINGUISTIC KNOWLEDGE

When you know a language, you can speak and be understood by others who know that language. This means you have the capacity to produce sounds that signify certain meanings and to understand or interpret the sounds produced by others. We are referring to normal-hearing individuals. Deaf persons produce and understand sign languages just as hearing persons produce and understand spoken languages.

Everyone knows a language. Five-year-old children are almost as proficient at speaking and understanding as are their parents. Yet the ability to carry out the simplest conversation requires profound knowledge that most speakers are unaware of. This is as true of speakers of Japanese as of English, of Armenian as of Navajo. A speaker of English can produce a sentence having two relative clauses without knowing what a relative clause is, like

> My goddaughter who was born in Sweden and who now lives in Vermont is named Disa, after a Viking queen.

In a parallel fashion, a child can walk without understanding or being able to explain the principles of balance and support, or the neurophysiological control mechanisms that permit one to do so. The fact that we may know something unconsciously is not unique to language.

What, then, do speakers of English or Quechua or French or Mohawk or Arabic know?   5

Knowledege of the Sound System

Knowing a language means knowing what sounds are in that language and what sounds are not. This unconscious knowledge is revealed by the way speakers of one language pronounce words from another language. If you speak only English, for example, you may substitute an English sound for a non-English sound when pronouncing "foreign" words. Most English speakers pronounce the name *Bach* with a final *k* sound because the sound represented by the letters *ch* in German is not an English sound. If you pronounce it as the Germans do, you are using a sound outside the English sound system. French people speaking English often pronounce words like *this* and *that* as if they were spelled *zis* and *zat*. The English sound represented by the initial letters *th* is not part of the French sound system, and the French mispronunciation reveals the speakers' unconscious knowledge of this fact.

Knowing the sound system of language includes more than knowing the **inventory** of sounds: it includes knowing which sounds may start a word, end a word, and follow each other. The name of a former president of Ghana was *Nkrumah,* pronounced with an initial sound identical to the sound ending the English word *sing* (for most Americans). Most speakers of English mispronounce it (by Ghanaian standards) by inserting a short vowel before or after the *n* sound. Similarly, the first name of the New Zealand mystery writer Ngaio Marsh is usually mispronounced in this way. The reason for these "errors" is that no word in English begins with the *ng* sound. Children who learn English discover this fact about our language, just as Ghanaian and Australian children learn that words in their language may begin with the *ng* sound. [. . .]

Knowledge of the Meaning of Words

The minute I set eyes on an animal I know what it is. I don't have to reflect a moment; the right name comes out instantly . . . I seem to know just by the shape of the creature and the way it acts what animal it is. When the dodo came along he [Adam] thought it was a wildcat . . . But I saved him . . . I just spoke up in a quite natural way . . . and said "Well, I do declare if there isn't the dodo!"   – MARK TWAIN, *Eve's Diary*

Knowing the sounds and sound patterns in our language constitutes only one part of our linguistic knowledge. In addition, knowing a language is knowing that certain sound sequences **signify** certain concepts or **meanings.** Speakers of English know what *boy* means and that it means something different from *toy* or *girl* or *pterodactyl*. Knowing a language is therefore knowing how to relate sounds and meanings.

If you do not know a language, the sounds spoken to you will be mainly incomprehensible, because the relationship between speech sounds and the meanings they represent is, for the most part, an **arbitrary** one. You have to learn (when you are acquiring the language) that the sounds represented by the letters *house* (in the written form of the language) signify the

concept ▢ ; if you know French, this same meaning is represented by *maison;* if you know Twi, it is represented by ɔdaŋ; if you know Russian,

by *dom;* if you know Spanish, by *casa.* Similarly, the concept ☞ is represented by *hand* in English, *main* in French, *nsa* in Twi, and *ruka* in Russian.

The following are words in some different languages. How many of   10
them can you understand?

   a. kyinii
   b. doakam
   c. odun
   d. asa
   e. toowq
   f. bolna
   g. wartawan
   h. inaminatu
   i. yawwa

Speakers of the languages from which these words are taken know that they have the following meanings:

   a. a large parasol (in a Ghanaian language, Twi)
   b. living creature (in the native American language, Papago)
   c. wood (in Turkish)
   d. morning (in Japanese)
   e. is seeing (in a California Indian language, Luiseño)
   f. to speak (in a Pakistani language, Urdu); to ache (in Russian)
   g. reporter (in Indonesian)
   h. teacher (in a Venezuelan Indian language, Warao)
   i. right on! (in a Nigerian language, Hausa)

These examples show that the sounds of words are only given meaning by the language in which they occur. Mark Twain satirizes the idea that something is called X because it looks like X or called Y because it sounds like Y in the quotation at the beginning of this section. Neither the shape nor the other physical attributes of objects determine their pronunciation in any language. [. . .]

This arbitrary relationship between the **form** (sounds) and **meaning** (concept) of a word in spoken language is also true of the sign languages used by the deaf. If you see someone using a sign language you do not know, it is doubtful that you will understand the message from the signs alone. A person who knows Chinese Sign Language would find it difficult to understand American Sign Language. Signs that may have originally been **mimetic** (similar to miming) or **iconic** (with a nonarbitrary relationship between form and meaning) change historically as do words, and the iconicity is lost. These signs become **conventional,** so knowing the shape or movement of the hands does not reveal the meaning of the gestures in sign languages.

There is, however, some **"sound symbolism"** in language—that is, words whose pronunciation suggests the meaning. A few words in most languages are **onomatopoeic**—the sounds of the words supposedly imitate the sounds of nature. Even here, the sounds differ from one language to another, reflecting the particular sound system of the language. In English, we say *cockadoodledoo* to represent the rooster's crow, but in Russian they say *kukuriku.*

Sometimes particular sound sequences seem to relate to a particular concept. In English many words beginning with *gl* relate to sight, such as *glare, glint, gleam, glitter, glossy, glaze, glance, glimmer, glimpse,* and *glisten.* However, such words are a very small part of any language, and *gl* may have nothing to do with "sight" in another language, or even in other words in English, such as *gladiator, glucose, glory, glycerine, globe,* and so on.

English speakers know the *gl* words that relate to sight and those that   15
do not; they know the onomatopoeic words, and all the words in the basic vocabulary of the language. There are no speakers of English who know all 450,000 words listed in *Webster's Third New International Dictionary;* but even if there were and that were all they knew, they would not know English. Imagine trying to learn a foreign language by buying a dictionary and memorizing the words. No matter how many words you learned, you would not be able to form the simplest phrases or sentences in the language or understand a native speaker. No one speaks in isolated words. (Of course, you could search in your traveler's dictionary for individual words to find out how to say something like "car—gas—where?" After many tries, a native might understand this question and then point in the direction of a gas station. If you were answered with a sentence, however, you probably would not understand what was said or be able to look it up, because you would not know where one word ended and another began.) [. . .]

The Creativity of Linguistic Knowledge

Knowledge of a language enables you to combine words to form phrases, and phrases to form sentences. You cannot buy a dictionary of any language with all its sentences, because no dictionary can list all the possible sentences. Knowing a language means being able to produce new sentences never spoken before and to understand sentences never heard before. The linguist Noam Chomsky refers to this ability as part of the "creative aspect" of language use. Not every speaker of a language can create great literature, but you, and all persons who know a language, can and do "create" new sentences when you speak and understand new sentences "created" by others.

This "creative ability" is due to the fact that language use is not limited to stimulus-response behavior. It's true that if someone steps on our toes we will "automatically" respond with a scream or gasp or grunt, but these sounds are really not part of language; they are involuntary reactions to stimuli. After we automatically cry out, we can say "That was some clumsy act, you big oaf" or "Thank you very much for stepping on my toe because I was afraid I had elephantiasis and now that I can feel it hurt I know it isn't so," or any one of an infinite number of sentences, because the particular sentence we produce is not controlled by any stimulus.

Even some involuntary cries like *ouch* are constrained by our own language system, as are filled pauses that are sprinkled through controversial speech—*er* or *uh* or *you know* in English. They contain only the sounds found in the language. French speakers, for example, often fill their pauses with the vowel sound that starts with their word for egg—*oeuf*—a sound that does not occur in English.

Knowing a language includes knowing what sentences are appropriate in various situations. Saying "Hamburger costs $2.00 a pound" after someone has just stepped on your toe would hardly be an appropriate response, although it would be possible.

Consider the following sentence: 20

> Daniel Boone decided to become a pioneer because he dreamed of pigeon-toed giraffes and cross-eyed elephants dancing in pink skirts and green berets on the wind-swept plains of the Midwest.

You may not believe the sentence; you may question its logic; but you can understand it, although you probably never heard or read it before now.

Knowledge of a language, then, makes it possible to understand and produce new sentences. If you counted the number of sentences in this book that you have seen or heard before, the number would be small. Next time you write an essay or a letter, see how many of your sentences are new. Few sentences are stored in your brain, to be "pulled out" to fit some situation or matched with some sentence that you hear. Novel sentences never spoken or heard before cannot be in your memory.

Simple memorization of all the possible sentences in a language is impossible in principle. If for every sentence in the language a longer sentence can be formed, then there is no limit to the length of any sentence and therefore no limit to the number of sentences. In English you can say:

This is the house.

or

This is the house that Jack built.

or

This is the malt that lay in the house that jack built.

or

This is the dog that chased the cat that killed the rat that ate the malt that lay in the house that Jack built.

and you need not stop there. How long, then, is the longest sentence? A speaker of English can say:

The old man came.

or

The old, old, old, old, old man came.

How many "olds" are too many? Seven? Twenty-three?

It is true that the longer these sentences become, the less likely we would be to hear or to say them. A sentence with 276 occurrences of "old" would be highly unlikely in either speech or writing, even to describe Methuselah; but such a sentence is theoretically possible. That is, if you know English, you have the knowledge to add any number of adjectives as modifiers to a noun.

All human languages permit their speakers to form indefinitely long sentences; "creativity" is a universal property of human language.

To memorize and store an infinite set of sentences would require an   25
infinite storage capacity. However, the brain is finite, and even if it were
not, we could not store novel sentences.

Knowledge of Sentences and Nonsentences

When you learn a language you must learn something finite—your vocabulary is finite (however large it may be)—and that can be stored. If sentences in a language were formed by putting one word after another in any order, then language could simply be a set of words. You can see that words are not enough by examining the following strings of words:

(1) a.   John kissed the little old lady who owned the shaggy dog.
      b.   Who owned the shaggy dog John kissed the little old lady.
      c.   John is difficult to love.
      d.   It is difficult to love John.
      e.   John is anxious to go.

    f.   It is anxious to go John.

    g.   John, who was a student, flunked his exams.

    h.   Exams his flunked student a was who John.

If you were asked to put a star or asterisk before the examples that seemed "funny" or "no good" to you, which ones would you star? Our "intuitive" knowledge about what is or is not an allowable sentence in English convinces us to star b, d, f, and h. Which ones did you star?

Would you agree with the following judgments?

(2) a.   What he did was climb a tree.

     b.   *What he thought was want a sports car.

     c.   Drink your beer and go home!

     d.   *What are drinking and go home?

     e.   I expect them to arrive a week from next Thursday.

     f.   *I expect a week from next Thursday to arrive them.

     g.   Linus lost his security blanket.

     h.   *Lost Linus security blanket his.

If you starred the same ones we did, then you agree that not all strings of words constitute sentences in a language, and knowledge of a language determines which are and which are not. Therefore, in addition to knowing the words of the language, linguistic knowledge must include "rules" for forming sentences and making judgments like those you made about the examples in (1) and (2). These rules must be finite in length and finite in number so that they can be stored in our finite brains; yet they must permit us to form and understand an infinite set of new sentences, as we discussed earlier. [. . .]

A language, then, consists of all the sounds, words, and possible sen-   30
tences. When you know a language, you know the sounds, the words, and the rules for their combination.

FOCUSING ON CONTENT

1. What, according to Fromkin and Rodman, distinguishes humans from other animals? Why is talk so important?

2. Explain specifically what it means to know a language.

3. In addition to a knowledge of the inventory of sounds, what does knowing the sound system of a language include? Explain your answer with several examples from English or another language you are familiar with.

4. What do Fromkin and Rodman mean when they say in paragraph 9 that the relationship between speech and meanings is arbitrary?

5. What is an onomatopoeic word? Give several examples.

6. In what ways is each of us creative in our use of language? What does this creativity reveal about language use?

FOCUSING ON WRITING

1. What is Fromkin and Rodman's thesis, and where is it stated? (Glossary: *Thesis*)

2. What is the function of paragraph 5 in the context of the essay?

3. Fromkin and Rodman are careful to use examples to clarify and explain many of their points. Identify several of their examples and explain why you find them effective.

4. In paragraph 22, writers claim that "simple memorization of all the possible sentences in a language is impossible in principle." How do they convince you of the validity of their claim?

5. How do Fromkin and Rodman organize their essay? You may find it helpful to make a scratch outline in answering this question. (Glossary: *Organization*)

LANGUAGE IN ACTION

Read the following English folktale, which is taken from Joseph Jacob's 1890 book *English Fairy Tales*. How does the story relate to the concept of arbitrariness, as explained by Fromkin and Rodman? (9).

FROM "MASTER OF ALL MASTERS"

A girl once went to a fair to be hired as a servant. At last a funny-looking old gentleman engaged her and took her home to his house. When she got there he told her he had something to teach her for in his house he had his own names for things.

He said to her: "What will you call me?"

"Master or Mister or whatever you please, sir."

"You must call me 'Master of Masters.' And what would you call this?" pointing to his bed.

"Bed or couch or whatever you please, sir."

"No, that's my barnacle. And what do you call these?" said he, pointing to his pants.

"Breeches or trousers or whatever you please, sir."

"You must call them squibs and crackers. And what do you call her?" pointing to the cat.

"Kit or cat or whatever you please, sir."

"You must call her 'white-faced simminy' And this now," showing the fire, "what would you call this?"

"Fire or flame or whatever you please, sir."

"You must call it 'hot cockalorum,' and what this?" he went on, pointing to the water.

"Water or wet or whatever you please, sir."

"No, 'pandalorum' is its name. And what do you call this?" asked he, as he pointed to the house.

"House or cottage or whatever you please, sir."

"You must call it 'high topper mountain.'"

That very night the servant woke her master up in a fright and said: "Master of all masters, get out of your barnacle and put on your squibs and crackers. For white-face simminy has got a spark of hot cockalorum on its tail, and unless you get some pandalorum high topper mountain will be all on hot cockalorum." . . . That's all.

WRITING SUGGESTIONS

1. (*Writing from Experience*) In paragraph 1, Fromkin and Rodman state that "We live in a world of language." What do you think they mean by this statement? Write an essay in which you discuss how the statement is borne out in your own memories and the way in which you relate to the world today. Be sure to illustrate your points with specific examples.

2. (*Writing from Reading*) The writers in this section have at least one thing in common: They all agree that using language is an indispensable aspect of being human. "Whatever else people do when they come together — whether they play, fight, make love, or make automobiles — they talk," say Victoria Fromkin and Robert Rodman in the first paragraph of their essay. But much of modern psychology and many New Age practices encourage us to really "feel" our emotions and "experience" the truth of those feelings. Does this idea conflict with the ideas of Fromkin and Rodman? Based on your reading of their article, write an essay about how you think Fromkin and Rodman would respond to the emotional thrust of modern psychology? Cite specific passages in their essay to support your views.

3. (*Writing from Research*) Research the process by which humans acquire a native language. The subject is known as "language acquisition" and is so classified in libraries and databases. You may wish to report on the latest research involving the inherent predisposition to acquire language, a concept developed by the noted linguist Noam Chomsky. Other possible topics include the role of imitation in language acquisition and the various stages that humans pass through as they acquire their native tongues.

Language and Thought

Susanne K. Langer

Susanne K. Langer was born in New York City in 1895 and attended Radcliffe College. There she studied philosophy, an interest she maintained until her death in 1985. She stayed in Cambridge, Massachusetts, as a tutor at Harvard University from 1927 to 1942. Langer then taught at the University of Delaware, Columbia University, and Connecticut College, where she remained from 1954 until the end of her distinguished teaching career. Her books include Philosophy in a New Key: A Study of the Symbolism of Reason, Rite, and Art *(1942),* Feeling and Form *(1953), and* Mind: An Essay in Human Feeling *(1967).*

In the following essay, which originally appeared in Ms. *magazine, Langer explores how language separates humans from the rest of the animal kingdom. She contends that the use of symbols—in addition to the use of signs that animals also use—frees humans not only to react to their environment but also to think about it. Moreover, symbols allow us to create imagery and ideas not directly related to the real world, so that we can plan, imagine, and communicate abstractions—to do, in essence, the things that make us human.*

WRITING TO DISCOVER: *Young children must often communicate—and be communicated to—without the use of language. To a child, for example, a danger sticker on a bottle can mean "don't touch," and a green traffic light might mean "the car will start again." Think back to your own childhood experiences. Write about how communication took place without language. What associations were you able to make?*

A symbol is not the same thing as a sign; that is a fact that psychologists and philosophers often overlook. All intelligent animals use signs; so do we. To them as well as to us sounds and smells and motions are signs of food, danger, the presence of other beings, or of rain or storm. Furthermore, some animals not only attend to signs but produce them for the benefit of others. Dogs bark at the door to be let in; rabbits thump to call each other; the cooing of doves and the growl of a wolf defending his kill are unequivocal signs of feelings and intentions to be reckoned with by other creatures.

We use signs just as animals do, though with considerably more elaboration. We stop at red lights and go on green; we answer calls and bells, watch the sky for coming storms, read trouble or promise or anger in each other's eyes. That is animal intelligence raised to the human level. Those of us who are dog lovers can probably all tell wonderful stories of

how high our dogs have sometimes risen in the scale of clever sign interpretation and sign using.

A sign is anything that announces the existence or the imminence of
some event, the presence of a thing or a person, or a change in the state
of affairs. There are signs of the weather, signs of danger, signs of future
good or evil, signs of what the past has been. In every case a sign is
closely bound up with something to be noted or expected in experience.
It is always a part of the situation to which it refers, though the reference
may be remote in space and time. In so far as we are led to note or expect
the signified event we are making correct use of a sign. This is the essence
of rational behavior, which animals show in varying degrees. It is entirely
realistic, being closely bound up with the actual objective course of
history—learned by experience, and cashed in or voided by further experience.

If man had kept to the straight and narrow path of sign using, he
would be like the other animals, though perhaps a little brighter. He
would not talk, but grunt and gesticulate the point. He would make his
wishes known, give warnings, perhaps develop a social system like that of
bees and ants, with such a wonderful efficiency of communal enterprise
that all men would have plenty to eat, warm apartments—all exactly alike
and perfectly convenient—to live in, and everybody could and would sit
in the sun or by the fire, as the climate demanded, not talking but just
basking, with every want satisfied, most of his life. The young would
romp and make love, the old would sleep, the middle-aged would do the
routine work almost unconsciously and eat a great deal. But that would
be the life of a social, superintelligent, purely sign-using animal.

To us who are human, it does not sound very glorious. We want to   5
go places and do things, own all sorts of gadgets that we do not absolutely need, and when we sit down to take it easy we want to talk.
Rights and property, social position, special talents and virtues, and above
all our ideas, are what we live for. We have gone off on a tangent that
takes us far away from the mere biological cycle that animal generations
accomplish; and that is because we can use not only signs but symbols.

A symbol differs from a sign in that it does not announce the presence of the object, the being, condition, or whatnot, which is its meaning, but merely *brings this thing to mind*. It is not a mere "substitute
sign" to which we react as though it were the object itself. The fact is that
our reaction to hearing a person's name is quite different from our reaction to the person himself. There are certain rare cases where a symbol
stands directly for its meaning: in religious experience, for instance, the
Host is not only a symbol but a Presence. But symbols in the ordinary
sense are not mystic. They are the same sort of thing that ordinary signs
are; only they do not call our attention to something necessarily present
or to be physically dealt with—they call up merely a conception of the
thing they "mean."

The difference between a sign and a symbol is, in brief, that a sign causes us to think or act *in face* of the thing signified, whereas a symbol causes us to think *about* the thing symbolized. Therein lies the great importance of symbolism for human life, its power to make this life so different from any other animal biography that generations of men have found it incredible to suppose that they were of purely zoological origin. A sign is always embedded in reality, in a present that emerges from the actual past and stretches to the future; but a symbol may be divorced from reality altogether. It may refer to what is not the case, to a mere idea, a figment, a dream. It serves, therefore, to liberate thought from the immediate stimuli of a physically present world; and that liberation marks the essential difference between human and nonhuman mentality. Animals think, but they think *of* and *at* things; men think primarily *about* things. Words, pictures, and memory images are symbols that may be combined and varied in a thousand ways. The result is a symbolic structure whose meaning is a complex of all their respective meanings, and this kaleidoscope of *ideas* is the typical product of the human brain that we call the "stream of thought."

The process of transforming all direct experience into imagery or into that supreme mode of symbolic expression, language, has so completely taken possession of the human mind that it is not only a special talent but a dominant, organic need. All our sense impressions leave their traces in our memory not only as signs disposing our practical reactions in the future but also as symbols, images representing our *ideas* of things; and the tendency to manipulate ideas, to combine and abstract, mix and extend them by playing with symbols, is man's outstanding characteristic. It seems to be what his brain most naturally and spontaneously does. Therefore his primitive mental function is not judging reality, but *dreaming his desires.*

Dreaming is apparently a basic function of human brains, for it is free and unexhausting like our metabolism, heartbeat, and breath. It is easier to dream than not to dream, as it is easier to breathe than to refrain from breathing. The symbolic character of dreams is fairly well established. Symbol mongering, on this ineffectual, uncritical level, seems to be instinctive, the fulfillment of an elementary need rather than the purposeful exercise of a high and difficult talent.

The special power of man's mind rests on the evolution of this special activity, not on any transcendently high development of animal intelligence. We are not immeasurably higher than other animals; we are different. We have a biological need and with it a biological gift that they do not share.

Because man has not only the ability but the constant need of *conceiving* what has happened to him, what surrounds him, what is demanded of him — in short, of symbolizing nature, himself, and his hopes and fears — he has a constant and crying need of *expression*. What he cannot express, he cannot conceive; what he cannot conceive is chaos, and fills him with terror.

If we bear in mind this all-important craving for expression we get a new picture of man's behavior; for from this trait spring his powers and his weaknesses. The process of symbolic transformation that all our experiences undergo is nothing more nor less than the process of *conception,* underlying the human faculties of abstraction and imagination.

When we are faced with a strange or difficult situation, we cannot react directly, as other creatures do, with flight, aggression, or any such simple instinctive pattern. Our whole reaction depends on how we manage to conceive the situation—whether we cast it in a definite dramatic form, whether we see it as a disaster, a challenge, a fulfillment of doom, or a fiat of the Divine Will. In words or dreamlike image, in artistic or religious or even in cynical form, we must *construe* the events of life. There is great virtue in the figure of speech, "I can *make* nothing of it," to express a failure to understand something. Thought and memory are processes of *making* the thought content and the memory image; the pattern of our ideas is given by the symbols through which we express them. And in the course of manipulating those symbols we inevitably distort the original experience, as we abstract certain features of it, embroider and reinforce those features with other ideas, until the conception we project on the screen of memory is quite different from anything in our real history.

Conception is a necessary and elementary process; what we do with our conceptions is another story. That is the entire history of human culture— of intelligence and morality, folly and superstition, ritual, language, and the arts—all the phenomena that set man apart from, and above, the rest of the animal kingdom. As the religious mind has to make all human history a drama of sin and salvation in order to define its own moral attitudes, so a scientist wrestles with the mere presentation of "the facts" before he can reason about them. The process of *envisaging* facts, values, hopes, and fears underlies our whole behavior pattern; and this process is reflected in the evolution of an extraordinary phenomenon found always, and only, in human societies—the phenomenon of language.

Language is the highest and most amazing achievement of the symbolistic human mind. The power it bestows is almost inestimable, for without it anything properly called "thought" is impossible. The birth of language is the dawn of humanity. The line between man and beast—between the highest ape and the lowest savage—is the language line. Whether the primitive Neanderthal man was anthropoid or human depends less on his cranial capacity, his upright posture, or even his use of tools and fire, than on one issue we shall probably never be able to settle— whether or not he spoke.

In all physical traits and practical responses, such as skills and visual judgments, we can find a certain continuity between animal and human

15

mentality. Sign using is an ever evolving, ever improving function throughout the whole animal kingdom, from the lowly worm that shrinks into his hole at the sound of an approaching foot, to the dog obeying his master's command, and even to the learned scientist who watches the movements of an index needle.

The continuity of the sign-using talent has led psychologists to the belief that language is evolved from the vocal expressions, grunts and coos and cries, whereby animals vent their feelings or signal their fellows; that man has elaborated this sort of communion to the point where it makes a perfect exchange of ideas possible.

I do not believe that this doctrine of the origin of language is correct. The essence of language is symbolic, not signific; we use it first and most vitally to formulate and hold ideas in our own minds. Conception, not social control, is its first and foremost benefit.

Watch a young child that is just learning to speak play with a toy; he says the name of the object, e.g.: "Horsey! horsey! horsey!" over and over again, looks at the object, moves it, always saying the name to himself or to the world at large. It's quite a time before he talks to anyone in particular; he talks first of all to himself. This is his way of forming and fixing the *conception* of the object in his mind, and around this conception all his knowledge of it grows. *Names* are the essence of language; for the *name* is what abstracts the conception of the horse from the horse itself, and lets the mere idea recur at the speaking of the name. This permits the conception gathered from one horse experience to be exemplified again by another instance of a horse, so that the notion embodied in the name is a general notion.

To this end, the baby uses a word long before he *asks* for the object; when he wants his horsey he is likely to cry and fret, because he is reacting to an actual environment, not forming ideas. He uses the animal language of *signs* for his wants; talking is still a purely symbolic process — its practical value has not really impressed him yet. 20

Language need not be vocal; it may be purely visual, like written language, or even tactual, like the deaf-mute system of speech; but it *must be denotative*. The sounds, intended or unintended, whereby animals communicate do not constitute a language because they are signs, not names. They never fall into an organic pattern, a meaningful syntax of even the most rudimentary sort, as all language seems to do with a sort of driving necessity. That is because signs refer to actual situations, in which things have obvious relations to each other that require only to be noted; but symbols refer to ideas, which are not physically there for inspection, so their connections and features have to be represented. This gives all true language a natural tendency toward growth and development, which seems almost like a life of its own. Languages are not invented; they grow with our need for expression.

In contrast, animal "speech" never has a structure. It is merely an emotional response. Apes may greet their ration of yams with a shout of "Nga!" But they do not say "Nga" between meals. If they could *talk about* their yams instead of just saluting them, they would be the most primitive men instead of the most anthropoid of beasts. They would have ideas, and tell each other things true and false, rational or irrational; they would make plans and invent laws and sing their own praises, as men do.

FOCUSING ON CONTENT

1. Define what Langer refers to as a sign. Define symbol. (Glossary: *Definition* and *Symbol*) Why is the distinction between the two so important?

2. What is the essential difference between the way animals "think" and the way humans think? How has that changed human mental function at an organic level? How has the biological change affected our development in relation to animals?

3. What does Langer mean when she says, "In words or dreamlike images . . . we must *construe* the events of life" (13)? How does this claim relate to the process of conception?

4. Comment on the statements Langer makes in paragraph 11. As she claims, do you feel the need to conceptualize and to express? Explain.

FOCUSING ON WRITING

1. What is Langer's thesis in this essay? Where does she state it? (Glossary: *Thesis*)

2. What examples of signs and symbols does Langer provide? (Glossary: *Examples*) How effective do you find her examples? What examples of signs and symbols can you provide?

3. In paragraph 11, Langer states: "What [man] cannot express, he cannot conceive; what he cannot conceive is chaos, and fills him with terror." Review the first ten paragraphs of the essay. How does Langer prepare the reader to accept this abstract and bold statement? (Glossary: *Concrete/Abstract* and *Organization*)

LANGUAGE IN ACTION

Review what Langer has to say about signs and symbols, particularly the differences she draws between them (6–7). Then examine the following graphics. What does each graphic mean? Which ones are signs, and which are symbols? Be prepared to defend your conclusions in a classroom discussion.

WRITING SUGGESTIONS

1. (*Writing from Experience*) Using symbols for expression need not involve explicit use of language. Within the framework of a particular society, many methods of symbolic communication are possible. When you walk across campus, for example, what do you want to communicate to others even if you do not speak to anyone? How do you communicate this message? For instance, how does your facial expression, clothing, hairstyle, or jewelry serve as a symbol? Write an essay in which you describe and analyze the nonlanguage symbols you use to communicate.

2. (*Writing from Reading*) It has often been said that language reveals the character of the person using it. Write an essay in which you analyze the character of a particular writer based on his or her use of language. You may want to comment on a writer in this text whose article you have read, such as Langer. Consider such areas as vocabulary range, sentence variety, slang, correct grammar, jargon, and tone. What do these elements tell you about the character of the person? (Glossary: *Jargon, Slang,* and *Tone*).

3. (*Writing from Research*) Research recent experiments involving animal communication. Some experiments, for example, reveal the gorilla's use of sign language; others show that dolphins have complex communication systems that we are only beginning to understand. Write a paper in which you summarize the research and discuss how it relates to Langer's ideas about human and animal use of signs and symbols. Did you find any evidence that certain animals can use basic symbols? Is there a possibility that gorillas and dolphins can think *about* things rather than simply *of* and *at* them?

A Brief History of English

PAUL ROBERTS

Paul Roberts (1917–1967) was a linguist, teacher, and writer. Born in California, he received his B.A. from San Jose State University and his M.A. and Ph.D. from the University of California at Berkeley. After teaching at San Jose Sate and then Cornell University, Roberts became director of language at the Center of American Studies in Rome. His books include Understanding Grammar *(1954),* Patterns of English *(1956),* Understanding English *(1958),* English Sentences *(1962), and* English Syntax *(1964).*

In the following selection from Understanding English, *Roberts recounts the major events in the history of England and discusses their relationship to the development of the English language. He tells how the people who invaded England influenced the language and how, in recent times, the rapid spread of English has resulted in its becoming a major world language.*

WRITING TO DISCOVER: *Think about a work you have read that was written in nonmodern English, such as those by Shakespeare, Chaucer, Swift, or their contemporaries. How difficult was it for you to understand the work? Write about what it taught you about the evolution of the English language?*

HISTORICAL BACKGROUNDS

No understanding of the English language can be very satisfactory without a notion of the history of the language. But we shall have to make do with just a notion. The history of English is long and complicated, and we can only hit the high spots.

The history of our language begins a little after A.D. 600. Everything before that is pre-history, which means that we can guess at it but can't prove much. For a thousand years or so before the birth of Christ our linguistic ancestors were savages wandering through the forests of northern Europe. Their language was a part of the Germanic branch of the Indo-European Family.

At the time of the Roman Empire — say, from the beginning of the Christian Era to around A.D. 400 — the speaker of what was to become English were scattered along the northern coast of Europe. They spoke a dialect of Low German. More exactly, they spoke several different dialects, since they were several different tribes. The names given to the tribes who got to England are *Angles, Saxons,* and *Jutes.* For convenience, we can refer to them as Anglo-Saxons.

The first contact with civilization was a rather thin acquaintance with the Roman Empire on whose borders they lived. Probably some of the Anglo-Saxons wandered into the Empire occasionally, and certainly Roman merchants and traders traveled among the tribes. At any rate, this period was the first of our many borrowings from Latin. Such words as *kettle, wine, cheese, butter, cheap, plum, gem, bishop, church* were borrowed at this time. They show something of the relationship of the Anglo-Saxons with the Romans. The Anglo-Saxons were learning, getting their first taste of civilization.

They still had a long way to go, however, and their first step was to   5
help smash the civilization they were learning from. In the fourth century the Roman power weakened badly. While the Goths were pounding away at the Romans in the Mediterranean countries, their relatives, the Anglo-Saxons, began to attack Britain.

The Romans had been the ruling power in Britain since A.D. 43. They had subjugated the Celts whom they found living there and had succeeded in setting up a Roman administration. The Roman influence did not extend to the outlying parts of the British Isles. In Scotland, Wales, and Ireland the Celts remained free and wild, and they made periodic forays against the Romans in England. Among other defense measures, the Romans built the famous Roman Wall to ward off the tribes in the north.

Even in England the Roman power was thin. Latin did not become the language of the country as it did in Gaul and Spain. The mass of people continued to speak Celtic, with Latin and the Roman civilization it contained in use as a top dressing.

In the fourth century, troubles multiplied for the Romans in Britain. Not only did the untamed tribes of Scotland and Wales grow more and more restive, but the Anglo-Saxons began to make pirate raids on the eastern coast. Furthermore, there was growing difficulty everywhere in the Empire, and the legions in Britain were siphoned off to fight elsewhere. Finally, in A.D. 410, the last Roman ruler in England, bent on becoming emperor, left the islands and took the last of the legions with him. The Celts were left in possession of Britain but almost defenseless against the impending Anglo-Saxon attack.

Not much is surely known about the arrival of the Anglo-Saxons in England. According to the best early source, the eighth-century historian Bede, the Jutes came in 449 in response to a plea from the Celtic king, Vortigern, who wanted their help against the Picts attacking from the north. The Jutes subdued the Picts but then quarreled and fought with Vortigern, and, with reinforcements from the Continent, settled permanently in Kent. Somewhat later the Angles established themselves in eastern England and the Saxons in the south and west. Bede's account is plausible enough, and these were probably the main lines of the invasion.

We do know, however, that the Angles, Saxons, and Jutes were a   10
long time securing themselves in England. Fighting went on for as long

as a hundred years before the Celts in England were all killed, driven into Wales, or reduced to slavery. This is the period of King Arthur, who was not entirely mythological. He was a Romanized Celt, a general, though probably not a king. He had some success against the Anglo-Saxons, but it was only temporary. By 550 or so the Anglo-Saxons were firmly established. English was in England.

OLD ENGLISH

All this is pre-history, so far as the language is concerned. We have no record of the English language until after 600, when the Anglo-Saxons were converted to Christianity and learned the Latin alphabet. The conversion began, to be precise, in the year 597 and was accomplished within thirty or forty years. The conversion was a great advance for the Anglo-Saxons, not only because of the spiritual benefits but because it reestablished contact with what remained of Roman civilization. This civilization didn't amount to much in the year 600, but it was certainly superior to anything in England up to that time.

It is customary to divide the history of the English language into three periods: Old English, Middle English, and Modern English. Old English runs from the earliest records—i.e., seventh century—to about 1100; Middle English from 1100 to 1450 or 1500; Modern English from 1500 to the present day. Sometimes Modern English is further divided into Early Modern, 1500–1700, and Late Modern, 1700 to the present.

When England came into history, it was divided into several more or less autonomous kingdoms, some of which at times exercised a certain amount of control over the others. In the century after the conversion the most advanced kingdom was Northumbria, the area between the Humber River and the Scottish border. By A.D. 700 the Northumbrians had developed a respectable civilization, the finest in Europe. It is sometimes called the Northumbrian Renaissance, and it was the first of the several renaissances through which Europe struggled upward out of the ruins of the Roman Empire. It was in this period that the best of the Old English literature was written, including the epic poem *Beowulf.*

In the eighth century, Northumbrian power declined, and the center of influence moved southward to Mercia, the kingdom of the Midlands. A century later the center shifted again, and Wessex, the country of the West Saxons, became the leading power. The most famous king of the West Saxons was Alfred the Great, who reigned in the second half of the ninth century, dying in 901. He was famous not only as a military man and administrator but also as a champion of learning. He founded and supported schools and translated or caused to be translated many books from Latin into English. At this time also much of the Northumbrian literature of two centuries earlier was copied in West Saxon. Indeed, the great bulk of Old English writing which has come down to us is in the West Saxon dialect of 900 or later.

In the military sphere, Alfred's great accomplishment was his successful   15
opposition to the Viking invasions. In the ninth and tenth centuries, the Norsemen emerged in their ships from their homelands in Denmark and the Scandinavian peninsula. They traveled far and attacked and plundered at will and almost with impunity. They ravaged Italy and Greece, settled in France, Russian, and Ireland, colonized Iceland and Greenland, and discovered America several centuries before Columbus. Nor did they overlook England.

After many years of hit-and-run raids, the Norsemen landed an army on the east coast of England in the year 866. There was nothing much to oppose them except the Wessex power led by Alfred. The long struggle ended in 877 with a treaty by which a line was drawn roughly from the northwest of England to the southeast. On the eastern side of the line Norse rule was to prevail. This was called the Danelaw. The western side was to be governed by Wessex.

The linguistic result of all this was a considerable injection of Norse into the English language. Norse was at this time not so different from English as Norwegian or Danish is now. Probably speakers of English could understand, more or less, the language of the newcomers who had moved into eastern England. At any rate, there was considerable interchange and word borrowing. Examples of Norse words in the English language are *sky, give, law, egg, outlaw, leg, ugly, scant, sly, crawl, scowl, take, thrust*. There are hundreds more. We have even borrowed some pronouns from Norse—*they, their,* and *them.* These words were borrowed first by the eastern and northern dialects and then in the course of hundreds of years made their way into English generally.

It is supposed also—indeed, it must be true—that the Norsemen influenced the sound structure and the grammar of English. But this is hard to demonstrate in detail.

A SPECIMEN OF OLD ENGLISH

We may now have an example of Old English. The favorite illustration is the Lord's Prayer, since it needs no translation. This has come to us in several different versions. Here is one:

Fæder ure,
þou þe eart on heofonum,
si þin nama gehalgod.
Tobecume þin rice.
Gewurþe ðin willa on eor ðan swa swa on heofenum.
Urne gedæghwamlican hlaf syle us to dæg.
And forgyf us ure gyltas, swa swa we forgyfa ðurum gyltendum.
And ne gelæd þu us on costnunge,
ac alys us of yfele. Soþlice.

Some of the differences between this and Modern English are merely   20
differences in orthography. For instance, the sign *æ* is what Old English
writers used for a vowel sound like that in modern *hat* or *and*. The *th*
sounds of modern *thin* or *then* are represented in Old English by þ or ð.
But of course there are many differences in sound too. *Ure* is the ancestor
of modern *our,* but the first vowel was like that in *too* or *ooze*. *Hlaf* is
modern *loaf;* we had dropped the *h* sound and changed the vowel, which
in *hlaf* was pronounced something like the vowel in *father*. Old English
had some sounds which we do not have. The sound represented by *y*
does not occur in Modern English. If you pronounce the vowel in *bit*
with your lips rounded, you may approach it.

In grammar, Old English was much more highly inflected than Modern English is. That is, there were more case endings for nouns, more person and number endings for verbs, a more complicated pronoun system,
various endings for adjectives, and so on. Old English nouns had four
cases — nominative, genitive, dative, accusative. Adjectives had five — all
these and an instrumental case besides. Present-day English has only two
cases for nouns — common case and possessive case. Adjectives now have
no case system at all. On the other hand, we now use a more rigid word
order and more structure words (prepositions, auxiliaries, and the like) to
express relationships than Old English did.

Some of this grammar we can see in the Lord's Prayer. *Heofonum,*
for instance, is a dative plural; the nominative singular was *heofon*. *Urne* is
an accusative singular; the nominative is *ure*. In *urum glytendum* both
words are dative plural. *Forgyfaþ* is the first person plural form of the
verb. Word order is different: "urne gedæghwamlican hlaf syle us" in
place of "Give us our daily bread." And so on.

In vocabulary Old English is quite different from Modern English.
Most of the Old English words are what we may call native English: that is,
words which have not been borrowed from other languages but which have
been a part of English ever since English was a part of Indo-European. Old
English did certainly contain borrowed words. We have seen that many
borrowings were coming in from Norse. Rather large numbers had been
borrowed from Latin, too. Some of these were taken while the Anglo-
Saxons were still on the Continent (*cheese, butter, bishop, kettle,* etc.); a large
number came into English after the conversion (*angel, candle, priest, mar-
tyr, radish, oyster, purple, school, spend,* etc.). But the great majority of Old
English words were native English.

Now, on the contrary, the majority of words in English are borrowed,
taken mostly from Latin and French. Of the words in *The American College
Dictionary* only about 14 percent are native. Most of these, to be sure, are
common, high-frequency words — *the, of, I, and, because, man, mother,
road,* etc.; of the thousand most common words in English, some 62 percent are native English. Even so, the modern vocabulary is very much Latinized and Frenchified. The Old English vocabulary was not.

MIDDLE ENGLISH

Sometime between the years 1000 and 1200 various important   25
changes took place in the structure of English, and Old English became
Middle English. The political event which facilitated these changes was
the Norman Conquest. The Normans, as the name shows, came originally from Scandinavia. In the early tenth century they established themselves in northern France, adopted the French language, and developed a
vigorous kingdom and a very passable civilization. In the year 1066, led
by Duke William, they crossed the Channel and made themselves masters
of England. For the next several hundred years, England was ruled by
kings whose first language was French.

One might wonder why, after the Norman Conquest, French did not
become the national language, replacing English entirely. The reason is
that the Conquest was not a national migration, as the earlier Anglo-
Saxon invasion had been. Great numbers of Normans came to England,
but they came as rulers and landlords. French became the language of the
court, the language of the nobility, the language of polite society, the
language of literature. But it did not replace English as the language of
the people. There must always have been hundreds of towns and villages
in which French was never heard except when visitors of high station
passed through.

But English, though it survived as the national language, was profoundly changed after the Norman Conquest. Some of the changes—in
sound structure and grammar—would no doubt have taken place
whether there had been a Conquest or not. Even before 1066 the case
system of English nouns and adjectives was becoming simplified; people
came to rely more on word order and prepositions than on inflectional
endings to communicate their meanings. The process was speeded up by
sound changes which caused many of the endings to sound alike. But no
doubt the Conquest facilitated the change. German, which didn't experience a Norman Conquest, is today rather highly inflected compared to its
cousin English.

But it is in vocabulary that the effects of the Conquest are most obvious. French ceased, after a hundred years or so, to be the native language
of very many people in England, but it continued—and continues still—
to be a zealously cultivated second language, the mirror of elegance and
civilization. When one spoke English, one introduced not only French
ideas and French things but also their French names. This was not only
easy but socially useful. To pepper one's conversation with French expressions was to show that one was well-bred, elegant, *au courant*. The
last sentence shows that the process is not yet dead. By using *au courant*
instead of, say, *abreast of things,* the writer indicates that he is no dull
clod who knows only English but an elegant person aware of how things
are done in *le haut monde.*

Thus French words came into English, all sorts of them. There were words to do with government: *parliament, majesty, treaty, alliance, tax, government;* church words: *parson, sermon, baptism, incense, crucifix, religion;* words for foods: *veal, beef, mutton, bacon, jelly, peach, lemon, cream, biscuit;* colors: *blue, scarlet, vermilion;* household words: *curtain, chair, lamp, towel, blanket, parlor;* play words: *dance, chess, music, leisure, conversation;* literary words: *story, romance, poet, literary;* learned words: *study, logic, grammar, noun, surgeon, anatomy, stomach;* just ordinary words of all sorts; *nice, second, very, age, bucket, gentle, final, fault, flower, cry, count, sure, move, surprise, plain.*

All these and thousands more poured into the English vocabulary be-   30 tween 1100 and 1500 until, at the end of that time, many people must have had more French words than English at their command. This is not to say that English became French. English remained English in sound structure and in grammar, though these also felt the ripples of French influence. The very heart of the vocabulary, too, remained English. Most of the high-frequency words—the pronouns, the prepositions, the conjunctions, the auxiliaries, as well as a great many ordinary nouns and verbs and adjectives—were not replaced by borrowings.

Middle English, then, was still a Germanic language, but it differed from Old English in many ways. The sound system and the grammar changed a good deal. Speakers made less use of case systems and other inflectional devices and relied more on word order and structure words to express their meanings. This is often said to be a simplification, but it isn't really. Languages don't become simpler; they merely exchange one kind of complexity for another. Modern English is not a simple language, as any foreign speaker who tries to learn it will hasten to tell you.

For us Middle English is simpler than Old English just because it is closer to Modern English. It takes three or four months at least to learn to read Old English prose and more than that for poetry. But a week of good study should put one in touch with the Middle English poet Chaucer. Indeed, you may be able to make some sense of Chaucer straight off, though you would need instruction in pronunciation to make it sound like poetry. Here is a famous passage from the *General Prologue to the Canterbury Tales,* fourteenth century:

> Ther was also a nonne, a Prioresse,
> That of hir smyling was ful symple and coy,
> Hir gretteste oath was but by Seinte Loy,
> And she was cleped* Madame Eglentyne.
> Ful wel she song the service dyvyne,
> Entuned in hir nose ful semely.
> And Frenshe she spak ful faire and fetisly,**

---

*named.
**elegantly.

After the scole of Stratford-atte-Bowe,
For Frenshe of Parys was to hir unknowe.

EARLY MODERN ENGLISH

Sometime between 1400 and 1600 English underwent a couple of sound changes which made the language of Shakespeare quite different from that of Chaucer. Incidentally, these changes contributed much to the chaos in which English spelling now finds itself.

One change was the elimination of a vowel sound in certain unstressed positions at the end of words. For instance, the words *name, stone, wine, dance* were pronounced as two syllables by Chaucer but as just one by Shakespeare. The *e* in these words became, as we say, "silent." But it wasn't silent for Chaucer; it represented a vowel sound. So also the words *laughed, seemed, stored* would have been pronounced by Chaucer as two-syllable words. The change was an important one because it affected thousands of words and gave a different aspect to the whole language.

The other change is what is called the Great Vowel Shift. This was a systematic shifting of half a dozen vowels and diphthongs in stressed syllables. For instance, the word *name* had in Middle English a vowel something like that in the modern word *father; wine* had the vowel of modern *mean; he* was pronounced something like modern *hey; mouse* sounded like *moose; moon* had the vowel of *moan.* Again the shift was thoroughgoing and affected all the words in which these vowel sounds occurred. Since we still keep the Middle English system of spelling these words, the differences between Modern English and Middle English are often more real than apparent.

The vowel shift has meant also that we have come to use an entirely different set of symbols for representing vowel sounds than is used by writers of such languages as French, Italian, or Spanish, in which no such vowel shift occurred. If you come across a strange word—say, *bine*—in an English book, you will pronounce it according to the English system, with the vowel of *wine* or *dine.* But if you read *bine* in a French, Italian, or Spanish book, you pronounce it with the vowel of *mean* or *seen.*

These two changes, then, produced the basic differences between Middle English and Modern English. But there were several other developments that had an effect upon the language. One was the invention of printing, an invention introduced into England by William Caxton in the year 1475. Where before books had been rare and costly, they suddenly became cheap and common. More and more people learned to read and write. This was the first of many advances in communication which have worked to unify languages and to arrest the development of dialect differences, though of course printing affects writing principally rather than speech. Among other things it hastened the standardization of spelling.

35

The period of Early Modern English — that is, the sixteenth and seventeenth centuries — was also the period of the English Renaissance, when people developed, on the one hand, a keen interest in the past and, on the other, a more daring and imaginative view of the future. New ideas multiplied, and new ideas meant new language. Englishmen had grown accustomed to borrowing words from French as a result of the Norman Conquest; now they borrowed from Latin and Greek. As we have seen, English had been raiding Latin from Old English times and before, but now the floodgates really opened, and thousands of words from the classical languages poured in. *Pedestrian, bonus, anatomy, contradict, climax, dictionary, benefit, multiply, exist, paragraph, initiate, scene, inspire* are random examples. Probably the average educated American today has more words from French in his vocabulary than from native English sources, and more from Latin than from French.

The greatest writer of the Early Modern English period is of course Shakespeare, and the best-known book is the King James Version of the Bible, published in 1611. The Bible (if not Shakespeare) has made many features of Early Modern English perfectly familiar to many people down to the present time, even though we do not use these features in present-day speech and writing. For instance, the old pronouns *thou* and *thee* have dropped out of use now, together with their verb forms, but they are still familiar to us in prayer and in Biblical quotations: "Whither thou goest, I will go." Such forms as *hath* and *doth* have been replaced by *has* and *does;* "Goes he hence tonight?" would now be "Is he going away tonight?"; Shakespeare's "Fie, on't, sirrah" would be "Nuts to that, Mac." Still, all these expressions linger with us because of the power of the works in which they occur.

It is not always realized, however, that considerable sound changes   40
have taken place between Early Modern English and the English of the present day. Shakespearian actors putting on a play speak the words, properly enough, in their modern pronunciation. But it is very doubtful that this pronunciation would be understood at all by Shakespeare. In Shakespeare's time, the word *reason* was pronounced like modern *raisin; face* had the sound of modern *glass;* the *l* in *would, should, palm* was pronounced. In these points and a great many others the English language has moved a long way from what it was in 1600.

RECENT DEVELOPMENTS

The history of English since 1700 is filled with many movements and countermovements, of which we can notice only a couple. One of these is the vigorous attempt made in the eighteenth century, and the rather half-hearted attempts made since, to regulate and control the English language. Many people of the eighteenth century, not understanding very well the forces which govern language, proposed to polish and prune and restrict English, which they felt was proliferating too wildly. There was much talk of an academy which would rule on what people could and could not say and write. The academy never came into being, but the eighteenth century did succeed in establishing certain attitudes which, though they haven't had much effect on the development of the language itself, have certainly changed the native speaker's feeling about the language.

In part, a product of the wish to fix and establish the language was the development of the dictionary. The first English dictionary was published in 1603; it was a list of 2,500 words briefly defined. Many others were published with gradual improvements until Samuel Johnson published his *English Dictionary* in 1755. This, steadily revised, dominated the field in England for nearly a hundred years. Meanwhile in America, Noah Webster published his dictionary in 1828, and before long dictionary publishing was big business in this country. The last century has seen the publication of one great dictionary: the twelve-volume *Oxford English Dictionary,* compiled in the course of seventy-five years through the labors of many scholars. We have also, of course, numerous commercial dictionaries which are as good as the public wants them to be if not, indeed, rather better.

Another product of the eighteenth century was the invention of "English grammar." As English came to replace Latin as the language of scholarship, it was felt that one should also be able to control and dissect it, parse and analyze it, as one could Latin. What happened in practice was that the grammatical description that applied to Latin was removed and superimposed on English. This was silly, because English is an entirely different kind of language, with its own forms and signals and ways of producing meaning. Nevertheless, English grammars on the Latin model were worked out and taught in the schools. In many schools they are still being taught. This activity is not often popular with school children, but it is sometimes an interesting and instructive exercise in logic. The principal harm in it is that it has tended to keep people from being interested in English and has obscured the real features of English structure.

But probably the most important force on the development of English in the modern period has been the tremendous expansion of English-speaking peoples. In 1500 English was a minor language, spoken by a few people on a small island. Now it is perhaps the greatest language of the world, spoken natively by over a quarter of a billion people and as a second language by many millions more. When we speak of English now, we must specify whether we mean American English, British English, Australian English, Indian English, or what, since the differences are considerable. The American cannot go to England or the Englishman to America confident that he will always understand and be understood. The Alabaman in Iowa or the Iowan in Alabama shows himself a foreigner every time he speaks. It is only because communication has become fast and easy that English in this period of its expansion has not broken into a dozen mutually unintelligible languages.

FOCUSING ON CONTENT

1. Why is Roberts careful to describe the relationship between historical events in England and the development of the English language? In what ways did the historical events affect the English language?

2. How would you characterize in social terms the French words that were brought into English by the Norman Conquest? In what areas of life did the French have the greatest influence?

3. Explain what changes the English language underwent as a result of the Great Vowel Shift. What is the importance of this linguistic phenomenon for the history of English?

4. Having read Roberts's essay, do you think it is helpful to your education to know something about the history of English? Why or why not?

FOCUSING ON WRITING

1. What is Roberts's thesis in this essay? (Glossary: *Thesis*) Where does he state it? Does he convince you of his thesis? Why or why not?

2. Roberts makes extensive use of examples. Why is his use of examples particularly appropriate for his topic? What did you learn about writing from reading an essay that is so reliant on examples?

3. Roberts wrote this essay in the 1950s, when people were less sensitive to racial and ethnic slurs in writing than they are today. (Glossary: *Biased Language*) Reread the first ten paragraphs, paying particular attention to Roberts's use of such words as *savages, untamed tribes,* and *civilization.* Do you find any of his diction offensive or see how others might find it so? (Glossary: *Diction*) Suggest specific ways to change Roberts's diction in order to improve the impression his writing makes on contemporary readers. How do you as a writer guard against biased writing?

LANGUAGE IN ACTION

The following passage from Frances Mayes's best-seller *Under the Tuscan Sun: At Home in Italy* (1996) refers to the etymology, or history, of the interesting word *boustrophedon.*

A few summers ago, a friend and I hiked in Majorca above Soller. We climbed across and through miles of dramatic, enormous olives on broad terraces. Up high, we came upon stone huts where the grove tenders sheltered themselves. Although we got lost and encountered a pacing bull in a meadow, we felt this immense peace all day, walking among those trees that looked and may have been a thousand years old. Walking these few curving acres here gives me the same feeling. Unnatural as it is, terracing has a natural feel to it. Some of the earliest methods of writing, called boustrophedon, run from right to left, then from left to right. If we were trained that way, it probably is a more efficient way to read. The etymology of the word reveals Greek roots meaning "to turn like an ox plowing." And that writing is like the rising terraces: The U-turn space required by an ox with plow suddenly loops up a level and you're going in the other direction.

Using your college dictionary, identify the language from which each of the following words was borrowed:

barbecue
buffalo
casino
decoy
ditto
fruit
hustle
marmalade
orangutan
posse
raccoon
veranda

WRITING SUGGESTIONS

1. (*Writing from Experience*) During its relatively brief four-hundred-year history, American English has consistently been characterized by change. How is American English still changing today? Write about the effects, if any, the Gulf War, the war in Kosovo, the NASA space program, the drug culture, computers and other new technology, the women's movement, the global economy and community, or recent waves of immigration have had on American English?

2. (*Writing from Reading*) In paragraph 1 Paul Roberts writes, "No understanding of the English language can be very satisfactory without a notion of the history of the language." What exactly does Roberts mean by *understanding*? Write an essay in which you dispute or substantiate his claim.

3. (*Writing from Research*) The English language is part of a larger family of languages known as the Germanic languages. These languages are, in turn, part of a larger family of languages known as the Indo-European languages, which are the supposed descendants of a hypothetical language known as Proto-Indo-European. Research what has been written about Proto-Indo-European and write an essay reporting your findings.

The Prescriptive Tradition

DAVID CRYSTAL

British linguist David Crystal was born on July 6, 1941, in Northern Ireland. He received his B.A. from the University of London in 1962, his Ph.D. in 1966, and taught at the University of Reading (England) as a professor of linguistics until 1985. He is the author or editor of many books on language and linguistics, including the Dictionary of Linguistics and Phonetics, *first published in 1980. In addition to his work as an author, lecturer, and reference-book editor, Crystal currently serves as the director of the Ucheldre Center.*

By the time most people graduate from high school they are familiar with the rules of English and the exceptions to those rules. These rules, it turns out, are the legacy of the prescriptive tradition in English that had its beginnings in the eighteenth century. In the following article from the Cambridge Encyclopedia of Language *(1987), Crystal traces the history of prescriptivism, an authoritarian tradition that sought to codify the principles of English and preserve the language's purity. This background information helps us understand the current philosophical debate between linguists who want to* prescribe *and those who want to* describe *the language, a debate that Crystal does not see as resolvable by an either-or solution.*

WRITING TO DISCOVER: *Think about your experiences as you were taught the rules of English. What were you taught and how were you taught? What is your current thinking about the rules of English? Write about whether they are necessary or arbitrary and unnecessary.*

PRESCRIPTIVISM

In its most general sense, prescriptivism is the view that one variety of language has an inherently higher value than others, and that this ought to be imposed on the whole of the speech community. The view is propounded especially in relation to grammar and vocabulary, and frequently with reference to pronunciation. The variety which is favored, in this account, is usually a version of the "standard" written language, especially as encountered in literature, or in the formal spoken language which most closely reflects this style. Adherents to this variety are said to speak or write "correctly"; deviations from it are said to be "incorrect."

All the main European languages have been studied prescriptively, especially in the 18th century approach to the writing of grammars and dictionaries. The aims of these early grammarians were threefold: (a) they wanted to codify the principles of their languages, to show that there was a system beneath the apparent chaos of usage, (b) they wanted a means of settling disputes over usage, (c) they wanted to point out what they felt to be common errors, in order to "improve" the language. The authoritarian nature of the approach is best characterized by its reliance on "rules" of grammar. Some usages are "prescribed," to be learned and followed accurately; others are "proscribed," to be avoided. In this early period, there were no half-measures: usage was either right or wrong, and it was the task of the grammarian not simply to record alternatives, but to pronounce judgment upon them.

These attitudes are still with us, and they motivate a widespread concern that linguistic standards should be maintained. Nevertheless, there is an alternative point of view that is concerned less with "standards" than with the *facts* of linguistic usage. This approach is summarized in the statement that it is the task of the grammarian to *describe*, not *prescribe* — to record the facts of linguistic diversity, and not to attempt the impossible tasks of evaluating language variation or halting language change. In the second half of the 18th century, we already find advocates of this view, such as Joseph Priestly, whose *Rudiments of English Grammar* (1761) insists that "the custom of speaking is the original and only just standard of any language." Linguistic issues, it is argued, cannot be solved by logic and legislation. And this view has become the tenet of the modern linguistic approach to grammatical analysis.

In our own time, the opposition between "descriptivists" and "prescriptivists" has often become extreme, with both sides painting unreal pictures of the other. Descriptive grammarians have been presented as people who do not care about standards, because of the way they see all forms of usage as equally valid. Prescriptive grammarians have been presented as blind adherents to a historical tradition. The opposition has even been presented in quasi-political terms — of radical liberalism vs elitist conservatism.

If these stereotypes are abandoned, we can see that both approaches   5
are important, and have more in common than is often realized — involving a mutual interest in such matters as acceptability, ambiguity, and intelligibility. The descriptive approach is essential because it is the only way in which the competing claims of different standards can be reconciled: when we know the facts of language use, we are in a better position to avoid the idiosyncrasies of private opinions, and to make realistic recommendations about teaching or style. The prescriptive approach provides a focus for the sense of linguistic values which everyone possesses, and which ultimately forms part of our view of social structure, and of our own place within it. After 200 years of dispute, it is perhaps sanguine to expect any immediate rapport to be achieved, but there are some grounds for optimism, now that sociolinguists are beginning to look

more seriously at prescriptivism in the context of explaining linguistic attitudes, uses, and beliefs.

THE ACADEMIES

Some countries have felt that the best way to look after a language is to place it in the care of an academy. In Italy, the *Accademia della Crusca* was founded as early as 1582, with the object of purifying the Italian language. In France, in 1635, Cardinal Richelieu established the *Académie française*, which set the pattern for many subsequent bodies. The statutes of the *Académie* define as its principal function:

> to labor with all possible care and diligence to give definite rules to our language, and to render it pure, eloquent, and capable of treating the arts and sciences.

The 40 academicians were drawn from the ranks of the church, nobility, and military—a bias which continues to the present day. The *Académie*'s first dictionary appeared in 1694.

Several other academies were founded in the 18th and 19th centuries. The Spanish Academy was founded in 1713 by Philip V, and within 200 years corresponding bodies had been set up in most South American Spanish countries. The Swedish Academy was founded in 1786; the Hungarian in 1830. There are three Arabic academies, in Syria, Iraq, and Egypt. The Hebrew Language Academy was set up more recently, in 1953.

In England, a proposal for an academy was made in the 17th century, with the support of such men as John Dryden and Daniel Defoe. In Defoe's view, the reputation of the members of this academy

> would be enough to make them the allowed judges of style and language; and no author would have the impudence to coin without their authority . . . There should be no more occasion to search for derivations and constructions, and it would be as a criminal then to coin words as money.

In 1712, Jonathan Swift presented his *Proposal for Correcting, Improving and Ascertaining the English Tongue*, in which he complains to the Lord Treasurer of England, the Earl of Oxford, that

> our language is extremely imperfect; that its daily improvements are by no means in proportion to its daily corruptions; that the pretenders to polish and refine it have chiefly multiplied abuses and absurdities; and that in many instances it offends against every part of grammar.

His academy would "fix our language for ever," for,

> I am of the opinion, it is better a language should not be wholly perfect, than it should be perpetually changing.

The idea received a great deal of support at the time, but nothing was done. And in due course, opposition to the notion grew. It became evident that the French and Italian academies had been unsuccessful in stopping the course of language change. Dr. Johnson, in the Preface to his Dictionary, is under no illusion about the futility of an academy, especially in England, where he finds "the spirit of English liberty" contrary to the whole idea:

> When we see men grow old and die at a certain time one after another, century after century, we laugh at the elixir that promises to prolong life to a thousand years; and with equal justice may the lexicographer be derided, who being able to produce no example of a nation that has preserved their words and phrases from mutability, shall imagine that his dictionary can embalm his language, and secure it from corruption, and decay, that it is in his power to change sublunary nature, or clear the world at once from folly, vanity, and affectation.

From time to time, the idea of an English Academy continues to be voiced, but the response has never been enthusiastic. A similar proposal in the USA was also rejected. By contrast, since the 18th century, there has been an increasing flow of individual grammars, dictionaries, and manuals of style in all parts of the English-speaking world.

LANGUAGE CHANGE

The phenomenon of language change probably attracts more public notice and criticism than any other linguistic issue. There is a widely held belief that change must mean deterioration and decay. Older people observe the casual speech of the young, and conclude that standards have fallen markedly. They place the blame in various quarters—most often in the schools, where patterns of language education have changed a great deal in recent years, but also in state public broadcasting institutions, where any deviations from traditional norms provide an immediate focus of attack by conservative, linguistically sensitive listeners. The concern can even reach national proportions, as in the widespread reaction in Europe against what is thought of as the "American" English invasion.

Unfounded Pessimism

It is understandable that many people dislike change, but most of the   10
criticism of linguistic change is misconceived. It is widely felt that the
contemporary language illustrates the problem at its worst, but this belief
is shared by every generation. Moreover, many of the usage issues recur
across generations: several of the English controversies which are the
focus of current attention can be found in the books and magazines of

the 18th and 19th centuries—the debate over *it's me* and *very unique*, for example. In *The Queen's English* (1863), Henry Alford, the Dean of Canterbury, lists a large number of usage issues which worried his contemporaries, and gave them cause to think that the language was rapidly decaying. Most are still with us, with the language not obviously affected. In the mid-19th century, it was predicted that British and American English would be mutually unintelligible within 100 years!

There are indeed cases where linguistic change can lead to problems of unintelligibility, ambiguity, and social division. If change is too rapid, there can be major communication problems, as in contemporary Papua, New Guinea—a point which needs to be considered in connection with the field of language planning. But as a rule, the parts of language which are changing at any given time are tiny, in comparison to the vast, unchanging areas of language. Indeed, it is because change is so infrequent that it is so distinctive and noticeable. Some degree of caution and concern is therefore always desirable, in the interests of maintaining precise and efficient communication; but there are no grounds for the extreme pessimism and conservatism which is so often encountered—and which in English is often summed up in such slogans as "Let us preserve the tongue that Shakespeare spoke."

The Inevitability of Change

For the most part, language changes because society changes. To stop or control the one requires that we stop or control the other—a task which can succeed to only a very limited extent. Language change is inevitable and rarely predictable, and those who try to plan a language's future waste their time if they think otherwise—time which would be better spent in devising fresh ways of enabling society to cope with the new linguistic forms that accompany each generation. These days, there is in fact a growing recognition of the need to develop a greater linguistic awareness and tolerance of change, especially in a multi-ethnic society. This requires, among other things, that schools have the knowledge and resources to teach a common standard, while recognizing the existence and value of linguistic diversity. Such policies provide a constructive alternative to the emotional attacks which are so commonly made against the development of new words, meanings, pronunciations, and grammatical constructions. But before these policies can be implemented, it is necessary to develop a proper understanding of the inevitability and consequences of linguistic change.

Some people go a stage further, and see change in language as a progression from a simple to a complex state—a view which was common as a consequence of 19th-century evolutionary thinking. But there is no evidence for this view. Languages do not develop, progress, decay, evolve, or act according to any of the metaphors which imply a specific endpoint and level of excellence. They simply change, as society changes. If a language dies out, it does so because its status alters in society, as other cultures and languages take over its role: it does not die because it has "got too old," or "becomes too complicated," as is sometimes maintained. Nor, when languages change, do they move in a predetermined direction. Some are losing inflections; some are gaining them. Some are moving to an order where the verb precedes the object; others to an order where the object precedes the verb. Some languages are losing vowels and gaining consonants; others are doing the opposite. If metaphors must be used to talk about language change, one of the best is that of a system holding itself in a state of equilibrium, while changes take place within it; another is that of the tide, which always and inevitably changes, but never progresses, while it ebbs and flows.

FOCUSING ON CONTENT

1. According to Crystal, what does it mean to be a language prescriptivist? How does a prescriptivist differ from a descriptivist?

2. What were the aims of the eighteenth-century English grammarians? What is the legacy of their work with language?

3. Why does Crystal believe that both prescriptive and descriptive approaches are important?

4. What was the purpose of the language academies? How successful were they in fulfilling their objectives? Why was an English academy never formed?

5. According to Crystal, what linguistic issue attracts the most public notice and criticisms? What are his views on this issue?

6. What are some of the commonly held misconceptions about language change? How does Crystal refute each? What metaphors does he believe are most appropriate when discussing language change? (Glossary: *Figures of Speech*) Do they seem appropriate to you? Why or why not?

FOCUSING ON WRITING

1. What is Crystal's purpose in this selection? (Glossary: *Purpose*)

2. How would you describe Crystal's tone? (Glossary: *Tone*) Is his tone appropriate for his subject, audience, and purpose? Explain.

3. How has Crystal organized his essay? (Glossary: *Organization*) The heads in the text highlight the three main sections of the essay. Could these three sections be reordered without losing anything? Why or why not?

4. Why do you think Crystal italicized *facts, describe,* and *prescribe* in paragraph 3?

5. In paragraph 8, Crystal quotes Dr. Samuel Johnson from the preface to his *Dictionary*. What function does this extensive quotation serve in the context of the paragraph in which it appears?

LANGUAGE IN ACTION

The following excerpt is from *The Elements of Style* (1959 edition) by William Strunk Jr. and E. B. White. Read the passage and determine whether its objective is to be prescriptive or descriptive. How do you know? What clues in the wording help you make your determination?

Insightful. The word is a suspicious overstatement for "perceptive." If it is to be used at all, it should be used for instances of remarkably penetrating vision. Usually, it crops up merely to inflate the commonplace.

> That was an insightful remark you made.

> That was a perceptive remark you made.

In terms of. A piece of padding usually best omitted.

> The job was unattractive in terms of salary.

> The salary made the job unattractive.

Interesting. An unconvincing word; avoid it as a means of introduction. Instead of announcing that what you are about to tell is interesting, make it so.

> An interesting story is told of

> (Tell the story without preamble.)

> In connection with the forthcoming visit of Mr. B. to America, it is interesting to recall that he

> Mr. B., who will soon visit America

> Also to be avoided in introduction is the word *funny*. Nothing becomes funny by being labeled so.

Irregardless. Should be *regardless*. The error results from failure to see the negative in *-less* and from a desire to get it in as a prefix, suggested by such word as *irregular, irresponsible,* and, perhaps especially, *irrespective.*

-ize. Do not coin verbs by adding this tempting suffix. Many good and useful verbs do end in *-ize: summarize, temporize, fraternize, harmonize, fertilize.* But there is a growing list of abominations: *containerize, customize, prioritize, finalize,* to name four. Be suspicious of *-ize;* let your ear and your eye guide you. Never tack *-ize* onto a noun to create a verb. Usually you will discover that a useful verb already exists. Why say "moisturize" when there is the simple, unpretentious word *moisten?*

WRITING SUGGESTIONS

1. *(Writing from Experience)* Write an essay in which you recount your early school experiences with English. Did your teachers hold a prescriptivist or descriptivist attitude toward language? Do you remember being taught grammar, spelling, and penmanship in school? In what ways did

these experiences help shape your current attitudes toward speaking, reading, and writing?

2. (*Writing from Reading*) Read the prefaces to two desk dictionaries, and write a report on the relative weight given to descriptivist and prescriptivist approaches in each dictionary. Be sure to quote particularly revealing passages from the prefaces to support your assessments.

3. (*Writing from Research*) After doing some library research, write an essay in which you highlight the essentials in the debate between descriptivists and prescriptivists. From what you can gather, why has this debate become so emotionally charged?

LANGUAGE IN USE:
Two Short Stories

Many of the fundamental elements of our lives are quite amazing, yet we usually take them for granted. Just getting out of bed in the morning requires a dizzyingly complex series of internal actions involving biochemistry, mechanical physics, kinesiology, and so on, but all of these actions occur at the subconscious level. In much the same way, communication becomes automatic, and we rarely think about the marvelous complexity of language and its use, even as we read and speak. The world of fiction, however, often illuminates the power of language and helps us to see our lives and our language from a new perspective.

The following selections, both by renowned authors writing from diverse cultural backgrounds, show how even simple stories can reveal the layers of meaning in the words we use and the way we communicate. "The Story of the Arrowmaker," from Native American writer N. Scott Momaday, includes both a story from Native American tradition and Momaday's commentary about how it reveals the nature of words, meaning, and language. "Snow," by Julia Alvarez, a writer from the Dominican Republic, shows how words, without knowledge and context, are arbitrary and malleable.

Although one story is written and the other is part of an oral storytelling tradition, both create a setting in which aspects of the power of language are easy to understand and appreciate. Both also carry the urgency of a life-and-death situation—one real, one potential—which serves to further magnify the importance of language.

WRITING TO DISCOVER: *As you were growing up, did you hear family stories being told? Were some of them repeated often, especially by the same family storyteller? What kinds of stories were they? Did they reveal any particular cultural influences? Did any of the stories have a special emphasis on language? Briefly recount one or two of the stories and speculate on their meaning.*

The Story of the Arrowmaker

N. SCOTT MOMADAY

Celebrated writer and educator N. Scott Momaday is a Kiowa Indian. He has based much of his writing on his Indian ancestry and is the author of several books, including House Made of Dawn *(1969), for which he won the Pulitzer Prize,* The Way to Rainy

Mountain (1969) and In the Bear's House *(1999). In "The Story of the Arrowmaker," which appeared in* Parabola *in 1995, the narrator tells a very simple but at the same time complex story of the human condition as it is based on the spoken word. The story goes to the heart of the function of language and to the responsibility we share in using it.*

When I was a child, my father told me the story of the arrowmaker, and he told it to me many times, for I fell in love with it. I have no memory that is older than that of hearing it. This is the way it goes:

If an arrow is well made, it will have tooth marks upon it. That is how you know. The Kiowas made fine arrows and straightened them in their teeth. Then they drew them to the bow to see that they were straight. Once there was a man and his wife. They were alone at night in their tipi. By the light of the fire the man was making arrows. After a while he caught sight of something. There was a small opening in the tipi where two hides had been sewn together. Someone was there on the outside, looking in. The man went on with his work, but he said to his wife, "Someone is standing outside. Do not be afraid. Let us talk easily, as of ordinary things." He took up an arrow and straightened it in his teeth: then, as it was right for him to do, he drew it to the bow and took aim, first in this direction and then in that. And all the while he was talking, as if to his wife. But this is how he spoke: "I know that you are there on the outside, for I can feel your eyes upon me. If you are a Kiowa, you will understand what I am saying, and you will speak your name." But there was no answer, and the man went on in the same way, pointing the arrow all around. At last his aim fell upon the place where his enemy stood, and he let go of the string. The arrow went straight to the enemy's heart.

Heretofore the story of the arrowmaker has been the private possession of a very few, a tenuous link in that ancient chain of language which we call the oral tradition: tenuous because the tradition itself is so; for as many times as the story has been told, it was always but one generation removed from extinction. But it was held dear, too, on that same account. That is to say, it has been neither more nor less durable than the human voice, and neither more nor less concerned to express the meaning of the human condition. And this brings us to the heart of the matter at hand: The story of the arrowmaker is also a link between language and literature. It is a remarkable act of the mind, a realization of words and the world that is altogether simple and direct, yet nonetheless rare and profound, and it illustrates more clearly than anything else in my own experience, at least, something of the essential character of the imagination—and in particular of that personification which in this instance emerges from it: the man made of words.

It is a fine story, whole, intricately beautiful, precisely realized. It is worth thinking about, for it yields something of value; indeed, it is full of provocation, rich with suggestion and consequent meaning. There is often an inherent danger that we might impose too much of ourselves upon it. It is informed by an integrity that bears examination easily and well, and in the process it seems to appropriate our own reality and experience.

It is significant that the story of the arrowmaker returns in a special way upon itself. It is about language, after all, and it is therefore part and parcel of its own subject; virtually, there is no difference between the telling and that which is told. The point of the story lies, not so much in what the arrowmaker does, but in what he says—and indeed that he says it. The principal fact is that he speaks, and in so doing he places his very life in the balance. It is this aspect of the story which interests me most, for it is here that the language becomes most conscious of itself; we are close to the origin and object of literature, I believe: our sense of the verbal dimension is very keen, and we are aware of something in the nature of language that is at once perilous and compelling. "If you are a Kiowa, you will understand what I am saying, and you will speak your name." Everything is ventured in this simple declaration, which is also a question and a plea. The conditional element with which it begins is remarkably tentative and pathetic; precisely at this moment is the arrowmaker realized completely, and his reality consists in language, and it is poor and precarious. And all of this occurs to him as surely as it does to us. Implicit in that simple occurrence is all of his definition and his destiny, and all of ours. He ventures to speak because he must; language is the repository of his whole knowledge and experience, and it represents the only chance he has for survival. Instinctively, and with great care, he deals in the most honest and basic way with words. "Let us talk easily, as of ordinary things," he says. And of the ominous unknown he asks only the utterance of a name, only the most nominal sign that he is understood, that his words are returned to him on the sheer edge of meaning. But there is no answer, and the arrowmaker knows at once what he has not known before; that his enemy is, and that he has gained an advantage over him. This he knows certainly, and the certainty itself is his advantage, and it is crucial; he makes the most of it. The venture is complete and irrevocable, and it ends in success. The story is meaningful. It is so primarily because it is composed of language, and it is in the nature of language in turn that it proceeds to the formulation of meaning. Moreover, the story of the arrowmaker, as opposed to other stories in general, centers upon his procession of words toward meaning. It seems in fact to turn upon the very idea that language involves the elements of risk and responsibility; and in this it seeks to confirm itself. In a word, it seems to say, everything is a risk. That may be true, and it may also be that the whole of literature rests upon that truth.

The arrowmaker is preeminently the man made of words. He has consummate being in language; it is the world of his origin and of his posterity, and there is no other. But it is a world of definite reality and of infinite possibility. I have come to believe that there is a sense in which the arrowmaker has more nearly perfect being than have other men, by and large, as he imagines himself, whole and vital, going on into the unknown darkness and beyond. And this last aspect of his being is primordial and profound.

And yet the story has it that he is cautious and alone, and we are given to understand that his peril is great and immediate, and that he confronts it in the only way he can. I have no doubt that this is true, and I believe that there are implications which point directly to the determination of our literary experience and which must not be lost upon us. A final word, then, on an essential irony which marks this story and gives peculiar substance to the man made of words. The storyteller is nameless and unlettered. From one point of view we know very little about him, except that he is somehow translated for us in the person of an arrowmaker. But, from another, that is all we need to know. He tells us of his life in language, and of the awful risk involved. It must occur to us that he is one with the arrowmaker and that he has survived, by word of mouth, beyond other men. We said a moment ago that, for the arrowmaker, language represented the only chance of survival. It is worth considering that he survives in our own time, and that he has survived over a period of untold generations.

Snow

JULIA ALVAREZ

Julia Alvarez is a writer-in-residence at Middlebury College. She has taught at the University of Vermont, George Washington University, and at the Breadloaf Writers' Conference. Her best-selling novels— How the Garcia Girls Lost Their Accents *(1991),* In the Time of the Butterflies *(1994), and* ¡Yo! *(1997)—have received many honors, including the American Library Association's Notable Book of the Year and finalist for the National Book Critics Circle Award. Her collection of personal essays* Something to Declare *appeared in 1998. In the following short story, taken from* How the Garcia Girls Lost Their Accents, *Alvarez writes about how a young Hispanic girl, newly arrived in the United States, mistakes her first snowflakes for the fallout from a nuclear attack.*

Our first year in New York we rented a small apartment with a Catholic school nearby, taught by the Sisters of Charity, hefty women in long black gowns and bonnets that made them look peculiar, like dolls in mourning. I liked them a lot, especially my grandmotherly fourth grade teacher, Sister Zoe. I had a lovely name, she said, and she had me teach the whole class how to pronounce it. *Yo-lan-da.* As the only immigrant in my class, I was put in a special seat in the first row by the window, apart from the other children so that Sister Zoe could tutor me without disturbing them. Slowly, she enunciated the new words I was to repeat: *laundromat, cornflakes, subway, snow.*

Soon I picked up enough English to understand holocaust was in the air. Sister Zoe explained to a wide-eyed classroom what was happening in Cuba. Russian missiles were being assembled, trained supposedly on New York City. President Kennedy, looking worried too, was on the television at home, explaining we might have to go to war against the Communists. At school, we had air-raid drills: an ominous bell would go off and we'd file into the hall, fall to the floor, cover our heads with our coats, and imagine our hair falling out, the bones in our arms going soft. At home, Mami and my sisters and I said a rosary for world peace. I heard new vocabulary: *nuclear bomb, radioactive fallout, bomb shelter.* Sister Zoe explained how it would happen. She drew a picture of a mushroom on the blackboard and dotted a flurry of chalkmarks for the dusty fallout that would kill us all.

The months grew cold, November, December. It was dark when I got up in the morning, frosty when I followed my breath to school. One morning as I sat at my desk daydreaming out the window, I saw dots in the air like the ones Sister Zoe had drawn—random at first, then lots and lots. I shrieked, "Bomb! Bomb!" Sister Zoe jerked around, her full black skirt ballooning as she hurried to my side. A few girls began to cry.

But then Sister Zoe's shocked look faded. "Why, Yolanda dear, that's snow!" She laughed. "Snow."

"Snow," I repeated. I looked out the window warily. All my life I   5
had heard about the white crystals that fell out of American skies in the winter. From my desk I watched the fine powder dust the sidewalk and parked cars below. Each flake was different, Sister Zoe said, like a person, irreplaceable and beautiful.

WRITING SUGGESTIONS: MAKING CONNECTIONS

1. As discussed in the introduction, language can become too automatic and is often taken for granted. The two stories you just read illustrate aspects of the power and complexity of language by making language use a central focus. In a short essay, react to the statement that language is underestimated in our day-to-day lives. Do you agree with this statement? If so, why do we tend to underestimate the profound role language can play in our lives? If not, defend your reasoning. Explain how people work to appreciate and understand language.

2. In both "The Story of the Arrowmaker" and "Snow," the authors draw upon their experiences and cultural heritage to present their stories. Based on your own experiences or cultural background, write a short story in which you convey the inherent power and complexity of some aspect of the English language. Remember that failures and mistakes in communication, as found in "Snow," can yield insights just as profound as those gained from the successful use of language, as found in "The Story of the Arrowmaker."

3. "The Story of the Arrowmaker" and "Snow" are written in English, but both authors approach their subjects from the perspective of other cultures and the knowledge of different languages and storytelling traditions. Choose a specific Native American or Caribbean culture—Momaday is a Kiowa Indian, and Alvarez is from the Dominican Republic—and use the resources in your library and on the Internet to research its literature and storytelling traditions. Write an essay in which you present your research. What are the purposes of storytelling within the culture you chose? What are the characteristics of the stories in that culture? What do the stories and their use of language reveal about the culture?

6

WRITERS
ON WRITING

WRITING: THE TRANSACTION

What Happens When People Write?

MAXINE HAIRSTON

*Maxine Hairston is Professor Emerita of Rhetoric and Compo-
sition at the University of Texas at Austin, where she served as
coordinator of advanced expository writing courses, director of first-
year English, and associate dean of humanities. She is a past chair
of the Conference on College Composition and Communication
and has written many articles on rhetoric and teaching writing.
She has also authored and coauthored several textbooks, including*
The Scott, Foresman Handbook for Writers, *5th ed. (1996) and*
The Riverside Reader, *5th ed. (1996).*

In the following selection, taken from Hairston's textbook Successful Writing *(1998), now in its fourth edition, she takes the mystery out of writing by giving an overview of the writing process. By
looking at the way professional writers work, she shows us how to establish realistic expectations of what should happen each time we sit
down to write. Next, Hairston focuses on the differences between
two major types of writing—explanatory and exploratory—that
writers should master and value equally. She explains how a
writer's writing process can change depending on the type of writing someone is doing.*

WRITING TO DISCOVER: *Think about what happens when you sit
down to write. Do you have one particular pen that you like to use, or
do you compose on a personal computer? Where do you like to write?*

Do you have any special rituals that you go through before settling into your task? Briefly describe the process you go through from the time you make the decision to put an idea in writing (or are given an assignment) to the time that you submit final copy. Is the process roughly the same for all the different types of writing that you do? Explain.

Many people who have trouble writing believe that writing is a mysterious process that the average person cannot master. They assume that anyone who writes well does so because of a magic mixture of talent and inspiration, and that people who are not lucky enough to have those gifts can never become writers. Thus they take an "either you have it or you don't" attitude that discourages them before they even start to write.

Like most myths, this one has a grain of truth in it, but only a grain. Admittedly the best writers are people with talent just as the best musicians or athletes or chemists are people with talent. But that qualification does not mean that only talented people can write well any more than it means that only a few gifted people can become good tennis players. Tennis coaches know differently. From experience, they know any reasonably well-coordinated and healthy person can learn to play a fairly good game of tennis if he or she will learn the principles of the game and work at putting them into practice. They help people become tennis players by showing them the strategies that experts use and by giving them criticism and reinforcement as they practice those strategies. In recent years, as we have learned more about the processes of working writers, many teachers have begun to work with their writing students in the same way.

AN OVERVIEW OF THE WRITING PROCESS

How Professional Writers Work

- Most writers don't wait for inspiration. They write whether they feel like it or not. Usually they write on a schedule, putting in regular hours just as they would on a job.
- Professional writers consistently work in the same places with the same tools—pencil, typewriter, or word processor. The physical details of writing are important to them so they take trouble to create a good writing environment for themselves.
- Successful writers work constantly at observing what goes on around them and have a system for gathering and storing material. They collect clippings, keep notebooks, or write in journals.
- Even successful writers need deadlines to make them work, just like everyone else.
- Successful writers make plans before they start to write, but they keep their plans flexible, subject to revision.

- Successful writers usually have some audience in mind and stay aware of that audience as they write and revise.
- Most successful writers work rather slowly; four to six double-spaced pages is considered a good day's work.
- Even successful writers often have trouble getting started; they expect it and don't panic.
- Successful writers seldom know precisely what they are going to write before they start, and they plan on discovering at least part of their content as they work. (See section below on explanatory and exploratory writing.)
- Successful writers stop frequently to reread what they've written and consider such rereading an important part of the writing process.
- Successful writers revise as they write and expect to do two or more drafts of anything they write.
- Like ordinary mortals, successful writers often procrastinate and feel guilty about it; unlike less experienced writers, however, most of them have a good sense of how long they can procrastinate and still avoid disaster.

Explanatory and Exploratory Writing

Several variables affect the method and speed with which writers work—how much time they have, how important their task is, how skilled they are, and so on. The most important variable, however, is the kind of writing they are doing. I am going to focus on two major kinds here: *explanatory* and *exploratory*. To put it briefly, although much too simply, explanatory writing *tends* to be about information; exploratory writing *tends* to be about ideas.

Explanatory writing can take many forms: a movie review, an explanation of new software, an analysis of historical causes, a report on a recent political development, a biographical sketch. These are just a few possibilities. The distinguishing feature of all these examples and other kinds of explanatory writing is that the writer either knows most of what he or she is going to say before starting to write or knows where to find the material needed to get started. A typical explanatory essay might be on some aspect of global warming for an environmental studies course. The material for such a paper already exists—you're not going to create it or discover it within your subconscious. Your job as a writer is to dig out the material, organize it, and shape it into a clearly written, carefully supported essay. Usually you would know who your readers are for an explanatory essay and, from the beginning, shape it for that audience. 5

Writers usually make plans when they are doing explanatory writing, plans that can range from a page of notes to a full outline. Such plans help them to keep track of their material, put it in some kind of order, and find a pattern for presenting it. For explanatory writing, many writers find that the traditional methods work well; assertion/support, cause and effect, process, compare/contrast, and so on. Much of the writing that students do in college is explanatory, as is much business writing. Many magazine articles and nonfiction books are primarily explanatory writing. It's a crucially important kind of writing, one that we depend on for information and education, one that keeps the machinery of business and government going.

Explanatory writing is not necessarily easy to do nor is it usually formulaic. It takes skill and care to write an accurate, interesting story about the physician who won a Nobel Prize for initiating kidney transplants or an entertaining and informative report on how the movie *Dick Tracy* was made. But the process for explanatory writing is manageable. You identify the task, decide what the purpose and who the audience are, map out a plan for finding and organizing information, then divide the writing itself into doable chunks and start working. Progress may be painful, and you may have to draft and revise several times to clarify points or get the tone just right, but with persistence, you can do it.

Exploratory writing may also take many forms: a reflective personal essay, a profile of a homeless family, an argument in support of funding for multimillion dollar science projects, or a speculative essay about the future of the women's movement. These are only a few possibilities. What distinguishes these examples and exploratory writing in general is that the writer has only a partially formed idea of what he or she is going to write before starting. A typical piece of exploratory writing might be a speculative essay on why movies about the Mafia appeal so much to the American public. You might hit on the idea of writing such a piece after you have seen several mob movies—*Goodfellas, Miller's Crossing,* and *Godfather III*—but not really know what you would say or who your audience would be. The material for such a paper doesn't exist; you would have to begin by reading, talking to people, and by drawing on the ideas and insights you've gleaned from different sources to reach your own point of view. And you would certainly expect some of your most important ideas—your own conclusions—to come to you as you wrote.

Because you don't know ahead of time exactly what you're going to say in exploratory writing, it's hard to make a detailed plan or outline; however, you can and should take copious notes as you prepare to write. You might be able to put down a tentative thesis sentence, for example, "American moviegoers are drawn to movies about the Mafia and mob violence because they appeal to a streak of lawlessness that has always been strong in American character." Such a sentence could be an anchor to get you started writing, but as a main idea, it could change or even disappear as the paper developed.

Many papers you write in college will be exploratory papers, for example, an interpretive paper in a literature course, an essay on the future of an ethnic community for a cultural anthropology course, or an argumentative paper for a government course proposing changes in our election laws. Many magazine articles and books are also exploratory, for example, an

10

article on the roots of violence in American cities or an autobiographical account of being tagged a "slow learner" early in one's school career. Both in and out of college, exploratory writing is as important as explanatory writing because it is the springboard and testing ground for new ideas.

Exploratory writing isn't necessarily harder to do than explanatory writing, but it is harder to plan because it resists any systematic approach. That makes it appeal to some writers, particularly those who have a reflective or speculative turn of mind. They like the freedom of being able just to write to see what is going to develop. But although exploratory writers start out with more freedom, eventually they too have to discipline themselves to organize their writing into clear, readable form. They also have to realize that exploratory writing usually takes longer and requires more drafts.

When you're doing exploratory writing, anticipate that your process will be messy. You have to tolerate uncertainty longer because ideas keep coming as you write and it's not always clear what you're going to do with them and how—or if—you can fit them into your paper. Exploratory writing is also hard to organize—sometimes you'll have to outline *after* you've written your first draft in order to get the paper under control. Finally, you also have to have confidence in your own instincts; now that you are focusing on ideas and reflections more than on facts, you have to believe that you have something worth writing about and that other people are interested in reading it.

Of course, not all writing can be easily classified as either explanatory or exploratory; sometimes you'll be working with information and ideas in the same paper and move from presenting facts to reflecting about their implications. For example, in an economics course you might report on how much Japan has invested in the United States economy over the last decade and where those investments have been made; then you could speculate about the long-range impact on American business. If you were writing a case study of a teenage mother for a social work class, you would use mostly explanatory writing to document the young woman's background, schooling, and important facts about her present situation; then you could go to exploratory writing to suggest how her options for the future can be improved.

In general, readers respond best to writing that thoughtfully connects facts to reflections, explanations to explorations. So don't hesitate to mix the two kinds of writing if it makes your paper stronger and more interesting. At this point, you might ask "Why do these distinctions matter to me?" I think there are several reasons.

First, it helps to realize that there isn't *a* writing process—there are   15
writing *processes,* and some work better than others in specific situations. Although by temperament and habit you may be the "just give me the facts, ma'am," kind of person who prefers to do explanatory writing, you also need to become proficient at exploratory writing in order to write the speculative, reflective papers that are necessary when you have to write about long-range goals or speculate about philosophical issues. If,

on the other hand, by temperament you'd rather ignore outlines and prefer to spin theories instead of report on facts, you also need to become proficient at explanatory writing. In almost any profession, you're going to have to write reports, summarize data, or present results of research.

Second, you'll become a more proficient and relaxed writer if you develop the habit of analyzing before you start, whether you are going to be doing primarily explanatory or exploratory writing. Once you decide, you can consciously switch into certain writing patterns and write more efficiently. For instance, when you're writing reports, case studies, research papers, or analyses, take the time to rough out an outline and make a careful list of the main points you need to make. Schedule time for research and checking facts; details are going to be important. Review some of the routine but useful patterns you could use to develop your paper: cause and effect, definition, process, narration, and so forth. They can work well when you have a fairly clear idea of your purpose and what you're going to say.

If you're starting on a less clearly defined, more open-ended paper—for example, a reflective essay about Picasso's portrayal of women for an art history course—allow yourself to be less organized for a while. Be willing to start without knowing where you're going. Look at some paintings to get your ideas flowing, talk to some other students, and then just start writing, confident that you'll find your content and your direction. Don't worry if you can't get the first paragraph right—it will come later. Your first goal with exploratory writing should be to generate a fairly complete first draft in order to give yourself something to work with. Remember to give yourself plenty of time to revise. You'll need it.

Finally, resist the idea that one kind of writing is better than another. It's not. Sometimes there's a tendency, particularly in liberal arts classes, to believe that people who do theoretical or reflective writing are superior; that exploratory writing is loftier and more admirable than writing in which people present facts and argue for concrete causes. That's not really the case. Imaginative, thoughtful writing about theories and opinions is important and interesting, but informative, factual writing is also critically important, and people who can do it well are invaluable. Anyone who hopes to be an effective, confident writer should cultivate the habits that enable him or her to do both kinds of writing well.

FOCUSING ON CONTENT

1. According to Hairston, in what ways is a writing teacher like a tennis coach? Does this analogy help you to view your writing teacher differently? (Glossary: *Analogy*) Explain.

2. Review the list of items that Hairston provides to explain how professional writers work. How many points on the list are you already doing? What items if any, surprised you?

3. What are the main differences between explanatory and exploratory writing? Which type do you usually find yourself doing? Is Hairston's essay explanatory, exploratory, or a combination of both types of writing?

FOCUSING ON WRITING

1. Carefully examine Hairston's diction or choice of words in this selection. (Glossary: *Diction*) Would you consider any of her words the technical language or jargon of writing teachers? (Glossary: *Technical Language*) Is her language appropriate for her intended audience? Explain.

2. Discuss how Hairston uses comparison and contrast to explain the differences between explanatory and exploratory writing. (Glossary: *Comparison and Contrast*) What examples does she use to illustrate her points? (Glossary: *Examples*)

3. What transitions does Hairston use to connect the ideas in paragraphs 15 and 16? (Glossary: *Transitions*) Briefly explain how her transitions work.

4. How would you describe Hairston's tone in this essay? (Glossary: *Tone*) Explain how her choice of words helps her create this tone. (Glossary: *Diction*) Use examples from the text to show what you mean. How important is tone to writers? To readers?

LANGUAGE IN ACTION

Consider the following cartoon from the *New Yorker*. What insights into the writing process does the cartoon give you? How does humor help people talk about situations that might otherwise be difficult to discuss? Explain.

"No wonder you can't write. You're not plugged in!"

WRITING SUGGESTIONS

1. (*Writing from Experience*) How well do you know yourself as a writer? Drawing on what you wrote in your Writing to Discover entry for this selection, write an essay in which you describe the process you normally follow in writing a composition. Do you begin by brainstorming for ideas, thinking before you write, or do you simply start writing, hoping that ideas will come to you as you write? How many drafts does it usually take before you have a piece of writing that satisfies you? What part of the process is the most difficult for you? The easiest for you?

2. (*Writing from Reading*) In list form, describe the processes for writing an explanatory and an exploratory essay. Discuss your lists with others in your class. What are the main differences between the two processes? Write an essay about these differences.

3. (*Writing from Research*) How useful do you find outlining? When in the writing process do you usually prepare an outline? Do your outlining practices vary according to the type of writing you are doing? What recommendations about outlining have your previous teachers made? Consult several texts in the library about outlining. Then, using the preceding questions as a starting point, compose a brief questionnaire about outlining practices and the benefits of outlining, and give the questionnaire to the other students in your writing class. What conclusions can you draw from your tabulated questionnaires? Based on your findings, write an essay arguing for or against the benefits of outlining.

Writing for an Audience

LINDA FLOWER

Linda Flower is professor of English at Carnegie-Mellon University, where she directed the Business Communication program for a number of years. She has been a leading researcher on the composing process, and the results of her investigations have shaped and informed her influential writing text Problem-Solving Strategies for Writing, *now in its fifth edition (1999).*

In this selection, which is taken from that text, Flower's focus is on audience — the people for whom we write. She believes that writers must establish a "common ground" between themselves and their readers, one that lessens their differences in knowledge, attitudes, and needs. Although we can never be certain who might read what we write, it is nevertheless important for us to have a target audience in mind. Many of the decisions that we make as writers are influenced by that real or imagined reader.

WRITING TO DISCOVER: *Imagine for a moment that you just received a speeding ticket for going sixty-five miles per hour in a thirty-mile-per-hour zone. How would you describe the episode to your best friend? To your parents? To the judge in court? Sketch out the three versions, and then write about how the three versions of your story differ. How do you account for these differences?*

The goal of the writer is to create a momentary common ground between the reader and the writer. You want the reader to share your knowledge and your attitude toward that knowledge. Even if the reader eventually disagrees, you want him or her to be able for the moment to *see things as you see them.* A good piece of writing closes the gap between you and the reader.

ANALYZE YOUR AUDIENCE

The first step in closing that gap is to gauge the distance between the two of you. Imagine, for example, that you are a student writing your parents, who have always lived in New York City, about a wilderness survival expedition you want to go on over spring break. Sometimes obvious differences such as age or background will be important, but the critical differences for writers usually fall into three areas: the reader's *knowledge* about the topic; his or her *attitude* toward it, and his or her personal or professional *needs.* Because these differences often exist, good writers do more than simply express their meaning; they pinpoint the critical differ-

ences between themselves and their reader and design their writing to reduce those differences. Let us look at these areas in more detail.

KNOWLEDGE.   This is usually the easiest difference to handle. What
does your reader need to know? What are the main ideas you hope to
teach? Does your reader have enough background knowledge to really
understand you? If not, what would he or she have to learn?

ATTITUDES.   When we say a person has knowledge, we usually refer
to his conscious awareness of explicit facts and clearly defined concepts.
This kind of knowledge can be easily written down or told to someone else.
However, much of what we "know" is not held in this formal, explicit way.
Instead it is held as an attitude or image — as a loose cluster of associations.
For instance, my image of lakes includes associations many people would
have, including fishing, water skiing, stalled outboards, and lots of kids
catching night crawlers with flashlights. However, the most salient or powerful parts of my image, which strongly color my whole attitude toward
lakes, are thoughts of cloudy skies, long rainy days, and feeling generally
cold and damp. By contrast, one of my best friends has a very different cluster of associations: to him a lake means sun, swimming, sailing, and happily
sitting on the end of a dock. Needless to say, our differing images cause us
to react quite differently to a proposal that we visit a lake. Likewise, one reason people often find it difficult to discuss religion and politics is that terms
such as "capitalism" conjure up radically different images.

As you can see, a reader's image of a subject is often the source of at-   5
titudes and feelings that are unexpected and, at times, impervious to mere
facts. A simple statement that seems quite persuasive to you, such as
"Lake Wampago would be a great place to locate the new music camp,"
could have little impact on your reader if he or she simply doesn't visual-
ize a lake as a "great place." In fact, many people accept uncritically any
statement that fits in with their own attitudes — and reject, just as uncritically, anything that does not.

Whether your purpose is to persuade or simply to present your perspective, it helps to know the image and attitudes that your reader already
holds. The more these differ from your own, the more you will have to
do to make him or her *see* what you mean.

NEEDS.   When writers discover a large gap between their own knowledge and attitudes and those of the reader, they usually try to change the
reader in some way. Needs, however, are different. When you analyze a
reader's needs, it is so that you, the writer, can adapt to him. If you ask a friend
majoring in biology how to keep your fish tank from clouding, you don't want
to hear a textbook recitation on the life processes of algae. You expect a friend
to adapt his or her knowledge and tell you exactly how to solve your problem.

The ability to adapt your knowledge to the needs of the reader is often crucial to your success as a writer. This is especially true in writing done on a job. For example, as producer of a public affairs program for a television station, 80 percent of your time may be taken up planning the details of new shows, contacting guests, and scheduling the taping sessions. But when you write a program proposal to the station director, your job is to show how the program will fit into the cost guidelines, the FCC requirements for relevance, and the overall programming plan for the station. When you write that report your role in the organization changes from producer to proposal writer. Why? Because your reader needs that information in order to make a decision. He may be *interested* in your scheduling problems and the specific content of the shows, but he *reads* your report because of his own needs as station director of the organization. He has to act.

In college, where the reader is also a teacher, the reader's needs are a little less concrete but just as important. Most papers are assigned as a way to teach something. So the real purpose of a paper may be for you to make connections between two historical periods, to discover for yourself the principle behind a laboratory experiment, or to develop and support your own interpretation of a novel. A good college paper doesn't just rehash the facts; it demonstrates what your reader, as a teacher, needs to know — that you are learning the thinking skills his or her course is trying to teach.

Effective writers are not simply expressing what they know, like a student madly filling up an examination bluebook. Instead they are *using* their knowledge: reorganizing, maybe even rethinking their ideas to meet the demands of an assignment or the needs of their reader. 10

FOCUSING ON CONTENT

1. How, according to Flower, does a competent writer achieve the goal of closing the gap between himself or herself and the reader? How does a writer determine what a reader's "personal or professional needs" (2) are?

2. What, for Flower, is the difference between knowledge and attitude? Why is it important for writers to understand this difference?

3. In paragraph 4, Flower discusses the fact that many words have both positive and negative associations. How do you think words come to have associations? (Glossary: *Connotation/Denotation*) Consider, for example, such words as *home, anger, royalty, welfare, politician,* and *strawberry shortcake.*

4. What does Flower believe constitutes a "good college paper" (9)? Do you agree with her assessment? Why or why not?

FOCUSING ON WRITING

1. Flower wrote this selection for college students. How well did she assess your knowledge, attitude, and needs about the subject of a writer's audience?

Does Flower's use of language and examples show a sensitivity to her audience? Provide specific examples to support your view. (Glossary: *Examples*)

2. Flower notes in paragraph 4 that many words often have "a loose cluster of associations." Explain how you can use this fact to advantage when writing an argument. A personal essay. An informative piece.

3. When using technical language in a paper on a subject you have thoroughly researched or are already familiar with, why is it important for you to know your audience? (Glossary: *Audience*) What language strategies might you use to adapt your knowledge to your audience? Explain. How could your classmates, friends, or parents help you?

LANGUAGE IN ACTION

Analyze the language of the advertisement on the following page for a hard drive workstation from Corporate Systems Center. Based on your own familiarity with computer language, identify those words that you consider computer jargon. (Glossary: *Technical Language*) Which words are appropriate for a general audience? An expert audience? For what kind of audience do you think this ad was written? Explain.

WRITING SUGGESTIONS

1. (*Writing from Experience*) Write an essay in which you discuss the proposition that honesty is a prerequisite of good writing. Ask yourself what it means to write honestly. What does dishonest writing look and sound like? Do you have a responsibility to be an honest writer? How is honesty in writing related to audience? Be sure to illustrate your essay with examples from your own experiences.

2. (*Writing from Reading*) In order to write well, a writer has to identify his or her audience. Choose a topic that is important to you, and taking into account what Flower calls your audience's knowledge, attitude, and needs, write a letter about that topic to your best friend. Then write a letter on the same topic to your instructor. How does your message differ from letter to letter? How does your diction change? (Glossary: *Diction*) What conclusions about audience can you draw from your two letters? How successful do you think you were in "closing the gap between you and the reader" in each letter?

3. (*Writing from Research*) When you become an expert or authority on a subject, you learn its special language or jargon. (Glossary: *Technical Language*) In your library or on the Internet, research the technical language of a field that interests you, such as the language of a college major, a sport, or a hobby. What is the function or purpose of the technical language you researched? Write an essay in which you discuss the benefits of technical language as well as the potential drawbacks of using it with inappropriate audiences.

The Case for Short Words

RICHARD LEDERER

A lifelong student of language, Richard Lederer taught for twenty-seven years at St. Paul's School in Concord, New Hampshire. Anyone who has read one of his nine books will know why he has been called "America's wittiest verbalist." Lederer loves language and enjoys writing about its marvelous richness. His books include Crazy English *(1998),* Anguished English *(1988),* The Play of Words *(1991),* Adventures of a Verbivore *(1994), and* Nothing Risqué, Nothing Gained *(1995). Lederer holds a doctorate from the University of New Hampshire and is currently vice president of SPELL, Society for the Preservation of English Language and Literature. He is a language commentator on New Hampshire public radio and writes a weekly column, "Looking at Language," for the* Concord Monitor.*

In the following selection, a chapter from The Miracle of Language *(1991), Lederer sings the praises of small words. Too often we think that someone is measuring the quality of our work by counting the number of long words we use. Nothing could be further from the truth. Lederer reminds us that well-chosen monosyllabic words can be a writer's best friends because they are functional and often pack a powerful punch.*

WRITING TO DISCOVER: *Are you impressed by writers who use long words with seeming ease? Do you consider long words to be more intelligent than short words? Clearer? How would you describe your own writing vocabulary? Explain how word length affects writing — your own and others.*

When you speak and write, there is no law that says you have to use big words. Short words are as good as long ones, and short, old words — like *sun* and *grass* and *home* — are best of all. A lot of small words, more than you might think, can meet your needs with a strength, grace, and charm that large words do not have.

Big words can make the way dark for those who read what you write and hear what you say. Small words cast their clear light on big things — night and day, love and hate, war and peace, and life and death. Big words at times seem strange to the eye and the ear and the mind and the heart. Small words are the ones we seem to have known from the time we were born, like the hearth fire that warms the home.

Short words are bright like sparks that glow in the night, prompt like the dawn that greets the day, sharp like the blade of a knife, hot like salt tears that scald the cheek, quick like moths that flit from flame to flame, and terse like the dart and sting of a bee.

Here is a sound rule: Use small, old words where you can. If a long word says just what you want to say, do not fear to use it. But know that our tongue is rich in crisp, brisk, swift, short words. Make them the spine and the heart of what you speak and write. Short words are like fast friends. They will not let you down.

The title of this chapter and the four paragraphs that you have just read   5 are wrought entirely of words of one syllable. In setting myself this task, I did not feel especially cabined, cribbed, or confined. In fact, the structure helped me to focus on the power of the message I was trying to put across.

One study shows that twenty words account for twenty-five percent of all spoken English words, and all twenty are monosyllabic. In order of frequency they are: *I, you, the, a, to, is, it, that, of, and, in, what, he, this, have, do, she, not, on,* and *they.* Other studies indicate that the fifty most common words in written English are each made of a single syllable.

For centuries our finest poets and orators have recognized and employed the power of small words to make a straight point between two minds. A great many of our proverbs punch home their points with pithy monosyllables: "Where there's a will, there's a way," "A stitch in time saves nine," "Spare the rod and spoil the child," "A bird in the hand is worth two in the bush."

Nobody used the short word more skillfully than William Shakespeare, whose dying King Lear laments:

> And my poor fool is hang'd! No, no, no life!
> Why should a dog, a horse, a rat have life,
> And thou no breath at all? . . .
> Do you see this? Look on her, look, her lips.
> Look there, look there!

Shakespeare's contemporaries made the King James Bible a centerpiece of short words — "And God said, Let there be light: and there was light. And God saw the light, that it was good." The descendants of such mighty lines live on in the twentieth century. When asked to explain his policy to Parliament, Winston Churchill responded with these ringing monosyllables: "I will say: it is to wage war, by sea, land, and air, with all our might and with all our strength that God can give us." In his "Death of the Hired Man" Robert Frost observes that "Home is the place where, when you go there,/They have to take you in." And William H. Johnson uses ten two-letter words to explain his secret of success: "If it is to be,/It is up to me."

You don't have to be a great author, statesman, or philosopher to tap   10 the energy and eloquence of small words. Each winter I ask my ninth graders at St. Paul's School to write a composition composed entirely of one-syllable words. My students greet my request with obligatory moans and groans, but, when they return to class with their essays, most feel that, with the pressure to produce high-sounding polysyllables relieved, they have created some of their most powerful and luminous prose. Here are submissions from two of my ninth graders:

> What can you say to a boy who has left home? You can say that he has done wrong, but he does not care. He has left home so that he will not have to deal with what you say. He wants to go as far as he can. He will do what he wants to do.
>
> This boy does not want to be forced to go to church, to comb his hair, or to be on time. A good time for this boy does not lie in your reach, for what you have he does not want. He dreams of ripped jeans, shorts with no starch, and old socks.
>
> So now this boy is on a bus to a place he dreams of, a place with no rules. This boy now walks a strange street, his long hair blown back by the wind. He wears no coat or tie, just jeans and an old shirt. He hates your world, and he has left it. — *Charles Shaffer*

> For a long time we cruised by the coast and at last came to a wide bay past the curve of a hill, at the end of which lay a small town. Our long boat ride at an end, we all stretched and stood up to watch as the boat nosed its way in.
>
> The town climbed up the hill that rose from the shore, a space in front of it left bare for the port. Each house was a clean white with sky blue or grey trim; in front of each one was a small yard, edged by a white stone wall strewn with green vines.
>
> As the town basked in the heat of noon, not a thing stirred in the streets or by the shore. The sun beat down on the sea, the land, and the back of our necks, so that, in spite of the breeze that made the vines sway, we all wished we could hide from the glare in a cool, white house. But, as there was no one to help dock the boat, we had to stand and wait.
>
> At last the head of the crew leaped from the side and strode to a large house on the right. He shoved the door wide, poked his head through the gloom, and roared with a fierce voice. Five or six men came out, and soon the port was loud with the clank of chains and creak of planks as the men caught ropes thrown by the crew, pulled them taut, and tied them to posts. Then they set up a rough plank so we could cross from the deck to the shore. We all made for the large house while the crew watched, glad to be rid of us. — *Celia Wren*

You too can tap into the vitality and vigor of compact expression. Take a suggestion from the highway department. At the boundaries of your speech and prose place a sign that reads "Caution: Small Words at Work."

FOCUSING ON CONTENT

1. In paragraph 4, Lederer offers us one rule for better writing: "Use small, old words where you can. If a long word says just what you want to say, do not fear to use it." Is this a rule that you can live with? Why or why not?

2. In the new millennium, do you think Lederer's case for using small words is still relevant? Explain. What did you think about small words before reading Lederer's essay? What public perceptions of small words does Lederer have to combat?

3. In paragraphs 7–9, Lederer presents a number of examples ranging from proverbs and biblical passages to quotations from well-known writers. What point about small words does he make with these examples?

FOCUSING ON WRITING

1. As you were reading Lederer's essay for the first time, were you surprised by his announcement in paragraph 5 that the preceding paragraphs contained only single-syllable words? If not, when were you first aware of what he was doing? What does Lederer's strategy in his opening paragraphs tell you about small words?

2. In paragraph 3, Lederer builds his case for small words with a series of similes. (Glossary: *Figures of Speech*) Explain how each of these similes works and how each affects your image of small words.

3. Carefully analyze the two student essays Lederer presents. In particular, circle all the main verbs that each student uses. What, if anything, do these verbs have in common? After studying the two essays, what conclusions can you draw about verbs and strong, powerful writing?

4. In paragraph 6, Lederer shifts from an emotional argument for small words to a logical one. How did his numerous examples affect you? (Glossary: *Examples*) Which examples made the greatest impact on you? Why?

LANGUAGE IN ACTION

In his 1990 book *The Play of Words*, Richard Lederer presents the following activity called "Verbs with Verve." What do you learn about the power of verbs from this exercise? Explain.

Researchers showed groups of test subjects a picture of an automobile accident and then asked this question: "How fast were the cars going when they———?" The blank was variously filled in with *bumped, contacted, hit, collided,* or *smashed.* Groups that were asked "How fast were the cars going when they smashed?" responded with the highest estimates of speed.

All of which proves that verbs create specific images in the mind's eye. Because verbs are the words in a sentence that express action and movement, they are the spark plugs of effective style. The more specific the verbs you choose in your speaking and writing, the more sparky will be the images you flash on the minds of your listeners and readers.

Suppose you write, "'No,' she said and left the room." Grammatically there is nothing wrong with this sentence. But because the verbs *say* and *leave* are among the most general and colorless in the English language, you have missed the chance to create a vivid word picture. Consider the alternatives:

SAID		LEFT	
apologized	jabbered	backed	sauntered
asserted	minced	bolted	skipped
blubbered	mumbled	bounced	staggered
blurted	murmured	crawled	stamped
boasted	shrieked	darted	stole
cackled	sighed	flew	strode
commanded	slurred	hobbled	strutted
drawled	snapped	lurched	stumbled
giggled	sobbed	marched	tiptoed
groaned	whispered	plodded	wandered
gurgled	whooped	pranced	whirled

If you had chosen from among these vivid verbs and had crafted the sentence "'No,' she sobbed, and stumbled out of the room," you would have created a powerful picture of something quite distraught.

Here are brief descriptions of twenty different people. Choosing from the two lists of synonyms for *said* and *left*, fill in the blanks of the sentence "'No,' he/she _____, and _____ the room." Select the pair of verbs that best create the most vivid picture of each person described. Throughout your answers try to use as many different verbs as you can:

1. an angry person	11. an excited person
2. a baby	12. a frightened person
3. a braggart	13. a happy person
4. a child	14. someone in a hurry
5. a clown	15. an injured person
6. a confused person	16. a military officer
7. a cowboy/cowgirl	17. a sneaky person
8. someone crying	18. a timid person
9. a drunkard	19. a tired person
10. an embarrassed person	20. a witch

WRITING SUGGESTIONS

1. (*Writing from Experience*) How would you characterize your own writing? Do you think of yourself as a short-word person or a long-word person? Write a paper analyzing several paragraphs of one of your essays to see whether or not your perception of your own writing is accurate. What patterns emerge? How does your use of long and short words affect the main point of your writing?

2. (*Writing from Reading*) Write an essay in which you argue for the importance of using a varied, extensive vocabulary in your writing. Be sure to anticipate and counter any objections you believe Lederer might have to your argument. You may find it helpful to read Malcolm X's "Coming to an Awareness of Language" (pp. 63–66) before starting to write.

3. (*Writing from Research*) Philosopher Ludwig Wittgenstein once said, "The limits of my language are the limits of my world." What do you think he meant? Have you ever been at a loss for words? Do you remember how it felt to be unable to express yourself the way you wanted to? Does a large, far-ranging vocabulary really expand one's world? Write an essay in which you support or argue against Wittgenstein's generalization. In developing your essay, use carefully selected examples from your own experience, interviews with peers, and research in the library or on the Internet to support your position.

How to Write with Style

Kurt Vonnegut Jr.

Kurt Vonnegut was born in 1922 in Indianapolis, Indiana. While he was a student at Cornell University, he joined the army to serve in World War II. He fought in the European campaign and was taken prisoner by the German army. He also witnessed the Allied firebombing of Dresden in 1945, a bloody and pointless incident that inspired his novel Slaughterhouse-Five *(1969). After the war, Vonnegut completed his education at the University of Chicago, and since 1950 he has worked full time as a writer. In addition to* Slaughterhouse-Five, *his best-known novels are probably* Player Piano *(1952) and* Cat's Cradle *(1963). Vonnegut's more recent novels are* Breakfast of Champions *(1973),* Galapagos *(1999),* Hocus Pocus *(1990), and* Timequake *(1993). Some of his short stories have been collected in* Welcome to the Monkey House *(1968).*

In the following selection, originally written in 1982 for the International Paper Company as part of a famous writers' series on good writing, Vonnegut shares his thoughts on the elements of style and on how writing style reflects the level of a writer's respect for his or her readers. He then offers simple yet practical suggestions for writing with style.

WRITING TO DISCOVER: *Has anyone ever commented on your style as a writer? If so, what did you think about the comments? How would you characterize your writing style? Does it reflect your style of speech? Your personality? Your degree of seriousness? Are you satisfied with your writing style as it is, or would you like to change it? Explain.*

Newspaper reporters and technical writers are trained to reveal almost nothing about themselves in their writings. This makes them freaks in the world of writers, since almost all of the other ink-stained wretches in that world reveal a lot about themselves to readers. We call these revelations, accidental and intentional, elements of style.

These revelations tell us as readers what sort of person it is with whom we are spending time. Does the writer sound ignorant or informed, stupid or bright, crooked or honest, humorless or playful—? And on and on.

Why should you examine your writing style with the idea of improving it? Do so as a mark of respect for your readers, whatever you're writing. If you scribble your thoughts any which way, your readers will surely feel that you care nothing about them. They will mark you down as an egomaniac or a chowderhead—or worse, they will stop reading you.

The most damning revelation you can make about yourself is that you do not know what is interesting and what is not. Don't you yourself like or dislike writers mainly for what they choose to show you or make you think about? Did you ever admire an empty-headed writer for his or her mastery of the language? No.

So your own winning style must begin with ideas in your head.   5

1. FIND A SUBJECT YOU CARE ABOUT

Find a subject you care about and which you in your heart feel others should care about. It is this genuine caring, and not your games with language, which will be the most compelling and seductive element in your style.

I am not urging you to write a novel, by the way—although I would not be sorry if you wrote one, provided you genuinely cared about something. A petition to the mayor about a pothole in front of your house or a love letter to the girl next door will do.

2. DO NOT RAMBLE, THOUGH

I won't ramble on about that.

3. KEEP IT SIMPLE

As for your use of language: Remember that two great masters of language, William Shakespeare and James Joyce, wrote sentences which were almost childlike when their subjects were most profound. "To be or not to be?" asks Shakespeare's Hamlet. The longest word is three letters long. Joyce, when he was frisky, could put together a sentence as intricate and as glittering as a necklace for Cleopatra, but my favorite sentence in his short story "Eveline" is this one: "She was tired." At the point in the story, no other words could break the heart of a reader as those three words do.

Simplicity of language is not only reputable, but perhaps even sacred. The   10
Bible opens with a sentence well within the writing skills of a lively fourteen-year-old: "In the beginning God created the heaven and the earth."

4. HAVE THE GUTS TO CUT

It may be that you, too, are capable of making necklaces for Cleopatra, so to speak. But your eloquence should be the servant of the ideas in your head. Your rule might be this: If a sentence, no matter how excellent, does not illuminate your subject in some new and useful way, scratch it out.

5. SOUND LIKE YOURSELF

The writing style which is most natural for you is bound to echo the speech you heard when a child. English was the novelist Joseph Conrad's third language, and much that seems piquant in his use of English was no doubt colored by his first language, which was Polish. And lucky indeed is the writer who has grown up in Ireland, for the English spoken there is so amusing and musical. I myself grew up in Indianapolis, where common speech sounds like a band saw cutting galvanized tin, and employs a vocabulary as unornamental as a monkey wrench.

In some of the more remote hollows of Appalachia, children still grow up hearing songs and locutions of Elizabethan times. Yes, and many Americans grow up hearing a language other than English, or an English dialect a majority of Americans cannot understand.

All these varieties of speech are beautiful, just as the varieties of butterflies are beautiful. No matter what your first language, you should treasure it all your life. If it happens not to be standard English, and if it shows itself when you write standard English, the result is usually delightful, like a very pretty girl with one eye that is green and one that is blue.

I myself find that I trust my own writing most, and others seem to   15
trust it most, too, when I sound most like a person from Indianapolis, which is what I am. What alternatives do I have? The one most vehemently recommended by teachers has no doubt been pressed on you, as well: to write like cultivated Englishmen of a century or more ago.

6. SAY WHAT YOU MEAN TO SAY

I used to be exasperated by such teachers, but am no more. I understand now that all those antique essays and stories with which I was to compare my own work were not magnificent for their datedness or foreignness, but for saying precisely what their authors meant them to say. My teachers wished me to write accurately, always selecting the most effective words, and relating the words to one another unambiguously, rigidly, like parts of a machine. The teachers did not want to turn me into an Englishman after all. They hoped that I would become understandable—and therefore understood. And there went my dream of doing with words what Pablo Picasso did with paint or what any number of jazz idols did with music. If I broke all the rules of punctuation, had words mean whatever I wanted them to mean, and strung them together higgledy-piggledy, I would simply not be understood. So you, too, had better avoid Picasso-style or jazz-style writing, if you have something worth saying and wish to be understood.

Readers want our pages to look very much like pages they have seen before. Why? This is because they themselves have a tough job to do, and they need all the help they can get from us.

7. PITY THE READERS

They have to identify thousands of little marks on paper, and make sense of them immediately. They have to *read,* an art so difficult that most people don't really master it even after having studied it all through grade school and high school—twelve long years.

So this discussion must finally acknowledge that our stylistic options as writers are neither numerous nor glamorous, since our readers are bound to be such imperfect artists. Our audience requires us to be sympathetic and patient teachers, even willing to simplify and clarify—whereas we would rather soar high above the crowd, singing like nightingales.

That is the bad news. The good news is that we Americans are gov-   20
erned under a unique Constitution, which allows us to write whatever we please without fear of punishment. So the most meaningful aspect of our styles, which is what we choose to write about, is utterly unlimited.

8. FOR REALLY DETAILED ADVICE

For a discussion of literary style in a narrower sense, in a more technical sense, I commend to your attention *The Elements of Style,* by William Strunk, Jr., and E. B. White (Macmillan, 1979). E. B. White is, of course, one of the most admirable literary stylists this country has so far produced.

You should realize, too, that no one would care how well or badly Mr. White expressed himself, if he did not have perfectly enchanting things to say.

FOCUSING ON CONTENT

1. Vonnegut believes that we like to read certain writers for what they "choose to show [us] or make [us] think about" (4). Why else do you read? Explain.

2. According to Vonnegut, what is the relationship between a writer's style and his or her audience? What responsibilities does he believe writers have to readers?

3. Which of Vonnegut's seven pointers on writing do you find most useful? Least useful? Why?

4. Teachers of writing often assign essays and stories for their students to read. What advantages does Vonnegut see in such reading? What, for you, is the connection between reading and writing?

FOCUSING ON WRITING

1. How would you characterize Vonnegut's style in this piece? Do you think he has followed his own advice? Explain.

2. Did you feel Vonnegut's respect for you as a reader as you read his essay? Specifically, what in his essay led you to this conclusion?

3. Identify several of the metaphors and similes that Vonnegut uses. (Glossary: *Figures of Speech*) How does each one work in the context of this selection? What advantages does figurative language afford the writer?

LANGUAGE IN ACTION

Read the following poem by New Englander James Hayford. What insights does it give you about style? Would Vonnegut be likely to agree or disagree with Hayford's view? How would you characterize Hayford's own style in this poem? Explain.

STYLE

As the cold currents of the brook
Render its sands and pebbles clear,
Just so does style in man or book
Brighten the content, bring it near.

WRITING SUGGESTIONS

1. (*Writing from Experience*) Have you read any of Vonnegut's novels? If so, write him a letter in which you share your reactions to his work. If not, write a letter to an author whose work you have read. Be sure that in writing your letter you follow Vonnegut's advice in this selection.

2. (*Writing from Reading*) How do you suppose Vonnegut would react to Richard Lederer's essay "The Case for Short Words" or William Zinsser's "Simplicity," which follows? Write an essay in which you explore some of the reasons why writers find it difficult to follow Vonnegut's third rule: Keep It Simple.

3. (*Writing from Research*) As Vonnegut suggests, look at a copy of Strunk and White's *The Elements of Style*. Does the size of the volume surprise you? Write an essay in which you argue for or against requiring this book for every incoming first-year student at your school. Support your position with references to Strunk and White and to other sources you discovered in the library or on the Internet.

Simplicity

WILLIAM ZINSSER

Born in New York City in 1922, William Zinsser was educated at Princeton University. After serving in the army in World War II, he worked at the New York Herald Tribune *as an editor, writer, and critic. During the 1970s he taught a popular course in nonfiction at Yale University, and from 1979 to 1987 he was general editor of the Book-of-the-Month Club. Zinsser has written more than a dozen books, including* The City Dwellers *(1962)* Pop Goes America *(1966),* Spring Training *(1989), and three widely used books on writing:* On Writing Well *(6ᵗʰ ed., 1998),* Writing with a Word Processor *(1983), and* Writing to Learn *(1988). Currently, he teaches at the New School in New York City, and his freelance writing regularly appears in some of our leading magazines.*

The following selection is taken from On Writing Well. *This book grew out of Zinsser's many years of experience as a professional writer and teacher. In this essay, Zinsser exposes what he believes is the writer's number one problem — "clutter." He sees Americans "strangling in unnecessary words, circular constructions, pompous frills, and meaningless jargon." His solution is simple: Writers must know what they want to say and must be thinking clearly as they start to compose. Then self-discipline and hard work are necessary to achieve clear, simple prose. No matter what your experience as a writer has been, you will find Zinsser's observations sound and his advice practical.*

WRITING TO DISCOVER: *Some people view writing as "thinking on paper." They believe that by seeing something written on a page they are better able to "see what they think." Write about the relationship, for you, between writing and thinking. Are you one of those people who likes to "see" ideas on paper while trying to work things out? Or do you like to think through ideas before writing about them?*

Clutter is the disease of American writing. We are a society strangling in unnecessary words, circular constructions, pompous frills, and meaningless jargon.

Who can understand the viscous language of everyday American commerce: the memo, the corporation report, the business letter, the notice from the bank explaining its latest "simplified" statement? What member of an insurance or medical plan can decipher the brochure explaining his costs and benefits? What father or mother can put together a child's toy from the instructions on the box? Our national tendency is to inflate and thereby sound important. The airline pilot who announces that he is presently anticipating experiencing considerable precipitation wouldn't think of saying it may rain. The sentence is too simple—there must be something wrong with it.

But the secret of good writing is to strip every sentence to its cleanest components. Every word that serves no function, every long word that could be a short word, every adverb that carries the same meaning that's already in the verb, every passive construction that leaves the reader unsure of who is doing what—these are the thousand and one adulterants that weaken the strength of a sentence. And they usually occur in proportion to education and rank.

During the 1960s the president of my university wrote a letter to mollify the alumni after a spell of campus unrest. "You are probably aware," he began, "that we have been experiencing very considerable potentially explosive expressions of dissatisfaction on issues only partially related." He meant the students had been hassling them about different things. I was far more upset by the president's English than by the students' potentially explosive expressions of dissatisfaction. I would have preferred the presidential approach taken by Franklin D. Roosevelt when he tried to convert into English his own government's memos, such as this blackout order of 1942:

> Such preparations shall be made as will completely obscure all Federal buildings and non-Federal buildings occupied by the Federal government during an air raid for any period of time from visibility by reason of internal or external illumination.

"Tell them," Roosevelt said, "that in buildings where they have to   5
keep the work going to put something across the windows."

Simplify, simplify. Thoreau said it, as we are so often reminded, and no American writer more consistently practiced what he preached. Open *Walden* to any page and you will find a man saying in a plain and orderly way what is on his mind:

> I went to the woods because I wished to live deliberately, to front only the essential facts of life, and see if I could not learn what it had to teach, and not, when I came to die, discover that I had not lived.

How can the rest of us achieve such enviable freedom from clutter? The answer is to clear our heads of clutter. Clear thinking becomes clear writing; one can't exist without the other. It's impossible for a muddy thinker to write good English. You may get away with it for a paragraph or two, but soon the reader will be lost, and there's no sin so grave, for the reader will not easily be lured back.

Who is this elusive creature, the reader? The reader is someone with an attention span of about 30 seconds—a person assailed by other forces competing for attention. At one time these forces weren't so numerous: newspapers, radio, spouse, home, children. Today they also include a "home entertainment center" (TV, VCR, tapes, CDs), pets, a fitness program, a yard and all the gadgets that have been bought to keep it spruce, and that most potent of competitors, sleep. The person snoozing in a chair with a magazine or a book is a person who was being given too much unnecessary trouble by the writer.

It won't do to say that the reader is too dumb or too lazy to keep pace with the train of thought. If the reader is lost, it's usually because the writer hasn't been careful enough. The carelessness can take any number of forms. Perhaps a sentence is so excessively cluttered that the reader, hacking through the verbiage, simply doesn't know what it means. Perhaps a sentence has been so shoddily constructed that the reader could read it in several ways. Perhaps the writer has switched pronouns in mid-sentence, or has switched tenses, so the reader loses track of who is talking or when the action took place. Perhaps Sentence B is not a logical sequel to Sentence A—the writer, in whose head the connection is clear, hasn't bothered to provide the missing link. Perhaps the writer has used an important word incorrectly by not taking the trouble to look it up. The writer may think "sanguine" and sanguinary" mean the same thing, but the difference is a bloody big one. The reader can only infer (speaking of big differences) what the writer is trying to imply.

Faced with such obstacles, readers are at first tenacious. They blame   10
themselves—they obviously missed something, and they go back over the mystifying sentence, or over the whole paragraph, piecing it out like an ancient rune, making guesses and moving on. But they won't do this for long. The writer is making them work too hard, and they will look for one who is better at the craft.

Writers must therefore constantly ask: What am I trying to say? Surprisingly often they don't know. Then they must look at what they have written and ask: Have I said it? Is it clear to someone encountering the subject for the first time? If it's not, some fuzz has worked its way into the machinery. The clear writer is someone clearheaded enough to see this stuff for what it is: fuzz.

I don't mean that some people are born clearheaded and are therefore natural writers, whereas others are naturally fuzzy and will never write well. Thinking clearly is a conscious act that writers must force upon themselves, as if they were working on any other project that requires logic: adding up a laundry list or doing an algebra problem. Good writing doesn't come naturally, though most people obviously think it does. Professional writers are constantly being bearded by strangers who say they'd like to "try a little writing sometime"—meaning when they retire from their real profession, which is difficult, like insurance or real estate. Or they say, "I could write a book about that." I doubt it.

Writing is hard work. A clear sentence is not accident. Very few sentences come out right the first time, or even the third time. Remember this in moments of despair. If you find that writing is hard, it's because it *is* hard. It's one of the hardest things people do.

FOCUSING ON CONTENT

1. What exactly is clutter? When do words qualify as clutter, and when do they not?

2. In paragraph 2, Zinsser states that "Our national tendency is to inflate and thereby sound important." What do you think he means by inflate? Provide several examples to illustrate how people use language to inflate.

3. In paragraph 9, Zinsser lists some of the language-based obstacles that a reader may encounter in carelessly constructed prose. Which of these problems most try your patience? Why?

4. One would hope that education would help in the battle against clutter, but, as Zinsser notes, wordiness "usually occur[s] in proportion to education and rank" (4). Do your own experiences or observations support Zinsser's claim? Discuss.

FOCUSING ON WRITING

1. What assumptions does Zinsser make about readers? According to Zinsser, what responsibilities do writers have to readers? How do these responsibilities manifest themselves in Zinsser's writing? How do you think Linda Flower (pp. 139–41) or Kurt Vonnegut (pp. 150–53) would respond to what Zinsser says about audience? (Glossary: *Audience*) Explain.

2. Zinsser believes that writers need to ask themselves two questions — "What am I trying to say?" and "Have I said it?" — constantly as they write. How would these questions help you eliminate clutter from your own writing? Give some examples from one of your essays.

3. In order "to strip every sentence to its cleanest components," we need to be sensitive to the words we use and know how they function within our sentences. For each of the "adulterants that weaken the strength of a sentence," which Zinsser identifies in paragraph 3, provide an example from your own writing.

4. Zinsser knows that sentence variety is an important feature of good writing. Locate several examples of the short sentences (seven or fewer words) he uses in this essay, and explain how each relates in length, meaning, and impact to the sentences around it.

LANGUAGE IN ACTION

The following two pages show a passage from Zinsser's final manuscript for this essay. Carefully study the manuscript, and discuss how Zinsser eliminated clutter in his own prose. Then, using Zinsser as a model, judiciously eliminate the clutter from several paragraphs in one of your papers.

5 --

is too dumb or too lazy to keep pace with the ~~writer's~~ train of thought. My sympathics are ~~entirely~~ with him.) ~~He's not so dumb.~~ (If the reader is lost, it is generally because the writer ~~of the article~~ has not been careful enough to keep him on the ~~proper~~ path.

This carelessness can take any number of ~~different~~ forms. Perhaps a sentence is so excessively ~~long and~~ cluttered that the reader, hacking his way through ~~all~~ the verbiage, simply doesn't know what *it* ~~the writer~~ means. Perhaps a sentence has been so shoddily constructed that the reader could read it in any of *several* ~~two or three different~~ ways. ~~He thinks he knows what the writer is trying to say, but he's not sure.~~ Perhaps the writer has switched pronouns in mid-sentence, or ~~perhaps he~~ has switched tenses, so the reader loses track of who is talking ~~to whom,~~ or ~~exactly~~ when the action took place. Perhaps Sentence B is not a logical sequel to Sentence A -- the writer, in whose head the connection is ~~perfectly~~ clear, has not *bothered to provide* ~~given enough thought to providing~~ the missing link. Perhaps the writer has used an important word incorrectly by not taking the trouble to look it up ~~and make sure.~~ He may think that "sanguine" and "sanguinary" mean the same thing, but) ~~I can assure you that~~ (the difference is a bloody big one ~~to the reader.~~ *The reader* ~~He~~ can only ~~try to~~ infer ~~what~~ (speaking of big differences) what the writer is trying to imply.

Faced with *these* ~~such a variety of~~ obstacles, the reader is at first a remarkably tenacious bird. He ~~tends to~~ blame*s* himself. ~~He~~ obviously missed something, ~~he thinks,~~ and he goes back over the mystifying sentence, or over the whole paragraph, piecing it out like an ancient rune, making guesses and moving on. But he won't do this for long. ~~He will soon run out of patience.~~ (The writer is making him work too hard ~~-- harder than he should have to work --~~ (and the reader will look for ~~a writer~~ *one* who is better at his craft.

6 --

The writer must therefore constantly ask himself: What am
I trying to say? ~~in this sentence?~~ (Surprisingly often, he
doesn't know.) ~~And~~ Then he must look at what he has ~~just~~
written and ask: Have I said it? Is it clear to someone
encountering ~~who is coming upon~~ the subject for the first time? If it's
not, ~~clear,~~ it is because some fuzz has worked its way into the
machinery. The clear writer is a person ~~who is~~ clear-headed
enough to see this stuff for what it is: fuzz.

I don't mean ~~to suggest~~ that some people are born
clear-headed and are therefore natural writers, whereas
others ~~other people~~ are naturally fuzzy and will ~~therefore~~ never write
well. Thinking clearly is ~~an entirely~~ conscious act that the
writer must force ~~keep forcing~~ upon himself, just as if he were
embarking ~~starting out~~ on any other ~~kind of~~ project that requires ~~calls for~~ logic:
adding up a laundry list or doing an algebra problem ~~or playing
chess.~~ Good writing doesn't ~~just~~ come naturally, though most
people obviously think it does. ~~it's as easy as walking.~~ The professional

WRITING SUGGESTIONS

1. (*Writing from Experience*) Think about what you do every time you write. Does your process differ from that described by Hairston (pp. 131–36) or Zinsser? Write an essay in which you discuss any differences you discover between your own writing process and those described by Hairston and Zinsser. Does your writing process change with the type of writing you are doing? Explain.

2. (*Writing from Reading*) Each of the essays in Chapter 6, "Writers on Writing," is concerned with the importance of writing well, of using language effectively and responsibly. Write an essay in which you explore one of the common themes (audience, revision, diction, simplicity) that is emphasized in two or more of the selections.

3. (*Writing from Research*) Visit your library and/or local bookstore and examine the reference books offering advice on writing. What kinds of books did you find? What does the large number of such books say to you about Americans' attitudes toward writing? Compare and contrast the approaches several books take and the audiences at which each book is aimed. What conclusions can you draw from your comparisons?

The Maker's Eye: Revising Your Own Manuscripts

Donald M. Murray

Born in Boston, Massachusetts, in 1924, Donald M. Murray taught writing for many years at the University of New Hampshire, his alma mater. He has served as an editor at Time *magazine, and he won the Pulitzer Prize in 1954 for editorials that appeared in the* Boston Globe. *Murray's published works include novels, short stories, poetry, and sourcebooks for teachers of writing, like* A Writer Teaches Writing *(1968),* The Craft of Revision *(1991), and* Learning by Teaching *(1982), in which he explores aspects of the writing process.* Write to Learn, *(6th ed,. 1998), a textbook for college composition courses, is based on Murray's belief that writers learn to write by writing, by taking a piece of writing through the whole process, from invention to revision.*

In the following essay, first published in the Writer *in October 1973 and later revised for this text, Murray discusses the importance of revision to the work of the writer. Most professional writers live by the maxim that "writing is rewriting." And to rewrite or revise effectively, we need to become better readers of our own work, open to discovering new meanings, and sensitive to our use of language. Murray draws on the experiences of many writers to make a compelling argument for careful revising and editing.*

WRITING TO DISCOVER: *Thinking back on your education to date, what did you think you had to do when teachers told you to revise a piece of your writing? How did the request to revise make you feel? Write about your earliest memories of revising some of your writing. What kinds of changes do you remember making?*

When students complete a first draft, they consider the job of writing done—and their teachers too often agree. When professional writers complete a first draft, they usually feel that they are at the start of the writing process. When a draft is completed, the job of writing can begin.

That difference in attitude is the difference between amateur and professional, inexperience and experience, journeyman and craftsman. Peter F. Drucker, the prolific business writer, calls his first draft "the zero draft"—after that he can start counting. Most writers share the feeling that the first draft, and all of those which follow, are opportunities to discover what they have to say and how best they can say it.

To produce a progression of drafts, each of which says more and says it more clearly, the writer has to develop a special kind of reading skill.

In school we are taught to decode what appears on the page as finished writing. Writers, however, face a different category of possibility and responsibility when they read their own drafts. To them the words on the page are never finished. Each can be changed and rearranged, can set off a chain reaction of confusion or clarified meaning. This is a different kind of reading which is possibly more difficult and certainly more exciting.

Writers must learn to be their own best enemy. They must accept the criticism of others and be suspicious of it; they must accept the praise of others and be even more suspicious of it. Writers cannot depend on others. They must detach themselves from their own pages so that they can apply both their caring and their craft to their own work.

Such detachment is not easy. Science-fiction writer Ray Bradbury   5 supposedly puts each manuscript away for a year to the day and then rereads it as a stranger. Not many writers have the discipline or the time to do this. We must read when our judgment may be at its worst, when we are close to the euphoric moment of creation.

Then the writer, counsels novelist Nancy Hale, "should be critical of everything that seems to him most delightful in his style. He should excise what he most admires, because he wouldn't thus admire it if he weren't . . . in a sense protecting it from criticism." John Ciardi, the poet, adds, "The last act of the writing must be to become one's own reader. It is, I suppose, a schizophrenic process, to begin passionately and to end critically, to begin hot and to end cold; and, more important, to be passion-hot and critic-cold at the same time."

Most people think that the principal problem is that writers are too proud of what they have written. Actually, a greater problem for most professional writers is one shared by the majority of students. They are overly critical, think everything is dreadful, tear up page after page, never complete a draft, see the task as hopeless.

The writer must learn to read critically but constructively, to cut what is bad, to reveal what is good. Eleanor Estes, the children's book author, explains: "The writer must survey his work critically, coolly, as though he were a stranger to it. He must be willing to prune, expertly and hard-heartedly. At the end of each revision, a manuscript may look . . . worked over, torn apart, pinned together, added to, deleted from, words changed and words changed back. Yet the book must maintain its original freshness and spontaneity."

Most readers underestimate the amount of rewriting it usually takes to produce spontaneous reading. This is a great disadvantage to the student writer, who sees only a finished product and never watches the craftsman who takes the necessary step back, studies the work carefully, returns to the task, steps back, returns, steps back, again and again. Anthony Burgess, one of the most prolific writers in the English-speaking world, admits, "I might revise a page twenty times." Roald Dahl, the popular children's writer, states, "By the time I'm nearing the end of a story, the first part will have been reread and altered and corrected at least 150 times. . . . Good writing is essentially rewriting. I am positive of this."

Rewriting isn't virtuous. It isn't something that ought to be done. It is simply something that most writers find they have to do to discover what they have to say and how to say it. It is a condition of the writer's life.

There are, however, a few writers who do little formal rewriting, primarily because they have the capacity and experience to create and review a large number of invisible drafts in their minds before they approach the page. And some writers slowly produce finished pages, performing all the tasks of revision simultaneously, page by page, rather than draft by draft. But it is still possible to see the sequence followed by most writers most of the time in rereading their own work.

Most writers scan their drafts first, reading as quickly as possible to catch the larger problems of subject and form, and then move in closer and closer as they read and write, reread and rewrite.

The first thing writers look for in their drafts is *information*. They know that a good piece of writing is built from specific, accurate, and interesting information. The writer must have an abundance of information from which to construct a readable piece of writing.

Next writers look for *meaning* in the information. The specifics must build to a pattern of significance. Each piece of specific information must carry the reader toward meaning.

Writers reading their own drafts are aware of *audience*. They put themselves in the reader's situation and make sure that they deliver information which a reader wants to know or needs to know in a manner which is easily digested. Writers try to be sure that they anticipate and answer the questions a critical reader will ask when reading the piece of writing.

Writers make sure that the *form* is appropriate to the subject and the audience. Form, or genre, is the vehicle which carries meaning to the reader, but form cannot be selected until the writer has adequate information to discover its significance and an audience which needs or wants that meaning.

Once writers are sure the form is appropriate, they must then look at the *structure,* the order of what they have written. Good writing is built on a solid framework of logic, argument, narrative, or motivation which runs through the entire piece of writing and holds it together. This is the time when many writers find it most effective to outline as a way of visualizing the hidden spine by which the piece of writing is supported.

The element on which writers may spend a majority of their time is *development*. Each section of a piece of writing must be adequately developed. It must give readers enough information so that they are satisfied. How much information is enough? That's as difficult as asking how much garlic belongs in a salad. It must be done to taste, but most beginning writers underdevelop, underestimating the reader's hunger for information.

As writers solve development problems, they often have to consider questions of *dimension*. There must be a pleasing and effective proportion among all the parts of the piece of writing. There is a continual process of subtracting and adding to keep the piece of writing in balance.

Finally, writers have to listen to their own voices. *Voice* is the force   20
which drives a piece of writing forward. It is an expression of the writer's authority and concern. It is what is between the words on the page, what glues the piece of writing together. A good piece of writing is always marked by a consistent, individual voice.

As writers read and reread, write and rewrite, they move closer and closer to the page until they are doing line-by-line editing. Writers read their own pages with infinite care. Each sentence, each line, each clause, each phrase, each word, each mark of punctuation, each section of white space between the type has to contribute to the clarification of meaning.

Slowly the writer moves from word to word, looking through language to see the subject. As a word is changed, cut, or added, as a construction is rearranged, all the words used before that moment and all those that follow that moment must be considered and reconsidered.

Writers often read aloud at this stage of the editing process, muttering or whispering to themselves, calling on the ear's experience with language. Does this sound right—or that? Writers edit, shifting back and forth from eye to page to ear to page. I find I must do this careful editing in short runs, no more than fifteen or twenty minutes at a stretch, or I become too kind with myself. I begin to see what I hope is on the page, not what actually is on the page.

This sounds tedious if you haven't done it, but actually it is fun. Making something right is immensely satisfying, for writers begin to learn what they are writing about by writing. Language leads them to meaning, and there is the joy of discovery, of understanding, of making meaning clear as the writer employs the technical skills of language.

Words have double meanings, even triple and quadruple meanings.   25
Each word has its own potential of connotation and denotation. And when writers rub one word against the other, they are often rewarded with a sudden insight, an unexpected clarification.

The maker's eye moves back and forth from word to phrase to sentence to paragraph to sentence to phrase to word. The maker's eye sees the need for variety and balance, for a firmer structure, for a more appropriate form. It peers into the interior of the paragraph, looking for coherence, unity, and emphasis, which make meaning clear.

I learned something about this process when my first bifocals were prescribed. I had ordered a larger section of the reading portion of the glass because of my work, but even so, I could not contain my eyes within this new limit of vision. And I still find myself taking off my glasses and bending my nose toward the page, for my eyes unconsciously flick back and forth across the page, back to another page, forward to still another, as I try to see each evolving line in relation to every other line.

When does this process end? Most writers agree with the great Russian writer Tolstoy, who said, "I scarcely ever reread my published writings, if by chance I come across a page, it always strikes me: all this must be rewritten; this is how I should have written it."

The maker's eye is never satisfied, for each word has the potential to ignite new meaning. This article has been twice written all the way through the writing process [. . .]. Now it is to be republished in a book. The editors made a few small suggestions, and then I read it with my maker's eye. Now it has been re-edited, re-revised, re-read, and re-re-edited, for each piece of writing to the writer is full of potential and alternatives.

A piece of writing is never finished. It is delivered to a deadline, torn out of the typewriter on demand, sent off with a sense of accomplishment and shame and pride and frustration. If only there were a couple more days, time for just another run at it, perhaps then . . .   30

FOCUSING ON CONTENT

1. How does Murray define *information* and *meaning* (13–14)? Why is the distinction between the two terms important?

2. According to Murray, at what point(s) in the writing process do writers become concerned about the individual words they are using? What do you think Murray means when he says in paragraph 24 that "language leads [writers] to meaning"?

3. The phrase "the maker's eye" appears in Murray's title and in several places throughout the essay. What do you suppose he means by this? Consider how the maker's eye could be different from the reader's eye.

4. According to Murray, when is a piece of writing finished? What, for him, is the function of deadlines?

FOCUSING ON WRITING

1. What does Murray see as the connection between reading and writing? How does reading help the writer? What should writers be looking for in their reading? What kinds of writing techniques or strategies does Murray use in his essay? Why should we read a novel or magazine article differently than we would a draft of one of our own essays?

2. According to Murray, writers look for information, meaning, audience, form, structure, development, dimension, and voice in their drafts. What rationale or logic do you see, if any, in the way Murray has ordered these items? Are these the kinds of concerns you have when reading your drafts? Explain.

3. What are the essential differences between revising and editing? What types of language concerns are dealt with at each stage? Why is it important to revise before editing?

4. Murray notes that writers often reach a stage in their editing where they read aloud, "muttering or whispering to themselves, calling on the ear's experience with language" (23). What exactly do you think writers are listening for when they read aloud? Try reading several paragraphs of Murray's essay aloud. Explain what you learned about his writing? Have you ever read your own writing aloud? If so, what did you discover?

5. Compared to the paragraphs of many other writers, Murray's paragraphs are short. Why do you suppose Murray chose to use short paragraphs? What, for example, would be lost if paragraphs 12–14 or 24–25 were joined together? Explain.

LANGUAGE IN ACTION

Carefully read the opening four paragraphs of Annie Dillard's "Living Like Weasels," which is taken from *Teaching a Stone to Talk* (1982). Using two different color pens, first circle the subject and underline the verb in each main clause in one color, and then circle the subject and underline the verb in each subordinate clause with the other. What does this exercise reveal about Dillard's diction (nouns and verbs) and sentence structure?

A weasel is wild. Who knows what he thinks? He sleeps in his underground den, his tail draped over his nose. Sometimes he lives in his den for two days without leaving. Outside, he stalks rabbits, mice, muskrats, and birds, killing more bodies than he can eat warm, and often dragging the carcasses home. Obedient to instinct, he bites his prey at the neck, either splitting the jugular vein at the throat or crunching the brain at the base of the skull, and he does not let go. One naturalist refused to kill a weasel who was socketed into his hand deeply as a rattlesnake. The man could in no way pry the tiny weasel off, and he had to walk half a mile to water, the weasel dangling from his palm, and soak him off like a stubborn label.

And once, says Ernest Thompson Seton—once, a man shot an eagle out of the sky. He examined the eagle and found the dry skull of a weasel fixed by the jaws to his throat. The supposition is that the eagle had pounced on the weasel and the weasel swiveled and bit as instinct taught him, tooth to neck, and nearly won. I would like to have seen that eagle from the air a few weeks or months before he was shot: was the whole weasel still attached to his feathered throat, a fur pendant? Or did the eagle eat what he could reach, gutting the living weasel with his talons before his breast, bending his beak, cleaning the beautiful airborne bones?

I have been reading about weasels because I saw one last week. I startled a weasel who startled me, and we exchanged a long glance.

Twenty minutes from my house, through the woods by the quarry and across the highway, is Hollins Pond, a remarkable piece of shallowness, where I like to go at sunset and sit on a tree trunk. Hollins Pond is also called Murray's Pond; it covers two acres of bottomland near Tinker Creek with six inches of water and six thousand lily pads. In winter, brown-and-white steers stand in the middle of it, merely dampening their hooves; from the distant shore they look like miracle itself, complete with miracle's nonchalance. Now, in summer, the steers are gone. The water lilies have blossomed and spread to a green horizontal plane that is terra firma to plodding blackbirds, and tremulous ceiling to black leeches, crayfish, and carp.

WRITING SUGGESTIONS

1. (*Writing from Experience*) According to Murray, many professional writers view first drafts as something they have to do before they can get started with the real work of writing—revision. How do you view your first drafts? Why do you suppose teachers report that revision is the most difficult stage in the writing process for their students? What is it about revision that makes it difficult, or at least makes people perceive it as being difficult? Write an essay in which you explore your own experiences with revision. You may find it helpful to review what you wrote for the Writing to Discover prompt at the beginning of this essay.

2. (*Writing from Reading*) What, for you, is the difference between revising and editing? Using information from Murray's essay as well as material from at least one other selection in this chapter, write an essay in which you highlight the distinctive characteristics of these two oft-confused stages in the writing process.

3. (*Writing from Research*) Writing about pressing social issues usually requires a clear statement of a particular problem and the precise definition of critical terms. For example, if you were writing about the increasing number of people being kept alive by machines, you would need to examine the debate surrounding the legal and medical definitions of the word *death*. Debates continue about the meanings of other controversial terms, such as *morality, minority* (ethnic), *alcoholism, racism, sexual harassment, life* (as in the abortion issue), *pornography, liberal, gay, censorship, conservative, remedial, insanity, literacy, political correctness, assisted suicide, lying, high crimes and misdemeanors,* and *kidnapping* (as in custody disputes). Select one of these words or one of your own. After carefully researching some of the controversial people, situations, and events surrounding your word, write an essay in which you discuss the problems associated with the term and its definition.

CASE IN POINT:
A Discussion of Usage

For more than three hundred years, a battle has been waging over what constitutes "good" English. Many Americans have insisted on the need for "correctness." Schools have traditionally taught the difference between *imply* and *infer,* that students should never split an infinitive, and that proper form is "between you and *me*" and not "between you and *I.*" Contemporary language critics admit that language changes over time, but they seem disturbed by the rapid changes that are occurring today: Many Americans pepper their speech with slang and jargon, others speak English only as a second language, and few people consistently speak what the purists call Standard English. Critics also point out that much of the writing produced in this country is error-ridden and ineffective.

The following three essays present different perspectives in the ongoing debate about the question of correct grammar and usage. In the first piece, "Its Academic, or Is It?" Charles R. Larson courageously and comically explores the ways in which Americans are misusing apostrophes. He believes that a decline in reading has led to a lack of knowledge about how to use this important punctuation mark. Further, he laments that few people are even concerned about it. In "Like I Said, Don't Worry," Patricia T. O'Conner discusses our national attitude toward grammar and usage from a different perspective than Larson. O'Conner is gentle and sympathetic with readers who have been intimidated by grammar, yet she doesn't devalue it. She recognizes that grammar serves a purpose but that the purpose is not to denigrate the speakers of the language. And in "A Rarity: Grammar Lessons from Dad," scientist Robert T. Klose openly discusses his concern for the language skills of his students. Rather than blaming the students, however, he levels the blame on our schools, the supposed "safe harbors for the standards of the English language."

Although these three writers take different viewpoints, each of them, with humor and without apology, affirms the strengths of a successful, long-standing linguistic system.

WRITING TO DISCOVER: *What has been your experience with grammar, punctuation, and usage in school? Did teachers ever intimidate you with their insistence on correct grammar and usage? How important to you is writing and speaking "correctly"? Recount an incident that helps to explain your current attitude toward correctness.*

Its Academic, or Is It?

CHARLES R. LARSON

A professor of literature at American University in Washington, D.C., since 1965, Charles R. Larson received both his B.A. and M.A. from the University of Colorado and his Ph.D. from Indiana University. After graduating from Colorado, he was among the first generation of Americans to join the Peace Corps, serving in Nigeria for two years. Larson has written several critical studies, including The Novel in the Third World *(1976) and* American Indian Fiction *(1978), and two works of fiction,* Academia Nuts *(1977) and* Arthur Dimmesdale *(1983). His articles, essays, and stories appear regularly in major magazines and newspapers.*

In the following essay, which first appeared as a "My Turn" column in Newsweek *in November 1995, Larson takes a stand for correct usage.*

If you're 35 years or older, you probably identify a common grammatical error in the heading on this page. Younger than that and, well, you likely have another opinion: "Its all relative"—except, of course, for the apostrophe. Unfortunately, age appears to be the demarcation here. For those in the older group, youth has already won the battle. I've been keeping a list of places where its is misused: newspapers, magazines, op-eds in major publications and, more recently, wall texts in museums. A few weeks ago I encountered the error in a book title: *St. Simons: A Summary of It's History,* by R. Edwin and Mary A. Green. My list is getting longer and longer.

Does it even matter that the apostrophe is going the way of the stop sign and the directional signal in our society? Does punctuation count any longer? Are my complaints the ramblings of an old goat who's taught English for too many years?

What's the big deal, anyway? Who cares whether it's its or it's? Editors don't seem to know when the apostrophe's necessary. (One of them confessed to me that people have always been confused about the apostrophe—better just get rid of it.) My university undergraduates are clearly befuddled by the correct usage. Too many graduate applications—especially those of students aspiring to be creative writers—provide no clue that the writer understands when an apostrophe is required. Even some of my colleagues are confused by this ugglesome contraction.

How can a three-letter word be so disarming, so capable of separating the men from the boys? Or the women from the girls? When in doubt use it both ways, as in a recent advertisement hyping improved, SAT, GRE, and LSAT scores: "Kaplan locations all over the U.S. are offering full-length exams just like the actual tests. It's a great way to test your

skills and get a practice score without the risk of your score being reported to schools. And now, for a limited time only, its absolutely free!"

And now, students, which one of the above spellings of the I word is   5
correct: (a) the first, (b) the second, (c) both, or (d) neither? Any wonder
why Educational Testing Services had to add 100 points to the revised
SAT exams?

It's been my recent experience that the apostrophe hasn't actually ex-
ited common usage; it's simply migrated somewhere later in the sentence.
Hence, "Shes lost her marble's" has become the preferred use of this irritating snippet of punctuation in current American writing. "Hes not lost his
hat; hes lost his brains'." "Theres gold in them there hill's." Or "It was the
best of times' and the worst of time's." The latter, of course, is from Charles
Dickens *A Tale of Two Cities'*. Or is it Charle's Dickens?

Where will this end? Virtual apostrophe's? At times I wonder if all
those missing apostrophes are floating somewhere in outer space. Don't
they have to be somewhere, if—as some philosophers tell us—nothing is
ever lost? Lately, I've seen the dirty three-letter word even punctuated as
its'. What's next?

I'ts? 'Its?

How complicated can this be? How difficult is it to teach a sixth
grader how to punctuate correctly?

Heaven knows I've tried to figure it out, agonized about it for years.   10
I remember being dismayed nearly 20 years ago when I was walking
around the neighborhood and discovered an enormous stack of books
that someone had put out on the curb, free for the taking. Most of the
titles were forgettable; hence the reason they'd been left for scavengers or
the next trash pickup. However, mixed among the flotsam and jetsam
was a brand-new hardback collegiate dictionary. How could this be, I
asked myself? Could someone have too many dictionaries? I think the
ideal would be one in every room.

Someone was sending me a signal. If words are unimportant, punctuation is something even more lowly. Why worry about such quodlibets?
When was the last time anyone even noticed? Certainly, no one at
Touchstone Books caught the errors in a recent ad for *Failing at Fairness: How Our Schools Cheat Girls,* by Myra and David Sadker. A testimonial for the book reads as follows: "Reader's will be stunned at the
overwhelming evidence of sexism the author's provide." You bet, and the
blurb writers' lack of grammatical correctness.

If editors at publishing houses can't catch these errors, who can? Errors
common to advertising copy have already spread into the books themselves. I dread walking into a bookstore a decade from now and encountering the covers of classics edited by a new generation of apostrophe-
challenged editors: *Father's and Sons', The Brothers' Karamazov, The Adventure's of Huckleberry Finn, The Postman Alway's Ring's Twice, A Mid-
summers' Night Dream.* (Who's wood's these are I think I know . . .)

The apostrophe is dead because reading is dead. Notice that I didn't say "The apostrophe's dead because reading's dead." That's far too complex an alteration. When in doubt simply write out the full sentence, carefully avoiding all possessives and contradictions. Soon, no one will be certain about grammatical usage anyway. Computers will come without an apostrophe key. Why bother about errors on the Internet? E-mail messages are often so badly written they make no sense. Fortunately, they get erased almost immediately. Everything pass'es too quickly.

Last week I went to a lamp store to purchase two new floor lamps for our living room: five rooms of lamps and hundreds of styles—except for one minor problem. Not one lamp was designed for reading. Virtually all the lamps illuminated the ceiling; all were designed for television addicts, not readers. So how is one supposed to read TV Guide? The place was so dark (was I expected to hold my book up to the ceiling?) I could hardly find my way out. And speaking of TV, what's the plural: TVs or TV's?

Time to stop this grumbling. Thing's fall apart. If I start making a list   15
only of the times the apostrophe is used properly, I won't even have to worry about it. I can already hear you say, "Your kidding."

Like I Said, Don't Worry

Patricia T. O'Conner

A former New York Times Book Review *editor, Patricia T. O'Conner has reviewed for the* Book Review *and written "On Language" guest columns for William Safire in the* New York Times Magazine. *She has also conducted a grammar course for* Times *employees. In her two books,* Woe Is I: The Grammar-phobe's Guide to Better English in Plain English *(1996) and* Words Fail Me: What Everyone Who Writes Should Know about Writing *(1999), O'Conner strives to demystify the realms of grammar, usage, and writing.*

In the following article, which first appeared as a "My Turn" column in Newsweek *in December 1996, O'Conner suggests that we lighten up about grammar and usage because we are all prone to occasional lapses. She believes that rather than being obsessed by error, we should nurture our "love [of] talking about words, about language."*

Now that I'm a grammar maven, everyone's afraid to talk to me. Well, not everyone. Since my grammar book was published this fall, my friends have discovered a new sport: gotcha! The object is to correct my speech, to catch me in the occasional "between you and I" (OK, I admit it). The winner gets to interrupt with a satisfied "aha!"

But people I meet for the first time often confess that speaking with an "authority" on language gives them the willies. Grammar, they say apologetically, was not their best subject. And they still don't get it: the subjunctives, the dependent clauses, the coordinating conjunctions. So their English is bound to be flawed, they warn, and I should make allowances. They relax when I tell them that I'm not perfect either, and that I don't use technical jargon when I write about grammar. You don't have to scare readers off with terms like *gerund* and *participle* to explain why an *-ing* word like *bowling* can play so many different roles in a sentence. With the intimidating terminology out of the way, most people express a lively, even passionate, interest in English and how it works. As a reader recently told me, "I don't need to know all the parts of a car to be a good driver."

Grammarians and hairsplitting wannabes have always loved to argue over the fine points of language. What surprises me these days is the number of grammatically insecure people who are discussing English with just as much fervor, though without the pedantry. As a guest author on radio call-in shows and online chats, I've found that the chance to air a linguistic grievance or pose a question in a nonjudgmental atmosphere often proves irresistible. "Is *irregardless* OK?" a caller hesitantly asks. "I hear it so much these days." (No.) Or, "Is *sprang* a word?" (Yes.) "Media *is* or media *are?*" (*Are,* for the time being.) I saw an ad with the word *alright,* spelled A-L-R-I-G-H-T. It is correct? (No, it's not all right.) "If I *was?* Or if I *were?*" (It depends.) I love it when people who say they hated grammar in school get all worked up over *like* versus *as,* or *convince* versus *persuade,* or *who* versus *whom.* Obviously it wasn't grammar per se that once turned them off. It was the needless pedagoguery — the tyranny of the pluperfects, the intransitives, and all the rest. The truth is that people love talking about words, about language. After years as an editor at *The New York Times Book Review,* I can vouch that almost everybody gets something wrong now and then — a dangler here, a spelling problem there, a runaway sentence, beastly punctuation. Those who regularly screw up would like to do better, and even the whizzes admit they'd like to get rid of a weakness or two.

So, is grammar back? Has good English become . . . cool?

Before you laugh, download this. Thanks to the computer, Americans are communicating with one another at a rate undreamed of a generation ago — and *in writing.* People who seldom wrote more than a memo or a shopping list are producing blizzards of words. Teenagers who once might have spent the evening on the phone are hunched over their computers, gossiping by e-mail and meeting in chat rooms. Wired college students are conferring with professors, carrying on romances, and writing home for money, all from computer terminals in their dorm rooms. Many executives who once depended on secretaries to "put it in English" are now clicking on REPLY and winging it.

The downside of all this techno-wizardry is that our grammar isn't quite up to the mark. We're writing more, and worse, than ever before. (If you don't believe this, check out a chat room or an electronic bulletin board. It's not a pretty sight.) The ease and immediacy of electronic communication are forcing the computer-literate to think about their grammar for the first time in years, if ever. It's ironic that this back-to-basics message should come from cyberspace. Or is it? Amid the din of the information revolution, bombarded on all sides by technological wonders, we can hardly be blamed for finding in grammar one small sign of order amid the chaos.

There is evidence of this return to order elsewhere in our society, too. Perhaps the "family values" mantra, for better or worse, is nothing more than a call for order in a culture that seems to have lost its moral bearings. At any rate, laissez-faire grammar bashers who used to regard good English as an impediment to spontaneity and creativity are seeing the light — and it's not spelled L-I-T-E.

But what about those of us whose "lex" education is a dim memory? The very word *grammar* evokes a visceral response — usually fear. If it makes your hair stand on end, you're part of a proud tradition. The earliest grammarians, bless their shriveled hearts, did English a disservice by appealing more to our feelings of inferiority than to our natural love of

5

words. They could never quite forgive our mongrel tongue for not being Latin, but felt that English could redeem itself somewhat by conforming to the rules of Latin grammar. The word *grammar,* in fact, originally meant "the study of Latin." All this may help explain a couple of silly no-nos from the past, discredited by the most respected twentieth-century grammarians: those inflexible rules against splitting an infinitive and ending a sentence with a preposition.

Surely no school subject has been more detested and reviled by its victims than grammar. Some people would rather have a root canal than define the uninflected root of a word. At the same time, the ability to use language well appeals to our need to be understood, to participate, to be one of the tribe. It's no wonder so many of the people I meet confess to being grammatically inadequate, yet fascinated by words.

My message to these people, delivered from the lofty heights of my   10
newly acquired mavenhood, is this: stop beating up on yourselves. It's only a grammatical error, not a drive-by shooting. Words are wonderful, but they're not sacred. And between you and I (aha!), nobody's perfect.

A Rarity: Grammar Lessons from Dad

ROBERT T. KLOSE

Robert T. Klose is a professor of biological sciences at the University of Maine in Orono. After graduating from Fairleigh Dickinson University in 1976 with a degree in marine biology, Klose served as a shipboard hospital corpsman and Spanish translator in the U.S. Navy, later returning to graduate school at the University of Maine. A published poet and prolific freelance writer, he is a regular contributor to the Christian Science Monitor, Maine Life, *the* Times Record, *and the* Bangor Daily News. *He writes on a variety of subjects ranging from the biological sciences to music—especially the clarinet—to language issues. His first book,* Adopting Alyosha: A Single Man Finds a Son in Russia, *appeared in 1999.*

In the following article, which first appeared in the Boston Globe *on September 4, 1996, Klose speaks out on the status of English language instruction in America. Surprised by a chance encounter with a former student and her inarticulateness about her recent trip to Europe, Klose cannot deny his concern for his students' English, including that of his son.*

If I am the only parent who still corrects his child's English, then perhaps my son is right: To him I am an oddity, a father making remarks about something that no longer seems to merit comment.

I think I got serious about this only recently, when I ran into one of my former students, fresh from two months in Europe. "How was it?" I asked, full of anticipation.

She nodded three or four times, searched the heavens for the right words, and then informed me, "It was, like, whoa."

And that was it. The glory of Greece and the grandeur of Rome summed up in a nonstatement. My student's "whoa" was exceeded only by my head-shaking woe.

As a biology teacher, perhaps I shouldn't be overly concerned with my students' English. After all, the traditional refuge of the science teacher is the hated multiple-choice exam, where students are asked to recognize, but not actually use, language. My English-teaching colleagues are, however, duty-bound to extract essays, compositions, and position papers from their charges. These products, I am told, are becoming increasingly awful. I still harbor the image of an English-teacher colleague who burst into my office one day in a sweat of panic. "Quick!" she commanded. "A dictionary!"

She tore through the book. "Just as I thought!" she exclaimed, pinning the entry with her finger. "It is spelled r-e-c-e-i-v-e."

Her point, whether she knew it or not, was that students make the same mistakes repeatedly. As for their teachers, they must read hundreds

5

and eventually thousands of errors, which in time become more familiar than the accepted forms, so that the instructors themselves become uncertain whether it's "recieve" or receive, "protien" or protein.

The one thing that stories about the demise of English in America have in common is that they're all true. And students usually bear the brunt of the infamy, because there is a sense that they should know better. The truth is that they are being misled everywhere they look and listen.

Supermarket aisles point them to the "stationary," even though the pads and notebooks are not nailed down; people "could care less," even when they couldn't; and, more and more, friends and loved ones announce that they've just "ate" when, in fact, they've eaten.

Blame must be laid (and lie, not lay, it does) somewhere, and I am   10
happy to place it squarely on the schools, which should be safe harbors for the standards of the English language. Instead, they don't teach grammar at all. Or syntax or vocabulary. In fact, the younger teachers themselves have little knowledge of these underpinnings of the language, because they also went without exposure to them.

The schools having affirmed poor or sloppy speech habits through their lack of attention to them, I am obligated to do the dirty work of gently ushering my son onto the path of competent communication. But, as the Wicked Witch of the West said in one of her rhetorical musings, "These things must be handled delicately." (Alyosha's patience is limited when his dad behaves like a teacher.)

The other day, I was driving to a nearby town with my son. As we set out on our 5-mile trip, he noticed a bird in eccentric flight and said, "It's flying so raggedly." Impressed with his description, I remarked, "Good adverb!"

He asked me what an adverb was. I explained that it's a word that tells you something about a verb, which led to his asking me what a verb was. I explained that it's an action word, giving him an example: "Dad drives the truck. 'Drives' is the verb," I told him, "because it's the thing Dad is doing."

He became intrigued with the idea of action words. So we listed a few more. Fly, swim, dive, run. And then, having fallen prey to his own curiosity, he asked me if other words had names. This led to a discussion of nouns, adjectives, and articles. The upshot of all this is that within the span of a 10-minute drive, he had learned—from scratch—to recognize the major parts of speech in a sentence.

It was painless and fun, but it's not being taught in the schools.   15
There seems to be a sense that as long as a student is making himself understood, all is well. Sort of like driving a junker that blows smoke and has a flat tire. If it gets you there, what's the problem?

Perhaps, then, language should be looked upon as a possession: keeping it clean and in repair shows concern and effort. It demonstrates attentiveness to detail and the accomplishment of a goal—clear, accurate, descriptive speech.

Just this morning my son and I were eating breakfast when I attempted to add milk to my tea. "Dad," he cautioned, "if I were you, I wouldn't do that. It's sour."

"Alyosha," I said, swelling with pride, "that's a grammatically perfect sentence. You used 'were' instead of 'was.'"

"I know, I know," he said with a degree of weary irritation. "It's the subjunctive mood."

I was, like, whoa.   20

WRITING SUGGESTIONS: MAKING CONNECTIONS

1. What effect does O'Conner believe e-mail is having on usage? How has e-mail affected your use of language and concern for grammar? Do you think Larson would agree with any of O'Conner's comments about e-mail? Write an essay in which you compare and contrast O'Conner's and Larson's views on e-mail and indicate where you stand with respect to these views.

2. Carefully read the following letter Ann Landers received from a reader in Wood Ridge, New Jersey, and her reply to that letter. Then write a response to E. E. in Wood Ridge that's informed by your understanding of the usage controversy and your reading of the essays by Larson, O'Connor, and Klose.

Using Improper Grammar Makes Anyone Look like a Fool

DEAR ANN LANDERS: Have Americans forgotten there is such a thing as verb tense? I am shocked when I hear people say "woulda came," "coulda went," "shoulda did," "woulda took," "had went," "hadn't came," and so on. Don't they realize "woulda" and "coulda" are slang versions of "would've" and "could've"—which are contractions for would have and could have?

I heard a narrator say, "I seen" in a political commercial, and a TV reporter say, "We haven't spoke." An attorney in a television show said, "The evidence do not," and a TV anchorwoman said, "had threw it" and "between you and I."

I was a secretary for almost 50 years and am thankful that with only a high school education my English is impeccable. You will do a lot of folks a big favor if you print this letter and bring it to their attention.—E. E., Wood Ridge, N.J.

DEAR E. E.: Thanks for taking the time and trouble to write. I shoulda thunk to tell them off myself.

3. O'Conner writes that there is no need to use technical jargon when discussing grammar. She believes that "with the intimidating terminology out of the way, most people express a lively, even passionate, interest in English and how it works" (2). From your own experience, is she correct? Write an essay in which you present some of your own encounters with grammar in school. What memories do you have of your teachers working with you on matters of grammar and vocabulary? Or do your experiences jibe with Klose's claim that schools "don't teach grammar at all. Or syntax or vocabulary" (10)?

4. After reading the pieces by Larson, O'Conner, and Klose, where do you stand on the question of usage? Write an essay in which you clearly articulate your position, showing how you agree or disagree with each of these writers.

5. Do some research on punctuation in your library or on the Internet. How did the individual marks come into use, and what does each mean? What's the difference, for example, between a colon (:) and a semicolon (;) or between a comma (,) and a dash (—)? The late Lewis Thomas wrote an excellent essay on the subject called "On Punctuation," which was published in his book *The Medusa and the Snail* (1979). That piece might provide a good starting point for your research. Write an essay in which you explain the history, meaning, and function of one or more marks of punctuation.

6. Klose makes the following statement in paragraph 8: "The one thing that stories about the demise of English in America have in common is that they're all true." How does he support this claim? Are you convinced that the English language is on the skids? Do some research in your library or on the Internet about "pop grammarians" like Edwin Newman and John Simon, who predicted the ruin of the English language starting in the 1960s. What evidence did they provide to document their claims? Write an essay in which you report on the current health of the English language.

7

NAMES AND NAMING

Naming Names: The Eponym Craze

CULLEN MURPHY

Cullen Murphy, managing editor of the Atlantic Monthly *since 1985, has had an interesting career in magazine journalism. Born in New Rochelle, New York, he was educated at Catholic schools in Greenwich, Connecticut, and Dublin, Ireland. After graduating from Amherst College with honors in medieval history in 1974, he went to work for both* Change, *an educational magazine, and the* Wilson Quarterly *before joining the* Atlantic Monthly. *Murphy's bestseller* Rubbish! (1992), *which he coauthored with William Rathje, examines what's really in our nation's landfills. In 1995 he published* Just Curious, *a collection of essays that first appeared in the* Atlantic Monthly *and* Harper's. *For several decades Cullen Murphy has also written the text for* Prince Valiant, *the popular comic strip his father draws.*

In the following essay, which first appeared in January 1997 in the online magazine Slate, *Murphy turns his attention to the eponym, a word formed from the name of a person, place, or thing. He estimates that there are at least thirty-five thousand eponyms in English. Although more and more eponyms are entering the language and quickly being spread by the media, Murphy believes that not all of them are destined to have a long life.*

WRITING TO DISCOVER: *Make up some new words for a type of person, a particular kind of action, or an object with special qualities,*

based on the name of the person associated with it. For example,
suppose you want to give a name to an especially good round of golf,
you might call it a Tiger, or use Tiger as a verb ("She tigered that
round!"), after the great young player Tiger Woods. After making
up one or two words and defining them, briefly sketch out the rea-
sons why your word should be commonly adopted.

The 1996 elections had no sooner sloughed into despond than I
came across the following sentence in an election-eve wrap-up by Michael
Lewis in the *New Republic.* "There is no denying," Lewis wrote, in the fi-
nale to an antic "Campaign Journal" series that saw him parting the
crowds around various presidential entourages with the prosthetic assistance of a television Steadycam on his shoulder, "that I was excited by
working alongside Ted Koppel, driven less by a Fallovian desire to inform
the public than a lust to become rich and famous."

The word popped out: *Fallovian.* Could I have been witnessing the
birth of an eponym — as wondrous a sight in its way as our recent glimpse
of an island-in-the-making off the coast of Hawaii? An eponym, of
course, is a word that has been formed from the name of a person, place,
or thing (*eponumos* is a Greek word meaning "named on"). For some
eponymous terms, the eponymy is obvious, or famous: *Caesarean section;*
graham cracker; Molotov cocktail; boycott; leotard; Luddite; silhouette; volt.
Many more eponyms, though familiar, are not so obviously eponymous.
Maudlin, for instance, comes from the name of Mary Magdalene, who in
painted and sculpted form is typically shown weeping. *Masochism* comes
from the name of the demented nineteenth-century novelist Leopold von
Sacher-Masoch, who described the relevant eponymous practices in his
writings. (Recently, a group in Ukraine has been attempting to raise a
monument to Masoch in his native city, Lviv.)

And *Fallovian?* In this case, the contextual evidence suggested that
Michael Lewis' coinage fell into the class of eponym known as a "deriva-
tive" — in this case, derived from a name, that of James Fallows, editor of
U.S. News & World Report, who has championed an approach to reporting that emphasizes hard analysis of serious issues and eschews the cult of
journalists as highly paid pundits, celebrities, or oddsmakers. Lewis confirmed that this meaning was precisely the one intended, and said that, as
far as he knew, his use of it in the *New Republic* marked this proper
noun's maiden voyage as an adjective. Fallows himself, affably abashed,
was unaware of previous appearances of the term.

Eponymous words have never needed much tending or encouragement. There are about thirty-five thousand of them in the ordinary stock
of the English language, a figure that does not include the many eponymous words in the specialized languages of science, engineering, and es-

pecially medicine. The use of eponyms in medicine is steeply on the decline, but ordinary eponyms, linguistic experts say, are enjoying a growth spurt these days. According to citations in recent newspapers and magazines, to *gump* through life is to make one's way by means of dumb luck. To espouse two positions at once is to *pull a Clinton*. To adopt the hairstyle popularized by the actress Jennifer Aniston on *Friends* is to *get a Rachel* or to *get a* Friends *do*. A *sagan* is a unit of quantity equivalent to "billions and billions" — the quotation an unintentionally self-parodic trademark of the late astronomer Carl Sagan. *Imeldific,* made possible by Imelda Marcos, refers to ostentatious grandiosity and extravagant bad taste. An *Iraqi manicure* is torture. *Waldheimer's disease* is a convenient lapse of memory.

To *kevork* someone is to assist him in the commission of suicide — an   5
eponym derived proximately, of course, from the work of Dr. Jack Kevorkian, but made possible by the prior success of the rhyming verb to *bork* (from the name Robert Bork, and meaning to use every means possible to sabotage a nominee to high office). An eponymous verb derived from the name O.J. Simpson — *to O.J.,* meaning "to slash" — shows some signs of acceptance among teen-agers (*O.J.* had a previous life as an eponym, denoting a big car of the kind Simpson drove in his commercials for Hertz. "Drive off in a def O.J.," went a line in a 1979 rap song by the Sugar Hill Gang.)

The verb *to bobbitt,* with its well-known specific connotation under the household-amputation rubric, has become so widely used as to have now acquired metaphoric senses. For instance, the verb is used to mean "to deprive of vigor" in this sentence from a letter to the editor of the conservative *Washington Times:* "Bravo to Tony Snow for exposing the bobbi[t]ting of the GOP leadership when confronted with Democratic tirades." (Linguistic note from abroad: The practice of *bobbitting,* according to an Asia correspondent of some years — my sister Cait, as it happens — is relatively frequent in Thailand. The local name for the practice is a Thai word that, when translated into English, means "feeding the ducks.")

The surge in eponyms is no doubt related, in part, to the efflorescence of metanames* in general. Pseudonyms have never been more widely employed than they are today, when millions of invented, incorporeal identities are in play in all kinds of electronic communication. The married woman who takes her husband's family name as a surname yet keeps her own family name as a middle name — Hillary Rodham Clinton, Sandra Day O'Connor — has unwittingly introduced a new form of patronymic,** which takes its place alongside the more traditional (Slavic, Scandinavian, Islamic, Hispanic) versions. Even anonymity,

---

*The flowering of names that transcend their original meanings.
**A name derived from that of the father or paternal ancestor.

owing to controversy [. . .] over the authorship of the novel *Primary Colors*, has had to endure an uncharacteristically high public profile [. . .]. I don't know what name future historians will bestow on our present age, but arguably the age deserves not a name but a nym.

Why more eponymy now? Some people, of course, have set out to make well-known eponymous terms of their names, as Donald Trump is doing with his new magazine *Trump Style*. The proliferation of commercial brand names is certainly a major factor: Consider *Nintendo neck*, the *Twinkie defense*, the *Teflon presidency*. For reasons that hardly need belaboring, it is easier today than ever before for any name—personal or commercial—to become widely known quickly, even if transiently. Memorable eponymous terms require memorable nominal roots and, in the English-speaking world, people's names are becoming more diverse and interesting as more cultures are demographically and linguistically annexed. Also, eponymous terms allow almost anyone to display competence, even brilliance, at coining useful and appropriate-sounding new words—thereby encouraging further attempts to do so.

Leona Helmsley. Mark Furhman. Alfonse D'Amato. Madonna. Roberto Alomar. Mother Teresa. Bill Gates. Oliver Stone. These and scores of other names cry out for eponyplasty. I look forward to your suggestions.

FOCUSING ON CONTENT

1. Murphy includes a number of eponyms in paragraph 2. Use your college dictionary or the Internet to determine who gave their names to the following terms and why: *Caesarean section, graham cracker, Molotov cocktail, boycott, leotard, Luddite, silhouette, volt.*

2. To whom does *Waldheimer* refer, and to what does *Waldheimer's disease* refer (4)? If you do not know, how might you find out?

3. In his final paragraph, Murphy says that the names he has just listed cry out for *eponyplasty*. What does he mean by that word? Is the word in the dictionary?

4. What reasons does Murphy give for the rise of eponyms? What else might account for this rise? Explain.

FOCUSING ON WRITING

1. What is Murphy's thesis in this essay? (Glossary: *Thesis*) Where is it stated?

2. Why do you think Murphy waits until his second paragraph to define *eponym*, the key term of his essay?

3. "Naming Names: The Eponym Craze" first appeared in the online magazine *Slate*. Assuming that this essay is typical of the style of that magazine, for

what type of audience is the magazine intended? On what specific stylistic clues do you base your answer? (Glossary: *Style*)

4. Why is Murphy's conclusion appropriate for his essay? How does he prepare the reader for this conclusion? (Glossary: *Beginnings and Endings*)

LANGUAGE IN ACTION

John Updike wrote the following poem about "some Frenchmen" who lent their names to our vocabulary. After reading the poem, consult your desk dictionary or another reference work to learn more about the actual contributions of these men. Summarize the inventions of each man, and comment on Updike's effectiveness in capturing the nature of each invention in poetry.

SOME FRENCHMEN

Monsieur Etienne de Silhouette
   Was slim and uniformly black;
His profile was superb, and yet
   He vanished when he turned his back.

Humane and gaunt, precise and tall
   Was Docteur J. I. Guillotin;
He had one tooth, diagonal
   And loose, which, when it fell, spelled *fin*.

André Marie Ampère, a spark,
   Would visit other people's homes
And gobble volts until the dark
   Was lit by his resisting ohms.

Another type, Daguerre (Louis),
   In silver salts would soak his head,
Expose himself to light, and be
   Developed just in time for bed.

WRITING SUGGESTIONS

1. (*Writing from Experience*) What eponyms do your friends and teacher use? Do you always know what they refer to? Is a generation gap sometimes at work in eponym usage? That is, do those who are older or younger than you use eponyms whose referents are unfamiliar to you? Write an essay on the generational differences in the use of eponyms that relies heavily on the examples you use and those used by older or younger people.

2. (*Writing from Reading*) When he spots the first use of the word *Fallovian*, Murphy gets, or pretends to get, rather excited about what he refers to as

"the birth of an eponym." He also admits that many of the eponyms being created today will not last. Write an essay in which you argue that it is not important to witness the birth of eponyms or to worry about their meanings until they become fixtures in the language.

3. (*Writing from Research*) Write an essay on so-called proprietary eponyms, those eponyms such as *xerox* and *scotch tape* that are trademarks or company-owned names but are also in general use. As a starting point for your research, you may want to read the comments and examples compiled by R. Krause at the following Web site: <http:www.prairienet.org/~rkrause/brands.html>.

"Hey, Cono!"

CHARLES GASPARINO

A staff reporter for the Wall Street Journal, *Charles Gasparino covers the financial beat. He writes articles on stocks, bonds, municipal finances, and retirement finances—subjects that require not only technical expertise but also the ability to put complex financial dynamics into everyday language. Prior to working for the* Journal, *he was a staff writer for* Newsday.

In the following article, which first appeared in the Journal *in November 1998, Gasparino turns his attention to an entirely different subject as he reports on a special group of Italian Americans who live in the Williamsburg section of the Bronx, one of New York City's five burroughs. These Italian Americans are all named "Cono" after Saint Cono, a Benedictine monk and the patron saint of Teggiano, a town in southern Italy. "There might be more men named Cono in Williamsburg than in any other place on earth, outside of Italy," writes Gasparino.*

WRITING TO DISCOVER: *If you suddenly found yourself in a strange town where everyone had the same first name, how would you react? Would you think you were a part of some science fiction story? You would certainly find it unusual, but would you think it humorous? How would you try to determine what was going on with the naming process in the town? What questions would you ask the inhabitants? Briefly describe the scene and explore your own thoughts about this imaginary town.*

Walk along Graham Avenue, past the salumerias and trattorias, and you'll run into plenty of guys with names like Anthony, Michael, Vincent, and Paul.

But here in Brooklyn's Williamsburg neighborhood, the most popular first name isn't one of the staples of Italian-American manhood. It's Cono, which means "cone" in English.

There might be more men named Cono in Williamsburg than in any other place on earth, outside Italy. There are delis, pizzerias, and restaurants with Cono in their names. There's a Cono club, located in an old synagogue on Ainslie Street, the heart of the neighborhood's Cono population, and a Cono festival each fall.

"There are Conos all over the world, but this is the capital," says Cono Natale, owner of Cono & Son's O'Pescatore restaurant on Graham Avenue. "Every family has a Cono, maybe two," he says. "It's still going strong."

Mr. Natale named his oldest son Cono. His recently married daughter, Anna Maria Natale-Darienzo, age 27, says she plans to keep the tradition 5

185

going by naming at least one of her children Cono, "even if it's a middle name," she says. "When you hear the name Cono, you think, 'Where did he get such an odd name?' But then you remember the connection."

That connection is the medieval mountain of Teggiano in southern Italy, the legendary birthplace of the first Cono. According to the local lore, Cono was born around 1100, became a Benedictine monk, and went on to perform numerous miracles. A 100-foot monument and statue of St. Cono, his head crowned with a golden halo, stands proudly in the town's piazza. Some of his remains, embedded in a statue of a sleeping Cono, are in the church of Santa Maria Maggiore.

Generations of Teggianese boys were named Cono, and the name spread as Teggianesi, fleeing the poverty of southern Italy's Mezzogiorno region, settled in Argentina, Brazil, Uruguay and, of course, in Brooklyn.

Williamsburg, a quiet working-class neighborhood of neat row houses and backyard gardens, became a favorite destination, a place where immigrants spoke southern Italian dialect and where the old customs—food and family and devotion to the Catholic Church—were always present.

"The name is particular to this neighborhood because of the devotion to St. Cono," says Msgr. David Cassato, of Our Lady of Mount Carmel Church. Msgr. Cassato says there are 100 to 150 men with the first name Cono living in the neighborhood. But the Cono population is even larger when you count middle names and confirmation names.

It isn't easy keeping track of all the Conos in Williamsburg. Locals   10
like to say there are more Conos here than in Teggiano. On Graham Avenue, across the street from Mr. Natale's popular fish place, there's S. (for Saint) Cono's Pizzeria. Down the block, Cono D'Alto runs a popular salumeria—or delicatessen—which offers some of the freshest pasta and homemade mozzarella around. A few storefronts down, Cono Colombo and his wife, Maria, run La Locanda, a trattoria specializing in homemade cavatelli—a shell-shaped pasta made from ricotta.

"Sometimes you get a whole bunch of Conos together and someone says, 'Hey, Cono!' and everyone turns around," Mr. D'Alto says. Customers often get confused between Mr. D'Alto's deli and Mr. Natale's restaurant. "My friend Cono (Natale) is always calling complaining that my customers call him for orders," Mr. D'Alto says.

Over the years, the Conos have come up with ways to differentiate themselves: An elderly Cono would be called "Conucio," (pronounced co-NOOCH-ee-o). A youthful Cono is affectionately called "Conocino" (co-noo-CHI-no), or little Cono, to distinguish him from his father or grandfather.

Mr. Natale concedes that it isn't easy being Cono. For years he has tried, without success, to get the state to correct a misspelling on his driver's license; it calls him "Como" instead of "Cono." "I tried a couple of times to get it changed, but it still came out Como," he says.

The confusion can get a bit more serious. Mr. Natale's son, Cono Natale Jr., recalls one time when he was pulled over by the police because, they said, he had several outstanding tickets. Turns out, however, they weren't after him—it was his cousin Cono they wanted. "I had to go to court to straighten it out," Mr. Natale says. "It wasn't easy." In another instance, yet another cousin named Cono was served with divorce papers from the younger Mr. Natale's wife. "The process server probably thought, 'Hey, both these guys are Italian, they look alike, and how many Conos can there be in the world?'" Mr. Natale says.

The San Cono di Teggiano Catholic Association—or the Cono club, as it is known in the neighborhood—is most certainly the center of Cono activity. Members meet in the hall to play cards, drink espresso, and reminisce. Every year, in late September, the club meets to celebrate the birthday of San (Italian for Saint) Cono, serving food native to Teggiano—fresh cavatelli with broccoli rabe sauteed in olive oil, and zeppole, fried dough covered with powdered sugar.

In 1997, the club, which has about 140 members, arranged for the statue of the sleeping Cono—800-year-old bones and all—to be flown to Brooklyn. A police escort led the bones and 75 of Cono's followers— including the mayor of Teggiano—back from Kennedy International Airport to the Cono hall on Ainslie Street. Old women guarded the statue day and night, until the celebration was over. "It was like the president was here," Ms. Colombo says.

The statue was safely returned, with many thanks, to Teggiano, with its 14 churches and five convents in the center of town. Mayor Angelo Mario Giffoni says that of the city's 8,600 inhabitants, 1,500 men have the name Cono. Mr. Giffoni, who named his son Cono, says Teggianesi believe St. Cono protects them from earthquakes, and they "even write poems about" him.

The man in whom they place their faith was born in Teggiano (it was then called Diano) near the end of the twelfth century to an elderly couple who thought they were sterile, regarded the child as a gift from God, and named him Cono after receiving some form of divine indication. Why "Cono"? Some say the child's head was shaped like a cone. The cone-head, so to speak, was a "symbol of perfection," representing the Holy Trinity.

The young Cono ran away from home and became a Benedictine monk—against the wishes of his parents, who wanted their only son to marry, have children, and carry on the family name. His parents ultimately gave up on their conventional ambitions for their child when they witnessed him praying, unscathed, in a burning oven.

The rest is history, or legend at the very least. Cono went on to perform miracles—by some accounts, he saved the town of Teggiano from invaders by catching a cannonball in his bare hands. He died when he was 18, but he continued to protect his flock with miracles—and the name of Cono spread. The Teggianese credit Cono with protecting them from Allied bombs during World War II. Cono is also believed to have healed the sick.

There's only one problem: St. Cono of Teggiano may not be a saint. At least not according to the Vatican, which says it "tolerates" him but that there are no records showing he was canonized. Msgr. Robert Sarno, in the Vatican's Congregation for the Causes of the Saints, in Rome, explains: "In a lot of local towns, people have their holy people, and they are called saints. No one is going to go back and investigate something from the eleventh or twelfth century. . . . They've been tolerated— that's all."

But in Williamsburg, there's really no debate about St. Cono— though the various Conos have a lot to say about living with this unusual name.

"When I first came here, (Americans) couldn't make heads or tails out of my name—they didn't know if it was my last name, or what," says Mr. D'Alto, 51, who arrived in the U.S. in 1957, when he was nine, and now owns Mamma Maria Salumeria on Graham Avenue. "They made me almost paranoid."

Cono Namorato, 56, says one of his Williamsburg elementary-school teachers recommended to his mother that she change his name from Cono to Conrad. "Back then, we had a lot of old-time Irish teachers who were concerned that I couldn't go into the business world with a name like Cono." His mother politely declined, choosing to take her chances on Cono.

Mr. Namorato, who went on to become an investigator for the Justice Department, and who now is one of the nation's top tax attorneys, says his name has become one of his "biggest assets" in attracting clients. "I get referrals from all over the country," he says. "They don't know how to spell my name, but they know the guy named Cono who does tax work."   25

But Rocco Manzolillo, president of the Cono club, fears the name is dying out as young Italian-Americans give up the old ways. When Mr. D'Alto recently asked his 20-something cousin what he was going to name his newborn son, Cono wasn't at the top of his list. "He said, 'I don't like the name,'" Mr. D'Alto recalls. "He's going to regret it."

Cono Natale Jr., 33, says he isn't sure whether he will hand the name down to his son. It was difficult venturing outside the friendly confines of Williamsburg with a name like Cono. "You should know what I went through," Cono Jr. says. Seated with his father one afternoon at the restaurant, beneath a picture of their beloved Teggiano, he recalls some of the gibes he took because of his name—some people "would call you Cano, some would call you Conrad. Would I want my son to go through that? I don't know." To which his father replies: "You better name your son Cono."

FOCUSING ON CONTENT

1. Who was the original Cono and why was he so named, as far as can be known? What is ironic about the status of St. Cono within the Catholic Church? (Glossary: *Irony*)

2. What special properties are associated with the name Cono that make people want to name their sons Cono?

3. What kinds of problems result from having so many people with the same first names in Williamsburg?

4. How do relatives, friends, and neighbors keep all the Conos straight?

5. How does Gasparino use the naming process to reveal Italian American culture?

FOCUSING ON WRITING

1. What examples does Gasparino use to show the importance of St. Cono to the Italian Americans who live in Williamsburg and elsewhere around the world? (Glossary: *Examples*)

2. How does Gasparino give his readers some sense of the character of the Williamsburg neighborhood? What Italian words does he use, and how does he help readers understand those words? (Glossary: *Diction*)

3. What is Gasparino's tone in this article? Serious? Bemused? Mocking? Reportorial? How does he create that tone? (Glossary: *Tone* and *Diction*) Is his tone appropriate for his topic and audience? Why or why not?

4. How important to the story are the interviews that Gasparino had with local citizens? Could he have obtained his information in some other way? Explain.

LANGUAGE IN ACTION

The following list compiled by Kate Monk shows names borrowed from English and other languages. What do you think of these words as first names for children? Would you consider using any of them for your own child? Why or why not? What do you suppose is the purpose behind the use of such names?

BORROWED WORDS

Male

Albino	Armani	Blade	Bryck	Cady	Clint
Alias	Arrow	Bleu	Buck	Canyon	Cloud
Allias	Auto	Brandy	Bucky	Chidi	Cologne'o
Aman	Baby Boy	Bric	Buddy	Ciclo	Corynthian
Amani	Babyboy	Brick	Buster	Cielo	Craig
Apache	Beau	Brother	Cachet	Clarion	Crescent

Dale	Genesis	Justyce	Merced	Porsche	Son
Dean	Genisis	Kalyx	Minus	Reality	Sonny
Dell	Gitano	Kashmir	Miracle	Refugio	Storm
Devotion	Glen	Kodiak	Novin	River	Suade
Dusty	Glyn	Lake	Numbers	Rusty	Sunny
Elegio	Grove	Largent	Ocean	Saber	Swade
Freedom	Hallelujah	Lawyer	Omni	Sabre	Tabor
Fronde	Idol	Lea	Paciano	Savon	Tuff
Future	Junior	Legend	Parahiso	Scout	Ukulele
Galleon	Justic	Librado	Phi	Sea-Land	Unknown
Garth	Justice	Marine	Polo	Secret	Victory
General	Justis	Maverick	Porche	Slate	Zen

Female

Amnesty	Celestia	Fini	Kosey	Oceana	Serepta
Angelic	Cerise	Fondea	Kylie	Oriel	Shadow
Angell	Cherish	Genesis	Leaf	Oshe'auna	Sherry
Angle	Cherubim	Gentry	Legacy	Pasjionette	Spirit
Angyl	Chianti	Gloriana	L'pree	Peripheral	Storie
Anjel	Coda	Glory	Luna	Phyre	Storm
Ashante	Colleen	Gloryana	Lyric	Porscha	Stormy
Aura	Daily	Golden	Lyrica	Posey	Story
Babi	Dale	Goldie	Lyrik	Precious	Sugar
Baby	Delicia	Harmony	Madra	Procopia	Sunnie
Baby Girl	Destry	Haven	Maison	Promise	Sunny
Babygirl	Dextra	Heaven	Mandolin	Pyxi	Sunshine
Blessyng	Diadema	Heavynne	Mardi	Quinte	Suthern
Bliss	Dimity	Honey	Mayda	Rain	Symetria
Blythe	Diva	Hosanna	Melodee	Rainbow	Symphony
Bonnie	Divine	Infinity	Melodie	Raine	Tarcy
Brandi	Divya	Iridian	Melody	Rainee	Tawny
Breez	Dovie	Iridiana	Merri	Rainey	Tempest
Breeze	Dreama	Journee	Mink	Rainna	Thunder
Brooke	Dreamy	Journey	Miracle	Rainy	Trinity
Cadence	Ebony	Jubilie	Misty	Raven-Skye	Truly
Cadonce	Ermine	Jurnee	Monita	Reason	Two Rain-
Cameo	Essence	Justicia	Moon	Rebel	bows Flying
Candy	Eternity	Kadence	Mysti	Rejoyce	Unique
Capriel	Fairelin	Kapriece	Noelle	Remedy	Velvet
Caresse	Fairyn	Kapriellc	Novclle	Romany	Whisper
Carmel	Fantasia	Karisma	Ocean	Rumor	Wilda
Castelly	Feather	Karma			

WRITING SUGGESTIONS

1. (*Writing from Experience*) What nicknames do you recall using when you were a child? Were you known by a particular nickname? Write an essay in which you discuss the various nicknames used by your friends and relatives

when you were growing up. How did the names come about, and what purposes did they serve. Do any of the names still exist?

2. (*Writing from Reading*) Cono Namorato, quoted in paragraph 24 of Gasparino's article, says that a school teacher recommended to his mother that she change his name to Conrad so that he would have an easier time going into business. Although his mother declined, Cono Namorato went on to become one of the country's top tax attorneys. Write an essay in which you explore the impulse to change your own name. What might be the benefits and the dangers of changing your name? Why might other people encourage you to do so? You may want to reread Edite Cunha's essay "Talking in the New Land," which appears on pages 74–83.

3. (*Writing from Research*) How common is it to find that some names are popular at particular points in time? As you have gone through school, have you found that many of your classmates share the same first name? One student, for example, said that in one of her courses there were six Jennifers. What accounts for the popularity of certain first names, or given names, at a particular time in history? Write an essay on trends in naming children. To research the frequency of first names in your state in any given year, try writing to the Bureau of Vital Statistics or the Department of Health. You can also search the Internet for national statistics, and some states have Web sites as well.

A World without Surnames

J. N. HOOK

Julius Nicholas Hook has authored or coauthored over thirty books on the history of American and British English and the teaching of English. Born in Macoupin County, Illinois, in 1913, Hook earned his Ph.D. from the University of Illinois at Urbana-Champaign, where he taught for many years. Now retired, he has shown a particular interest in names and the naming process and has published The Book of Names *(1983) and* All Those Wonderful Names *(1991).*

The following selection, which takes us back to when there were no surnames and shows us why they developed, is from another of Hook's books, Family Names: How Our Surnames Came to America *(1982). Of* Family Names, *he writes, "This book is a distillate of what I have learned about surnames and their role in America's development. It's a love story, really, and it's unabashedly sentimental at times. My love affair with surnames has intensified my affection for America. These names represent what America was and is, hint at what it can be."*

WRITING TO DISCOVER: *Reflect on your surname or family name and write about it. What does your family name mean? Does it reflect your ancestry? Is your name descriptive in any way?*

When the world's population was small and even a city might hold only a few thousand people, and when most folks never got more than ten or fifteen miles from their birthplace (usually walking), and when messages were sent by personal messenger rather than by impersonal post, there was hardly a necessity for more than one name. Even kings got by with a single name. When someone referred to King David, there was no need to ask David who?

No one knows who first felt the need to apply any name at all to himself or any of his fellows. According to Pliny, some ancient tribes were *anonymi* (nameless) and it is barely possible that a few *anonymi* may still exist in remote corners of the world. But for the most part personal names of some sort exist wherever there are human beings. As British onomatist* C. L. Ewen has said,

> The most general custom among the savage tribes was to give a child the name of a deceased ancestor, but any descriptive word which might indicate sex, order of birth, race, caste, office, physical feature, god,

---

*An expert in names and the naming process.

historical fact, or a more fanciful concept, served the purpose of a distinguishing label.

"A distinguishing label" — that of course is what a name is. It differentiates one person from another, allowing a mother to single out one child's attention, helping an officer to address a command to an individual, assisting any of us to carry out our daily tasks that depend on distinguishing one person from another.

Customs in naming have varied considerably, and some seem strange to us. Ewen mentioned an African tribe in which young boys had names that were changed to something else at puberty, and another tribe in which a father took a new name when his first child was born, his virility having thus been confirmed. Members of other tribes change their names after serious illness or when they get old. Some American Indians had different names for different seasons. People of Dahomey, in East Africa, once had several names, including some that named guardian spirits and others that were kept secret except from intimates. Some names have been very long: *The Encyclopedia of Religion and Ethics* mentions a Babylonian name that can be translated "O Ashur, the lord of heaven and earth, give him life." To this day, the Balinese have no surnames, and as youngsters many often change their personal names. They do have caste and birth-order designations that stay with them all their lives.

The ancient Greeks generally used only single names (Sophocles and   5
Plato, for example), but occasionally employed additional phrases for further identification. Thus Alexander, whom we describe as "the Great," was Alexandros o Philippon, Alexander the son of Phillip.

During Rome's centuries of greatness, Romans — especially those of the upper classes — were likely to have three names, like Gaius Julius Caesar. The *praenomen* (Gaius) corresponded to our given names. The *nomen* or *nomen gentilium* (Julius) identified the clan or tribe (*gens*), which usually consisted of a number of families sharing this name. The *cognomen* (Caesar) designated the particular family within the *gens*. There might even be a fourth name, called an *agnomen*, which could be a mark of distinction (like "Africanus" bestowed on Scipio after military victories in Africa), or just an additional mark of identification (for instance, Emperor Octavian, born Gaius Octavius, added the name Julius Caesar after Gaius, but retained Octavianus as an *agnomen*). During the period of Rome's decline, some persons adopted or were given even more names — as many as thirty-six.

In Roman times the *cognomens* were most like our surnames. They were hereditary, and they usually fell into the same classifications as English and Continental names. Some indicated the place from which the family had come or with which it was associated: Gnaeus Marcius Coriolanus, about whom Shakespeare wrote a play, is said to have won the battle of Corioli in 493 B.C. A few names are those of ancestors:

Agrippa, the family name of some of the descendants of Herod the Great. Some plebeians bore *cognomens* that named their occupations, as Metellus (servant), Missor (archer). The Romans especially liked descriptive *cognomens,* as Sapiens (the wise), Crassus (the fat), or Marcellus (the little hammer).

After the fall of Rome, multiple names largely disappeared for a few centuries throughout Europe, although compound names were fairly frequent in some places. Thus Irish Faolchadh was a compound of *wolf* and *warrior,* and the German Gerhard was compounded of *spear* and *firm.*

In the tenth century Venetian noblemen began to adopt hereditary family names. This custom was to be followed later by the Irish, the French, the English, and then the Germans and other Europeans.

Suppose that you were living in England in the Middle Ages. Suppose further that your name was John. Not John Something—just John. The Somethings did not yet exist in England. King or commoner, you were just John. [10]

Your male ancestors had also been John, or Thomas, Robert, Harold, Richard, William, or more anciently Eadgar or Eadwine or Aelfred, and their wives may have been Alice, Joan, Berthe, Blanche, Beatrice, Margaret, Marie, Inga, or Grette. Most names of your day were Norman French, since the descendants of William the Conqueror and his followers ruled the land. Huntingdon, for instance, had only 1 percent recognizably Anglo-Saxon names in A.D. 1295.

The number of different names was not large. The same Huntingdon list shows that 18 percent of all males in that county were called William, 16 percent John, 10 percent Richard, and 7 percent Robert, and that only 28 other names made up the remainder. So over half of these men shared only 4 names. In Yorkshire in the fourteenth century, in a list of 19,600 mixed male and female names, C. L. Ewen found that John accounted for 17 percent of the total, followed by William, Thomas, and Robert, with Alice (5 percent) and Joan (4 percent in various spellings) the most popular names for women. There were some biblical names other than John—almost 2 percent Adam, for example— but the popularity of Peter, Paul, Abraham, David, and others was still in the future.

England, like other countries in the Middle Ages, was mainly a rural and male-dominated society. There were no large cities. Some groups of people lived within the walls of a castle or nearby; still others clustered in villages from which workers trudged short distances each day to tend the crops or the livestock, or where they remained to do their smithing, wagon making, tailoring, or other tasks. Women often worked beside the men in the fields, and in a family wealthy enough to have its own cow or a few pigs or sheep, the women were likely to be responsible for the animals' care. Women's liberation was centuries away and largely undreamed of—although older England had had some strong queens, and Shakespeare's plays would later reflect some influence of women on medieval national affairs. In general, women were subservient, and their subservience was to be shown in the naming processes getting under way.

Almost all the occupational names, for example, refer to work done mainly or entirely by men in the Middle Ages, and countless fathers but few mothers were memorialized in names that would become family names. Had women's prestige been higher we would today have many persons with names like Milkmaid, Buxom, and Margaretson.

If the Middle Ages had been urbanized, no doubt the use of second names would have accelerated. If a city has three thousand Williams, ways must be found to indicate which William one talks about. A typical medieval village, though, might have had only five or ten Williams, a similar number of Johns, and maybe two or three Roberts or Thomases.

Even so, distinctions often needed to be made. If two villages were talking about you (John, you remember, is who you are), misunderstandings would arise if each had a different John in mind. So qualifications were added, as in imaginary bits of conversation like these:

"A horse stepped on John's foot."
"John from the hill?"
"No. John of the dale."

"John the son of William?"
"No. John the son of Robert"

"John the smith?"
"No. John the tailor."

"John the long?"
"No. John the bald."

In the rush of conversation the little, unimportant words could drop out or be slurred over so that John from the hill became John hill, and the other person's could be John dale, John William's son, John Robert's son, John smith, John tailor, John long, and John bald (or ballard, which means *the bald one*). The capital letters that we now associate with surnames are only scribal conventions introduced later on.

Distinctions like those illustrated in the conversations were a step toward surnames. But the son of John the smith might be Robert the wainwright (wagon maker). That is, he did not inherit the designation *smith* from his father. There were no true English surnames—family names— until Robert the son of John smith became known as Robert smith (or Smith) even though his occupation was a wainwright, a fletcher (arrow maker), a tanner or barker (leather worker), or anything else. Only when the second name was passed down from one generation to the next did it become a surname.

That step did not occur suddenly or uniformly, although throughout most of Europe it was a medieval development. Ewen has described the details of the development in England, basing his scholarly analysis on thousands of entries in tax rolls, court records, and other surviving documents. He has pointed out that before the fourteenth century most of the differentiating adjuncts were prefaced by *filius* (son of), as in Adam fil'Gilberti (Adam, son of Gilbert), by *le* (the), as in Beaudrey le Teuton, by *de* (of, from), as in Rogerius de Molis (Roger from the mills), or by *atta* (at the), as in John atte Water (John at the water), which later might be John Atwater. These particles often dropped out. Thus a fourteenth-century scribe began writing his name as David Tresruf, but other evidence shows that Tresruf was simply a place name and that David de Tresruf was the way the scribe earlier wrote his name.

Almost all English and Continental surnames fall into the four categories I have illustrated: 20

Place names	John Hill, John Atwater
Patronyms (or others based on personal names)	John Robertson, John Williams, John Alexander
Occupational names	John Smith, John Fletcher
Descriptive names	John Long, John Armstrong

With a few exceptions the million-plus surnames that Americans bear are of these four sorts. If we were mainly an Oriental or an African nation, the patterns would be different. But we are primarily European in our origins, and in Europe it seemed natural to identify each person during the surname-giving period according to location, parentage, occupation, appearance, or other characteristics.

It never used to occur to me that my name and almost everyone   22 else's name has a meaning, now often unknown even to its possessors. My own name, I found, is a place name. A *hook* is a sharp bend in a stream or a peninsula or some odd little corner of land. My paternal ancestors, who came from Somerset in southern England, lived on such a hook, probably one of the many irregularly shaped bits of land in Somerset. The numerous Hookers, like General Joseph Hooker in the Civil War, lived in similar places in the name-giving period. Hocking(s), Hoke(r), Horn(e), and Horman(n) are other English or German names that share the meaning of Hook, so they are my cousins, by semantics though not by blood. So are the Dutch Hoekstra, van Hoek, and Haack, who lived in their own odd little corners in the Netherlands.

By coincidence, my mother's father (part Finnish, mostly German) bore a name that also referred to a bend or angle. He was Engel, and his ancestors had lived in Angeln, in Schleswig in northern Germany. The Angles who came in the fifth century to the British Isles with the Saxons, Jutes, and Frisians to help the Celts against the savage Picts (but eventually drove their hosts to the western and northern reaches of the islands) took their name from the same German area, and England—Angle-land historically—is named for them. Angeln got its name because it was shaped somewhat like a fishhook; the word is obviously related to *angle* and the sport of *angling.*

The fourfold identification of people by place, ancestry, occupation, or description has worked well, and only science fiction writers today ever suggest that our names may or should be replaced by numbers or number-letter combinations. Even an ordinary name like William Miller, George Rivers, or Anne Armstrong can acquire an individuality and a remember-able quality hard to imagine for 27–496–3821 or Li94T8633. I'd proba-bly not enjoy a love affair with American names that looked like mere license plate identifications.

The proportion in each category of names may vary from one Euro-   25
pean language to another. Thus 70 percent or more of Irish, Welsh, and Scandinavian surnames are patronyms. Spanish families have also pre-ferred patronyms, but place names are not far behind. In France patro-nyms lead once more, but names of occupations are in second place. In Germany, however, patronyms of the simple English sort are relatively few, although hereditary combinative descriptions like the previously mentioned Gerhard are common, occupational names are frequent, and place names not uncommon. In most countries personal descriptive sur-names lag behind the others.

Elsdon Smith analyzed seven thousand of our most common Ameri-can surnames and found these proportions:

	Percentage
Place names	43.13
Patronyms	32.23
Occupational names	15.16
Nicknames (descriptives)	9.48

In an analysis that I made of several hundred American surnames of English origin, I obtained the following percentages:

	Percentage
Place names	35.49
Patronyms	32.37
Occupational names	19.66
Personal descriptors	12.47

The fact that large numbers of American surnames are derived from En-gland is reflected in the similarities between Smith's percentages and mine.

Often, superficially different American surnames turn out to be essen-tially the same name in meaning when translated from the foreign language into English. . . . Place names, often unique or nearly so, are not likely to be internationally duplicated except when they refer to geographically common features like bodies of water or land masses. We may illustrate the possibilities with the English surname Hill, whose German equivalent may be Buhl, Buehler, Knor(r), or Piehl, paralleled by Dutch Hoger and Hoogland (literally *high land*), French Depew and Dumont, Italian Costa and Colletti, Finnish Maki (one of Finland's most common names), Hungarian Hegi, Scandinavian Berg, Bergen, Bagge, and Haugen, and Slavic Kopec, Kopecky, and Pagorak, all of which mean *hill* or *small mountain*.

Differences in size or in skin or hair coloration are international, as many of our personal descriptive surnames confirm. English Brown and Black, for instance, may refer to either dark skin or brown or black hair. (*Black*, however, sometimes comes from the Old English *blac*, related to our *bleach* and meaning *white* or *light*, so Mr. Black's ancestors may have been either fair or dark.) Blake is a variant of Black. The French know the dark person as Le Brun or Moreau, the Germans as Braun, Brun, Mohr, or Schwartz, the Italians as Bruno, the Russians as Chernoff. Pincus refers to a dark-skinned Jew, Mavros to a dark Greek. Dark Irishmen may be named, among other possibilities, Carey, Duff, Dunn(e), Dolan, Dow, or Kearns. Hungarian Fekete has a dark skin. Czechoslovakian Cerny or Czerny (black) reveals his linguistic similarity to Polish Czarnik, Czarniak, or Czarnecki and Ukrainian Corney. Spanish Negron is a very dark person.

Many names spelled identically are common to two or more languages, and a considerable number of such names have more than a single meaning. So Gray, although usually an English name meaning *gray haired,* in a few instances is French for a person from Gray (the estate of Gradus) in France. Gray must therefore be classified both as a personal descriptor and a place name. Hoff is usually German for a farm or an enclosed place, but less often is English for Hoff (pagan temple), a place in Westmoreland. Many Scandinavian names are identical in Denmark, Norway, and Sweden, although spelling variants such as *-sen* and *-son* suggest the likelihood of one country rather than another. In general a person must know at least a little about his or her ancestry before determining with assurance the nationality and most likely meaning of his or her name.

A small percentage of names, few of them common in the United States, is derived from sources other than the basic four. For example, a few Jewish names are based on acronyms or initials. Thus Baran or Baron sometimes refers to *Ben Rabbi Nachman,* and Brock to *Ben Rabbi Kalman.* Zak, abbreviating *zera kedoshim* (the seed of martyrs), is often respelled Sack, Sacks, or Sachs, although these may also be place names for people from Saxony. Katz is sometimes based on *kohen tzedek* (priest of righteousness), and Segal (in several spellings) can be *segan leviyyah* (member of the tribe of Levi).

Other Jewish names are somewhat arbitrary German or Yiddish pairings, usually with pleasant connotations, like Lowenthal (lions' valley),

30

Gottlieb (God's love), or Finkelstein (little finch stone). Some modern Swedes have replaced their conventional patronyms (Hanson, Jorgenson, etc.) with nature words or pairings of nature words, like Lind (linden), Lindstrom (linden stream), Asplund (aspen grove), or Ekberg (oak mountain).

Numerous Norwegian surnames are a special variety of place names called farm names. Many Norwegian farms have held the same name for hundreds of years, and people from a given farm have come to be known by its name. So Bjornstad, for instance, means *Bjorn's farm,* and Odega(a)rd means *dweller on uncultivated land.*

Japanese names are comparable to some of the Jewish and Swedish names mentioned a moment ago, in that they frequently combine two words, one or both of which may refer to nature. So Fujikawa combines two elements meaning *wisteria* and *river,* Hayakawa is *early, river,* Tanaka is *rice-field, middle,* Inoue is *well* (noun), *upper,* and Kawasaki is *river, headland.*

Chinese surnames are very few—perhaps nine or ten hundred in all—and endlessly repeated. A few dozen of them are especially widely used, like the familiar Wong, which may mean either *field* or *large body of water,* Chin (the name of the first great dynasty, of more than two thousand years ago), Wang (*yellow* or *prince*), Le (*pear tree*), and Yee (*I*).   35

The names given foundlings could readily provide material for a full chapter. Bastard as an appellation was once freely applied to foundlings or any illegitimate children even among royalty and the nobility, but today the name is opprobrious and there are few if any Bastards listed in American directories. Italian Esposito is the same as Spanish Exposita, for which the Italian spelling is generally substituted. Other Italian names suggest the blessedness or holiness of the foundling: De Benedictis, De Angelis, De Santis, and della Croce (one who lives near the cross).

The English Foundling Hospital authorities once conferred noble or famous names on foundlings, who thus might be named Bedford, Marlborough, Pembroke, or the like, or sometimes Geoffrey Chaucer, John Milton, Francis Bacon, Oliver Cromwell, or even Peter Paul Rubens. Some names were taken from fiction: Tom Jones, Clarissa Harlowe, Sophia Western. Other foundlings were given the names of places where they were found: e.g., Lawrence because the infant was found in St. Lawrence. A little girl found in a waiting room of the Southern Railway was named Frances Southern.

Not more than one American surname in twenty, however, can be classified with assurance in any category other than the big four: places, patronyms, occupations, and descriptors.

FOCUSING ON CONTENT

1. What, according to Hook, is a name? In your own words, describe the naming system used by upper-class Romans.

2. How, according to Hook, did England get its name?

3. How is the subservience of women in the Middle Ages borne out in the naming process?

4. Hook says that almost all English and Continental surnames fall into four categories. What are those categories? What is a *patronym*?

5. In what way are Japanese names comparable to some Jewish and Swedish names?

6. What is a foundling? How were foundlings frequently named?

7. How do American surnames reveal our country's history?

FOCUSING ON WRITING

1. When discussing the various aspects of a language, a writer often needs to use a great many examples, as Hook has done. What special demands does the need for numerous examples place on the writer? (Glossary: *Examples*)

2. How does Hook personalize his essay? Provide a few examples that show his personal involvement in what he's writing.

3. What kinds of evidence does Hook use to support his statements about how surnames arose in the Middle Ages? (Glossary: *Evidence*) Do you find his evidence convincing? Explain.

4. What is the function of Hook's concluding sentence? (Glossary: *Beginnings and Endings*)

LANGUAGE IN ACTION

Comment on the relationship of the following Ann Landers column to J. N. Hook's essay.

***

REFUSAL TO USE NAME IS THE ULTIMATE INSULT

DEAR ANN LANDERS: Boy, when you're wrong, you're really wrong. Apparently, you have never been the victim of a hostile, nasty, passive-aggressive person who refuses to address you by name. Well, I have.

My husband's mother has never called me by my name in the 21 years I've been married to her son. Nor has she ever said "please" or "thank you," unless someone else is within hearing distance. My husband's children by his first wife are the same way. The people they care about are always referred to by name, but the rest of us are not called anything.

If you still think this is a "psychological glitch," as you said in a recent column, try speaking to someone across the room without addressing that person by name. To be nameless and talked at is the ultimate put-down, and I wish you had said so. — "Hey You" in Florida

DEAR FLORIDA: Sorry I let you down. Your mother-in-law's refusal to call you by name is, I am sure, rooted in hostility. Many years ago, Dr. Will Menninger said, "The sweetest sound in any language is the sound of your own name." It can also be a valuable sales tool. My former husband, one of the world's best salesmen, said if you want to make a sale, get the customer's name, use it when you make your pitch, and he will be half sold. His own record as a salesman proved him right.

WRITING SUGGESTIONS

1. (*Writing from Experience*) Is your surname very common in American society, very rare, or somewhere in between? Do others have difficulty pronouncing or spelling it? Write an essay in which you reflect on the way your surname has affected your life and the way people react to you. Be sure to give examples of the role your name plays in day-to-day life. For example, a John Smith may yearn for a more distinctive name or may find security in a name that is very common and thus attracts little attention.

2. (*Writing from Reading*) Hook states that most surnames derive from occupations or associations with male figures. As he writes, "Had women's prestige been higher we would today have many persons with names like Milkmaid, Buxom, and Margaretson." Also, traditional practice in American society dictates that a woman assume her husband's surname at marriage. Write an essay in which you discuss the current issues that have developed regarding women's desires to retain their surnames after marriage and pass them along to their own children. Do you think this trend is a positive one? How would you implement a naming system that does not discriminate against one gender or the other?

3. (*Writing from Research*) Write an essay in which you discuss the history of your surname. You might want to start by using the information from your Writing to Discover entry for this selection. Interview your relatives to discover what they may know about your family name. Did it change over time? How do you know? What was the reason for the change(s)? To supplement your inquiry, look in J. N. Hook's *Family Names: How Our Surnames Came to America,* the book from which the preceding essay is taken. Hook includes chapters on the names of the British and northern Europeans, southern Europeans, eastern Europeans, Africans, Koreans, Chinese, Arabs, and many other peoples of the world. Equally valuable is the chapter on the sources of his research, which may help you extend your own research. Your study should be not only an exciting exploration for you but something you will want to pass on to members of your family.

What's in a Name?

BONNIE WACH

In the following magazine article, originally published in Health *magazine in September 1992, writer Bonnie Wach explores the impact names can have on people. As anyone who has faced teasing about an unusual name can attest, children bear the consequences of the names their parents choose. "To be sure," writes Wach, "in the search for uncommon names, some parents have gone off the deep end. The living, breathing results are kids named Fuzzy, Whisper, Pitbull, Demon, Nausea, and Mischief, to name just a few recent examples." As Wach notes, however, at least one researcher believes that an unusual name may be beneficial because it increases a person's recognition factor. Whether such names are harmful or helpful, parents should act thoughtfully when naming a child. Our names, after all, are inseparable from our identities.*

WRITING TO DISCOVER: *Reflect on your first name, your last name, or your name taken in its entirety. Jot down answers to some of these questions: Do you regard your name as common or uncommon? Why? Aside from the fact that it is your name, does it have any special significance? In other words, were you named after someone or something? Does your name reveal your heritage? What overtones does your name carry for you? What overtones do you think it carries for others?*

A person with a bad name is already half-hanged, an old proverb goes. But in modern times, we reserve the right to buck convention — and the fates be damned. Not that we don't believe in the power of names. The problem is that when it comes time to name our offspring, we discover that bucking convention isn't so easy.

Take, for instance, the plight of Ty and Dione Affleck in Seattle, whose efforts to pick the right monikers for their two children became a major project:

"We looked through lists of Old English or Gaelic names to tie in with Affleck, and then scanned lists of the most popular names and nixed anything above seventieth place," Dione says. The couple — she's a physical therapist, he's a doctor — considered McKenzie, Paige, Ethan, Calvin, Blake, Keith, and Kevin, but feared they were becoming overused. Finally, a few years ago, after poring over the book *10,000 Baby Names,* they settled on Chelsea for their daughter and, more recently, Ryan for their son. Unfortunately, they soon found they were hardly alone.

"Little did we know. Here we were trying so desperately to be individual and unique, and now we already know dozens of Chelseas and Ryans," says Dione. To top it off, now there's a Chelsea in the White House.

So it goes. For girls, such "unusual" names as Ashley, Amanda, 5 Samantha, and Jessica have all been in the top ten since 1988. Brittany, with a push from TV's "thirtysomething," hit number one in 1989 and stayed there. Common baby boomer names like Susan and Linda didn't even make the top 50 last year. Boys' names tend to be a bit more stable: Census figures show that Michael, Christopher, Matthew, David, and Andrew have held their top spots for more than a decade. But Ethan, Nicholas, and Tyler have jumped in popularity.

What's so awful about having a common name? Edwin (don't call him Eddie) Lawson, a psychology professor emeritus at State University of New York in Fredonia, puts it this way: "Imagine that you've got a special outfit and you wear it out to dinner. You won't like it if another woman is wearing the same outfit."

And so the quest for one-of-a-kind "outfits" takes some inventive turns. For the most part, the days when hip parents named their children Moon Unit and Nirvana are gone. In their place, geographical names such as Paris, Madison, and Dakota have become chic (actresses Melanie Griffith and Melissa Gilbert-Brinkman both have children named Dakota), as have ones that sound like they belong to someone's grandparents, like Nell and Gus.

Many parents are suddenly rediscovering—or simply inventing—their roots, according to Cleveland Kent Evans, a psychology professor at Bellevue College in Nebraska who's spent years tracking name trends. Upper-middle-class Jewish couples have started looking to their ancestral heritage for nineteenth century immigrant names like Max or Hannah. Working-class African American parents fashion ethnic-sounding names with the prefixes La and Sha or with suffixes such as isha, onda, ita, or ika, as in LaToya and Shandrika. And educated, upper-middle-class couples of various ethnic backgrounds have taken to bestowing gender-neutral family names, such as Jordan and Taylor, on their daughters.

"People are trying harder and harder to be more original," says Leonard Ashley, an onomastician (that's someone who studies names) at Brooklyn College. "But they shouldn't try to be too original. When people give their daughter a name like Tempest, it's like making her wear a spangled rhinestone dress to the supermarket. It's not for everyday wear."

To be sure, in the search for uncommon names, some parents have 10 gone off the deep end. The living, breathing results are kids named Fuzzy, Whisper, Pitbull, Demon, Nausea, and Mischief, to name just a few recent examples.

Some say there's a danger such names could become self-fulfilling prophesies. After all, in the seventies, a New York psychologist looked into the subject and found 180 examples of people whose names seemed to lead them down a particular career path, including Bacon Chow the nutritionist, Lionel Tiger the animal behavior researcher, and Cardinal Sin, the archbishop. Does it follow that the girl whose parents dubbed her Fayle (pronounced *fail*) is destined to flop?

"A name like that can handicap and scar you for life," says Albert Mehrabian, a UCLA psychology professor who isn't fond of being called Al. "I think children have enough pressure on them without the additional disadvantage of an unpleasant name."

Mehrabian cites studies like the one in which researchers asked teachers to grade identical essays titled "What I Did Last Sunday." The ones signed by a "David" or "Lisa" consistently got better grades than those by an "Elmer" or "Bertha." In another study, researchers asked college students at Tulane University to pick a beauty queen from six photos of women who had previously been judged equally attractive. The photos marked Jennifer, Kathy, and Christine consistently beat out the ones labeled Gertrude, Harriet, and Ethel.

"A bad name affects how a person is perceived by friends, coworkers, and total strangers. It's like forcing someone to walk around all their life with blue-colored hair," Mehrabian says.

But what exactly is a "bad" name? To find out, Mehrabian surveyed   15
2,000 people, asking them to judge a slew of first names. "I told people, 'You're about to meet somebody for the first time and you know only their name and their sex. Tell me what that person is going to be like.'" The respondents rated each name in terms of success, morality, health, warmth, cheerfulness, and masculinity or femininity.

The survey results, published in *The Name Game*, "a comprehensive guide to first names," confirm what we already know: Some names carry definite stereotypes. Bunny and DiDi, for example, scored high on feminity but bombed on success and morality. Brunhilde was a loser in all categories. For boys, John, Rick, Chad, and Buck all had high success and masculinity scores. Melvin, on the other hand, scored zero in the health category, which includes characteristics like popularity, athleticism, good looks, confidence, and assertiveness.

So what about Mel Gibson?

"This is a statistical relationship," Mehrabian says. "Not everyone with a bad name will be unsuccessful."

Nicknames didn't fare well in Mehrabian's survey, either. Robert did better in all categories than Bob. Jacqueline scored the highest among girls' names under success, but Jackie did only about half as well. Mehrabian says that people with nicknames are often not taken seriously. (Don't tell Johnny Carson or Tip O'Neill.)

"Names aren't as important as people think," Evans says. "If you just   20
have a name to react to, you're bound to come up with a prejudiced judgment. But when you add a real person to the name, it's not that much of an influence." He points out that surveys singling out suppos-

edly undesirable names say nothing about how those names actually influence a person's self-image.

In fact, researchers have tried for decades to link unusual or less desirable names to everything from psychological maladjustment to criminal misdeeds. For the most part, they've come up empty-handed. One 1948 study, for example, set out to test the then-current opinion that there was a greater likelihood of success in marriage if a man "selects a girl with a common name." Of 414 women at a black college, those with uncommon names such as Florenda, Janafea, Honthalena, and Aluesta were found to be no more neurotic—and thus less marriageable—than women with names like Mary, Helen, Susie, Ethel, and Daisy.

More recent research suggests that if unusual names have *any* effect on social or psychological development, it may very well be a positive one: A 1980 study of Wesleyan University students found that women with unusual names actually scored higher in "sociability" and "social presence" on psychological tests than women with more common names.

Nevertheless, Mehrabian's heard enough sad stories—from a man named Jack Daniels to a woman called Latrina—to be convinced that, for some people at least, an unusual name spells trouble. "Parents can be very egocentric when it comes to naming their children. They pick names that make an intellectual statement, like Alpha or Beta, or ones, like Ima Hogg and Ura Hogg, that they think are kind of funny. It's not funny for the child."

His advice to expectant parents: Think before you dub. "Remember, you're tagging your child with something that will become a permanent part of his or her identity," he says.

FOCUSING ON CONTENT

1. Wach begins her article with the proverb "A person with a bad name is already half-hanged." What point is Wach making about onomastics? (Glossary: *Onomastics*) How does her use of this proverb influence your reading of the rest of the article?

2. According to Wach, what were the trends in children's names during the 1990s? How do her observations compare to what you have observed about your own age group? How have names changed since you were born?

3. Mel Gibson is obviously not handicapped by his "bad" name. Explain why, based on the conclusions that Albert Mehrabian and Cleveland Evans draw from their studies. What other people have succeeded in spite of what you might consider "bad" names?

FOCUSING ON WRITING

1. Look through Wach's essay for examples of questions that she asks the reader. For what purpose(s) does Wach use those questions? Do you ever use questions in your own essays? Explain.

2. It is clear from her essay that Wach has interviewed people with regard to the power of names. How has she used quotations from her interviews to develop her essay? (Glossary: *Examples*)

3. Describe Wach's style in this essay. Study Wach's particular use of words, sentence construction, and transitions to help you do your assessment. (Glossary: *Diction, Style,* and *Transitions*) Is her style appropriate for her audience and subject matter? Explain.

LANGUAGE IN ACTION

Explain the relationship you see, if any, between Wach's essay and the following report by Lois B. Morris, which is taken from the March 1999 issue of *Allure*.

NAMING NAMES

Some parents believe that old-fashioned names for their daughters sound beautiful. But according to a new study, women with these names are at a disadvantage when it comes to first impressions. In several studies, psychologist Andrew N. Christopher of the University of Florida in Gainesville asked a total of 316 men and women to describe their reactions to female names from three categories — those that were popular earlier in the century (such as Betty, Alice, Gloria, and Phyllis); contemporary favorites (including Jennifer, Theresa, and Michelle); and familiar but uncommon names (Holly, Jill, and Vanessa). Christopher found that men who evaluated identical personal ads from women with a variety of names invariably rejected the Ediths, Eleanors, and other "oldies." In another test, both men and women who evaluated identical résumés of female job applicants gave the lowest potential employment ratings to those with old-fashioned monikers. Such names evoke unfavorable and probably unconscious biases against old people, says Christopher, and that can affect first impressions when other information is limited.

WRITING SUGGESTIONS

1. (*Writing from Experience*) A major part of learning in any field involves becoming familiar with the names for ideas and things that characterize the subject. For example, photographers need to know the meaning of wide angle, 35 mm, single-lens reflex, frame, focal length, shutter speed, ASA, exposure, large format, F-stop, contact sheet, fixer, red eye, and so forth. Choose a subject you are familiar with, such as your major, a hobby, or a sport, and write an essay in which you discuss the terms that are most important to that subject. Be sure to include information about how you learned the critical terms, what can go wrong if you don't know them, and what you are unable to do if you are unfamiliar with them.

2. (*Writing from Reading*) Do a study of the names of the people in your dormitory or in one of your social groups. Analyze those names in light of Bonnie Wach's essay. In your opinion, are any of the names unusual? Why? Do they sound strange? Do they represent a culture different from your own? Do they remind you of another word that you find humorous? Which of the names are rather common sounding? Write an essay in which you discuss your findings. Make sure that you don't simply describe the names you found. Instead, build a context for your essay and provide a thesis for your comments. (Glossary: *Thesis*)

3. (*Writing from Research*) The names of cities, towns, rivers, and mountains provide clues to settlement and migration patterns and reflect local history as well. After examining a map of your state or region, select six place names and write a report in which you discuss the origin of each name and what it tells of local history. To begin this research, look in your library or on the Internet for any comprehensive books or articles about the place names in your area. If none exists, inquire in the municipal offices or libraries of the places you have chosen to study.

The Names of Women

LOUISE ERDRICH

Born in Minnesota in 1954 to Ralph and Rita Erdrich, who both worked for the Bureau of Indian Affairs, Louise Erdrich grew up in North Dakota and belongs to the Turtle Mountain band of Chippewa Native Americans. She received her B.A. from Dartmouth College and M.A. from Johns Hopkins University. Author of numerous poems, novels, and short stories, Erdrich won the National Book Critics Circle Award in 1984 for her novel Love Medicine. *Her other novels include* The Beet Queen *(1986),* Tracks *(1988),* The Bingo Palace *(1994),* The Antelope Wife *(1998), and with her late husband Michael Dorris* The Crown of Columbus *(1991). She has also written two collections of poetry,* Jacklight *(1984) and* Baptism of Desire *(1990).*

"The Names of Women," originally published in Erdrich's book The Blue Jays *(1995), is about both personal discovery and an entire culture that has been swept away over time. The essay reveals parts of Erdrich's own heritage, and it gives readers a glimpse at some of what was lost when Native American cultures were diluted and then died out.*

WRITING TO DISCOVER: *If you had a descriptive name, as do many Native Americans, what would you like it to be? Why? Write about your hypothetical name. Would there be any advantages or disadvantages in having a descriptive name?*

Ikwe is the word for woman in the language of the Anishinabe, my mother's people, whose descendants, mixed with and married to French trappers and farmers, are the Michifs of the Turtle Mountain reservation in North Dakota. Every Anishinabe *Ikwe*, every mixed-blood descendent like me, who can trace her way back a generation or two, is the daughter of a mystery. The history of the woodland Anishinabe—decimated by disease, fighting Plains Indian tribes to the west and squeezed by European settlers to the east—is much like most other Native American stories, a confusion of loss, a tale of absences, of a culture that was blown apart and changed so radically in such a short time that only the names survive.

And yet, those names.

The names of the first women whose existence is recorded on the rolls of the Turtle Mountain Reservation, in 1892, reveal as much as we can ever recapture of their personalities, complex natures, and relationships. These names tell stories, or half stories, if only we listen closely.

There once were women named *Standing Strong, Fish Bones, Different Thunder*. There once was a girl called *Yellow Straps*. Imagine what it was like to pick berries with *Sky Coming Down*, to walk through a storm with *Lightning Proof*. Surely, she was struck and lived, but what about the person next to her? People always avoided *Steps Over Truth*, when they wanted a straight answer, and *I Hear*, when they wanted to keep a secret. *Glittering* put coal on her face and watched for enemies at night. The woman named *Standing Across* could see things moving far across the lake. The old ladies gossiped about *Playing Around*, but no one dared say anything to her face. *Ice* was good at gambling. *Shining One Side* loved to sit and talk to *Opposite the Sky*. They both knew *Sounding Feather, Exhausted Wind*, and *Green Cloud*, daughter of *Seeing Iron*. *Center of the Sky* was a widow. *Rabbit, Prairie Chicken*, and *Daylight* were all little girls. *She Tramp* could make great distance in a day of walking. *Cross Lightning* had a powerful smile. When *Setting Wind* and *Gentle Woman Standing* sang together the whole tribe listened. *Stop the Day* got her name when at her shout the afternoon went still. *Log* was strong, *Cloud Touching Bottom* weak and consumptive. *Mirage* married *Wind*. Everyone loved *Musical Cloud*, but children hid from *Dressed in Stone*. *Lying Down Grass* had such a gentle voice and touch, but no one dared to cross *She Black of Heart*.

We can imagine something of these women from their names.   5
Anishinabe historian Basil Johnston notes that "such was the mystique and force of a name that it was considered presumptuous and unbecoming, even vain, for a person to utter his own name. It was the custom for a third person, if present, to utter the name of the person to be identified. Seldom, if ever, did either husband or wife speak the name of the other in public."

Shortly after the first tribal roll, the practice of renaming became an ecclesiastical exercise, and, as a result, most women in the next two generations bear the names of saints particularly beloved by the French. *She Knows the Bear* became Marie. *Sloping Cloud* was christened Jeanne. *Taking Care of the Day* and *Yellow Day Woman* turned into Catherines. Identities are altogether lost. The daughters of my own ancestors, *Kwayzancheewin—Acts Like a Boy* and *Striped Earth Woman*—go unrecorded, and no hint or reflection of their individual natures comes to light through the scattershot records of those times, although they must have been genetically tough in order to survive: there were epidemics of typhoid, flu, measles, and other diseases that winnowed the tribe each winter. They had to have grown up sensible, hard-working, undeviating in their attention to their tasks. They had to have been lucky. And if very lucky, they acquired carts.

It is no small thing that both of my great-grandmothers were known as women with carts.

The first was Elise Eliza McCloud, the great-granddaughter of *Striped Earth Woman*. The buggy she owned was somewhat grander than a cart. In her photograph, Elise Eliza gazes straight ahead, intent, elevated in her pride. Perhaps she and her daughter Justine, both wearing reshaped felt fedoras, were on their way to the train that would take them from Rugby, North Dakota, to Grand Forks, and back again. Back and forth across the upper tier of the plains, they peddled their hand-worked tourist items — dangling moccasin brooches and little beaded hats, or, in the summer, the wild berries, plums, and nuts that they had gathered from the wooded hills. Of Elise Eliza's industry there remains in the family only an intricately beaded pair of buffalo horns and a piece of real furniture, a "highboy," an object once regarded with some awe, a prize she won for selling the most merchandise from a manufacturer's catalogue.

The owner of the other cart, Virginia Grandbois, died when I was nine years old: she was a fearsome and fascinating presence, an old woman seated like an icon behind the door of my grandparents' house. Forty years before I was born, she was photographed on her way to fetch drinking water at the reservation well. In the picture she is seated high, the reins in her fingers connected to a couple of shaggy fetlocked draft ponies. The barrel she will fill stands behind her. She wears a man's sweater and an expression of vast self-pleasure. She might have been saying *Kaygoh*, a warning, to calm the horses. She might have been speaking to whomever it was who held the camera, still a novel luxury.

Virginia Grandbois was known to smell of flowers. In spite of the   10
potato picking, water hauling, field and housework, she found the time and will to dust her face with pale powder, in order to look more French. She was the great-great-granddaughter of the daughter of the principal leader of the *A-waus-e*, the Bullhead clan, a woman whose real name was never recorded but who, on marrying a Frenchman, was "recreated" as Madame Cadotte. It was Madame Cadotte who acted as a liaison between her Ojibway relatives and her husband so that, even when French influence waned in the region, Jean-Baptiste Cadotte stayed on as the only trader of importance, the last governor of the fort at Sault St. Marie.

By the time I knew Virginia Grandbois, however, her mind had darkened, and her body deepened, shrunk, turned to bones and leather. She did not live in the present or in any known time at all. Periodically, she would awaken from dim and unknown dreams to find herself seated behind the door in her daughter's house. She then cried out for her cart and her horses. When they did not materialize, Virginia Grandbois rose with great energy and purpose. Then she walked towards her house, taking the straightest line.

That house, long sold and gone, lay over one hundred miles due east and still Virginia Grandbois charged ahead, no matter what lay in her path — fences, sloughs, woods, the yards of other families. She wanted home, to get home, to be home. She wanted her own place back, the place she had made, not her daughter's, not anyone else's. Hers. There was no substitute, no kindness, no reality that would change her mind. She had to be tied to the chair, and the chair to the wall, and still there was no reasoning with Virginia Grandbois. Her entire life, her hard-won personality, boiled down in the end to one stubborn, fixed, desperate idea.

I started with the same idea—this urge to get home, even if I must walk straight across the world. Only, for me, the urge to walk is the urge to write. Like my great-grandmother's house, there is no home for me to get to. A mixed-blood, raised in the Sugarbeet Capital, educated on the Eastern seaboard, married in a tiny New England village, living now on a ridge directly across from the Swan Range in the Rocky Mountains, my home is a collection of homes, of wells in which the quiet of experience shales away into sweet bedrock.

Elise Eliza pieced the quilt my mother slept under, a patchwork of shirts, pants, other worn-out scraps, bordered with small rinsed and pressed Bull Durham sacks. As if in another time and place, although it is only the dim barrel of a four-year-old's memory, I see myself lying wrapped under smoky quilts and dank green army blankets in the house in which my mother was born. In the fragrance of tobacco, some smoked in home-rolled cigarettes, some offered to the Manitous whose presence still was honored, I dream myself home. Beneath the rafters, shadowed with bunches of plants and torn calendars, in the nest of a sagging bed, I listen to mice rustle and the scratch of an owl's claws as it paces the shingles.

Elise Eliza's daughter-in-law, my grandmother Mary LeFavor, kept   15
that house of hand-hewed and stacked beams, mudded between. She managed to shore it up and keep it standing by stuffing every new crack with disposable diapers. Having used and reused cloth to diaper her own children, my grandmother washed and hung to dry the paper and plastic diapers that her granddaughters bought for her great-grandchildren. When their plastic-paper shredded, she gathered them carefully together and one day, on a summer visit, I woke early to find her tamping the rolled stuff carefully into the cracked walls of that old house.

It is autumn in the Plains, and in the little sloughs ducks land, and mudhens, whose flesh always tastes greasy and charred. Snow is coming soon, and after its first fall there will be a short, false warmth that brings out the sweet-sour odor of highbush cranberries. As a descendant of the women who skinned buffalo and tanned and smoked the hides, of women who pounded berries with the dried meat to make winter food, who made tea from willow bark and rosehips, who gathered snakeroot, I am affected by the change of seasons. Here is a time when plants consolidate their tonic and drop seed, when animals store energy and grow thick fur. As for me, I start keeping longer hours, writing more, working harder, though I am obviously not a creature of a traditional Anishinabe culture. I was not raised speaking the old language, or adhering to the cycle of religious ceremonies that govern the Anishinabe spiritual relationship to the land and the moral order within human configurations. As the wedding of many backgrounds, I am free to do what simply feels right.

My mother knits, sews, cans, dries food and preserves it. She knows how to gather tea, berries, snare rabbits, milk cows, and churn butter. She can grow squash and melons from seeds she gathered the fall before. She is, as were the women who came before me, a repository of all of the homey virtues, and I am the first in a long line who has not saved the autumn's harvest in birch bark *makuks* and skin bags and in a cellar dry and cold with dust. I am the first who scratches the ground for pleasure, not survival, and grows flowers instead of potatoes. I record rather than practice the arts that filled the hands and days of my mother and her mother, and all the mothers going back into the shadows, when women wore names that told us who they were.

FOCUSING ON CONTENT

1. Erdrich begins her essay with the Anishinabe word for woman, *Ikwe*. Why is this word important? What does Erdrich accomplish by introducing it at the beginning of her essay?

2. The quotation from Basil Johnston in paragraph 5 mentions the "mystique and force" of Anishinabe names. Why did the names have such mystique? What happened to the Anishinabe culture when the French made naming an ecclesiastical exercise?

3. Summarize Erdrich's descriptions of her great-grandmothers in one or two sentences. Why do you think Erdrich describes them at length? How do their stories represent what happened to the Anishinabe culture as a whole?

4. In paragraph 4, why do you think Erdrich makes associations with so many Anishinabe names? What does this list tell you about the culture that was lost? Provide some alternative associations for ten of the names. How do you think your ethnocentricity, your immersion in a particular culture, influences the way you interpret names? (Glossary: *Ethnocentricity*)

FOCUSING ON WRITING

1. What does Erdrich mean when she writes in paragraph 13, "I started with the same idea — this urge to get home, even if I must walk straight across the world. Only, for me, the urge to walk is the urge to write"? How is writing like walking? Do you think Erdrich "gets home" in this essay? What in her style leads you to your answer? (Glossary: *Style*)

2. Erdrich's paragraphs are well developed. Although most are of average length or a bit longer, she includes several paragraphs (2, 3, and 7) that are shorter than normal. What is the function of each of those paragraphs?

3. In paragraph 16, Erdrich begins the last section of her essay with the following description: "It is autumn in the Plains, and in the little sloughs ducks land, and mudhens, whose flesh always tastes greasy and charred. Snow is coming soon, and after its first fall there will be a short, false warmth that brings out the sweet-sour odor of highbrush cranberries." Why do you think Erdrich includes this description of place? How does it tie in with her heritage?

LANGUAGE IN ACTION

Show-business people often change their names to further their careers. Here are the professional names and the original names of a number of celebrities. Discuss with your classmates the significance of the names and the reasons they might have been changed.

Professional Names	Original Names
Tony Curtis	Bernard Schwartz
Mick Jagger	Michael Philip
Simone Signoret	Simone Kaminker
Roy Rogers	Leonard Sly
Raquel Welch	Raquel Tejada
James Garner	James Bumgarner
Bob Dylan	Robert Zimmerman
Doris Day	Doris von Kappelhoff
Fred Astaire	Frederick Austerlitz
John Wayne	Marion Michael Morrison
Cyd Charisse	Tula Finklea
Anne Bancroft	Annemaria Italiano
Michael Caine	Maurice J. Micklewhite
Jack Benny	Benjamin Kubelsky
Connie Francis	Concetta Franconero
Ringo Starr	Richard Starkey
Hugh O'Brian	Hugh J. Krampe

WRITING SUGGESTIONS

1. (*Writing from Experience*) In an essay entitled "Going Home," write with the same general purpose that Louise Erdrich has written "The Names of Women," not about names necessarily but about the way writing can create a home or a number of homes. Before you write, think about the implications of Erdrich's metaphor and consider the various kinds of writing experiences that constitute going home. How does the creative process of writing

provide not only a sense of power and control but also a sense of the familiarity and comfort of home?

2. (*Writing from Reading*) Write an essay in which you compare and/or contrast Erdrich's essay with Katherine Whittemore's "Endangered Languages" (pp. 348–50). How do both essays enlighten us about what is really lost when a whole language disappears or when even a portion of a language is no longer available to us? In what ways does Whittemore provide a grander context for Erdrich's reflections, and in what ways does Erdrich cast the spotlight on a special part of the problem?

3. (*Writing from Research*) As a general subject area for further research and writing, Native American languages are varied and interesting. With the renaissance of interest in Native American studies, especially over the past few decades, there is a vast quantity of information from which to draw. Choose an area of Native American languages that interests you and, using library and Internet research, write an essay explaining your findings to other students who may not know about that area. Following are some possible general subjects: the migration patterns of early North American native peoples and the influence of those patterns on language, genetic research tracing the movement of tribes, the use of carbon-dating techniques to verify the age of antiquities, languages that existed but are now extinct, the various strategies being used to save native languages, and the grammatical structure of a particular native language.

Giving Things Names

S. I. HAYAKAWA AND ALAN R. HAYAKAWA

S. I. Hayakawa (1906–1992), a former senator from California and honorary chair of the English-only movement, wrote the influential semantics text Language in Thought and Action *in 1941. With the help of his son Alan, he brought out the fifth edition of the book in 1991. Born in Vancouver, Canada, to Japanese parents, Hayakawa attended the University of Manitoba, McGill University, and the University of Wisconsin before beginning a career as a professor of English. He later became president of San Francisco State University. Hayakawa's other language books include* Our Language and Our World *(1959) and* Symbol, Status, and Personality *(1963).*

Alan Hayakawa was born in Chicago on July 16, 1946, and received a B.A. in mathematics from Reed College in 1970. He began his writing career as a reporter for the Oregonian *in Portland, Oregon, in 1975, and he moved to Washington, D.C., in 1987 as the* Oregonian's Washington *correspondent. He is now the manager of the InsideLine, a telephone news and information service, at the* Patriot-News *in Harrisburg, Pennsylvania. In addition to coauthoring the fifth edition of* Language in Thought and Action, *Hayakawa has coauthored* The Blair Handbook *(1999), now in its third edition, and the* College Writer's Reference *(1998), now in its second edition.*

In the following selection, taken from Language in Thought and Action, *the Hayakawas reveal the power that words can have over thoughts. The terms we use to classify things—whether people, objects, or concepts—can and do affect our reactions to them. As the Hayakawas make clear, words can be powerful tools for prejudice and stereotyping.*

WRITING TO DISCOVER: *We like to use words to classify things and, in particular, other people. Think about your classmates. You have probably classified people you do not know well—"He's a nerd," "She's a preppie," "He's a jock," and so on. Write about why you think such labeling is so common. What are its advantages? What problems do you think labeling can create?*

The figure on page 216 shows eight objects, let us say animals, four large and four small, a different four with round heads and another four with square heads, and still another four with curly tails and another four with straight tails. These animals, let us say, are scampering about your village, but since at first they are of no importance to you, you ignore them. You do not even give them a name.

One day, however, you discover that the little ones eat up your grain, while the big ones do not. A differentiation sets itself up, and, abstracting the common characteristics of A, B, C, D, you decide to call these *gogo*; E, F, G, and H you decide to call *gigi*. You chase away the *gogo*, but leave the *gigi* alone. Your neighbor, however, has had a different experience; he finds that those with square heads bite, while those with round heads do not. Abstracting the common characteristics of B, D, F, and H, he calls them *daba*, and A, C, E, and G, he calls *dobo*. Still another neighbor discovers, on the other hand, that those with curly tails kill snakes, while those with straight tails do not. He differentiates them, abstracting still another set of common characteristics: A, B, E, and F are *busa*, while C, D, G, and H are *busana*.

Now imagine that the three of you are together when E runs by. You say, "There goes the *gigi*"; your first neighbor says, "There goes the *dobo*"; your other neighbor says, "There goes the *busa*." Here, immediately, a great controversy arises. What is it *really*, a *gigi*, a *dobo*, or a *busa*? What is the *right name*? You are quarreling violently when along comes a fourth person from another village who calls it a *muglock*, an edible animal, as opposed to *uglock*, an inedible animal—which doesn't help matters a bit.

Of course, the question, "What is it *really*?" "What is its *right name*?" is a nonsense question. By a nonsense question is meant one that is not capable of being answered. Things can have "right names" only if there is a necessary connection between symbols and things symbolized, and we have seen that there is not. That is to say, in the light of your interest in protecting your grain, it may be necessary for you to distinguish the animal E as *gigi*; your neighbor, who doesn't like to be bitten, finds it practical to distinguish it as a *dobo*; your other neighbor, who likes to see snakes killed, distinguishes it as a *busa*. What we call things and where we draw the line between one class of things and another depend upon the interests we have and the purposes of the classification. For example, animals are classified in one way by the meat industry, in a different way by the leather industry, in another different way by the fur industry, and in a

still different way by the biologist. None of these classifications is any more final than any of the others; each of them is useful for its purpose.

This holds, of course, regarding everything we perceive. A table "is" a table to us, because we can understand its relationship to our conduct and interests; we eat at it, work on it, lay things on it. But to a person living in a culture where no tables are used, it may be a very strong stool, a small platform, or a meaningless structure. If our culture and upbringing were different, that is to say, our world would not look the same to us.

Many of us, for example, cannot distinguish between pickerel, pike, salmon, smelt, perch, crappie, halibut, and mackerel; we say that they are "just fish, and I don't like fish." To a seafood connoisseur, however, these distinctions are real, since they mean the difference to him between one kind of a good meal, a very different kind of good meal, or a poor meal. To a zoologist, who has other and more general ends in view, even finer distinctions assume great importance. When we hear the statement, then, "This fish is a specimen of pompano, *Trachinotus carolinus*," we accept this as being "true," even if we don't care, not because that is its "right name," but because that is how it is *classified* in the most complete and most general system of classification that people scientifically interested in fish have evolved.

When we name something, then, we are classifying. *The individual object or event we are naming, of course, has no name and belongs to no class until we put it in one.* To illustrate again, suppose that we were to give the extensional meaning of the word "Korean." We would have to point to all "Koreans" living at a particular moment and say, "The word 'Korean' denotes at the present moment these persons: $A_1, A_2, A_3, \ldots A_n$." Now, let us say, a child, whom we shall designate as Z, is born among these "Koreans." *The extensional meaning of the word "Korean," determined prior to the existence of Z, does not include Z.* Z is a new individual belonging to no classification, since all classifications were made without taking Z into account. Why, then, is Z also a "Korean"? *Because we say so.* And, saying so—fixing the classification—we have determined to a considerable extent future attitudes toward Z. For example, Z will always have certain rights in Korea; in other nations he will be regarded as an "alien" and will be subject to laws applicable to "aliens."

In matters of "race" and "nationality," the way in which classifications work is especially apparent. For example, I am by birth a "Canadian," by "race" a "Japanese," and am now an "American." Although I was legally admitted to the United States on a Canadian passport as a "non-quota immigrant," I was unable to apply for American citizenship until after 1952. Until 1965, American immigration law used classifications based on "nationality" and on "race." A Canadian entering the United States as a permanent resident had no trouble getting in, unless he happened to be of Oriental extraction, in which case his "nationality" became irrelevant and he was classified by "race." If the quota for his

5

"race"—for example, Japanese—was filled (and it often was), and if he could not get himself classified as a non-quota immigrant, he was not able to get in at all. (Since 1965, race and national origin have been replaced with an emphasis on "family reunification" as the basis for American immigration law, and race is no longer explicitly mentioned.) Are all these classifications "real"? Of course they are, *and the effect that each of them has upon what he may or may not do constitutes their "reality."*

I have spent my entire life, except for short visits abroad, in Canada and the United States. I speak Japanese haltingly, with a child's vocabulary and an American accent; I do not read or write it. Nevertheless, because classifications seem to have a kind of hypnotic power over some people, I am occasionally credited with (or accused of) having an "Oriental mind." Since Buddha, Confucius, General Tojo, Mao Tse-tung, Pandit Nehru, Rajiv Gandhi, and the proprietor of the Golden Pheasant Chop Suey House all have "Oriental minds," it is difficult to know whether to feel complimented or insulted.

When is a person "black"? By the definition once widely accepted in   10
the United States, any person with even a small amount of "Negro blood"—that is, whose parents or ancestors were classified as "Negroes"—is "black." *It would be exactly as justifiable to say that any person with even a small amount of "white blood" is "white."* Why say one rather than the other? Because the former system of classification *suits the convenience of those making the classification.* (The classification of blacks and other minorities in this country has often suited the convenience of whites.) Classification is not a matter of identifying "essences." It is simply a reflection of social convenience or necessity—and different necessities are always producing different classifications.

There are few complexities about classifications at the level of dogs and cats, knives and forks, cigarettes and candy, but when it comes to classifications at high levels of abstraction, for example, those describing conduct, social institutions, philosophical and moral problems, serious difficulties occur. When one person kills another, is it an act of murder, an act of temporary insanity, an act of homicide, an accident, or an act of heroism? As soon as the process of classification is completed, our attitudes and our conduct are, to a considerable degree, determined. We hang the murderer, we treat the insane, we absolve the victim of circumstance, we pin a medal on the hero.

THE BLOCKED MIND

We need not concern ourselves here with the injustices done to "Jews," "Roman Catholics," "Republicans," "redheads," "chorus girls," "sailors," "Southerners," "Yankees," and so on, by snap judgments or, as it is better to call them, fixed reactions. "Snap judgments" suggest that such errors can be avoided by thinking more slowly; this, of course, is not the case, for some people think very slowly with no better results. What we are concerned with is the way in which we block the development of our own minds by automatic reactions.

In the grip of such reactions some people may say, "A Jew's a Jew. There's no getting around that"—confusing the denoted, extensional Jew with the fictitious "Jew" inside their heads. Such persons, the reader will have observed, can usually be made to admit, on being reminded of certain "Jews" whom they admire—perhaps Albert Einstein, Sandy Koufax, Jascha Heifetz, Benny Goodman, Woody Allen, Henry Kissinger, or Kitty Dukakis—that "there are exceptions, of course." They have been compelled by experience, that is to say, to take cognizance of at least a few of the multitude of Jews who do not fit their preconceptions. At this point, however, they continue triumphantly, "But exceptions only prove the rule?"[1]—which is another way of saying, "Facts don't count."

People who "think" in this way may identify some of their best friends as "Jewish"; but to explain this they may say, "I don't think of them as Jews at all. They're just friends." In other words, the fictitious "Jew" inside their heads remains unchanged *in spite of their experience.*

People like this may be said to be impervious to new information. 15 They continue to vote Republican or Democratic, no matter what the Republicans or Democrats do. They continue to object to socialists, no matter what the socialists propose. They continue to regard mothers as sacred, no matter who the mother. A woman who had been given up on both by physicians and psychiatrists as hopelessly insane was being considered by a committee whose task it was to decide whether or not she should be committed to an asylum. One member of the committee doggedly refused to vote for commitment. "Gentlemen," he said in tones of deepest reverence, "you must remember that this woman is, after all, a mother." Similarly, some people continue to hate Protestants or Catholics, no matter which Protestant or Catholic. Ignoring characteristics left out in the process of classification, they overlook—when the term Republican is applied to the party of Abraham Lincoln, the party of Warren Harding, the party of Richard Nixon, and the party of Ronald Reagan—the rather important differences among them.

COW₁ IS NOT COW₂

How do we prevent ourselves from getting into such intellectual blind alleys, or, finding we are in one, how do we get out again? One way is to remember that practically all statements in ordinary conversation,

---

1. This extraordinarily fatuous saying originally meant, "The exception tests the rule"—*Exception probat regulum*. This older meaning of the word "prove" survives in such an expression as "automobile proving ground."

debate, and public controversy taking the form "Republicans are Republicans," "Business is business," "Boys will be boys," "Women drivers are women drivers," and so on, are *not true*. Let us put one of these blanket statements back into a context in life.

> "I don't think we should go through with this deal, Bill. Is it altogether fair to the railroad company?"
> "Aw, forget it! *Business is business,* after all."

Such an assertion, although it looks like a "simple statement of fact," is not simple and is not a statement of fact. The first "business" *denotes* the transaction under discussion; the second "business" invokes the *connotations* of the word. The sentence is a *directive*, saying, "Let us treat this transaction with complete disregard for considerations other than profit, as the word 'business' suggests." Similarly, when a father tries to excuse the mischief done by his sons, he says, "Boys will be boys"; in other words, "Let us regard the actions of my sons with that indulgent amusement customarily extended toward those whom we call 'boys,'" though the angry neighbor will say, of course, "Boys, my eye! They're little hoodlums; that's what they are!" Such assertions are not informative statements but directives, directing us to classify the object or event under discussion in given ways, in order that we may feel or act as suggested by the terms of the classification.

There is a simple technique for preventing such directives from having their harmful effect on our thinking. It is the suggestion made by Korzybski that we add "index numbers" to our terms, thus: Englishman$_1$, Englishman$_2$ . . . ; cow$_1$, cow$_2$, cow$_3$ . . . ; communist$_1$, communist$_2$, communist$_3$. The terms of the classification tell us what the individuals in that class have in common; *the index numbers remind us of the characteristics left out*. A rule can then be formulated as a general guide in all our thinking and reading: police officer$_1$ *is not* police officer$_2$; mother-in-law$_1$ *is not* mother-in-law$_2$, and so on. This rule, if remembered, prevents us from confusing levels of abstraction and forces us to consider the facts on those occasions when we might otherwise find ourselves leaping to conclusions which we may later have cause to regret.

"TRUTH"

Many semantic problems are, ultimately, problems of classification and nomenclature. Take, for example, the extensive debate over abortion. To opponents of legalized abortion, the unborn entity within a woman's womb is a "baby." Because abortion foes *want* to end abortion, they insist that the "baby" *is* a human being with its own legal rights and that therefore *"abortion is murder."* They call themselves "pro-life" to emphasize their position. Those who *want* individual women to be able to choose whether or not to end a pregnancy call that same unborn entity a "fetus" and insist that a "fetus" *is not* a viable human being capable of living on its own, and claim that a woman has a "right" to make such a choice. Partisans of either side have accused the other of "perverting the meanings of words" and of "not being able to understand plain English."

The decision finally rests not upon appeals to past authority, but upon *what society wants*. In the case *Roe v. Wade*, the Supreme Court found that a "right"—specifically, a right to privacy—permits women to make a private, medical decision before a certain stage of pregnancy. If society again wants doctors prosecuted for performing abortions, as they often were before 1973, it will obtain a new decision from Congress or the Supreme Court that abortion "is" murder or that the unborn entity "is" a human being. Either way, society will ultimately get the decision it collectively wants, even if it must wait until the present members of the Supreme Court are dead and an entirely new court is appointed. When the desired decision is handed down, people will say, "Truth has triumphed." *Society, in short, regards as "true" those systems of classification that produce the desired results.* 20

The scientific test of "truth," like the social test, is strictly practical, except for the fact that the "desired results" are more severely limited. The results desired by society may be irrational, superstitious, selfish, or humane, but the results desired by scientists are only that our systems of classification produce predictable results. Classifications, as amply indicated already, determine our attitudes and behavior toward the object or event classified. When lightning was classified as "evidence of divine wrath," no courses of action other than prayer were suggested to prevent one's being struck by lightning. But after Benjamin Franklin classified it as "electricity," a measure of control over it was achieved by the invention of the lightning rod. Certain physical disorders were formerly classified as "demonic possession," and this suggested that we "drive the demons out" by whatever spells or incantations we could think of. The results were uncertain. But when those disorders were classified as "bacillus infections," courses of action were suggested that led to more predictable results. Science seeks only the *most generally useful* systems of classification; these it regards for the time being, until more useful classifications are invented, as "true."

FOCUSING ON CONTENT

1. According to the authors, "What we call things and where we draw the line between one class of things and another depend upon the interests we have and the purposes of the classification" (4). They cite the different methods of

animal classification by the meat, leather, and fur industries as one example of what they mean. Choose a popular song, motion picture, or book, and list four or five terms that could be used to classify it. Who would be likely to use each of these terms, and why?

2. The Hayakawas remind us that the United States once defined "any person with even a small amount of 'Negro blood' . . . as 'black'" (10). Why do you think this system of classification suited the convenience of American whites? What were some of the implications of this system for those individuals so classified?

3. What do the authors mean by "the blocked mind" (12–15)? Provide some examples that are not mentioned in the essay.

4. According to the Hayakawas, is there any such thing as a "true" system of classification? Can language convey "truth"? How does the idea of ethnocentricity enter into your answer? (Glossary: *Ethnocentricity*) Explain.

FOCUSING ON WRITING

1. How do the Hayakawas make their fairly abstract subject matter clear to the reader? For example, do they use induction, deduction, or both to develop their explanation of the relationship between naming and classifying? (Glossary: *Deduction* and *Induction*)

2. What is the relationship that you as a writer see between concreteness and abstraction in writing? (Glossary: *Concrete/Abstract*) Why is the ability to move up and down the ladder of abstraction an essential writing skill? Are there any guidelines that tell writers when to be concrete or abstract in their writing? Explain.

3. Discuss the authors' use of examples as evidence. Are their examples concrete, abstract, or both? Why are examples so important in this particular selection? (Glossary: *Examples*)

LANGUAGE IN ACTION

The accompanying drawing is a basic exercise in classification. By determining the features that the figures have in common, establish the general class to which they all belong. Next, establish subclasses by determining the distinctive features that distinguish one subclass from another. Then place each figure in an appropriate subclass within your classification system. You may wish to compare your classification system to those developed by other members of your class and to discuss any differences that exist. Finally, discuss this exercise in light of the Hayakawa's comments regarding the dynamics and importance of classification.

WRITING SUGGESTIONS

1. (*Writing from Experience*) Write an essay in which you discuss Korzybski's idea of using index numbers (18) to avoid confusion and misunderstanding. Although the Hayakawas give a number of examples that show how such indexing can be helpful, try to come up with your own examples for your paper. If possible, explain how not understanding the indexing principle has created problems for you.

2. (*Writing from Reading*) Review what you have learned from reading the Hayakawas' essay. Then explain in an essay how naming things is not merely attaching labels to them but an action that reflects and affects our fundamental thought processes.

3. (*Writing from Research*) Alfred Korzybski (1879–1950) was a Polish-born linguist who is credited with creating the field of general semantics. In 1933 he published *Science and Sanity*, which helped to make the field very popular, especially in the United States. Write an essay on Korzybski and the principles of general semantics. Discuss how general semantics has contributed to our understanding of the way language affects our lives. As you begin your research, you may want to consult *Science and Sanity* or the Hayakawas' *Language in Thought and Action*.

Rah, Rah, Ruffians!

Bil Gilbert

Bil Gilbert was born in Michigan in 1927, attended Northwestern University and Michigan State University, and earned his B.A. at Georgetown University. He later did graduate work in zoology. A free-lance journalist for the past fifty years, Gilbert has written for a number of publications, among them Sports Illustrated *and* Smithsonian. *He is also the author of ten books, including* How to Talk to Anyone, Anytime, Anywhere: The Secrets of Good Conversation *(1995), which he coauthored with Larry King.*

In the following essay, which first appeared in Smithsonian *magazine in October 1998, Gilbert classifies and analyzes the nicknames, mascot names, and logos of many colleges and universities. With more than a touch of dismay in his voice, Gilbert notes that "No article I have written has generated more mail than this one, with about one-third of it angry. Some readers, ridiculously offended by my poking fun at those nicknames, and theirs in particular, went so far as to threaten to cancel their subscriptions to* Smithsonian.*"*

WRITING TO DISCOVER: *Consider your school's nickname or the name of your mascot or logo. Jot down your impressions of how those names affect fans. What effects do the names have on you as a student and on students in general at your school? Are the names generally positive or negative? Explain.*

There has been much talk of late about sportsmanship good and bad, the idea being to encourage the former and discourage the latter. It is unlikely that much progress is going to be made at the college and university level, however, until someone does something about those terrible names.

I'm referring to the nicknames, logos, and mascots many of our 3,700-plus institutions of higher learning have chosen to represent themselves. Nearly half have selected animals, emphasizing traits—bloodthirstiness, viciousness, and so forth—that cannot possibly improve the moral character of young men and women. The most popular beasts are the supposedly dangerous felines—tigers, lions, wildcats, and such—who denote more than 200 schools. They are closely followed by flocks of hunting or scavenging birds; packs of wolves and reputedly ferocious breeds of domestic dogs (among them more than 40 bulldogs); bears and members of the weasel and Mustelidae family (six wolverines and three badgers) who have especially nasty reputations. There are also many teams named after hoofed beasts so powerful and unruly that they are usually found only in wild or well-fenced places because of the personal or property damage they can cause in settlements. In this Thundering Herd (Marshall University, Huntington, West Virginia) are Bison, Bulls, Rams, Razorbacks, Mustangs, and a Mastodon (Indiana University-Purdue University, Ford Wayne, Indiana).

Cold-blooded fauna are represented, athletically, by multiple Gators, Cobras, Rattlers, and a Gila Monster (Eastern Arizona College, Thatcher, Arizona). About 50 academic institutions are affiliated with swarms of hornets, wasps, and yellow jackets. Except for the Terrapins (University of Maryland, College Park, Maryland) and perhaps the Horned Frogs (Texas Christian University, Fort Worth, Texas), creatures in these categories are ones that in real life people would avoid like poison, as in fact some of them are.

The humanoid totems adopted by 500 or so colleges and universities are potentially more dangerous than the animals. Misguided youths may come to admire the reputed ferocity of, say, a Wolverine (Grove City College, Grove City, Pennsylvania) but cannot actually behave like one, as they might in the case of the Savages (Southeastern Oklahoma State University, Durant, Oklahoma). Good productive people used as collegiate symbols are vastly outnumbered by mean, violent thugs and rascals. Shockingly, there are more than 40 Buccaneers, Corsairs, and Pirates. There is even a Keel-hauler (California State University-Maritime Academy, Vallejo, California). Closely allied are 30-odd Vikings. These berserks were professional killers, arsonists, pillagers, rapists and often very disagreeable drunks. Representing several accredited institutions along with these sea goons is a virtual regiment of Knights, Lancers, Marauders, Musketeers, Raiders, Swordsmen, Spartans, Tartars and other paramilitary bullies, robbers, and terrorists. It's true that some may have been dupes and mercenaries of wicked masters, but none of this bloody gang should be advertised to youths as dashing heroes.

Less dangerous but still violent and disruptive are the ordinary brawlers   5 with whom some otherwise reputable schools have seen fit to associate themselves. Perhaps the most prominent are the Fighting Illini and the Fighting Irish, but this pair would probably get the stuffing kicked out of them by the several collegiate Fighting Scots. The Ragin' Cajuns (University of Southwestern Louisiana, Lafayette, Louisiana) would no doubt give a good account of themselves in any such melee. More disturbing in regards to domestic tranquillity are two Battling Bishops (North Carolina Wesleyan College, Rocky Mount, North Carolina, and Ohio Wesleyan University, Delaware, Ohio), the Fighting Parsons (Nyack College, Nyack, New York), and the Fightin' Christians (Elon College, Elon College, North Carolina).

Some worry nowadays about the spread of satanic influences. The most obvious sources of this unholy promotion are the 20-odd colleges and universities that blatantly represent themselves, athletically, as Devils, including a number of Blue and Red ones. The others are colorless and of restricted distribution — for example, the Delta Devils (Mississippi Valley State University, Itta Bena, Mississippi). For evil measure there are also a half-dozen Demons, and the Trolls (Trinity Christian College, Palos Heights, Illinois).

Clearly, character building is not a top priority for educators who send out their athletes as princes and princesses of darkness—as the Scalping Braves and Ladybraves (Alcorn State University, Lorman, Mississippi) or the Vandals (University of Idaho, Moscow, Idaho).

And what of the impressionable students? One must consider the impact of some names on behavior. It must be difficult to establish honor codes and prevent cribbing and plagiarism when students are encouraged to root for sneaks and cheats, such as the Claim Jumpers (Columbia College, Sonora, California), Land Sharks (Landmark College, Putney, Vermont), Rustlers (Central Wyoming College, Riverton, Wyoming), and Sooners (University of Oklahoma, Norman, Oklahoma).

Many colleges and universities chose their nicknames, logos, and mascots before they had female athletes and teams. A few adjusted to the post-Title IX era with good sense and grace. To be commended are, for example, the Anchormen and Anchorwomen (Rhode Island College, Providence, Rhode Island), Gentlemen and Ladies (Centenary College, Shreveport, Louisiana), and Lords and Ladies (Kenyon College, Gambier, Ohio). The Trojans and Women of Troy (University of Southern California, Los Angeles, California) and the Yeomen and Yeowomen (Oberlin College, Oberlin, Ohio) may cause some merriment but are honest efforts. The most creative and/or surreal are the Lights and Skylights (Montana State University-Northern, Havre, Montana). For reasons of tradition and local usage the several Cowboys and Cowgirls may be acceptable, but definitely not are the Lumberjacks and Lumberjills (Northland College, Ashland, Wisconsin), Vikings and Vi Queens (Augustana College, Rock Island, Illinois), Wildcats and Kittens (Wiley College, Marshall, Texas).

It appears that no teams currently in action are named after cows, ewes, mares, or sows. But a goodly number of schools have done much worse by identifying their sportswomen with unnatural creatures: Lady Rams, for example, or the equally unlikely Lady Barons, Lady Dons, Lady Knights, and Lady Lumberjacks.

Existing athletic governing bodies have amply demonstrated that they lack the will and/or wit to deal effectively with these grave concerns. As to who might: a new federal Nomenclature Regulatory Agency (NRA) seems necessary. As a first step the NRA should scientifically examine the behavioral impact of all current sporting names, logos, and mascots. Those certified as being beneficial or at least value-neutral may be retained. Substandard institutions and franchises could be given a year to select replacements from among several approved categories.

Trees, for example, are big, distinguished, durable beings that can provide a forest full of classy monikers. Presently this resource is being exploited only by a relative few: the Buckeyes (Ohio State University, Columbus, Ohio), the Maple Leafs (Goshen College, Goshen, Indiana), the Oaks (Menlo College, Atherton, California), and the Sycamores (Indiana State University, Terre Haute, Indiana). In one fell swoop most of those disgusting Blue Devils and Red Devils could be undone by requiring them to become Blue Spruces and Red Maples.

Foodstuffs could also provide yeasty names. Why not transform the Scalping Braves and Ladybraves of Alcorn into the Breads? Other improvements would be: the Alaska Bakes, Boston Cream Pies, Charlotte Russes, Idaho Potatoes, Kentucky Fried Chickens, Louisiana Po' Boys, Rice Pilafs, Vermont Syrups, Virginia Hams, Wisconsin Cheddars, and Worcester State Sauces.

Actually, there's one Arizona school that's far ahead of the pack in this regard. For teams with heart, nobody beats the Scottsdale Community College Artichokes.

FOCUSING ON CONTENT

1. Does Gilbert really think that college nicknames are "terrible names" (1)? Explain.

2. Why does Gilbert consider a name such as Savages to be worse than Wolverines?

3. In paragraph 9, Gilbert suggests that not all schools adjusted well when it came to incorporating female athletes into their nomenclature. From his examples, when does this not work well? What examples can you add from your own experience?

4. What do you think of Gilbert's suggestion for a new federal agency, the Nomenclature Regulatory Agency (NRA) (11)? His suggestion to use names based on trees (12) or foodstuffs (13)?

FOCUSING ON WRITING

1. What is Gilbert's thesis in this essay? Where does he state it? (Glossary: *Thesis*) Do you think his thesis is a serious one? If not, what is its purpose?

2. Into what categories does Gilbert classify the nicknames, logos, and mascot names of colleges and universities? Do your college's nicknames fit into his classification system? (Glossary: *Division and Classification*) Why do you think Gilbert uses the strategy of classification to develop his essay?

3. Gilbert humorously concludes his essay with a reference to the Scottsdale Community College Artichokes. What characteristics of an artichoke make it an appropriate foodstuff for a college nickname? How do you think the reference works as a conclusion? (Glossary: *Beginnings and Endings*)

LANGUAGE IN ACTION

The following Web page includes a few mascots with purposes other than the promotion of college sports. Consider the purpose of each. What feelings do you think each mascot is supposed to inspire? What kinds of behavior are suggested by the character, costume, and posture of each mascot? Do these suggestions seem effective? In other words, does each mascot seem to achieve its purpose?

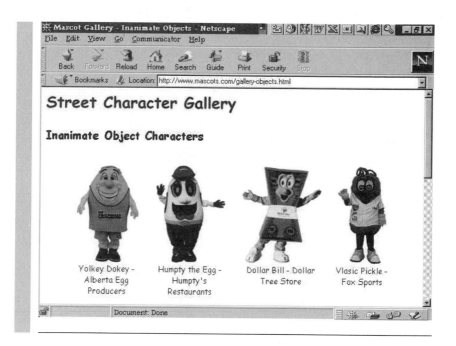

WRITING SUGGESTIONS

1. (*Writing from Experience*) If you are a student at one of the colleges or universities that Gilbert mentions, what are your reactions to his comments? Write an essay in which you briefly inform your readers of his argument and then explain why you support or oppose his position on school nicknames. If you are not a student at one of the colleges he mentions, consider your school's own nickname or mascot in the light of this essay.

2. (*Writing from Reading*) Gilbert writes, "One must consider the impact of some names on behavior" (8). Do you think that school nicknames actually cause problems with students' behavior? If you believe in the positive power of some names, do you also believe in the negative impact of others? Write an essay on the power of school nicknames. Discuss how nicknames help to build school spirit, or detract from it, in the very competitive atmosphere of collegiate sports.

3. (*Writing from Research*) Write an essay on your school's nickname, the name of your mascot, or your school's logo. Research the history of the name. Try to find out how it originated, when it was first used, and when it became an official name. Discuss the power you think the name has for students, alumni, faculty, and staff.

CASE IN POINT:
How the Business World Uses Names

Naming is one of the most important things humans do. Naming gives us a measure of power over people, plants and animals, ideas, and material objects. To name is to differentiate, to compare and contrast, to recognize, to value, and to validate. Names can be colorful, descriptive, magical, prosaic, poetic and uplifting, familiar and warm, formal and rigid, ambiguous and razor-edged. Names can remind us of where we've been and where we'd like to go.

The two essays in this casebook take us into a world of naming that is very specialized but very familiar, the sea of names for the products we use. In "A Name So Smooth, the Product Glides In," J. C. Herz looks at the world of video games and explains how a professional naming company infuses life and poetry into the name of a hot new product. In her essay "Why Big Businesses Break Spelling Rules," Alleen Pace Nilsen discusses the reasoning behind misspelled names such as *Aspercreme, Fantastik, DieHard,* and *Playskool.*

> **WRITING TO DISCOVER:** *After spending countless hours slaving over spelling tests and dictionaries, students leave school and go to the "Kwik Mart" and stroll past the "Lite" beer to buy a tube of "Ultra Brite." Or they go to the "Tastee Freez" to enjoy a "Creemee." Do such spellings bother you? Write about why you think companies deliberately misspell words. What advantages might there be in such misspellings?*

A Name So Smooth, the Product Glides In

J. C. HERZ

Born in 1971, "vid kid" J. C. Herz has established herself as the preeminent chronicler of the world of video games, the $6 billion electronic-entertainment industry. A clever and inventive writer, Herz explores the dark nether regions of the Internet and the mysteries of online discussions with cyberpunks and hackers. She also analyzes such cultural phenomena as Myst, Super Mario, Pac Man, Frogger, *and* Doom. *Her very popular books are* Surfing on the Internet *(1995) and* Joystick Nation *(1997).*

The following selection was originally published in the "Games Theory" column of the New York Times *on November 26, 1998. Here Herz explores the creation of the name* Nuon, *a new video game.*

Nuon. Say it a few times. Roll it around on your tongue. Nnnnnnn. Nnnnnnuon. Nuuuu-on. Ooooooh.

Hmmmm . . . .

How does that feel? Does it feel cutting edge? Does it feel futuristic? Does it feel authentic? Would you drive it? Would you buy running tights made out of it? Would you order it in a bar? Would you use it to charge a major purchase? Would you take it for a migraine? Would you play video games with it?

If you answered yes to the last question, you've justified a five-figure fee paid to Lexicon, a professional naming agency, by VM Labs, a technology company whose microchip, the newly christened Nuon, will be powering DVD players and set-top boxes in 1999.

The idea behind Nuon is to piggyback a video game platform on top 5 of a digital video system so people who might never buy a Nintendo 64 or Playstation will suddenly find themselves in possession of a video game machine. And once they own it, why not buy a game or two, just for kicks? The Nuon audience (Nuonites?) are not hard-core gamers. But then, neither are the hundreds of thousands of people who made Deer Hunter the best-selling computer game in North America.

But if a rose is a rose is a rose, a consumer electronics device by any other name does not smell as sweet. There are, in the patois of marketing, "branding considerations."

For instance, the name of this new product needs to be short because it has to fit inside a stamp-size space, along with a logo, on the front of a smallish device. "We needed something under five letters to make a good graphic impact on the front of the panel," said Greg Labrec, VM Labs' vice president for marketing, describing the name game as a high-stakes corporate crossword puzzle. "Under five letters, describes our chip and the operating system and the architecture as a whole. Something that somebody would want to have in a high-tech device."

"We had a bunch of combinations like Intervision, which combined interactive and vision, and Active DVD, which sort of gave a sense of active as opposed to passive DVD. On our own, we hit about 400 different names over the course of a year and a half. Actually, there were at least double that—I disqualified a lot of them. Like, there was one that everybody really, really liked, Actavid. And after I said it sounded like an aspirin, no one could get that out of their mind. As soon as I said that, it was like, boom, off the list."

After 18 months of beer-fueled brainstorming marathons, the team determined that it could not shuffle the English language skillfully enough to produce the magic moniker, the golden open-sesame word whose very sound would persuade consumers to part with hundreds of dollars.

Clearly, this was a job for professionals. Namely, the squad of lin- 10 guists at Lexicon, who named Intel's Pentium chip, Oldsmobile's Alero sports coupe, Vibrance shampoo, Slates dress slacks, Embassy Suite Hotels, an osteoporosis drug called Evista, and a sassy clear malt beverage for the younger set. Yes — Zima.

"The process is very simple," said David Placek, Lexicon's chief executive, whose vocal timbre and speech rhythms bear a strong resemblance to Dana Carvey's caricature of George Bush. "You make up some word. Let's say we take a word like zoka. Z-o-k-a, zoka. Now we'll just change one letter in there. We'll change zoka to vaka to loka, and m and n. And we'll show four or five names, all from that similar zoka structure. And we'll tell someone: 'Think about pain relief. Think that you have a headache right now. Now, you can take any one of these for that aspirin. Pick it, whether it's zoka, voka, whatever, pick it.' And then you probe why. What is it? Is it faster? Is it harder?"

"Then we take those same names, and we go to another group of people and say: 'Think about a sports car. I'm going to give you one of these sports cars. Which one are you going to take?' And you probe again as to why. And if you do that with enough people in enough languages, you can begin to identify certain phonetic properties. For example, I can tell you that 'z' is one of the fastest sounds in the alphabet. So if speed would have been the only important thing, we might have ended up with zunos or something like that. I can tell you that the sound of p and b, as in Powerbook, another brand we created, those are very dependable sound properties. So if you're out there with a lightweight portable, one of the underlying requirements will be dependability, reliability. If it drops, will it work again. So those sound properties go to work for you.

"In the case of Nuon, the word starts with an n and it ends with an n," Placek continued.

"That's called consonant harmony. It has a quick start and a quick stop to it. Nuon. And that, we felt, gave it precision. So we started working with that n in front and the n on the back. And we wanted to open it up. O is one of the fullest sounds, so we started experimenting with that. And we took a look at that 'nu' for newness there, which is quite appropriate and convenient, and we took that 'on,' as in interactive, as in playing a game, and we put them together. And interestingly enough, there's a very tiny elementary particle called a muon. And then there's neon, which is this bright gas. And then you also have things like proton and neutron. So we felt that it would deliver performance."

In that respect, Nuon is a phonetic sibling to Xeon, Intel's high-performance workstation chip, which Lexicon also named. "You have a *faster* thing there," Placek explained, emphasizing the linguistic nuance. "You have the x there, pronounced like z, so it's fast. It's got a lot of *power* there. That was about power versus — you can see how Nuon was more interactive, a little subtler, a little more approachable."

And indeed it is. If Nuon were a car, it would be a small, egg-shaped, electric one, a mid-21st-century version of the Dodge Neon, whose name

15

includes an exuberant squeal (eeeeee!!!!) between the friendly edges of beveled n's. It's fun to say. Nnnnnn. Oooooooh. Noodle. It's tooth-some. Sounds consumable. It's new!

I'm sold, and Orwell was dead wrong. The language isn't being crushed under the weight of oppression. It is experiencing an algal bloom of new vocabulary. Synthetic words. Words with no history—and no his-torical baggage. Words that are globally palatable, bred as they are in the petri dish of international market research. Words that make new things, especially technology and pharmaceuticals, seem tasty.

Words that are about pleasure (Viagra), health (Slimfast) and enter-tainment (Web TV). Words that have no meaning outside the commer-cial sphere.

Our language, like our food supply, has become a triumph of genetic engineering and synthetic additives. Pehaps a video game machine is the epitome of this process, this shift to a virtual economy and a virtual lan-guage. Because video games are a product whose material existence is vestigial: ones and zeroes stored on a disk, for now, until that goes away and they become streams of code on a network: pure experience, purely spatial and kinesthetic and imaginary, and beyond language.

Why Big Businesses Break Spelling Rules

ALLEEN PACE NILSEN

A specialist in children's literature and the study of sexist language, Alleen Pace Nilsen is a professor at Arizona State University, where she has also served as assistant vice-president of academic affairs. Her books on language study include Pronunciation Contrasts in English *(1971),* Language Play: An Introduction to Linguistics *(1983),* The Language of Humor/The Humor of Language *(1983), and* Living Language: Reading, Thinking, and Writing *(1999).*

Not all corporate strategies are bottom-line driven, as Nilsen demonstrates in the following 1994 essay, which was originally published in the English Journal. *The misspellings we see throughout the business world—such as* Skilsaw, Dunkin' Donuts, *and* Ziploc—*result from a demand for uniqueness, not correctness. Nilsen explains how legal, economic, and social needs all affect the naming of products.*

While English teachers try to teach students not only the specifics of spelling but also a respect for "correct" spelling, advertisements for commercial products are filled with such "incorrect" spellings as *tek* for *tech,* *brite* for *bright,* and *plak* for *plaque.* It's not that the business world is unaware of the differences brought about by one or two letters. As the following discussion shows, advertisers and naming companies realize full well what they are doing as they adapt English spelling to meet their legal, economic, and social needs.

LEGAL REASONS FOR MISSPELLINGS

The main reason that companies create product names with strange spellings is so that the name can be registered and protected as a trademark. One of the most successful brand names of the 20th century is *Jell-o,* which Mary Wait, the wife of the manufacturer, coined in 1897. Ungenerous historians have conjectured that she might have thought *gelatin* was spelled with a *j,* but it's more likely that she was simply ahead of her time in creating a distinctive neologism, which today is an increasingly popular method of naming products and companies.

Today's companies are forced to create new words to use as product names because the United States Trademark Office has approximately 750,000 live registrations with another 150,000 under review. Because this is more entries than are in some dictionaries, chances are high that whatever name a company tries to register will already have been registered by someone else. Also, consultants advise against making a name from a commonplace description of a product or service as in *Affordable Cleaners, Secretary Services, One-Hour Photo, Best Printing, Roofing Specialists,* and *Computer Mart.* Even though these names might be accepted trademark registration, a second company could begin using the same or a very similar name without registering it. If the first company sued the second company for trademark infringement, it would probably lose the case based on the reasoning that the chosen name honestly described the second company's product or service.

Trademark laws are designed to protect unique names, not to prevent people from using ordinary words. This is why we see such product names as those on the left instead of the correctly spelled words on the right:

Registered Trademark	*Description in Standard Spelling*
Aspercreme	Aspirin cream
BernzOmatic	Burns automatically (propane tanks)
DresSports	Dress and sports (shoes)
Dunkin' Donuts	Dunking doughnuts
E-Z-on	Easy on (boots)
Fantastik cleanser	Fantastic cleanser
Gotta Have It	Got to have it (sportswear)
Haggar Expand-o-matic	Haggar automatically expanding (slacks)
Jasco termin-8	Jasco terminate (wood preservative)
Krylon Kalifornia Kolors	Krylon California colors (spray paints)
Kwik Kopy	Quick copy (printing services)
Playskool	Play school (toys)
Ry-Krisp	Rye crisp (crackers)
Sof-Streets	Soft streets (shoes)
Thermolite	Thermal light (insulation)
Toys/Kids "Я" Us	Toys/Kids are us (stores)
Whataburger	What a hamburger
Wolverine Durashocks	Wolverine durable shock-resistant (boots)

There are no set rules for how deviant a word needs to be in order to become a unique name. The company who first marketed *lite beer* went to court claiming to have an original and unique trademark that other companies should not be able to use. However the judge ruled that *lite* was a variant spelling of *light* rather than a unique name; hence a multitude of companies now make not only *lite* drinks, but *lite* baked goods, *lite* canned foods, and *lite* snacks.

5

EVERY SPACE COUNTS

Another reason that companies use deviant spellings is to shorten their names. During the 1970s, hyphenated names were in fashion, as in *Tidy-Bowl* toilet cleaner, *Not-So-Hot* cotton panty, *Cup-A-Soup* instant soup in individual packets, *Forget-Me-Not* perfume, *Soap-On-A-Rope* hanging shower soap, *Silence-Is-Golden* cough medicine, and *Janitor-In-A-Drum* cleaning compound. Hyphenated names aren't created as often today: first, because the technique was overused, and second, because such long names proved cumbersome in computer print-outs and advertising layouts. Especially on foods and drugs, new federal regulations require so much information to be printed on the labels that there's little room left for the name.

Thus every letter counts, and so instead of using whole words, today's name makers create new words from morphemes, the smallest units of sound that carry, or at least suggest, meaning. For example, *gen* as in "genetics," *tech* or *tek* as in "technology," *Amer* as in "American," and *micro* as in "microprocessing." One naming company has created a list of 6,000 morphemes that it works with, but it might also use short words that are in some way associated with the product or syllables taken from the generic name of the item or from the names of two or more companies that are merging.

When morphemes are put together, a single word can do the work of phrases or even sentences. For example, the name of *Advil* tablets may be considered shorthand for a message about the "advantages" of being "well," while *Allerest* is shorthand for something like "rest your allergies," and *Mexsana* powder suggests that it will work against heat rash even in someplace as hot as Mexico. *Mylanta* is a persuasive name in making customers ask for something like "my antacid." It also has positive connotations and is easy to pronounce because of its similarity to "Atlanta." *Efferdent* is the name of an "effervescent" cleanser for "dentures," while *Slimnastics* is a "gymnastics" program designed to make people "slim." *Danskin* is a blending of "dance" and "skin," *Nyquil* of "night" and "tranquil," and *Sunkist* of "sun" and "kissed."

This latter example is especially effective in providing an emotionally appealing reference to the Sunbelt states where oranges are grown. The "correctly" spelled "sun kissed" as part of a description would have taken ten spaces as compared to seven; plus it could not have been protected as a trademark. Similarly, if Sears *DieHard* battery were two words instead of one, it would have been a description rather than one of the most successful trademarks of our era.

CONNECTIONS BETWEEN SPELLING AND PRONUNCIATION

The question of when the wrong spelling of an old word changes   10
into the right spelling of a new word bears resemblance to the argument between a police officer and a driver. The officer was giving the driver a ticket for parking on the wrong side of the street, but the driver was arguing that he had parked on the correct side of the street but just a little far from the curb. For our purposes, the answer doesn't really matter.

What's relevant to questions about spelling is that whether we have old words with altered spellings or brand new words, the spelling is going to be streamlined. Such brand names as the following may indicate the future of English spelling in that their pronunciations are clear in spite of—or perhaps because of—the streamlining which has dropped silent letters, deleted spaces between words, and substituted single letters for combinations.

Evenflo (baby products)
Hi-Tec SWAT (boots)
Kloz (children's clothing)
Miracle Gro (plant fertilizer)
Mop & Glo (floor cleaner)
Scotch-gard (fabric protector)
Sew n' Vac (repair shop)
Skilsaw (power tools)
Titebond (glue)
Ziploc (storage bags)

If the *Led Zeppelin* rock group has spelled the first word of its name correctly, *lead,* a lot of people might have missed the contradictory image because *lead* (to rhyme with *red*) and *lead* (to rhyme with *reed*) are homographs. When faced with homographs, our minds have been trained to pick the most likely pronunciation and meaning—something that in this case the *Led Zeppelin* folks didn't want us to do.

The name became so well known that a generation of students grew up thinking that the *lead* in "lead pencils" and "lead oxide" should be spelled *led,* and they probably weren't at all surprised by the spelling of *Def Leppard* as a name for a 1980s rock group. Although this group has a unique name, it nevertheless bears both sound and graphic similarities to *Led Zeppelin,* and in relation to spelling goes it one better in that both words are deviant.

Companies who advertise extensively on television and radio might make themselves stand out from the crowd by having a name whose pronunciation doesn't match its spelling. *Nike* shoes is an example. If we hadn't seen dozens of commercials, few of us would have known that *Nike* rhymes with *Mikey.* However, most companies cannot afford this much advertising, and so while they may not spell according to the rules of the dictionary, they are very careful to spell according to common expectations for pronunciation. This is especially true for the manufacturers of cigarettes and alcohol who cannot teach people how to pronounce their names because they cannot advertise on television or radio.

THE VALUE OF AMBIGUITY

Although we warn students to spell words carefully to avoid possibilities of confusion, advertisers might want ambiguous names that only suggest meanings. When the Honda Company of Japan named its *Acura* car

15

to sell to an American market, it worked with Name Lab, a San Francisco company. President Ira Bachrach explained in a 1993 National Public Radio interview that the goal was to find a name that would make people think of high quality engineering. They wanted to counterbalance the image of shoddy workmanship connected in consumers' minds with cheaply made and easily-broken toys, which in the 1950s were identified by "Made in Japan" labels. Bachrach's company worked with the French *acutesse,* the Italian *acutezza,* and the English *accurate* and *acumen,* all with meanings related to intelligence, sharpness, and acuteness. The name that was finally chosen has all of these positive connotations for speakers of various languages, and yet there is nothing for the company to prove since it hasn't made an overt claim.

In other examples, the Nissan *Altima* was taken from Latin "altus" suggesting a higher order, as in English "altitude." The creators also hoped it would make buyers think of "ultimate." The Oldsmobile company wanted a car name that would appeal to "achievers," but to name a car *Achiever* or *Achievement* seemed too obvious, and so the term was softened to *Achieva.* In a similar way, the Volkswagen *Jetta* is a vague reminder of the power of a jet airplane, while the Nissan *Maxima* suggests "maximum" and the *Sentra* may make people think of a "sentry" standing guard. The Mitsubishi *Precis* suggests "precise," and the Honda *Integra* suggests "integrity," while the Chevrolet *Lumina* has the positive connotations of a "luminary" or of something "luminous."

Cars aren't the only product whose manufacturers want to suggest more than they can promise. The makers of a portable toilet can't really guarantee sanitary conditions but they can suggest them with the name *Sani Pottie.* Similarly, the makers of plastic bandage strips can't promise a cure, but they can suggest one with the name *Curad.* Relationships between the verb "lug" and the noun "luggage" reveal the negative feelings that most of us have about suitcases, but the Samsonite company gives us hope with its *Ultralite* bags. In a similar way, the makers of *Kaopectate* hint that their product will "K-O" or "knock out" problems with peptic acids, while *Sinex* gives us hope for "X-ing out" sinus problems and *Sominex* for "X-ing out" insomnia. Helped by the success of such names as *Xerox, Exxon, Kleenex, Kotex,* and *Clorox,* X has become a popular addition to product and company names where it implies a connection to science or technology. Car names with X include *Mazda RX-7, Honda CRX* and *Accord XL, Nissan Maxima GXE* and *Pulsar NX, Hyundai Excel,* and *Ford Ranger XLT.* A northern California medical laboratory named itself *Immunex* from "immune" and "experiments," while another one named itself *Xoma* from X as the biochemical symbol for the cross-linking of proteins and *oma* as the Greek word for "tumor." Popular drugs, in addition to *Sominex* and *Sinex,* include *Comtrex* cold tablets and *Drixoral* decongestant tablets.

INTERNATIONAL INFLUENCES

In 1904, *Post Toasties,* one of the great American product names, was created out of desperation by American businessman C. W. Post, who had invented a ready-to-eat cereal that he named *Elijah's Manna.* The British government refused to register such a trademark because they thought it sacrilegious to use a Biblical miracle to sell corn flakes.

The history of advertising is filled with examples of such adjustments — or the needs for such adjustments — as people from different cultures interrelate. When the *Triad Semiconductors International* company learned that in some far eastern languages *triad* is used similarly to the way Americans use the term "mafia," it changed its name to *Music,* an acronym for *Multi User Specialty Integrated Circuits.* The *Exxon* corporation was first going to use *Enco* until learning that in Japan its name would be translated as "car trouble." Managers didn't want to repeat the sad experience of the Chevrolet Company which learned too late that in Spanish the name of their *Nova* model means "won't go."

Among the reasons that the U.S. Office of Trademark Registration has so many names on file is that applications from foreign countries have increased dramatically. For example in 1988, Canadians filed 2,447 applications; in 1990 they filed 3,701, with the estimate for 1995 being 10,000. In a similar fashion for the same time period, Mexican applications jumped from 120 to 140 to 1,500; and Japanese applications from 1,010 to 2,412 to 9,000 (*Wall Street Journal,* Jan. 14, 1992).

While people usually react negatively to thinking that their culture is being changed from the outside, advertisers try to soften attitudes by treating the changes playfully. When a bank merger brought the *Sanwa* bank into California, it was the fifth largest bank in the world but was virtually unknown to its potential clients. The first clue that there was a problem with name recognition came in the phone pad messages that were left at the bank's advertising agency. The receptionist taking the phone calls wrote down such garbled names as *San Juan Bank* and *Sanyo Bank.* This inspired the ad agency to devise a set of commercials poking fun at the bank's name, including a play on *Sanwa Barbara* (*Los Angeles Times,* Jan. 23, 1990).

The idea that languages change when cultures interact is usually illustrated through lists of word borrowings, but broader changes can also be traced. One such change is the influence that Americans had on the naming of Japanese cars and more recently the influence that the Japanese have had on the naming of American cars. Katsumi Tobino, a 1993-94 visiting scholar at Arizona State University from Kyoto, Japan, explained that the Japanese view cars as a western invention and so think it's appropriate for their names to be written in English. Even if a Japanese car is given a Japanese name, it will be spelled in English rather than written with Japanese characters.

If we compare the names of American cars before the late 1960s, when sales of foreign cars grew from 5.5 percent to 23 percent, to the names we have today we can see evidence of a Japanese influence not only on the type of cars manufactured in America but also on the names we give them. American manufacturers traditionally aimed their cars at a male market and gave them such "macho" names as the Oldsmobile *Cutlass,* the Buick *LeSabre,* the Mercury *Bobcat* and *Lynx,* the Plymouth *Fury* and *Barracuda,* the Chevrolet *Stingray,* the Dodge *Lancer* and *Rampage,* and the Ford *Cobra.* The Japanese, who were not so wedded to the English language and to American sales tactics, felt much freer to experiment with new names and different sales approaches. They brought not only new kinds of cars but new kinds of marketing to the automobile industry. One illustration is how many names of recent cars —maufactured by both Japanese and American companies—end in *-a,* which is considered to be a feminine ending and was therefore studiously avoided in the "old" days: *Acura, Altima, Berreta, Celica, Cordia, Corolla, Cressida, Festiva, Integra, Lumina, Maxima, Micra, Previa, Sentra, Stanza,* and *Supra.*

Whether we consider these misspellings or new words, they illustrate a changed attitude about the freedom that speakers feel in putting letters together. Perhaps the most dramatic illustration of changed attitudes toward both vehicles and names is the success of the Chevrolet company in the 1980s with its pickup truck named *Luv*—a small name for a small truck—both of which went against the "rules" of the game.

CONCLUSION

Advertisers have always been creative in changing spelling for purposes of wordplay in which they create or clarify puns, but here we see the rules of spelling being broken for legal reasons. Business people are creating neologisms to make it easier to acquire and keep trademark protection for the names of their companies or products. When they create their new names, they save space by dropping extra letters and crunching words or morphemes together. And although they may break standard spelling rules, they are careful to match spelling to pronunciation because they want names that people can easily say and remember. The many factors that must be taken into account when drugs are named illustrate some of the complexities faced by all name makers in this era of worldwide marketing controlled by government regulations and professional standards. And finally, in what comes close to the kinds of language play that we're accustomed to from poets and punsters, we see how name makers choose combinations of letters that suggest or hint at more than a company can actually promise.

25

WRITING SUGGESTIONS: MAKING CONNECTIONS

1. Many product names are chosen for their connotative or suggestive values. For example, the name *Tide* for the detergent suggests the power of the ocean tides and the rhythmic surge of cleansing waters; the name *Pride* for the wax suggests how the user will feel after using the product; and the name *Taurus* for the car suggests the strength and durability of a bull. Taking into account what you've learned from the essays by Herz and Nilsen, write an essay about how the connotations of brand names enhance the appeal of various products. Base your essay on the brand names in *one* of the following categories: cosmetics, deodorants, candy, paint, car batteries, motorcycles, fast-food sandwiches, greeting cards, disposable diapers, video games, or cat food.

2. In the concluding sentence to her essay, Nilsen writes, "[I]n what comes close to the kinds of language play that we're accustomed to from poets and punsters, we see how name makers choose combinations of letters that suggest or hint at more than a company can actually promise." In Herz's essay, we see how wordsmiths worked to give VM Labs' latest microchip, the Nuon, a name that implied precision and performance. Write an essay in which you take *one* of the following positions:

   a. The clever names of products lead most people to expect more of products than they can deliver.
   b. You are not at all deceived by the clever names of products, and you don't think most consumers are.
   c. We are all subconsciously deceived by product names that "hint at more than a company can actually promise."

3. Based on what you have learned from the essays by Nilsen and Herz, analyze how some famous products have been named. Be sure to choose products that are not discussed in the preceding essays. To start your research, you may want to consult some histories of how products got their names, such as *Names That Sell: How to Create Great Names for Your Company, Product, or Service* by Fred Barrett; *Great American Brands* by David Powers Cleary; *Brand Strategy* by John M. Murphy; or *Crafting the Perfect Name: The Art and Science of Naming a Company or Product* by George Burroughs Blake and Nancy Blake-Bohne. You will probably also want to search the Internet for sites on product names and naming.

8

PREJUDICE, STEREOTYPES, AND LANGUAGE

The Language of Prejudice

GORDON ALLPORT

Gordon Allport was born in Montezuma, Indiana, in 1897. He attended Harvard College and graduated Phi Beta Kappa in 1919 with majors in philosophy and economics. During his undergraduate years, he also became interested in psychology, and a meeting with Sigmund Freud in Vienna in 1920—during which the founder of psychoanalysis failed to impress him—had a profound influence on him. After studying and teaching abroad, Allport returned to Harvard to teach social ethics and to pursue his Ph.D., which he received in 1922. He went on to become a full professor at Harvard in 1942, served as chairman of the psychology department, and received the Gold Medal Award of the American Psychological Foundation in 1963. He died in 1967.

Allport became known for his outspoken stances regarding racial prejudice, and he was hopeful about efforts being made to eradicate it. His book The Nature of Prejudice *(1954) is still regarded as one of the most important and influential texts on the subject. The following excerpt from that book analyzes the connections between language and prejudice and explains some of the specific ways in which language can induce and shape prejudice.*

WRITING TO DISCOVER: *While in high school and college, many students are associated with groups that bring together people of disparate racial and religious backgrounds but whose labels still carry* *with them positive or negative associations. You may have made such associations yourself without thinking twice about it, as in "He's just a jock," or "She's with the popular crowd—she'll never go out with me." To what group, if any, did you belong in high school? Briefly write about the effects on you and your classmates of cliques in your school. How did the labels associated with the different groups influence how you thought about the individual members of each group?*

Without words we should scarcely be able to form categories at all. A dog perhaps forms rudimentary generalizations, such as small-boys-are-to-be avoided—but this concept runs its course on the conditioned reflex level, and does not become the object of thought as such. In order to hold a generalization in mind for reflection and recall, for identification and for action, we need to fix it in words. Without words our world would be, as William James said, an "empirical sand-heap."

NOUNS THAT CUT SLICES

In the empirical world of human beings there are some two and a half billion grains of sand corresponding to our category "the human race." We cannot possibly deal with so many separate entities in our thought, nor can we individualize even among the hundreds whom we encounter in our daily round. We must group them, form clusters. We welcome, therefore, the names that help us to perform the clustering.

The most important property of a noun is that it brings many grains of sand into a single pail, disregarding the fact that the same grains might have fitted just as appropriately into another pail. To state the matter technically, a noun *abstracts* from a concrete reality some one feature and assembles different concrete realities only with respect to this one feature. The very act of classifying forces us to overlook all other features, many of which might offer a sounder basis than the rubric we select. Irving Lee gives the following example:

> I knew a man who had lost the use of both eyes. He was called a "blind man." He could also be called an expert typist, a conscientious worker, a good student, a careful listener, a man who wanted a job. But he couldn't get a job in the department store order room where employees sat and typed orders which came over the telephone. The personnel man was impatient to get the interview over. "But you're a blind man," he kept saying, and one could almost feel his silent assumption that somehow the incapacity in one aspect made the man incapable in every other. So blinded by the label was the interviewer that he could not be persuaded to look beyond it.

Some labels, such as "blind man," are exceedingly salient and powerful. They tend to prevent alternative classification, or even cross-classification. Ethnic labels are often of this type, particularly if they refer to some highly visible feature, e.g., Negro, Oriental. They resemble the labels that point to some outstanding incapacity—*feeble-minded, cripple, blind man*. Let us call such symbols "labels of primary potency." These symbols act like shrieking sirens, deafening us to all finer discriminations that we might otherwise perceive. Even though the blindness of one man and the darkness of pigmentation of another may be defining attributes for some purposes, they are irrelevant and "noisy" for others.

Most people are unaware of this basic law of language—that every   5 label applied to a given person refers properly only to one aspect of his nature. You may correctly say that a certain man is *human, a philanthropist, a Chinese, a physician, an athlete*. A given person may be all of these; but the chances are that *Chinese* stands out in your mind as the symbol of primary potency. Yet neither this nor any other classificatory label can refer to the whole of a man's nature. (Only his proper name can do so.)

Thus each label we use, especially those of primary potency, distracts our attention from concrete reality. The living, breathing, complex individual—the ultimate unit of human nature—is lost to sight. As in the figure, the label magnifies one attribute out of all proportion to its true significance, and masks other important attributes of the individual. . . .

A category, once formed with the aid of a symbol of primary potency, tends to attract more attributes than it should. The category labeled *Chinese* comes to signify not only ethnic membership but also reticence, impassivity, poverty, treachery. To be sure, . . . there may be genuine ethnic-linked traits, making for a certain *probability* that the member of an ethnic stock may have these attributes. But our cognitive process is not cautious. The labeled category, as we have seen, includes indiscriminately the defining attribute, probable attributes, and wholly fanciful, nonexistent attributes.

Even proper names—which ought to invite us to look at the individual person—may act like symbols of primary potency, especially if they arouse ethnic associations. Mr. Greenberg is a person, but since his name is Jewish, it activates in the hearer his entire category of Jews-as-a-whole.

LABELS OF PRIMARY POTENCY

BLIND MAN   CHINESE   NEGRO

An ingenious experiment performed by Razran shows this point clearly, and at the same time demonstrates how a proper name, acting like an ethnic symbol, may bring with it an avalanche of stereotypes.

> Thirty photographs of college girls were shown on a screen to 150 students. The subjects rated the girls on a scale from one to five for *beauty, intelligence, character, ambition, general likability.* Two months later the same subjects were asked to rate the same photographs (and fifteen additional ones introduced to complicate the memory factory). This time five of the original photographs were given Jewish surnames (Cohen, Kantor, etc.), five Italian (Valenti, etc.), and five Irish (O'Brien, etc.); and the remaining girls were given names chosen from the signers of the Declaration of Independence and from the Social Register (Davis, Adams, Clark, etc.).
>
> When Jewish names were attached to photographs there occurred the following changes in ratings:
> decrease in liking
> decrease in character
> decrease in beauty
> increase in intelligence
> increase in ambition
> For those photographs given Italian names there occurred:
> decrease in liking
> decrease in character
> decrease in beauty
> decrease in intelligence

Thus a mere proper name leads to prejudgments of personal attributes. The individual is fitted to the prejudice ethnic category, and not judged in his own right.

While the Irish names also brought about depreciated judgment, the depreciation was not as great as in the case of the Jews and Italians. The falling of likability of the "Jewish girls" was twice as great as for "Italians" and five times as great as for "Irish." We note, however, that the "Jewish" photographs caused higher ratings in *intelligence* and in *ambition.* Not all stereotypes of out-groups are unfavorable.

The anthropologist, Margaret Mead, has suggested that labels of primary potency lose some of their force when they are changed from nouns into adjectives. To speak of a Negro soldier, a Catholic teacher, or a Jewish artist calls attention to the fact that some other group classifications are just as legitimate as the racial or religious. If George Johnson is spoken of not only as a Negro but also as a *soldier,* we have at least two attributes to know him by, and two are more accurate than one. To depict him truly as an individual, of course, we should have to name many more attributes. It is a useful suggestion that we designate ethnic and religious membership where possible with *adjectives* rather than *nouns.*

EMOTIONALLY TONED LABELS

Many categories have two kinds of labels—one less emotional and one   10
more emotional. Ask yourself how you feel, and what thoughts you have,
when you read the words *school teacher,* and then *school marm.* Certainly
the second phrase calls up something more strict, more ridiculous, more
disagreeable than the former. Here are four innocent letters: m-a-r-m.
But they make us shudder a bit, laugh a bit, and scorn a bit. They call up
an image of a spare, humorless, irritable old maid. They do not tell us
that she is an individual human being with sorrows and troubles of her
own. They force her instantly into a rejective category.

In the ethnic sphere even plain labels such as Negro, Italian, Jew,
Catholic, Irish-American, French-Canadian may have emotional tone for a
reason that we shall soon explain. But they all have their higher key equiva-
lents: nigger, wop, kike, papist, harp, canuck. When these labels are employed we can be almost certain that the speaker *intends* not only to
characterize the person's membership, but also to disparage and reject him.

Quite apart from the insulting intent that lies behind the use of certain labels, there is also an inherent ("physiognomic") handicap in many
terms designating ethnic membership. For example, the proper names
characteristic of certain ethnic memberships strike us as absurd. (We compare them, of course, with what is familiar and therefore "right.") Chinese names are short and silly; Polish names intrinsically difficult and
outlandish. Unfamiliar dialects strike us as ludicrous. Foreign dress
(which, of course, is a visual ethnic symbol) seems unnecessarily queer.

But of all of these "physiognomic" handicaps the reference to color,
clearly implied in certain symbols, is the greatest. The word Negro comes
from the Latin *niger* meaning black. In point of fact, no Negro has a black
complexion, but by comparison with other blonder stocks, he has come to be
known as a "black man." Unfortunately *black* in the English language is a
word having a preponderance of sinister connotations: the outlook is black,
blackball, blackguard, black-hearted, black death, blacklist, blackmail, Black
Hand. In his novel *Moby Dick,* Herman Melville considers at length the remarkably morbid connotations of black and the remarkably virtuous connotations of white.

Nor is the ominous flavor of black confined to the English language. A
cross-cultural study reveals that the semantic significance of black is more or
less universally the same. Among certain Siberian tribes, members of a priv-
ileged clan call themselves "white bones," and refer to all others as "black
bones." Even among Uganda Negroes there is some evidence for a white
god at the apex of the theocratic hierarchy; certain it is that a white cloth,
signifying purity, is used to ward off evil spirits and disease.

There is thus an implied value-judgment in the very concept of *white*   15
race and *black race.* One might also study the numerous unpleasant connotations of *yellow,* and their possible bearing on our conception of the
people of the Orient.

Such reasoning should not be carried too far, since there are undoubtedly, in various contexts, pleasant associations with both black and yellow. Black velvet is agreeable, so too are chocolate and coffee. Yellow tulips are well liked; the sun and moon are radiantly yellow. Yet it is true that "color" words are used with chauvinistic overtones more than most people realize. There is certainly condescension indicated in many familiar phrases: dark as a nigger's pocket, darktown strutters, white hope (a term originated when a white contender was sought against the Negro heavyweight champion, Jack Johnson), the white man's burden, the yellow peril, black boy. Scores of everyday phrases are stamped with the flavor of prejudice, whether the user knows it or not.

We spoke of the fact that even the most proper and sedate labels for minority groups sometimes seem to exude a negative flavor. In many contexts and situations the very terms *French-Canadian, Mexican,* or *Jew,* correct and nonmalicious though they are, sound a bit opprobrious. The reason is that they are labels of social deviants. Especially in a culture where uniformity is prized, the name of *any* deviant carries with it *ipso facto* a negative value-judgment. Words like *insane, alcoholic, pervert* are presumably neutral designations of a human condition, but they are more: they are finger-pointing at a deviance. Minority groups are deviants, and for this reason, from the very outset, the most innocent labels in many situations imply a shading of disrepute. When we wish to highlight the deviance and denigrate it still further we use words of a higher emotional key: crackpot, soak, pansy, greaser, Okie, nigger, harp, kike.

Members of minority groups are often understandably sensitive to names given them. Not only do they object to deliberately insulting epithets, but sometimes see evil intent where none exists. Often the word Negro is spelled with a small *n,* occasionally as a studied insult, more often from ignorance. (The term is not cognate with white, which is not capitalized, but rather with Caucasian, which is.) Terms like "mulatto," or "octoroon" cause hard feeling because of the condescension with which they have often been used in the past. Sex differentiations are objectionable, since they seem doubly to emphasize ethnic difference: why speak of Jewess and not of Protestantess, or of Negress and not of whitess? Similar overemphasis is implied in the terms like Chinamen or Scotchman; why not American man? Grounds for misunderstanding lie in the fact that minority group members are sensitive to such shadings, while majority members may employ them unthinkingly.

THE COMMUNIST LABEL

Until we label an out-group it does not clearly exist in our minds. Take the curiously vague situation that we often meet when a person wishes to locate responsibility on the shoulders of some out-group whose nature he cannot specify. In such a case he usually employs the pronoun "they" without an antecedent. "Why don't they make these sidewalks wider?" "I hear they are going to build a factory in this town and hire a lot of foreigners." "I won't pay this tax bill; they can just whistle for their money." If asked "who?" the speaker is likely to grow confused and embarrassed. The common use of the orphaned pronoun *they* teaches us that people often want and need to designate out-groups (usually for the purpose of venting hostility) even when they have no clear conception of the out-group in question. And so long as the target of wrath remains vague and ill-defined specific prejudice cannot crystallize around it. To have enemies we need labels.

Until relatively recently [late 1940s]—strange as it may seem— 20 there was no agreed-upon symbol for *communist*. The word, of course, existed but it had no special emotional connotation, and did not designate a public enemy. Even when, after World War I, there was a growing feeling of economic and social menace in this country, there was no agreement as to the actual source of the menace.

A content analysis of the Boston *Herald* for the year 1920 turned up the following list of labels. Each was used in a context implying some threat. Hysteria had overspread the country, as it did after World War II. Someone must be responsible for the postwar malaise, rising prices, uncertainty. There must a villain. But in 1920 the villain was impartially designated by reporters and editorial writers with the following symbols:

> alien, agitator, anarchist, apostle of bomb and torch, Bolshevik, communist, communist laborite, conspirator, emissary of false promise, extremist, foreigner, hyphenated-American, incendiary, IWW, parlor anarchist, parlor pink, parlor socialist, plotter, radical, red, revolutionary, Russian agitator, socialist, Soviet, syndicalist, traitor, undesirable.

From this excited array we note that the *need* for an enemy (someone to serve as a focus for discontent and jitters) was considerably more apparent than the precise *identity* of the enemy. At any rate, there was no clearly agreed upon label. Perhaps partly for this reason the hysteria abated. Since no clear category of "communisn" existed there was no true focus for the hostility.

But following World War II this collection of vaguely interchangeable labels became fewer in number and more commonly agreed upon. The out-group menace came to be designated almost always as *communist* or *red*. In 1920 the threat, lacking a clear label, was vague; after 1945 both symbol and thing became more definite. Not that people knew precisely what they meant when they said "communist," but with the aid of the term they were at least able to point consistently to *something* that inspired fear. The term developed the power of signifying menace and led to various repressive measures against anyone to whom the label was rightly or wrongly attached.

Logically, the label should apply to specifiable defining attributes, such as members of the Communist Party, or people whose allegiance is with the Russian system, or followers, historically, of Karl Marx. But the label came in for far more extensive use.

What seems to have happened is approximately as follows. Having suffered through a period of war and being acutely aware of devastating revolutions abroad, it is natural that most people should be upset, dreading to lose their possessions, annoyed by high taxes, seeing customary moral and religious values threatened, and dreading worse disasters to come. Seeking an explanation for this unrest, a single identifiable enemy is wanted. It is not enough to designate "Russia" or some other distant land. Nor is it satisfactory to fix blame on "changing social conditions." What is needed is a human agent near at hand: someone in Washington, someone in our schools, in our factories, in our neighborhood. If we *feel* an immediate threat, we reason, there must be a near-lying danger. It is, we conclude, communism, not only in Russia but also in America, at our doorstep, in our government, in our churches, in our colleges, in our neighborhood.

Are we saying that hostility toward communism is prejudice? Not necessarily. There are certainly phases of the dispute wherein realistic social conflict is involved. American values (e.g., respect for the person) and totalitarian values as represented in Soviet practice are intrinsically at odds. A realistic opposition in some form will occur. Prejudice enters only when the defining attributes of *communist* grow imprecise, when anyone who favors any form of social change is called a communist. People who fear social change are the ones most likely to affix the label to any persons or practices that seem to them threatening.

For them the category is undifferentiated. It includes books, movies, preachers, teachers who utter what for them are uncongenial thoughts. If evil befalls — perhaps forest fires or a factory explosion — it is due to communist saboteurs. The category becomes monopolistic, covering almost anything that is uncongenial. On the floor of the House of Representatives in 1946, Representative Rankin called James Roosevelt a communist. Congressman Outland replied with psychological acumen, "Apparently everyone who disagrees with Mr. Rankin is a communist."

When differentiated thinking is at a low ebb — as it is in times of social crises — there is a magnification of two-valued logic. Things are perceived as either inside or outside a moral order. What is outside is likely to be called communist. Correspondingly — and here is where damage is done — whatever is called communist (however erroneously) is immediately cast outside the moral order.

This associative mechanism places enormous power in the hands of a demagogue. For several years Senator McCarthy managed to discredit many citizens who thought differently from himself by the simple device of calling them communist. Few people were able to see through this trick and many reputations were ruined. But the famous senator has no monopoly on the device. As reported in the Boston *Herald*: on November 1, 1946, Representative Joseph Martin, Republican leader in the House, ended his election campaign against his Democratic opponent by saying, "The people will vote tomorrow between chaos, confusion, bankruptcy, state socialism or communism, and the preservation of our American life, with all its freedom and its opportunities." Such an array of emotional labels placed his opponent outside the accepted moral order. Martin was re-elected. . . .

Not everyone, of course, is taken in. Demagogy, when it goes too   30
far, meets with ridicule. Elizabeth Dilling's book, *The Red Network*, was so exaggerated in its two-valued logic that it was shrugged off by many people with a smile. One reader remarked, "Apparently if you step off the sidewalk with your left foot you're a communist." But it is not easy in times of social strain and hysteria to keep one's balance, and to resist the tendency of a verbal symbol to manufacture large and fanciful categories of prejudiced thinking.

VERBAL REALISM AND SYMBOL PHOBIA

Most individuals rebel at being labeled, especially if the label is uncomplimentary. Very few are willing to be called *fascistic, socialistic,* or *anti-Semitic.* Unsavory labels may apply to others; but not to us.

An illustration of the craving that people have to attach favorable symbols to themselves is seen in the community where white people banded together to force out a Negro family that had moved in. They called themselves "Neighborly Endeavor" and chose as their motto the Golden Rule. One of the first acts of this symbol-sanctified band was to sue the man who sold property to Negroes. They then flooded the house which another Negro couple planned to occupy. Such were the acts performed under the banner of the Golden Rule.

Studies made by Stagner and Hartmann show that a person's political attitudes may in fact entitle him to be called a fascist or a socialist, and yet he will emphatically repudiate the unsavory label, and fail to endorse any movement or candidate that overtly accepts them. In short, there is a *symbol phobia* that corresponds to *symbol realism.* We are more inclined to the former when we ourselves are concerned, though we are much less critical when epithets of "fascist," "communist," "blind man," "school marm" are applied to others.

When symbols provoke strong emotions they are sometimes regarded no longer as symbols, but as actual things. The expressions "son of a bitch" and "liar" are in our culture frequently regarded as "fighting words." Softer and more subtle expressions of contempt may be accepted. But in these particular cases, the epithet itself must be "taken back." We certainly do not change our opponent's attitude by making him take back a word, but it seems somehow important that the word itself be eradicated.

Such verbal realism may reach extreme length.   35

> The City Council of Cambridge, Massachusetts, unanimously passed a resolution (December, 1939) making it illegal "to possess, harbor, sequester, introduce or transport, within the city limits, any book, map, magazine, newspaper, pamphlet, handbill, or circular containing the words Lenin or Leningrad."

Such naiveté in confusing language with reality is hard to comprehend unless we recall that word-magic plays an appreciable part in human thinking. The following examples, like the one preceding, are taken from Hayakawa.

> The Malagasy soldier must eschew kidneys, because in the Malagasy language the word for kidney is the same as that for "shot"; so shot he would certainly be if he ate a kidney.

> In May, 1937, a state senator of New York bitterly opposed a bill for the control of syphilis because "the innocence of children might be corrupted by a widespread use of the term. . . . This particular word creates a shudder in every decent woman and decent man."

This tendency to reify words underscores the close cohesion that exists between category and symbol. Just the mention of "communist," "Negro," "Jew," "England," "Democrats," will send some people into a panic of fear or a frenzy of anger. Who can say whether it is the word or the thing that annoys them? The label is an intrinsic part of any monopolistic category. Hence to liberate a person from ethnic or political prejudice it is necessary at the same time to liberate him from *word fetishism*. This fact is well known to students of general semantics who tell us that prejudice is due in large part to verbal realism and to symbol phobia. Therefore any program for the reduction of prejudice must include a large measure of semantic therapy.

FOCUSING ON CONTENT

1. Nouns, or names, provide an essential service in making categorization possible. Yet according to Allport, nouns are also words that "cut slices." What does he mean by that term? What is inherently unfair about nouns?

2. What are "labels of primary potency" (4)? Why does Allport equate them with "shrieking sirens"? Why are such labels important to his essay?

3. What does the experiment with the nonlabeled and labeled photos demonstrate? How do labels affect the way the mind perceives reality?

4. What does Allport mean by the "orphaned pronoun *they*" (19)? Why is it used so often in conversation?

5. What does Allport mean by *symbol phobia* (33)? How does this concept illustrate the unfairness of labeling others?

FOCUSING ON WRITING

1. What is Allport's thesis, and where is it stated? (Glossary: *Thesis*)

2. In paragraph 2, why do you think Allport uses a metaphorical image—grains of sand—to represent people? (Glossary: *Figurative Language*) How does this metaphor help him present his point?

3. In paragraph 3, Allport uses Irving Lee's story of a blind man who was unable to get a job as an example of how powerful certain labels can be. (Glossary: *Examples*) What other quotations does he use as examples? What is the purpose of each one? Do you think they are effective? Why or why not?

4. Allport wrote "The Language of Prejudice" in the early 1950s. does this help explain why he devotes many paragraphs to the evolution of the label *communist*? What are the connotations of the word *communist* today? (Glossary: *Connotation/Denotation*)

LANGUAGE IN ACTION

Read the following brief article, which appeared in the *New York Times* on December 13, 1968. Then make a list of the arguments for and against the UN action. Do you think it's possible to legislate tolerance and tone down prejudice through the use—or nonuse—of language?

UN GROUP URGES DROPPING OF WORDS WITH RACIST TINGE

In an effort to combat racial prejudice, a group of United Nations experts is urging sweeping revision of the terminology used by teachers, mass media, and others dealing with race.

Words such as *Negro, primitive, savage, backward, colored, bushman,* and *uncivilized* would be banned as either "contemptuous, unjust, or inadequate." They were described as aftereffects of colonialism.

The report said that the terms were "so charged with emotive potential that their use, with or without conscious pejorative intent, to describe or characterize certain ethnic, social, or religious groups, generally provoked an adverse reaction on the part of these groups."

The report said further that even the term *race* should be used with particular care since its scientific validity was debatable and that it "often served to perpetuate prejudice." The experts suggested that the word *tribe* should be used as sparingly as possible, since most of the "population groups" referred to by this term have long since ceased to be tribes or are losing their tribal character. A *native* should be called *inhabitant,* the group advised, and instead of *paganism* the words *animists, Moslems, Brahmans,* and other precise words should be used. The word *savanna* is preferable to *jungle,* and the new countries should be described as *developing* rather than *underdeveloped,* the experts said.

WRITING SUGGESTIONS

1. (*Writing from Experience*) Make an extensive list of the labels that have been or could be applied to you at this time. Write an essay in which you discuss the labels that you find "truly offensive," those you can "live with," and those that you "like to be associated with." Explain your reasons for putting particular labels in each of these categories.

2. (*Writing from Reading*) Allport states, "Especially in a culture where uniformity is prized, the name of any deviant carries with it *ipso facto* a negative value-judgment" (17). This was written in the 1950s. Since then, the turbulent 1960s, the political correctness movement of the 1980s and 1990s, and the mainstreaming of "alternative" cultures have all attempted to persuade people to accept differences and be more tolerant. Write an essay in which you consider Allport's statement today. Which labels that identify someone as different still carry a negative association? Have the social movements of the past decades changed in a fundamental way how we think about others? Do you think there is more acceptance of nonconformity today, or is a nonconformist or member of a minority still subjected to negative, though perhaps more subtle, labeling? Support your conclusions with examples from your own experience and from the depiction of current events in the popular media.

3. (*Writing from Research*) Allport wrote *The Nature of Prejudice* before the civil rights movement began in earnest, though he did live to see it grow and reach its climax at the famous 1963 march on Washington. (See Martin Luther King's celebrated "I Have a Dream" speech on p. 302.) Obviously, part of the civil rights movement was in the arena of language, and its leaders often used impressive rhetoric to confront the language of prejudice. Write an essay in which you analyze how the kinds of labels and symbols identified by Allport were used in speeches and documents both to justify the continuation of segregation and prejudice and to decry it. How did the leaders of the civil rights movement use language to their advantage? To what emotions or ideas did the language of the opposition appeal? The Internet and your library have vast information about the movement's genesis and history, so it may be difficult at first to decide on a specific area of research. Start by looking at how language was used by both sides in the battle over civil rights.

Words with Built-in Judgments

S. I. HAYAKAWA AND ALAN R. HAYAKAWA

S. I. Hayakawa (1906–1992), a former senator from California and honorary chair of the English-only movement, wrote the influential semantics text Language in Thought and Action *in 1941. With the help of his son Alan, he brought out the fifth edition of the book in 1991. Born in Vancouver, Canada, to Japanese parents, Hayakawa attended the University of Manitoba, McGill University, and the University of Wisconsin before beginning a career as a professor of English. He later became president of San Francisco State University. Hayakawa's other language books include* Our Language and Our World *(1959) and* Symbol, Status, and Personality *(1963).*

Alan Hayakawa was born in Chicago on July 16, 1946, and received a B.A. in mathematics from Reed College in 1970. He began his writing career as a reporter for the Oregonian *in Portland, Oregon, in 1975, and he moved to Washington, D.C., in 1987 as the* Oregonian's *Washington correspondent. He is now the manager of the InsideLine, a telephone news and information service, at the* Patriot-News *in Harrisburg, Pennsylvania. In addition to coauthoring the fifth edition of* Language in Thought and Action, *Hayakawa has coauthored* The Blair Handbook *(1999), now in its third edition, and the* College Writer's Reference *1998), now in its second edition.*

In Language in Thought and Action, *from which the following selection is taken, the Hayakawas explore the complex relationships that exist between reality and the language we use to describe it. They demonstrate the power that some words — especially those associated with "race, religion, political heresy, and economic dissent" — have to evoke strong emotional responses. As Japanese Americans, they have felt this power firsthand. The Hayakawas explain how an awareness of the power of words can help writers and speakers avoid both stirring up traditional prejudices and unintentionally giving offense.*

WRITING TO DISCOVER: *People often use labels such as* teenager, Iranian, blind, senior citizen, liberal, *and* Japanese *to describe other people quickly. Spend some time carefully listening to the labels you use, and make a list of them. Do these labels give an accurate picture of a whole person? Do they carry implied judgments? Explain.*

The fact that some words simultaneously arouse both informative and affective connotations gives a special complexity to discussions involving religious, racial, national, and political groups. To many people, the word "communist" has both the informative connotation of "one who believes in communism" and the affective connotation of "one whose ideals and purposes are altogether repellent." Words applying to occupations of which one disapproves ("pickpocket," racketeer," "prostitute") and those applying to believers in philosophies of which one disapproves ("atheist," "radical," "heretic," "materialist," "fundamentalist") likewise often communicate *simultaneously* a fact and a judgment on that fact. Such words may be called "loaded"—that is, their affective connotations may strongly shape people's thoughts.

In some parts of the United States, there is a strong prejudice against certain ethnic groups, such as Mexican Americans, whether immigrant or American-born. The strength of this prejudice is revealed by the fact that polite people and the press have stopped using the word "Mexican," using the term "Hispanic" instead to avoid any negative connotations. There are also terms such as "Chicano" and "Latino" that Mexican American and Spanish-speaking groups have chosen to describe themselves.

Names that are "loaded" tend to influence behavior toward those to whom they are applied. Currently, the shop doorways and freeway underpasses of American cities are sheltering tens of thousands of people who have no work and no homes. These people used to be referred to as "bums"—a word that suggests not only a lack of employment but a lack of desire to work, people who are lazy, satisfied with little, and who have no desire to enter the mainstream of the American middle class or subscribe to its values. Thus, to think of these people as "bums" is to think that they are only getting what they deserve. With the search for new names for such people— "street people," "homeless," "displaced persons"—we may find new ways of thinking about their situation that may in turn suggest new ways of helping deal with it. Similarly, "problem drinker" has replaced "drunkard" and "substance abuser" has replaced "junkie." "Developmentally disabled" has replaced "retarded," which in turn replaced "idiot."

The negative connotations of words sometimes change because of deliberate changes in the way they are used. Michael Harrington, the American socialist, has said that "socialist" became a political dirty word in the 1930s and 1940s in the United States when opposing politicians and editorialists repeatedly linked "socialism" and "communism," obscuring what adherents to the two philosophies saw as distinctions between them. In the 1964 presidential campaign, it was said by his opponents that Senator Barry Goldwater was "too conservative" to be made president. The negative connotations of "conservative" had receded by 1988; in that presidential campaign, then Vice President George Bush repeatedly amplified the negative connotations of the word "liberal" and then accused his opponent, Michael Dukakis, of being one.

The meaning of words also changes from speaker to speaker, from hearer to hearer, and from decade to decade. An elderly Japanese woman of

5

my acquaintance used to squirm at the mention of the word "Jap." "Whenever I hear that word," she used to say, "I feel dirty all over." She was reacting to the negative connotations as it was used during the Second World War and earlier. More recently, "JAP" is an acronym for "Jewish American princess," heard as an insult by an entirely different ethnic group.

A black friend of mine recalls hitchhiking as a young man in the 1930s through an area of the country where very few blacks lived. He was given a ride by a white couple, who fed him and gave him a place to sleep in their home. However, they kept referring to him as "little nigger," which upset him profoundly. He finally asked them not to call him by that "insulting term," a request they had difficulty understanding, as they had not meant to offend him. One way my friend might have explained his point further would have been to say, "Excuse me, but in the part of the country I come from, white people who wish to show contempt for my race call us 'niggers.' I assume this is not your intention."

In recent times, the negative connotations of the word "nigger" are more widely understood. This is partly the result of efforts by black Americans and others to educate the public. Early in 1942, when I was living in Chicago and teaching at the Illinois Institute of Technology, I was invited to become a columnist for the *Chicago Defender*—at that time the most militant of Negro newspapers. I say "Negro" rather than "black" because this was 1942 and it was the mission of that newspaper to make people proud of being "Negro." The word "Negro" at that time was used with dignity and pride. In its editorial policy, the *Defender* saw to it that the word was used in that way. It was always capitalized. Later, during the civil rights movement of the 1950s and 1960s, a wider effort was made to make just this point in the mind of the American public as a whole, first substituting "Negro" for "colored," "nigger," "nigrah," and, later, substituting "black" for "Negro." "Black" is now the word most frequently chosen by people of African origin in the United States to describe themselves, and the word "Negro" is considered by many to be old-fashioned, and condescending. Most recently, it has been proposed that "African American" be substituted for "black." *Those who believe that the meaning of a word is innately part of the word risk offending or being offended because of having ignored differences in context or current usage.*

The conflicts that erupt over words are invariably an index to social concerns over the reality that the words refer to. Much debate has arisen over the issue of sexual discrimination in language. Is it fair, many people ask, that the word "man" should stand for all human beings, male and female? Should we say, "Everyone should cast his vote," when half the voters are women? Are there biases that are unfair to women — and to men — built into the English language? If so, what can or should be done about it?

The problem can be better understood if we look at the disputed words in the contexts in which they appear. In some contexts, the extensional meaning of "man" as a synonym for the species *Homo sapiens* covers both sexes, without any discrimination implied: men, women, and children; Englishmen, Chinese, Eskimos, Aborigines, next-door neighbors, and so forth. In other contexts, "man" refers only to the male: "There is a man at the door." The problems with connotation occur in a context such as: "The work team is short ten men." In such a case the employer may be inclined to look for ten more males to hire, even when the work can be done equally well by women.

The Chinese ideograph [人], also used in Japanese, stands for "man"   10
in the generic sense: "person," "human being." A different ideograph [男] is used for "man" in the sense of "male human being." Since women traditionally have been assigned subordinate roles in both Chinese and Japanese cultures, discrimination against women cannot be said to be due solely to the peculiarities of language.

For those who have no difficulty with the different meanings of "man," or who like the maleness they find in the generic term, the language needs no modification. But what about those who are dissatisfied with the masculine connotations of "man"? What about the woman on the softball team who insists on being called "first baseperson" or the committee leader who styles herself "chairperson"? What about the woman named "Cooperman" who wanted to change her name to "Cooperperson" and petitioned a court to legalize the change? (Her petition was denied.) Can the language accommodate them?

Fortunately, the language is flexible enough for people to make personal adjustments to meet their own standards. "Human beings" or "humans" or "people" are acceptable substitutes for the generic "man," though rhetorically they may not always sound as good. Instead of saying "Man is a tool-using animal," we can say, "Human beings are tool-using animals."

Once it becomes apparent that we can construct any sentence we please without incurring possible sexual stereotypes, a further question remains: Should we demand that all writers adopt a "nonsexist" vocabulary and always use it — for example, the neutral plural? On this point history offers some guidance.

Most of the attempts made to force living language into a doctrinaire program have failed resoundingly. Jonathan Swift once spoke out acidly against the use of the word "mob" as a corrupt shortening of the Latin term *mobile vulgus*. Dr. Samuel Johnson resisted, to no avail, the admission of the word "civilization" into his dictionary because it seemed to him a barbarism, despite its respectable Latin root. In this century, Mussolini tried to eliminate the informal *tu* in Italian (the second person singular pronoun, whose English counterpart, "thou," has disappeared in ordinary English usage). He covered Italy with posters commanding Italians to use the *voi* form instead. His campaign failed. The social forces that created the words in the first place could not be changed by logic, fiat, or program. Language has usually proven stronger than the individual.

It must not be forgotten that language, created over centuries and   15
inherited with our culture, does not exert its tyranny uniformly over all
who use it. In the novel *Kingsblood Royal* by Sinclair Lewis, actually a
tract against racial prejudice, the central character is a vicious racial
bigot—but he is careful never to use the word "nigger."

Similarly, an individual who uses "sexist" terms uncritically may have
all kinds of discriminatory attitudes towards women, or he—or she—
may be entirely free of them. The presence or absence of such terms has
no necessary connection with the presence or absence of the corresponding attitudes.

This does not mean that writers who are sensitive to sexual bias in
language should resign themselves to what they consider a sorry state of
affairs. They can carry out their own programs within their own speech
and writing. These efforts are not without risk of accidentally engender-
ing new, unintended meanings. For example, in revising the words of
hymns, the Episcopal Church changed "Christian Men, Rejoice!" to
"Christian Friends, Rejoice!" However, as Sara Mosle pointed out in *The
New Republic,* the theological implications of extending joy only to
friends—what about Christian enemies, or even strangers?—were entirely inappropriate to the message of the hymn. "How long would it be
before Christmas cards read 'Peace on Earth, good will towards friends?'
A different proposition altogether from the brotherly (or sisterly) bene-
diction to all mankind."

The calling of attention to sex discrimination contained within language, a campaign conducted in a similar way to that by which "Negro"
and then "black" were successfully substituted for "colored," has served
to raise society's awareness of the problem of built-in bias in language,
even though it has not yet transformed the language. Even if such efforts
fail to dislodge all forms of gender bias in the language, the effort to correct the problem is, in itself, worthwhile. As the poet John Ciardi has observed:

> In the long run the usage of those who do not think about the language
> will prevail. Usages I resist will become acceptable. It will not do to re-
> sist uncompromisingly. Yet those who care have a duty to resist.
> Changes that occur against such resistance are tested changes. The lan-
> guage is better for them—and for the resistance.

One other curious fact needs to be recorded about the words we
apply to such hotly debated issues as race, religion, political heresy, and
economic dissent. Every reader is acquainted with people who, according
to their own flattering descriptions of themselves, "believe in being
frank" and like to "tell it like it is." By "telling it like it is," such people
usually mean calling anything or anyone by the term which has the
strongest and most disagreeable affective connotations. Why people
should pin medals on themselves for "candor" for performing this nasty

feat has often puzzled me. Sometimes it is necessary to violate verbal taboos as an aid to clearer thinking, but, more often, to insist upon "telling it like it is" is to provide our minds with a greased runway down which we may slide back into unexamined and reactive patterns of evaluation and behavior.

FOCUSING ON CONTENT

1. In the beginning of the essay, what do the Hayakawas mean by an informative connotation? An affective connotation? (Glossary: *Connotation/Denotation*) What do the Hayakawas mean when they characterize words that have both connotations as "loaded"?

2. How can names "influence behavior toward those to whom they are applied" (3)? What is the difference in affective connotation between calling someone a "bum" and saying that a person is "homeless"?

3. What do the Hayakawas mean when they say, "*Those who believe that the meaning of a word is innately part of the word risk offending or being offended because of having ignored differences in context or current usage*" (7)?

4. What does history tell us about attempts to force changes on a living language?

5. Is a person who uses sexist terms necessarily sexist? (Glossary: *Sexist Language*) Explain.

FOCUSING ON WRITING

1. Trace one of the examples given by the Hayakawas in paragraph 3 regarding how potentially loaded words have evolved over the years, such as the evolution of the term *idiot*. How effective do you find their use of examples in general and this example in particular? (Glossary: *Examples*)

2. The Hayakawas structure paragraphs 11 and 12 as a question-and-answer segment. In paragraph 11, they ask if the language is able to accommodate those who seek to remove sexist or gender-specific references in everyday words. Paragraph 12 answers in the affirmative, concluding that gender-neutral substitutions are acceptable even though "they may not always sound as good." Why do you think the Hayakawas structure their discussion of gender-specific references in this way? What does it indicate about their intended audience? (Glossary: *Audience*)

3. In what is a rather academic and straightforward piece, the Hayakawas introduce the image of a "greased runway" at the very end of their discussion. To what does the greased runway refer? Do you find it an effective image? Do you think it's appropriate to introduce such a metaphor so late in the piece? (Glossary: *Figurative Language*) Why or why not?

LANGUAGE IN ACTION

Sometimes a word can become so loaded that it irrevocably affects other valid words. The following article by Steven Pinker, which first appeared in the *New York Times* on February 2, 1999, reveals how this can happen. Consider the plight of David Howard, whose correct, nonpejorative use of the word *niggardly* set off a firestorm of controversy and cost him his job. Jot down your reactions to the situation? Do you think Howard should have been fired? Do you agree that the word *niggardly* should be removed from the vocabulary of our society, regardless of its actual meaning and derivation? Explain your answers.

RACIST LANGUAGE,
REAL AND IMAGINED

Last week David Howard, an aide to the Mayor of Washington, resigned after a staff meeting in which he called his budget "niggardly." A colleague thought he had used a racial epithet, though in fact "niggard" is a Middle English word meaning "miser." It has nothing to do with the racial slur based on Spanish for "black," which came into English centuries later.

This is not the first time the inaccurate parsing of an innocent remark has led to confusion. Remember, in "Annie Hall," how Woody Allen thinks he has been the target of an anti-Semitic slur from two people on a New York street? One person had asked, "Dj'ou eat yet?" and his companion had replied, "No, dj'ou?"

Last week's misunderstanding was of a different sort. "Niggardly" may be unexceptionable on etymological grounds, but given what we know about how the mind deals with language, the word was a disaster waiting to happen.

Most words and parts of words have many meanings, and when we listen to someone speak, our brains have to find the right ones. Some recent laboratory experiments indicate that this is a two-stage process.

First, all the meanings of a word, including inappropriate ones, light up willy-nilly in the brain. When we hear about "spiders, roaches, and bugs," the thought of surveillance devices flashes through our minds for a few hundredths of a second—until that misinterpretation is repressed by our analysis of the context.

Thus it is impossible for anyone to hear "niggardly" without thinking, if only for a moment, of the ethnic slur.

Worse, the context is of little help in squelching the wrong meaning. Everyone is an amateur linguist, and we all strive for a logical—though sometimes incorrect—parsing of what we hear. This is why folk etymologies are rampant in dialects, like "sparrowgrass" (asparagus) and "very-close" (varicose) veins.

Many phrases have become standard English, like chaise lounge (from the French chaise longue or "long chair"), cockroach (from the Spanish cucaracha) and bridegroom (originally bridgome, Middle English for "bride man").

"Niggardly" is easy to mis-parse. English grammar allows a "d" or "ed" to be stuck on a noun to form an adjective (as in "hook-nosed" and "left-handed"), and it allows "ly" to be put on an adjective to form an adverb.

Thus we get "absent-mindedly," "good-humoredly," "half-heartedly," "markedly," "otherworldly," "pointedly," "shame-facedly," and "single-handedly."

The "a" is not much help, because "ar" often substitutes for "er"—as in "beggar," "burglar," "hangar," and "scholar."

Worst of all, the deducible meaning makes all-too-good linguistic sense. Terms for stinginess and duplicitousness are among the most common examples of racist language: "to gyp" (probably from gypsy), "to welsh" (perhaps from Welsh), "Dutch treat," "Indian giver."

Does this mean a perfectly innocent word is doomed? It would not be the first time. Words are often sacrificed when they take on secondary, emotionally charged meanings. "Queer," for example is now problematic, and many animals (like donkeys) are losing their fine old Anglo-Saxon names.

If you find yourself vaguely offended thinking of the other words I could have included here, you should have some sympathy for David Howard's audience.

Still, Mr. Howard should get his job back. Though "niggardly" begs to be misunderstood, the misunderstanding can be overruled. After the various associates of a word light up in the mental dictionary, the rest of the brain can squelch the unintended ones, thanks to the activity that psycholinguists call "post-lexical-access processing" and that other people call "common sense."

WRITING SUGGESTIONS

1. (*Writing from Experience*) The Hayakawas' discussion of loaded words reflects a national movement and debate—termed *political correctness*—that, among other goals, seeks to aggressively remove loaded words from common use. Such terms as *chairperson, physically challenged,* and *sanitation technician* have become part of our everyday vocabulary. Still, many argue that political correctness has gone too far, and some even parody the movement: Should short people, for example, be termed *vertically challenged?* What do you think about political correctness? How has it changed the way you speak and the level of awareness—and respect—you have for others who are different from you? Write an essay in which you discuss your experiences with political correctness and how important you believe it is. Has it gone too far, making it too easy for some people to take offense at just about anything you say? Or is it helpful in eliminating loaded terms that imply disrespect?

2. (*Writing from Reading*) Reread the quote from John Ciardi (18). He has a pessimistic view when he says, "In the long run the usage of those who do not think about the language will prevail." What does he mean by this statement? Write an essay in which you agree or disagree with his view. How does language change? How can those who do not care about it affect its change? What can those who do care about it do to fulfill what Ciardi calls their "duty to resist"?

3. (*Writing from Research*) The Hayakawas explore gender bias in language, an important topic to many people. Unfortunately, many of the fundamental conventions, constructions, and expressions of our language were established within what is now considered a very sexist and patriarchal society. Changing or eliminating them is more challenging than changing other prejudicial language because male predominance is woven into the English language, not

added on. Research the current thinking about gender bias in language and the attempts being made to overcome it. There are many books and Internet sources on this topic, but the books *Breaking the Patriarchal Code: The Linguistic Basis of Sexual Bias* (1996) by Louise Goueffic and *Road to Equity: Gender, Equity and Language* (1995) by Brian Lee Crowley provide good starting points. Write a paper in which you first provide background information on the gender bias debate and then present an argument about what should be done to address the situation. What are the fundamental issues related to gender bias in language? How are they being addressed by the experts and linguists? Based on your research and personal views, what is your opinion about the issue? Do you think gender bias in language is exaggerated and that the issue is being blown out of proportion? Do you think it is part of the foundation of sexist thought and needs to be addressed more aggressively? Or are the current efforts to modify the language appropriate and sufficient? Explain your reasoning.

The Borders of Words

LARRY SMITH

Poet, essayist, and educator Larry Smith was born in 1943, in Mingo Junction, Ohio, and has remained close to his roots in his work. He received his M.A. and Ph.D. from Kent State University and now teaches English and humanities at Firelands College of Bowling Green State University. Smith also directs publications at Bottom Dog Press, which he describes as being "dedicated to writing of the Midwest and working class." His many publications include six collections of poetry; two literary biographies; Beyond Rust *(1995), a collection of stories; and* Working It Out *(1998), a novel. Smith has received numerous awards for his writing, including an Ohioana Citation for Poetry, a National Endowment for the Humanities Fellowship, a Fulbright Lectureship, and an Ohio Arts Council Individual Artist Fellowship in criticism.*

In the following selection, originally published in the Humanist *in 1995, Smith explores the power words and language have to close our minds and limit our thinking. As Smith explains, words all too easily become tools of exclusion that divide the world into "us" and "them"; it is possible, though, to escape the cage of language and pursue understanding in a way that is inclusive of the diversity that surrounds us.*

WRITING TO DISCOVER: *People often say that they made a decision with their heart, not their head, meaning that they were swayed more by emotion than by logic or intellect. Write about whether you consider yourself more of a thinking person or an emotional person. How do you separate the two? Do you think emotional and intellectual responses are mutually exclusive? Why or why not?*

For me, one of the most powerful and passionate scenes in American theater comes in William Gibson's *The Miracle Worker*, when young Helen Keller, blind, deaf, and mute from birth, speaks her first word—not as a concept but as a reality.

Her teacher, Annie Sullivan, stands at the well, pumping water onto Helen and saying the word into her palm again and again until Helen at last mouths the word "Wa-ter"—not as a piece of language to be used but as a cool, clear, ringing fact. She had come to realize the truth inside of words, with all the power and vision that opens to her. Sullivan declares it: "That words can be her eyes, to everything in the world outside her, and inside too, what is she without words? With them she can think, have ideas, be reached, there's not a thought or fact in the world that can't be hers." I believe in that.

I also know what I do not believe in: the practice of using language for inclusion and exclusion. Though discrimination may be basic to our sensory-psychological processes and can help us tell the difference between the sound of a cow and a sheep, between the odor of human food and human waste, when discrimination is enlarged to separate us from others or from the natural world, it becomes a human evil. It becomes a limitation that walls us off from ourselves and all that we are. When we begin to mark and label our experience, our language—that tool for communication and expression—can become a block to the heart.

"It's only human!" "That's just human nature." I'm tired of this lame excuse for human abuse when "being human" should mean having the ability to see beyond such limitations. Denial—in whatever sense we use it—is always a denial of self, and from it come the "shadows" that fall across our lives. Clearly we are all parts of groups—our families, our tribes, our communities; they all have their names—but shouldn't this recognition of human connection be extended to others? Could there be a path of inclusion that does not also exclude? I know the few man-to-man talks my father ever gave me and my brother in our cluttered basement were about this. Leaning on his tool table, he advised us in simple terms about treating all women as sisters, about extending family blood to everyone. Back then it seemed both natural and right.

It still does.

What brought on all this concern about boundaries? It truly arises not as a "reaction" but as a "realization"—as a "sensing" more than a "knowledge." In my fifties, I look around and begin to see the slowness of progress and the all-too-familiar obstacles of ignorance, violence, coercion, fear, and denial. Added to and integral with those is the human capacity to restrict, to cast labels and draw lines. Sadly, the specifics of discrimination are easy to cite: Nazism, fascism, and other nationalisms which start wars and institutionalize oppression; the patterns of class division, of haves and have-nots, which foster social injustice and unrest; the antisocial notice that we are not welcome here. Human history abounds with our records of such abuse and denial.

At rare times we make efforts to rise above such sham, as in the "Universal Declaration of Human Rights," adopted in 1948 by the U.N. General Assembly. Recognizing human potential as well as human rights, nations had met and drafted a way out of our patterned injustices—a declaration of our common rights:

> **Article 12**—No one shall be subjected to arbitrary interference with his privacy, family, home, or correspondence, nor to attacks upon his honor and reputation. Everyone has the right to the protection of the law against such interference or attacks. . . .

Article 23—

1. Everyone has the right to work, to free choice of employment, to just and favorable conditions of work, and to protection against unemployment.
2. Everyone, without any discrimination, has the right to equal pay for equal work.
3. Everyone who works has the right to just and favorable remuneration ensuring for himself and his family an existence worthy of human dignity, and supplemented, if necessary, by other means of social protection.
4. Everyone has the right to form and join trade unions for the protection of his interests.

Here is language put to its ultimate good, and I go back to these clear statements to correct my own vision of the world. They are my corrective lenses, reminders of what we are capable of doing as well as how we have failed. The idealism may sound tinny to young ears, but that is only because young people live amidst our failures and the clatter of words. I sense that our young still want to see us all live up to such values. They're just more disgusted with our lack of progress and with the sacrifice of their own innocence. However, this copy of the "Universal Declaration of Human Rights" comes today from fundamentally a youth-supported organization—Amnesty International. We are all young and old together.

To get this closer to home, to our personal ways of exclusion, we need only ask what makes us draw those lines between ourselves and others—the color of their skin, their origins, their way of speech or dress, where they live and with whom, how they grow their hair or grass. What makes us sense them as different and therefore outside of ourselves? And what gives us this right to exclude? Walk into a crowded room and you can read the body language—the diverted eyes, the turned shoulders, the silences that speak. Blacks in America are well practiced at reading these signs, as are Native Americans and other minority ethnic groups.

But so are women and the poor, young and old. In fact, we are all   10 part of the process—both excluded and excluder. All of us are in and outside of lines; all of us draw those lines around ourselves and our groups. When we sanctify the process with language, it becomes a way of seeing and being, and a tragic loss of life—for us all.

As a teacher, I walk into a lot of rooms, and what I find is myself standing up in front while others choose their seats and associations— whom they accept into their circle, whom they will talk with. In one class, it may be a best friend; in another, someone from home or someone who now lives in the dorm, someone who is old or black or female. And yet our circles are not fixed; we have the capacity to extend them infinitely. That is our hope—to open the nets.

I believe that the cause of this divisiveness is twofold: fear and its shadow, powerlessness. Because we deny and doubt our own feelings, we are afraid; feeling powerless, we create the fictive power of withdrawal. Like a small child, we choose not to recognize or respond to these others. We place them beneath us, or render them invisible through the infantile power of denial. And we end with what? A divided heart making boundaries that abuse ourselves as much as others. Mimicking our social culture, we separate our life into compartments—dividing our day into work and play, business and home, struggle and recreation . . . the words are there. And so we separate the sacred and secular, home and education, commerce and nature until we end with a fractured and fragmented vision. To maintain the unreasonable nature of our boundaries, we create the divided self.

As a teacher and writer, this realization of the tyranny of language came as something of a shock, yet it is something I had suspected for a long time. This semester it struck me as I asked my students to write on the issue of "poverty in America." As I wrote the words "the poor" across the board, I faced my students and was struck dumb with a triple realization: that some of them live below the "poverty line"; that no clear definition exists for the words "the poor"; and that, if I began to pretend that there were, I would be teaching a lie. The minute we point at "the poor," they are other, and so I was pushed through a long birth canal to the realization: we are the poor, all of us. We are also the rich, the wicked, the kind, and the unkind. I told them that as I was telling it to myself. Grounded in truth, the discussion grew and blossomed in some of their best writings.

A further realization came in another lesson I had been doing on "Writing Towards Wholeness." It begins with the question of how we come to know the world—how we receive it into ourselves. The answers are so basic, it's hard to see their importance. I begin by asking them, "Point to where you are inside your body." They, of course, point to their head or heart or eyes, or they sit in a confused silence. I draw a large circle on the board and begin to intersect it with lines drawn through the middle. At the top, I write, "Thought (the head)" and at the opposite end I write, "Emotions (the heart)." We have a long discussion on each as a way of knowing, and I ask how many of them are more of a "thinking" person and how many consider themselves a "feeling" person. It is usually about half and half. I do the same for other points on the grid—"Senses and Intuition," "Rational and Irrational"—usually ending with "Literal and Spiritual." After some practice, I hand them a poem—William Stafford's "Driving Through the Dark"—and ask them to read and mark what aspects of the person are called forth in the words. It's a good exercise and yet all wrong.

Somewhere into the fourth or fifth time I was teaching it I realized: 15
these are not polarities; these are all integral parts of the self. We learn the simplest things again and again. We need not divide ourselves but must remain integrated and whole. Thereafter, for each of the aspects of the self I drew arrows, and all of them were pointing to the center, where the real

wholeness lies. I'm reminded that the Japanese have a single word that means both "head and heart"—a more accurate reflection of how we live.

Beware of dualistic thinking, I tell myself; but also more specifically now, beware of starting any sentence with a collective noun. The second I start to say, "Blacks . . ." or "Students today . . ." or "American women . . ." I know that I am wrong. Not only am I destined to stereotype for convenience but I am also treating a word as though it were a reality—and that reality, in turn, controls my perception. This is more than political correctness; it has become a necessary way of maintaining fairness and power over our own minds and hearts. If we want these things, we must strive for the holistic view.

In Scott Russell Sanders' recent article for *Parabola,* I find assurance. He points out the beauty of the mandala symbol, in which the four pointed crosses or squares designating the four elements embrace the wholeness of the circle. To Carl Jung he attributes the recognition that such mandalas "symbolize the search for a center, outwardly in the cosmos and inwardly in the psyche." Happily, such symbols of inclusiveness are there if we search them out. Sanders also recognized rightly that "any description of the world is a net thrown over a flood; no matter how fine the mesh, the world leaks through" and advises us that "no single alphabet can express the full range of our knowledge." Inside this open system, all can live free; the search for understanding is continuous and dependent upon diversity. We can all take comfort in that.

Another place where I find comfort is in the gentle guidance of Jack Kornfield's *A Path with Heart:* "Compassion allows life to pass through our hearts with its great paradoxes of life, love, joy, and pain. When compassion opens in us, we give what we can to stop the war, to heal the environment, to care for the poor, to care for people with AIDS, to save the rain forests." Most of this happens without words, though a kind and mindful word is always a way of converting karma. Zen student Trudi Jinpu Hirsch tells the story of visiting a friend with AIDS. On one visit, a doctor told her bluntly, "Your friend is a dead person. You may as well face it." Hirsch confesses, "As soon as that happened, conditioning set in. When I went back to see this person . . . I'm now looking at a dead person. I mean . . . what that can do. . . . I mean I'm killing him with my mind." We become slaves to our perception, yet the way to avoid becoming encaged in language and labels is to recognize that we walk into that cage ourselves. And if we empower ourselves, we can walk back out; it's our own mind, after all. As Octavio Paz reminds us, even an enslaved man is free if he can close his eyes and think.

Ultimately, the power to resist and envision still rests within each of us. Why should we be slaves when we can transform the world? Language may be a way to divide us and our world. But if we can keep our hearts and eyes open to each other, our language can become a way to connect us and set us free.

FOCUSING ON CONTENT

1. What does "being human" mean to Smith (4)? Why is denial necessarily a denial of self?

2. What is represented by the "Universal Declaration of Human Rights"? How do the statements in the Declaration serve as "corrective lenses" for Smith (8)?

3. According to Smith, what causes the divisiveness that plagues us? How does it ultimately affect our everyday lives?

4. Why does Smith describe the exercise with the circle and William Stafford's poem as "a good exercise and yet all wrong" (14)?

5. Where does Smith find reassurance as he strives for "the holistic view (16)"? How do these sources comfort and encourage him?

FOCUSING ON WRITING

1. Smith introduces his topic with a scene from *The Miracle Worker*. (Glossary: *Beginnings and Endings*) What concept does he introduce? Do you find the scene an appropriate introduction to the idea of using language for inclusion and exclusion? Why or why not?

2. What does Smith mean when he says "We are all young and old together" at the conclusion of paragraph 8? How does this sentence serve to tie together the content of the paragraph that precedes it? (Glossary: *Paragraph*)

3. What is Smith's overall purpose in his essay? (Glossary: *Purpose*) Quote the passage that you think best summarizes his purpose.

4. Smith gives explicit references to his experiences as a teacher to help explain the insidious nature of inclusion and exclusion in language. How effective are these anecdotes about teaching? How does his interaction with students serve to educate him—and, by extension, his readers—about language and thinking beyond the classroom?

LANGUAGE IN ACTION

Jack Kornfield, whose book is quoted by Smith in paragraph 18, holds a Ph.D. in clinical psychology and was also trained as a Buddhist monk in Thailand, Burma, and India. As you can tell from the following interview, which first appeared in the *Sounds True Catalog* (1995) and is now available on the Internet, his point of view is based on Eastern thought (ST is *Sounds True*). How does Kornfield's understanding and teaching of Buddhist philosophy tie in with Smith's sense that we need to transcend our tendency to divide and exclude? How can Kornfield's teachings help us use language to, as Smith says, open our nets?

ST: *How would you describe the essence of Buddhist psychology?*

JK: The essence of Buddhist psychology is practical and transformative. It offers a way to understand the heart and mind so that we can be free, authentically compassionate, and happy in the midst of all the things that change in our world. Buddhist psychology provides tools and practices for true happiness in the midst of praise and blame, gain and loss, pleasure and pain.

It is also an old psychology—thousands of years old—so it's very well developed. There is an understanding of the nature of the senses, the body, and the mind taught in monasteries whose details are as sophisticated as an M.I.T. course on cybernetics. And at the same time it leads to direct ways of transforming our relationship to the world so that we are free. Just as all the great oceans have but one taste—the taste of salt—so all of the teachings of the Buddhas are said to have but one taste, which is the sweet taste of freedom in the heart.

ST: *What do you mean by that—"freedom of the heart"? Is that something we can actually have in our lives on a daily basis?*

JK: Freedom is possible for each of us. It is the capacity and birthright of every human being. The circumstances of our lives cannot always be changed, yet even in the midst of the greatest difficulties we have within us a longing to be more loving, to be open, to not be so caught up and reactive. And this freedom in the face of fear, anger, addiction, and confusion connects us to what we really know to be true in ourselves. This can be cultivated and awakened through a wise practice and understanding.

ST: *What are the practices of Buddhist psychology?*

JK: They are initially practices of sacred attention—to reconnect the body and mind. We begin by learning to know our breath and our body intimately. Then we expand our attention to the world of our senses; to sight, sound, taste, and smell, to understand the life of the senses and the body. From this we begin to examine the nature of mind and how our moods and inner stories affect all the relationships that we have as the world changes around us.

From this point, there comes the possibility of the practices of the spacious heart of forgiveness: of letting go, of inner abundance and ease. With these we shift from the "body of fear," from the small-self stories that we've identified with, to our Buddha nature: an inherent happiness.

Within this set of teachings are practices for reawakening our natural loving-kindness; for cultivation of profound forgiveness; practices of compassion and joy and the practice of equanimity—which brings a sense of divine equilibrium, or sacred ease in the midst of all things of life.

WRITING SUGGESTIONS

1. (*Writing from Experience*) Everyone faces experiences in which they must break out of a particular "group"—such as a group based on ethnic heritage, social status, or hobbies—in order to accomplish something or because they find themselves "out of their element." Write an essay in which you describe how you broke away from a group that was important to you. Why did you do it? How did you feel about it? Do you think the experience opened your mind or reinforced old stereotypes? Did you have some of Smith's sense of opening up your "net" or "circle"? Or did the experience make you feel more apart from others than you did before? Did it have any

long-term impact on how you view yourself in the context of the rest of the world?

2. (*Writing from Reading*) In paragraph 16, Smith says, "beware of starting any sentence with a collective noun. . . . This is more than political correctness; it has become a necessary way of maintaining fairness and power over our own minds and hearts." Write an essay in which you analyze this statement. How unexclusionary can one be? After all, as Allport said in his essay on pages 243–52, there are billions of grains of sand (people) in the world, and it is impossible to consider and accommodate every individual. Is it possible to categorize without perpetuating stereotypes of "loaded" associations? If so, how? If not, what can people do to be more inclusive in thinking about and dealing with others?

3. (*Writing about Research*) Using a keyword search, look on the Internet to find a copy of the United Nations' "Universal Declaration of Human Rights" from 1948, which Smith quotes in his essay. After studying the Declaration, write an essay in which you support or argue with Smith's characterization of it as "language put to its ultimate good." How effective is such language? After all, Amnesty International poignantly demonstrates each year that human rights cannot be taken for granted in most regions of the world even now, more than fifty years after the Declaration was made. Is language that encourages us to seek a higher level of conduct sufficient? How should language be tied to concrete actions and results?

The Meanings of a Word

GLORIA NAYLOR

Novelist and essayist Gloria Naylor was born in New York City in 1950. She worked as a missionary for the Jehovah's Witnesses from 1967 to 1975 and then as a telephone operator until 1981, the year she graduated from Brooklyn College. Naylor later started a graduate program in African American studies at Yale University. In her fiction, she explores the lives of African American women, drawing freely from her own experiences and those of her extended family. As Naylor has stated, "I wanted to become a writer because I felt that my presence as a black woman and my perspective as a woman in general had been underrepresented in American literature." She received the American Book Award for First Fiction for The Women of Brewster Place *(1982), a novel that was later adapted for television. This success was followed by* Linden Hills *(1985),* Mama Day *(1988),* Bailey's Cafe *(1993) and* The Men of Brewster Place *(1998). Naylor's short fiction and essays have appeared widely, and she has also edited* Children of the Night: Best Short Stories by Black Writers, 1967– *(1995).*

More than any other form of prejudiced language, racial slurs are intended to wound and shame. In the following essay, which first appeared in the New York Times *in 1986, Naylor remembers a time when a third-grade classmate called her a nigger. By examining the ways in which words can take on meaning depending on who uses them and to what purpose, Naylor concludes that "words themselves are innocuous; it is the consensus that gives them power."*

WRITING TO DISCOVER: *Have you or someone you know ever been called a derogatory name? Write about how this made you feel.*

Language is the subject. It is the written form with which I've managed to keep the wolf away from the door and, in diaries, to keep my sanity. In spite of this, I consider the written word inferior to the spoken, and much of the frustration experienced by novelists is the awareness that whatever we manage to capture in even the most transcendent passages falls far short of the richness of life. Dialogue achieves its power in the dynamics of a fleeting moment of sight, sound, smell, and touch.

I'm not going to enter the debate here about whether it is language that shapes reality or vice versa. That battle is doomed to be waged whenever we seek intermittent reprieve from the chicken and egg dispute. I will simply take the position that the spoken word, like the written word, amounts to a nonsensical arrangement of sounds or letters without a consensus that assigns "meaning." And building from the meanings of what we hear, we order reality. Words themselves are innocuous; it is the consensus that gives them true power.

I remember the first time I heard the word *nigger*. In my third-grade class, our math tests were being passed down the rows, and as I handed the papers to a little boy in back of me, I remarked that once again he had received a much lower mark than I did. He snatched his test from me and spit out that word. Had he called me a nymphomaniac or a necrophiliac, I couldn't have been more puzzled. I didn't know what a nigger was, but I know that whatever it meant, it was something he shouldn't have called me. This was verified when I raised my hand, and in a loud voice repeated what he had said and watched the teacher scold him for using a "bad" word. I was later to go home and ask the inevitable question that every black parent must face—"Mommy, what does *nigger* mean?"

And what exactly did it mean? Thinking back, I realize that this could not have been the first time the word was used in my presence. I was part of a large extended family that had migrated from the rural South after World War II and formed a close-knit network that gravitated around my maternal grandparents. Their ground-floor apartment in one of the buildings they owned in Harlem was a weekend mecca for my immediate family, along with countless aunts, uncles, and cousins who brought along assorted friends. It was a bustling and open house with assorted neighbors and tenants popping in and out to exchange bits of gossip, pick up an old quarrel, or referee the ongoing checkers game in which my grandmother cheated shamelessly. They were all there to let down their hair and put up their feet after a week of labor in the factories, laundries, and shipyards of New York.

Amid the clamor, which could reach deafening proportions—two or three conversations going on simultaneously, punctuated by the sound of a baby's crying somewhere in the back rooms or out on the street—there was still a rigid set of rules about what was said and how. Older children were sent out of the living room when it was time to get into the juicy details about "you-know-who" up on the third floor who had gone and gotten herself "p-r-e-g-n-a-n-t!" But my parents, knowing that I could spell well beyond my years, always demanded that I follow the others out to play. Beyond sexual misconduct and death, everything else was considered harmless for our young ears. And so among the anecdotes of the triumphs and disappointments in the various workings of their lives, the word *nigger* was used in my presence, but it was set within contexts and inflections that caused it to register in my mind as something else.

In the singular, the word was always applied to a man who had distinguished himself in some situation that brought their approval for his strength, intelligence, or drive:

"Did Johnny *really* do that?"

"I'm telling you, that nigger pulled in $6,000 of overtime last year. Said he got enough for a down payment on a house."

When used with a possessive adjective by a woman — "my nigger" — it became a term of endearment for her husband or boyfriend. But it could be more than just a term applied to a man. In their mouths it became the pure essence of manhood — a disembodied force that channeled their past history of struggle and present survival against the odds into a victorious statement of being: "Yeah, that old foreman found out quick enough — you don't mess with a nigger."

In the plural, it became a description of some group within the community that had overstepped the bounds of decency as my family defined it. Parents who neglected their children, a drunken couple who fought in public, people who simply refused to look for work, those with excessively dirty mouths or unkempt households were all "trifling niggers." This particular circle could forgive hard times, unemployment, the occasional bout of depression — they had gone through all of that themselves — but the unforgivable sin was a lack of self-respect.

A woman could never be a "nigger" in the singular, with its connotation of confirming worth. The noun *girl* was its closest equivalent in that sense, but only when used in direct address and regardless of the gender doing the addressing. *Girl* was a token of respect for a woman. The one-syllable word was drawn out to sound like three in recognition of the extra ounce of wit, nerve, or daring that the woman had shown in the situation under discussion.

"G-i-r-l, stop. You mean you said that to his face?"

But if the word was used in a third-person reference or shortened so that it almost snapped out of the mouth, it always involved some element of communal disapproval. And age became an important factor in these exchanges. It was only between individuals of the same generation, or from any older person to a younger (but never the other way around), that *girl* would be considered a compliment.

I don't agree with the argument that use of the word *nigger* at this social stratum of the black community was an internalization of racism. The dynamics were the exact opposite: the people in my grandmother's living room took a word that whites used to signify worthlessness or degradation and rendered it impotent. Gathering there together, they transformed *nigger* to signify the varied and complex human beings they knew themselves to be. If the word was to disappear totally from the mouths of even the most liberal of white society, no one in that room was naive enough to believe it would disappear from white minds. Meeting the word head-on, they proved it had absolutely nothing to do with the way they were determined to live their lives.

So there must have been dozens of times that *nigger* was spoken in front of me before I reached the third grade. But I didn't "hear" it until it was said by a small pair of lips that had already learned it could be a way to humiliate me. That was the word I went home and asked my mother about. And since she knew that I had to grow up in America, she took me in her lap and explained.

FOCUSING ON CONTENT

1. How, according to Naylor, do words get meanings?

2. Why does the boy sitting behind Naylor call her a nigger (3)? Why is she confused by this name-calling?

3. When Naylor was growing up, what two meanings did the word *girl* convey? How were those meanings defined by the speaker? In what way was age an important factor in the correct uses of *girl*?

4. Why does Naylor disagree with the notion that the use of the word *nigger* within her community was an internalization of racism?

FOCUSING ON WRITING

1. Naylor begins her essay with an abstract discussion about how words derive their meaning and power. How does this introduction tie in with her anecdote and discussion of the word *nigger*? (Glossary: *Abstract/Concrete*) Why is the introduction vital to the overall message of her essay?

2. Naylor says she must have heard the word *nigger* many times while she was growing up; yet she "heard" it for the first time when she was in the third grade (15). How does she explain this seeming contradiction? (Glossary: *Paradox*)

3. Define what *nigger* means to Naylor in the context of her family. (Glossary: *Definition*) Why do you suppose she offers so little in the way of definition of her classmate's use of the word?

4. How would you characterize Naylor's tone in her essay? (Glossary: *Tone*) Is she angry, objective, cynical, or something else? Cite examples of her diction to support your answer. (Glossary: *Diction*)

LANGUAGE IN ACTION

Naylor's essay discusses how those in her community used the word *nigger* for their own purposes and "rendered it impotent" (14). Nevertheless, the word still has a lot of negative power, as revealed in the following 1995 essay by Keith Woods, which was published by the Poynter Institute for Media Studies.

The consensus to which Naylor refers—here represented by Mark Fuhrman—gives the word that power, making news organizations report it in euphemisms or as a deleted expletive. In preparation for class discussion, think about your position on the following questions: What should be done about the word *nigger*? Should African Americans use it and try to "render it impotent" by creating their own prevailing context for it? Should the word be suppressed, forced into the fringes of racist thought, and represented in euphemisms? Or is there another way to address the word's negative power?

AN ESSAY ON A WICKEDLY
POWERFUL WORD

When I heard Mark Fuhrman's voice saying the word "nigger," I heard a lynch mob. I saw the grim and gleeful faces of murderous white men. I felt the coarse, hairy rope. I smelled the sap of the hangin' tree and saw Billie Holiday's "strange fruit" dangling from its strongest limb.

What a wickedly powerful word, nigger. So many other slurs could have slithered from Fuhrman's tongue and revealed his racism without provoking those images.

Jiggaboo.

Spade.

Coon.

I hear the hatred in those words, but I don't feel the fire's heat the way I do when this white former policeman says nigger. Somewhere in that visceral reflex is the reason news organizations had to use that word this time around.

Somewhere in the sting of seeing it, hearing it, feeling it is the reason they should think hard before using it the next time.

In context, there is no other way to report what Mark Furhman said. "Racial epithet" doesn't quite get it, does it? "Spearchucker" is a racial epithet, but it doesn't make you see burnt crosses and white sheets. Just rednecks.

The "n-word" sounds silly, childish, something you'd say when you don't want your 3-year-old to know what you're talking about. And "n-----?" What does that accomplish other than to allow newspapers the dubious out of saying, "Well, it's actually the reader who's saying nigger, not us."

When Mark Fuhrman or any person armed with a club or a gun or a bat or a judicial robe or a teaching certificate or any measure of power says "nigger," it's more than an insult. It summons all the historic and modern-day violence that is packed into those six letters.

Nigger is "Know your place."

Nigger is, "I am better than you."

Nigger is, "I can frame you or flunk you or beat you or kill you because . . ."

Nigger is, "I own you."

You just can't convey that definition with n-dash dash-dash-dash-dash. You can't communicate it with bleeps or blurbs or euphemisms. The problem is that sometimes the only way to do your job as a journalist is to say or write the word that furthers the mission of racists.

I'd like to believe that there's some lessening of harm every time the word sees the light of day. I once fantasized about a day when a group of black rappers or comedians would appropriate the white sheets and hoods of the KKK and go gallivanting across MTV or HBO and forever render that image so utterly ridiculous that no self-respecting racist would ever wear it again.

But then, Richard Pryor tried to appropriate nigger, didn't he? Took it right from the white folks and turned it into a career before he thought better of it. So did the rappers NWA ("Niggas With Attitudes"). So did my friends on the streets of New Orleans. So has a generation of young black people today.

Still, the definition didn't change.

Dick Gregory tried it. In the dedication of his autobiography, "Nigger," the comedian-turned-activist wrote: "Dear Momma—Wherever you are, if ever you hear the word "nigger" again, remember they are advertising my book."

He wrote that 31 years ago, but if Lucille Gregory were here to hear Mark Fuhrman, she'd surely know he wasn't talking about her son's novel. The definition doesn't change. It doesn't hurt any less after three decades. No less after three centuries.

It's the same word, spiked with the same poison, delivering the same message of inferiority, degradation, hatred, and shame. The same word whether it's Fuhrman saying it or Huck Finn or Def Comedy Jam or Snoop Doggy Dogg or my old friends from Touro Street (Because, they do call themselves nigger, you know).

It hurts every time it's in the paper or on the air or in the street. Every time. Sometimes there's no way around using it in the media, but only sometimes.

Could there come a day when you see it or read it or hear it from the home-boys so much that you hardly notice? When your eyebrow doesn't arch as often or your jaw suddenly drop when the six o'clock anchor plops the word onto your living room coffee table?

Maybe. And you might even say, that day, "Oh, they're just talking about niggers again."

Are we better off then?

WRITING SUGGESTIONS

1. (*Writing from Experience*) Write an essay in which you describe the process through which you became aware of prejudice, either toward yourself or toward another person or group of people. Did a specific event spark your awareness, such as that detailed in your Writing to Discover entry? Or did you become aware of prejudice in a more gradual way? Did you learn about prejudice primarily from your peers, your parents, or someone else? How did your new awareness affect you? How have your experience(s) shaped the way you think and feel about prejudice today?

2. (*Writing from Reading*) In addition to discussing the word *nigger*, Naylor talks about the use of *girl*, a word with far less negative baggage but one that can still be offensive when used in an inappropriate context. Write an essay in which you discuss your use of a contextually sensitive word. What is its strict definition? How do you use it? In what context(s) might its use be inappropriate? Why is the word used in different ways?

3. (*Writing from Research*) Read Gloria Naylor's signature book, *The Women of Brewster Place*. Write an essay in which you compare the world Naylor creates in Brewster Place to the one she sketches in "The Meaning of a Word." What are the women of Brewster Place like? How do they use language? How do their interactions among themselves and within their community contrast with the ones they have with the outside world? (Glossary: *Comparison and Contrast*) What elements of the book do you think may be autobiographical in nature? Explain your reasoning.

"I'll Explain It to You": Lecturing and Listening

DEBORAH TANNEN

Deborah Tannen, professor of linguistics at Georgetown University, was born in Brooklyn, New York, and earned her Ph.D. in linguistics at the University of California, Berkeley. Tannen specializes in the study of the ways people talk to each other. Her first book, That's Not What I Meant *(1986) catapulted her into the public spotlight, and subsequently she has appeared on talk shows discussing the differences between male and female conversation patterns. In 1990 she published the best-selling book* You Just Don't Understand: Women and Men in Conversation *(1990).* Talking from 9 to 5: How Women's and Men's Conversational Styles Affect Who Gets Heard, Who Gets Credit *(1994), and* What Gets Done at Work *(1995) focuses on the workplace, seeking to make the corporate boardroom a place where both sexes can be heard and understood. Her sixteenth book,* The Argument Culture, *was published in 1998 and discusses Americans' growing fascination with arguing and arguments. Tannen's extensive writings also include academic books and articles, short stories, and poetry.*

In the following selection from You Just Don't Understand, *Tannen examines the differing ways that men and women use language in conversing with one another: Men, by lecturing, reinforce their independence and establish or test their status; women, by listening, establish rapport and closeness through self-revelation. Tannen concludes that "Women and men both can gain by understanding the other's gender style, and by learning to use it on occasion."*

WRITING TO DISCOVER: *What differences do you notice between your conversations with men and those with women. Jot down the kinds of things women like to talk about. How do these compare to the things men like to talk about? When a man and a woman are talking about the same topic, do you find their approaches similar? Explain.*

At a reception following the publication of one of my books, I noticed a publicist listening attentively to the producer of a popular radio show. He was telling her how the studio had come to be built where it was, and why he would have preferred another site. What caught my attention was the length of time he was speaking while she was listening. He was delivering a monologue that could only be called a lecture, giving her detailed information about the radio reception at the two sites, the architecture of the sta-

278

tion, and so on. I later asked the publicist if she had been interested in the information the producer had given her. "Oh, yes," she answered. But then she thought a moment and said, "Well, maybe he did go on a bit." The next day she told me, "I was thinking about what you asked. I couldn't have cared less about what he was saying. It's just that I'm so used to listening to men go on about things I don't care about, I didn't even realize how bored I was until you made me think about it."

I was chatting with a man I had just met at a party. In our conversation, it emerged that he had been posted in Greece with the RAF during 1944 and 1945. Since I had lived in Greece for several years, I asked him about his experiences: What had Greece been like then? How had the Greek villagers treated the British soldiers? What had it been *like* to be a British soldier in wartime Greece? I also offered information about how Greece had changed, what it is like now. He did not pick up on my remarks about contemporary Greece, and his replies to my questions quickly changed from accounts of his own experiences, which I found riveting, to facts about Greek history, which interested me in principle but in the actual telling left me profoundly bored. The more impersonal his talk became, the more I felt oppressed by it, pinned involuntarily in the listener position.

At a showing of Judy Chicago's jointly created art work *The Dinner Party*, I was struck by a couple standing in front of one of the displays: The man was earnestly explaining to the woman the meaning of symbols in the tapestry before them, pointing as he spoke. I might not have noticed this unremarkable scene, except that *The Dinner Party* was radically feminist in conception, intended to reflect women's experiences and sensibilities.

While taking a walk in my neighborhood on an early summer evening at twilight, I stopped to chat with a neighbor who was walking his dogs. As we stood, I noticed that the large expanse of yard in front of which we were standing was aglitter with the intermittent flickering of fireflies. I called attention to the sight, remarking on how magical it looked. "It's like the Fourth of July," I said. He agreed, and then told me he had read that the lights of fireflies are mating signals. He then explained to me details of how these signals work—for example, groups of fireflies fly at different elevations and could be seen to cluster in different parts of the yard.

In all these examples, the men had information to impart and they were imparting it. On the surface, there is nothing surprising or strange about that. What is strange is that there are so many situations in which men have factual information requiring lengthy explanations to impart to women, and so few in which women have comparable information to impart to men.

The changing times have altered many aspects of relations between women and men. Now it is unlikely, at least in many circles, for a man to

5

say, "I am better than you because I am a man and you are a woman." But women who do not find men making such statements are nonetheless often frustrated in their dealings with them. One situation that frustrates many women is a conversation that has mysteriously turned into a lecture, with the man delivering the lecture to the woman, who has become an appreciative audience.

Once again, the alignment in which women and men find themselves arrayed is asymmetrical. The lecturer is framed as superior in status and expertise, cast in the role of teacher, and the listener is cast in the role of student. If women and men took turns giving and receiving lectures, there would be nothing disturbing about it. What is disturbing is the imbalance. Women and men fall into this unequal pattern so often because of the differences in their interactional habits. Since women seek to build rapport, they are inclined to play down their expertise rather than display it. Since men value the position of center stage and the feeling of knowing more, they seek opportunities to gather and disseminate factual information.

If men often seem to hold forth because they have the expertise, women are often frustrated and surprised to find that when they have the expertise, they don't necessarily get the floor.

FIRST ME, THEN ME

I was at a dinner with faculty members from other departments in my university. To my right was a woman. As the dinner began, we introduced ourselves. After we told each other what departments we were in and what subjects we taught, she asked what my research was about. We talked about my research for a little while. Then I asked her about her research and she told me about it. Finally, we discussed the ways that our research overlapped. Later, as tends to happen at dinners, we branched out to others at the table. I asked a man across the table from me what department he was in and what he did. During the next half hour, I learned a lot about his job, his research, and his background. Shortly before the dinner ended there was a lull, and he asked me what I did. When I said I was a linguist, he became excited and told me about a research project he had conducted that was related to neurolinguistics. He was still telling me about his research when we all got up to leave the table.

This man and woman were my colleagues in academia. What happens when I talk to people at parties and social events, not fellow researchers? My experience is that if I mention the kind of work I do to women, they usually ask me about it. When I tell them about conversational style or gender differences, they offer their own experiences to support the patterns I describe. This is very pleasant for me. It puts me at center stage without my having to grab the spotlight myself, and I frequently gather anecdotes I can use in the future. But when I announce my line of work

10

to men, many give me a lecture on language—for example, about how people, especially teenagers, misuse language nowadays. Others challenge me, for example questioning me about my research methods. Many others change the subject to something they know more about.

Of course not all men respond in this way, but over the years I have encountered many men, and very few women, who do. It is not that speaking in this way is *the* male way of doing things, but that it is *a* male way. There are women who adopt such styles, but they are perceived as speaking like men.

IF YOU'VE GOT IT, FLAUNT IT—OR HIDE IT

I have been observing this constellation in interaction for more than a dozen years. I did not, however, have any understanding of *why* this happens until fairly recently, when I developed the framework of status and connection. An experimental study that was pivotal in my thinking shows that expertise does not ensure women a place at center stage in conversation with men.

Psychologist H. M. Leet-Pellegrini set out to discover whether gender or expertise determined who would behave in what she terms a "dominant" way—for example, by talking more, interrupting, and controlling the topic. She set up pairs of women, pairs of men, and mixed pairs, and asked them to discuss the effects of television violence on children. In some cases, she made one of the partners an expert by providing relevant factual information and time to read and assimilate it before the videotaped discussion. One might expect that the conversationalist who was the expert would talk more, interrupt more, and spend less time supporting the conversational partner who knew less about the subject. But it wasn't so simple. On the average, those who had expertise did talk more, but men experts talked more than women experts.

Expertise also had a different effect on women and men with regard to supportive behavior. Leet-Pellegrini expected that the one who did not have expertise would spend more time offering agreement and support to the one who did. This turned out to be true—*except* in cases where a woman was the expert and her nonexpert partner was a man. In this situation, the women experts showed support—saying things like "Yeah" and "That's right"—far *more* than the nonexpert men they were talking to. Observers often rated the male nonexpert as more dominant than the female expert. In other words, the women in this experiment not only didn't wield their expertise as power, but tried to play it down and make up for it through extra assenting behavior. They acted as if their expertise were something to hide.

And perhaps it was. When the word *expert* was spoken in these experimental conversations, in all cases but one it was the man in the conversation   15 who used it, saying something like "So, you're the expert." Evidence of the woman's superior knowledge sparked resentment, not respect.

Furthermore, when an expert man talked to an uninformed woman, he took a controlling role in structuring the conversation in the beginning *and* the end. But when an expert man talked to an uninformed man, he dominated in the beginning but not always in the end. In other words, having expertise was enough to keep a man in the controlling position if he was talking to a woman, but not if he was talking to a man. Apparently, when a woman surmised that the man she was talking to had more information on the subject than she did, she simply accepted the reactive role. But another man, despite a lack of information, might still give the expert a run for his money and possibly gain the upper hand by the end.

Reading these results, I suddenly understood what happens to me when I talk to women and men about language. I am assuming that my acknowledged expertise will mean I am automatically accorded authority in the conversation, and with women this is generally the case. But when I talk to men, revealing that I have acknowledged expertise in this area often invites challenges. I *might* maintain my position if I defend myself successfully against the challenges, but if I don't, I may lose ground.

One interpretation of the Leet-Pellegrini study is that women are getting a bum deal. They don't get credit when it's due. And in a way, this is true. But the reason is not—as it seems to many women—that men are bums who seek to deny women authority. The Leet-Pellegrini study shows that many men are inclined to jockey for status, and challenge the authority of others, when they are talking to men too. If this is so, then challenging a woman's authority as they would challenge a man's could be a sign of respect and equal treatment, rather than lack of respect and discrimination. In cases where this is so, the inequality of the treatment results not simply from the men's behavior alone but from the differences in men's and women's styles: Most women lack experience in defending themselves against challenges, which they misinterpret as personal attacks on their credibility.

Even when talking to men who are happy to see them in positions of status, women may have a hard time getting their due because of differences in men's and women's interactional goals. Just as boys in high school are not inclined to repeat information about popular girls because it doesn't get them what they want, women in conversation are not inclined to display their knowledge because it doesn't get them what they are after. Leet-Pellegrini suggests that the men in this study were playing a game of "Have I won?" while the women were playing a game of "Have I been sufficiently helpful?" I am inclined to put this another way: The game women play is "Do you like me?" whereas the men play "Do you respect me?" If men, in seeking respect, are less liked by women, this is an unsought side effect, as is the effect that women, in seeking to be liked, may lose respect. When a woman has a conversation with a man, her efforts to emphasize their similarities and avoid showing off can easily be interpreted, through the lens of status, as relegating her to a one-down position, making her appear either incompetent or insecure.

A SUBTLE DEFERENCE

Elizabeth Aries, a professor of psychology at Amherst College, set   20
out to show that highly intelligent, highly educated young women are no longer submissive in conversations with male peers. And indeed she found that the college women did talk more than the college men in small groups she set up. But what they said was different. The men tended to set the agenda by offering opinions, suggestions, and information. The women tended to react, offering agreement or disagreement. Furthermore, she found that body language was as different as ever: The men sat with their legs stretched out, while the women gathered themselves in. Noting that research has found that speakers using the open-bodied position are more likely to persuade their listeners, Aries points out that talking more may not ensure that women will be heard.

In another study, Aries found that men in all-male discussion groups spent a lot of time at the beginning finding out "who was best informed about movies, books, current events, politics, and travel" as a means of "sizing up the competition" and negotiating "where they stood in relation to each other." This glimpse of how men talk when there are no women present gives an inkling of why displaying knowledge and expertise is something that men find more worth doing than women. What the women in Aries's study spent time doing was "gaining a closeness through more intimate self-revelation."

It is crucial to bear in mind that both the women and the men in these studies were establishing a camaraderie, and both were concerned with their relationships to each other. But different aspects of their relationships were of primary concern: their place in a hierarchical order for the men, and their place in a network of intimate connections for the women. The consequence of these disparate concerns was very different ways of speaking.

Thomas Fox is an English professor who was intrigued by the differences between women and men in his freshman writing classes. What he observed corresponds almost precisely to the experimental findings of Aries and Leet-Pellegrini. Fox's method of teaching writing included having all the students read their essays to each other in class and talk to each other in small groups. He also had them write papers reflecting on the essays and the discussion groups. He alone, as the teacher, read these analytical papers.

To exemplify the two styles he found typical of women and men, Fox chose a woman, Ms. M, and a man, Mr. H. In her speaking as well as her

writing, Ms. M. held back what she knew, appearing uninformed and un-
interested, because she feared offending her classmates. Mr. H. spoke and
wrote with authority and apparent confidence because he was eager to
persuade his peers. She did not worry about persuading; he did not worry
about offending.

In his analytical paper, the young man described his own behavior in   25
the mixed-gender group discussions as if he were describing the young
men in Leet-Pellegrini's and Aries's studies:

> In my sub-group I am the leader. I begin every discussion by stating my
> opinions as facts. The other two members of the sub-group tend to sit
> back and agree with me. . . . I need people to agree with me.

Fox comments that Mr. H. reveals "a sense of self, one that acts to
change himself and other people, that seems entirely distinct from Ms.
M's sense of self, dependent on and related to others."

Calling Ms. M's sense of self "dependent" suggests a negative view
of her way of being in the world—and, I think, a view more typical of
men. This view reflects the assumption that the alternative to independence is dependence. If this is indeed a male view, it may explain why so
many men are cautious about becoming intimately involved with others:
It makes sense to avoid humiliating dependence by insisting on independence. But there is another alternative: *inter*dependence.

The main difference between these alternatives is symmetry. Dependence is an asymmetrical involvement: One person needs the other, but
not vice versa, so the needy person is one-down. Interdependence is symmetrical: Both parties rely on each other, so neither is one-up or one-
down. Moreover, Mr. H's sense of self is also dependent on others. He
requires others to listen, agree, and allow him to take the lead by stating
his opinions first.

Looked at this way, the woman and man in this group are both dependent on each other. Their differing goals are complementary, although neither understands the reasons for the other's behavior. This
would be a fine arrangement, except that their differing goals result in
alignments that enhance his authority and undercut hers.

DIFFERENT INTERPRETATIONS—AND
MISINTERPRETATIONS

Fox also describes differences in the way male and female students in
his classes interpreted a story they read. These differences also reflect assumptions about the interdependence or independence of individuals.
Fox's students wrote their responses to "The Birthmark" by Nathaniel
Hawthorne. In the story, a woman's husband becomes obsessed with a
birthmark on her face. Suffering from her husband's revulsion at the sight

of her, the wife becomes obsessed with it too and, in a reversal of her initial impulse, agrees to undergo a treatment he has devised to remove the birthmark — a treatment that succeeds in removing the mark, but kills her in the process.

Ms. M interpreted the wife's complicity as a natural response to the   30
demand of a loved one: The woman went along with her husband's lethal schemes to remove the birthmark because she wanted to please and be appealing to him. Mr. H blamed the woman's insecurity and vanity for her fate, and he blamed her for voluntarily submitting to her husband's authority. Fox points out that he saw her as individually responsible for her actions, just as he saw himself as individually responsible for his own actions. To him, the issue was independence: The weak wife voluntarily took a submissive role. To Ms. M, the issue was interdependence: The woman was inextricably bound up with her husband, so her behavior could not be separated from his.

Fox observes that Mr. H saw the writing of the women in the class as spontaneous — they wrote whatever popped into their heads. Nothing could be farther from Ms. M's experience as she described it: When she knew her peers would see her writing, she censored everything that popped into her head. In contrast, when she was writing something that only her professor would read, she expressed firm and articulate opinions.

There is a striking but paradoxical complementarity to Ms. M's and Mr. H's styles, when they are taken together. He needs someone to listen and agree. She listens and agrees. But in another sense, their dovetailing purposes are at cross-purposes. He misinterprets her agreement, intended in a spirit of connection, as a reflection of status and power: He thinks she is "indecisive" and "insecure." Her reasons for refraining from behaving as he does — firmly stating opinions as facts — have nothing to do with her attitudes toward her knowledge, as he thinks they do, but rather result from her attitudes toward her relationships with her peers.

These experimental studies by Leet-Pellegrini and Aries, and the observations by Fox, all indicate that, typically, men are more comfortable than women in giving information and opinions and speaking in an authoritative way to a group, whereas women are more comfortable than men in supporting others. [. . .]

LISTENER AS UNDERLING

Clearly men are not always talking and women are not always listening. I have asked men whether they ever find themselves in the position of listening to another man giving them a lecture, and how they feel about it. They tell me that this does happen. They may find themselves talking to someone who presses information on them so insistently that they give in and listen. They say they don't mind too much, however, if the information is interesting. They can store it away for future use, like remembering a joke to tell others later. Factual information is of less interest to women because it is of less use to them. They are unlikely to try to pass on the gift of information, more likely to give the gift of being a good audience.

Men as well as women sometimes find themselves on the receiving end of a lecture they would as soon not hear. But men tell me that it is most likely to happen if the other man is in a position of higher status. They know they have to listen to lectures from fathers and bosses. 35

That men can find themselves in the position of unwilling listener is attested to by a short opinion piece in which A. R. Gurney bemoans being frequently "cornered by some self-styled expert who harangues me with his considered opinion on an interminable agenda of topics." He claims that this tendency bespeaks a peculiarly American inability to "converse" — that is, engage in a balanced give-and-take — and cites as support the French observer of American customs Alexis de Tocqueville, who wrote, "An American . . . speaks to you as if he was addressing a meeting." Gurney credits his own appreciation of conversing to his father, who "was a master at eliciting and responding enthusiastically to the views of others, though this resiliency didn't always extend to his children. Indeed, now I think about it, he spoke to us many times as if he were addressing a meeting."

It is not surprising that Gurney's father lectured his children. The act of giving information by definition frames one in a position of higher status, while the act of listening frames one as lower. Children instinctively sense this — as do most men. But when women listen to men, they are not thinking in terms of status. Unfortunately, their attempts to reinforce connections and establish rapport, when interpreted through the lens of status, can be misinterpreted as casting them in a subordinate position — and are likely to be taken that way by many men.

WHAT'S SO FUNNY?

The economy of exchanging jokes for laughter is a parallel one. In her study of college students' discussion groups, Aries found that the students in all-male groups spent a lot of time telling about times they had played jokes on others, and laughing about it. She refers to a study in which Barbara Miller Newman found that high school boys who were not "quick and clever" became the targets of jokes. Practical joking — playing a joke *on* someone — is clearly a matter of being one-up: in the know and in control. It is less obvious, but no less true, that *telling* jokes can also be a way of negotiating status.

Many women (certainly not all) laugh at jokes but do not later remember them. Since they are not driven to seek and hold center stage in a group, they do not need a store of jokes to whip out for this purpose. A woman I will call Bernice prided herself on her sense of humor. At a cocktail party, she met a man to whom she was drawn because he seemed at first to share this trait. He made many funny remarks, which she spontaneously laughed at. But when she made funny remarks, he seemed not to hear. What had happened to his sense of humor? Though telling jokes and laughing at them are both reflections of a sense of humor, they are very different social activities. Making others laugh gives you a fleeting power over them: As linguist Wallace Chafe points out, at the moment of laughter, a person is temporarily disabled. The man Bernice met was comfortable only when he was making her laugh, not the other way around. When Bernice laughed at his jokes, she thought she was engaging in a symmetrical activity. But he was engaging in an asymmetrical one.

A man told me that sometime around tenth grade he realized that he   40
preferred the company of women to the company of men. He found that his female friends were more supportive and less competitive, whereas his male friends seemed to spend all their time joking. Considering joking an asymmetrical activity makes it clearer why it would fit in with a style he perceived as competitive. [. . .]

MUTUAL ACCUSATIONS

Considering these dynamics, it is not surprising that many women complain that their partners don't listen to them. But men make the same complaint about women, although less frequently. The accusation "You're not listening" often really means "You don't understand what I said in the way that I meant it," or "I'm not getting the response I wanted." Being listened to can become a metaphor for being understood and being valued.

In my earlier work I emphasized that women may get the impression men aren't listening to them even when the men really are. This happens because men have different habitual ways of showing they're listening. As anthropologists Maltz and Borker explain, women are more inclined to ask questions. They also give more listening responses — little words like *mhm, uh-uh,* and *yeah* — sprinkled throughout someone else's talk, providing a running feedback loop. And they respond more positively and enthusiastically, for example by agreeing and laughing.

All this behavior is doing the work of listening. It also creates rapport-talk by emphasizing connection and encouraging more talk. The corresponding strategies of men — giving fewer listener responses, making statements rather than asking questions, and challenging rather than agreeing — can be understood as moves in a contest by incipient speakers rather than audience members.

Not only do women give more listening signals, according to Maltz and Borker, but the signals they give have different meanings for men and women, consistent with the speaker/audience alignment. Women use "yeah" to mean "I'm with you, I follow," whereas men tend to say "yeah" only when they agree. The opportunity for misunderstanding is clear. When a man is confronted with a women who has been saying "yeah," "yeah," "yeah," and then turns out not to agree, he may conclude that she has been insincere, or that she was agreeing without really listening. When a woman is confronted with a man who does *not* say "yeah"—or much of anything else—she may conclude that *he* hasn't been listening. The men's style is more literally focused on the message level of talk, while the women's is focused on the relationship or metamessage level.

To a man who expects a listener to be quietly attentive, a woman giving a stream of feedback and support will seem to be talking too much for a listener. To a woman who expects a listener to be active and enthusiastic in showing interest, attention, and support, a man who listens silently will seem not to be listening at all, but rather to have checked out of the conversation, taken his listening marbles, and gone mentally home. 45

Because of these patterns, woman may get the impression that men aren't listening when they really are. But I have come to understand more recently, that it is also true that men listen to women less frequently than women listen to men, because the act of listening has different meanings for them. Some men really *don't* want to listen at length because they feel it frames them as subordinate. Many women do want to listen, but they expect it to be reciprocal—I listen to you now; you listen to me later. They become frustrated when they do the listening now and now and now, and later never comes.

MUTUAL DISSATISFACTION

If women are dissatisfied with always being in the listening position, the dissatisfaction may be mutual. That a woman feels she has been assigned the role of silently listening audience does not mean that a man feels he has consigned her to that role—or that he necessarily likes the rigid alignment either.

During the time I was working on this book, I found myself at a book party filled with people I hardly knew. I struck up a conversation with a charming young man who turned out to be a painter. I asked him about his work and, in response to his answer, asked whether there has been a return in contemporary art to figurative painting. In response to my question, he told me a lot about the history of art—so much that when he finished and said, "That was a long answer to your question," I had long since forgotten that I had asked a question, let alone what it was. I had not minded this monologue—I had been interested in it—but I realized, with something of a jolt, that I had just experienced the dynamic that I had been writing about.

I decided to risk offending my congenial new acquaintance in order to learn something about his point of view. This was, after all, a book party, so I might rely on his indulgence if I broke the rules of decorum in the interest of writing a book. I asked whether he often found himself talking at length while someone else listened. He thought for a moment and said yes, he did, because he liked to explore ideas in detail. I asked if it happened equally with women and men. He thought again and said, "No, I have more trouble with men." I asked what he meant by trouble. He said, "Men interrupt. *They* want to explain to *me*."

Finally, having found this young man disarmingly willing to talk   50 about the conversation we had just had and his own style, I asked which he preferred: that a woman listen silently and supportively, or that she offer opinions and ideas of her own. He said he thought he liked it better if she volunteered information, making the interchange more interesting.

When men begin to lecture other men, the listeners are experienced at trying to sidetrack the lecture, or match it, or derail it. It this system, making authoritative pronouncements may be a way to begin an *exchange* of information. But women are not used to responding in that way. They see little choice but to listen attentively and wait for their turn to be allotted to them rather than seizing it for themselves. If this is the case, the man may be as bored and frustrated as the woman when his attempt to begin an exchange of information ends in his giving a lecture. From his point of view, she is passively soaking up information, so she must not have any to speak of. One of the reasons men's talk to women frequently turns into lecturing is *because* women listen attentively and do not interrupt with challenges, sidetracks, or matching information.

In the conversations with male and female colleagues that I recounted at the outset of this chapter, this difference may have been crucial. When I talked to the woman, we each told about our own research in response to the other's encouragement. When I talked to the man, I encouraged him to talk about his work, and he obliged, but he did not encourage me to talk about mine. This may mean that he did not want to hear about it—but it also may not. In her study of college students' discussion groups, Aries found that women who did a lot of talking began to feel uncomfortable; they backed off and frequently drew out quieter members of the group. This is perfectly in keeping with women's desire to keep things balanced, so everyone is on an equal footing. Women expect their conversational partners to encourage them to hold forth. Men who do not typically encourage quieter members to speak up, assume that anyone who has something to say will volunteer it. The men may be equally disappointed in a conversational partner who turns out to have nothing to say.

Similarly, men can be as bored by women's topics as women can be by men's. While I was wishing the former RAFer would tell me about his personal experiences in Greece, he was probably wondering why I was boring him with mine and marveling at my ignorance of the history of a country I had lived in. Perhaps he would have considered our conversation a success if I had challenged or topped his interpretation of Greek history rather than listening dumbly to it. When men, upon hearing the kind of work I do, challenge me about my research methods, they are inviting me to give them information and show them my expertise — something I don't like to do outside of the classroom or lecture hall, but something they themselves would likely be pleased to be provoked to do.

The publicist who listened attentively to information about a radio station explained to me that she wanted to be nice to the manager, to smooth the way for placing her clients on his station. But men who want to ingratiate themselves with women are more likely to try to charm them by offering interesting information than by listening attentively to whatever information the women have to impart. I recall a luncheon preceding a talk I delivered to a college alumni association. My gracious host kept me entertained before my speech by regaling me with information about computers, which I politely showed interest in, while inwardly screaming from boredom and a sense of being weighed down by irrelevant information that I knew I would never remember. Yet I am sure he thought he was being interesting, and it is likely that at least some male guests would have thought that he was. I do not wish to imply that all women hosts have entertained me in the perfect way. I recall a speaking engagement before which I was taken to lunch by a group of women. They were so attentive to my expertise that they plied me with questions, prompting me to exhaust myself by giving my lecture over lunch before the formal lecture began. In comparison to this, perhaps the man who lectured to me about computers was trying to give me a rest.

The imbalance by which men often find themselves in the role of lec- 55
turer, and women often find themselves in the role of audience, is not the creation of only one member of an interaction. It is not something that men do to women. Neither is it something that women culpably "allow" or "ask for." The imbalance is created by the difference between women's and men's habitual styles. [. . .]

HOPE FOR THE FUTURE

What is the hope for the future? Must we play out our assigned parts to the closing act? Although we tend to fall back on habitual ways of talking, repeating old refrains and familiar lines, habits can be broken. Women and men both can gain by understanding the other gender's style, and by learning to use it on occasion.

Women who find themselves unwillingly cast as the listener should practice propelling themselves out of that position rather than waiting patiently for the lecture to end. Perhaps they need to give up the belief that they must wait for the floor to be handed to them. If they have something to say on a subject, they might push themselves to volunteer it. If they are bored with a subject, they can exercise some influence on the conversation and change the topic to something they would rather discuss.

If women are relieved to learn that they don't always have to listen, there may be some relief for men in learning that they don't always have to have interesting information on the tips of their tongues if they want to impress a woman or entertain her. A journalist once interviewed me for an article about how to strike up conversations. She told me that another expert she had interviewed, a man, had suggested that one should come up with an interesting piece of information. I found this amusing, as it seemed to typify a man's idea of a good conversationalist, but not a woman's. How much easier men might find the task of conversation if they realized that all they have to do is listen. As a woman who wrote a letter to the editor of *Psychology Today* put it, "When I find a guy who asks, 'How was your day?' and really wants to know, I'm in heaven."

FOCUSING ON CONTENT

1. Why was the scene Tannen saw at the showing of *The Dinner Party* so striking (3)? Why is the image an effective one for her to use to introduce her topic?

2. Tannen writes that the Leet-Pellegrini study was "pivotal" in her thinking (12). What in particular about that study made it so?

3. According to Tannen, a fundamental difference exists between the goals of women and men in conversation. What do women wish to achieve? What do men wish to achieve? How does this difference contribute to the difficulties men and women have in communicating with one another?

4. In what ways do the listening styles of women and men differ? How can these differences create profound misunderstandings?

5. According to Tannen, how do men and women use jokes differently in their conversations?

6. What conversational strategies do men use when their attempts to lecture other men meet with opposition? Would these same strategies work for women in similar situations? Explain.

FOCUSING ON WRITING

1. As a woman writing about the different communication styles of women and men, Tannen carries with her an unavoidable bias: She more readily understands the female point of view and must learn about the male point of view.

In order for her work to be welcomed by a wide audience, however, she must try not to show bias in her presentation. Identify passages in which Tannen presents her findings even-handedly, particularly in regard to male tendencies. What techniques does she use to make her conclusions acceptable to both male and female readers?

2. Tannen intersperses her writing with findings from academic research, such as the Leet-Pellegrini study, and personal anecdotes that illustrate the point she is making. Do you find her anecdotal evidence effective in illustrating her points? (Glossary: *Evidence*) Why or why not?

3. Tannen says, "Once again, the alignment in which women and men find themselves arrayed is asymmetrical" (7). What does she mean? Why do you think she uses the concepts of symmetry and asymmetry, terms more often associated with geometry, to describe male-female interaction? Why is her choice of words effective? (Glossary: *Diction*)

4. What is Tannen's tone in this essay? How do you think she achieves it? (Glossary: *Tone*)

LANGUAGE IN ACTION

Tannen's book *Talking from 9 to 5* (1994) deals with how to handle the different ways men and women communicate in a business setting. Problems at work that are created through gender-based misunderstandings can be significant, as indicated in the following excerpt from a communication seminar run by P. J. Poole, a company that specializes in such seminars. Using information in Tannen's essay, make a list of the specific problems gender-communication awareness can solve in work situations. What kinds of miscommunications might occur between men and women in the workplace? How might such communication create "systemic barriers—barriers that negatively impact individual productivity, morale, and job satisfaction"?

GENDER COMMUNICATION AWARENESS

Communication is a key issue facing today's organizations. Differences in gender communication styles can affect what gets done, how it gets done, who gets heard, who gets acknowledged, and who gets credit.
Consider that:

- Men and women communicate, approach work place challenges, solve problems, and provide leadership in remarkably different ways. What is interpreted as assertive in a man, can be viewed as aggressive in a woman.
- Not understanding these differences creates systemic barriers—barriers that negatively impact individual productivity, morale, and job satisfaction. Not to mention that inhibiting employee contribution has a negative impact on your organization's bottom line.

Misunderstandings and miscommunications between men and women happen every day for two reasons. First, we have different communication styles. Second, and more importantly, we do not know it—we think that everyone communicates in the same way.

Awareness, understanding, and valuing our different communication styles removes barriers created by misunderstandings. It ensures that men and women are flexible and able to adapt to different situations. It impacts their ability to work together, as well as their ability to get ahead in the organization. In other words, it affects their productivity.

Understanding and valuing our different communication styles will result in:

- successful communications,
- the reduction of gender conflicts,
- the improvement of working relationships, and
- increased productivity.

WRITING SUGGESTIONS

1. (*Writing from Experience*) Write an essay in which you discuss how closely your own experience mirrors Tannen's information. How valid are her findings, in your opinion? Do you conform to the gender styles presented in her essay, both in how you speak and how you listen? Do your friends? Have you ever thought about the motivations behind your conversational style, such as trying to be competitive or conciliatory? Have you ever had trouble communicating with a member of the opposite sex, especially someone with whom you had a close relationship? What happened? Does Tannen's article help you understand some of the communication pitfalls you have already experienced? Explain.

2. (*Writing from Reading*) Throughout her article, Tannen talks about the general classifications of "men" and "women" and the differences in how men and women communicate. Other essays in this chapter, however, indicate that using such broad classifications or labels may be dangerous or prejudicial. Drawing on the information in this chapter, write an essay in which you assess the pros and cons of making general characterizations for two such diverse groups as men and women. On the one hand, many studies show that there *are* profound differences in how the two genders approach the world and communicate. Understanding these differences may, in fact, help people get along with one another. On the other hand, such generalizations don't take individual variation into account. Consequently, they may encourage people to make judgments that don't necessarily apply to their specific situations. Do you think generalizations about gender can be harmful? Can they actually help fuel sexism, gender discrimination, and animosity between men and women? What is your opinion of the popular psychology books on this topic, such as John Gray's *Men Are from Mars, Women Are from Venus?* Do you think such books are helpful, or do you think they can do as much harm as good? Explain.

3. (*Writing from Research*) Over a period of several weeks, gather data about how men and women speak and interact. Record as many conversations as

you can in a variety of settings, including casual conversations over a meal, classroom discussions, informal chats, and one-on-one conversations. Be sure to include conversations from large as well as small groups and from same-gender and mixed-gender groups. It's also essential to let others know that you are writing down their conversations. As you record what people say, try to observe their general body language and movement patterns. When you have collected enough data, try to classify the various interactions, paying particular attention to the similarities and differences between men and women. (Glossary: *Division and Classification*) Who spoke the most? What did the men talk about? What did the women talk about? What were the differences between the mixed-gender settings and the same-gender settings? Write a paper in which you summarize your findings; then compare them to those of Tannen and the researchers cited in her essay. Do your findings support Tannen's claims concerning the prevalent nature of lecturer-listener interaction? Do you think men seek to establish hierarchy and women seek connection?

Gender Wars in Cyberspace

NATHAN COBB

Born in Newton, Massachusetts, on June 16, 1943, journalist Nathan Cobb began his writing career after graduating from Pennsylvania State University in 1965 with a B.A. in English. He joined the staff of the Boston Globe *in 1969 and has remained there as a feature writer for the Living and Sunday magazine sections. He is the coauthor of two books:* Love and Hate on the Tennis Court *(1977) and* Cityside/Countryside *(1980), a collection of his columns from the* Boston Globe.

Although recent studies have identified significant differences in the way men and women communicate, the advent of the Internet seemed to signal a change—an anonymous, gender-neutral forum in which men and women could express themselves without traditional forms of gender association. In the following selection, originally published in the Boston Globe *in March 1995, Cobb discusses how and why the gender-neutral ideal of Internet communication remains elusive.*

WRITING TO DISCOVER: *How do you communicate? Would you characterize yourself as confrontational or as conciliatory when you enter into a potential conflict? To what extent do your online communications—e-mails, chat-room dialogues, and so on—reflect your face-to-face communication style? Write about an instance or two of conflict, and relate your reactions, classifying them as best you can.*

Consider the Yo alert.

Yo?

Yo. Subscribers to ECHO, a small online service based in Manhattan, use the greeting to signify important messages when they converse with one another via computer. But there's a difference between those who Yo and those who don't.

"What we've found is that men tend to 'Yo' a lot more than women," says Stacy Horn, who founded ECHO five years ago. "And they're much more likely to 'Yo' strangers. Women simply do not 'Yo' strangers."

But wait. Isn't cyberspace supposed to be gender neutral, a place where women can feel empowered and men don't think they have to flex their pecs? Aren't the Internet and its commercial online siblings supposed to go beyond the notion that men are men and women are women, washing away this pre-Infobahn concept with rivers of sexless text? "Online, we don't know gender," declares Newton-based Internet analyst Daniel Dern.

5

A growing group of people beg to differ, no small number of them women. They contend not only that there are differences between male and female 'Netiquette—a.k.a. online manners—but also differences in the overall conversational styles used by men and women who "talk" via computer.

"Although a lot of people have said that online communication removes cues about gender, age, and background, that's not true," argues Laurel Sutton, a graduate student in linguistics at the University of California at Berkeley who has studied online discourse. "Everything that you communicate about yourself when you communicate face-to-face comes through when you communicate online. So men talk like men and women talk like women."

STILL A MAN'S CYBERWORLD

Statistically speaking, of course, it's still a man's cyberworld out there. Among the major online services, CompuServe estimates that 83 percent of its users are men, while America Online pegs its male subscribers at 84 percent. Prodigy claims a 60/40 male/female ratio among users. Nobody keeps figures for the Internet, the vast web of interconnected computer networks that is owned and operated by no single entity, but estimates of female participation run from 10 to 35 percent. Indeed, most of the computer culture is male-dominated.

If you don't think there's a shortage of women online, listen to the dialogue one recent evening inside an America Online "chat" room known as the Romance Connection, a kind of digital dating bar. When the lone female in the room departed—assuming she really was female—after entertaining the other 22 members of the group with a bit of soft-core titillation, there was an awkward pause.

"What are we going to do now?" one participant typed.   10

"Who wants to play the naked female?" someone else asked.

"Not me," came a response.

"Not me, either," came another.

"Well, if you can't fake it, don't volunteer," offered the first.

Most women who go online quickly learn that many such chat areas   15
and certain Internet newsgroups—places where cyberians sharing similar interests can post messages to one another—are spots where testosterone-based life-forms are likely to harass them, inquiring about their measurements and sexual preferences as if they've phoned 1–900–DIALSEX. "It's like walking into a real bad '70s disco," says David Fox, the author of *Love Bytes,* a new book about online dating. "The fact that people can be anonymous is a major factor. I mean, a 13-year-old can go around living his teenage fantasy of picking up women."

As a result, many women adopt gender-neutral screen names, switching from, say, Victoria to VBG, Nova to Vanity, and Marcia to Just Being Me.

"This way, if some jerk comes along you can always say you're a man," says Pleiades (real name: Phyllis), whose screen handle refers to the seven daughters of Atlas and Pleione but is apparently enough to throw off pursuers.

Almost everyone also agrees that men "flame" more than women, meaning they are more prone to firing off missives that are intended as insults or provocations. "For men, the ideal of the Internet is that it should be this exchange of conflicting views," says Susan Herring, a linguistics professor at University of Texas at Arlington who has written extensively about women's participation on computer networks. "But women are made uncomfortable by flaming. As little girls, women are taught to be nice. Little boys are taught to disagree and argue and even fight."

A recent case in point: Entering a debate on smoking in restaurants that was taking place in a newsgroup on the Internet, a user named Colleen politely staked out her position as a question. "Why is it necessary to smoke inside a restaurant?" she asked. In reply, a user named Peter instantly flamed. He announced he would not pay good money to eat if he couldn't smoke at the same time. "You people are complete and utter morons!" he declared.

"Women come online more to build relationships, to talk about issues," contends Susan William DeFife, the founding partner of Women's Leadership Connection (WLC), an online service linked to Prodigy.

Ask Rebecca Shnur of Easton, Pa., a WLC subscriber who effusively likens being online to an "all-night college bull session. It's been a long time since I've talked like this with women," she says.   20

Men tend to be less concerned about making permanent connections. "I think they're much more willing to just jump online and see where it goes," says DeFife. "And, of course, to flame."

If men tend to be flamers, do women tend to be flamees? Nancy Tamosaitis, a New York author who has written several books about the online world, thinks they do. "By expressing any kind of strong opinion, women tend to get flamed a lot more than men do," Tamosaitis says. "There's a real strong culture on Internet. Men feel they own it. It's like an old boys' club. They don't want women or newcomers, especially female newcomers."

When Tamosaitis is flamed, she points out, it's almost always by a man. "I can count the flames I've gotten from women on the fingers of both hands," she says. "And men seem to bring it to a personal level. A woman will say, 'You're out of place!' A man will say, 'You're ugly!'"

CONFRONTATION WORKS

But women who seek a softer, gentler information superhighway may find themselves sending messages into the wind. Says Sherry Terkle, an MIT professor and an authoritative voice on the subject of sociology and technology: "If you send out an online message that's inclusive, that includes many points of view, or that's conciliatory, you may get no response. And women are more likely to make that kind of communication, whereupon no message comes back.

"But if you make a controversial statement, maybe even an exaggeration, you're more likely to get responses. So the medium pushes people toward a controversial style. It rewards the quick jab. It encourages a kind of confrontational style, which men are more comfortable with." [25]

When Susan Herring, the University of Texas linguist, disseminated an electronic questionnaire on 'Netiquette, even some of the online comments about the survey itself took on male/female styles. "I hope this doesn't sound terribly rude, but a survey is one of the last things I want to see in my mailbox," apologized one woman in declining to respond. A man who also had better things to do was less polite. "What bothers me most," he declared, "are abuses of networking such as yours: unsolicited, lengthy, and intrusive postings designed to further others' research by wasting my time."

WOMEN ARE "LURKERS"

Meanwhile, research shows that women who go online tend to send fewer messages per capita than do men and that their messages are shorter. There is also a widespread belief that more women than men are "lurkers": people who go online to read other people's messages rather than to participate. "It's the same way you find many women sitting in physics class and acting like wallpaper," Terkle says, referring to male-dominated science classrooms. "They're just not comfortable because it matters who's in charge. It matters who seems to be in a position of power."

Even Michael O'Brien, an Internet magazine columnist who is by no means convinced that there is much difference between the online sexes ("I see fewer differences on the Internet than in everyday life"), allows that women "usually come across as the voice of reason. You almost never see a female counterflame. Men flame back and forth. Usually women just shut up and go away."

In her best-selling 1990 book, *You Just Don't Understand: Women & Men in Conversation,* Georgetown University linguist Deborah Tannen described men as being comfortable with the language of confrontation and women comfortable with consensus. A self-described e-mail junkie, Tannen sees much of the same behavior online. "Actually, I would say that the differences that typify men's and women's [offline] style actually get *exaggerated* online," she says. "I subscribe to very few universals, but one I believe in is that men are more likely to use opposition, or fighting, or even warlike images. Women are not as likely to do that. They're more likely to take things as a nasty attack."

Tannen recalls coming across a seemingly angry online message writ-   30
ten by a male graduate student that concluded with the command to
"get your hands off my Cyberspace!"

"I had an exchange with the fellow about it because it struck me, a
woman, as being fairly hostile and inappropriate," Tannen recalls. "But
then I realized I was overinterpreting the hostility of what to him was a
fairly ritualized and almost playful statement."

Nancy Rhine wishes more women would adopt this type of playful-
ness in cyberspace. Slightly more than a year ago, Rhine founded
Women's Wire, a minuscule online service (1,500 subscribers compared
to, say, American Online's 2 million), because she believed women
weren't participating enough online. Between 90 and 95 percent of her
subscribers are female, she says, and she contends that Women's Wire is a
more polite and less flame-filled place than other services.

"But there's a pro and con to that," she concedes "On the one hand,
this is a very comfortable environment. On the other hand, I sometimes
wish there were more characters posting things that were thought-
provoking and stimulating.

"Women are conditioned to be nice, to be the caretakers, and that's
the way it feels online here," Rhine says. "But I'd like to see us take more
risks. I'd like to see women be more outrageous online."

FOCUSING ON CONTENT

1. What is the "Yo alert" (1–4)? Why is it particularly relevant to Cobb's essay?

2. In what ways are chat areas and newsgroups like a "real bad '70s disco" (15)?
   How does harassment influence how people communicate on the Internet?

3. According to the experts quoted by Cobb, why are men far more likely than
   women to flame? How does this tendency reflect the different goals men and
   women have when they communicate over the Internet?

4. What is a "lurker" (27)? Why do many women choose to lurk?

5. What can result when the members of a group of Internet subscribers are almost entirely female? What are the advantages of all-female communication?
   What are the disadvantages?

FOCUSING ON WRITING

1. Cobb begins his essay with an unusual three-sentence sequence. "Consider
   the Yo alert. Yo? Yo." Why is "Yo" an effective subject with which to open
   his essay? Do you find the beginning of the essay effective in capturing your
   attention? (Glossary: *Beginnings and Endings*) Why or why not?

2. Look at the essay again, paying close attention to the credentials of the experts Cobb quotes to support his arguments. (Glossary: *Evidence*) What do
   they have in common? Why do you think Cobb chooses them for his essay?

3. Cobb's essay has a light tone, despite the fact that it addresses two potentially controversial subjects. First, as he acknowledges, the assumption that the Internet is gender blind is still prevalent, so his argument may not be well received by some people. Second, gender differences are always a volatile topic. How does Cobb attempt to present his material in a nonthreatening fashion? Identify several passages in which Cobb establishes his tone. (Glossary: *Tone*)

4. There has been much investigation of the new vocabulary spawned by the growth of the Internet. Even terms such as *e-mail* and *cyberspace*, which seem so ordinary now, were specialized terms in the early 1990s. Identify the Internet-specific vocabulary that Cobb uses in his piece. (Glossary: *Technical Language*) What does the use of such language indicate about Cobb's audience? (Glossary: *Audience*)

LANGUAGE IN ACTION

Several studies have explored how the different genders participate in various online discussions. The results of these studies agree with Cobb's anecdotal data—that men tend to post more, and longer, messages and that they tend to be more aggressive about promoting their views. Read the following excerpt from a 1993 study by S. C. Herring. Then jot down your thoughts about each posting. How did each make you react? Would you be more likely to respond to one or the other? Why? Discuss your reactions with your class. Why do you think gender is still so important in academic Internet discussion groups? How might women overcome the supposed "handicaps" of their communication style when participating in online discourse?

TABLE 1 Features of Women's and Men's Language

Women's Language	Men's Language
Attenuated assertions	Strong assertions
Apologies	Self-promotion
Explicit justifications	Presuppositions
Questions	Rhetorical questions
Personal orientation	Authoritative orientation
Supports others	Challenges others
	Humor/sarcasm

The examples below, taken from messages posted during the LINGUIST "issues" discussion, illustrate some of the features of each style.

Female Contributor: I am intrigued by your comment that work such as that represented in WFDT may not be as widely represented in LSA as other work because its argumentation style doesn't lend itself to falsification à la Popper. Could you say a bit more about what you mean here? I am interested because I think similar mismatches in argumentation are at stake in other areas of cognitive science, as well as because I study argumentation as a key (social and cognitive) tool for human knowledge construction.
[personal orientation, attenuation, questions, justification]

Male Contributor: It is obvious that there are two (and only two) paradigms for the conduct of scientific inquiry into an issue on which there is no consensus. One is [. . .]. But, deplorable as that may be, note that either paradigm (if pursued honestly) will lead to truth anyway. That is, whichever side is wrong will sooner or later discover that fact on its own. If, God forbid, autonomy and/or modularity should turn out to be His truth, then those who have other ideas will sooner or later find this out.

[authoritative orientation, strong assertions, sarcasm]

WRITING SUGGESTIONS

1. (*Writing from Experience*) One of the important aspects of Internet communications—and a reason many assume the Internet is gender neutral—is anonymity. Participants in online discourse are judged by their words alone and may reveal only as much about themselves as they wish. Think about your own Internet correspondence, whether via e-mail, chat rooms, newsgroups, or other online forums. Write an essay in which you explore how the anonymity of Internet correspondence affects you. Are you more willing to be confrontational or provocative in online communication? Have you developed an online persona that differs from your typical personality? Or does your online voice closely resemble your actual personality and face-to-face communication style? Do you think your gender influences how you use the Internet? Explain your reasoning.

2. (*Writing from Reading*) Consider the following quote from Nancy Tamosaitis: "There's a real strong culture on the Internet. Men feel they own it. It's like an old boys' club. They don't want women or newcomers, especially female newcomers" (22). Since 1995, when Cobb wrote his article, the Internet has become much less the domain of technology experts and far more a part of everyday life. Do you think Tamosaitis's quote is still valid? Write an essay in which you assess the current state of Internet communications and predict where they will go. Is there a chance that these communications can become the gender-neutral, inclusive forum so eagerly promoted by online service providers? Use Cobb's essay and your own observations to support your position.

3. (*Writing from Research*) Cobb quotes Nancy Rhine as wishing her woman-friendly online service, Women's Wire, contained more thought-provoking and controversial dialogue. Now, however, women have far more resources on the Web than they did even a few years ago. Investigate several sites that are specifically tailored for women. Sites such as The Electra Pages, Feminist.com, the National Organization for Women Web site, and the Women Homepage (MIT) are good places to start and have links for further inquiry. Compare the content and tone of the sites to some that are not gender specific or do not cater to a female audience. Write an essay in which you present your findings. What differences did you find among the various types of sites? Are the differences striking or subtle? Do you agree with Rhine's assessment of how women choose to communicate on the Web? Do the sites reflect an increased comfort level for women using the Web? Explain.

LANGUAGE IN USE:
The Language of Unity

Few things are more tedious than having to sit through a long, boring speech. On the other hand, few things are more inspiring than a good speech given by an eloquent speaker. A skilled orator is a performer, much like a musician. Instead of a beat, though, the speaker makes words flow and resonate. Instead of a melody, the message communicates rich images and compelling thoughts. The words of a speaker are more alive than those of a writer because the speaker can directly communicate the passion and conviction of the words to his or her audience. Nevertheless, the transcript of a good speech can still capture our attention.

The two speeches that follow have remarkable parallels, despite the fact that they were delivered more than one hundred years apart. Both writers were gifted public speakers, and both made compelling statements against racial injustice. Both used parallel constructions to help them deliver their messages and inspired their audiences with visions of a brighter future.

Sojourner Truth and Martin Luther King Jr. used their eloquence to blunt the prejudice and fear of their foes. Language was their weapon, and their intelligence, dignity, and conviction still resonate from their words. King's speech in particular has become part of our cultural consciousness.

WRITING TO DISCOVER: *Have you ever heard a speech that you found particularly inspiring or moving? Make some notes about why the speech or the speaker was so effective. How did the speech affect the way you now think about the speaker's subject?*

I Have a Dream
MARTIN LUTHER KING JR.

Martin Luther King Jr., son of a Baptist minister, was born in 1929 and ordained at the age of eighteen. King went on to study at Morehouse College, Crozer Theological Seminary, Boston University, and Chicago Theological Seminary. He first came to prominence in 1955 when he led a successful boycott against the segregated bus system of Montgomery, Alabama. As the first president of the Southern Christian Leadership Conference, King promoted a policy of massive but nonviolent resistance to racial injustice. The leading spokesman for the civil rights movement during the 1950s and 1960s, he also championed women's rights and protested the Vietnam War. In 1964 his efforts won him the Nobel Peace Prize. King was assassinated in April 1968 after he spoke at a rally in Memphis, Tennessee.

King delivered "I Have a Dream" in 1963 from the steps of the Lincoln Memorial to more than two hundred thousand people who had come to Washington, D.C., to demonstrate for civil rights. In this mighty sermon — replete with allusions to the Bible, the Negro spiritual tradition, and great documents and speeches of the past — King presented his indictment of the present and his vision of the future.

I am happy to join with you today in what will go down in history as the greatest demonstration for freedom in the history of our nation.

Five score years ago, a great American, in whose symbolic shadow we stand today, signed the Emancipation Proclamation. This momentous decree came as a great beacon light of hope to millions of Negro slaves who had been seared in the flames of withering injustice. It came as a joyous daybreak to end the long night of their captivity. But one hundred years later, the Negro still is not free. One hundred years later, the life of the Negro is still sadly crippled by the manacles of segregation and the chains of discrimination. One hundred years later, the Negro lives on a lonely island of poverty in the midst of a vast ocean of material prosperity. One hundred years later, the Negro is still anguished in the corners of American society and finds himself in exile in his own land. And so we have come here today to dramatize a shameful condition.

In a sense we have come to our nation's capital to cash a check. When the architects of our republic wrote the magnificent words of the Constitution and the Declaration of Independence, they were signing a promissory note to which every American was to fall heir. This note was the promise that all men — yes, Black men as well as white men — would be guaranteed the inalienable rights of life, liberty, and the pursuit of happiness.

It is obvious today that America has defaulted on this promissory note insofar as her citizens of color are concerned. Instead of honoring this sacred obligation, America has given the Negro people a bad check, a check which has come back marked "insufficient funds." But we refuse to believe that the bank of justice is bankrupt. We refuse to believe that there are insufficient funds in the great vaults of opportunity of this nation; and so we have come to cash this check, a check that will give us upon demand the riches of freedom and the security of justice.

We have also come to this hallowed spot to remind America of the   5
fierce urgency of *now*. This is no time to engage in the luxury of cooling off or to take the tranquilizing drug of gradualism. *Now* is the time to make real the promises of democracy. *Now* is the time to rise from the

dark and desolate valley of segregation to the sunlit path of racial justice. *Now* is the time to lift our nation from the quicksands of racial injustice to the solid rock of brotherhood. *Now* is the time to make justice a reality for all of God's children.

It would be fatal for the nation to overlook the urgency of the moment. This sweltering summer of the Negro's legitimate discontent will not pass until there is an invigorating autumn of freedom and equality. Nineteen sixty-three is not an end, but a beginning. And those who hope that the Negro needed to blow off steam and will now be content will have a rude awakening if the nation returns to business as usual. There will be neither rest nor tranquility in America until the Negro is granted his citizenship rights. The whirlwinds of revolt will continue to shake the foundations of our nation until the bright day of justice emerges.

But there is something that I must say to my people who stand on the warm threshold which leads into the palace of justice. In the process of gaining our rightful place, we must not be guilty of wrongful deeds. Let us not seek to satisfy our thirst for freedom by drinking from the cup of bitterness and hatred. We must forever conduct our struggle on the high plane of dignity and discipline. We must not allow our creative protest to degenerate into physical violence. Again and again we must rise to the majestic heights of meeting physical force with soul force. And the marvelous new militancy which has engulfed the Negro community must not lead us to a distrust of all white people; for many of our white brothers, as evidenced by their presence here today, have come to realize that their destiny is tied up with our destiny, and they have come to realize that their freedom is inextricably bound to our freedom.

We cannot walk alone. And as we walk we must make the pledge that we shall always march ahead. We cannot turn back. There are those who are asking the devotees of civil rights, "When will you be satisfied?" We can never be satisfied as long as the Negro is the victim of the unspeakable horrors of police brutality. We can never be satisfied as long as our bodies, heavy with the fatigue of travel, cannot gain lodging in the motels of the highways and the hotels of the cities. We cannot be satisfied as long as the Negro's basic mobility is from a smaller ghetto to a larger one. We can never be satisfied as long as our children are stripped of their selfhood and robbed of their dignity by signs stating "For Whites Only." We cannot be satisfied as long as the Negro in Mississippi cannot vote and a Negro in New York believes he has nothing for which to vote. No, no, we are not satisfied, and we will not be satisfied until justice rolls down like waters and righteousness like a mighty stream.

I am not unmindful that some of you have come here out of great trials and tribulations. Some of you have come fresh from narrow jail cells. Some of you have come from areas where your quest for freedom left you battered by the storms of persecution and staggered by the winds of police brutality. You have been the veterans of creative suffering. Continue to work with the faith that unearned suffering is redemptive.

Go back to Mississippi, and go back to Alabama. Go back to South Carolina. Go back to Georgia. Go back to Louisiana. Go back to the slums and ghettos of our Northern cities, knowing that somehow this situation can and will be changed. Let us not wallow in the valley of despair.   10

I say to you today, my friends, even though we face the difficulties of today and tomorrow, I still have a dream. It is a dream deeply rooted in the American dream. I have a dream that one day this nation will rise up and live out the true meaning of its creed: "We hold these truths to be self-evident, that all men are created equal." I have a dream that one day, on the red hills of Georgia, sons of former slaves and the sons of former slave owners will be able to sit down together at the table of brotherhood. I have a dream that one day even the state of Mississippi, a state sweltering with the heat of injustice, sweltering with the heat of oppression, will be transformed into an oasis of freedom and justice. I have a dream that my four little children will one day live in a nation where they will not be judged by the color of their skin, but by the content of their character.

I have a dream today. I have a dream that one day down in Alabama —with its vicious racists, with its governor's lips dripping with the words of interposition and nullification—one day right there in Alabama, little Black boys and Black girls will be able to join hands with little white boys and white girls as sisters and brothers.

I have a dream today. I have a dream that one day every valley shall be exalted and every hill and mountain shall be made low, the rough places will be made plain and the crooked places will be made straight, and the glory of the Lord shall be revealed, and all flesh shall see it together.

This is our hope. This is the faith that I go back to the South with. And with this faith we will be able to hew out of the mountain of despair a stone of hope. With this faith we will be able to transform the jangling discords of our nation into a beautiful symphony of brotherhood. With this faith we will be able to work together, to play together, to struggle together, to go to jail together, to stand up for freedom together, knowing that we will be free one day.

And this will be the day—this will be the day when all of God's children will be able to sing with new meaning: 15

> My country, 'tis of thee,
> Sweet land of liberty,
>   Of thee I sing;
> Land where my fathers died,
> Land of the Pilgrims' pride,
> From every mountainside
>   Let freedom ring.

And if America is to be a great nation, this must become true.

And so let freedom ring from the prodigious hilltops of New Hampshire. Let freedom ring from the mighty mountains of New York. Let freedom ring from the heightening Alleghenies of Pennsylvania. Let freedom ring from the snow-capped Rockies of Colorado. Let freedom ring from the curvaceous slopes of California.

But not only that. Let freedom ring from Stone Mountain of Georgia. Let freedom ring from Lookout Mountain of Tennessee. Let freedom ring from every hill and molehill of Mississippi. "From every mountainside let freedom ring."

And when this happens—when we allow freedom to ring, when we let it ring from every village and every hamlet, from every state and every city—we will be able to speed up that day when all of God's children, Black men and white men, Jews and Gentiles, Protestants and Catholics, will be able to join hands and sing in the words of the old Negro spiritual: "Free at last! Free at last! Thank God Almighty. We are free at last!"

And Ain't I a Woman?

SOJOURNER TRUTH

Sojourner Truth was born a slave named Isabella in Ulster County, New York, in 1797. Freed by the New York State Emancipation Act of 1827, she went to New York City and underwent a profound religious transformation. She worked as a domestic servant and, in her active evangelism, tried to reform prostitutes. Adopting the name Sojourner Truth in 1843, she became a traveling preacher and abolitionist.

Although she remained illiterate, Truth's compelling presence gripped her audience as she spoke eloquently about emancipation and women's rights. After the Civil War, she worked to provide education and employment for emancipated slaves until her death in 1883.

Well, children, where there is so much racket there must be something out of kilter. I think that 'twixt the Negroes of the South and the women at the North, all talking about rights, the white men will be in a fix pretty soon. But what's all this here talking about?

That man over there says that women need to be helped into carriages, and lifted over ditches, and to have the best place everywhere. Nobody ever helps me into carriages, or over mud puddles, or gives me any best place! And ain't I a woman? Look at me! Look at my arm. I have plowed and planted, and gathered into barns, and no man could head me! And ain't I a woman? I could work as much and eat as much as a man—when I could get it—and bear the lash as well! And ain't I a woman? I have borne thirteen children, and seen them most all sold off to slavery, and when I cried out with my mother's grief, none but Jesus heard me! And ain't I a woman?

Then they talk about this thing in the head; what's this they call it? [Intellect, someone whispers.] That's it, honey. What's that got to do with women's rights or Negro's rights? If my cup won't hold but a pint, and yours holds a quart, wouldn't you be mean not to let me have my little half-measure full?

Then that little man in black there, he says women can't have as much rights as men, 'cause Christ wasn't a woman! Where did your Christ come from? Where did your Christ come from? From God and a woman! Man had nothing to do with him.

If the first woman God ever made was strong enough to turn the world upside down all alone, these women together ought to be able to turn it back, and get it right side up again! And now they is asking to do it, the men better let them.

Obliged to you for hearing me, and now old Sojourner ain't got nothing more to say.

5

MAKING CONNECTIONS: WRITING SUGGESTIONS

1. King and Truth spoke out about the injustice they saw around them. What social cause do you find the most compelling today? Human rights? AIDS awareness? Prevention of domestic abuse? Ending racial prejudice? Imagine that you have been asked to make a speech that will be heard not only by those involved with your cause but by a large general audience. Using the techniques of Truth and King (brevity, powerful metaphors, vivid imagery, parallelism, and so on), write a speech that addresses your topic of concern. Be prepared to give your speech to your class.

2. The speeches of both King and Truth hold out hope for the future. They both envision a future in which the status quo is, as Truth states, turned upside down. And what they envisioned did, to some extent, come to pass. Write an essay in which you project how Truth and King would react to the world as we know it today. What do you think would please them? Disappoint them? How might their reactions differ, given their different eras and experiences? What do you think they would want to change in our society? Explain your reasoning.

3. Like King and Truth, Abraham Lincoln spoke persuasively and forcefully about the problems of his time, especially when he faced the challenge of healing a sharply divided country after the Civil War. Read Lincoln's "Second Inaugural Address" (pp. 558–59) and his "Gettysburg Address" (pp. 563–64). Then write an essay in which you compare and contrast the rhetorical strategies of these three orators. (Glossary: *Comparison and Contrast*)

4. Sojourner Truth's journey from slave to activist, to speaker, and, posthumously, to cultural icon was an arduous and circuitous one. Research her life. There are several biographies about her, including Nell Irvin Painter's acclaimed *Sojourner Truth: A Life, a Symbol,* which can offer a foundation for your research. Write an essay in which you present background information about her life and assess her strengths and weaknesses. How was she able to overcome and transcend the deprivations and indignities of her early years? What role did religion play in her life and accomplishments? Consider what she might have done had she lived during the era of Martin Luther King Jr. Do you think her abilities and beliefs would be effective in an age of mass media? Why or why not?

9

LANGUAGE
AND CULTURE

Shakespeare in the Bush

LAURA BOHANNAN

Are people alike everywhere? Are all peoples subject to the same feelings, driven by the same motivations? Do great stories of human endeavor carry identical messages to every audience, regardless of its background? Laura Bohannan, a retired anthropologist from the University of Illinois at Chicago, believed in the universality of human experience until she attempted to retell the story of Hamlet to members of a tribe in West Africa. She found that it was very difficult indeed to translate a classic tale from one language and culture to another. An audience that has no concept of ghosts, is accustomed to chiefs who have many wives, and ascribes madness to witchcraft must necessarily reinterpret Hamlet in ways so fundamental that the thrust of the original story is lost. In both word and concept, Shakespeare's vision of human tragedy becomes unrecognizable when its "true meaning" is interpreted by the wise elders of a distant, illiterate tribe whose existence he could not have imagined. Bohannan's article was first published in Natural History *magazine in 1966.*

WRITING TO DISCOVER: *Ponder the question of whether all peoples are essentially the same or fundamentally different, and write down your thoughts. If we are all human, aren't we the same? If we are fundamentally the same, though, why is there so much emphasis on the differences—both positive and negative—among cultures?*

Just before I left Oxford for the Tiv in West Africa, conversation turned to the season at Stratford. "You Americans," said a friend, "often have difficulty with Shakespeare. He was, after all, a very English poet, and one can easily misinterpret the universal by misunderstanding the particular."

I protested that human nature is pretty much the same the whole world over; at least the general plot and motivation of the greater tragedies would always be clear—everywhere—although some details of custom might have to be explained and difficulties of translation might produce other slight changes. To end an argument we could not conclude, my friend gave me a copy of *Hamlet* to study in the African bush: it would, he hoped, lift my mind above its primitive surroundings, and possibly I might, by prolonged meditation, achieve the grace of correct interpretation.

It was my second field trip to that African tribe, and I thought myself ready to live in one of its remote sections—an area difficult to cross even on foot. I eventually settled on the hillock of a very knowledgeable old man, the head of a homestead of some hundred and forty people, all of whom were either his close relatives or their wives and children. Like the other elders of the vicinity, the old man spent most of his time performing ceremonies seldom seen these days in the more accessible parts of the tribe. I was delighted. Soon there would be three months of enforced isolation and leisure, between the harvest that takes place just before the rising of the swamps and the clearing of new farms when the water goes down. Then, I thought, they would have even more time to perform ceremonies and explain them to me.

I was quite mistaken. Most of the ceremonies demanded the presence of elders from several homesteads. As the swamps rose, the old men found it too difficult to walk from one homestead to the next, and the ceremonies gradually ceased. As the swamps rose even higher, all activities but one came to an end. The women brewed beer from maize and millet. Men, women, and children sat on their hillocks and drank it.

People began to drink at dawn. By midmorning the whole homestead was singing, dancing, and drumming. When it rained, people had to sit inside their huts: there they drank and sang or they drank and told stories. In any case, by noon or before, I either had to join the party or retire to my own hut and my books. "One does not discuss serious matters when there is beer. Come, drink with us." Since I lacked their capacity for the thick native beer, I spent more and more time with *Hamlet*. Before the end of the second month, grace descended on me. I was quite sure that *Hamlet* had only one possible interpretation, and that one universally obvious.

Early every morning, in the hope of having some serious talk before the beer party, I used to call on the old man at his reception hut—a circle of posts supporting a thatched roof above a low mud wall to keep out wind and rain. One day I crawled through the low doorway and

5

found most of the men of the homestead sitting huddled in their ragged cloths on stools, low plank beds, and reclining chairs, warming themselves against the chill of the rain around a smoky fire. In the center were three pots of beer. The party had started.

The old man greeted me cordially. "Sit down and drink." I accepted a large calabash full of beer, poured some into a small drinking gourd, and tossed it down. Then I poured some more into the same gourd for the man second in seniority to my host before I handed my calabash over to a young man for further distribution. Important people shouldn't ladle beer themselves.

"It is better like this," the old man said, looking at me approvingly and plucking at the thatch that had caught in my hair. "You should sit and drink with us more often. Your servants tell me that when you are not with us, you sit inside your hut looking at a paper."

The old man was acquainted with four kinds of "papers": tax receipts, bride price receipts, court fee receipts, and letters. The messenger who brought him letters from the chief used them mainly as a badge of office, for he always knew what was in them and told the old man. Personal letters for the few who had relatives in the government or mission stations were kept until someone went to a large market where there was a letter writer and reader. Since my arrival, letters were brought to me to be read. A few men also brought me bride price receipts, privately, with requests to change the figures to a higher sum. I found moral arguments were of no avail, since in-laws are fair game, and the technical hazards of forgery difficult to explain to an illiterate people. I did not wish them to think me silly enough to look at any such papers for days on end, and I hastily explained that my "paper" was one of the "things of long ago" of my country.

"Ah," said the old man. "Tell us."   10

I protested that I was not a storyteller. Story telling is a skilled art among them; their standards are high, and the audiences critical — and vocal in their criticism. I protested in vain. This morning they wanted to hear a story while they drank. They threatened to tell me no more stories until I told them one of mine. Finally, the old man promised that no one would criticize my style "for we know you are struggling with our language." "But," put in one of the elders, "you must explain what we do not understand, as we do when we tell you our stories." Realizing that here was my chance to prove *Hamlet* universally intelligible, I agreed.

The old man handed me some more beer to help me on with my storytelling. Men filled their long wooden pipes and knocked coals from the fire to place in the pipe bowls; then, puffing contentedly, they sat back to listen. I began in the proper style, "Not yesterday, not yesterday, but long ago, a thing occurred. One night three men were keeping watch outside the homestead of the great chief, when suddenly they saw the former chief approach them."

"Why was he no longer their chief?"

"He was dead," I explained. "That is why they were troubled and afraid when they saw him."

"Impossible," began one of the elders, handing his pipe on to his neighbor, who interrupted, "Of course it wasn't the dead chief. It was an omen sent by a witch. Go on."   15

Slightly shaken, I continued. "One of these three was a man who knew things" — the closest translation for scholar, but unfortunately it also meant witch. The second elder looked triumphantly at the first. "So he spoke to the dead chief saying, 'Tell us what we must do so you may rest in your grave,' but the dead chief did not answer. He vanished, and they could see him no more. Then the man who knew things — his name was Horatio — said this event was the affair of the dead chief's son, Hamlet."

There was a general shaking of heads round the circle. "Had the dead chief no living brothers? Or was this son the chief?"

"No," I replied. "That is, he had one living brother who became the chief when the elder brother died."

The old men muttered: such omens were matters for chiefs and elders, not for youngsters; no good could come of going behind a chief's back; clearly Horatio was not a man who knew things.

"Yes, he was," I insisted, shooing a chicken away from my beer. "In our country the son is next to the father. The dead chief's younger brother had become the great chief. He had also married his elder brother's widow only about a month after the funeral."   20

"He did well," the old man beamed and announced to the others, "I told you that if we knew more about Europeans, we would find they really were very like us. In our country also," he added to me, "the younger brother marries the elder brother's widow and becomes the father of his children. Now, if your uncle, who married your widowed mother, is your father's full brother, then he will be a real father to you. Did Hamlet's father and uncle have one mother?"

His question barely penetrated my mind; I was too upset and thrown too far off balance by having one of the most important elements of *Hamlet* knocked straight out of the picture. Rather uncertainly I said that I thought they had the same mother, but I wasn't sure — the story didn't say. The old man told me severely that these genealogical details made all the difference and that when I got home I must ask the elders about it. He shouted out the door to one of his younger wives to bring his goatskin bag.

Determined to save what I could of the mother motif, I took a deep breath and began again. "The son Hamlet was very sad because his mother had married again so quickly. There was no need for her to do so, and it is our custom for a widow not to go to her next husband until she has mourned for two years."

"Two years is too long," objected the wife, who had appeared with the old man's battered goatskin bag. "Who will hoe your farms for you while you have no husband?"

"Hamlet," I retorted without thinking, "was old enough to hoe his   25
mother's farms himself. There was no need for her to remarry." No one
looked convinced. I gave up. "His mother and the great chief told Hamlet
not to be sad, for the great chief himself would be a father to Hamlet.
Furthermore, Hamlet would be the next chief: therefore he must stay to
learn the things of a chief. Hamlet agreed to remain, and all the rest went
off to drink beer."

While I paused, perplexed at how to render Hamlet's disgusted soliloquy to an audience convinced that Claudius and Gertrude had behaved
in the best possible manner, one of the younger men asked me who had
married the other wives of the dead chief.

"He had no other wives," I told him.

"But a chief must have many wives! How else can he brew beer and
prepare food for all his guests?"

I said firmly that in our country even chiefs had only one wife, that they
had servants to do their work, and that they paid them from tax money.

It was better, they returned, for a chief to have many wives and sons   30
who would help him hoe his farms and feed his people; then everyone loved
the chief who gave much and took nothing—taxes were a bad thing.

I agreed with the last comment, but for the rest fell back on their favorite way of fobbing off my questions: "That is the way it is done, so
that is how we do it."

I decided to skip the soliloquy. Even if Claudius was here thought
quite right to marry his brother's widow, there remained the poison
motif, and I knew they would disapprove of fratricide. More hopefully I
resumed, "That night Hamlet kept watch with the three who had seen
his dead father. The dead chief again appeared, and although the others
were afraid, Hamlet followed his dead father off to one side. When they
were alone, Hamlet's dead father spoke."

"Omens can't talk!" The old man was emphatic.

"Hamlet's dead father wasn't an omen. Seeing him might have been
an omen, but he was not." My audience looked as confused as I sounded.
"It *was* Hamlet's dead father. It was a thing we call a 'ghost.'" I had to
use the English word, for unlike many of the neighboring tribes, these
people didn't believe in the survival after death of any individuating part
of the personality.

"What is a 'ghost'? An omen?"   35

"No, a 'ghost' is someone who is dead but who walks around and
can talk, and people can hear him and see him but not touch him."

They objected. "One can touch zombies."

"No, no! It was not a dead body the witches had animated to sacrifice
and eat. No one else made Hamlet's dead father walk. He did it himself."

"Dead men can't walk," protested my audience as one man.

I was quite willing to compromise. "A 'ghost' is the dead man's   40
shadow."

But again they objected. "Dead men cast no shadows."

"They do in my country," I snapped.

The old man quelled the babble of disbelief that arose immediately and told me with that insincere, but courteous, agreement one extends to the fancies of the young, ignorant, and superstitious, "No doubt in your country the dead can also walk without being zombies." From the depths of his bag he produced a withered fragment of kola nut, bit off one end to show it wasn't poisoned, and handed me the rest as a peace offering.

"Anyhow," I resumed, "Hamlet's dead father said that his own brother, the one who became chief, had poisoned him. He wanted Hamlet to avenge him. Hamlet believed this in his heart, for he did not like his father's brother." I took another swallow of beer. "In the country of the great chief, living in the same homestead, for it was a very large one, was an important elder who was often with the chief to advise and help him. His name was Polonius. Hamlet was courting his daughter, but her father and her brother . . . [I cast hastily about for some tribal analogy] warned her not to let Hamlet visit her when she was alone on her farm, for he would be a great chief and so could not marry her."

"Why not?" asked the wife, who had settled down on the edge of the   45
old man's chair. He frowned at her for asking stupid questions and growled, "They lived in the same homestead."

"This was not the reason," I informed them. "Polonius was a stranger who lived in the homestead because he helped the chief, not because he was a relative."

"Then why couldn't Hamlet marry her?"

"He could have," I explained, "but Polonius didn't think he would. After all, Hamlet was a man of great importance who ought to marry a chief's daughter, for in his country a man could have only one wife. Polonius was afraid that if Hamlet made love to his daughter, then no one else would give a high price for her."

"That might be true," remarked one of the shrewder elders, "but a chief's son would give his mistress's father enough presents and patronage to more than make up the difference. Polonius sounds like a fool to me."

"Many people think he was," I agreed. "Meanwhile Polonius sent his   50
son Laertes off to Paris to learn the things of the country, for it was the homestead of a very great chief indeed. Because he was afraid that Laertes might waste a lot of money on beer and women and gambling, or get into trouble by fighting, he sent one of his servants to Paris secretly, to spy out what Laertes was doing. One day Hamlet came upon Polonius's daughter Ophelia. He behaved so oddly he frightened her. Indeed" — I was fumbling for words to express the dubious quality of Hamlet's madness — "the chief and many others had also noticed that when Hamlet talked one could understand the words but not what they meant. Many people thought that he had become mad." My audience suddenly became much more attentive. "The great chief wanted to know what was wrong with Hamlet, so he sent

for two of Hamlet's age mates [school friends would have taken long explanation] to talk to Hamlet and find out what troubled his heart. Hamlet, seeing that they had been bribed by the chief to betray him, told them nothing. Polonius, however, insisted that Hamlet was mad because he had been forbidden to see Ophelia, whom he loved."

"Why," inquired a bewildered voice, "should anyone bewitch Hamlet on that account?"

"Bewitch him?"

"Yes, only witchcraft can make anyone mad, unless, of course, one sees the beings that lurk in the forest."

I stopped being a storyteller, took out my notebook and demanded to be told more about these two causes of madness. Even while they spoke and I jotted notes, I tried to calculate the effect of this new factor on the plot. Hamlet had not been exposed to the beings that lurk in the forests. Only his relatives in the male line could bewitch him. Barring relatives not mentioned by Shakespeare, it had to be Claudius who was attempting to harm him. And, of course, it was.

For the moment I staved off questions by saying that the great chief   55
also refused to believe that Hamlet was mad for the love of Ophelia and nothing else. "He was sure that something much more important was troubling Hamlet's heart."

"Now Hamlet's age mates," I continued, "had brought with them a famous storyteller. Hamlet decided to have this man tell the chief and all his homestead a story about a man who had poisoned his brother because he desired his brother's wife and wished to be chief himself. Hamlet was sure the great chief could not hear the story without making a sign if he was indeed guilty, and then he would discover whether his dead father had told him the truth."

The old man interrupted, with deep cunning, "Why should a father lie to his son?" he asked.

I hedged: "Hamlet wasn't sure that it really was his dead father." It was impossible to say anything, in that language, about devil-inspired visions.

"You mean," he said, "it actually was an omen, and he knew witches sometimes send false ones. Hamlet was a fool not to go to one skilled in reading omens and divining the truth in the first place. A man-who-sees-the-truth could have told him how his father died, if he really had been poisoned, and if there was witchcraft in it; then Hamlet could have called the elders to settle the matter."

The shrewd elder ventured to disagree. "Because his father's brother   60
was a great chief, one-who-sees-the-truth might therefore have been afraid to tell it. I think it was for that reason that a friend of Hamlet's father—a witch and an elder—sent an omen so his friend's son would know. Was the omen true?"

"Yes," I said, abandoning ghosts and the devil; a witch-sent omen it would have to be. "It was true, for when the storyteller was telling his tale before all the homestead, the great chief rose in fear. Afraid that Hamlet knew his secret, he planned to have him killed."

The stage set of the next bit presented some difficulties of translation. I began cautiously. "The great chief told Hamlet's mother to find out from her son what he knew. But because a woman's children are always first in her heart, he had the important elder Polonius hide behind a cloth that hung against the wall of Hamlet's mother's sleeping hut. Hamlet started to scold his mother for what she had done."

There was a shocked murmur from everyone. A man should never scold his mother.

"She called out in fear, and Polonius moved behind the cloth. Shouting, 'A rat!' Hamlet took his machete and slashed through the cloth." I paused for dramatic effect. "He had killed Polonius!"

The old men looked at each other in supreme disgust. "That Polonius   65 truly was a fool and a man who knew nothing! What child would not know enough to shout, 'It's me!'" With a pang, I remembered that these people are ardent hunters, always armed with bow, arrow, and machete; at the first rustle in the grass an arrow is aimed and ready, and the hunter shouts "Game!" If no human voice answers immediately, the arrow speeds on its way. Like a good hunter Hamlet had shouted, "A rat!"

I rushed in, to save Polonius's reputation. "Polonius did speak. Hamlet heard him. But he thought it was the chief and wished to kill him earlier that evening. . . ." I broke down, unable to describe to these pagans, who had no belief in individual after-life, the difference between dying at one's prayers and dying "unhousell'd, disappointed, unaneled."

This time I had shocked my audience seriously. "For a man to raise his hand against his father's brother and the one who has become his father—that is a terrible thing. The elders ought to let such a man be bewitched."

I nibbled at my kola nut in some perplexity, then pointed out that after all the man had killed Hamlet's father.

"No," pronounced the old man, speaking less to me than to the young men sitting behind the elders. "If you father's brother has killed your father, you must appeal to your father's age mates; *they* may avenge him. No man may use violence against his senior relative." Another thought struck him, "But if his father's brother had indeed been wicked enough to bewitch Hamlet and make him mad that would be a good story indeed, for it would be his fault that Hamlet, being mad, no longer had any sense and thus was ready to kill his father's brother."

There was a murmur of applause. *Hamlet* was again a good story to   70 them, but it no longer seemed quite the same story to me. As I thought over the coming complications of plot and motive, I lost courage and decided to skim over dangerous ground quickly.

"The great chief," I went on, "was not sorry that Hamlet had killed Polonius. It gave him a reason to send Hamlet away, with his two treacherous mates, with letters to a chief of a far country, saying that Hamlet should be killed. But Hamlet changed the writing on their papers, so that the chief killed his age mates instead." I encountered a reproachful glare from one of the men whom I had told undetectable forgery was not merely immoral but beyond human skill. I looked the other way.

"Before Hamlet could return, Laertes came back for his father's funeral. The great chief told him Hamlet had killed Polonius. Laertes swore to kill Hamlet because of this, and because his sister Ophelia, hearing her father had been killed by the man she loved, went mad and drowned in the river."

"Have you already forgotten what we told you?" The old man was reproachful. "One cannot take vengeance on a madman; Hamlet killed Polonius in his madness. As for the girl, she not only went mad, she was drowned. Only witches can make people drown. Water itself can't hurt anything. It is merely something one drinks and bathes in."

I began to get cross. "If you don't like the story, I'll stop."

The old man made soothing noises and himself poured me some more beer. "You tell the story well, and we are listening. But it is clear that the elders of your country have never told you what the story really means. No, don't interrupt! We believe you when you say your marriage customs are different, or your clothes and weapons. But people are the same everywhere; therefore, there are always witches and it is we, the elders, who know how witches work. We told you it was the great chief who wished to kill Hamlet, and now your own words have proved us right. Who were Ophelia's male relatives?"

"There were only her father and her brother." *Hamlet* was clearly out of my hands.

"There must have been many more; this also you must ask of your elders when you get back to your country. From what you tell us, since Polonius was dead, it must have been Laertes who killed Ophelia, although I do not see the reason for it."

We had emptied one pot of beer, and the old men argued the point with slightly tipsy interest. Finally one of them demanded of me, "What did the servant of Polonius say on his return?"

With difficulty I recollected Reynaldo and his mission. "I don't think he did return before Polonius was killed."

"Listen," said the elder, "and I will tell you how it was and how your story will go, then you may tell me if I am right. Polonius knew his son would get into trouble, and so he did. He had many fines to pay for fighting, and debts from gambling. But he had only two ways of getting money quickly. One was to marry off his sister at once, but it is difficult to find a man who will marry a woman desired by the son of a chief. For if the chief's heir commits adultery with your wife, what can you do? Only a fool calls a case against a man who will someday be his judge. Therefore Laertes had to take the second way: he killed his sister by witchcraft, drowning her so he could secretly sell her body to the witches."

I raised an objection. "They found her body and buried it. Indeed Laertes jumped into the grave to see his sister once more—so, you see, the body was truly there. Hamlet, who had just come back, jumped in after him."

"What did I tell you?" The elder appealed to the others. "Laertes was up to no good with his sister's body. Hamlet prevented him, because the chief's heir, like a chief, does not wish any other man to grow rich and powerful. Laertes would be angry, because he would have killed his sister without benefit to himself. In our country he would try to kill Hamlet for that reason. Is this not what happened?"

"More or less," I admitted. "When the great chief found Hamlet was still alive, he encouraged Laertes to try to kill Hamlet and arranged a fight with machetes between them. In the fight both young men were wounded to death. Hamlet's mother drank the poisoned beer that the chief meant for Hamlet in case he won the fight. When he saw his mother die of poison, Hamlet, dying, managed to kill his father's brother with his machete."

"You see, I was right!" exclaimed the elder.

"That was a very good story," added the old man, "and you told it   85
with very few mistakes. There was just one more error, at the very end. The poison Hamlet's mother drank was obviously meant for the survivor of the fight, whichever it was. If Laertes had won, the great chief would have poisoned him, for no one would know that he arranged Hamlet's death. Then, too, he need not fear Laertes' witchcraft; it takes a strong heart to kill one's only sister by witchcraft.

"Sometime," concluded the old man, gathering his ragged toga about him, "you must tell us some more stories of your country. We, who are elders, will instruct you in their true meaning, so that when you return to your own land your elders will see that you have not been sitting in the bush, but among those who know things and who have taught you wisdom."

FOCUSING ON CONTENT

1. In the opening paragraph, Bohannan quotes her English friend as saying that "one can easily misinterpret the universal by misunderstanding the particular." How does this comment relate to Bohannan's own interpretation of *Hamlet*? How does it relate to the response to *Hamlet* of her African audience?

2. Why does Bohannan agree to tell the story of *Hamlet* to the tribespeople? (Glossary: *Purpose*)

3. Bohannan intersperses her retelling of *Hamlet* with a narrative about the behavior of the tribal members listening to the story. Why do you think she includes

details about their sharing the beer and the kola nut? Why does she bring in the commentary of the old man's wife (45) and that of the "shrewd" elder (60)?

4. What familiar English words and cultural concepts is Bohannan unable to translate directly into the language of her audience? What are some of the misunderstandings that arose as a result? How else might Bohannan have tried to translate the words or explain the concepts?

5. At one point (54), Bohannan abandons *Hamlet* for a few moments in order to take notes. Both she and the elders are authorities in their own cultures. When it comes to storytelling, however, they behave very differently. Discuss these differences and the reasons for them.

6. Near the end of the essay (75), the old man remarks that "people are the same everywhere." How does this comment reflect Bohannan's theme? Why is it ironic? (Glossary: *Irony*) What do both the comment and the theme have to do with language?

FOCUSING ON WRITING

1. The tone of the essay is humorous throughout. (Glossary: *Tone*) How does humor serve Bohannan's purpose?

2. "Shakespeare in the Bush" is really more than one narrative: Shakespeare's story is one narrative, Bohannan's retelling is another, and the chief's interpretation is yet another. How does Bohannan organize the three narratives so that readers don't get confused? (Glossary: *Narration* and *Organization*)

3. How effective is Bohannan's conclusion? Do you think the story needs more of a resolution? Why or why not? (Glossary: *Endings*)

LANGUAGE IN ACTION

Spanglish is the result of the impulse to bridge two languages and cultures: Spanish and English. The following excerpt is from "It's the Talk of Nueva New York: The Hybrid Called Spanglish," by Lizette Alvarez, which first appeared in the *New York Times* on March 25, 1997. Study both examples of Spanglish and Alvarez's translations of them, and then write about your own reactions to Spanglish. Do you think a hybrid language might have helped Bohannan convey more accurately the story of *Hamlet* to the Tiv people?

TALKING THE TALK

Of the two basic forms of Spanglish, borrowing—saying English words "Spanish style" and spelling them accordingly—is more common among first-generation speakers; later generations tend to switch back and forth. Here are examples of the hybrid language—often spoken with a sense of humor—that has vaulted from streets to talk shows to the pages of magazines like *Latina* and *generation ñ*.

bacuncliner: vacuum cleaner
biper: beeper, pager
boyla: boiler
chileando: chilling out
choping: shopping
fafu: fast food
jangear: hang out

joldoperos: muggers, holdup artists
liqueo: leak
maicrogüey: microwave oven
pulóver: T-shirt
roofo: roof
sangüiche: sandwich
tensén: 10-cent store, like Kmart or Woolworth's

Spanglish

EL Oye, me estoy frisando y el estin está broken—close the door. ¿Vamos a lonchar, or what? I need to eat before I go to my new job as a chiroquero.

ELLA ¿Quieres que te cocine some rice en la jitachi, or should I just get you some confley con leche? By the way, you embarkated me el otro día. ¿What did you do, pick up some fafu en vez de ir al restaurante where I was waiting? Eres tan chipero.

Translation

HE Hey, I'm freezing and the steam [or heat] is broken—close the door. Are we going to have lunch or what? I need to eat before I go to my new job as a Sheetrocker.

SHE Do you want me to cook you some rice in the Hitachi [catchall term for all steam cookers], or should I just get you some cornflakes [ditto for any kind of cereal] with milk? By the way, you stood me up the other day. What did you do, pick up some fast food instead of going to the restaurant where I was waiting? You're so cheap.

WRITING SUGGESTIONS

1. (*Writing from Experience*) Laura Bohannan may have been "quite sure that *Hamlet* had only one possible interpretation, and that one universally obvious," but she is not the only interpreter of the play to struggle with her audience over concepts such as ghosts, madness, and incest. English-speaking audiences experience some of the same problems with a four-hundred-year-old story about a quasi-historical event obscured in the mists of medieval Europe, though not to the extent that the Tiv did. There are several excellent versions of *Hamlet* available on film, notably those featuring the performances of Laurence Olivier, Mel Gibson, and Kenneth Branagh. View the Olivier version, followed by either or both of the others. Then write a paper analyzing the actors' different interpretations of the concepts of ghosts, madness, and incest.

2. (*Writing from Reading*) The Tiv elders in Laura Bohannan's essay occupy a place of major importance within the community. Write a brief paper describing the powers and responsibilities the elders possess, and discuss what groups of people in our own society approximate the role of the native storyteller.

3. (*Writing from Research*) Before printed language was widely available, the bard, minstrel, and troubadour played a role in Western culture somewhat analogous to that of the storyteller in an oral culture. Research and write an essay about the roles of minstrels in early Greece or in Europe during the Middle Ages. Explore how that role has affected contemporary America.

Are Accents Out? Hey, Dude, Like NEH-oh Way!

Patrick Cooke

Patrick Cooke was born in Rochester, New York, in 1952. A graduate of Georgetown University, he has written for many newspapers and magazines, including the New York Times Magazine, *the* Washington Post, Vogue, *and* New York. *Formerly a contributing editor to* Health *magazine and a senior editor at* Men's Journal, *Cooke is now the executive editor of* Forbes FYI, *a lifestyle magazine. Cooke's concerns about the future of media and their growing tendency to refer to writers as "content providers" has led him to seek other outlets for his writing talents. He is currently living in San Francisco and working on several screenplays.*

In the following article, which first appeared in the New York Times Magazine *in November 1989, Cooke gives a resounding "No!" to the question "Are accents out?" Despite fears that television would homogenize the speech of all Americans, regional and social variations of American English continue to thrive. If you listen carefully to the way people speak, you can often identify the differences in pronunciation, vocabulary, and grammar that mark the richness of language heritage.*

WRITING TO DISCOVER: *Do you think of yourself as speaking with an accent? If so, write about when and where you first became aware of your accent. If not, write about why you think your speech lacks an accent. Has your thinking about accents changed since you entered college?*

I have never much liked the way I talk. In upstate New York, where I was raised, people said things like "Lemme have a HEE-am SEEN-wich" and "You scared the BEE-JEES-us outa me." It had no grace. Nowhere in our local speech was there the hint of a drawl, or any majestic New England tones, or even a trace of down-state Brooklynese—which can sound almost poetic if you are in the right mood. No, up in the lovely glens of New York we went around loudly meowing through our noses, saying "Everything's gist FEE-an-TEE-astic, FEE-ab-ulos!" and scaring the bejesus out of one another.

If American mobility and television have conspired to dilute regional accents, as language critics have been insisting for most of this century, word never reached *my* old hometown. Nor, according to linguists of the American Dialect Society, have accents been much corrupted anywhere else. We are not all beginning to sound the same—despite what some people believe.

A couple of years ago, the novelist Thomas Williams wrote that "in the last thirty years I've seen the very speech of my own state, New Hampshire, change gradually toward something like Middle Western standard, as though the last generation learned as much of its tongue from Captain Kangaroo and Johnny Carson as it did from its parents and grandparents." That's probably easy enough to believe these days. The nation is seemingly becoming more homogenized, and if a Big Mac tastes the same in Hollywood, Florida, as it does in Hollywood, California, it is not unreasonable to presume that we all sound like Ronald McDonald.

But consider this: A few years ago a cargo handler for Pan-American World Airways named Paul Prinzivalli was suspected of having phoned in bomb threats to the airline's offices in Los Angeles. The charge was based on tapes made of the caller, who, officials thought, had a heavy East Coast accent similar to Prinzivalli's. It wasn't until William Labov, a linguist at the University of Pennsylvania, testified that the caller had a Boston accent—and Prinzivalli had a metropolitan New York accent— that the charges were dropped. "I had to fly out there," says Labov, who has spent nearly thirty years listening to gibbering Americans from coastal Massachusetts to the bone-dry Southwest, "and explain to a room full of Californians that not everybody on the East Coast sounds the same."

The truth is, say linguists, that various regions of the country are sounding increasingly different from one another. Yes, certain words have vanished—seldom do you hear a worm called a john-jumper any more. But accents? Hardly.   5

Every American has one. New dialects spring up where they are least expected; familiar ones change continually but remain potent enough to define us or betray us. And we are pegged for our origins every time we do something as innocent as order a ham sandwich.

Those origins can be traced back to the day the English carried their bags ashore at Jamestown, Va., in 1607, and at Massachusetts thirteen years later. The accent they brought along was part Elizabethan London and part rural speech from counties like Yorkshire and Lancashire. Those sounds—particularly the vowels—became the basis for the American English that was spoken in early Colonial settlements such as Boston, New York City, and Charleston.

Dialects tend to burrow in these "focal areas," as linguists call such cities of influence, and soon more and more of them began to dot the landscape. In fact, America quickly became something of a shattered mirror of focal areas as waves of ethnic groups began grabbing land and building cities—the Dutch in New York, the Irish and Italians in New England, and the Ulster Scots and Germans in the South (where present-day stresses on words like "IN-surance" and "JU-ly" are relics of Germanic constructions).

The American English that began to move west during the nineteenth century came from the Eastern inland parts of the country—

people along the Eastern seaboard did not participate in western migration as readily as those further inland, beach-front property being what it
is. The dialect of Southern inland regions such as northern Georgia and
the western Carolinas spread as far west as Texas, and established a few
new focal areas, like Nashville and Little Rock, Arkansas, along the way.
When this dialect collided with the Spanish influence in the Southwest, it
then veered north into the Rockies.

"At the same time, there were all kinds of Northerners moving   10
west," says Lee Pederson, a linguist at Emory University who has studied
both Northern and Southern accents. "The dialect of Chicago, for example, is purely Northern inland. It came from western New England
and Hartford, Connecticut, and became the basis for what you hear now
around Cleveland, Detroit, and the Great Lakes."

By the time prairie schooners came to a halt at the Pacific Ocean in
the mid-1800s, the English they carried was a mixture of sundry Eastern
dialects, mingled with foreign influences from the immigrants who were
picked up en route. It retained little of its Colonial origins. Then, too,
these California settlers discovered that not only had a few coastal North-
easterners beaten them around Cape Horn and planted their own brand
of Northern accent in San Francisco and Los Angeles, but they also had
claimed most of the good beachfront property.

Today's state boundaries—and often even city borders—are all but
useless for determining who speaks what. Within Boston, for example,
where ethnic communities have remained closely knit, you hear differences between the English spoken by the Italian Americans, Irish Americans, and Americans who speak Yiddish. Even outside the East Coast, in
those provinces thought to speak only dreary, standard American, regional peculiarities persist. In Pittsburgh, the football team is called the
"STILL-ers"; in Idaho, the locals call the capital "BOY-see"; in Wisconsin, the big town by the lake is "Muh-WAUK-ee"; in New Mexico, they
say "cheat" for sheet, and in Chicago it seems one Daley or another has
always been the "Mare."

Dialects change with all the speed of a john-jumper, but they do
change. It is quite possible that you do not speak precisely the way your
grandfather does, although you both grew up on the same street. Linguists used to record those slight generational dissimilarities and then
lament the demise of a regional dialect. Starting in the 1960s, however,
socio-linguists began wondering why sounds change at all, and whether
there might be some clues to social behavior behind the variances.

In 1963, for example, William Labov discovered that there were two
distinct ways of speaking among year-round residents on Martha's Vineyard off the coast of Massachusetts—though it all sounded Yankee to
outsiders. The older residents, who planned to remain on the island, had
somehow reinforced their dialect as a way of distancing themselves from
the mainlanders, who had begun buying up large portions of the island.

The younger residents, who planned to leave the island, spoke more like the mainlanders than the people who had raised them.

Just as the islanders perceived outsiders as a threat to local life, so   15
too, it appears, have established groups in the large cities viewed the wave of new ethnic groups—blacks, Hispanics, and Asians—that have flooded into their communities since World War II. Using dialect has been one way of circling the wagons.

"Many of the things that people struggle for in this world, particularly jobs and houses, they achieve through their connections within the local community," says Labov. Language changes are often a defensive reaction against newcomers who seem to threaten these rights and privileges.

Sometimes these changes come in the form of new vocabulary; more often, linguists have learned, it is the vowel sounds that are affected. In the mid-1970s, Labov began studying the Northern dialect region from New England to the Great Lakes. He recorded the range of speech across three generations, and compared his findings with earlier linguistic surveys from the 1940s. He was startled to discover that a wholesale shifting of the short vowel sounds had occurred.

The shift essentially worked this way: Imagine that the numbers on the face of a clock are replaced by vowels. Whether because of a defensive reaction to new groups entering the territory or some other unknown factors, the vowel *a* at one o'clock begins crowding the vowel *e* at two o'clock. That then begins nudging *i* and so on, until the whole face has shifted slightly.

Linguists are uncertain why the chain reaction begins at a particular vowel, but in the North—especially in Chicago, Detroit, Cleveland, Buffalo, Rochester, and my old hometown—they found that among many speakers the word "John" was now pronounced "Jan." The word "Ann" had become "Ian," and the word "ham" had somehow wandered over into "Lemme have a HEE-am SEEN-wich."

Meanwhile, other shifts were discovered elsewhere in the East, but   20
with different sets of vowels pressuring one another. In Philadelphia, "crayon" and "crown" were both said as "crayon"; "bounce" and "balance" both came out as "balance." In the Southern states, "pen" and "pin" had become homophonous. So cramped were other Southern vowels that people had begun to break words like "bed" into two syllables: "BEE-id."

Researchers found that these shifts in pronunciation generally behave like a slow-moving virus. Occasionally, though, the speed picks up dramatically. "In 1976 in Eastern Pennsylvania, we found that 5 percent of the kids we studied had merged the words 'caught' and 'cot' so that both were said as 'cot,'" says Labov. "Last year we went back and found that 80 percent are now doing it."

As accents continue to evolve, certain regions, principally the North and South, are finding it progressively difficult to understand one

another. For example, when Labov's research team played a tape record-
ing of a Chicago speaker to forty lifelong residents of Birmingham, Alabama, the sentence "He hadda wear socks" was interpreted correctly by
only two people. The rest guessed that he said "He hadda wear slacks" or
maybe it was "sacks." The sentence "When we had the busses with the
antennas on the top" sounded for all the world to some Alabamans like
"When we had the bosses Whitney antennas on the top."

There was another surprising and disturbing discovery. In none of
these areas have lower-class blacks adopted the regional dialect changes.
"One of the things we found, to our astonishment, was how similar black
speech is throughout the country," says Labov. The reason, researchers
say, is that while white middle-class residents of these areas look to the
local community for their rewards, blacks, long denied those local rewards, view themselves as a national group with national aspirations. The
result, says Labov, is that blacks and whites continue to grow further
apart in the way each group speaks the language.

Some Americans, hoping perhaps to identify with a particular group—
or conversely, to not be identified with a group—are desperate to purge
any trace of their origins. And who could blame them? We are all instinctively aware of the stereotypes that arise the moment a person begins to
speak. When television needs a hick with a heart of gold, it looks southward for a twangy moron like Ernest, the comedian of commercial fame:
"Hey, Vern!" When a cold-hearted killer is called for, it's a Brooklynese
speaker croaking "youse guys"—a surviving Irish pronunciation that
[former] New York City Mayor David Dinkins would like to hear shifted
into oblivion.

Beverly Inman-Ebel, a speech pathologist in Chattanooga, Ten-   25
nessee, has spent [. . .] a number of years teaching Southerners—house-
wives and beauty queens, businessmen and politicians—how to reduce
their regional dialects. "People come to me seeking a voice that doesn't
stand out," she says. "When I ask clients whom they admire and would
love to sound like, the men say Ronald Reagan and the women say Diane
Sawyer."

For $75 to $175 an hour, Inman-Ebel helps clients untangle features
of the Southern vowel shift, making "ten" and "tin" two separate sounds
again. Sounding regional, she says, is increasingly a barrier to success.
"One company just sent me three executives for accent reduction," she
says. "One of them will become the C.E.O. How they speak is certainly
not the only criterion for the promotion, but it is a factor."

Still, despite the best efforts of speech pathologists, most of us are
pretty much stuck with our accents by the time we reach the age of thirteen. With that in mind, think of how often you've heard a sixteen-year-
old say, "Hey, dude, like NEH-oh way!" Spooky, isn't it?

A couple of years ago, James W. Hartman, a linguist at the University
of Kansas, started wondering about these sounds that teenagers make.

He had heard Moon Unit Zappa's gag-me-with-a-spoon routine, which parodied the way kids talk in the San Fernando Valley, about 1,500 miles west in Los Angeles County. Why was he hearing something disturbingly similar in the high school halls and shopping malls of Lawrence, Kansas? In Shakespeare's time, a fist fight between two boys might have started with the words "I yuke to pringle with you!" Now, it was something closer to "Yer rilly gonna fill, like, SEH-oh bad in a minute, man." Could English still be on the correct evolutionary path?

Hartman first detected this phenomenon in 1983, while doing research for the Dictionary of American Regional English. He noticed that some young people were using certain vowel sounds that were not features of the areas where they grew up.

"The most mystifying aspect of all is why some sounds are chosen   30
and others are not," says Hartman of the new accent, which appears to be a mix of various Northern and Southern dialects. "It's almost as though these kids all sat down at a meeting and agreed that these are the features we're going to use."

The "fronted O" sound, for example, which comes out as GEH-oh and NEH-oh, had long been a feature in the Baltimore area, but Hartman observed that something happened when it was picked up by kids in the Los Angeles area, kids who had no connection whatever to Baltimore. They added it to, among other things, a softening of vowels that fall before the letter *l* (words like "sale" were being pronounced "sell").

Hartman's research, still in its preliminary stages, has shown that the young people making these new noises appear to be between sixteen and twenty-five years old; they typically come from upwardly mobile families and are college bound. That would make this latest phenomenon more of a social dialect—much like the Boston Brahmin accent—than a regional dialect.

In fact, what's most remarkable about the new dialect is how widespread it has become. Strongest in Southern California, where it seems to have started, the dialect apparently traveled across the United States from west to east roughly along Route 70. It is the first American dialect ever to move in that direction, which has prompted the name Sun-Belt Speak. But so far, the engine pumping it through young channels remains something of a mystery.

The influence of television has mostly been ruled out, simply because TV has little, if any, effect on an accent. "Peer pressure, school, or anything you have an involvement in affects language—not television," says Donna Christian, director of the research division at the Center for Applied Linguistics in Washington. "What matters is who will judge you or whom you're trying to impress in some way. There's no reason to become more like the television."

There's probably nothing to fear from Sun-Belt Speak. It will prove   35
no better at uprooting entrenched regional accents than Johnny Carson has been. Like any other new dialect that has passed over the continent in

the last four centuries, a vowel here or a word there may survive. But in eighty years, these, too, will become but a faint addition to the drawls and quacks we hear around us. Right?

"I don't have a clue," says Hartman. "But I will say that since I started looking into this, people have sent me tapes from all over the country, and Sun-Belt Speak is more widespread than I'd first thought. It has appeared in northern Ohio and southern Florida, for example. I wouldn't even be surprised if it showed up soon in a place like, say, up-state New York."

FOCUSING ON CONTENT

1. According to Cooke, who believes that we are all sounding more and more the same? Who refutes this position? Where does Cooke himself stand on this issue?

2. How have accents changed in recent years? How does the discussion of accents on Martha's Vineyard (14) illustrate a way in which an accent can change over time? (Glossary: *Examples*)

3. According to Cooke, why haven't many African Americans participated in this recent shift in regional dialects (23)? (Glossary: *Dialect*) Why do linguists think this is a cause for concern?

4. What characterizes Sun-Belt Speak? In what specific ways does it differ from other U.S. dialects? Explain.

FOCUSING ON WRITING

1. Cooke chose a rather startling, though recognizable, illustration of an accent for the title of his essay. Based on the title, what did you expect the tone of his essay to be? (Glossary: *Tone*) Does the essay achieve this tone? Why or why not? Cite specific passages from the essay that help establish its overall tone.

2. Coke begins his essay by offering a personal point of view. (Glossary: *Point of View*) Do you think his use of personal experience is an effective way to begin the essay? (Glossary: *Beginnings and Endings*) Why or why not? Do you ever use the first person in your writing? If so, when and why do you use it?

3. Cooke's article concerns itself with the spoken dialects of English. When, if ever, is it acceptable to use dialects in writing? Do dialectical differences in pronunciation, grammar, or vocabulary often appear in writing? Explain.

4. What Cooke calls Sun-Belt Speak could be considered a demographic dialect rather than a geographic accent because its use was common in a specific age group from a shared socioeconomic background, not in a specific region. It therefore differs rather markedly from other regional accents Cooke discusses. Why do you think Cooke uses Sun-Belt Speak as an example of a developing dialect in his essay? (Glossary: *Examples*) Do you find his use of it as an example effective? Explain.

LANGUAGE IN ACTION

Read the following story from Marguerite Wolf's 1998 book *A Window on Vermont*. With your classmates, discuss the story in light of what you learned about slang expressions in the Cooke article.

POINT OF VIEW

When I was a teenager I thought octogenarians were as strange as octopi. It was inconceivable that I would ever be *that* old. Now that I am one—octogenarian, not octopus—I'm beginning to think that teenagers may be the strange ones. They wear pants three sizes too big that fold and drag around their heels like mufflers. They poke holes in sensitive parts of their anatomy. Their speech is limited to "No way!" or "Right," and they use "like" and "y'know" in place of commas and periods. "We went downtown like cruising y'know and hung like all afternoon y'know" No, I don't know.

Girls favor black for prom dresses, either mid-thigh or floor length, but for every other occasion grunge is in. Boys own thirty-nine t-shirts (I counted my grandson's), twenty-five caps worn backwards and never removed, and five pairs of trail boots, casuals, and sneakers in various stages of disintegration. [. . .]

They know how to ski and snowboard, ride mountain bikes, and surf the net, but they don't know a salad fork from a pitchfork. I'm not sure they know what a pitchfork is, either. They know how to set up a program for the computer, but they don't know how to spell the words. They don't need to. The computer will do it for them. They don't know how to write a thank you note or any reason why they should write one.

I have three grandsons. They are great, and not all of my remarks apply to them. They do thank me by telephone. I admire their technical skills, their athletic ability, their cavity-free teeth (thanks to fluoride), and their strong muscles. They are not nearly as tongue-tied as their peers, and they don't say "like" or "y'know" every other word, at least not to me. And their speech is not sprinkled with four letter words—again, at least not to me.

[. . .] Do I look as weird to teenagers as they sometimes look to me? Of course I do. Who am I kidding? Would I want to be their age again? NO WAY! I don't want another ride on that roller coaster or the years of doubt and discovery. They may never have heard of Will Rogers, Caruso, ration books, or Marlene Dietrich, but for years I didn't know that The Who was a band or what teams were playing in the Super Bowl.

WRITING SUGGESTIONS

1. (*Writing from Experience*) Reread your Writing to Discover entry, and think about what is recognizable about your accent. Has anyone ever commented on it? Now think about how you would like your speech to sound. Write an essay in which you consider what you would do if you could change your

accent. Are you content with the way you speak, or is there a person whose accent you would like to emulate? Why? What do you think are the positive and negative aspects of your speech? Would the negative aspects be eliminated if you sounded like your chosen person? How do you think your accent might affect your pursuit of social and career goals once you finish your education?

2. (*Writing from Reading*) Cooke's essay argues that regional accents are actually becoming stronger, despite the prevailing sense that cultural homogenization, through television and other mass media, should weaken such accents over time. Television is dismissed because it does not require a response, thus offering no incentive for people to emulate the way the actors speak. Yet the quick spread of Sun-Belt Speak after Moon Unit Zappa's gag-me-with-a-spoon routine seems to indicate that mass media can influence how some people sound. Write an essay in which you consider the media's influence on accents and dialects. Do you agree or disagree with Cooke and the experts he quotes that the media are not having an effect? Or do you think people are influenced by what they hear and see even if they don't have to respond to it?

3. (*Writing from Research*) Whether or not the mass media *affect* how people express themselves, there is no question that the mass media *reflect* how people speak. Do some research into the world of mass media by paying close attention to how people talk in movies and on TV and radio shows that are aimed at a young-adult audience (ages fifteen to twenty-four or so) or that are meant to realistically depict how young adults speak. Examples include *Dawson's Creek, Party of Five, Friends,* and just about anything on MTV for television; *Clueless, Good Will Hunting,* and *Ten Things I Hate about You* for movies; and your local alternative-rock or college-radio-station disc jockeys. Also look for written material that contains what you consider realistic dialogue. Assemble a large enough sampling so that you can write a paper presenting what, if any, recent patterns of speech have replaced the Sun-Belt Speak Cooke describes. How does one sound hip today? Do geographic regions still play a role in young-adult accents and expressions? Present your findings using specific examples of speech you heard or read during your research.

English Belongs to Everybody

ROBERT MACNEIL

Born in Montreal, Canada, Robert MacNeil is probably best known as the former coanchor of the Public Broadcasting Service's MacNeil/Lehrer NewsHour, *which was broadcast from 1975 to 1995 and which continues to this day under Jim Lehrer's tutelage. During MacNeil's long career in broadcasting and journalism, he covered many major events in American history, including the John F. Kennedy assassination, the 1968 Democratic National Convention, and the 1973 Senate Watergate hearings. MacNeil's publications include* The People Machine: The Influence of Television on American Politics *(1968), which examines the frailties of television news organizations;* The Right Place at the Right Time *(1982), which recounts his experiences as a journalist;* Wordstruck *(1989), an autobiography; and* The Story of English *(1986), which he originally created as a PBS series on the history and development of the English language. In 1998 he published* Breaking News, *a fictional attack on the media's handling of an Oval Office sex scandal. MacNeil is now at work on another novel as well as a television series on Shakespeare.*

In the following essay from Wordstruck, *MacNeil asserts that the supposed demise of English today is actually healthy change. As much as it may disturb grammarians, the ability of English to change keeps it strong and dynamic.*

WRITING TO DISCOVER: *Do you change the way you use language in different situations? If you are like most people, you probably do. Write about how your use of language changes and why. How is your spoken English different from your written English?*

This is a time of widespread anxiety about the language. Some Americans fear that English will be engulfed or diluted by Spanish and want to make it the official language. There is anxiety about a crisis of illiteracy, or a crisis of semiliteracy among high school, even college, graduates.

Anxiety, however, may have a perverse side effect: experts who wish to "save" the language may only discourage pleasure in it. Some are good-humored and tolerant of change, others intolerant and snobbish. Language reinforces feelings of social superiority or inferiority; it creates insiders and outsiders; it is a prop to vanity or a source of anxiety, and on both emotions the language snobs play. Yet the changes and the errors that irritate them are no different in kind from those which have shaped our language for centuries. As Hugh Kenner wrote of certain British critics in *The Sinking Island,* "They took note of language only when it annoyed them." Such people are killjoys: they turn others away from an interest in the language, inhibit their use of it, and turn pleasure off.

Change is inevitable in a living language and is responsible for much of the vitality of English; it has prospered and grown because it was able to accept and absorb change.

As people evolve and do new things, their language will evolve too. They will find ways to describe the new things and their changed perspective will give them new ways of talking about the old things. For example, electric light switches created a brilliant metaphor for the oldest of human experiences, being *turned on* or *turned off.* To language conservatives those expressions still have a slangy, low ring to them; to others they are vivid, fresh-minted currency, very spendable, very "with-it."

That tolerance for change represents not only the dynamism of the   5
English-speaking peoples since the Elizabethans, but their deeply rooted ideas of freedom as well. This was the idea of the Danish scholar Otto Jespersen, one of the great authorities on English. Writing in 1905, Jespersen said in his *Growth and Structure of the English Language:*

> The French language is like the stiff French garden of Louis XIV, while the English is like an English park, which is laid out seemingly without any definite plan, and in which you are allowed to walk everywhere according to your fancy without having to fear a stern keeper enforcing rigorous regulations. The English language would not have been what it is if the English had not been for centuries great respecters of the liberties of each individual and if everybody had not been free to strike out new paths for himself.

I like that idea and do not think it just coincidence. Consider that the same cultural soil, the Celtic-Roman-Saxon-Danish-Norman amalgam, which produced the English language also nourished the great principles of freedom and rights of man in the modern world. The first shoots sprang up in England and they grew stronger in America. Churchill called them "the joint inheritance of the English-speaking world." At the very core of those principles are popular consent and resistance to arbitrary authority; both are fundamental characteristics of our language. The English-speaking peoples have defeated all efforts to build fences around their language, to defer to an academy on what was permissible English and what was not. They'll decide for themselves, thanks just the same.

Nothing better expresses resistance to arbitrary authority than the persistence of what grammarians have denounced for centuries as "errors." In the common speech of English-speaking peoples—Americans, Englishmen, Canadians, Australians, New Zealanders, and others—these usages persist, despite rising literacy and wider education. We hear them every day:

Double negative: "I don't want none of that."

Double comparative: "Don't make that any more heavier!"

Wrong verb: "Will you learn me to read?"

These "errors" have been with us for at least four hundred years, because you can find each of them in Shakespeare.

Double negative: in *Hamlet,* the King says:

Nor what he spake, though it lack'd form a little,
Was not like madness.

Double comparative: In *Othello,* the Duke says:

Yet opinion . . . throws a more safer voice on you.

Wrong verb: In *Othello,* Desdemona says:

My life and education both do learn me how to respect you.

I find it very interesting that these forms will not go away and lie down. They were vigorous and acceptable in Shakespeare's time; they are far more vigorous today, although not acceptable as standard English. Regarded as error by grammarians, they are nevertheless in daily use all over the world by a hundred times the number of people who lived in Shakespeare's England.

It fascinates me that *axe,* meaning "ask," so common in black Ameri- 10
can English, is standard in Chaucer in all forms—*axe, axen, axed:* "and *axed* him if Troilus were there." Was that transmitted across six hundred years or simply reinvented?

English grew without a formal grammar. After the enormous creativity of Shakespeare and the other Elizabethans, seventeenth- and eighteenth-century critics thought the language was a mess, like an overgrown garden. They weeded it by imposing grammatical rules derived from tidier languages, chiefly Latin, whose precision and predictability they trusted. For three centuries, with some slippage here and there, their rules have held. Educators taught them and written English conformed. Today, English-language newspapers, magazines, and books everywhere broadly agree that correct English obeys these rules. Yet the wild varieties continue to threaten the garden of cultivated English and, by their numbers, actually dominate everyday usage.

Nonstandard English formerly knew its place in the social order. Characters in fiction were allowed to speak it occasionally. Hemingway believed that American literature really did not begin until Mark Twain, who outraged critics by reproducing the vernacular of characters like Huck Finn. Newspapers still clean up the grammar when they quote the ungrammatical, including politicians. The printed word, like Victorian morality, has often constituted a conspiracy of respectability.

People who spoke grammatically could be excused the illusion that their writ held sway, perhaps the way the Normans thought that French had conquered the language of the vanquished Anglo-Saxons. A generation ago, people who considered themselves educated and well-spoken might have had only glancing contact with nonstandard English, usually in a well-understood class, regional, or rural context.

It fascinates me how differently we all speak in different circumstances. We have levels of formality, as in our clothing. There are very formal occasions, often requiring written English: the job application or the letter to the editor—the dark-suit, serious-tie language, with everything pressed and the lint brushed off. There is our less formal out-in-the-world language—a more comfortable suit, but still respectable. There is language for close friends in the evenings, on weekends—blue-jeans-and-sweatshirt language, when it's good to get the tie off. There is family language, even more relaxed, full of grammatical short cuts, family slang, echoes of old jokes that have become intimate shorthand—the language of pajamas and uncombed hair. Finally, there is the language with no clothes on; the talk of couples—murmurs, sighs, grunts—language at its least self-conscious, open, vulnerable, and primitive.

Broadcasting has democratized the publication of language, often at its   15
most informal, even undressed. Now the ears of the educated cannot escape the language of the masses. It surrounds them on the news, weather, sports, commercials, and the ever-proliferating talk and call-in shows.

This wider dissemination of popular speech may easily give purists the idea that the language is suddenly going to hell in this generation, and may explain the new paranoia about it.

It might also be argued that more Americans hear more correct, even beautiful, English on television than was ever heard before. Through television more models of good usage reach more American homes than was ever possible in other times. Television gives them lots of colloquial English, too, some awful, some creative, but that is not new.

Hidden in this is a simple fact: our language is not the special private property of the language police, or grammarians, or teachers, or even great writers. The genius of English is that is has always been the tongue of the common people, literate or not.

English belongs to everybody: the funny turn of phrase that pops into the mind of a farmer telling a story; or the traveling salesman's dirty joke; or the teenager saying, "Gag me with a spoon"; or the pop lyric— all contribute, are all as valid as the tortured image of the academic, or the line the poet sweats over for a week.

Through our collective language sense, some may be thought beauti-   20
ful and some ugly, some may live and some may die; but it is all English and it belongs to everyone—to those of us who wish to be careful with it and those who don't care.

FOCUSING ON CONTENT

1. Who does MacNeil describe as "killjoys" (2)? Why does MacNeil believe their influence is destructive to the vitality of the English language?

2. Why does MacNeil claim that various examples of "improper" English are not likely to go away soon? Whose work does he cite to reinforce his conclusion? (Glossary: *Examples*)

3. When was standardization imposed on the English language? Why was it thought necessary to do so?

4. React to MacNeil's statement that English "has always been the tongue of the common people" (18). What does he mean? What does the statement imply to you?

5. What does MacNeil say is the real reason behind the recent perception that American English is undergoing a sudden turn for the worse? What role do television and other forms of mass media play in the modern evolution of the language?

FOCUSING ON WRITING

1. In paragraph 2, MacNeil says the current anxiety about language may lead to a "perverse side effect." What is this side effect? Why does MacNeil describe it as perverse? What other words could he have used to describe it? What impact would the use of a word other than *perverse* have on the overall tone of the essay? (Glossary: *Tone*)

2. In paragraph 4, MacNeil uses the terms *turned on* and *turned off* as examples of how modern influences can contribute to new language metaphors. He characterizes these expressions as being very "with it." What does he mean? Why do you think he uses one slang term to describe other such terms? Do you find this an effective part of his argument? Why or why not?

3. What simile does Otto Jesperson use in the passage quoted by MacNeil (5)? (Glossary: *Figures of Speech*) Do you find it an effective image? MacNeil adopts the simile and uses it later in the essay. Is it an appropriate simile for MacNeil's argument? Why or why not?

4. What terms does MacNeil use to describe those who favor a rigid grammar and a correct, unchanging use of English? How does he describe the way they react to the current use of the language? What point is he making?

LANGUAGE IN ACTION

English is a dynamic language, but even MacNeil would probably concede that "pushing the envelope" of acceptable speech can be overdone, as the following selection demonstrates. This excerpt is taken from the Web page "Jargon, Weasel Words, and Gobbledygook" by G. Jay Christensen. (You may also want to check Christensen's Web site at <http://www.csun.edu/~vcecn006/public1.htm>.) How careful do you think you should be in using the English language? Should there be a balance between dynamic change and consistent, coherent structure and diction? Discuss your answers with your class.

PARAGRAPHS OF BUZZWORDS BUZZ LOUDLY

Dr. Michael Wunsch from Northern Arizona University offered some delightful parodies about how buzzwords are taking over our language. With his permission I quote some of the paragraphs he gave at a recent business communication conference.

Now that we have talked the talk and viably interfaced in a politically correct, huge attempt to jump start, kick start, downsize, rightsize, bash, or showcase something, may I have, my fellow Americans, some of your cutting-edge, walk-the-walk, super input that will hopefully debut and impact somebody's bottom line as we speak while we are on a mission to dig deeper and then move up to the next level, and beyond that, to take care of business on the information superhighway and earn bragging rights?

I knew that you would turn this perceived worst-case scenario around and echo somebody by responding with "Exactly!" Let's be honest, a person doesn't have to be a rocket scientist or heart surgeon to know the big news that you are a happy camper who is cool and great, you know, despite your cautious optimism. No question, you are a warm-and-fuzzy, world-class, wave-of-the-future, state-of-the-art, high-tech, totally awesome, less-than-slow-lane, more-than-happy, user-friendly, outrageously key dude who can and will give much, much more. (In an ad, the point at which the copywriter ran out of hype!) The huge upside is that you are arguably neither a wimp nor a sucker. In my mind, I'm proactively fed up with hanging around; therefore, my agenda is that I am reactively out of here, under condition of anonymity, in an effort to put it all together to bring everybody up to speed. Let's rumble on a big-time roll at a huge 110 percent effort to make things happen at crunch time by advocating zero tolerance! There you go! Have a nice day!

As Bill Maher is fond of saying on *Politically Incorrect,* the previous information has been "satirized" for your protection. Are you convinced to be careful how you use the English language?

WRITING SUGGESTIONS

1. (*Writing from Experience*) MacNeil contends that television makes all forms of English accessible to everyone. It does broadcast "bad" English, but it also brings a lot of correct, elegant English into viewers' homes. Think about the language usage on the television shows you watch and the radio stations you listen to. How do they handle slang, dialogue, and other word usage? For example, the show *Seinfeld* was very aggressive in coining clever phrases and word associations, and *NYPD Blue* sometimes uses vocabulary that many consider profane. Also, how does your favorite form of music use language? Are the lyrics poetic or direct? Do they include a lot of slang? Write an essay in which you examine the influence television and radio have had on your own language. Do you and your peers incorporate expressions from these sources into your own speech?

2. (*Writing from Reading*) MacNeil uses *gag me with a spoon,* the familiar phrase from Sun-Belt Speak that was also identified by Cooke (p. 327) as an example of a contribution to the English language. Think about other recent contributions to the language that you have heard—and perhaps even used

yourself. Write an essay in which you argue for or against MacNeil's contention that such new phrases or uses of the language contribute to English as a whole. What advantages or features do they offer? What dangers do they pose to the integrity of the language? As a writer, how do you regard such changes?

3. (*Writing from Research*) Choose a magazine in your library for which you can access back issues from the 1930s, 1940s, or 1950s. The magazine should be one intended for a general audience. Choose three issues: one from one of the three decades mentioned previously, one from the 1970s, and one from the 1990s. In each issue, select four or five articles, preferably on a variety of topics—news, entertainment, technology, and so on. With MacNeil's essay in mind, thoroughly examine the articles. How have the language and style of writing changed over the years? Write an essay in which you summarize your findings, identifying specific examples of word usage as well as general characteristics. To what extent do modern innovations and contemporary spoken slang affect the language in the articles? Do any of the articles deviate from Standard English? If so, what is the author's purpose in using nonstandard English?

Black Children, Black Speech

Dorothy Z. Seymour

Dorothy Z. Seymour began her career as an elementary school teacher, which eventually led her to write children's books. Some of these books actually originated as stories for her own first-grade class. A native of Cleveland, Ohio, she received both her B.S. and M.S. from Case Western Reserve University. After more than a decade in teaching, Seymour went to work as an editor and free-lance writer. She has traveled widely and has discovered that different cultures give her "a new perspective on America and the assumptions of Americans about life and how to lead it."

In this essay, which first appeared in the November 19, 1971, issue of Commonweal Magazine, *Seymour discusses an important question facing present-day educators: How does one approach the conflict between the patterns of a nonstandard dialect, which the child learns either at home or from other children, and the equivalent patterns of Standard English? The issue is highly controversial and emotional. Seymour first analyzes the distinguishing features of Black English and then considers the impact of Black English on American schools before making her case for a program of bidialectism. She believes that teachers and parents need to be informed about nonstandard language in order to implement such a program in U.S. schools.*

WRITING TO DISCOVER: *Write about what you think and feel when you hear someone speak English differently than you do. Do you always understand what that person means? Do you think others should learn to speak the way you do? Should you speak the way they do?*

"Cmon, man, les git goin'!" called the boy to his companion. "Dat bell ringing'. It say, 'Git in rat now!'" He dashed into the school yard.

"Aw, f'get you," replied the other. "Whe' Richuh? Whe' da' muvvuh? He be goin' to schoo'."

"He in de' now, man!" was the answer as they went through the door.

In the classroom they made for their desks and opened their books. The name of the story they tried to read was "Come." It went:

Come, Bill, come
Come with me.

Come and see this.
See what is here.

The first boy poked the second. "Wha' da' wor'?"
    "Da' wor' *is,* you dope."   5
    "*Is?* Ain't no wor' *is.* You jivin' me? Wha' da' wor' mean?"
    "Ah dunno. Jus' *is.*"
    To a speaker of Standard English, this exchange is only vaguely comprehensible. But it's normal speech for thousands of American children. In addition it demonstrates one of our biggest educational problems: children whose speech style is so different from the writing style of their books that they have difficulty learning to read. These children speak Black English, a dialect characteristic of many inner-city Negroes. Their books are, of course, written in Standard English. To complicate matters, the speech they use is also socially stigmatized. Middle-class whites and Negroes alike scorn it as low-class poor people's talk.
    Teachers sometimes make the situation worse with their attitudes toward Black English. Typically, they view the children's speech as "bad English" characterized by "lazy pronunciation," "poor grammar," and "short, jagged words." One result of this attitude is poor mental health on the part of the pupils. A child is quick to grasp the feeling that while school speech is "good," his own speech is "bad," and that by extension he himself is somehow inadequate and without value. Some children react to this feeling by withdrawing; they stop talking entirely. Others develop the attitude of "F'get you, honky." In either case, the psychological results are devastating and lead straight to the dropout route.
    It is hard for most teachers and middle-class Negro parents to accept   10
the idea that Black English is not just "sloppy talk" but a dialect with a form and structure of its own. Even some eminent black educators think of it as "bad English grammar" with "slurred consonants" (Professor Nick Aaron Ford of Morgan State College in Baltimore) and "ghettoese" (Dr. Kenneth B. Clark, the prominent educational psychologist).
    Parents of Negro school children generally agree. Two researchers of Columbia University report that the adults they worked with in Harlem almost unanimously preferred that their children be taught Standard English in school.
    But there is another point of view, one held in common by black militants and some white liberals. They urge that middle-class Negroes stop thinking of the inner-city dialect as something to be ashamed of and repudiated. Black author Claude Brown, for example, pushes this view.
    Some modern linguists take a similar stance. They begin with the premise that no dialect is intrinsically "bad" or "good," and that a nonstandard speech style is not defective speech but different speech. More important, they have been able to show that Black English is far from being a careless way of speaking the Standard; instead, it is a rather rigidly

constructed set of speech patterns, with the same sort of specialization in sounds, structure, and vocabulary as any other dialect.

THE SOUNDS OF BLACK ENGLISH

Middle-class listeners who hear black inner-city speakers say "dis" and "tin" for "this" and "thin" assume that the black speakers are just being careless. Not at all; these differences are characteristic aspects of the dialect. The original cause of such substitutions is generally a carryover from one's original language or that of his immigrant parents. The interference from that carryover probably caused the substitution of /d/ for the voiced *th* in *this*, and /t/ for the unvoiced *th* sound in *thin*. (Linguists represent language sounds by putting letters within slashes or brackets.) Most speakers of English don't realize that the two *th* sounds of English are lacking in many other languages and are difficult for most foreigners trying to learn English. Germans who study English, for example, are surprised and confused about these sounds because the only Germans who use them are the ones who lisp. These two sounds are almost nonexistent in the West African languages which most black immigrants brought with them to America.

Similar substitutions used in Black English are /f/, a sound similar to the unvoiced *th*, in medial word-position, as in *birfday* for *birthday*, and in final word-position, as in *roof* for *Ruth* as well as /v/ for the voiced *th* in medial position, as in *bruvver* for *brother*. These sound substitutions are also typical of Gullah, the language of black speakers in the Carolina Sea Islands. Some of them are also heard in Caribbean Creole.

Another characteristic of the sounds of Black English is the lack of /l/ at the end of words, sometimes replaced by the sound /w/. This makes words like *tool* sound like *too*. If /l/ occurs in the middle of a Standard English word, in Black English it may be omitted entirely: "I can hep you." This difference is probably caused by the instability and sometimes interchangeability of /l/ and /r/ in West African languages.

One difference that is startling to middle-class speakers is the fact that Black English words appear to leave off some consonant sounds at the end of words. Like Italian, Japanese, and West African words, they are more likely to end in vowel sounds. Standard English *boot* is pronounced *boo* in Black English. *What* is *wha*. *Sure* is *sho*. *Your* is *yo*. This kind of difference can make for confusion in the classroom. Dr. Kenneth Goodman, a psycholinguist, tells of a black child whose white teacher asked him to use *so* in a sentence — not "sew a dress" but "the other *so*." The sentence the child used was "I got a *so* on my leg."

A related feature of Black English is the tendency in many cases not to use sequences of more than one final consonant sound. For example, *just* is pronounced *jus'*, *past* is *pass*, *mend* sounds like *men* and *hold* like

15

hole. *Six* and *box* are pronounced *sick* and *bock*. Why should this be? Perhaps because West African languages, like Japanese, have almost no clusters of consonants in their speech. The Japanese, when importing a foreign word, handle a similar problem by inserting vowel sounds between every consonant, making *baseball* sound like *besuboru*. West Africans probably made a simpler change, merely cutting a series of two consonant sounds down to one. Speakers of Gullah, one linguist found, have made the same kind of adaptation of Standard English.

Teachers of black children seldom understand the reason for these differences in final sounds. They are apt to think that careless speech is the cause. Actually, black speakers aren't "leaving off" any sounds; how can you leave off something you never had in the first place?

Differences in vowel sounds are also characteristic of the nonstandard   20
language. Dr. Goodman reports that a black child asked his teacher how to spell rat. "R-a-t," she replied. But the boy responded. "No ma'am, I don't mean rat mouse, I mean rat now." In Black English, *right* sounds like *rat*. A likely reason is that in West African languages, there are very few vowel sounds of the type heard in the word *right*. This type is common in English. It is called a glided or dipthongized vowel sound. A glided vowel sound is actually a close combination of two vowels; in the word *right* the two parts of the sound "eye" are actually "ah-ee." West African languages have no such long, two-part, changing vowel sounds; their vowels are generally shorter and more stable. This may be why in Black English, *time* sounds like *Tom*, *oil* like *all*, and *my* like *ma*.

LANGUAGE STRUCTURE

Black English differs from Standard English not only in its sounds but also in its structure. The way the words are put together does not always fit the description in English grammar books. The method of expressing time, or tense, for example, differs in significant ways.

The verb *to be* is an important one in Standard English. It's used as an auxiliary verb to indicate different tenses. But Black English speakers use it quite differently. Sometimes an inner-city Negro says "He coming"; other times he says "He be coming." These two sentences mean different things. To understand why, let's look at the tenses of West African languages; they correspond with those of Black English.

Many West African languages have a tense which is called the habitual. This tense is used to express action which is always occurring and it is formed with a verb that is translated as *be*. "He be coming" means something like "He's always coming," "He usually comes," or "He's been coming."

In Standard English there is no regular grammatical construction for such a tense. Black English speakers, in order to form the habitual tense in English, use the word *be* as an auxiliary: *He be doing it. My Momma be working. He be running.* The habitual tense is not the same as the present tense, which is constructed in Black English without any form of the verb *to be: He do it. My Momma working. He running.* (This means the action is occurring right now.)

There are other tense differences between Black English and Standard English. For example, the nonstandard speech does not use changes in grammar to indicate the past tense. A white person will ask, "What did your brother say?" and the black person will answer, "He say he coming." (The verb *say* is not changed to *said.*) "How did you get there?" "I walk." This style of talking about the past is paralleled in the Yoruba, Fante, Hausa, and Ewe languages of West Africa.

Expression of plurality is another difference. The way a black child will talk of "them boy" or "two dog" makes some white listeners think Negroes don't know how to turn a singular word into a plural word. As a matter of fact, it isn't necessary to use an *s* to express plurality. In Chinese and Japanese, singular and plural are not generally distinguished by such inflections; plurality is conveyed in other ways. For example, in Chinese it's correct to say "There are three book on the table." This sentence already has two signals of the plural, *three* and *are;* why require a third? This same logic is the basis of plurals in most West African languages, where nouns are often identical in the plural and the singular. For example, in Ibo, one correctly says *those man,* and in both Ewe and Yoruba one says *they house.* American speakers of Gullah retain this style; it is correct in Gullah to say *five dog.*

Gender is another aspect of language structure where differences can be found. Speakers of Standard English are often confused to find that the nonstandard vernacular often uses just one gender of pronoun, the masculine, and refers to women as well as men as *he* or *him.* "He a nice girl," even "Him a nice girl" are common. This usage probably stems from West African origins, too, as does the use of multiple negatives, such as "Nobody don't know it."

Vocabulary is the third aspect of a person's native speech that could affect his learning of a new language. The strikingly different vocabulary often used in Negro Nonstandard English is probably the most obvious aspect of it to a casual white observer. But its vocabulary differences don't obscure its meaning the way different sounds and different structure often do.

Recently there has been much interest in the African origins of words like *goober* (peanut), *cooter* (turtle), and *tote* (carry), as well as others that are less certainly African, such as *to dig* (possibly from the Wolof *degan,* "to understand"). Such expressions seem colorful rather than low-class to many whites; they become assimilated faster than their black originators do. English professors now use *dig* in their scholarly articles, and current advertising has enthusiastically adopted *rap.*

Is it really possible for old differences in sound, structure, and vocabulary to persist from the West African languages of slave days into

25

30

present-day inner-city Black English? Easily. Nothing else really explains such regularity of language habits, most of which persist among black people in various parts of the Western Hemisphere. For a long time scholars believed that certain speech forms used by Negroes were merely leftovers from archaic English preserved in the speech of early English settlers in America and copied by their slaves. But this theory has been greatly weakened, largely as the result of the work of a black linguist, Dr. Lorenzo Dow Turner of the University of Chicago. Dr. Turner studied the speech of Gullah Negroes in the Sea Islands off the Carolina coast and found so many traces of West African languages that he thoroughly discredited the archaic-English theory.

When anyone learns a new language, it's usual to try speaking the new language with the sounds and structure of the old. If a person's first language does not happen to have a particular sound needed in the language he is learning, he will tend to substitute a similar or related sound from his native language and use it to speak the new one. When Frenchman Charles Boyer said "Zees ees my heart," and when Latin American Carmen Miranda sang "Souse American way," they were simply using sounds of their native languages in trying to pronounce sounds of English. West Africans must have done the same thing when they first attempted English words. The tendency to retain the structure of the native language is a strong one, too. That's why a German learning English is likely to put his verb at the end: "May I a glass beer have?" The vocabulary of one's original language may also furnish some holdovers. Jewish immigrants did not stop using the word *bagel* when they came to America; nor did Germans stop saying *sauerkraut*.

Social and geographical isolation reinforces the tendencies to retain old language habits. When one group is considered inferior, the other group avoids it. For many years it was illegal to give any sort of instruction to Negroes, and for slaves to try to speak like their masters would have been unthinkable. Conflict of value systems doubtless retards changes, too. As Frantz Fanon observed in *Black Skin, White Masks,* those who take on white speech habits are suspect in the ghetto, because others believe they are trying to "act white." Dr. Kenneth Johnson, a black linguist, put it this way: "As long as disadvantaged black children live in segregated communities and most of their relationships are confined to those within their own subculture, they will not replace their functional nonstandard dialect with the nonfunctional standard dialect."

Linguists have made it clear that language systems that are different are not necessarily deficient. A judgment of deficiency can be made only in comparison with another language system. Let's turn the tables on Standard English for a moment and look at it from the West African point of view. From this angle, Standard English: (1) is lacking in certain language sounds, (2) has a couple of unnecessary language sounds for which others may serve as good substitutes, (3) doubles and drawls some of its vowel sounds in sequences that are unusual and difficult to imitate, (4) lacks a method of forming an important tense, (5) requires an unnecessary number of ways to indicate tense, plurality, and gender, and (6) doesn't mark negatives sufficiently for the result to be a good strong negative statement.

Now whose language is deficient?

How would the adoption of this point of view help us? Say we accepted the evidence that Black English is not just a sloppy Standard but an organized language style which probably has developed many of its features on the basis of its West African heritage? What would we gain?

The psychological climate of the classroom might improve if teachers understood why many black students speak as they do. But we still have not reached a solution of the main problem. Does the discovery that Black English has pattern and structure mean that it should not be tampered with? Should children who speak Black English be excused from learning the Standard in school? Should they perhaps be given books in Black English to learn from?

Any such accommodation would surely result in a hardening of the new separatism being urged by some black militants. It would probably be applauded by such people as Roy Innis, Director of C.O.R.E., who is currently recommending dual autonomous education systems for white and black. And it might facilitate learning to read, since some experiments have indicated that materials written in Black English syntax aid problem readers from the inner city.

But determined resistance to the introduction of such printed materials into schools can be expected. To those who view inner-city speech as bad English, the appearance in print of sentences like "My mamma, she work" can be as shocking and repellent as a four-letter word. Middle-class Negro parents would probably mobilize against the move. Any stratagem that does not take into account such practicalities of the matter is probably doomed to failure. And besides, where would such a permissive policy on language get these children in the larger society, and in the long run? If they want to enter an integrated America they must be able to deal with it on its own terms. Even Professor Toni Cade of Rutgers, who doesn't want "ghetto accents" tampered with, advocates mastery of Standard English because, as she puts it, "if you want to get ahead in this country, you must master the language of the ruling class." This has always been true, wherever there has been a minority group.

The problem then appears to be one of giving these children the ability to speak (and read) Standard English without denigrating the vernacular and those who use it, or even affecting the ability to use it. The only way to do this is to officially espouse bidialectism. The result would be the ability to use either dialect equally well—as Dr. Martin Luther King did—depending on the time, place, and circumstances. Pupils would have to learn enough about Standard English to use it when necessary, and teachers would have to learn enough about the inner-city dialect to understand and accept it for what it is—not just a "careless" version of Standard English but a different form of English that's appropriate in certain times and places.

Can we accomplish this? If we can't, the result will be continued   40
alienation of a large section of the population, continued dropout trouble with consequent loss of earning power and economic contribution to the nation, but most of all, loss of faith in America as a place where a minority people can at times continue to use those habits that remind them of their link with each other and with their past.

FOCUSING ON CONTENT

1. What, according to Seymour, is the consequence of people assuming that Black English is "lazy" or "bad" English? Why do these assumptions persist?

2. What are some of the characteristics of Black English pronunciation? Where do such pronunciation patterns originate?

3. What are the key characteristics of Black English grammar and verb tense?

4. Seymour concludes that Black English retains many aspects of West African languages, despite the fact that the West African influences would have had to persist for nearly 150 years. How does she defend her theory? How is it possible for such influences to overshadow Standard English in black communities for so long?

5. Why do you think it is important to make the distinction between a person's language being "different" and it being "defective"? In what ways is this distinction relevant to Seymour's argument about language?

6. How does Seymour propose that society accommodate students who speak Black English? How would her solution address the needs of the students, their parents and teachers, and society at large? Do you find her proposal a reasonable one? Why or why not?

FOCUSING ON WRITING

1. Seymour begins her essay by quoting an exchange between black students in Black English. (Glossary: *Beginnings and Endings*) What does she achieve by introducing Black English to the reader at the beginning of the essay? How does the content of the dialogue help introduce the purpose of the essay? (Glossary: *Purpose*)

2. When Seymour wrote her article in 1971, writers commonly used the male pronoun *he* to refer to both genders. Identify several sentences in which Seymour uses *he* in this selection, and try to eliminate the bias by rewriting the sentences. (Glossary: *Sexist Language*)

3. Seymour introduces three major components of her argument by asking a question to begin paragraphs 30, 35, and 40. Do you find this an effective

way for her to introduce the topic in each case? Why or why not? Why do you think Seymour uses this technique?

4. How would you characterize Seymour's tone in this essay? (Glossary: *Tone*) What words in particular lead you to characterize it this way? (Glossary: *Diction*) Do you find her tone appropriate for her argument? Why or why not?

LANGUAGE IN ACTION

In the mid-1990s, the Oakland, California, school system created a firestorm of controversy by proposing to teach Ebonics (what Seymour calls Black English) in the schools. Following is a carefully crafted academic response to this very emotional and volatile issue. Analyze the 1997 document approved by the Linguistics Society of America. What techniques do the authors use to define the issue and present their position? How do they avoid entering the broader—and very contentious—societal debate over the use of Ebonics?

LINGUISTICS SOCIETY OF AMERICA (LSA) RESOLUTION ON THE OAKLAND "EBONICS" ISSUE

Whereas there has been a great deal of discussion in the media and among the American public about the 18 December 1996 decision of the Oakland School Board to recognize the language variety spoken by many African American students and to take it into account in teaching Standard English, the Linguistic Society of America, as a society of scholars engaged in the scientific study of language, hereby resolves to make it known that:

a. The variety known as "Ebonics," "African American Vernacular English" (AAVE), and "Vernacular Black English," and by other names is systematic and rule-governed like all natural speech varieties. In fact, all human linguistic systems—spoken, signed, and written—are fundamentally regular. The systematic and expressive nature of the grammar and pronunciation patterns of the African American vernacular has been established by numerous scientific studies over the past thirty years. Characterizations of Ebonics as "slang," "mutant," "lazy," "defective," "ungrammatical," or "broken English" are incorrect and demeaning.

b. The distinction between "languages" and "dialects" is usually made more on social and political grounds than on purely linguistic ones. For example, different varieties of Chinese are popularly regarded as "dialects," though their speakers cannot understand each other, but speakers of Swedish and Norwegian, which are regarded as separate "languages," generally understand each other. What is important from a linguistic and educational point of view is not whether AAVE is called a "language" or a "dialect" but rather that its systematicity be recognized.

c. As affirmed in the LSA Statement of Language Rights (June 1996), there are individual and group benefits to maintaining vernacular speech varieties and there are scientific and human advantages to linguistic diversity. For those living in the United States there are also benefits in acquiring Standard English and resources should be made available to all who aspire to mastery of Standard English. The

Oakland School Board's commitment to helping students master Standard English is commendable.

d. There is evidence from Sweden, the U.S., and other countries that speakers of other varieties can be aided in their learning of the standard variety by pedagogical approaches which recognize the legitimacy of the other varieties of a language. From this perspective, the Oakland School Board's decision to recognize the vernacular of African American students in teaching them Standard English is linguistically and pedagogically sound.

WRITING SUGGESTIONS

1. (*Writing from Experience*) Seymour proposes accepting bidialectism, which would reinforce respect for Black English while the teaching of Standard English continued in the schools. According to Seymour, bidialectism would allow children to emulate Martin Luther King Jr., who was masterful in using both dialects. It could be said that most young people, even those who have mastered Standard English, practice a form of bidialectism. Think about how you speak with your parents and teachers, and how you speak when you are with your friends. Write a short essay in which you summarize the differences between the two situations. What are the differences in vocabulary? In sentence structure? Why do you tailor your speech according to the situation?

2. (*Writing from Reading*) According to Seymour, when children are made to feel ashamed of their language, they become ashamed of themselves, and they tend to react with defiance or capitulation. Seymour characterizes the results as "devastating" and states outright that they "lead straight to the dropout route" (9). Do you agree with Seymour's presumption? Write an essay in which you discuss your perception of how people's attitudes toward others are affected by the way they speak. What, for you, is the nature of the relationship between language and self-worth?

3. (*Writing from Research*) The preceding Language in Action section presented a resolution from academic linguists supporting the Oakland school board's decision to use Ebonics in the classroom. Using your library's media sources and the Internet, research the other arguments for and against the use of Ebonics in the schools. Write an essay in which you summarize the situation in the Oakland schools, the reasoning behind the adoption of Ebonics, and the arguments against using nonstandard English in education. Then write a three- or four-sentence position statement for or against Oakland's decision to use Ebonics. Base your position statement on the situation in the Oakland schools at the time, the nature of the instruction proposed, and your perception regarding what would have been gained and lost by implementing Ebonics instruction.

Endangered Languages

Katharine Whittemore

Magazines as diverse as Smithsonian, Audubon, Seventeen, New England Monthly, Lingua Franca, Self, *and* Adirondack Life *have published the work of Katharine Whittemore, a freelance writer and editor from Cambridge, Massachusetts. A graduate of Trinity College in Hartford, Connecticut, Whittemore later edited the* American Retrospective Series, *producing anthologies of articles that were originally written for* Harper's *magazine. She found working on these books, including* Voices in Black & White: Writings on Race in America from Harper's Magazine *(1992) and* Turning Toward Home: Reflections on the Family from Harper's Magazine *(1993), fascinating because of their broad historical record of life in America. Whittemore has said about writing, "If you are curious about the world, it's the best profession possible, because you get to alight in universes that aren't normally open to you." Whittemore currently reviews books for* Salon *magazine online.*

The following essay first appeared in "Ideas," a column Whittemore wrote for the Boston Globe *from 1994 to 1995. She makes readers aware of the rapid acceleration in language extinction. As global communications become easier and standardization more attractive, it is becoming difficult for small cultures to retain their languages. Whittemore's essay discusses the reasons behind the disappearance of so many languages and explains what the world loses when a language dies out.*

WRITING TO DISCOVER: *Most of us think of English as a subject in school and a means of communication — we seldom take the time to consider its impact on who we are and the way we see the world. Imagine if English were outlawed — if all English-language writing were destroyed and you had to learn a completely different language in six months. Write about how you would feel and what would be lost along with the demise of the English language.*

Brute statistic: some 90 percent of the world's languages will be extinct by the century's close. Here in America, this means no more Mandan, Osage, or Tuscarora, as well as the end of maybe 20 Alaskan languages, like Ainu, Eyak, and the fantastic Ubykh, with its 80 tongue-pretzeling consonants. Almost all of Australia's 250 aboriginal dialects are dying. Even languages with hundreds of thousands of speakers, such as Basque and Breton, are threatened. (Children aren't learning them these days.)

We work feverishly to save endangered species, yet we let these exquisite products of human culture disappear. As linguist Michael Krauss thunders: "Should we mourn the loss of Eyak or Ubykh any less than the loss of the panda or California condor?"

Krauss, of the University of Alaska, was the keynote speaker at "Endangered Languages: Current Issues and Future Prospects," a conference held in February [1995] at Dartmouth College, in Hanover, New Hampshire. It was organized by two Dartmouth faculty members, Lindsay Whaley, assistant professor of linguistics and classics (who speaks French, Spanish, German, Kinyarwanda, Swahili, ancient Greek, and Latin), and Lenore Grenoble, assistant professor of Russian language and literature (and speaker of Russian, German, Serbo-Croatian, and old-church Slavic, plus minimal Italian and Japanese and "badly accented French").

Linguists, of course, deplore the passing of any language. "As professionals," says Whaley, "we can't bear to watch 90 percent of our database disappear." Yes, but should the rest of us care? Isn't it easier, honestly, if the Tower of Babel slowly crumbles? Melting pot and all that? "When you lose a language," Grenoble explains, "you don't just lose words and sounds but a whole way of looking at the world."

Having mastered a dozen languages between them, Whaley and Grenoble are asked to demonstrate how a language beams forth "a way of looking at the world." They warm to the task. "Think of words like *ennui*, which are perfect, yet untranslatable," Grenoble says. Whaley laughs, and adds *Weltschmerz* to the list, that oh-so-Teutonic nod to vague despair, and "anything Yiddish, like *schlemiel, mensch.*" 5

In Russian, Grenoble says, there is a verb, *dostat'*, which means "to get," but not in painless fashion, as with a gift, but "to get with difficulty." It's used all the time, to denote getting one dented tin of sardines, say, after waiting on line for hours in uncomfortable shoes. "*Dostat'* shows a singular Soviet-style agony," Grenoble says. In Kinyarwanda, which is spoken in Rwanda, you can rejigger the emphasis through use of transitive verbs. "With a sentence like 'The doctor healed the patients,'" explains Whaley, "you can say the same thing, but switched around, so it literally translates as 'The patients healed the doctor.' It still means the doctor did the healing, but the patients' role is highlighted."

Native American languages are full of what linguists call evidentials, Grenoble says. Each verb, depending on how it is intoned, indicates what source of knowledge is being called upon in the statement. If a Nez Perce Indian says, "The day will be stormy," the "will be" might mean the speaker saw clouds gathering, or that someone else told her it would storm, or that she had a vision in which a storm was imminent. The attitudes of entire civilizations are nestled in that beautiful complexity.

In Japanese, there isn't just one set of numbers, as in English; there are different numbers used to count different objects and shapes. If you tote up sheets of paper, for instance, you apply certain numerals, while others are employed to tabulate stones. Surely, this tells us something about the precision of Japanese society. "A language says what it needs to say," as Grenoble puts it. In other words, each language expresses the heart and mind of its adherents.

Lovely, but haven't languages been dying for as long as people have walked on the earth? Yes, but today's mortality rate makes a mockery of natural attrition. Why are things so bad now? There's what Krauss calls the "cultural nerve gas" of television, which is broadcast only in predominant languages. Then there is the irony of increased literacy: As more native people receive formal education, schools cannot print textbooks in every language. Hegemony matters, too: Under Spanish colonial rule, for example, there wasn't room for the Mayan language; in the new Germany, there's no place for upper and lower Sorbian (it's spoken in parts of East Germany). "In the past, regular attrition was outstripped by growing diversity," says Whaley. "But today," Grenoble chimes in, "languages are not evolving, they're being *replaced*."

There are ways of staunching the ruin. Linguists are desperately try-   10
ing to locate the last elderly speakers of various languages and get them on video and audiotape. Apprenticeships, in which an elderly speaker is matched with a younger student to pass the torch, are being established at a frantic pace. When there is a large population to support them, immersion schools are making good headway. In northern Quebec, the Kanaweha Mohawks have set up an elementary school that offers its curriculum in the native language. Grenoble knows a linguist who pulled up at the school yard and was overjoyed to hear little boys cursing at each other in Mohawk.

The Navajo have been particularly skillful at keeping their language alive. In order to get their Anglicized kids to see that Navajo is worth knowing, tribe educators work on giving it cachet. Administrators bring hip, Navajo-speaking artists and musicians to school regularly, to drive home the notion that "speaking Navajo is cool," as Whaley says. Some tribes, like western Canada's Salishan family (it includes the Montana and the Idaho tribes), have even set up language camps for kids in the summertime.

And in the end, it's not the linguists but these would-be heirs who prize their world of words most. "It's an extremely emotional issue," says Whaley. "My students think attachment to language is a kind of nostalgia. But it's much more than that. When someone's ancestral language dies, they're not just sad, they feel a crushing loss." Grenoble nods, then adds: "They say it's a kind of agony."

FOCUSING ON CONTENT

1. What do the languages mentioned by Whittemore in the first paragraph have in common? What does this imply about the languages that are most threatened with extinction in the near future?

2. According to Whaley and Grenoble, what is lost when a language dies out? Why are linguists fighting to save languages?

3. What is notable about the way the Japanese count (8)? What does this attribute say about Japanese society?

4. According to Whittemore and the experts she quotes, what has accelerated the loss of languages in recent years? In what way has the process changed?

5. How are the Navajo people combating the loss of their language (11)? Why does their approach work?

FOCUSING ON WRITING

1. Write a short definition of the term *endangered language,* basing your definition on Whittemore's essay. (Glossary: *Definition*) What associations can you make from the term? Do you think it's an appropriate term for her to use? Why or why not?

2. In paragraph 9, Whittemore uses the words of Krauss to label television as a "cultural nerve gas." Her opinion of television is obvious, but why do you think she chooses the pejorative quotation rather than simply say that she does not like the effect of television? What exactly does she wish to communicate with her specific choice of words? (Glossary: *Diction*)

3. Most of Whittemore's specific examples are quotations from her discussion with Grenoble and Whaley. (Glossary: *Examples*) How does their continued "presence" in the essay assist Whittemore in arguing her thesis? (Glossary: *Thesis*) Why is the support of expert linguists so important for her essay?

4. Whittemore ends her essay on a somewhat depressing note. Indeed, the last word is *agony.* (Glossary: *Beginnings and Endings*) What does she achieve in her last paragraph? With what thoughts and emotions does she wish to leave her readers? Explain.

LANGUAGE IN ACTION

The following excerpt, from *Revitalizing Indigenous Languages* (1999), demonstrates the importance of language to the cultural identity of the Iñupiaq Eskimos. What is your "cultural spirit"? How easy is it for you to identify with a specific culture or heritage? If your heritage were assaulted by "an all-pervasive modern individualistic, materialistic, and hedonistic technological culture," what aspects of your heritage would you try to retain?

FROM THE INTRODUCTION TO
SOME BASICS OF INDIGENOUS LANGUAGE REVITALIZATION

In the United States there is an "English-Only" political movement that questions the value of teaching languages other than English, including indigenous languages. Throughout the symposiums there has been a theme of how language and culture are intimately entwined and cannot be separated. The importance of cultural retention, and thus indigenous language retention, was brought home to me at the third symposium in Anchorage, Alaska, when I picked up a card describing Iñupiaq Eskimo values. One side of the card read:

> Every Iñupiaq is responsible to all other Iñupiaq for the survival of our cultural spirit, and the values and traditions through which it survives.
> Through our extended family, we retain, teach, and live our Iñupiaq way.

The other side read, "With guidance and support from Elders, we must teach our children Iñupiaq values" and then the card listed the values of "knowledge of language, sharing, respect for others, cooperation, respect for elders, love for children, hard work, knowledge of family tree, avoidance of conflict, respect for nature, spirituality, humor, family roles, hunter success, domestic skills, humility, [and] responsibility to tribe." The card concluded with "OUR UNDERSTANDING OF OUR UNIVERSE AND OUR PLACE IN IT IS A BELIEF IN GOD AND A RESPECT FOR ALL HIS CREATIONS." I have kept this card in my wallet as a reminder that indigenous language revitalization is part of a larger attempt by indigenous peoples to retain their cultural strengths in the face of the demoralizing assaults of an all-pervasive modern individualistic, materialistic, and hedonistic technological culture. The card reminds me of why it is so important to do everything we can to help the efforts of any person or group that wants to work to preserve their language.

WRITING SUGGESTIONS

1. (*Writing from Experience*) Whittemore asserts that the French word *ennui* cannot be translated well into English. When you watch foreign movies, you have probably noticed that the subtitle dialogue often seems uninspired — something has been lost in translation. On the other hand, think about a hip American movie being translated into other languages. How well do you think the dialogue in *Clueless* (or another movie with considerable slang) would fare in translation? Write an essay about the unique words and qualities of English. What does English have going for it, in your opinion? What do you consider its weaknesses? Explain your views.

2. (*Writing from Reading*) Grenoble says, "When you lose a language, you don't just lose words and sounds but a whole way of looking at the world." This statement assumes that language actively reinforces large aspects of each culture. Write an essay on this subject, considering the following questions: How much impact do you think language has on culture? What is the relationship between language and culture? Do you agree with the idea that each language helps to create a specific way of looking at the world? Why couldn't this way of looking at the world be translated and, over time, adequately expressed in another language? Do you think a lot of effort should be put into saving the languages that are dying out?

3. (*Writing from Research*) Using Internet and library resources, research a language that is either extinct or is threatened with extinction. Choose one that is prominent in linguistic studies. Write an essay about why the language died out or is seriously threatened. What language and culture are replacing it? What has been lost by its speakers and what, if anything, has been gained?

The Language We Know

SIMON ORTIZ

Award-winning writer Simon Ortiz was born in the Acoma Pueblo in New Mexico in 1941. His experiences at the Bureau of Indian Affairs day school—where he learned English but where expression of his native language was suppressed and punished—introduced him to the struggle between Native Americans and the U.S. government, a prominent subject in his writing to the present day. Ortiz has taught Native American literature and creative writing at the Institute of Native American Arts, the University of New Mexico, Navajo Community College, Sinte Gleska College, San Diego State University, Colorado College, the College of Marin, and Lewis and Clark College. His published works include Naked in the Wind *(1971),* Going for the Rain *(1976),* Fight Back: For the Sake of the People, For the Sake of the Land *(1980), and the more recent* After and Before Lightning *(1994). Ortiz has also become an important voice for tribal issues and concerns, having served his tribe as interpreter and first lieutenant governor.*

In the following essay, first published in 1987 in I Tell You Now: Autobiography Essays by Native American Writers, *Ortiz discusses his relationship with language and the effects his two primary languages have had on his life and writing style. He makes it clear that his inspiration to write still comes from the struggle of the Acoma Pueblo people and his desire to preserve their ancient culture and traditions.*

WRITING TO DISCOVER: *Jot down a story you know that was passed along to you verbally. It could, for example, be a family story, something you heard at school, or part of a performance you saw. What did the story gain from your having heard it rather than read it? What did it teach you? Why was it memorable? If it were written, how might it be different?*

I don't remember a world without language. From the time of my earliest childhood, there was language. Always language, and imagination, speculation, utters of sound. Words, beginnings of words. What would I be without language? My existence has been determined by language, not only the spoken but the unspoken, the language of speech and the language of motion. I can't remember a world without memory. Memory, immediate and far away in the past, something in the sinew, blood, ageless cell. Although I don't recall the exact moment I spoke or tried to speak, I know the feeling of something tugging at the core of the mind, something unutterable uttered into existence. It is language that brings us into existence. It is language that brings us into being in order to know life.

My childhood was the oral tradition of the Acoma Pueblo people—Aaquumeh hano—which included my immediate family of three older sisters, two younger sisters, two younger brothers, and my mother and father. My world was our world of the Aaquumeh in McCartys, one of the two villages descended from the ageless mother pueblo of Acoma. My world was our Eagle clan-people among other clans. I grew up in Deetziyamah, which is the Aaquumeh name for McCartys, which is posted at the exit off the present interstate highway in western New Mexico. I grew up within a people who farmed small garden plots and fields, who were mostly poor and not well schooled in the American system's education. The language I spoke was that of a struggling people who held ferociously to a heritage, culture, language, and land despite the odds posed them by the forces surrounding them since A.D.1540, the advent of Euro-American colonization. When I began school in 1948 at the BIA (Bureau of Indian Affairs) day school in our village, I was armed with the basic ABC's and the phrases "Good morning, Miss Oleman" and "May I please be excused to go to the bathroom," but it was an older language that was my fundamental strength.

In my childhood, the language we all spoke was Acoma, and it was a struggle to maintain it against the outright threats of corporal punishment, ostracism, and the invocation that it would impede our progress towards Americanization. Children in school were punished and looked upon with disdain if they did not speak and learn English quickly and smoothly, and so I learned it. It has occurred to me that I learned English simply because I was forced to, as so many other Indian children were. But I know, also, there was another reason, and this was that I loved language, the sound, meaning, and magic of language. Language opened up vistas of the world around me, and it allowed me to discover knowledge that would not be possible for me to know without the use of language. Later, when I began to experiment with and explore language in poetry and fiction, I allowed that a portion of that impetus was because I had come to know English through forceful acculturation. Nevertheless, the underlying force was the beauty and poetic power of language in its many forms that instilled in me the desire to become a user of language as a writer, singer, and storyteller. Significantly, it was the Acoma language, which I don't use enough of today, that inspired me to become a writer. The concepts, values, and philosophy contained in my original language and the struggle it has faced have determined my life and vision as a writer.

In Deetziyamah, I discovered the world of the Acoma land and people firsthand through my parents, sisters, and brothers, and my own perceptions, voiced through all that encompasses the oral tradition, which is ageless for any culture. It is a small village, even smaller years ago, and like other Indian communities it is wealthy with its knowledge of daily event, history, and social system, all that make up a people who have a many-dimensioned heritage. Our family lived in a two-room home (built by my grandfather some years after he and my grandmother moved with their daughters from Old Acoma), which my father added rooms to later. I remember by father's work at enlarging our home for our growing family. He was a skilled stoneworker, like many other men of an older Pueblo generation who worked with sandstone and mud mortar to build their homes and pueblos. It takes time, persistence, patience, and the belief that the walls that come to stand will do so for a long, long time, perhaps even forever. I like to think that by helping to mix mud and carry stone for my father and other elders I managed to bring that influence into my consciousness as a writer.

Both my mother and my father were good storytellers and singers (as   5
my mother is to this day—my father died in 1978), and for their generation, which was born soon after the turn of the century, they were relatively educated in the American system. Catholic missionaries had taken both of them as children to a parochial boarding school far from Acoma, and they imparted their discipline for study and quest for education to us children when we started school. But it was their indigenous sense of gaining knowledge that was most meaningful to me. Acquiring knowledge about life was above all the most important item; it was a value that one had to have in order to be fulfilled personally and on behalf of his community. And this they insisted upon imparting through the oral tradition as they told their children about our native history and our community and culture and our "stories." These stories were common knowledge of act, event, and behavior in a close-knit pueblo. It was knowledge about how one was to make a living through work that benefited his family and everyone else.

Because we were a subsistence farming people, or at least tried to be, I learned to plant, hoe weeds, irrigate and cultivate corn, chili, pumpkins, beans. Through counsel and advice I came to know that the rain which provided water was a blessing, gift, and symbol and that it was the land which provided for our lives. It was the stories and songs which provided the knowledge that I was woven into the intricate web that was my Acoma life. In our garden and our cornfields I learned about the seasons, growth cycles of cultivated plants, what one had to think and feel about the land; and at home I became aware of how we must care for each other: All of this was encompassed in an intricate relationship which had to be maintained in order that life continue. After supper on many occasions my father would bring out his drum and sing as we, the children, danced to themes about the rain, hunting, land and people. It was all that is contained within the language of oral tradition that made me explicitly aware of a yet unarticulated urge to write, to tell what I had learned and was learning and what it all meant to me.

My grandfather was old already when I came to know him. I was only one of his many grandchildren, but I would go with him to get wood for our households, to the garden to chop weeds, and to his sheep camp to help care for his sheep. I don't remember his exact words, but I know they were about how we must sacredly concern ourselves with the people and the holy earth. I know his words were about how we must regard ourselves and others with compassion and love; I know that his knowledge was vast, as a medicine man and an elder of his kiva, and I listened as a boy should. My grandfather represented for me a link to the past that is important for me to hold in my memory because it is not only memory but knowledge that substantiates my present existence. He and the grandmothers and grandfathers before him thought about us as they lived, confirmed in their belief of a continuing life, and they brought our present beings into existence by the beliefs they held. The consciousness of that belief is what informs my present concerns with language, poetry, and fiction.

My first poem was for Mother's Day when I was in the fifth grade, and it was the first poem that was ever published, too, in the Skull Valley School newsletter. Of course I don't remember how the juvenile poem went, but it must have been certain in its expression of love and reverence for the woman who was the most important person in my young life. The poem didn't signal any prophecy of my future as a poet, but it must have come from the forming idea that there were things one could do with language and writing. My mother, years later, remembers how I was a child who always told stories — that is, tall tales — who always had explanations for things probably better left unspoken, and she says that I also liked to perform in school plays. In remembering, I do know that I was coming to that age when the emotions and thoughts in me began to moil to the surface. There was much to experience and express in that age when youth has a precociousness that is broken easily or made to flourish. We were a poor family, always on the verge of financial disaster, though our parents always managed to feed us and keep us in clothing. We had the problems, unfortunately ordinary, of many Indian families who face poverty on a daily basis, never enough of anything, the feeling of a denigrating self-consciousness, alcoholism in the family and community, the feeling that something was falling apart though we tried desperately to hold it all together.

My father worked for the railroad for many years as a laborer and later as a welder. We moved to Skull Valley, Arizona, for one year in the early 1950s, and it was then that I first came in touch with a non-Indian, non-Acoma world. Skull Valley was a farming and ranching community, and my younger brothers and sisters and I went to a one-room school. I had never really had much contact with white people except from a careful and suspicious distance, but now here I was, totally surrounded by them, and there was nothing to do but bear the experience and learn from it. Although I perceived there was not much difference between *them* and *us* in certain respects, there was a distinct feeling that we were not the same either. This thought had been inculcated in me, especially by an Acoma expression— *Gaimuu Mericano*—that spoke of the "fortune" of being an American. In later years as a social activist and committed writer, I would try to offer a strong positive view of our collective Indianness through my writing. Nevertheless, my father was an inadequately paid laborer, and we were far from our home land for economic-social reasons, and my feelings and thoughts about that experience during that time would become a part of how I became a writer.

Soon after, I went away from my home and family to go to boarding   10
school, first in Santa Fe and then in Albuquerque. This was in the 1950s, and this had been the case for the past half-century for Indians: We had to leave home in order to become truly American by joining the mainstream, which was deemed to be the proper course of our lives. On top of this was termination, a U.S. government policy which dictated that Indians sever their relationship to the federal government and remove themselves from their lands and go to American cities for jobs and education. It was an era which bespoke the intent of U.S. public policy that Indians were no longer to be Indians. Naturally, I did not perceive this in any analytical or purposeful sense; rather, I felt an unspoken anxiety and resentment against unseen forces that determined our destiny to be un-Indian, embarrassed and uncomfortable with our grandparents' customs and strictly held values. We were to set our goals as American working men and women, singlemindedly industrious, patriotic, and unquestioning, building for a future which ensured that the United States was the greatest nation in the world. I felt fearfully uneasy with this, for by then I felt the loneliness, alienation, and isolation imposed upon me by the separation from my family, home and community.

Something was happening; I could see that in my years at Catholic school and the U.S. Indian school. I remembered my grandparents' and parents' words: Educate yourself in order to help your people. In that era and the generation who had the same experience I had, there was an unspoken vow: We were caught in a system inexorably, and we had to learn that system well in order to fight back. Without the motive of a fightback we would not be able to survive as the people our heritage had lovingly bequeathed us. My diaries and notebooks began then, and though none have survived to the present, I know they contained the varied moods of a youth filled with loneliness, anger, and discomfort that seemed to have unknown causes. Yet at the same time, I realize now, I was coming to know myself clearly in a way that I would later articulate in writing. My love of language, which allowed me to deal with the world, to delve into it, to experiment and discover, held for me a vision of awe and wonder, and by then grammar teachers had noticed I was a good speller, used verbs and tenses correctly, and wrote complete sentences. Although I imagine that they might have surmised this as unusual for an Indian student whose original language was not English, I am grateful for their perception and attention.

During the latter part of that era in the 1950s of Indian termination and the Cold War, a portion of which still exists today, there were the beginnings of a bolder and more vocalized resistance against the current U.S. public policies of repression, racism, and cultural ethnocide. It seemed to be inspired by the civil rights movement led by black people in the United States and by decolonization and liberation struggles worldwide. Indian people were being relocated from their rural homelands at an astonishingly devastating rate, yet at the same time they resisted the U.S. effort by maintaining determined ties with their heritage, returning often to their native communities, and establishing Indian centers in the cities they were removed to. Indian rural communities, such as Acoma Pueblo, insisted on their land claims and began to initiate legal battles in the areas of natural and social, political and economic human rights. By the retention and the inspiration of our native heritage, values, philosophies, and language, we would know ourselves as a strong and enduring people. Having a modest and latent consciousness of this as a teenager, I began to write about the experience of being Indian in America. Although I had only a romanticized image of what a writer was, which came from the pulp rendered by American popular literature, and I really didn't know anything about writing, I sincerely felt a need to say things, to speak, to release the energy of the impulse to help my people.

My writing in my late teens and early adulthood was fashioned after the American short stories and poetry taught in the high schools of the 1940s and 1950s, but by the 1960s, after I had gone to college and dropped out and served in the military, I began to develop topics and themes from my Indian background. The experience in my village of Deetziyamah and Acoma Pueblo was readily accessible. I had grown up within the oral tradition of speech, social and religious ritual, elders' counsel and advice, countless and endless stories, everyday event, and the visual art that was symbolically representative of life all around. My mother was a potter of the well-known Acoma clayware, a traditional art form that had been passed to her from her mother and the generations of mothers before. My father carved figures from wood and did beadwork. This was not unusual, as Indian people know; there was always some kind of artistic endeavor that people set themselves to, although they did not necessarily articulate it as "Art" in the sense of Western civilization. One lived and expressed an artful life, whether it was in ceremonial singing and dancing, architecture, painting, speaking, or in the way one's social-cultural life was structured. When I turned my attention to my own heritage, I did so because this was my identity, the substance of who I was, and I wanted to write about what that meant. My desire was to write about the integrity and dignity of an Indian identity, and at the same time I wanted to look at what this was within the context of an America that had too often denied its Indian heritage.

To a great extent my writing has a natural political-cultural bent simply because I was nurtured intellectually and emotionally within an atmosphere of Indian resistance. Aacquu did not die in 1598 when it was burned and razed by European conquerors, nor did the people become hopeless when their children were taken away to U.S. schools far from home and new ways were imposed upon them. The *Aaquumeh hano,* despite losing much of their land and surrounded by a foreign civilization, have not lost sight of their native heritage. This is the factual case with most other Indian peoples, and the clear explanation for this has been the fight-back we have found it necessary to wage. At times, in the past, it was outright armed struggle, like that of present-day Indians in Central and South America with whom we must identify; currently, it is often in the legal arena, and it is in the field of literature. In 1981, when I was invited to the White House for an event celebrating American poets and poetry, I did not immediately accept the invitation. I questioned myself about the possibility that I was merely being exploited as an Indian, and I hedged against accepting. But then I recalled the elders going among our people in the poor days of the 1950s, asking for donations—a dollar here and there, a sheep, perhaps a piece of pottery—in order to finance a trip to the nation's capital. They were to make another countless appeal on behalf of our people, to demand justice, to reclaim lost land even though there was only spare hope they would be successful. I went to the White House realizing that I was to do no less than they and those who had fought in the Pueblo Revolt of 1680, and I read my poems and sang songs that were later described as "guttural" by a Washington, D.C., newspaper. I suppose it is more or less understandable why such a view of Indian literature is held by many, and it is also clear why there should be a political stand taken in my writing and those of my sister and brother Indian writers.

The 1960s and afterward have been an invigorating and liberating   15
period for Indian people. It has been only a little more than twenty years since Indian writers began to write and publish extensively, but we are writing and publishing more and more; we can only go forward. We come from an ageless, continuing oral tradition that informs us of our values, concepts, and notions as native people, and it is amazing how much of this tradition is ingrained so deeply in our contemporary writing, considering the brutal efforts of cultural repression that was not long ago outright U.S. policy. We were not to speak our languages, practice our spiritual beliefs, or accept the values of our past generations; and we were discouraged from pressing for our natural rights as Indian human beings. In spite of the fact that there is to some extent the same repression today,

we persist and insist in living, believing, hoping, loving, speaking, and writing as Indians. This is embodied in the language we know and share in our writing. We have always had this language, and it is the language, spoken and unspoken, that determines our existence, that brought our grandmothers and grandfathers and ourselves into being in order that there be a continuing life.

FOCUSING ON CONTENT

1. What aspects of language captivated Ortiz, even as a child? What inspired him to become a writer?

2. What is significant about Ortiz's family home? What does it demonstrate about Acoma culture?

3. In what ways did Ortiz's parents and grandparents pass along Acoma traditions and values to him? How have these traditions and values affected his writing?

4. What are the problems associated with the Acoma Pueblo? What relationship do its residents have with non-Acoma Americans?

5. What effect did the American policy of termination have on Ortiz and his family? What impact did it have on the way Ortiz viewed himself in the world?

6. Why was Ortiz reluctant to attend the White House celebration of American poets and poetry? Why did he eventually go?

FOCUSING ON WRITING

1. Although Ortiz expresses many strong emotions in his essay, what would you say is his overall tone? (Glossary: *Tone*) Identify specific passages that establish the tone, and explain their importance.

2. In paragraph 3, Ortiz describes language as "magic." What other words does he use to convey his love of language? (Glossary: *Diction*) Why do you think he communicates this love, even as he documents the painful manner in which he was indoctrinated into the English-speaking American mainstream?

3. What does Ortiz mean when he says in paragraph 13 that Indians "lived and expressed an artful life"? How does the Indian definition of *art* differ from the European-American definition? (Glossary: *Definition*)

4. How does Ortiz respond to the characterization of his poetry and singing at the White House as "guttural"? To what does the term refer? Why is this characterization, and his response, important to the purpose of his essay? (Glossary: *Purpose*)

5. A number of Ortiz's paragraphs are long by contemporary standards. Analyze paragraph 14. Do you think the paragraph should be divided? If so, where would you divide it? If not, what does the author accomplish by writing such a long paragraph? (Glossary: *Unity and Organization*)

LANGUAGE IN ACTION

The struggles between Native Americans and the U.S. government are on-going, although, as Ortiz indicates, they now tend to take place in legislatures and courthouses rather than on battlefields. The following excerpt is a summary by Karen M. Strom from the Ward Alan Minge book, *Ácoma, Pueblo in the Sky* (1991). It reveals how the Ácoma view their relationship both to the land and to the state and federal governments. How would you characterize the language used by the Ácoma people? What does the language reveal about their relationship with the land?

ÁCOMA OPPOSITION TO THE
EL MALPAIS NATIONAL MONUMENT

The Ácoma Pueblo voiced strong opposition over the entire period that the creation of the **El Malpais National Monument** was under consideration. The Ácoma reservation not only bordered on but extended into the proposed National Monument area because of several recent land purchases which were made by the Pueblo specifically to acquire religious shrines and water sources.

> Many times through the motions of the political world, we as the first inhabitants of this area are neglected by the greater society. We do not feel that the designation of wilderness can aid us as Ácoma people in any beneficial manner now or in the future. We urge that this position [be] not accepted as one comment; but rather giving due consideration to the government-to-government relationship and the number of people that the tribal government is representative of. This information has been presented to our tribal members at various community meetings through the past three years and rest assured that they support our position ["Malpais Lava Flow Belongs to the Ácoma Pueblo, Indian Leaders tell BLM." *Albuquerque Tribune,* May 23, 1979.]

Nonetheless, in 1986 House Resolution 3684, to establish El Malpais National Monument was introduced, without even recognizing the existence of Ácoma objections. Hearings were held in Grants [NM] where local residents could comment upon the proposal . [. . .]

During these meetings, Governor Paytiamo of Ácoma stated the Ácoma position:

> The Pueblo of Ácoma people retain vested interest in these lands considered as a national monument. These lands always remain Ácoma's aboriginal lands in spite of its designation as Bureau of Land Management land and/or as state school lands. Federal and state laws may take away our lands under newly instituted laws but our people remain intact with the land, as our Ácoma elders say, "We are already underneath the land."

The Governor then listed the specific points disputed by the Ácoma Pueblo:

1. Ácoma did not want to be constrained in any future development of its property adjacent to El Malpais.
2. Ácoma must be assured continued access to the reservation.

3. Ácoma would protect its water rights, both for her private deeded lands and for the surface and subsurface waters reaching the reservation.
4. Ácoma wanted the religious shrines protected under the Indian Religious Freedom Act.
5. Ácoma objected to attracting more tourists who would trespass on tribal lands or damage property.
6. Ácoma considered the prehistoric ruins as sacred and objected to visitors disturbing them in any manner.

The bill was revised to exclude private and deeded lands, including those owned by the Ácoma Pueblo. However the boundary of the proposed monument extended to the Ácoma Reservation boundary, therefore preventing them from enlarging the reservation any further toward the west. The Ácoma wished the monument boundary to end on the west side of State Road 117. The Ácoma offered to purchase the 12,385 acres east of State Road 117. The bill was passed by the House in the revised form without taking the Ácoma position into account . [. . .]

[After several unsuccessful appeals in the Senate], the Ácoma Tribal Council authorized the Governor to take the Abraham Lincoln cane, the symbol of trust between the tribe and the federal government, back to Washington and break it. The Council concluded that the federal government felt that their tribal lands were all public domain, that their religious shrines were no longer accepted as sacred, and that their water rights had no protection. The Council felt that the return of the Lincoln cane would best demonstrate the way they felt they had been treated yet again. Although there was some last minute activity attempting to placate the Ácoma people, the answer was always that the bill was too far along for any changes to be made at this point. President Reagan refused to see Governor Paytiamo. The Tribal Council again complained to the New Mexico delegation:

> Ácoma is hurt by the fact that laws made by the dominant society continue to oppress native people. We can no longer be pushed and required to yield to the injustice being done to us. We can only see how the whiteman's laws are so often used to the detriment of our sacred lands. We must insist that this act is unjust.

The Council then again repeated their request that the 12,385 acres east of State Road 117 be returned to the tribe.

Last minute help from Senator Daniel Inouye was unavailing due to the opposition of the New Mexico Congressional delegation. The Senate unanimously approved the bill on December 17, 1987. President Reagan signed the bill on Governor Paytiamo's last day in office, Dec. 31, after ignoring a letter from the Governor requesting an audience to discuss the bill in the presence of the Lincoln cane.

WRITING SUGGESTIONS

1. (*Writing from Experience*) Ortiz's parents and grandparents made it clear that he should get a good education. They wanted him to assimilate into mainstream American culture. Then, they reasoned, he could be effective in working to improve the plight of his people. This is a responsibility that Ortiz has

obviously handled with skill and dedication, but it is nonetheless a burden in some ways. What do your parents want you to achieve, and why do they have particular goals for you? Write an essay in which you discuss your background, your current perception of how you fit in mainstream culture, and where you believe you will end up. How hard do your parents push you? How much of an obligation do you feel toward them and, through them, toward your personal heritage? Are your personal goals in conflict with or compatible with those of your parents?

2. (*Writing from Reading*) In paragraph 10, Ortiz states, "We were to set our goals as American working men and women, singlemindedly industrious, patriotic, and unquestioning, building for a future which ensured that the United States was the greatest nation in the world." Write an essay in which you consider the meaning of *industrious, patriotic,* and *unquestioning* in the context of the quotation. How does each quality help the United States retain its national strength and identity? Why would the government try so hard to instill such qualities in those outside of mainstream society, including recent immigrants and, ironically, those native to the land? To what extent do you agree with Ortiz's characterization of the U.S. policy of termination?

3. (*Writing from Research*) There has been an intense effort in recent years to record Native American folklore and stories and put them in print for the first time. Using your library and Internet resources, find several collections of such stories. Read several selections from one tribe. If you can find enough Acoma tales, use those. Otherwise, select a tribe from New Mexico that has a large enough collection of folklore. Write an essay in which you discuss what the stories demonstrate about the tribe. How do the members view their place in the world? From what is expressed in their stories, what aspects of life are the most important to them? Do the stories teach values similar to those espoused by Ortiz's grandfather? In your opinion, how do the priorities and values expressed in the stories conflict with mainstream American culture?

The Dilemma of Black English

KEN PARISH PERKINS

Chicago native Ken Parish Perkins graduated from Southern Illinois University with degrees in journalism and African American studies. He began his writing career as a sports writer for several newspapers in Illinois and then became the culture critic for Dollars & Sense *magazine in Chicago. Several years later he joined the* Dallas Morning News *as an entertainment and general news reporter, eventually taking over as the newspaper's television critic. In 1993 he won two Griot Awards, which honor outstanding journalism covering African Americans. Perkins is currently a columnist for the* Fort Worth Star-Telegram.

The following selection originally appeared in the Star-Telegram *on July 13, 1998. Here Perkins uses basketball star Magic Johnson's failed attempt at hosting a talk show to explore various issues associated with Black English.*

WRITING TO DISCOVER: *Whether or not we are speakers of Black English, we can see all around us its influence on the way we talk. Write about how Black English has influenced your speech. Do you use it all the time or only in certain situations? Do you use only a few Black-English terms now and then, or do you not use this dialect at all?*

A lifelong friend of mine called the other day to shoot the breeze and we began, as we often do, to delve into, dissect, and dispose of subjects large and small with speedy efficiency.

Before long we'd been transported back to our Chicago enclave, and it wasn't until my live-in looked on in perplexed horror that I was aware of our slippage into the netherworld of diction and cultural expression.

He: "What it be like, brah?"

Me: "Just kickin', ma man. Wassup in A-Town?"

He: "Same-o sam-o, knowwhatI'msayin'? I gotta wait for some mo' months before they come through on that promotion."

Me: "So, wassup wit that? Thought dat was promised."

He: "Just another means in keepin' a brother down, youknowwhat-I'msayin'?"

My friend Daryl is college-educated with a weighty resume of fine work in banking, and, sure, I know exactly what he's saying. Many may not, my loved one included. She often uses my bilingual services as interpreter when Daryl and I are on one of our verbal rolls, which is almost any time we're within each other's space.

Ours is, to be precise, a black vernacular from the urban section of the Midwest region, a kind of pacing of melodic rhythms weaving speech

365

and expression, where metaphors, similes, and nouns are literally turned into verbs, and the rest is merely tossed in for primitive simplicity.

I explain this in part to be serious and amusing because the whole   10
issue of "Ebonics," or "black English," took center stage a couple of years back when an Oakland, Calif. school board pushed for permission to teach black English not as a cultural dialect but as a genetically based second language equal in stature to ordinary English. The board figured it was the only way students could academically progress.

But many African-Americans were insulted. Criticism mounted, and the resolution crashed and burned.

Buried under the rubble was a muffled debate about whether critics of "black English" are merely wannabe-white black folk seeking assimilation into the dominant culture.

Well, such a debate has resurfaced, albeit in the underground railroad of black thought (Internet, radio, black barbershops), conjured by a former basketball player who never would have thought he'd be part of a philosophical discussion on cultural linguistics.

Surely you know the dude. Earvin "Magic" Johnson. A former college b-baller who bolted out of Michigan State University early for NBA riches.

A businessman and millionaire many times over, Johnson is also a   15
brother from around the way and speaks that language accordingly. After harsh, though relatively quiet, criticism of his language skills during a brief stint as a sports commentator, Johnson knew he had to be better prepared for his latest battle.

He has been dutifully taking speech and diction lessons to better communicate with his interviewees, his live audience, and the viewers his show desperately needs to survive in the competitive late-night arena.

Of course, he slips. Johnson's way of saying "dis" for the word "this," "dat" for "that," "I shoulda," and "all's I want to do" has a good number of African-Americans rolling on the floor while others cringe in the embarrassment of a black man butchering the English language.

And that's where the debate begins. Some believe that black critics of black dialect are practicing a form of self-hatred, choosing a white culture over their own, and embracing what they call a slave mentality. Johnson is perfectly fine, since he's just talkin' like a brotha, ya know?

Besides, there's a reason for this. Johnson's dialect, as is mine, is a mixture of accent and sentence construction handed down from enslaved Africans who didn't speak English and weren't taught it. Before you dismiss this as nonsense, consider that slaves picked up words from masters intent on condemning them to a devastating cycle among the lower rungs of society. Some have made it out over the years, while many have not.

Daryl and I grew up in a poor, all-black neighborhood and were edu-   20
cated in cash-strapped all-black schools—my first "educated" peer was a white college roommate from a wealthy suburb whose word usage was

jarring to me but considered standard English by my professors. He could barely understand a word I said, and I had to adjust if my plans were to make it through journalism school.

For phone conversations with Daryl, black English is our adopted mode of speech, a vernacular chosen with the knowledge that we're both able to employ a more standardized language at will. Call us sellouts if you so please, but our social mobility and respect (from blacks as well as others) hinges on it, even though I have yet to master "ask" without saying "ax," and my editor often appears confused when I'm excited and speaking quickly.

In some ways it's like we're doomed. Past experience keeps black Americans gravely suspicious of anyone wanting to change anything about a way of life that's exclusive and therefore empowering. Our radars will remain keen as long as we witness, for instance, the dilution of the Spanish language in California (bilingual classes will be no more) and other ills.

Still, to adhere to such broken English for the sake of holding onto cultural heritage is false hope and complete nonsense. It's unfortunate that we continue to engage in "who's blacker than whom" contests, attaching the preservation of one's cultural history and identity to, of all things, poor grammar.

Johnson's talk show will go down in flames not because of dis and dat but because he is charming but not entertaining, and late-night television simply isn't his thing. While I've never talked with Johnson, I could see our private conversations dipping into the black vernacular, both of us feeling quite comfortable with the proceedings.

There is, in some ways, a sadness to this truth. But I'll settle for the 25 beauty of this exclusivity when it comes, particularly from strangers. Like the other day. Upon leaving the office, a black male city worker emptying the meters noticed me and said quickly, "Wassup, brah?"

"Nothin' much, ma man," I told him "Nothin' much."

FOCUSING ON CONTENT

1. What is Perkins's thesis in his article? (Glossary: *Thesis*) Do you agree with it? Explain.

2. Perkins writes that he has still not mastered the English language. What still troubles him in speaking Standard English? Why do you think he feels it is necessary to mention his difficulties?

3. According to Perkins, why didn't Magic Johnson's television show succeed? Do you agree with his explanation?

4. As Perkins sees it, what allowed him to succeed in journalism school?

5. Ultimately, Perkins doesn't seem to consider the black English–Standard English issue a problem. Why, then, do you think he chooses to write about it? (Glossary: *Purpose*)

FOCUSING ON WRITING

1. Early in his article Perkins includes some dialogue between him and his friend Daryl. What purpose does this dialogue serve? (Glossary: *Examples*)
2. Analyze the black vernacular that Perkins uses in his dialogue with Daryl. What techniques does he use to capture the nature of black speech in his writing?
3. What is the meaning of Perkins's conclusion? (Glossary: *Beginnings and Endings*) How does his conclusion reflect on the dialogue he had with Daryl? Do you think the conclusion is an effective one? Why or why not?
4. Perkins does not use Standard English exclusively in his writing. Where does he deviate from it? Why do you think he does so? (Glossary: *Diction* and *Style*)

LANGUAGE IN ACTION

Carefully read the following article by student Simone Brown, which originally appeared in the March 1997 edition of Princeton University's official multicultural publication, *The Vigil*. Based on your understanding of Ebonics, comment on the exchange between Simone Brown and Mr. Boogie. Do you find Brown's position on the issue convincing? Explain why or why not.

EBONICS DISCUSSION

One day I had a brilliant idea. Having nothing else to occupy my time, I became creative and decided to see what the Net had to offer. Looking at an endless expanse of possibilities, I decided to visit the *Essence* website in order to get their address so I could persuade them to do a makeover on the upwardly mobile young African-American woman that I am. So while looking through the features with that one goal in mind, my eyes fell upon the word "Ebonics." I was like, "Oh my goodness! Don't tell me *Essence* has succumbed to the temptation of joining the debate about Ebonics." They had. At the end of the article, there was a place where you could send in comments, opinions, jokes, whatever. I couldn't resist. Something else just took me over and made me write a couple of lines basically saying I thought the whole thing was a waste of time that should be spent thinking of ways I can pay for my education. So I made my little contribution, felt my little release, and went on with my life.

Lo and behold, the next day I get an e-mail from this random person calling himself "Boogie." I thought "Oh my goodness! It's probably another one of those people looking for a long lost friend whose first name is Simone and they think I'm the person because they saw my name on the Net." It's happened before. So I read it and was bombarded with sentence after sentence criticizing my opinion of Ebonics, discrediting my knowledge of the subject, and questioning my "cultural priorities."

Being the open-minded and forgiving person that I am, I read through this random person's argument. The main points [. . .] were as follows:

- The origin of the Ebonics style of speech is not rooted in ignorance but rather in African speech patterns which utilize a wholly different method of language organization.
- Ebonics as a term is a part of our reclamation of our African heritage.
- The variations in Ebonics are characteristic of African-based language systems. It could in fact be said to be a superior system, as it is context-based, not concrete-based.

My thoughts on the whole issue which I tactfully expressed to Mr. Boogie are as follows:

- Ebonics, also referred to as Black English, is not a language. There is no Ebonics culture and no Ebonics tribe. I am a black person (quite obviously), and I do not speak Ebonics and could not even if I wanted to. It is not an inherent characteristic of being black.
- Ebonics is best defined as being a bit more than a dialect. Having distinctly American origins and spoken largely by the portion of the black population whose ancestors came from Africa over two hundred years ago, any traces of "African speech patterns" have been greatly diluted and mutated by American English.
- Speaking Ebonics is not a way for me to reclaim my African heritage. I can understand reclaiming one's culture by speaking a true African language in addition to learning about various African cultures. But simply speaking a dialect of English is not the way to go.

[. . .] By refusing to give such a large place to Ebonics as an important part of the development of the African-American culture I am in no way denying my culture, race, or ancestry. That has been done enough by others in the past. I recognize that the formation of the distinctly African-American culture appreciated by many today results from myriad influences which have contributed to the development of various features of the culture including, but not limited to, language. Some people choose to call this hybrid formation Ebonics. So be it.

What bothers me mostly is the amount of time that has been spent arguing back and forth over this issue. It has served to be a divisive factor among the African-American community as people are forced to choose whether they are pro-Ebonics or not. And what is even worse is that people who are pro-Ebonics view anti-Ebonics behavior as an affront to their culture and a vehicle to deny one's "blackness." I see the overemphasizing of Ebonics as a method of taking attention from more important issues in African-American society and society in general. [. . .] In light of all of the other problems with violence, education, and finances that our communities are facing, it seems ridiculous that so much media time and argumentative effort is spent on little (in the big scheme of things) inconsequential Ebonics.

WRITING SUGGESTIONS

1. (*Writing from Experience*) What is your impression of Black English, or, as it is more often referred to in academic circles, Black English Vernacular (BEV)

or African American Vernacular English (AAVE)? If you speak Black English, in what circumstances do you use it? At home? With friends? In school? What determines when you use it? If you do not speak Black English, where do you hear it used? Write an essay in which you discuss your experience with Black English and the ways it has influenced your speech. Before you begin, refer to your Writing to Discover entry for this article.

2. (*Writing from Reading*) In paragraph 18, Perkins writes the following: "And that's where the whole debate begins. Some believe that black critics of black dialect are practicing a form of self-hatred, choosing a white culture over their own, and embracing what they call a slave mentality. Johnson is fine, since he's just talkin' like a black brotha, ya know?" Later, in paragraph 23, he writes, "Still, to adhere to such broken English for the sake of holding onto cultural heritage is false hope and complete nonsense." Which side of the argument do you support, or do you have a different interpretation of the issues? Write a letter to Perkins explaining your point of view. Once you have completed the assignment, you may even want to e-mail him a copy of your essay: kperkins@Star-telegram.com.

3. (*Writing from Research*) The concept of Standard English has caused much misunderstanding and debate. For many Americans, *standard* implies that one variety of English is more correct or more functional than others. Investigate the history of the concept of Standard English and write an essay based on your findings. How did it develop? How do various linguists define it? Is Standard English a social dialect? What role does Standard English play in the language-arts curricula of our schools? What exactly is the power or mystique of Standard English?

Southernisms Are as Numerous as Fleas on a Lazy, Old Mutt

MICHAEL LOLLAR

Michael Lollar was born in middle Tennessee in 1948. He grew up in Maryville in east Tennessee, near the Smoky Mountains, and attended the University of Tennessee, Knoxville, graduating with a B.S. degree in communications in 1970. Lollar writes: "I spent summers as a child with my grandparents on a farm in middle Tennessee and loved the sayings I heard as part of 'normal' conversation. After dinner, my grandmother would say she was 'fuller than a tick.' My aunt used to talk about friends who were 'poorer than a snake.' I thought she meant they had no money, but later learned she meant that they were skinny. That kind of introduction to language and feelings, I think, must have made me gravitate to the newspaper business." In the following selection, Lollar presents a catalog of some of the humorous and vivid expressions that have come to be associated with southern American culture. The article first appeared on January 7, 1997, in the Commercial Appeal, *the daily newspaper in Memphis where Lollar works as a writer and editor.*

WRITING TO DISCOVER: *Do your parents and grandparents, and the friends and relatives of their generations, sometimes use colorful expressions that you do not understand? Make a list of as many of these expressions as you can. What in particular characterizes these expressions? Why are they so colorful and memorable for you?*

It was at the Republican National Convention that GOP chairman Haley Barbour, a Mississippian, said that bringing competing elements of the party into a single platform is like "trying to load dogs into a wheelbarrow."

A fellow Southerner, President Clinton, often uses similar images. Imagine his fellow Rhodes scholars' reactions when Clinton promises that Republicans will "squeal like a pig stuck under a gate." Or, as he said at the '92 convention, that he'd fight alongside his supporters "'til the last dog dies."

But Southernisms aren't limited to politics by any means. And it's not what Southerners say so much as how they say it that makes many of them, including Toya Powell of Memphis, "proud to be a Southerner. The language has always been a source of joy for me. It becomes almost a spiritual thing."

Instead of announcing that they have had enough or too much to eat, Southerners might push back from the table, rub their stomachs and announce: "I'm fuller'n a tick."

That's among hundreds of phrases readers called in when the *Com-*   5
mercial Appeal recently invited its Memphis readers to give up their favorite old sayings. Some wrote to tell how they'd been "rode hard and
put up wet," or how they're "grinning like a mule eating briers," or how
they're "broker than the Ten Commandments."

For Powell, 39, a nuclear medicine technologist at Baptist Memorial
Hospital in Memphis, such phrases bring back memories of "a whole
mess" of friends and relatives whose language has helped define the region. When she repeats a phrase once used by someone else, Powell sees
the faces and hears the voices of grandparents, parents, neighbors, and
people who have moved away or died.

She and her mother once visited one of her mother's former teachers
in a nursing home. "She's dead now, but I can still see and hear that
sweet lady saying, 'Honey, that's too much sugar for a dime,' meaning
that somebody wanted something for nothing."

"Now that phrase will live forever in me. She will never be forgotten,
and I'll plant the seed for another generation. It's a way to transcend history, cultural mores, and the deaths of people that were important to us,"
says Powell.

In Nesbit, Miss., Evelyn Bearden, formerly of Arkansas, says she has an
aunt in Waynesboro, Tenn., whose language is so colorful "you can see it
when she talks, like word pictures. She once said that somebody came to fix
her hair and when they got through it 'looked like a Brillo pad.'"

Bearden's favorite expression came from the same aunt, who de-   10
scribed a man as "so crooked that when he died they didn't have to dig a
grave, they just screwed him into the ground like an auger."

Many of the phrases and sayings in the South are what University of
Memphis English professor and linguistics coordinator Marvin K. L.
Ching calls "relic expressions" or holdovers from life on farms and in
rural areas.

Joan Weatherly, a University of Memphis English professor and co-
executive secretary with Ching on the Southeastern Conference on Linguistics, says Southerners tend to think their language is richer in
expression and imagery than that of other regions. While it's difficult to
prove, Weatherly suspects it's true. And it seems to have become even
more pronounced as the region becomes more diverse, she says. "I think
people deliberately do this to put people on. I think Faulkner did it . . .
to shock people and make them realize they're in the South."

Like the man who was so crooked he didn't need a grave, crooks
have an entire subculture of language built around them. "He was
crooked as a barrel of snakes," says Memphian Jean Crump. "Crooked as
a jaybird's hind leg," says Greenville, Miss., stockbroker John Black.
"Crooked as a barrel of fish hooks," says Toya Powell.

Many expressions seem to try to outdo an original one. If you've had
a kitchen that was "too little to cuss a cat in," try this one from Mae

Donahoo of rural Tipton County, Tenn.: 'My kitchen is so small, if you cussed a cat in it you'd get hair in your mouth."

For those who aren't satisfied at being fuller'n a tick, try "tighter   15
than a tick on a bloodhound" or "fuller'n a tick on a yellow yard dog."

You've probably heard of somebody "bigger than the broad side of a barn" or "bigger than the broad side of a barn door," but Memphian Peggy Rolfes likes this one: "He's big enough to go bear hunting with a stick." Jean Crump says a large woman may look "like a feather bed tied in the middle."

People who are tight with money are rich targets of old sayings. Several said they grew up hearing about someone "tighter than Dick's hatband." Jean Crump adds this one: "He's so stingy he'd skin a flea for his hide and tallow." And this variation: "She was so stingy you couldn't get a flax seed up her bloomer leg."

In West Memphis, Ark., Oldsmobile-GMC dealer Sam C. Hudson says most of his favorite sayings came from his hometown of Brooksville, Miss. He likes, "Every tub should sit on its own bottom," meaning people are responsible for solving their own problems.

Like many others, Hudson grew up where people sometimes ran around "like a duck after a June bug," didn't "put all their eggs in the same basket" and "could cuss you out more ways than a farmer can go to town."

In the winter, it could be "colder than a well digger's butt" or in   20
summer "hotter'n a cowboy's pistol" or "hotter'n a depot stove five minutes before train time." In rural Mississippi, Hudson says, depots, like clockwork, stoked up their pot-bellied stoves just before the next train was due.

Another Arkansan, Sallie Streeter, says her husband, cotton consultant Jan Streeter, confounded a group of Australians during a recent trip. "They were asking what kind of food we eat, and he said, 'We eat every part of the hawg except the squeal, and we give that to mamas whose babies can't cry.'"

A lot of Southerners have found ways to cast aspersions about someone's mental prowess. "Dumb as an ox," "dumb as a post" or "dumb as a box of rocks" will get you started. But if you want to be more pointed, retired schoolteacher Grace D. Gary of Union City, Tenn., suggests, "He was so dumb he couldn't tell a cow pile from second base."

Brenda Smithson, a waitress at Dixie Cafe in Memphis, says, "If you put your brains in a bird, it would fly backward." In Hernando, Miss., casino administrator L. E. Johnson Jr. says his father used to say, "If your brains was dynamite, you wouldn't have enough to blow your nose." Ernestine Claydon, retired from Welcome Wagon, heard of someone who "didn't have the sense God allowed a louse."

Mark Twain once described something as being "dark as the inside of a cow." For Margaret Lewis, a former Arkansan, a similar expression came from an old boyfriend: "It was our first date, and, returning to my house after a dance, he said, 'It's darker than midnight under a skillet out here.'"

Lewis also has an expression about nervous people. While many re-   25
called "nervous as a long-tail cat in a room full of rocking chairs," she re-
calls "nervous as a pregnant nun." And Patty Woodruff says her grandmother used to say "nervous as Lot's wife in a rainstorm."

If someone looks puzzled or is experiencing something for the first time, Sara Erwin, a retired English teacher in Huntsville, Ala., says the person is "like a cow looking at a new gate." To avoid looking puzzled when you don't know the answer, Memphis elementary school teacher Elaine Johnson suggests this: "You've asked me too soon."

Several people like the expressions "busier than a one-armed paper-hanger" and "busier than a one-legged man in a butt-kicking contest." But Jackie Sanderlin, a retired secretary from McKesson Drug Co., added a twist: "I'm busier than a one-armed paperhanger with the seven-year itch."

And Gwynneth Green likes a pun her grandmother used in Alabama. "She said, 'Flattery is softsoap, and softsoap is 90 percent lye.'"

For Memphians, one of the most recognizable Southernisms is from a native son: "Thank you. Thank you very much." Even if you didn't rec-ognize that as an Elvis Presley expression, you would have no trouble rec-ognizing another Elvis-ism that has evolved into a broader meaning through the years:

"Ladies and gentlemen, Elvis has left the building."   30

FOCUSING ON CONTENT

1. What is the literal meaning of "I'm fuller than a tick" (4)? Why is a tick used in this expression?

2. Why does Professor Marvin K. L. Ching refer to southernisms as "relic ex-pressions" (11)? If such expressions no longer originate in rural circum-stances, why do people continue to use them and even invent new ones?

3. Speculate on how our nation's changing demographics may affect the use of southernisms. Will we see more of them in the future? Less of them? Why?

4. Why do you think people become nostalgic when they use or hear the kinds of expressions Lollar discusses? What, aside from their literal and metaphoric meanings, do such expressions convey?

5. In paragraph 3, Lollar quotes Toya Powell as saying that southern language "becomes almost a spiritual thing." Why do you think she might feel this way?

FOCUSING ON WRITING

1. What kinds of figures of speech are represented in Lollar's catalog of south-ernisms? (Glossary: *Figures of Speech*)

2. Lollar's thesis is that southernisms pervade southern culture. How does he present his examples to illustrate that idea? (Glossary: *Examples*)

3. In what ways would Lollar's southernisms and his comments about them be helpful to fiction writers who were basing their work in the South or who used southern characters? (Glossary: *Dialogue*)

4. Lollar ends his article with a discussion of Elvis Presley and the expressions "Thank you. Thank you very much." and "Ladies and gentlemen, Elvis has left the building." What is the meaning of his conclusion? In your opinion, how effective is it? (Glossary: *Beginnings and Endings*)

LANGUAGE IN ACTION

Regional expressions such as those Lollar has presented allow us to make generalizations about the people who use them and about the areas in which they live. Study the following expressions, which are taken from Wolfgang Meider's *As Strong as a Moose: New England Expressions* (1997). Then, drawing on these expressions, jot down some generalizations about New England and New Englanders.

It's so cold you have to milk the cows with wire pliers.
As strong as a moose.
He's so miserly he crawls under the door to save the hinges.
She's as sweet as maple sugar.
He doesn't know enough to pour water out of a boot with the directions written
   on the heel.
As white as a snow bank.
She's dainty as a cow with snowshoes on.
As naked as a peeled apple.
As clean as a New England kitchen.
She makes pancakes so thin they have but one side.
As steady as an old plow horse.

WRITING SUGGESTIONS

1. (*Writing from Experience*) Write an essay about the regional expressions that are common in the area where you grew up or where you are presently attending school. What aspects of life in your area do they reveal? Are the expressions from your region as colorful as the southernisms that Lollar writes about in his article?

2. (*Writing from Reading*) By sharing southernisms in his article, Lollar helps build a sense of identity among southerners and teaches people some regional expressions they may have never heard before. Some people, however, may prefer to ignore such regional expressions and to lose their local

identity. Write an essay in which you take a stand for either cultivating regional expressions in one's speech and writing or suppressing such expressions.

3. (*Writing from Research*) Write a report on *The Dictionary of Regional American English* (DARE), explaining what its mission is, how the compilers go about their work, and what they have accomplished thus far. If you visit DARE's Web site, you will be able to gain valuable background information. Be sure to also visit your school's library to become familiar with the volumes of DARE that have been published thus far. The following statement from DARE's Web site should get you started on your research:

> *The Dictionary of American Regional English* (DARE) is a reference tool unlike any other. Its aim is not to prescribe how Americans should speak, or even to describe the language we use generally, the "standard" language. Instead, it seeks to document the varieties of English that are not found everywhere in the United States — those words, pronunciations, and phrases that vary from one region to another, that we learn at home rather than at school, or that are part of our oral rather than our written culture. Although American English is remarkably homogeneous considering the tremendous size of the country, there are still many thousands of differences that characterize the various dialect regions of the United States. It is these differences that DARE records. Learn more about what DARE is, and who uses it; what is published; how to purchase it; DARE's funding; and how to contact us: <http://polyglot.lss.wisc.edu/dare/dare.html>.

CASE IN POINT:
The English-Only Controversy

Since Great Britain gained control over what is now the United States, English has been the dominant language in our country. Despite the multitude of cultures and ethnicities that comprise the United States, English has been a common thread linking them together. It may be somewhat surprising, then, that there is no official U.S. language. Now, even as English literacy becomes a necessity for people in many parts of the world, some people in the United States believe its primacy is being threatened right at home. Much of the current controversy focuses on Hispanic communities with large Spanish-speaking populations, who may feel little or no pressure to learn English. Yet in order for everyone to participate in our society, some way must be found to bridge the communication gap.

Recent government efforts in this regard have included bilingual programs in schools, on ballots, for providing emergency notices, and so on. The goal of the programs is to maintain a respect for the heritage and language of the non-English speakers while they learn the English language. The programs have come under fire, however, from those who believe that the U.S. government should conduct itself only in English. If people come here, the argument goes, they should take the responsibility to learn the native language as quickly as possible. And, English-only proponents reason, if immigrants do not or are not willing to learn English, the government should not accommodate them in another language. Moreover, there should be a mandate that the official language of the United States is English and that the government will conduct business in no other language. Many state governments have, in fact, already made such a declaration.

The other side of the argument has two components. One is the belief that it is discriminatory to mandate English because those who do not speak it are then denied basic rights until they learn the language. The second part of this argument is that the current situation is nothing new: There have always been groups of immigrants that were slow to assimilate into American culture, but they all eventually integrated, and the controversy will resolve itself. Furthermore, English is not threatened, and its use does not need to be legislated. Indeed, according to English-only critics, declaring English the official U.S. language could create far more problems than it solves.

The following selections address the issue from opposite sides. Robert King asks "Should English Be the Law?" in the context of our history and that of countries around the world. He notes that compared to similar situations in other countries, including the French Canadian separatist crisis just to our north, the problems here seem almost trivial. If being American still means anything unique, he concludes, we should be able to enjoy our linguistic diversity rather than be threatened by it. S. I. Hayakawa's "Bilingualism in America: English Should Be the *Only* Language" obviously comes to the opposite conclusion. Hayakawa, a former U.S. Senator from California and co-founder of U.S. English, an organization formed to promote English-only legislation, finds the recent policies accommodating bilingualism in schools and government alarming and presents a forceful argument in favor of establishing English as the official language of the United States.

> **WRITING TO DISCOVER:**   *It is now possible to go many places in the world and get along pretty well in English, no matter what other languages are spoken in the host country. If you were to emigrate, how hard would you work to learn the predominant language of your chosen country? What advantages would there be in learning that language, even if you could get by in English? How would you feel if the country had a law that forced you to learn its language as quickly as possible? Write down your thoughts about these questions.*

Should English Be the Law?

ROBERT D. KING

Scholar and teacher Robert D. King was born in Mississippi in 1936. He graduated from the Georgia Institute of Technology in 1959 with a degree in mathematics, beginning a distinguished and diverse career in academe. After a brief stint at IBM, King went to the University of Wisconsin, receiving a Ph.D. in German linguistics in 1965. He was hired by the University of Texas at Austin to teach German that same year and has spent more than three decades there teaching linguistics and Asian studies in addition to German. He also served as the dean of the College of Liberal Arts from 1979 until 1989 and currently holds the Audre and Bernard Rapoport Regents Chair of Liberal Arts. Indian studies have captured his attention lately, and his most recent book is Nehru and the Language Politics of India, *published in 1996.*

The language politics of the United States has become a hot topic in recent years as well. In the following selection, first published in the April 1997 issue of the Atlantic, *King provides historical background and perspective on the English-only debate.*

We have known race riots, draft riots, labor violence, secession, anti-war protests, and a whiskey rebellion, but one kind of trouble we've never had:

a language riot. Language riot? It sounds like a joke. The very idea of language as a political force — as something that might threaten to split a country wide apart — is alien to our way of thinking and to our cultural traditions.

This may be changing. On August 1 of last year [1996] the U.S. House of Representatives approved a bill that would make English the official language of the United States. The vote was 259 to 169, with 223 Republicans and thirty-six Democrats voting in favor and eight Republicans, 160 Democrats, and one independent voting against. The debate was intense, acrid, and partisan. On March 25 of last year the Supreme Court agreed to review a case involving an Arizona law that would require public employees to conduct government business only in English. Arizona is one of several states that have passed "Official English" or "English Only" laws. The appeal to the Supreme Court followed a 6-to-5 ruling, in October of 1995, by a federal appeals court striking down the Arizona law. These events suggest how divisive a public issue language could become in America — even if it has until now scarcely been taken seriously.

Traditionally, the American way has been to make English the national language — but to do so quietly, locally, without fuss. The Constitution is silent on language: the Founding Fathers had no need to legislate that English be the official language of the country. It has always been taken for granted that English *is* the national language, and that one must learn English in order to make it in America.

To say that language has never been a major force in American history of politics, however, is not to say that politicians have always resisted linguistic jingoism. In 1753 Benjamin Franklin voiced his concern that German immigrants were not learning English: "Those [Germans] who come hither are generally the most ignorant Stupid Sort of their own Nation. . . . they will soon so out number us, that all the advantages we have will not, in My Opinion, be able to preserve our language, and even our government will become precarious." Theodore Roosevelt articulated the unspoken American linguistic-melting-pot theory when he boomed, "We have room for but one language here, and that is the English language, for we intended to see that the crucible turns our people out as Americans, of American nationality, and not as dwellers in a polyglot boarding house." And: "We must have but one flag. We must also have but one language. That must be the language of the Declaration of Independence, of Washington's Farewell address, of Lincoln's Gettysburg speech and Second Inaugural."

OFFICIAL ENGLISH

TR's linguistic tub-thumping long typified the tradition of American politics. That tradition began to change in the wake of the anything-goes attitudes and the celebration of cultural differences arising in the 1960s. A 1975 amendment to the Voting Rights Action of 1965 mandated the "bilingual ballot" under certain circumstances, notably when the voters of selected language groups reached five percent or more in a voting district. Bilingual education became a byword of educational thinking during the 1960s. By the 1970s linguists had demonstrated convincingly—at least to other academics—that black English (today called African-American vernacular English or Ebonics) was not "bad" English but a different kind of authentic English with its own rules. Predictably, there have been scattered demands that black English be included in bilingual-education programs.

It was against this background that the movement to make English the official language of the country arose. In 1981 Senator S. I. Hayakawa, long a leading critic of bilingual education and bilingual ballots, introduced in the U.S. Senate a constitutional amendment that not only would have made English the official language but would have prohibited federal and state laws and regulations requiring the use of other languages. His English Language Amendment died in the Ninety-seventh Congress.

In 1983 the organization called U.S. English was founded by Hayakawa and John Tanton, a Michigan ophthalmologist. The primary purpose of the organization was to promote English as the official language of the United States. (The best background readings on America's "neolinguisticism" are the books *Hold Your Tongue*, by James Crawford, and *Language Loyalties*, edited by Crawford, both published in 1992.) Official English initiatives were passed by California in 1986, by Arkansas, Mississippi, North Carolina, North Dakota, and South Carolina in 1987, by Colorado, Florida, and Arizona in 1988, and by Alabama in 1990. The majorities voting for these initiatives were generally not insubstantial: California's, for example, passed by 73 percent.

It was probably inevitable that the Official English (or English Only—the two names are used almost interchangeably) movement would acquire a conservative, almost reactionary undertone in the 1990s. Official English is politically very incorrect. But its cofounder John Tanton brought with him strong liberal credentials. He had been active in the Sierra Club and Planned Parenthood, and in the 1970s served as the national president of Zero Population Growth. Early advisers of U.S. English resist ideological pigeonholing: they included Walter Annenberg, Jacques Barzun, Bruno Bettelheim, Alistair Cooke, Denton Cooley, Walter Cronkite, Angier Biddle Duke, George Gilder, Sidney Hook, Norman Podhoretz, Arnold Schwarzenegger, and Karl Shapiro. In 1987 U.S. English installed as its president Linda Chávez, a Hispanic who had been prominent in the Reagan Administration. A year later she resigned her position, citing "repugnant" and "anti-Hispanic" overtones in an internal memorandum written by Tanton. Tanton, too, resigned, and Walter Cronkite, describing the affair as "embarrassing," left the advisory board. One board member, Norman Cousins, defected in 1986, alluding to the "negative symbolic significance" of California's Official English initiative, Proposition 63. The current chairman of the board and CEO of U.S. English is Mauro E. Mujica, who claims that the organization has 650,000 members.

The popular wisdom is that conservatives are pro and liberals con. True, conservatives such as George Will and William F. Buckley Jr. have written columns supporting Official English. But would anyone characterize as conservatives the present and past U.S. English board members Alistair Cooke, Walter Cronkite, and Norman Cousins? One of the strongest opponents of bilingual education is the Mexican-American writer Richard Rodriguez, best known for his eloquent autobiography, *Hunger of Memory* (1982). There is a strain of American liberalism that defines itself in nostalgic devotion to the melting pot.

For several years relevant bills awaited consideration in the U.S. House of Representatives. The Emerson Bill (H.R. 123), passed by the House last August, specifies English as the official language of government, and requires that the government "preserve and enhance" the official status of English. Exceptions are made for the teaching of foreign languages; for actions necessary for public health, international relations, foreign trade, and the protection of the rights of criminal defendants; and for the use of "terms of art" from languages other than English. It would, for example, stop the Internal Revenue Service from sending out income-tax forms and instructions in languages other than English, but it would not ban the use of foreign languages in census materials or documents dealing with national security. *"E Pluribus Unum"* can still appear on American money. U.S. English supports the bill.

What are the chances that some version of Official English will become federal law? Any language bill will face tough odds in the Senate, because some western senators have opposed English Only measures in the past for various reasons, among them a desire by Republicans not to alienate the growing number of Hispanic Republicans, most of whom are uncomfortable with mandated monolingualism. Texas Governor George W. Bush, too, has forthrightly said that he would oppose any English Only proposals in his state. Several of the Republican candidates for President in 1996 (an interesting exception is Phil Gramm) endorsed versions of Official English, as has Newt Gingrich. While governor of Arkansas, Bill Clinton signed into law an English Only bill. As President, he has described his earlier action as a mistake.

Many issues intersect in the controversy over Official English: immigration (above all), the rights of minorities (Spanish-speaking minorities in particular), the pros and cons of bilingual education, tolerance, how best to educate the children of immigrants, and the place of cultural diversity in school curricula and in American society in general. The question that lies at the root of most of the uneasiness is this: Is America threatened by the preservation of languages other than English? Will

10

America, if it continues on its traditional path of benign linguistic neglect, go the way of Belgium, Canada, and Sri Lanka—three countries
among many whose unity is gravely imperiled by language and ethnic
conflicts?

LANGUAGE AND NATIONALITY

Language and nationalism were not always so intimately intertwined.
Never in the heyday of rule by sovereign was it a condition of employment that the King be able to speak the language of his subjects. George
I spoke no English and spent much of his time away from England, attempting to use the power of his kingship to shore up his German possessions. In the Middle Ages nationalism was not even part of the picture:
one owed loyalty to a lord, a prince, a ruler, a family, a tribe, a church, a
piece of land, but not to a nation and least of all to a nation as a language
unit. The capital city of the Austrian Hapsburg empire was Vienna, its
ruler a monarch with effective control of peoples of the most varied and
incompatible ethnicities, and languages, throughout Central and Eastern
Europe. The official language, and the lingua franca as well, was German.
While it stood—and it stood for hundreds of years—the empire was an
anachronistic relic of what for most of human history had been the normal relationship between country and language: none.

The marriage of language and nationalism goes back at least to Romanticism and specifically to Rousseau, who argued in his *Essay on the Origin
of Languages* that language must develop before politics is possible and
that language originally distinguished nations from one another. A little-
remembered aim of the French Revolution—itself the legacy of Rousseau—
was to impose a national language on France, where regional languages
such as Provençal, Breton, and Basque were still strong competitors against
standard French, the French of the Ile de France. As late as 1789, when the
Revolution began, half the population of the south of France, which spoke
Provençal, did not understand French. A century earlier the playwright
Racine said that he had had to resort to Spanish and Italian to make himself
understood in the southern French town of Uzès. After the Revolution na-
tionhood itself became aligned with language.

In 1846 Jacob Grimm, one of the Brothers Grimm of fairy-tale fame   15
but better known in the linguistic establishment as a forerunner of modern comparative and historical linguists, said that "a nation is the totality
of people who speak the same language." After midcentury, language was
invoked more than any other single criterion to define nationality. Language as a political force helped to bring about the unification of Italy
and of Germany and the secession of Norway from its union with Sweden
in 1905. Arnold Toynbee observed—unhappily—soon after the First
World War that "the growing consciousness of Nationality had attached

itself neither to traditional frontiers nor to new geographical associations but almost exclusively to mother tongues."

The crowning triumph of the new desideratum was the Treaty of Versailles, in 1919, when the allied victors of the First World War began redrawing the map of Central and Eastern Europe according to nationality as best they could. The magic word was "self-determination," and none of Woodrow Wilson's Fourteen Points mentioned the word "language" at all. Self-determination was thought of as being related to "nationality," which today we would be more likely to call "ethnicity"; but language was simpler to identify than nationality or ethnicity. When it came to drawing the boundary lines of various countries—Czechoslovakia, Yugoslavia, Romania, Hungary, Albania, Bulgaria, Poland—it was principally language that guided the draftsman's hand. (The main exceptions were Alsace-Lorraine, South Tyrol, and the German-speaking parts of Bohemia and Moravia.) Almost by default language became the defining characteristic of nationality.

And so it remains today. In much of the world, ethnic unity and cultural identification are routinely defined by language. To be Arab is to speak Arabic. Bengali identity is based on language in spite of the division of Bengali-speakers between Hindu India and Muslim Bangladesh. When eastern Pakistan seceded from greater Pakistan in 1971, it named itself Bangladesh: *desa* means "country"; *bangla* means not the Bengali people or the Bengali territory but the Bengali language.

Scratch most nationalist movements and you find a linguistic grievance. The demands for independence of the Baltic states (Latvia, Lithuania, and Estonia) were intimately bound up with fears for the loss of their respective languages and cultures in a sea of Russianness. In Belgium the war between French and Flemish threatens an already weakly fused country. The present atmosphere of Belgium is dark and anxious, costive; the metaphor of divorce is a staple of private and public discourse. The lines of terrorism in Sri Lanka are drawn between Tamil Hindus and Sinhalese Buddhists—and also between the Tamil and Sinhalese languages. Worship of the French language fortifies the movement for an independent Quebec. Whether a united Canada will survive into the twenty-first century is a question too close to call. Much of the anxiety about language in the United States is probably fueled by the "Quebec problem": unlike Belgium, which is a small European country, or Sri Lanka, which is halfway around the world, Canada is our close neighbor.

Language is a convenient surrogate for nonlinguistic claims that are often awkward to articulate, for they amount to a demand for more political and economic power. Militant Sikhs in India call for a state of their own: Khalistan ("Land of the Pure" in Punjabi). They frequently couch this as a demand for a linguistic state, which has a certain simplicity about it, a clarity of motive—justice, even, because states in India are normally linguistic states. But the Sikh demands blend religion, economics, language, and retribution for sins both punished and unpunished in a country where old sins cast long shadows.

Language is an explosive issue in the countries of the former Soviet Union. The language conflict in Estonia has been especially bitter. Ethnic Russians make up almost a third of Estonia's population, and most of them do not speak or read Estonian, although Russians have lived in Estonia for more than a generation. Estonia has passed legislation requiring knowledge of the Estonian language as a condition of citizenship. Nationalist groups in independent Lithuania sought restrictions on the use of Polish—again, old sins, long shadows. 20

In 1995 protests erupted in Moldova, formerly the Moldavian Soviet Socialist Republic, over language and the teaching of Moldovan history. Was Moldovan history a part of Romanian history or of Soviet history? Was Moldova's language Romanian? Moldovan—earlier called Moldavian—*is* Romanian, just as American English and British English are both English. But in the days of the Moldavian SSR, Moscow insisted that the two languages were different, and in a piece of linguistic nonsense required Moldavian to be written in the Cyrillic alphabet to strengthen the case that it was not Romanian.

The official language of Yugoslavia was Serbo-Croatian, which was never so much a language as a political accommodation. The Serbian and Croatian languages are mutually intelligible. Serbian is written in the Cyrillic alphabet, is identified with the Eastern Orthodox branch of the Catholic Church, and borrows its high-culture words from the east—from Russian and Old Church Slavic. Croatian is written in the Roman alphabet, is identified with Roman Catholicism and borrows its high-culture words from the west—from German, for example, and Latin. One of the first things the newly autonomous Republic of Serbia did, in 1991, was to pass a law decreeing Serbian in the Cyrillic alphabet the official language of the country. With Croatia divorced from Serbia, the Croatian and Serbian languages are diverging more and more. Serbo-Croatian has now passed into history, a language-museum relic from the brief period when Serbs and Croats called themselves Yugoslavs and pretended to like each other.

Slovakia, relieved now of the need to accommodate to Czech cosmopolitan sensibilities, has passed a law making Slovak its official language. (Czech is to Slovak pretty much as Croatian is to Serbian.) Doctors in state hospitals must speak to patients in Slovak, even if another language would aid diagnosis and treatment. Some 600,000 Slovaks—more than 10 percent of the population—are ethnically Hungarian. Even staff meetings in Hungarian-language schools must be in Slovak. (The government dropped a stipulation that church weddings be conducted in Slovak after heavy opposition from the Roman Catholic Church.) Language inspectors are told to weed out "all sins perpetrated on the regular Slovak language." Tensions between Slovaks and Hungarians, who had been getting along, have begun to arise.

The twentieth century is ending as it began—with trouble in the Balkans and with nationalist tensions flaring up in other parts of the globe. (Toward the end of his life Bismarck predicted that "some damn fool thing in the Balkans" would ignite the next war.) Language isn't always part of the problem. But it usually is.

UNIQUE OTHERNESS

Is there no hope for language tolerance? Some countries manage to   25
maintain their unity in the face of multilingualism. Examples are Finland, with a Swedish minority, and a number of African and Southeast Asian countries. Two others could not be more unlike as countries go: Switzerland and India.

German, French, Italian, and Romansh are the languages of Switzerland. The first three can be and are used for official purposes; all four are designated "national" languages. Switzerland is politically almost hyperstable. It has language problems (Romansh is losing ground), but they are not major, and they are never allowed to threaten national unity.

Contrary to public perception, India gets along pretty well with a host of different languages. The Indian constitution officially recognizes nineteen languages, English among them. Hindi is specified in the constitution as the national language of India, but that is a pious postcolonial fiction: outside the Hindi-speaking northern heartland of India, people don't want to learn it. English functions more nearly than Hindi as India's lingua franca.

From 1947, when India obtained its independence from the British, until the 1960s blood ran in the streets and people died because of language. Hindi absolutists wanted to force Hindi on the entire country, which would have split India between north and south and opened up other fracture lines as well. For as long as possible Jawaharlal Nehru, independent India's first Prime Minister, resisted nationalist demands to redraw the capricious state boundaries of British India according to language. By the time he capitulated, the country had gained a precious decade to prove its viability as a union.

Why is it that India preserves its unity with not just two languages to contend with, as Belgium, Canada, and Sri Lanka have, but nineteen? The answer is that India, like Switzerland, has a strong national identity. The two countries share something big and almost mystical that holds each together in a union transcending language. That something I call "unique otherness."

The Swiss have what the political scientist Karl Deutsch called   30
"learned habits, preferences, symbols, memories, and patterns of landholding": customs, cultural traditions, and political institutions that bind them closer to one another than to people of France, Germany, or Italy

living just across the border and speaking the same language. There is Switzerland's traditional neutrality, its system of universal military training (the "citizen army"), its consensual allegiance to a strong Swiss franc—and fondue, yodeling, skiing, and mountains. Set against all this, the fact that Switzerland has four languages doesn't even approach the threshold of becoming a threat.

As for India, what Vincent Smith, in the *Oxford History of India,* calls its "deep underlying fundamental unity" resides in institutions and beliefs such as caste, cow worship, sacred places, and much more. Consider *dharma, karma,* and *maya,* the three root convictions of Hinduism; India's historical epics; Gandhi; *ahimsa* (nonviolence); vegetarianism; a distinctive cuisine and way of eating; marriage customs; a shared past; and what the Indologist Ainslie Embree calls "Brahmanical ideology." In other words, "We are Indian; we are different."

Belgium and Canada have never managed to forge a stable national identity; Czechoslovakia and Yugoslavia never did either. Unique otherness immunizes countries against linguistic destabilization. Even Switzerland and especially India have problems; in any country with as many different languages as India has, language will never *not* be a problem. However, it is one thing to have a major illness with a bleak prognosis; it is another to have a condition that is irritating and occasionally painful but not life-threatening.

History teaches a plain lesson about language and governments: there is almost nothing the government of a free country can do to change language usage and practice significantly, to force its citizens to use certain languages in preference to others, and to discourage people from speaking a language they wish to continue to speak. (The rebirth of Hebrew in Palestine and Israel's successful mandate that Hebrew be spoken and written by Israelis is a unique event in the annals of language history.) Quebec has since the 1970s passed an array of laws giving French a virtual monopoly in the province. One consequence—unintended, one wishes to believe—of these laws is that last year kosher products imported for Passover were kept off the shelves, because the packages were not labeled in French. Wise governments keep their hands off language to the extent that it is politically possible to do so.

We like to believe that to pass a law is to change behavior; but passing laws about language, in a free society, almost never changes attitudes or behavior. Gaelic (Irish) is living out a slow, inexorable decline in Ireland despite enormous government support of every possible kind since Ireland gained its independence from Britain. The Welsh language, in contrast, is alive today in Wales in spite of heavy discrimination during its history. Three out of four people in the northern and western counties of Gwynedd and Dyfed speak Welsh.

I said earlier that language is a convenient surrogate for other national problems. Official English obviously has a lot to do with concern   35 about immigration, perhaps especially Hispanic immigration. America may be threatened by immigration; I don't know. But America is not threatened by language.

The usual arguments made by academics against Official English are commonsensical. Who needs a law when, according to the 1990 census, 94 percent of American residents speak English anyway? (Mauro E. Mujica, the chairman of U.S. English, cites a higher figure: 97 percent.) Not many of today's immigrants will see their first language survive into the second generation. This is in fact the common lament of first-generation immigrants: their children are not learning their language and are losing the culture of their parents. Spanish is hardly a threat to English, in spite of isolated (and easily visible) cases such as Miami, New York City, and pockets of the Southwest and southern California. The everyday language of south Texas is Spanish, and yet south Texas is not about to secede from America.

But empirical, calm arguments don't engage the real issue: language is a symbol, an icon. Nobody who favors a constitutional ban against flag burning will ever be persuaded by the argument that the flag is, after all, just a "piece of cloth." A draft card in the 1960s was never merely a piece of paper. Neither is a marriage license.

Language, as one linguist has said, is "not primarily a means of communication but a means of communion." Romanticism exalted language, made it mystical, sublime—a bond of national identity. At the same time, Romanticism created a monster: it made of language a means for destroying a country.

America has that unique otherness of which I spoke. In spite of all our racial divisions and economic unfairness, we have the frontier tradition, respect for the individual, and opportunity; we have our love affair with the automobile; we have in our history a civil war that freed the slaves and was fought with valor; and we have sports, hot dogs, hamburgers, and milk shakes—things big and small, noble and petty, important and trifling. "We are Americans; we are different."

If I'm wrong, then the great American experiment will fail—not be-   40
cause of language but because it no longer means anything to be an American; because we have forfeited that "willingness of the heart" that F. Scott Fitzgerald wrote was America; because we are not long joined by Lincoln's "mystic chords of memory."

We are not even close to the danger point. I suggest that we relax and luxuriate in our linguistic richness and our traditional tolerance of language differences. Language does not threaten American unity. Benign neglect is a good policy for any country when it comes to language, and it's a good policy for America.

Bilingualism in America: English Should Be the Only Language

S. I. HAYAKAWA

Samuel Ichiye Hayakawa was born to Japanese parents in Vancouver, British Columbia, in 1906. Educated at the University of Manitoba, McGill University, and the University of Wisconsin at Madison, Hayakawa had a distinguished career as a professor of linguistics and pioneer in semantics. He authored several books on language theory, including Our Language and Our World *in 1959. During his last teaching position at San Francisco State University, he was introduced to the political arena when he was named interim president of the college to deal with student rioters in 1968. His strict suppression of the uprising endeared him to conservatives throughout the country, and he went on to serve as a U.S. senator from California for one term (1977–1983).*

After leaving the Senate, Hayakawa became a leading figure in the effort to install English as the official language of the United States. In the following selection, first published in USA Today *in July 1989, he presents a concise argument that summarizes his position on the issue. Hayakawa died on February 27, 1992.*

During the dark days of World War II, Chinese immigrants in California wore badges proclaiming their original nationality so they would not be mistaken for Japanese. In fact, these two immigrant groups long had been at odds with each other. However, as new English-speaking generations came along, the Chinese and Japanese began to communicate with one another. They found they had much in common and began to socialize. Today, they get together and form Asian-American societies.

Such are the amicable results of sharing the English language. English unites us as American-immigrants and native-born alike. Communicating with each other in a single, common tongue encourages trust, while reducing racial hostility and bigotry.

My appreciation of English has led me to devote my retirement years to championing it. Several years ago, I helped to establish U.S. English, a Washington, D.C.-based public interest group that seeks an amendment to the U.S. Constitution declaring English our official language, regardless of what other languages we may use unofficially.

As an immigrant to this nation, I am keenly aware of the things that bind us as Americans and unite us as a single people. Foremost among these unifying forces is the common language we share. While it is certainly true that our love of freedom and devotion to democratic principles help to unite and give us a mutual purpose, it is English, our common language, that enables us to discuss our views and allows us to maintain a well-informed electorate, the cornerstone of democratic government.

Because we are a nation of immigrants, we do not share the characteristics of race, religion, ethnicity, or native language which form the common bonds of society in other countries. However, by agreeing to learn and use a single, universally spoken language, we have been able to forge a unified people from an incredibly diverse population.

Although our 200-year history should be enough to convince any skeptic of the powerful unifying effects of a common language, some still advocate the official recognition of other languages. They argue that a knowledge of English is not part of the formula for responsible citizenship in this country.

Some contemporary political leaders, like the former mayor of Miami, Maurice Ferre, maintain that "Language is not necessary to the system. Nowhere does our Constitution say that English is our language." He also told the *Tampa Tribune* that, "Within ten years there will not be a single word of English spoken [in Miami]—English is not Miami's official language—[and] one day residents will have to learn Spanish or leave."

The U.S. Department of Education also reported that countless speakers at a conference on bilingual education "expounded at length on the need for and eventually of, a multilingual, multicultural United States of America with a national language policy citing English and Spanish as the two 'legal languages.'"

As a former resident of California, I am completely familiar with a system that uses two official languages, and I would not advise any nation to move in such a direction unless forced to do so. While it is true that India functions with ten official languages, I haven't heard anyone suggest that it functions particularly well because of its multilingualism. In fact, most Indians will concede that the situation is a chaotic mess which has led to countless problems in the government's efforts to manage the nation's business. Out of necessity, English still is used extensively in India as a common language.

Belgium is another clear example of the diverse effects of two officially recognized languages in the same nation. Linguistic differences between Dutch- and French-speaking citizens have resulted in chronic political instability. Consequently, in the aftermath of the most recent government collapse, legislators are working on a plan to turn over most of its powers and responsibilities to the various regions, a clear recognition of the diverse effects of linguistic separateness.

There are other problems. Bilingualism is a costly and confusing bureaucratic nightmare. The Canadian government has estimated its bilingual costs to be nearly $400,000,000 per year. It is almost certain that these expenses will increase as a result of a massive expansion of bilingual services approved by the Canadian Parliament in 1988. In the United States, which has ten times the population of Canada, the cost of similar bilingual services easily would be in the billions.

We first should consider how politically infeasible it is that our nation ever could recognize Spanish as a second official language without opening the floodgates for official recognition of the more than 100 languages spoken in this country. How long would it take, under such an arrangement, before the United States started to make India look like a model of efficiency?

Even if we can agree that multilingualism would be a mistake, some would suggest that official recognition of English is not needed. After all, our nation has existed for over 200 years without this, and English as our common language has continued to flourish.

I could agree with this sentiment had government continued to adhere to its time-honored practice of operating in English and encouraging newcomers to learn the language. However, this is not the case. Over the last few decades, government has been edging slowly towards policies that place other languages on a par with English.

In reaction to the cultural consciousness movement of the 1960s and 15 1970s, government has been increasingly reluctant to press immigrants to learn the English language, lest it be accused of "cultural imperialism." Rather than insisting that it is the immigrant's duty to learn the language of this country, the government has acted instead as if it has a duty to accommodate an immigrant in his native language.

A prime example of this can be found in the continuing debate over Federal and state policies relating to bilingual education. At times, these have come dangerously close to making the main goal of this program the maintenance of the immigrant child's native language, rather than the early acquisition of English.

As a former U.S. senator from California, where we spend more on bilingual education programs than any other state, I am very familiar with both the rhetoric and reality that lie behind the current debate on bilingual education. My experience has convinced me that many of these programs are shortchanging immigrant children in their quest to learn English.

To set the record straight from the start, I do not oppose bilingual education *if it is truly bilingual*. Employing a child's native language to teach him (or her) English is entirely appropriate. What is not appropriate is continuing to use the children of Hispanic and other immigrant groups as guinea pigs in an unproven program that fails to teach English efficiently and perpetuates their dependency on their native language.

Under the dominant method of bilingual education used throughout this country, non-English-speaking students are taught all academic subjects such as math, science, and history exclusively in their native language. English is taught as a separate subject. The problem with this method is that there is no objective way to measure whether a child has learned enough English to be placed in classes where academic instruction is entirely in English. As a result, some children have been kept in native language classes for six years.

Some bilingual education advocates, who are more concerned with maintaining the child's use of their native language, may not see any problem with such a situation. However, those who feel that the most important goal of this program is to get children functioning quickly in English appropriately are alarmed.

In the Newhall School District in California, some Hispanic parents are raising their voices in criticism of its bilingual education program, which relies on native language instruction. Their children complain of systematically being segregated from their English-speaking peers. Now in high school, these students cite the failure of the program to teach them English first as the reason for being years behind their classmates.

Even more alarming is the Berkeley (Calif.) Unified School District, where educators have recognized that all-native-language instruction would be an inadequate response to the needs of their non-English-speaking pupils. Challenged by a student body that spoke more than four different languages and by budgetary constraints, teachers and administrators responded with innovative language programs that utilized many methods of teaching English. That school district is now in court answering charges that the education they provided was inadequate because it did not provide transitional bilingual education for every non-English speaker. What was introduced 20 years ago as an experimental project has become—despite inconclusive research evidence—the only acceptable method of teaching for bilingual education advocates.

When one considers the nearly 50 percent dropout rate among Hispanic students (the largest group receiving this type of instruction), one wonders about their ability to function in the English-speaking mainstream of this country. The school system may have succeeded wonderfully in maintaining their native language, but if it failed to help them to master the English language fully, what is the benefit?

ALTERNATIVES

If this method of bilingual education is not the answer, are we forced to return to the old, discredited, sink-or-swim approach? No, we are not, since, as shown in Berkeley and other school districts, there are a number of alternative methods that have been proven effective, while avoiding the problems of all-native-language instruction.

Sheltered English and English as a Second Language (ESL) are just two programs that have helped to get children quickly proficient in English. Yet, political recognition of the viability of alternate methods has been slow in coming. In 1988, we witnessed the first crack in the

monolithic hold that native language instruction has had on bilingual education funds at the Federal level. In its reauthorization of Federal bilingual education, Congress voted to increase the percentage of funds
available for alternate methods from four to 25 percent of the total. This
is a great breakthrough, but we should not be satisfied until 100 percent
of the funds are available for any program that effectively and quickly can
get children functioning in English, regardless of the amount of native
language instruction it uses.

My goal as a student of language and a former educator is to see all
students succeed academically, no matter what language is spoken in
their homes. I want to see immigrant students finish their high school education and be able to compete for college scholarships. To help achieve
this goal, instruction in English should start as early as possible. Students
should be moved into English mainstream classes in one or, at the very
most, two years. They should not continue to be segregated year after
year from their English-speaking peers.

Another highly visible shift in Federal policy that I feel demonstrates
quite clearly the eroding support of government for our common language is the requirement for bilingual voting ballots. Little evidence ever
has been presented to show the need for ballots in other languages. Even
prominent Hispanic organizations acknowledge that more than 90 percent of native-born Hispanics currently are fluent in English and more
than half of that population is English monolingual.

Furthermore, if the proponents of bilingual ballots are correct when
they claim that the absence of native language ballots prevents non-
English-speaking citizens from exercising their right to vote, then current
requirements are clearly unfair because they provide assistance to certain
groups of voters while ignoring others. Under current Federal law, native
language ballots are required only for certain groups: those speaking
Spanish, Asian, or Native American languages. European or African immigrants are not provided ballots in their native language, even in jurisdictions covered by the Voting Rights Act.

As sensitive as Americans have been to racism, especially since the
days of the Civil Rights Movement, no one seems to have noticed the
profound racism expressed in the amendment that created the "bilingual
ballot." Brown people, like Mexicans and Puerto Ricans; red people, like
American Indians; and yellow people, like the Japanese and Chinese, are
assumed not to be smart enough to learn English. No provision is made,
however, for non-English-speaking French-Canadians in Maine or Vermont, or Yiddish-speaking Hasidic Jews in Brooklyn, who are white and
thus presumed to be able to learn English without difficulty.

Voters in San Francisco encountered ballots in Spanish and Chinese   30
for the first time in the elections of 1980, much to their surprise, since
authorizing legislation had been passed by Congress with almost no debate, roll-call vote, or public discussion. Naturalized Americans, who had

taken the trouble to learn English to become citizens, were especially angry and remain so. While native language ballots may be a convenience to some voters, the use of English ballots does not deprive citizens of their right to vote. Under current voting law, non-English-speaking voters are permitted to bring a friend or family member to the polls to assist them in casting their ballots. Absentee ballots could provide another method that would allow a voter to receive this help at home.

Congress should be looking for other methods to create greater access to the ballot box for the currently small number of citizens who cannot understand an English ballot, without resorting to the expense of requiring ballots in foreign languages. We cannot continue to overlook the message we are sending to immigrants about the connection between English language ability and citizenship when we print ballots in other languages. The ballot is the primary symbol of civic duty. When we tell immigrants that they should learn English—yet offer them full voting participation in their native language—I fear our actions will speak louder than our words.

If we are to prevent the expansion of policies such as these, moving us further along the multilingual path, we need to make a strong statement that our political leaders will understand. We must let them know that we do not choose to reside in a "Tower of Babel." Making English our nation's official language *by law* will send the proper signal to newcomers about the importance of learning English and provide the necessary guidance to legislators to preserve our traditional policy of a common language.

WRITING SUGGESTIONS: MAKING CONNECTIONS

1. The selections from King and Hayakawa address immigrant assimilation from an academic viewpoint, but it is a highly personal subject for those who come here. After all, they must confront their English-language deficiencies right from the start. When American students study a foreign language at school, however, almost all of the speaking and instruction is in English until they progress far enough to understand instruction and detailed conversations in the other language. Think about your classroom experience in learning a foreign language and your interactions with nonnative English speakers. What are the most difficult challenges for you in language studies? Are you comfortable expressing yourself in the language? If you absolutely needed to communicate in that language, how well could you do it? Would you be willing to use pidgin Spanish (or French, German, Russian, or other language) to a native speaker? How do you respond to people who are just learning English? Do you get impatient with them or assume that they are poorly educated? Write an essay about how well you think you would do if suddenly you had to function in another country with a different language. How would you deal with those who were impatient with your language skills or dismissive of you? How self-conscious do you think you would be?

2. Read the following poem by Maria Mazziotti Gillan, which depicts how non-English speakers were treated in previous generations.

Public School No. 18: Paterson, New Jersey

Miss Wilson's eyes, opaque
as blue glass, fix on me:
"We must speak English.
We're in America now."
I want to say, "I am American,"
but the evidence is stacked against me.

My mother scrubs my scalp raw, wraps
my shining hair in white rags
to make it curl; Miss Wilson
drags me to the window, checks my hair
for lice. My face wants to hide.

At home, my words smooth in my mouth,
I chatter and am proud. In school,
I am silent; I grope for the right English
words, fear the Italian word will sprout
from my mouth like a rose.

I fear the progression of teachers
in their sprigged dresses,
their Anglo-Saxon faces.

Without words, they tell me
to be ashamed.
I am.
I deny that booted country
even from myself,
want to be still
and untouchable
as these women
who teach me to hate myself.

Years later, in a white
Kansas City house,
the psychology professor tells me
I remind him of the Mafia leader
on the cover of *Time* magazine.
My anger spits
venomous from my mouth:

I am proud of my mother,
dressed all in black,
proud of my father
with his broken tongue,
proud of the laughter
and noise of our house.

Remember me, ladies,
the silent one?
I have found my voice
and my rage will blow
your house down.

Think about the poem in the context of the selections by Hayakawa and King. Then consider the following three statements:

a. At this time, it is highly unlikely that Congress will legislate that English is the official language of the United States.
b. Immigrants should learn English as quickly as possible after arriving in the United States.
c. The cultures and languages of immigrants should be respected and valued so that the bitterness and resentment exhibited in Gillan's poem will not be fostered, even as immigrants are assimilated into American society.

What is the best way to assimilate non-English speaking immigrants into our society? Write an essay in which you propose how the United States, as a nation, can make the two latter statements a reality without resorting to an English-only solution. How can we deal with the transition for immigrants without provoking the rage so eloquently expressed by Gillan?

3. The two essays in this section provide a good look at how the same piece of information can be used as evidence for opposing viewpoints. King, an expert in Indian language politics, asserts in his essay, "Contrary to public perception, India gets along pretty well with a host of different languages." Hayakawa, on the other hand, contends, "In fact, most Indians will concede that the situation [multilingualism] is a chaotic mess which has led to countless problems in the government's efforts to manage the nation's business." Do some research of your own about India's language situation. A good place to start would be King's book, *Nehru and the Language Politics of India*. Other sources include *India: National and Language Problem* by B. I. Kluyev and *Language, Language, Language in a Plural Society* by Lachman M. Khubchandani. Information is available in a variety of Internet sources as well. From your research, what is your perception of India's language situation? Write an essay in which you present your opinion about how well the country functions with nineteen officially recognized languages. In your essay, consider the other side of the argument as well. How are both King and Hayakawa able to portray India's situation to fit their own opposing viewpoints?

10

LANGUAGE
AND THE MEDIA

Selection, Slanting, and Charged Language

NEWMAN P. BIRK AND GENEVIEVE B. BIRK

The more we learn about language and how it works, the more abundantly clear it becomes that our language shapes our perceptions of the world. Because most people have eyes to see, ears to hear, noses to smell, tongues to taste, and skins to feel, it seems as though our perceptions of reality should be pretty similar. We know, however, that this is not the case, and language, it seems, makes a big difference in how we perceive our world. In effect, language acts as a filter, heightening certain perceptions, dimming others, and totally voiding still others.

In the following selection from their book Understanding and Using Language *(1972), Newman and Genevieve Birk discuss how we use words, especially the tremendous powers that slanted and charged language wields. As a writer, you will be particularly interested to learn just how important your choice of words is. After reading what the Birks have to say, you'll never read another editorial, watch another commercial, or listen to another politician in quite the same way.*

WRITING TO DISCOVER: *Choose three different people and write a description of a person, an object, or an event from each of their perspectives. Consider how each would relate to the subject you chose, what details each would focus on, and the attitude each would have toward your subject.*

A. THE PRINCIPLE OF SELECTION

Before it is expressed in words, our knowledge, both inside and outside, is influenced by the principle of selection. What we know or observe depends on what we notice; that is, what we select, consciously or unconsciously, as worthy of notice or attention. As we observe, the principle of selection determines which facts we take in.

Suppose, for example, that three people, a lumberjack, an artist, and a tree surgeon, are examining a large tree in the forest. Since the tree itself is a complicated object, the number of particulars or facts about it that one could observe would be very great indeed. Which of these facts a particular observer will notice will be a matter of selection, a selection that is determined by his interests and purposes. A lumberjack might be interested in the best way to cut the tree down, cut it up and transport it to the lumber mill. His interest would then determine his principle of selection in observing and thinking about the tree. The artist might consider painting a picture of the tree, and his purpose would furnish his principle of selection. The tree surgeon's professional interest in the physical health of the tree might establish a principle of selection for him. If each man were now required to write an exhaustive, detailed report on every thing he observed about the tree, the facts supplied by each would differ, for each would report those facts that his particular principle of selection led him to notice.[1]

The principle of selection holds not only for the specific facts that people observe but also for the facts they remember. A student suddenly embarrassed may remember nothing of the next ten minutes of class discussion but may have a vivid recollection of the sensation of the blood mounting, as he blushed, up his face and into his ears. In both noticing and remembering, the principle of selection applies, and it is influenced not only by our special interest and point of view but by our whole mental state of the moment.

The principle of selection then serves as a kind of sieve or screen through which our knowledge passes before it becomes our knowledge. Since we can't notice everything about a complicated object or situation or action or state of our own consciousness, what we do notice is determined by whatever principle of selection is operating for us at the time we gain the knowledge.

It is important to remember that what is true of the way the principle   5
of selection works for us is true also for the way it works for others. Even

---

1. Of course, all three observers would probably report a good many facts in common — the height of the tree, for example, and the size of the trunk. The point we wish to make is that each observer would give us a different impression of the tree because of the different principle of selection that guided his observation.

before we or other people put knowledge into words to express meaning, that knowledge has been screened or selected. Before an historian or an economist writes a book, or before a reporter writes a news article, the facts that each is to present have been sifted through the screen of a principle of selection. Before one person passes on knowledge to another, that knowledge has already been selected and shaped, intentionally or unintentionally, by the mind of the communicator.

B. THE PRINCIPLE OF SLANTING

When we put our knowledge into words, a second process of selection, the process of slanting, takes place. Just as there is something, a rather mysterious principle of selection, which chooses for us what we will notice, and what will then become our knowledge, there is also a principle which operates, with or without our awareness, to select certain facts and feelings from our store of knowledge, and to choose the words and emphasis that we shall use to communicate our meaning.[2] Slanting may be defined as the process of selecting (1) knowledge — factual and attitudinal; (2) words; and (3) emphasis, to achieve the intention of the communicator. Slanting is present in some degree in all communication: one may *slant for* (favorable slanting), *slant against* (unfavorable slanting), or *slant both ways* (balanced slanting). [. . .]

C. SLANTING BY USE OF EMPHASIS

Slanting by use of the devices of emphasis is unavoidable,[3] for emphasis is simply the giving of stress to subject matter, and so indicating what is important and what is less important. In speech, for example, if we say that Socrates was *a wise old man,* we can give several slightly different meanings, one by stressing *wise,* another by stressing *old,* another by giving equal stress to *wise* and *old,* and still another by giving chief stress to *man.* Each different stress gives a different slant (favorable or unfavorable or balanced) to the statement because it conveys a different attitude toward Socrates or a different judgement of him. Connectives and word order also slant by the emphasis they give: consider the difference in

---

2. Notice that the "principle of selection" is at work as *we take in* knowledge, and that slanting occurs as *we express* our knowledge in words.

3. When emphasis is present — and we can think of no instance in the use of language in which it is not — it necessarily influences the meaning by playing a part in the favorable, unfavorable, or balanced slant of the communicator. We are likely to emphasize by voice stress, even when we answer *yes* or *no* to simple questions.

slanting or emphasis produced by *old but wise, old and wise, wise but old.* In writing, we cannot indicate subtle stresses on words as clearly as in speech, but we can achieve our emphasis and so can slant by the use of more complex patterns of word order, by choice of connectives, by underlining heavily stressed words, and by marks of punctuation that indicate short or long pauses and so give light or heavy emphasis. Question marks, quotation marks, and exclamation points can also contribute to slanting.[4] It is impossible either in speech or in writing to put two facts together without giving some slight emphasis or slant. For example, if we have in mind only two facts about a man, his awkwardness and his strength, we subtly slant those facts favorably or unfavorably in whatever way we may choose to join them.

More Favorable Slanting	*Less Favorable Slanting*
He is awkward and strong.	He is strong and awkward.
He is awkward but strong.	He is strong but awkward.
Although he is somewhat awkward, he is very strong.	He may be strong, but he's very awkward.

With more facts and in longer passages it is possible to maintain a delicate balance by alternating favorable emphasis and so producing a balanced effect.

All communication, then, is in some degree slanted by the *emphasis* of the communicator.

D. SLANTING BY SELECTION OF FACTS

To illustrate the technique of slanting by selection of facts, we shall examine three passages of informative writing which achieve different effects simply by the selection and emphasis of material. Each passage is made up of true statements or facts about a dog, yet the reader is given three different impressions. The first passage is an example of objective writing or balanced slanting, the second is slanted unfavorably, and the third is slanted favorably.

1. Balanced Presentation

Our dog, Toddy, sold to us as a cocker, produces various reactions in various people. Those who come to the back door she usually growls and barks at (a milkman has said that he is afraid of her); those who

---

4. Consider the slanting achieved by punctuation in the following sentences: He called the Senator an honest man? *He* called the Senator an honest man? He called the Senator an honest man! He said one more such "honest" senator would corrupt the state.

come to the front door, she whines at and paws; also she tries to lick people's faces unless we have forestalled her by putting a newspaper in her mouth. (Some of our friends encourage these actions; others discourage them. Mrs. Firmly, one friend, slaps the dog with a newspaper and says, "I know how hard dogs are to train.") Toddy knows and responds to a number of words and phrases, and guests sometimes remark that she is a "very intelligent dog." She has fleas in the summer, and she sheds, at times copiously, the year round. Her blonde hairs are conspicuous when they are on people's clothing or on rugs or furniture. Her color and her large brown eyes frequently produce favorable comment. An expert on cockers would say that her ears are too short and set too high and that she is at least six pounds too heavy.

The passage above is made up of facts, verifiable facts,[5] deliberately   10
selected and emphasized to produce a *balanced* impression. Of course not all the facts about the dog have been given — to supply *all* the facts on any subject, even such a comparatively simple one, would be an almost impossible task. Both favorable and unfavorable facts are used, however, and an effort has been made to alternate favorable and unfavorable details so that neither will receive greater emphasis by position, proportion, or grammatical structure.

2. Facts Slanted Against

That dog put her paws on my white dress as soon as I came in the door, and she made so much noise that it was two minutes before she had quieted down enough for us to talk and hear each other. Then the gas man came and she did a great deal of barking. And her hairs are on the rug and on the furniture. If you wear a dark dress they stick to it like lint. When Mrs. Firmly came in, she actually hit the dog with a newspaper to make it stay down, and she made some remark about training dogs. I wish the Birks would take the hint or get rid of that noisy, short-eared, overweight "cocker" of theirs.

This unfavorably slanted version is based on the same facts, but now these facts have been selected and given a new emphasis. The speaker, using her selected facts to give her impression of the dog, is quite possibly unaware of her negative slanting.

Now for a favorably slanted version:

---

5. *Verifiable facts* are facts that can be checked and agreed upon and proved to be true by people who wish to verify them. That a particular theme received a failing grade is a verifiable fact; one needs merely to see the theme with the grade on it. That the instructor should have failed the theme is not, strictly speaking, a verifiable fact, but a matter of opinion. That women on the average live longer than men is a verifiable fact; that they live better is a matter of opinion, *a value judgement.*

3. Facts Slanted For

What a lively and responsible dog! When I walked in the door, there she was with a newspaper in her mouth, whining and standing on her hind legs and wagging her tail all at the same time. And what an intelligent dog. If you suggest going for a walk, she will get her collar from the kitchen and hand it to you, and she brings Mrs. Birk's slippers whenever Mrs. Birk says she is "tired" or mentions slippers. At a command she catches balls, rolls over, "speaks," or stands on her hind feet and twirls around. She sits up and balances a piece of bread on her nose until she is told to take it; then she tosses it up and catches it. If you are eating something, she sits up in front of you and "begs" with those big dark brown eyes set in that light, buff-colored face of hers. When I got up to go and told her I was leaving, she rolled her eyes at me and sat up like a squirrel. She certainly is a lively and intelligent dog.

Speaker 3, like Speaker 2, is selecting from the "facts" summarized in balanced version 1, and is emphasizing his facts to communicate his impression.

All three passages are examples of *reporting* (i.e., consist only of verifiable facts), yet they give three very different impressions of the same dog because of the different ways the speakers slanted the facts. Some people say that figures don't lie, and many people believe that if they have the "facts," they have the "truth." Yet if we carefully examine the ways of thought and language, we see that any knowledge that comes to us through words has been subjected to the double screening of the principle of selection and the slanting of language. [. . .]

Wise listeners and readers realize that the double screening that is   15
produced by the principle of selection and by slanting takes place even when people honestly try to report the facts as they know them. (Speakers 2 and 3, for instance, probably thought of themselves as simply giving information about a dog and were not deliberately trying to mislead.) Wise listeners and readers know too that deliberate manipulators of language, by mere selection and emphasis, can make their slanted facts appear to support almost any cause.

In arriving at opinions and values we cannot always be sure that the facts that sift into our minds through language are representative and relevant and true. We need to remember that much of our information about politics, governmental activities, business conditions, and foreign affairs comes to us selected and slanted. More than we realize, our opinions on these matters may depend on what newspaper we read or what news commentator we listen to. Worthwhile opinions call for knowledge of reliable facts and reasonable arguments for and against—and such opinions include beliefs about morality and truth and religion as well as about public affairs. Because complex subjects involve knowing and dealing with many facts on both sides, reliable judgements are at best difficult to arrive at. If we want to be fairminded, we must be willing to subject our opinions to continual testing by new knowledge, and must realize that after all they *are* opinions, more or less trustworthy. Their trustworthiness will depend on the representativeness of our facts, on the quality of our reasoning, and on the standard of values that we choose to apply.

We shall not give here a passage illustrating the unscrupulous slanting of facts. Such a passage would also include irrelevant facts and false statements presented as facts, along with various subtle distortions of fact. Yet to the uninformed reader the passage would be indistinguishable from a passage intended to give a fair account. If two passages (2 and 3) of casual and unintentional slanting of facts about a dog can give such contradictory impressions of a simple subject, the reader can imagine what a skilled and designing manipulation of facts and statistics could do to mislead an uninformed reader about a really complex subject. An example of such manipulation might be the account of the United States that Soviet propaganda has supplied to the average Russian. Such propaganda, however, would go beyond the mere slanting of the facts: it would clothe the selected facts in charged words and would make use of the many other devices of slanting that appear in charged language.

E. SLANTING BY USE OF CHARGED WORDS

In the passages describing the dog Toddy, we were illustrating the technique of slanting by the selection and emphasis of facts. Though the facts selected had to be expressed in words, the words chosen were as factual as possible, and it was the selection and emphasis of facts and not of words that was mainly responsible for the two distinctly different impressions of the dog. In the passages below we are demonstrating another way of slanting — by the use of charged words. This time the accounts are very similar in the facts they contain; the different impressions of the subject, Corlyn, are produced not by different facts but by the subtle selection of charged words.

The passages were written by a clever student who was told to choose as his subject a person in action, and to write two descriptions, each using the "same facts." The instructions required that one description be slanted positively and the other negatively, so that the first would make the reader favorably inclined toward the person and the action, and the second would make him unfavorably inclined.

Here is the favorably charged description. Read it carefully and form   20
your opinion of the person before you go on to read the second description.

Corlyn

Corlyn paused at the entrance to the room and glanced about. A well-cut black dress draped subtly about her slender form. Her long blonde hair gave her chiseled features the simple frame they required. She smiled an engaging smile as she accepted a cigarette from her escort. As he lit it for her she looked over the flame and into his eyes. Corlyn had that rare talent of making every male feel that he was the only man in the world.

She took his arm and they descended the steps into the room. She walked with an effortless grace and spoke with equal ease. They each took a cup of coffee and joined a group of friends near the fire. The flickering light danced across her face and lent an ethereal quality to her beauty. The good conversation, the crackling logs, and the stimulating coffee gave her a feeling of internal warmth. Her eyes danced with each leap of the flames.

Taken by itself this passage might seem just a description of an attractive girl. The favorable slanting by use of charged words has been done so skillfully that it is inconspicuous. Now we turn to the unfavorable slanted description of the "same" girl in the "same" actions:

Corlyn

Corlyn halted at the entrance to the room and looked around. A plain black dress hung on her thin frame. Her stringy bleached hair accentuated her harsh features. She smiled an inane smile as she took a cigarette from her escort. As he lit it for her she stared over the lighter and into his eyes. Corlyn had a habit of making every male feel that he was the last man on earth.

She grasped his arm and they walked down the steps and into the room. Her pace was fast and ungainly, as was her speed. They each reached for some coffee and broke into a group of acquaintances near the fire. The flickering light played across her face and revealed every flaw. The loud talk, the fire, and the coffee she had gulped down made her feel hot. Her eyes grew more red with each leap of the flames.

When the reader compares these two descriptions, he can see how charged words influence the reader's attitude. One needs to read the two descriptions several times to appreciate all the subtle differences between them. Words, some rather heavily charged, others innocent-looking but lightly charged, work together to carry to the reader a judgement of a person and a situation. If the reader had seen only the first description of Corlyn, he might well have thought that he had formed his "own judgement on the basis of the facts." And the examples just given only begin to suggest the techniques that may be used in heavily charged language. For one thing, the two descriptions of Corlyn contain no really good example of the use of charged abstractions; for another, the writer was obliged by the assignment to use the same set of facts and so could not slant by selecting his material.

F. SLANTING AND CHARGED LANGUAGE

[. . .] When slanting of facts, or words, or emphasis, or any combination of the three *significantly influences* feelings toward, or judgements about, a subject, the language used is charged language. [. . .]

Of course communications vary in the amount of charge they carry and in their effect on different people; what is very favorably charged for one person may have little or no charge, or may even be adversely charged, for others. It is sometimes hard to distinguish between charged and uncharged expression. But it is safe to say that whenever we wish to convey any kind of inner knowledge—feelings, attitudes, judgements, values—we are obliged to convey that attitudinal meaning through the medium of charged language; and when we wish to understand the inside knowledge of others, we have to interpret the charged language that they choose, or are obliged to use. Charged language, then, is the natural and necessary medium for the communication of charged or attitudinal meaning. At times we have difficulty in living with it, but we should have even greater difficulty in living without it.

Some of the difficulties in living with charged language are caused by 25
its use in dishonest propaganda, in some editorials, in many political speeches, in most advertising, in certain kinds of effusive salesmanship, and in blatantly insincere, or exaggerated, or sentimental expressions of emotion. Other difficulties are caused by the misunderstandings and misinterpretations that charged language produces. A charged phrase misinterpreted in a love letter; a charged word spoken in haste or in anger; an acrimonious argument about religion or politics or athletics or fraternities; the frustrating uncertainty produced by the effort to understand the complex attitudinal meaning in a poem or play or a short story—these troubles, all growing out of the use of charged language, may give us the feeling that Robert Louis Stevenson expressed when he said, "The battle goes sore against us to the going down of the sun."

But however charged language is abused and whatever misunderstandings it may cause, we still have to live with it—and even by it. It shapes our attitudes and values even without our conscious knowledge; it gives purpose to, and guides, our actions; through it we establish and maintain relations with other people and by means of it we exert our greatest influence on them. Without charged language, life would be but half life. The relatively uncharged language of bare factual statement, though it serves its informative purpose well and is much less open to abuse and to misunderstanding, can describe only the bare land of factual knowledge; to communicate knowledge of the turbulencies and the calms and the deep currents of the sea of inner experience we must use charged language.

FOCUSING ON CONTENT

1. What is the principle of selection, and how does it work?
2. According to the Birks, how is slanting different from the principle of selection? What devices can a speaker or writer use to slant knowledge? When is it appropriate, if at all, to slant language?
3. What exactly are charged words? Demonstrate your understanding of charged language by picking some examples from the two descriptions of Corlyn.

4. Why is it important for writers and others to be aware of charged words? What can happen if you use charged language unknowingly? What are some of the difficulties in living in a world with charged language?

FOCUSING ON WRITING

1. What is the Birks's purpose in this essay? (Glossary: *Purpose*) Do they seem more intent on explaining or on arguing their position? Point to specific language that they use that led you to your conclusion. (Glossary: *Diction*)

2. Do you find the examples about Toddy the dog and Corlyn particularly helpful? (Glossary: *Examples*) Why or why not? What would have been lost, if anything, had the examples not been included?

3. How do the Birks organize their essay? (Glossary: *Organization*) Do you think the organizational pattern is appropriate given their subject matter and purpose? Explain.

4. How do the authors use transitional words and expressions to guide readers through the essay? (Glossary: *Transitions*) Mention some specific transitions.

5. The Birks wrote this essay in 1972, when people were not as sensitive to sexist language as they are today. (Glossary: *Sexist Language*) Reread several pages of their essay, paying particular attention to the Birks's use of pronouns and to the gender of the people in their examples. Suggest ways in which the Birks's diction could be changed so as to eliminate any sexist language.

LANGUAGE IN ACTION

According to the editors of *Newsweek,* the March 8, 1999, "Voices of the Century: Americans at War" issue "generated more than two hundred passionate responses from civilians and veterans." The following five letters are representative of those the editors received and published in the issue of March 29, 1999. Carefully read each letter, looking for slanting and charged language. Point out the verifiable facts you find. How do you know these facts are verifiable?

Kudos for your March 8 issue, "Voices of the Century: Americans at War." This issue surely ranks among the best magazines ever published. As a military historian, I gained a better perspective of this turbulent century from this single issue than from many other sources combined. The first-person accounts are the genius of the issue. And your selection of storytellers was truly inspired. The "Voices of the Century" is so powerful that I will urge all of my friends to read it, buying copies for those who are not subscribers. Many persons today, especially those born after WWII, do not comprehend or appreciate the defining events of this century. How can we be more confident that they will be aware of our vital past when making important social and political decisions during the next century? I have great confidence in the American spirit and will, but this missing perspective is my principal concern as I leave this nation to the ministry of my daughters, my grandchildren, and their generation. Why not publish "Voices of the Century" as a booklet and make it readily available to all young people? Why not urge every school system to make it required reading prior to graduation from high school?

–ALAN R. McKIE, Springfield, VA

Your March 8 war issue was a powerfully illustrated essay of the men and women who have served our country and the people of other lands in so many capacities. But it was the photos that touched my soul and made me cry all over again for the human loss, *my* loss. As I stared at the pictures of the injured, dead, dying, and crying, I felt as though I were intruding on their private hell. God bless all of them, and my sincere thanks for a free America.

–DEBORAH AMES, Sparks, NV

I arrived in this country at 15 as a Jewish refugee from Nazism. I became an American soldier at 19 and a U.S. Foreign Service officer at 29. As a witness to much of the history covered in your special issue, I wanted to congratulate *Newsweek* on a superb job. In your excellent introduction, I found only one word with which I take issue: that "after the war Rosie and her cohort *happily* went back to the joys of motherhood and built the baby boom." Rosie and her cohort were forced back into their traditional gender roles, and it took the women's movement another generation or two to win back the gains achieved during the war.

–LUCIAN HEICHLER, Frederick, MD

Editor's note: The word "happily" was carefully chosen. Contemporary surveys indicated that most of the American women who joined the work force because of World War II were glad to get back to family life when it was over.

On the cover of your "Americans at War" issue, you have the accompanying text "From WWI to Vietnam: The Grunts and the Great Men—In Their Own Words." In each of these wars, the grunts *were* the great men.

–PAULA S. McGUIRE, Charlotte, NC

Your March 8 issue was painful for me and other members of my family as a result of the photograph you included on page 62 showing a wounded soldier being dragged from the line of fire during the Tet Offensive. My family had previously confirmed with the photographer that the soldier was my youngest brother, Marine Cpl. Robert Mack Harrelson. His bullet-riddled body fought hard to survive and, with the assistance of many excellent, caring members of our U.S. Military Medical Staff, he was able to regain some degree of normalcy after his return. But the injuries he received were too great to overcome, resulting in the military funeral he had requested. The rekindled grief brought on by your photo is keenly felt throughout our large family, and especially so by our dear 85-year-old mother, who still speaks of Bob as though he might reappear at any time. In spite of the photo, I sincerely congratulate your fine publication for reminding the world of the tragedy of war.

–LOWELL L. HARRELSON, Bay Minette, AL

WRITING SUGGESTIONS

1. (*Writing from Experience*) Describe a day at your school or university. Begin with details that help you create a single dominant impression. Be careful to select only details that support the attitude and meaning you wish to convey. Once you've finished, compare your essay to those of your peers. In what ways do the essays differ? How are they the same? How does this writing exercise reinforce the Birks's discussion of the principle of selection?

2. (*Writing from Reading*) When used only positively or only negatively, charged words can alienate the reader and bring the author's reliability into question. Consider the Birks's two examples of Corlyn. In the first example Corlyn can do no wrong, and in the second she can do nothing right. Using these two examples as a guide, write your own multiparagraph description of a person you know well. Decide on the overall impression you want to convey to your readers, and use charged words—both positive and negative—to create that impression.

3. (*Writing from Research*) Find a newspaper or magazine editorial on a subject that you have strong opinions about. Analyze the writer's selection of facts and use of charged language. How well does the writer present different viewpoints? Is the editorial convincing? Why or why not? After researching the topic further in your library or on the Internet, write a letter to the editor in response to the editorial. In your letter, use information from your research to make a point about the subject. Also comment on any charged or slanted language the editor used. Mail your letter to the editor.

Read All about It! (But Don't Believe It)

CARYL RIVERS

A frequent contributor to Saturday Review, Glamour, McCall's, Boston Magazine, *and the* New York Times Magazine, *Caryl Rivers was born in Washington, D.C., in 1947. A graduate of Trinity College in Washington, D.C., and Columbia University's School of Journalism, she is professor of journalism at Boston University and the author of a number of nonfiction books and novels including* She Works, He Works: How Two-Income Families Are Happier, Healthier, and Better Off *(1996),* More Joy Than Rage: Crossing Generations with the New Feminism *(1991), and* Camelot *(1998). As a writer and journalist, she often comments on American society and popular culture, as evidenced by her 1996 book* Slick Spins and Fractured Facts: How Cultural Myths Distort the News. *Frequently, she focuses on women's issues.*

The following essay first appeared in the Boston Globe *in May 1996. Here she cautions us not to believe every headline that we read, especially when the headline speaks of women and their problems. In debunking many of the myths of womanhood that the media perpetuates, Rivers helps us see how journalists can misrepresent the facts, thus filling the news with distorted pictures of reality.*

WRITING TO DISCOVER: *Do you tend to believe most things that you see in print? If not, how do you know when to question what you read? Do you think some printed sources are more reliable than others? Find a few examples of printed materials you do not necessarily believe and explain why you are skeptical of their claims.*

The headlines, it seems, are everywhere. "PMS Affects Millions!," declares one. "Do Women Lack a Math Gene?," asks another. Then there's "Super-mom Gives Up!," — not to mention "Women Over 35 — Old Maids Forever?"

Such headlines, examples printed in mainstream newspapers and magazines, can be found in the American press nearly any day of the week. If your only source of information about women was the media, you'd expect to find the psych wards crammed with stressed-out working women, the streets littered with the bodies of victims of terminal PMS, desperate women over 30 rushing to the altar with the nearest available male, and women leaving the work force in droves, eager to emulate June Cleaver in that '60s sitcom "Leave It to Beaver."

The American press greatly exaggerates the problems of women — especially working women. The result is that women may be experiencing undeserved guilt and worry.

An examination of hundreds of articles reveals two myths about women—myths that are polar opposites and that exist simultaneously in what might be called Mediaspace: the Myth of Female Weakness and the Myth of Female Strength.

Both fictions have deep roots in culture and mythology. The Myth of   5
Female Weakness dates to Eve, who, the Bible says, couldn't resist eating the apple and so got humans kicked out of paradise. In the Middle Ages, sages wondered if woman had a soul. In the 19th century, it was accepted medical dogma that a woman's brain and her reproductive system could not develop at the same time.

The Myth of Female Strength shows up in the Bible and in Greek mythology: One glimpse of Medusa and a man was turned to stone; the sirens lured sailors to watery graves with their songs; and, of course, Delilah stole Samson's strength by cutting his hair.

The modern counterparts of these legends keep popping up in the press. Premenstrual syndrome, for example, got 1,810 mentions in the press during 1994 and '95, while pneumonia got 20. We all know that PMS kills more people than pneumonia, right?

If a woman's hormones aren't the problem, maybe it's her brain. The "math gene" story that suggested women were simply not biologically fit for doing mathematics was a big seller in the 1980s. It lingers still, despite critics' complaints that there is no evidence for a purely male "math gene." In fact, when you filter out a handful of geniuses, men and women perform very much alike on tests of mathematical ability.

What you don't see very often, however, is a headline such as this: "Do Caucasian males lack a math gene?" The same test that provoked the headline about women's math problems also showed that Asian males scored far better than Caucasians on the Scholastic Assessment Test. There was barely a whisper of this, however, in the media.

Politicians keep dredging up old ideas about female weakness. House   10
Speaker Newt Gingrich suggested that women aren't suited for combat because men are programmed to hunt giraffe, and GOP presidential hopeful Pat Buchanan wrote that women aren't aggressive enough for modern competitive capitalism. (Fortunately, that isn't stopping women from applying to West Point or the MBA program at Harvard.) The hunting argument is still being used against women, even though historians say that the all-male, big-game hunt emerged fairly late in human history. It was gathering by males and females that took us across the line into humanhood. But a bunch of gals and guys carrying salad choppers for pulverizing roots doesn't quite have the sex appeal of the guy with the spear.

If women aren't too weak, then just maybe they are too strong. The images of women with power are tinged with dread—from Glenn Close, the nutty woman in "Fatal Attraction," to Demi Moore in "Disclosure," to Hillary Rodham Clinton.

Consider the language used in the media about Clinton. There were more than 50 references to her as Lady Macbeth. Who has she murdered lately? She's also been called a witch, a liar, and a harridan, and there were several comparisons of her to Lorena Bobbitt. As I remember, Mrs. Clinton stood by her man through bad times, while Mrs. Bobbitt took a sharp-edged instrument to her husband's anatomy. Why the comparison?

Such dark images are not often applied to males in politics. Gingrich's unfavorable rating may [have been] sky-high, but nobody's [called] him a warlock. Nobody [called] him Macbeth.

It wasn't only Hillary Clinton, of course, who got labeled. Nancy Reagan was vilified as being "meddlesome," Rosalynn Carter was called the "steel magnolia," and Kitty Dukakis was called a "dragon lady." When Texas Gov. Ann Richards gave a very sensible speech to young women graduates about standing on their own two feet and not waiting for Mr. Right to support them, she was called a "man-basher." [. . .]

Some women get hit with both mythologies at the same time. Anita   15
Hill, for example, was portrayed as either a poor weak, besotted woman desperately in love and so naive that she was used by Democrats as a tool to attack Supreme Court nominee Clarence Thomas—or as a steely feminist Joan of Arc who spent her weekends reading obscenity cases so she could discover Long Dong Silver. Take your choice.

There's another myth that influences the media's presentation of women: the notion that when women leave home and hearth, chaos descends upon us. That notion—which shaped news coverage as far back as the days of women's suffrage—still plays like elevator music in the background of today's coverage of women. Working women are pictured as stress-ridden candidates for heart attacks—despite the fact that for two decades, nearly all the studies show working women as healthier than homemakers, and there has been no rise in coronary symptoms among working women.

The suspicion that if women are too ambitious they will be damaged in some way was the strong undercurrent of a news story that reported that women over age 35 have a greater chance of getting killed by a terrorist than getting married. There was absolutely no truth to the story— but it ended up on the covers of *Newsweek* and *People* magazines anyway.

Here's the story: Demographers say there is a general tendency for women to marry men two years their senior. It's also true that during the baby boom, each year brought an increasing number of babies; the baby crop in 1955 was larger than that in 1953, for example. So a 35-year-old woman who refused to marry anyone but a man two years her senior would find fewer such men. But if she married a man her own age, or a younger man, there was no shortage at all. This is a cover story? No.

Then there are the "trend stories" about women returning to hearth and home. One analyst noted that, in 1994, there was a dip among young women entering the labor force; at the same time, mortgage rates dipped, prompting the analyst to suggest that women were leaving their jobs and, with their husbands, buying homes where they could start families. This "news" garnered these headlines around the U.S.:

- The Return of the Single Breadwinner
- Number of Stay-At-Home Moms on the Rise
- Mothers Jilt Jobs for Homes, Families
- More Women Choose to Stay Home

But as it turned out, there was no such trend. If the analyst had 20 looked at the figures for men entering the labor force, he would have found that there was an even bigger dip among men. Were they running off to have babies? Or did the figure simply reflect a lousy job market?

And while there actually were lower mortgage rates, a story in the *New York Times* noted that young couples were carrying a much larger debt than in past years. Indeed, women may have been buying houses with their mates, but the debt on those houses would have tended to keep them in the job market. Once again, a phony story that leapt into the headlines.

Will it ever change? Don't hold your breath. The first woman started out with lousy press, and the daughters of Eve seem to have inherited her public relations problem. As long as old myths continue to play in our heads, as long as we accept a distorted view of women through history as passive, intellectually inferior, and weak (except when they are snipping off men's private parts), we will keep on seeing exaggerated headlines about women and their problems.

So the next time you see a story about how women hate their jobs and want to go home, or how women with good jobs are miserable wrecks, or how some brain or body part makes women unfit to be chief executive officers, take it with a grain of salt. You may not be hearing the cool, "objective" voice of journalism, but the old, endlessly replaying tapes of myth.

FOCUSING ON CONTENT

1. Rivers starts her essay by citing four newspaper and magazine headlines that greatly exaggerate the problems of women. What myths about women do these headlines illustrate?

2. Rivers's examination of hundreds of newspaper and magazine articles uncovered "the Myth of Female Weakness and the Myth of Female Strength" (4). How does she explain the fact that these seemingly contradictory myths exist side-by-side in what she calls Mediaspace? Do these two myths place women in a kind of no-win situation? Explain.

3. Rivers introduces a third myth in paragraph 16. How is this myth related, if at all, to the first two myths? To what ends does the press utilize this third myth?

4. Although Rivers doesn't provide a direct answer to the lack of press about men's problems, why do you suppose we don't find headlines like "Do Caucasian Males Lack a Math Gene?" or "More Men Choose to Stay Home"?

5. Does Rivers give us much cause to hope that the media will soon become more accurate in reporting on women's problems? What advice does she have for us as readers?

FOCUSING ON WRITING

1. What do you suppose Rivers's purpose is in writing this essay? (Glossary: *Purpose*) Did you think she is simply trying to convey information, or is she trying to persuade you to her position?

2. In paragraph 3, Rivers asserts her thesis that "The American press greatly exaggerates the problems of women—especially working women." (Glossary: *Thesis*) She then adds the corollary that "The result is that women may be experiencing undeserved guilt and worry." How does she support each of these claims? Is she able to convince you of the validity of each claim? Explain.

3. How does Rivers establish her authority on the topic of the misrepresentation of women and their problems in the media? What types of sources does she use to illustrate the three myths about women? (Glossary: *Examples*) Which examples work best for you? Explain why.

4. Rivers concludes paragraph 7 with a question that she doesn't expect us to answer. (Glossary: *Rhetorical Question*) How does this question function in the context of the essay? What is the tone of her question? (Glossary: *Tone*) Where else in the essay do you find her using this tone?

5. How does Rivers organize her essay? Do you find the introduction of a third myth in paragraph 16 troublesome after she has stated earlier that there are two myths? Why or why not?

LANGUAGE IN ACTION

Carefully read the following letter to the editor of the *New York Times*, which was published on November 19, 1992. In it Nancy Stevens, president of a small Manhattan advertising agency, argues against using the word *guys* to address women. How do you think Rivers would react to the use of the word *guys* to refer to women? Do you find such usage objectionable? Which one of the myths that Rivers discusses does Stevens's argument illustrate? Explain.

WOMEN AREN'T GUYS

A young woman, a lawyer, strides into a conference room. Already in attendance, at what looks to be the start of a high-level meeting, are four smartly dressed women in their 20's and 30's. The arriving woman plunks her briefcase down at the head of the polished table and announces, "O.K., guys, let's get started."

On "Kate and Allie," a television show about two women living together with Kate's daughter and Allie's daughter and son, the dialogue often runs to such phrases as, "Hey, you guys, who wants pizza?" All of the people addressed are female, except for Chip, the young son. "Come on, you guys, quit fighting," pleads one of the daughters when there is a tiff between the two women.

Just when we were starting to be aware of the degree to which language affects people's perceptions of women and substitute "people working" for "men working" and "humankind" for "mankind," this "guy" thing happened. Just when people have started becoming aware that a 40-year-old woman shouldn't be called a girl, this "guy" thing has crept in.

Use of "guy" to mean "person" is so insidious that I'll bet most women don't notice they are being called "guys," or, if they do, find it somehow flattering to be one of them.

Sometimes, I find the courage to pipe up when a bunch of us are assembled and are called "guys" by someone of either gender. "We're not guys," I say. Then everyone looks at me funny.

One day, arriving at a business meeting where there were five women and one man, I couldn't resist. "Hello, ladies," I said. Everyone laughed embarrassedly for the blushing man until I added, "and gent." Big sigh of relief. Wouldn't want to call a guy a "gal" now, would we?

Why is it not embarrassing for a woman to be called "guy?" We know why. It's the same logic that says women look sexy and cute in a man's shirt, but did you ever try your silk blouse on your husband and send him to the deli? It's the same mentality that holds that anything male is worthy (and to be aspired toward) and anything female is trivial.

We all sit around responding, without blinking, "black with one sugar, please," when anyone asks. "How do you guys like your coffee?"

What's all that murmuring I hear?

"Come on, lighten up."

"Be a good guy."

"Nobody means anything by it."

Nonsense.

WRITING SUGGESTIONS

1. (*Writing from Experience*) Write a narrative about a time that you or someone you know was judged by a cultural or societal stereotype similar to the ones described by Rivers (e.g., the myth of the macho male or the myth of the dumb blonde). What exactly was the situation? What myth was involved?

2. (*Writing from Reading*) Do you share Rivers's belief that the American press is unlikely to change its ways any time soon, or are you more optimistic about the situation? In an essay, support or refute Rivers's position (22) that "we will keep on seeing exaggerated headlines about women and their problems."

3. (*Writing from Research*) Select several popular general-readership magazines (*Time, People, Newsweek, U.S. News and World Report,* or others), and analyze the nonfiction stories they contain. How many articles discuss "women's problems?" How many deal with the issues of working women? How would you characterize the headlines that accompany each of the articles about women? Write an essay in which you use your analysis of the articles and headlines about women to support or refute Rivers's conclusions.

The Bias of Language, the Bias of Pictures

NEIL POSTMAN AND STEVE POWERS

A native of Brooklyn, New York, Neil Postman is a graduate of the State University of New York at Fredonia and Columbia University. He has authored eighteen books on language, education, the media, and communication theory. His books Discovering Your Language *(1996) and* Exploring Your Language *(1996) helped usher in an era of linguistic inquiry. He displays his skills as a media critic and cultural commentator in* The Disappearance of Childhood *(1982),* Amusing Ourselves to Death *(1985), and* Conscientious Objections *(1988). Postman's articles appear in the* New York Times Magazine, *the* Atlantic Monthly, *and the* Harvard Education Review, *and he is contributing editor to the* Nation. *Currently, he is University Professor and Paulette Goddard Chair of Media Ecology at New York University.*

Steve Powers was born in New York City in 1934. A graduate of Bernard M. Baruch College of the City University of New York, Powers has had a dual career as a professional musician and as a news correspondent for Fox Television News and the ABC Information Radio Network. Returning to New York University for a graduate degree in the 1980s, Powers started teaching at St. John's University in 1993. His interest in media literacy led him to team up with Postman to write the insightful and provocative book How to Watch a Television News Show *(1992).*

In the following selection, taken from that book, Postman and Powers look closely at what we as viewers are getting when we watch the news on television. They conclude that unless we come to television news with a "prepared mind [. . .] a news program is only a kind of rousing light show."

WRITING TO DISCOVER: *Where or how do you get news of what is happening in the world? Do you read a newspaper or watch network news programs on a regular basis? Do you read a weekly news magazine like* Time *or* Newsweek? *Write about which news sources you prefer and why.*

When a television news show distorts the truth by altering or manufacturing facts (through re-creations), a television viewer is defenseless even if a re-creation is properly labeled. Viewers are still vulnerable to misinformation since they will not know (at least in the case of docudramas) what parts are fiction and what parts are not. But the problems of verisimilitude posed by re-creations pale to insignificance when compared to the problems viewers face when encountering a straight (no-monkey-business) show. All news shows, in a sense, are re-creations in that what we hear and see on them are attempts to represent actual events, and are not the events themselves. Perhaps, to avoid ambiguity, we might call all news shows "re-presentations" instead of "re-creations." These re-presentations come to us in two forms: language and pictures. The question then arises: what do viewers have to know about language and pictures in order to be properly armed to defend themselves against the seductions of eloquence (to use Bertrand Russell's apt phrase)?

Let us take language first. Below are three principles that, in our opinion, are an essential part of the analytical equipment a viewer must bring to any encounter with a news show.

1. WHATEVER ANYONE SAYS SOMETHING IS, IT ISN'T.

This sounds more complex—and maybe more pretentious—than it actually is. What it means is that there is a difference between the world of events and the world of words about events. The job of an honest reporter is to try to find words and the appropriate tone in presenting them that will come as close to evoking the event as possible. But since no two people will use exactly the same words to describe an event, we must acknowledge that for every verbal description of an event, there are multiple possible alternatives. You may demonstrate this to your own satisfaction by writing a two-paragraph description of a dinner you had with at least two other people, then asking the others who were present if each of them would also write, independently, a two-paragraph description of the "same" dinner. We should be very surprised if all of the descriptions include the same words, in the same order, emphasize the same things, and express the same feelings. In other words, "the dinner itself" is largely a nonverbal event. The words people use to describe this event are not the event itself and are only abstracted re-presentations of the event. What does this mean for a television viewer? It means that the viewer must never assume that the words spoken on a television news show are exactly what happened. Since there are so many alternative ways of describing what happened, the viewer must be on guard against assuming that he or she has heard "the absolute truth."

2. LANGUAGE OPERATES AT VARIOUS LEVELS OF ABSTRACTION.

This means that there is a level of language whose purpose is to *describe* an event. There is also a level of language whose purpose is to *evaluate* an event. Even more, there is a level of language whose purpose is to *infer* what is unknown on the basis of what is known. The usual way to make these distinctions clear is through sentences such as the following three:

Manny Freebus is 5'8" and weighs 235 pounds.
Manny Freebus is grossly fat.
Manny Freebus eats too much.

The first sentence may be said to be language as pure description. It involves no judgments and no inferences. The second sentence is a description of sorts, but is mainly a judgment that the speaker makes of the "event" known as Manny Freebus. The third sentence is an inference based on observations the speaker has made. It is, in fact, a statement about the unknown based on the known. As it happens, we know Manny Freebus and can tell you that he eats no more than the average person but suffers from a glandular condition which keeps him overweight. Therefore, anyone who concluded from observing Manny's shape that he eats too much has made a false inference. A good guess, but false nonetheless.

You can watch television news programs from now until doomsday and never come across any statement about Manny Freebus. But you will constantly come across the three kinds of statements we have been discussing—descriptions, judgments, and inferences. And it is important for a viewer to distinguish among them. For example, you might hear an anchor introduce a story by saying: "Today Congress ordered an investigation of the explosive issue of whether Ronald Reagan's presidential campaign made a deal with Iran in 1980 to delay the release of American hostages until after the election." This statement is, of course, largely descriptive, but includes the judgmental word "explosive" as part of the report. We need hardly point out that what is explosive to one person may seem trivial to another. We do not say that the news writer has no business to include his or her judgment of this investigation. We do say that the viewer has to be aware that a judgment has been made. In fact, even the phrase "made a deal" (why not "arranged with Iran"?) has a somewhat sleazy connotation that implies a judgment of sorts. If, in the same news report, we are told that the evidence for such a secret deal is weak and that only an investigation with subpoena power can establish the truth, we must know that we have left the arena of factual language and have moved into the land of inference. An investigation with subpoena power may be a good idea but whether or not it can establish the truth is a guess on the journalist's part, and a viewer ought to know that.

3. ALMOST ALL WORDS HAVE CONNOTATIVE MEANINGS.

This suggests that even when attempting to use purely descriptive language, a journalist cannot avoid expressing an attitude about what he or she is saying. For example, here is the opening sentence of an anchor's report about national examinations: "For the first time in the nation's history, high-level education policymakers have designed the elements for a national examination system similar to the one advocated by President Bush." This sentence certainly looks like it is pure description although it is filled with ambiguities. Is this the first time in our history that this has been done? Or only the first time that high-level education policymakers have done it? Or is it the first time something has been designed that is similar to what the President has advocated? But let us put those questions aside. (After all, there are limits to how analytical one ought to be.) Instead, we might concentrate on such words as "high-level," "policymakers," and "designed." Speaking for ourselves, we are by no means sure that we know what a "high-level policymaker" is, although it sounds awfully impressive. It is certainly better than a "low-level policymaker," although how one would distinguish between the two is a bit of a mystery. Come to think of it, a low-level "policymaker" must be pretty good, too, since anyone who makes policy must be important. It comes as no surprise, therefore, that what was done was "designed." To design something usually implies careful thought, preparation, organization, and coherence. People design buildings, bridges, and furniture. If your experience has been anything like ours, you will know that reports are almost never designed; they are usually "thrown together," and it is quite a compliment to say that a report was designed. The journalist who paid this compliment was certainly entitled to do it even though he may not have been aware of what he was doing. He probably thought he had made a simple description, avoiding any words that would imply favor or disfavor. But if so, he was defeated in his effort because language tends to be emotion-laden. Because it is people who do the talking, the talk almost always includes a feeling, an attitude, a judgment. In a sense, every language contains the history of a people's feelings about the world. Our words are baskets of emotion. Smart journalists, of course, know this. And so do smart audiences. Smart audiences don't blame anyone for this state of affairs. They are, however, prepared for it.

It is not our intention to provide here a mini-course in semantics. Even if we could, we are well aware that no viewer could apply analytic principles all the time or even much of the time. Anchors and reporters talk too fast and continuously for any of us to monitor most of their sentences. Besides, who would want to do that for most of the stories on a news show? If you have a sense of what is important, you will probably judge most news stories to be fluff, or nonsense, or irrelevancies, not worthy of your analytic weaponry. But there are times when stories appear that are of major significance from your point of view. These are the times when your level of attention will reach a peak and you must call upon your best powers of interpretation. In those moments, you need to draw on whatever you know about the relationship between language and reality; about the distinctions among statements of fact, judgment, and inference; about the connotative meanings of words. When this is done properly, viewers are no longer passive consumers of news but active participants in a kind of dialogue between a news show and themselves. A viewer may even find that he or she is "talking back to the television set" (which is the title of a book by former FCC commissioner Nicholas Johnson). In our view, nothing could be healthier for the sanity and well-being of our nation than to have ninety million viewers talking back to their television news shows every night and twice on Sunday.

Now we must turn to the problem of pictures. It is often said that a picture is worth a thousand words. Maybe so. But it is probably equally true that one word is worth a thousand pictures, at least sometimes — for example, when it comes to understanding the world we live in. Indeed, the whole problem with news on television comes down to this: all the words uttered in an hour of news coverage could be printed on one page of a newspaper. And the world cannot be understood in one page. Of course, there is a compensation: television offers pictures, and the pictures move. Moving pictures are a kind of language in themselves, but the language of pictures differs radically from oral and written language, and the differences are crucial for understanding television news.

To begin with, pictures, especially single pictures, speak only in particularities. Their vocabulary is limited to concrete representation. Unlike words and sentences, a picture does not present to us an idea or concept about the world, except as we use language itself to convert the image to idea. By itself, a picture cannot deal with the unseen, the remote, the internal, the abstract. It does not speak of "man," only of *a* man; not of "tree," only of *a* tree. You cannot produce an image of "nature," any more than an image of "the sea." You can only show a particular fragment of the here-and-now — a cliff of a certain terrain, in a certain condition of light; a wave at a moment in time, from a particular point of view. And just as "nature" and "the sea" cannot be photographed, such larger abstractions as truth, honor, love, and falsehood cannot be talked about in the lexicon of individual pictures. For "showing of" and "talking about" are two very different kinds of processes: individual pictures give us the world as object; language, the world as idea. There is no such thing in nature as "man" or "tree." The universe offers no such categories or simplifications; only flux and infinite variety. The picture documents and celebrates the particularities of the universe's infinite variety. Language makes them comprehensible.

Of course, moving pictures, video with sound, may bridge the gap by juxtaposing images, symbols, sound, and music. Such images can present emotions and rudimentary ideas. They can suggest the panorama of nature and the joys and miseries of humankind.

Picture — smoke pouring from the window, cut to people coughing, an ambulance racing to a hospital, a tombstone in a cemetery.

Picture — jet planes firing rockets, explosions, lines of foreign soldiers surrendering, the American flag waving in the wind.

Nonetheless, keep in mind that when terrorists want to prove to the world that their kidnap victims are still alive, they photograph them holding a copy of a recent newspaper. The dateline on the newspaper provides the proof that the photograph was taken on or after that date. Without the help of the written word, film and videotape cannot portray temporal dimensions with any precision. Consider a film clip showing an aircraft carrier at sea. One might be able to identify the ship as Soviet or American, but there would be no way of telling where in the world the carrier was, where it was headed, or when the pictures were taken. It is only through language—words spoken over the pictures or reproduced in them—that the image of the aircraft carrier takes on specific meaning.

Still, it is possible to enjoy the image of the carrier for its own sake.   15
One might find the hugeness of the vessel interesting; it signifies military power on the move. There is a certain drama in watching the planes come in at high speeds and skid to a stop on the deck. Suppose the ship were burning: that would be even more interesting. This leads to an important point about the language of pictures. Moving pictures favor images that change. That is why violence and dynamic destruction find their way onto television so often. When something is destroyed violently it is altered in a highly visible way; hence the entrancing power of fire. Fire gives visual form to the ideas of consumption, disappearance, death—the thing that burned is actually taken away by fire. It is at this very basic level that fires make a good subject for television news. Something was here, now it's gone, and the change is recorded on film.

Earthquakes and typhoons have the same power. Before the viewer's eyes the world is taken apart. If a television viewer has relatives in Mexico City and an earthquake occurs there, then he or she may take a special interest in the images of destruction as a report from a specific place and time; that is, one may look at television pictures for information about an important event. But film of an earthquake can be interesting even if the viewer cares nothing about the event itself. Which is only to say, as we noted earlier, that there is another way of participating in the news—as a spectator who desires to be entertained. Actually to see buildings topple is exciting, no matter where the buildings are. The world turns to dust before our eyes.

Those who produce television news in America know that their medium favors images that move. That is why they are wary of "talking heads," people who simply appear in front of a camera and speak. When talking heads appear on television, there is nothing to record or document, no change in process. In the cinema the situation is somewhat different. On a movie screen, close-ups of a good actor speaking dramatically can sometimes be interesting to watch. When Clint Eastwood narrows his eyes and challenges his rival to shoot first, the spectator sees the cool rage of the Eastwood character take visual form, and the narrowing of the eyes is dramatic. But much of the effect of this small movement depends on the size of the movie screen and the darkness of the theater, which make Eastwood and his every action "larger than life."

The television screen is smaller than life. It occupies about 15 percent of the viewer's visual field (compared to about 70 percent for the movie screen). It is not set in a darkened theater closed off from the world but in the viewer's ordinary living space. This means that visual changes must be more extreme and more dramatic to be interesting on television. A narrowing of the eyes will not do. A car crash, an earthquake, a burning factory are much better.

With these principles in mind, let us examine more closely the structure of a typical newscast, and here we will include in the discussion not only the pictures but all the nonlinguistic symbols that make up a television news show. For example, in America, almost all news shows begin with music, the tone of which suggests important events about to unfold. The music is very important, for it equates the news with various forms of drama and ritual—the opera, for example, or a wedding procession—in which musical themes underscore the meaning of the event. Music takes us immediately into the realm of the symbolic, a world that is not to be taken literally. After all, when events unfold in the real world, they do so without musical accompaniment. More symbolism follows. The sound of teletype machines can be heard in the studio, not because it is impossible to screen this noise out, but because the sound is a kind of music in itself. It tells us that data are pouring in from all corners of the globe, a sensation reinforced by the world map in the background (or clocks noting the time on different continents). The fact is that teletype machines are rarely used in TV news rooms, having been replaced by silent computer terminals. When seen, they have only a symbolic function.

Already, then, before a single news item is introduced, a great deal has been communicated. We know that we are in the presence of a symbolic event, a form of theater in which the day's events are to be dramatized. This theater takes the entire globe as its subject, although it may look at the world from the perspective of a single nation. A certain tension is present, like the atmosphere in a theater just before the curtain goes up. The tension is represented by the music, the staccato beat of the teletype machines, and often the sight of news workers scurrying around typing reports and answering phones. As a technical matter, it would be no problem to build a set in which the newsroom staff remained off camera, invisible to the viewer, but an important theatrical effect would be lost. By being busy on camera, the workers help communicate urgency about the events at hand, which suggests that situations are changing so rapidly that constant revision of the news is necessary.

The staff in the background also helps signal the importance of the person in the center, the anchor, "in command" of both the staff and the news. The anchor plays the role of host. He or she welcomes us to the newscast and welcomes us back from the different locations we visit during the filmed reports.

Many features of the newscast help the anchor to establish the impression of control. These are usually equated with production values in broadcasting. They include such things as graphics that tell the viewer what is being shown, or maps and charts that suddenly appear on the screen and disappear on cue, or the orderly progression from story to story. They also include the absence of gaps, or "dead time," during the broadcast, even the simple fact that the news starts and ends at a certain hour. These common features are thought of as purely technical matters, which a professional crew handles as a matter of course. But they are also symbols of a dominant theme of television news: the imposition of an orderly world—called "the news"—upon the disorderly flow of events.

While the form of a news broadcast emphasizes tidiness and control, its content can best be described as fragmented. Because time is so precious on television, because the nature of the medium favors dynamic visual images, and because the pressures of a commercial structure require the news to hold its audience above all else, there is rarely any attempt to explain issues in depth or place events in their proper context. The news moves nervously from a warehouse fire to a court decision, from a guerrilla war to a World Cup match, the quality of the film most often determining the length of the story. Certain stories show up only because they offer dramatic pictures. Bleachers collapse in South America: hundreds of people are crushed—a perfect television news story, for the cameras can record the face of disaster in all its anguish. Back in Washington, a new budget is approved by Congress. Here there is nothing to photograph because a budget is not a physical event; it is a document full of language and numbers. So the producers of the news will show a photo of the document itself, focusing on the cover where it says "Budget of the United States of America." Or sometimes they will send a camera crew to the government printing plant where copies of the budget are produced. That evening, while the contents of the budget are summarized by a voice-over, the viewer sees stacks of documents being loaded into boxes at the government printing plant. Then a few of the budget's more important provisions will be flashed on the screen in written form, but this is such a time-consuming process—using television as a printed page—that the producers keep it to a minimum. In short, the budget is not televisable, and for that reason its time on the news must be brief. The bleacher collapse will get more time that evening.

While appearing somewhat chaotic, these disparate stories are not just dropped in the news program helter-skelter. The appearance of a scattershot story order is really orchestrated to draw the audience from one story to the next—from one section to the next—through the commercial breaks to the end of the show. The story order is constructed to hold and build the viewership rather than place events in context or explain issues in depth.

Of course, it is a tendency of journalism in general to concentrate on the surface of events rather than underlying conditions; this is as true for   25 the newspaper as it is for the newscast. But several features of television undermine whatever efforts journalists may make to give sense to the world. One is that a television broadcast is a series of events that occur in sequence, and the sequence is the same for all viewers. This is not true for a newspaper page, which displays many items simultaneously, allowing readers to choose the order in which they read them. If newspaper readers want only a summary of the latest tax bill, they can read the headline and the first paragraph of an article, and if they want more, they can keep reading. In a sense, then, everyone reads a different newspaper, for no two readers will read (or ignore) the same items.

But all television viewers see the same broadcast. They have no choices. A report is either in the broadcast or out, which means that anything which is of narrow interest is unlikely to be included. As NBC News executive Reuven Frank once explained:

> A newspaper, for example, can easily afford to print an item of conceivable interest to only a fraction of its readers. A television news program must be put together with the assumption that each item will be of some interest to everyone that watches. Every time a newspaper includes a feature which will attract a specialized group it can assume it is adding at least a little bit to its circulation. To the degree a television news program includes an item of this sort . . . it must assume that its audience will diminish.

The need to "include everyone," an identifying feature of commercial television in all its forms, prevents journalists from offering lengthy or complex explanations, or from tracing the sequence of events leading up to today's headlines. One of the ironies of political life in modern democracies is that many problems which concern the "general welfare" are of interest only to specialized groups. Arms control, for example, is an issue that literally concerns everyone in the world, and yet the language of arms control and the complexity of the subject are so daunting that only a minority of people can actually follow the issue from week to week and month to month. If it wants to act responsibly, a newspaper can at least make available more information about arms control than most people want. Commercial television cannot afford to do so.

But even if commercial television could afford to do so, it wouldn't. The fact that television news is principally made up of moving pictures prevents it from offering lengthy, coherent explanations of events. A television news show reveals the world as a series of unrelated, fragmentary moments. It does not—and cannot be expected to—offer a sense of coherence or meaning. What does this suggest to a TV viewer? That the viewer must come with a prepared mind—information, opinions, a sense of proportion, an articulate value system. To the TV viewer lacking such mental equipment, a news program is only a kind of rousing light show. Here a falling building, there a five-alarm fire, everywhere the world as an object, much without meaning, connections, or continuity.

FOCUSING ON CONTENT

1. Why do Postman and Powers consider all news shows "re-creations" (1)? What do they believe viewers need to know about language and pictures in order to view television news properly?

2. In what ways does the language of pictures differ from spoken and written language? Why, according to Postman and Powers, are these differences important for understanding television news?

3. Why do scenes of violence and dynamic destruction have such appeal to viewers? Why do television producers avoid "talking heads"? In comparison to the movies, why must visual changes "be more extreme and more dramatic [. . .] on television"?

4. In what ways can television news be considered a form of theater? According to Postman and Powers, how are news telecasts staged? What is the one dominant theme of television news, and how is this theme orchestrated?

5. What features of television news tend to undermine journalists' efforts to give context, depth, or sense to the world? What advantages do newspaper readers have over television viewers? Explain.

FOCUSING ON WRITING

1. What is Postman and Powers's main point about television news? (Glossary: *Thesis*) Where do they state their position? What changes, if any, do they want to see readers and viewers make as a result of reading this article?

2. What kinds of evidence do Postman and Powers provide to support their position? (Glossary: *Evidence*) Which evidence do you find most persuasive? Least persuasive? Explain.

3. How do Postman and Powers organize their argument? (Glossary: *Organization*) What is the function of paragraphs 2–8, and how are they related to the rest of the essay?

4. Examine the writers' diction in the opening paragraph. (Glossary: *Diction*) What is their attitude toward television news? (Glossary: *Attitude*) What about their language led you to this conclusion? Does their diction throughout the essay support the impression created in the opening paragraph?

LANGUAGE IN ACTION

Postman and Powers suggest that moving pictures of destruction are entertaining because they show rapid and large-scale change. This, in turn, implies that pictures are chosen for the emotional effect they may have. Discuss your response to this photograph in terms of its emotional effect. Keep in mind both the feeling the scene itself creates and that created by the destruction that is the implied aftermath of the soldiers' action. Postman and Powers also say that images can be converted to ideas. What ideas does this photograph convey about war? Explain how language could translate this image into different ideas about war or the military. How do such "translations" illustrate Postman and Powers's main point about language and pictures?

WRITING SUGGESTIONS

1. (*Writing from Experience*) Select several pictures from a photo album — of a wedding, or graduation, or pictures from a recent trip you took with friends. Do the pictures capture or tell the story of the event, or did you really have to be there to get the whole story? If a video of the event is available, watch it for the sake of comparison. Write an essay in which you discuss the limitations of still photographs in capturing an event.

2. (*Writing from Reading*) Watch (and videotape, if possible) at least two networks' versions of the same day's evening news. How are the news shows the same? Different? To what extent do the news telecasts support the analysis of news programs presented by Postman and Powers? Report your findings in an essay.

3. (*Writing from Research*) During the 1990s, what was the impact of television news reporting on the Gulf War, the O. J. Simpson trial, the death and funeral of Princess Diana, the president's impeachment trial, the NATO bombing of Yugoslavia, the death of John F. Kennedy Jr., or another newsworthy event? Research the event you chose in your library or on the Internet. Be sure to read accounts of your event in newspapers and magazines at the time it was happening. As you write an essay about the event, consider the following questions: To what extent can it be said that television news actually creates rather than reports the news? What impact do you think live coverage of events has on our perceptions of them? In what ways is live coverage different from an anchor's retelling of the news?

It's Up Close and Misleading

RITA BRAVER

Rita Braver is a national correspondent for CBS News and a senior correspondent for Sunday Morning. *She spent four years as CBS News' chief White House correspondent, covering a broad range of domestic and foreign issues. She has won five Emmy Awards, including one for investigative reporting and two for her coverage of the assassination of Israeli president Yitzhak Rabin. A graduate of the University of Wisconsin at Madison, Braver started her career in broadcast journalism with CBS affiliate WWL-TV in New Orleans. She joined the Washington bureau in 1972 as a news desk editor and has worked as a producer and editor as well as a reporter.*

In the following selection, which first appeared as an op-ed piece in the Washington Post *on March 14, 1996, Braver takes a close look at how the world of journalism is portrayed in the movie* Up Close *and* Personal, *starring Michelle Pfeiffer and Robert Redford. As one of the leading women broadcast journalists who has worked her way up through the ranks, Braver is particularly disturbed by the misinformation the movie gives viewers.*

WRITING TO DISCOVER: *What new movie was your favorite in the past year? What about this movie appeals to you? Write about how accurately the movie reflects your perception of the real world. Is it important to you that movies present an accurate picture of how the world works? Why or why not?*

I went to see *Up Close and Personal* the other night. It wasn't billed as a horror movie, but it sure scared the heck out of me. Gorgeous, sexy Michelle Pfeiffer plays ingenue television reporter Tally Atwater. Tally is really named Sally, but for some reason she can't pronounce her own name, so the Robert Redford–type news director who hires her (who just happens to be played by Redford) orders her to substitute "T" for "S" so she won't get caught up on a little detail like saying who she is.

Redford, who believe it or not is named "Warren Justice" in the movie, is a former network White House correspondent who resigns over a matter involving his honor and journalistic integrity. This, however, does not stop him from hiring Sally/Tally, even though he knows that she has sent him a faked resume tape, which includes a clip of her wearing a really bad suit and telling prospective news directors that they should hire her because "I'm going to be a star." Redford/Justice agrees, offering Sally/Tally a job because she is so telegenic she "eats the lens."

Now here's the scary part: Because of the movie I am going to be besieged by even more desperately ambitious young women who aren't much interested in the news but who think they want jobs like mine. They will be like the beautiful, perfectly coiffed intern whom CBS executives asked me to talk to a few years ago.

"So," I opened the conversation, "you're interested in journalism?" Her contact lens green eyes grew wide. "Oh, no," she gasped. "I just want to do on-cameras, like you do."

I saw *Up Close and Personal* at a benefit screening where I was on a   5
panel of journalists asked to talk about what it's like to be a real TV reporter who also happens to be a woman. Carole Simpson of ABC News and Margaret Warner of PBS' *NewsHour with Jim Lehrer* were on the panel, along with moderator Linda Werthheimer of National Public Radio.

I listened to their stories of taking crummy assignments, working nights and weekends, and constantly having to prove themselves. I told a few tales of my own.

But mainly I was struck by the fact that what drew all of us to become reporters was that we wanted to understand the world and help explain it. We were curious. We wanted to talk to people about their lives. We wanted to expose the differences between what public officials said and what they did.

In fact, we wanted to do all the same things that good male reporters wanted to do. But because we all came of age in a less-enlightened time, we women had to pry open a lot of news executives' doors that were slammed in our faces.

Which brings us to the other scary part of *Up Close and Personal*. It says that women are dopes who can succeed only if older, wiser men direct their every move.

Not only does Warren Justice tell Sally/Tally what to think and what   10
to say, he also tells her what to wear. He takes her shopping and charges her clothes to the station. True, she does have a few spunky moments, and she has enough good sense to propose to Warren. But Tally is incapable of covering stories without him at her side. She leaves Warren in Miami to take a new job in Philadelphia, but she's so inexperienced that she bombs. Never fear, Warren flies in to the rescue.

Finally, Tally ends up covering a prison riot, all by herself. Sort of. We'll skip the part about how she gets into the prison without making the 60 or 70 set-up calls a real reporter would have to make. We won't dwell on the fact she and her trusty cameraman are magically able to broadcast from inside the prison without any of the necessary technical equipment. And we're not even going to try to explain how delectable Tally avoids being held hostage, raped, or even threatened by the rampaging prisoners who kill eight of their fellow inmates.

The point is that just as the going gets tough, Warren arrives on the scene to speak slowly and steadily into Tally's earpiece and lead her through her live shots. Of course, rather than crouching down in the corner and letting the camera show the action transpiring in the prison the way any normal reporter would do, Tally thinks the way to cover the riot is to shove her mug in front of the camera and talk. But she only gets the guts to speak when Warren voices encouragement.

And, in a turn of events that is destined to send thousands of Tally wannabes stampeding out to their local prisons, Sally's Warren-managed performance results in her becoming a famous network anchorwoman. Her crowning achievement in her new roll? She actually stands up in front of a huge audience of television executives and delivers a speech without using a teleprompter!

I know that films are make-believe. But too many women TV reporters have paid too many dues to let Tally Atwater stand as their symbol. She succeeds without ever working the phones, developing a source, covering a beat or even a single story for more than a few hours. It's true that Redford and Pfeiffer were nice to watch, especially in those steamy love scenes. But their fun is over. I'm going to be sending all the starry-eyed job-seekers to them.

FOCUSING ON CONTENT

1. Why does Rita Braver, as a broadcast journalist, find the movie *Up Close and Personal* scary?

2. From Braver's synopsis of the movie's plot, how would you describe the relationship between television reporter Tally Atwater and her boss, news director Warren Justice. What does Braver find scary about this relationship?

3. In the first two paragraphs, we learn that the real name of Michelle Pfeiffer's character Tally is Sally and that Redford's character is named Warren Justice. What do you suppose the writers of the screenplay intended with these names?

FOCUSING ON WRITING

1. Braver grabs her readers' attention in her first two sentences. (Glossary: *Beginnings and Endings*) In what ways do these sentences serve to set up the rest of her essay?

2. Braver uses a number of words from the world of television and journalism. What do terms like *resume tape, clip, on-cameras, set-up calls,* and *teleprompter* add to her essay? Do you think such diction is appropriate for an audience that would be reading the op-ed page of the *Washington Post*? (Glossary: *Diction* and *Technical Language*) Explain.

3. In paragraphs 5 through 8, Braver explains that she attended a benefit screening of *Up Close and Personal* and was part of a panel of women with careers in broadcast journalism who discussed what it is like to be a woman in that profession. What would have been lost had Braver not included those paragraphs? In what ways do these paragraphs support Braver's position on both the movie and television reporting? (Glossary: *Examples*)

4. When writing about a movie, television program, or book—especially one people have not seen or read—we are confronted with the problem of making a point without simply rehashing or summarizing the plot. What specifically does Braver do to communicate plot essentials to her readers while at the same time advancing her thesis?

LANGUAGE IN ACTION

During the summer of 1999, the movie *South Park* hit the nation's theaters. In July, the *New York Times* carried a full-page advertisement for the movie in its Arts & Entertainment section. The ad used the bold headline, "Uh-oh. The critics love it!" Within the ad itself, however, only two reviewers— Richard Corliss of *Time* magazine and David Ansen of *Newsweek*—were quoted to promote the movie. The material quoted from their respective reviews reads as follows:

> "*South Park* is inspired comic rudeness. You may laugh yourself sick at this ruthlessly funny movie."
>
> —RICHARD CORLISS

> "*South Park* has a gag-to-laugh ratio even higher than the new *Austin Powers.*"
>
> —DAVID ANSEN

After reading the two quotations used in the advertisement, what is your impression of the movie? Now read the complete reviews by Corliss and Ansen, which are reprinted here. How accurately do you think the advertisement represents the reviewers' opinions? What can happen when a quotation is taken out of its original context?

SICK AND INSPIRED: THE *SOUTH PARK* MOVIE HAS A MEAN STREAK—AND A SONG IN ITS HEART

Some people should probably skip *South Park: Bigger, Longer & Uncut,* the new feature based on the Comedy Central cartoon series. A short list would include celebrities teased in the movie: the Baldwin brothers (they are killed en masse by the Royal Canadian Air Force); Conan O'Brien (he commits suicide by jumping from the GE Building); Winona Ryder (she performs an unusual exercise with Ping Pong balls); Bill Gates (he is shot dead because Windows 98 isn't fast enough); Saddam Hussein (he has a gay affair with Satan and toys shamelessly with the Horned One's affections); Barbra Streisand (for all the old reasons); Liza Minnelli (don't ask); and God (who is vilified by one of the movie's guest kid heroes). Also anyone who lacks a bottomless tolerance for inspired comic rudeness.

For the *South Park* film is that happy surprise, an idea that is enriched as it expands from 20 minutes of TV time to 80 movie minutes. It confounds those who suspected that the explosive blips of the *South Park* fad were ready to flatline and that a feature film — likely to bore the faithful and annoy everyone else — was the surest way to do a Conan off the window ledge of the show's fading notoriety.

The kids are still here: Stan, Kyle, Kenny, and Cartman, the quartet of cut-out third-graders in the "quiet little red-neck podunk white-trash mountain town" of South Park, Colo. A bit more is at stake this time: the fate of the world. The lads see a movie starring their favorite Canadian gross-out comics, Terrence and Phillip, and parrot the naughty language. The South Park moms blame Canada, and in a trice we're war-ready. Meanwhile, Kenny (the dead one) goes to hell, where Satan and Saddam lurk. It takes a children's crusade — La Resistance — to get to the final rainbow.

All that and a gigantic talking clitoris should be enough for a short feature. But director Trey Parker (who wrote the film with Matt Stone and Pam Brady) figured he'd turn *South Park* into a wall-to-wall musical: 14 tunes, each evoking a familiar Broadway style. Cartman's perky *Kyle's Mom's a Bitch* echoes *Chitty Chitty Bang Bang*, with choruses in fake Chinese, Dutch, and French. Saddam could be an Arabic fiddler on the roof as he struts his seedy charm in *I Can Change*. Satan has a hilariously solemn ballad in the Disney-cartoon mode; like the Little Mermaid, he wants to be *Up There*. There's a dexterous quartet of musical themes, à la *Les Miz*. And though a song whose refrain is, more or less, "Shut your flicking face, Uncle Flicka" would seem to have little room for musical wit, ace arranger Marc Shaiman turns it into an *Oklahoma* hoedown, with kids chirping like obscene Chipmunks.

Did we say obscene? Be warned: the raunch is nonstop and often noxious. Kids who take their parents (or Liza or the Baldwins) should be prepared for some gasps and a scolding. As Cartman says of the Terrence and Phillip epic, "This movie has warped my fragile little mind." To viewers with sturdier cerebellums, here's another warning: you may laugh yourself sick — as sick as this ruthlessly funny movie is.   —RICHARD CORLISS

TAKE THAT!

THE CRÈME DE LA CRUDE

To find out how obscenities save the world from Satan and Saddam Hussein; to understand why the United States has declared war on Canada; to hear the best (and only) song written in praise of Brian Boitano, and to witness the violent demise of Bill Gates, there is only one place to turn: *South Park: Bigger, Longer & Uncut*. Every bit as tasteless, irreverent, silly, and smart as the Comedy Central cartoon that catapulted creators Trey Parker and Matt Stone into the Hollywood catbird seat, *South Park* has a gag-to-laugh ratio even higher than the new *Austin Powers*.

And it's filled with roof-raising musical numbers. That may be the biggest difference from the half-hour show. Otherwise, all the familiar, strangely fatherless little devils are on hand: lovelorn Stan, still pining and puking for Wendy; obtuse Cartman, making anti-Semitic cracks at the neurotic Kyle, and the parka-shrouded, incomprehensible Kenny, who dies this time when a surgeon replaces his heart with a baked potato. How did he end up in surgery in the first place? He went up in flames in a failed attempt to light a fart.

Oh yes, flatulence is central to *South Park's* adolescent appeal, but also to the movie's plot—and its sly politics. The trouble begins when the kids sneak into an obscenity-filled Canadian movie, *Asses of Fire,* starring the infamous Terrence and Phil. Soon they are mimicking the stars' every dirty word, and just as soon Kyle's outraged mom is leading a campaign to protect the children of the nation. ("Blame Canada" is one of Parker and Marc Shaiman's rousing musical anthems.) A kind of crackpot Madeleine Albright, she soon has Clinton's ear. When the Canadians, protesting the arrest and imminent execution of Terrence and Phil, bomb the entire Baldwin family to oblivion, the hellhounds of war are unleashed. Better dead bodies than dirty words, the voices of morality decree, as Parker and Stone gleefully hurl satirical poop at the MPAA and all who have tried to muzzle *South Park's* wicked tongue. This raunchy assault on authority, coming in the midst of the nation's increasingly surreal debate on the pernicious influence of the media, couldn't be more timely. It cuts through the pious finger pointing like, well, we shouldn't really say.   —DAVID ANSEN

WRITING SUGGESTIONS

1. (*Writing from Experience*) Think about a movie or a television program that oversimplified or perhaps even misrepresented a subject that you have considerable knowledge of. Write a letter to the film's or program's director, producer, or writer in which you express your distress with the show and suggest ways that he or she might have dealt with the subject in question.

2. (*Writing from Reading*) Do you think Braver makes a legitimate point about the movie *Up Close and Personal?* Why or why not? How realistic do you think movies should be? Write an essay in which you either agree or disagree with Braver's position. You may find it helpful to review your Writing to Discover entry and to read the next essay—"Information, Please" by Caryn James—before you start writing.

3. (*Writing from Research*) Using Braver's essay as a model, write a review of a movie, television program, or book for a major newspaper. Before you start writing, be sure that you have a specific main point you want to make and that you have selected particular scenes or passages to illustrate what you want to say. Also do some research in the library or on the Internet to learn what others have said about what you're reviewing. Depending on their comments, you may want to argue against their views or use their opinions to support your main point.

Information, Please

CARYN JAMES

Caryn James is the chief television critic of the New York Times. *For six years she was a* Times *film reviewer, and she remains a frequent film and book critic. Her first novel* Glorie *was published in 1999.*

    In the following selection, which first appeared in the "Culture Zone" column of the New York Times Magazine *on March 29, 1998, James looks at the way facts and other nonfiction elements are "flooding into entertainment," particularly into popular television dramas and novels. She wonders whether viewers are becoming more informed with the factual information that bombards them, or whether we are becoming a "culture of pseudo-experts."*

WRITING TO DISCOVER: *What are your favorite television shows, and what is it that you receive from them? Write about whether television is simply another form of entertainment for you or whether you find it educational. Explain.*

Watch a few television dramas and you can become an expert on summary-judgment hearings (*The Practice*), motions to suppress evidence (*Law and Order*), fractured fibulae (*E.R.*), or Rasmussen's encephalitis (*Chicago Hope*). Pick a novel from the best-seller list and you can learn to act like a noble lawyer (John Grisham's *Street Lawyer*) or a crooked lawyer (John Grisham's *Partner*). Go to the movies and Will Hunting (Matt Damon in *Good Will Hunting*) will prove complex mathematical theories so fast even Robin Williams can't keep up, but then Will is exceptional. In this era of information overload, only a certified genius is allowed to stay so far ahead of the audience.

It is fashionable to complain about fictional elements creeping into nonfiction; after John Berendt recently admitted that he invented a phone call for *Midnight in the Garden of Good and Evil,* some critics treated him like a capital offender. Meanwhile, an equally significant but less noted trend is moving in the opposite direction: facts are flooding into entertainment.

This is happening partly because so many nonfiction sources exist today. With endless legal analysis on Court TV and health information ranging from medical journals to quack cures on the Internet, the audience simply knows more. Jargon is picked up rapidly. How long will it be before the noun "proffer"—not exactly a household word until Monica Lewinsky's lawyer, William Ginsburg, started tossing it around on television—becomes as familiar as "judge" or "jury" on a legal drama like *Law and Order*? (In the early days of the Lewinsky story, reporters explained that the proffer was the statement offering what she would tell the special prosecutor in exchange for immunity; now the term often floats by, already added to the pool of common knowledge.)

The trend of fiction absorbing fact has little to do with the heritage of great realists like Émile Zola and everything to do with that of popular entertainers like James Michener. The common explanation for Michener's success was that readers were learning something from his novels: the entire history of Hawaii or Poland wrapped in a family saga. Such easy-listening knowledge is the equivalent of playing language tapes while you sleep: no pain, some gain.

They may not be art, but such popular fictions have an immense, sometimes ludicrous, impact. Armed with a little knowledge from Grisham or *The Practice* and a little from the nightly news, television viewers spar with defense attorneys and prosecutors on call-in shows. CNN, Fox News, MSNBC, and Court TV thrive on such entertainments posing as news, as we become a culture of pseudo-experts.

But there are valuable side effects as well. Helpful, even lifesaving information may be picked up. *E.R.* has dealt with testicular cancer, and *Chicago Hope* with genetic testing for breast cancer. And there may be a more subtle, more profound social change going on, too. The medical and legal professions in particular are being demystified through entertainment, a process that fosters a healthy questioning of authority. When fictional heroes are shown making choices, some of them disastrous, the doctor-as-God syndrome (and its sibling, the lawyer-as-God) suffers a well-deserved blow.

This dynamic is most evident in medical dramas, the fictions that touch the widest range of people. There is still plenty of mystification, of course. "Get a cbc, ABG, Chem 20" doesn't have to mean more than "Do a bunch of tests." But an important message is that doctors and lawyers don't always have the answers. On *E.R.*, when a chemical spill forces the evacuation of the emergency room, a heart patient insists she feels fine and sends the doctors to care for sicker patients; she dies and the doctors question their judgment. This doesn't happen weekly, just often enough to suggest that professionals are people who possess diplomas, not infallible answers.

As the image of doctors subtly changes, the means of sending medical information through entertainment becomes more complicated. Both *E.R.* and *Chicago Hope* have spawned similar weekly health reports for the late local news. "Following *E.R.*" is a segment produced by the Johns Hopkins School of Public Health and WBAL-TV and sent to NBC stations around the country; "Living With Hope" is produced by WJZ in Baltimore in consultation with Johns Hopkins School of Medicine and distributed to CBS affiliates. Both report on real-life examples of a medical case from that week's episode. This puts *E.R.* and *Chicago Hope* in the center of a cycle: medical facts are turned into television drama, then reported on the news as facts again.

All the medical and legal dramas are vetted by experts—a necessity, considering the series' influence. Last year, a study of regular viewers

5

measured the impact of *E.R.* (The study was sponsored by the Kaiser Family Foundation, which finances "Following *E.R.*") Fifty-three percent of viewers said they learned about "important health care issues" from the show. But the most crucial findings may concern television itself. The study focused on an *E.R.* episode in which a victim of date rape is given a morning-after pill. Among those who were aware of emergency contraception before seeing that episode, 63 percent said that they had learned about it from television; only 11 percent got their information from a doctor or a clinic.

It would be dangerous if viewers relied on fictional doctors. Luckily,   10
television drama trades in personal dilemmas, not actual health decisions. In the best, facts are dropped into dialogue casually, serving the story first. On *Chicago Hope* a woman with H.I.V. wants to get pregnant and is told there is an 8 percent chance her child would be infected. Two doctors argue about whether that is too high. As one says, deftly passing the information along to us, "There are things we can do to reduce the risk: artificial insemination, AZT for the mother during pregnancy and for the baby postpartum." There are no simple answers to the characters' questions. When fiction handles fact well, the judgments are surrendered to the audience.

FOCUSING ON CONTENT

1. How does James account for the fact that nonfictional elements are cropping up everywhere in the world of popular entertainment, especially in television dramas, the movies, and best-selling novels?

2. What is James's attitude toward programming in which fictional elements creep into nonfiction? Does she believe entertainment should be kept separate from the news? Explain.

3. Part of the appeal of hospital and courtroom dramas is the specialized language or jargon that characters use, language that is often picked up and used by viewers. Why do you suppose viewers find such language so attractive? Do you share James's fear that we are becoming "a culture of pseudo-experts" (5)?

4. What does James see as the valuable side effects of the trend of fact invading fiction (6–7)?

5. In James's view, the writers of the best medical dramas insert facts unobtrusively into the flow of dialogue because they are promoting the story first (10). If you can, illustrate her point with an example from a show that you watched recently.

FOCUSING ON WRITING

1. What is James's purpose in this essay—to inform, to express personal thoughts and feelings, to argue a point? (Glossary: *Purpose*) What in her essay led you to this conclusion?

2. Reread James's opening paragraph. How effective do you find the opening? (Glossary: *Beginnings and Endings*) As a writer, how does she try to engage her readers?

3. What evidence does James supply to support her claim in paragraph 6 that "The medical and legal professions in particular are being demystified through entertainment, a process that fosters a healthy questioning of authority"? (Glossary: *Examples*) How convincing do you find her evidence? What else, if anything, could she have presented to strengthen her argument? Explain.

LANGUAGE IN ACTION

In the light of James's discussion of medical dramas like *E.R.* and *Chicago Hope,* consider the following cartoon from *The Get Well Book* (1998) by John McPherson. What, for you, is the source of McPherson's humor? What point do you think he is making? Do you think James would agree with McPherson's point? Why or why not?

"Stop the tape! See what George Clooney is
doing with that catheter? That's the procedure
I think we should try with Mr. Simkins."

WRITING SUGGESTIONS

1. (*Writing from Experience*) We are all aware that we are living in the Information Age. We are bombarded with facts and statistics on a daily basis and may sometimes feel there is an overload of information. What have been your experiences with the easy availability of information today? Has it made your life easier or more stressful? Write an essay in which you explore several personal encounters with the Information Age.

2. (*Writing from Reading*) James claims that hospital dramas like *E.R.* and *Chicago Hope* have helped to "demystify" the medical profession. Watch several episodes of each show, taking good notes about the medical issues presented and the portrayal of doctors, nurses, and other hospital personnel. Then write an essay in which you support or refute James's claim. Be sure to document your points with well-chosen examples from the episodes you watched.

3. (*Writing from Research*) In paragraph 10, James writes that "It would be dangerous if [television] viewers relied on fictional doctors." And indeed it would. Using material found in your library or on the Internet, write an essay about where you think most people get their information about health or medical issues today. What self-help health resources are available in print or online? Which magazines and newspapers carry regular health columns? You may find it helpful to limit your research to a single health or medical issue, such as nutrition and diet, contraception, AIDS, or mental illness.

Talk Shows and the Dumbing of America

TOM SHACHTMAN

Award-winning documentarian and author, Tom Shachtman was born in 1942 in New York City. After graduating with a B.A. from Tufts University in 1963 and an M.A. from Carnegie-Mellon University in 1966, he pursued a career as a freelance writer, producer, and director for television, writing the widely acclaimed trilogy "Children of Poverty," "Children of Trouble," and "Children of Violence" in the 1970s. Shachtman has taught writing at Harvard's Extension School and at New York University. He is the author of both fiction and nonfiction works, including Absolute Zero *(1999),* Video Power *(1988),* Skyscraper Dreams: The Great Real Estate Dynasties of New York *(1991), and* Around the Block: The Business of a Neighborhood *(1997).*

The following selection is taken from his book The Inarticulate Society: Eloquence and Culture in America *(1995). In this excerpt, Shachtman examines eight popular syndicated television talk shows to discover the impact these shows are having on the language and minds of viewers. He provides convincing evidence that talk shows are dumbing down or debasing the English language rather than helping American society deal with its increasing inarticulateness.*

WRITING TO DISCOVER: *Whether or not you watch television talk shows, you have heard of some popular hosts and their shows—Oprah Winfrey, Jenny Jones, Jerry Springer, Ricki Lake, Regis Philbin and Kathie Lee Gifford, Jane Whitney, and Sally Jessy Raphael, to name just a few. Jot down your thoughts or observations about these hosts and their shows. Is your impression of talk shows generally positive? Negative? Indifferent? Explain.*

On an Oprah Winfrey broadcast, when a young doctor confessed that he was something of a romantic, he reportedly received 40,000 letters from women wishing to share his life. While not every talk program can generate that amount of attention, collectively talk shows have an enormous audience, as many as 80 million viewers daily, and as the doctor's story makes clear, it is an audience that pays close attention to what is being said on the programs. To learn more about how language is being modeled for us on talk shows, on November 9, 1993, I spent the day watching and listening to snippets of eight mainstream syndicated talk shows.

At nine in the morning in New York, while NBC and some other channels carry game shows and cartoons, and while Mr. Rogers holds forth on public television, there are three talk shows in head-to-head competition: Jane Whitney on CBS, Montel Williams on the Fox network, and Regis Philbin and Kathie Lee Gifford on ABC.

Jane Whitney features a man whose problem is that he has two girlfriends. Tina and Jim are the guests in the first segment. She is angry about the situation, while he seems as contented as the cat who swallowed the cream. We later learn that Jim called the program and offered to appear with his two girlfriends, ostensibly to resolve their predicament. Jane Whitney's questioning demonstrates that she knows the terms "psychobabble," "avoiding commitment," "relationship," and "monogamous," but most of her queries are monosyllabic: "Some people, like, sleep with only one person at a time."

Jim's two lovers have never met. Now, to applause, the second young woman emerges from behind a curtain, and then, under Jane's questioning, the two comment on how they are and are not alike.

> JANE   Do you feel you have anything in common with her?
>
> SECOND   Him.
>
> TINA   How do you know he loves you? He loves me!
>
> JANE   You're playing, like, seniority here. Like, bookends.

Montel Williams's guests are six couples made up of older women and   5
younger men. Each woman introduces her young man, using such terms as "hunk," "sex appeal," and "perfect specimen of humanity," and making sure to announce his birth date, for the men are a decade or two younger than the women. The couples behave as though they are in the first flushes of affairs. We learn that the Montel Williams show arranged and taped a party at which these people were first introduced to one another, in exchange for promises to appear on the program. The basic subject of the program is sex. Queried by the host, one young man speaks of "not having to work for it" and another confides about older women, "they tell you what they want," which prompts an admission from one that "we want a little pleasure for ourselves." Titles over the screen inform us that "JOHN/ Likes women of all ages" and "NICK/Loves older women." The snickering quotient of the program is high. At the transition to commercials, footage of the mixer party is followed by a snippet from tomorrow's show, "Two sisters, one man. . . . You'd be surprised at how often this happens." At least one set of sisters are twins. During a later segment of the broadcast, a ponytailed male therapist comments on the couples, using such phrases as "comfort . . . not expected to last . . . emotional ties are suspended." The therapist is then questioned by the panel, which induces Montel to tell about his own experiences with older women. A billboard asks us at home, "Are You a Mom Who Wishes Her Son Would Stop Dating Tramps?" Those who can answer "yes" are to call the show.

"Born to Be Unfaithful," Jane Whitney's next program, will feature people who have been unfaithful and are the offspring of unfaithful parents. The subject after that is "Mothers who allow their teenage daughters to have sex in the house"; on videotape, one such mother says she prefers her daughter and the daughter's boyfriend to have sex at home "where I know that they're safe."

Barbara Walters visits Regis and Kathie Lee to impart backstage chatter about the celebrities she has interviewed for her latest special, to be broadcast that evening. In a clip, Barbara tries to learn from Julia Roberts whether the movie star thinks her husband of a few months is ugly or just differently handsome. Julia opts for handsome. In the studio Barbara and Kathie Lee brush cheeks and make hand motions to convey that they must phone one another for a lunch date very soon.

Fred Rogers visits a pretzel bakery. In an apron and baker's hat, he observes the various processes of the assembly line and kneads some dough with his own hands. His conversation with the bakers, aimed at an audience of preschool children, employs almost as large a vocabulary as that of the nine o'clock talk shows.

Not yet ready to make conclusions from such a small sample, later that day I watch segments of five more talk shows: Joan Rivers on CBS and, on NBC, Jerry Springer, Maury Povich, Sally Jessy Raphael, and Phil Donahue.

"How going back to the trauma of birth will help you clear up present problems" is the way Joan Rivers touts the subject of her program, but before discussing that she chats with a gossip columnist about the recent birth of Marla Maples's child, in which "aroma therapy" was used, and welcomes a pair of married guests to talk about "past-life therapy." The couple maintains that they were actually married in a previous life. The wife says that through reliving and understanding an incident in Roman times, she has been cured:

10

> GUEST   All that anger drained away. . . . My heart got tender. I got compassionate.
>
> JOAN   All this in one session?

[. . .] Then we are finally introduced to a female "prenatal psychologist." To investigate "early traumas . . . impressed on the psyche," this woman helps patients to go back to the moment of birth, even to the moment of conception. She has brought along some patients, whom Joan Rivers introduces: "My next guests have all been reborn, not through religion." These guests include another ponytailed male psychologist, who has been rescued by regression therapy from suicidal impulses, and a mother-and-daughter pair, similarly rescued from allergies. We shortly see a videotape of a volunteer who has gone through the therapy backstage. After the tape is shown, the volunteer comes onto the set and comments on reliving the attempt to get out of the birth canal: "I was engaged in some sort of battle."

From Boston, Jerry Springer features several trios, each consisting of a grandmother, her teenage daughter, and the daughter's infant. The infants have been born out of wedlock, one to a girl who became pregnant at twelve, the others to girls who were thirteen and fourteen. The teenagers had all considered abortion but had decided against it. Jerry asks about birth control. [. . .] A new grandmother allows that in retrospect she does "feel guilty" at not having given her daughter birth control instruction. "At thirteen, I didn't think she was going to be—you know—actively having sex with her boyfriend," who was nineteen; "I was in denial." Jerry Springer nods, and in general his treatment of an important subject, the epidemic of teenage pregnancies, is evenhanded. He questions the women sympathetically and with dignity, although he never refers to them by their names but says "Mom" and "Grandmom." He asks a woman in the latter category if the sensation of becoming a grandmother could have been a proud one, given the circumstances. She says, "I don't know; it's like, I was in the delivery with her, and it's like— 'Memories.'" Audience members express their belief that the fathers should be arraigned on charges of statutory rape, but the new mothers and grandmothers all agree that would not help anyone. [. . .]

Maury Povich has gone to Texas for "Return to Waco: Answers in the Ashes." In front of an audience of former cult members and Waco residents, Povich questions Mark Breault, who left the Branch Davidians in 1989; Breault's complaints to the authorities have been blamed by some survivors for instigating the raids. [. . .]

The government's lead pathologist then summarizes his team's findings about the thirty-two people who died in the bunker. In the most literate language I have heard all day, language that is compassionate, direct, and precise, he details the manner and cause of death: So many had gunshot wounds, so many died of asphyxiation; a gunshot wound in the mouth may have been self-inflicted, but a wound in the back of the head almost certainly was not. His findings, being made public for the first time, devastate the people in the audience and on the set whose relatives died in that bunker—as we at home are forced to learn because the cameras focus on their faces so that we become privy to their emotions. While the pathologist tells the story, Maury Povich approaches one panel member whose face fills the screen and asks, "Is this what you think, Stan, happened to your family?"

"Could your sex life use a pick-me-up?" asks the announcer of the   15
Phil Donahue show. Then voice and tape display aphrodisiacs, love potions, and an acupuncturist at work, and a panelist comments that "I'm getting turned on just by watching."

That, of course, is just what was intended.

Sally Jessy Raphael's program on November 9, 1993, deals with two 1986 cyanide poisoning deaths in the Seattle area, for which the wife of one of the victims was convicted and imprisoned. Of all the programs of this day, it is the worst exemplar in terms of use of language. First, Sally encapsulates the story for us in emotional kindergarten language: "Some family members say Stella was railroaded. 'She's innocent. Poor Stella.' Some say her daughter Cynthia was really the mastermind behind the deaths." A journalist has written a book about the case. He has corralled the guest panelists, but during the course of the program he must frequently interpret and augment what these guests say, for the guests prove remarkably unable to present their thoughts coherently or even clothed in words that aptly convey their meaning.

> STELLA'S NIECE   I didn't think that—there wasn't enough problems that would institute her to kill my uncle . . .
>
> STELLA'S FRIEND   She was somebody that would've taken a gun and shot him point-blank, instead of being sneaky and committed murder in the way that she was convicted.

When one guest is entirely unable to convey her meaning, Sally is forced to correct her in order that the audience can understand the story:

> FORMER HOUSEMATE   She used me as a scapegoat.
>
> SALLY   As a screen.
>
> AUDIENCE MEMBER   Maybe Cynthia was child-abused.

As with my student's use of "emitted" for "admitted," these poor grammatical, vocabulary, and word usages are evidence of the sort of misperception of language that can only come from learning language in a secondarily oral way. Pop psychology terms aside, the discourse of the moderators, the guests, the experts, and most of the studio audience members of all these programs mixes grade-school vocabulary and grammar with a leavening of naughty language. Granted, there is no pretense of trying to be articulate, but neither are there many accidental instances of felicitous phrasing. Vocabulary levels are depressingly low, more in line with the spoken-word corpus than might be presumed, since parts of the programs are scripted, and since the guests and stars of these programs are not speaking in private but in rather public circumstances, in front of viewing audiences numbered in the tens of millions.

Talk-show language has become almost completely detached from   20
the literate base of English. It is as though the program-makers have concluded that literate English has nothing to do with the emotive, real-life concerns of human beings, and therefore cannot be used to describe or analyze them. As a result, talk shows exist in the realm of vocabularies limited to the few hundred most commonly used words in the spoken language, augmented by a few terms pirated from the sublanguage of therapy. To talk of "Mothers who allow their teenage daughters to have sex in the house," or to inquire "Are You a Mom Who Wishes Her Son Would Stop Dating Tramps?" is to speak down to the audience, not even

to address the audience on its own level. These lines employ a vocabulary not much beyond that of a nine- or ten-year-old; the facts show that the daytime viewing audience is chronologically older and better educated than that. [. . .] But the programming elites seem to have nothing but contempt for their audiences composed of average Americans—for "the people we fly over," as one executive called them. Rather, the programmers embrace the fuzzy McLuhanesque belief that a world dominated by new electronic media will wholehcartedly share tribal emotions.

Walter Ong asserts [in *Rhetoric, Romance and Technology,* 1971] that the culture of secondary orality may mean a return to the primacy of the unconscious for those within it. That culture's gestation period is being shortened by the practices of today's news programs and talk shows, which encourage the audience to acquire information principally through images, and through a lexicon that mimics the oral rather than the literate language. The limited vocabulary, constrained syntax, unknowing or deliberate misuses of language, affectation of minor wit, constant reference to base emotions, and chronic citation of pop cultural icons in attempts to bond with the audience—these characteristic elements of news and talk programs constitute an enfeebled discourse.

The antidote is well known, since most of the people who create news programs and talk shows are themselves literate and fully capable of using the literate-based language. That antidote is to use the power of words to haul these programs back up to a literate level they once attained. Purveyors of talk shows currently reject such a goal as not commensurate with their objective of gaining the largest audience. However, there is no evidence of which I am aware that demonstrates any inverse relationship between the shows' popularity and the vocabulary and articulateness levels of talk show hosts and hostesses (and that of their carefully screened guests). Precisely the opposite may be true: Articulate behavior is part of the hosts' and hostesses' attractiveness. Phil Donahue and Oprah Winfrey are articulate as well as charismatic people. Rush Limbaugh's ability to deflate liberal icons and to create telling puns—"femi-nazis" for strident feminists—have attracted him a wide following. All three, and many others among the talk-show stars, possess good vocabularies, but they have yet to employ them to best use. All too often, they reach for thc simple instead of using their tremendous abilities to make complicated matters exciting and understandable. Given these stars' large talents and capacities to enthrall, audiences would undoubtedly follow them up the scale of literacy as gladly (and in just as large numbers) as they have followed them down the scale.

As for news broadcasts, the transformation could be even simpler. News broadcasts need to take a pledge to not only convey information but to set aside time in the broadcast to have that information illuminated by the minds and vocabularies of the reporters. Permit reporters once again to do the tasks of synthesis and analysis of information, as well as the job of being on the spot to collect it. Utilize television's fabulous educative ability. Employ vocabularies that may once in a while send an audience member scurrying to a dictionary—or, better yet, set a goal of encouraging the audience to incorporate interesting words into their own vocabularies. During the Gulf War, millions of Americans learned a new word when Peter Jennings of ABC News spoke of oil as a "fungible" commodity, which he explained meant that a unit of it from one source was essentially the same as a unit of it from another source. Network news divisions could improve the articulateness levels of their viewers by raising the vocabulary and sentence-structure levels of their own broadcasts and by taking the pledge to use "fungible" and other such marvelous if unfamiliar words when they are clearly appropriate. How about one new word a day? Such a practice would be unlikely to provoke viewers to turn away from their favorite newscasters and to the competition.

We need for our broadcasters once again to champion and employ the power of words as well as the power of images. This is not only in the public interest, but in their own. Informative broadcasting relies, in the end, on an audience that places some premium on the value of ideas. If its discourse is increasingly impoverished, then the audience will retreat from information-based programs into the wholly pictorial realm of video games and interactive fictional programming, where the audience has the illusion of deciding what happens. Then there will be no more market for television news or talk shows. What the informative shows are doing by embracing images and diminished language is the equivalent of a restaurant slowly poisoning all of its customers.

FOCUSING ON CONTENT

1. How would you characterize the subjects of the talk-show programs that Shachtman watched? Do there seem to be any differences between the morning and afternoon talk shows? Why do you think so many people find such topics worth watching?

2. In what ways does the Maury Povich show about the Branch Davidians contrast with the other shows? What does it have in common with them?

3. In paragraph 19, what does Shachtman mean when he hypothesizes that many of the talk-show guests' "poor grammatical, vocabulary, and word usages [. . .] can only come from learning language in a secondarily oral way"? How does Walter Ong's description of the culture of secondary orality (21) support Shachtman's claim?

4. What is Shachtman's solution for what he considers the deplorable state of language on television talk shows? Do you think his solution is realistic? He praises newscaster Peter Jennings for introducing viewers to the word *fungible* (23). What does *fungible* mean? How does Jennings's action support Shachtman's views?

5. Why does Shachtman believe that today's broadcasters need "to champion and employ the power of words as well as the power of images" (24)? What does he fear will happen if our discourse becomes increasingly impoverished?

FOCUSING ON WRITING

1. In paragraph 1, what is the point of Shachtman's example of the young doctor on Oprah Winfrey's show? How effective is this story as an opening? (Glossary: *Beginnings and Endings*) Explain.

2. In paragraph 8, Shachtman discusses the content of *Mr. Rogers*. Explain the purpose this paragraph serves in the context of the essay.

3. How does Shachtman organize his essay? (Glossary: *Organization*) Explain how paragraphs 1–18 are related to paragraphs 19–24.

4. How would you characterize Shachtman's style—his vocabulary, sentence structure, paragraph length—in paragraphs 19–24? (Glossary: *Style*) What stylistic differences do you see between this group of paragraphs and the first 18 paragraphs? Discuss how the two styles reflect both the content and the purpose of each section of the essay.

5. What is Shachtman's attitude toward each of the talk-show topics he uses in his examples? How does his word choice help him to convey this attitude? (Glossary: *Diction* and *Attitude*)

LANGUAGE IN ACTION

In a chapter on the importance of words in his popular book *The Word-a-Day Vocabulary Builder* (1963), Bergen Evans gives the following account of two events in history that turned on the choice of a particular word. Discuss the ways in which these examples support Shachtman's call for broadcasters and talk-show hosts to model literate-based language for viewers.

Some of history's great disasters have been caused by misunderstood directions. The heroic but futile charge of the Light Brigade at Balaclava in the Crimean War is a striking example. "Someone had blundered," Tennyson wrote. That was true, and the blunder consisted of the confusion over one word, which meant one thing to the person speaking but another to the persons spoken to.

The brigade was ordered to charge "the guns." The man who gave the order was on a hilltop and had in mind a small battery which was very plain to him but was concealed from the soldiers in the valley by a slight rise. The only guns *they* could see were the main Russian batteries at the far end of the valley. Therefore they assumed that "the guns" referred to the batteries *they* saw. The command seemed utter madness, but it was a command and the leader of the Brigade, after filing a protest, carried it out. [. . .]

[. . .] When [. . .] America and Russia confronted each other during the Cuban crisis in 1962, and the world hovered for a few days on the brink of disaster, the use of the word *quarantine* instead of *blockade* was extremely important.

A *blockade* is an act of war. No one knew quite what a *quarantine* meant, under the circumstances. But the very use of the word indicated that, while we were determined to protect ourselves, we wanted to avoid war. It was all a part of giving Russia some possibility of saving face. We wanted her missiles and planes out of Cuba and were prepared to fight even a nuclear war to get them out. But we certainly preferred to have them removed peacefully. We did not want to back Russia into a corner from which there could have been no escape except by violence.

Thus the use of *quarantine,* a purposefully vague word, was part of our strategy. Furthermore, it had other advantages over *blockade.* It is commonly associated with a restriction imposed by all civilized nations on people with certain communicable diseases to prevent them from spreading their disease throughout the community. It is a public health measure which, for all the inconvenience that it may impose on the afflicted individual, serves the public welfare. Thus, whereas a blockade would have been an announcement that we were proceeding aggressively to further our own interests, regardless of the rights of others, quarantine suggested a concern for the general welfare. In addition, it suggested that what was going on in Cuba was a dangerous disease which might spread.

WRITING SUGGESTIONS

1. (*Writing from Experience*) How would you characterize your own vocabulary? Have you ever felt limited or restricted by your command of the English language when speaking in class or addressing some other audience? Using examples from your own experience or observations, write an essay in which you show how your vocabulary has helped you or restricted you.

2. (*Writing from Reading*) The lexicographer Bergen Evans once wrote, "A vocabulary is a tool which one uses in formulating the important questions of life, the questions which must be asked before they can be answered. To a large extent, vocabulary shapes all the decisions we make. [. . .] Words are one of our chief means of adjusting to all the situations of life. The better control we have over words, the more successful our adjustment is likely to be." In short, Evans, like Shachtman, believes that if our vocabulary is impoverished our lives will be as well. Write a letter to a television network executive in which you support Shachtman's call for broadcasters "to champion and employ the power of words as well as the power of images." Within your letter, you may want to quote or refer to the comments of other writers in this book, such as Malcolm X (pp. 63 68).

3. (*Writing from Research*) In an effort to see whether or not talk shows have changed since Shachtman watched and listened to eight shows on November 9, 1993, watch or videotape all of the mainstream syndicated shows for a single day or a week's worth of a single talk show. Analyze the shows in terms of the subjects presented, the guests who appear, and the level of language used by hosts and guests alike. Then write an essay based on your research. According to your analysis, is the language used on the shows better, worse, or about the same as the language Shachtman describes hearing in 1993? Has the subject matter changed or improved? After analyzing current talk shows, what advice do you have for their producers and hosts?

LANGUAGE IN USE:
The Passing of Joe DiMaggio

From the time that he first stepped on the playing field in a New York Yankees' uniform on May 3, 1936, Joe DiMaggio captured the imagination of the American public. He hit with power and consistency, made plays in the field with grace and ease, threw the ball accurately and with authority, and ran the bases with finesse. In a word, he was the "complete" ballplayer. When DiMaggio died on March 8, 1999, at the age of eighty-four, the tributes poured in from all the media. He was remembered as an American hero, a cultural icon who in 1969 had been named "Baseball's Greatest Living Player." He was also remembered as a loner, a man who had once been married to Marilyn Monroe, and someone who had been immortalized in the lyrics of a Paul Simon song. The following three news stories about the death of Joe DiMaggio appeared in three different magazines— *Newsweek, Time,* and *Sports Illustrated.* Carefully read each article, looking for slanting and charged language. Point out the verifiable facts. On what points do the three articles agree? Disagree? You may want to reread the Birks's essay "Selection, Slanting, and Charged Language" (pp. 397–405) before you read these news stories.

WRITING TO DISCOVER: *Who are your heroes from the worlds of politics, entertainment, sports, science, business, or the arts? What is it about these figures that you admire? Write about how your heroes have been treated by the print and broadcast media. Do you consider the treatment fair? Why or why not?*

Joe DiMaggio: No Ordinary Joe
RON FIMRITE

Veteran sportswriter Ron Fimrite has covered baseball for Sports Illustrated *for over twenty-five years. His name is almost synonymous with the annual fall classic, baseball's World Series. Fimrite's many sports books include* Three Weeks in October: The Great Earthquake Series of '89 *(1990) and* Sports Illustrated: The World Series *(1996).*

Fimrite's tribute to baseball legend Joe DiMaggio first appeared in Sports Illustrated *on March 15, 1999.*

He had fame that transcended mere celebrity. For nearly half a century after his playing days had ended, Joe DiMaggio remained a regal presence in the public eye, a species of American aristocrat. And this in an age when the limelight shines too brightly and fades all too swiftly on an undeserving too many. But DiMaggio's renown never really disappeared, even in his relatively subdued final years.

I've known people who couldn't tell an infield fly from a household pest who nevertheless held the Yankee Clipper in awe. DiMaggio himself was fond of telling how, when he was introduced to the British royal couple on their 1983 visit to San Francisco, Prince Philip stopped dead in his tracks and noisily exclaimed, "Are you *the* Joe DiMaggio?"

Of course, Joe always looked like somebody important. Tall (until age and infirmity stooped him) and darkly handsome in a horse-faced way, dressed always with impeccable taste, consistently maintaining a discreet distance from his adoring public, he cut a most dignified figure. At the same time, this is just a ballplayer we're talking about here, the son of a fisherman, a man of so little formal education that his friends from the old San Francisco neighborhood say that he walked in one door at Galileo High School and out the other, all in his first day, never to be seen in that particular grove of academe again.

He was not at all articulate, although, like his contemporary Joe Louis, he was capable of the occasional pithy observation. "Joe, you've never heard such cheering," DiMaggio's then wife, Marilyn Monroe, famously told him in 1954 on returning from entertaining troops overseas. "Yes," said Joe, "I have."

DiMaggio was uncomfortable with strangers. In his playing days he did have some newspaper friends (most notably the columnist Jimmy Cannon), but he submitted to precious few interviews after he retired. Then again, Joe not only knew enough to keep his mouth shut in public, he made reticence a veritable art form.

He was a bundle of contradictions, though. He was an intensely private man who nevertheless married two actresses (the first was Dorothy Arnold), neither of whom was noticeably embarrassed by publicity and one of whom was an international sex symbol. He was fiercely protective of his dignity, but he was not above selling coffeemakers or the services of a bank in television commercials. He was capable of warm friendships, but, like another of his contemporaries, Frank Sinatra, he could end them abruptly and for reasons often trivial and usually unexplained.

So what did we all see in him? He was, beyond question, a magnificent ballplayer, some still say the best ever. And he played in the nation's media capital on some of the game's greatest teams. But ballplayers come and go, and athletic fame in these days of the blinking public eye is as fleeting as it is for any entertainer. For that matter, there may be nothing sadder than an old baseball player, unless, as Ring Lardner once suggested, it's an old baseball writer.

Surely there must be something else, some inner nobility that we all must have sensed. I don't pretend to have any unusual insights here, but

5

because DiMaggio and I, fellow San Franciscans, had some friends in common, I've been fortunate to see, largely through them, something of what it was that made this man so special.

One such friend was Joe Vetrano, who had been a placekicker and halfback for the original 1946 San Francisco 49ers and thereafter an immensely popular man about town. Born in New Jersey, he had gone to college at Southern Mississippi and had somehow melded the dialects of both regions into his own inimitable patois. He was a charming man, fond of recalling his football past, and he had a deep-throated laugh that had the unnerving intonation of a man strangling.

He and the Clipper had been golfing and drinking buddies for years   10
when DiMaggio inexplicably cut him off. Vetrano was hurt and mystified, but the rift in no way damaged his affection for his old pal. Then, again without explanation, DiMaggio welcomed him back into the fold. And, if anything, their friendship grew even stronger. It was as if nothing had ever happened between them.

In the mid-'90s Vetrano got very sick. His heart had failed him, and after some weeks in the hospital he was, for all intents and purposes, sent home to die. When he learned of Vetrano's illness, DiMaggio hurried back to the Bay Area from his new home in Florida. No one outside of his own and Vetrano's family knew he was back in town. Vetrano's son, Joe Jr., told me of the two friends' last moments together.

"They were sitting on the porch, laughing and telling old stories the way they always did. Then my dad turned to Joe and whispered, 'I'm going now, Joe.' And Joe said, 'Going? Where?' Dad just smiled at this and then put his head down. He died in Joe DiMaggio's arms."

It is said we are a people who need heroes. Joe DiMaggio did his best to fill that daunting role, first as the superb player he was, then as someone who kept alive his own legacy. But it may well be far more important that in small ways not publicly known, he was actually a pretty damn nice guy.

The Joe DiMaggio Nobody Knew

Richard Ben Cramer

A graduate of Johns Hopkins University and Columbia University, Richard Ben Cramer started his career as a reporter for the Baltimore Sun *and later worked for the* Philadelphia Inquirer. *Today he is a freelance journalist and writer. His books include* Ted Williams: The Season of the Kid *(1991),* What It Takes: The Way to the White House *(1992), and* Joe DiMaggio: A Hero's Life *(1999).*

The following article, which Cramer adapted from his biography of DiMaggio, appeared in Newsweek *on March 22, 1999.*

In the end, he was free of the crowds that cheered and revered him, the crowds that made his fortune and that he detested. He always hated it when fans would interrupt him in restaurants, stop him on the street, ask him to sign. Now, at last, with the help of a roaring squadron of San Francisco motorcycle cops, Joe DiMaggio would make his last trip on earth nonstop, beyond all annoyance, in perfect privacy. Perfection was always the goal. Joe's brother Dominic, the old Red Sox center fielder, ruled that only family could say goodbye in the grand old church. Dom said that's what Joe would have wanted. Yet even among those 60 mourners, there were many whom Joe had pushed away in life. There were aunts, uncles, cousins, second cousins, whom he'd walked away from 50 years ago when he thought they wanted too much from him. That pallbearer with the gray ponytail—that was Joe DiMaggio Jr., whom Big Joe bitterly cut out of his life. Father and son never spoke. Even Dommie, the youngest and sole surviving brother, didn't speak with Joe for years. Only as lung cancer was killing Joe at 84 did the brothers try to repair the breach.

Still, Dominic knew him cold. In the vast, empty, echoing Church of Sts. Peter and Paul, Dominic made the eulogy . . . and filled it with the records of which Joe was so proud: the MVP years, batting crowns, home-run championships, and World Series winners. After all, it was Joe himself who insisted for the past 30 years that he be introduced (*last*—always last) as *Baseball's Greatest Living Player.* That couldn't be said anymore, of course. But to ignore the stiff pride would have missed this man.

Dominic made another point—this not as a fellow player, but as a brother, and once again a bull's-eye—that Brother Joe, for all the pride, for all the fame, all the love of the crowd, never found his life's partner. And that was his sadness. Dommie didn't have to say the rest—how in this very church, 60 years before, while 10,000 of his townsmen cheered, Joe took his bride Dorothy Arnold. That marriage ended in a nasty divorce. And certainly Dommie would never bring up Joe's other wife, Marilyn Monroe, whose death sealed Joe's solitary fate forever. He always thought it was the crowd and the Kennedys, the hero machine, Hollywood and its hangers-on, who were responsible — they killed his girl. Joe wouldn't permit mention of her name in his life — why would he now, in death?

That was the point: he died as he lived . . . without intimates of any sort, an object of feverish curiosity, in impenetrable secrecy, swaddled in myth, without even a formalistic nod to the public's right to know. Dominic was correct: that's what Joe would have wanted . . . as the family in the church, the fans in the morning chill on the street who politely applauded his casket, as the nation as a whole looking in on TV . . . said goodbye to the loneliest hero we have ever had.

There was actually a vote for the greatest living player, in '69, base-   5
ball's centennial year. By that time, Ruth, Cobb, and Gehrig were gone. But Ted Williams, the last man to hit .400, was very much alive in memory and in person. The voters all had fresher visions of the modern greats — Musial and Mantle had recently retired, Mays and Clemente were still All-Stars. Still, it wasn't even close. Even dimmed by two decades' distance, one name, one man stood out alone. Joe DiMaggio walked away with the honor, as he'd won every other accolade in baseball — without apparent strain.

What was it about DiMaggio that set him apart — not just from players with whom he shared the field, but from every mortal who ever played the game?

There was, for a start, unequaled talent. There is an old dictum that a baseball player must do five things passably well: run, field, throw, hit, and hit for power. There are players who can do one of these brilliantly, who make millions every year in the major leagues. There are players who were brilliant at two in the Hall of Fame. DiMaggio — like no one else who'd ever played the game — was brilliant at five out of five.

But the men who played with him and against him didn't talk so much about those splendid abilities (what was there to say?) . . . but about what he couldn't do. He couldn't misjudge a fly ball in that vast Yankee Stadium center field; couldn't look bad on a low, slow curveball; couldn't ever rile an umpire against him, or act in an unbecoming way toward opponents. He never seemed to throw to the wrong base, never ran the base paths stupidly — he just *couldn't*. Or maybe there's a sixth talent, which is thinking — a constant, critical awareness on the ballfield . . . in which case, DiMaggio had six out of six.

There was another attribute (the only one Joe would mention in public), which was DiMaggio-as-Winner. In his 13 years, his Yankees won 10 pennants and 9 world championships. That is a record unmatched by any player from any other club in history. (For purposes of comparison: the Atlanta Braves, juggernaut of the '90s, have won four pennants and one world series.)

And it wasn't just Octobers, or the weight of winning over decades,   10
judged in numbers after the fact: it was every springtime when the papers

would fill with speculation about the new, stronger Indians, or Tigers or Red Sox ("Yeah, but the Yanks still got DiMag") . . . it was every late-inning, Yankees behind, when fans would glance at their scorecards to be sure Joe D. had another at-bat ("Don't worry, the Clipper'll get us even") . . . every time a Yankee pitcher looked over his shoulder, and knew he could throw this guy a strike ("There's room out there — Dago'll catch it") . . . it was every day or every night, every inning that DiMaggio could take the field. "You'd just see him," as Phil Rizzuto said, "and you knew you had a pretty good chance to win."

DiMaggio was famed for his prodigies: three MVP years, two years when he led the league in home runs, two when he led for average and of course, May, June, July of '41, when he hit safely in 56 straight, and the nation was literally singing his name. But DiMaggio was the best player on the field, no matter which day or year, no matter the opponent, no matter the score.

He never made a fuss about a game-winning hit, a run-saving hook-slide, an impossible catch amid the monuments in left-center . . . he knew he could do it. He seemed to play without mortal fear: when pitchers threw at his head, he wouldn't bail out, wouldn't hit the dirt, wouldn't *move his feet* — he'd lift his chin, let the ball pass beneath, and never even change his expression. It's often said (for want of better) that Joe D. was "a natural." In fact, he was the un-natural: for 13 years, he stood against the humbling nature of the game. He excelled and continued to excel, against injury and age, against the mounting "natural" odds. He exceeded, withal, the cruelest expectations: He was expected to lead and to win — and he did. He was expected to be the best — and he was. He was expected to be the exemplar of dignity, class, grace — expected even to *look* the best. And he looked perfect.

DiMaggio set the standard for the game, when the game was the standard for the nation. When DiMaggio broke in with the Yankees, in '36, baseball stood above any other national endeavor. It wasn't just American but wholesome, successful, a point of excellence and glamour in a country that didn't have many such points to enjoy. Every president since Taft came to throw out the first pitch in April. The only real professional sports (as measured by the real American standards — big-time hype and money) were baseball and boxing. And Joe Louis could fight Schmeling only once a year. But baseball was big news every day, as present as the weather — and as much discussed.

In Joe, the nation found a mirror for its best self. In the hard-knuckled '30s, he was the Sicilian immigrant's son who came from nothing, made it big. As the war drew nearer, he was our can-do poster boy, getting hits every day through the summer of '41. In the war, he sacrificed his best years but came back as a winner — bigger than ever. In postwar wealth and ease, he was our Broadway Joe, squiring Miss Americas at the Stork Club . . . until he wooed and won, in Marilyn Monroe, the most beautiful girl America could dream up. And even when he lost that girl for good, in 1962, he was us, at the start of our decade of assassination and bereavement. He was, at every turn, our idea of the American hero—one man we could look at, who made us feel good. For it was always about how we *felt* . . . with Joe. That's how it worked. No wonder we strove, for six decades—the nation, its presidents, its citizens, almost everyone—to give Joe the hero's life. It was always about us.

And, of course, that he knew.   15

DiMaggio's Father thought the boy was lazy—Joe would never help on the fishing boat. Joe was so tongue-tied that his sisters thought him slow-witted. For his part, Joe thought he'd never get free of his father's life, the grinding labor at Fisherman's Wharf . . . or never get out of his neighborhood—North Beach, in San Francisco. How could he get out?

He made it through elementary and grammar school: he was moved along with the other kids—why not?—Joe didn't make any trouble. But he never read, never said a word in class. And when he got to Galileo High School, the jig was up. The teachers might as well have been talking Chinese. Joe and his friends—all fishing folk—didn't understand a thing. He wasn't quite 16 years old when he simply stopped going to school. It was months before anybody noticed.

He still showed up to work every day, selling papers—at the corner of Sansome and Sutter. Joe sold The Call at three cents a copy and kept one penny. On a good day he might earn two or three bucks—and brought it home: his parents were strict about money. In 1932, there weren't many other jobs to choose from. He stacked wooden slats at Pacific Box. He tried squeezing oranges, but that was worse. He never lasted at any job for more than a week. There wasn't anything he wanted to do, except to have a few bucks in his pocket—and that was going to take a miracle. But that's what he found. Or, you could say, the miracle found him.

There was a myth that grew up around DiMaggio, after he'd become an American hero and needed a hero's story. The myth held that Joe only wanted to play baseball: that's why he wouldn't fish with his father, because he only loved the American game. But the fact was Joe had given up on baseball. What was the point? There wasn't any money in it. Still, when the neighborhood boys found a sponsor for their own semipro team—Rossi Olive Oil—they wanted Joe. He could smack that ball!

At first, they had to make him play—they'd go to his house and get   20
him out of bed, to make sure he'd show up. Within months, he'd moved on from Rossi Olive Oil. Another team would pay him a couple of dollars—and then he was offered five bucks a game! Within a year, the local pro teams offered tryouts. Joe was on his way.

By 18, he had a contract with the San Francisco Seals, in the Pacific Coast League—just a notch below the majors. By 21, he was a star with the Yankees, the toast of New York and a hero of Italian-Americans across the country. Now he had money and plenty of it—though he never seemed to sign a contract without a bitter fight for more. He bought his family a big new house and invested in a restaurant that his oldest brother could run. He had a splendid car before he could drive. The newspapers offered money, too—they wanted his autobiography. But they'd have to fill in the story themselves. Last time Joe looked, he was a kid selling papers at Sansome and Sutter.

It was more than athletic talent pushing Joe to the fore—though he had that in abundance. It was beauty, or something akin—classicism, grace—that set him apart. That's not to say he had poster-boy good looks. Especially in his younger years, he was hawk-nosed and buck-toothed. But no one who saw him move around a ballfield could forget him. There was the way he stepped up to hit—with thorough self-possession, not one extra twitch. Just one cock of the bat toward the pitcher and then all was still, balanced, perfect—like a statue . . . until the ball was almost in the catcher's glove, at which point Joe would smash it on a hard line, somewhere. There was the way he patrolled center field—never dove for a ball, never ran into a wall, never even ran out from under his cap. The ball would come down (no matter where) and Joe would be there. You could watch a whole season and never notice him running hard in the field—though that was illusion. Tommy Henrich, who played next to Joe in right for 11 years, said: "When that big sonofabuck ran, you could feel it in the ground."

Joe courted the same illusion of nonchalance off the field. But that was harder. He hadn't the gift of small talk with writers, the ready glad hand for fans. Whenever he could, he simply hid. After games, he'd sit in the clubhouse for hours, legs crossed on his stool, smoking and staring at nothing—waiting till even the diehard kids with autograph books had given up and gone home. The only place you might see him in New York was the corner table at Toots Shor's saloon, where the owner, staff, and a ring of idolators would make sure "The Dago" wasn't bothered.

The irony was, he had no chance of escaping our gaze. He might as well have tried to declare himself an Irishman. DiMaggio was our first modern media star—the first public person for the nation as a whole. It wasn't really his doing—but he came along just as we found the means to peer into our heroes' lives.

Of course, there had been big stars before . . . But Joe (so abstemious, so shy) was in a million parlors—big as Life, the new magazine that debuted the same year as he. We knew his face, his form (in stop-action photos!) down to the horrid scars on his heels where doctors tried to hack away the bone spurs. And then, too, the radio started airing every game. So it wasn't five thousand guys in straw hats who saw his exploits at the park. It was hundreds of thousands every day—millions in October—everywhere, they witnessed him.

25

And subtler changes, for DiMaggio, were worse. Radio meant interview shows: his voice, his feelings, the state of his famous and fragile body—all were known. And play-by-play forced the writers to change: it wasn't enough to tell what happened—We knew that, already!—the sports page had to show the players *up close*. Competition spurred columns—gossip, nightlife—what DiMaggio did off-hours was news, now, too. That was the cosmic joke on Joe: he got to the top and the country changed beneath him—the attitudes, appetites. We didn't just want a center fielder. We wanted him to be a personality for us. We wanted him, personally . . . which was his dread.

By his second year in the big leagues DiMaggio was name enough to be inveigled into the movies—a bit part in *Manhattan Merry Go Round*. It was on that movie set that Joe met a Minnesota blonde who called herself Dorothy Arnold. When they married, two years later, the ceremony made national news and set off the biggest party San Francisco had ever seen. The church was packed, and the park outside, and the streets for several blocks around. No one could get in, no one could get out—least of all, Joe.

By the end of June 1941, when Joe's consecutive hitting streak had climbed into the 40s, and he passed the record, DiMaggio had almost squeezed Hitler off the front page. The wires were running bulletins on The Yankee Clipper's every at-bat, and flashes (ten bells!) when he got that day's hit. Times Square was graced with a 30-foot-high Joe, announcing that Camels never irritated his throat, and Les Brown was climbing toward the top spot on *Your Hit Parade* with his new tune that had America singing along:

> He started baseball's famous streak,
> That's got us all aglow.
> He's just a man and not a freak—
> Joltin' Joe DiMaggio . . .

And in the middle of it all, Joe was evermore set apart. He was more and more estranged from his pregnant wife; save for his road roomie, Lefty Gomez, and the coterie at Shor's, he was friendless; he was moody, irritable or silent, chain-smoking, coffee-jangled, unable to sleep, working up an ulcer . . . and lonely. Withal, at 26, his shyness had turned to something harder: now, you dealt with Joe D. on his terms, or (more often) not at all; you wrote him up with hero-puff, or he'd cut you off for life.

It was Gomez who complained aloud: "Here we are, eleven and a half games ahead, and they're trying to ring in a war on us! If we were in third place, they wouldn't even mention it." But it was Joe who seethed when he had to give up the Yankees pinstripes after the '42 season and spend three years in a uniform of olive drab. As wars are measured, his wasn't that tough: mostly he played center field for the Seventh Army Air Force, in Hawaii. When he wasn't at the ballpark, he'd hang around his

30

Quonset hut. He had a lot of thinking to do — about Dorothy. She'd filed for divorce in 1943. She said Joe was cold, moody, silent, and almost never around for her and their little son, Joe Jr. Big DiMaggio was too proud to contest her suit. What could he do about it in Hawaii? Joe told one Army teammate, an old San Francisco friend, Dario Lodigiani: "They're gonna pay me for missing these years."

In fact, they did pay handsomely, after Joe came back in '46. The country was trying on its postwar affluence, and the nasty contract battles that marked DiMaggio's early years were all put behind. Baseball was booming, and the Yankees had new high-rolling ownership. In the course of the next five years, DiMaggio would become baseball's first hundred-thousand-dollar man.

Joe resumed the bachelor habits he held all his life — trains, planes, hotels. Even when he had a place of his own, it looked like a hotel room — there was nothing of his. What he had was a lot of money, some good clothes, his baseball records . . . and mostly, overwhelmingly, that image, the persona that had burned into the American brainpan, and into his. It was like his name — who he was supposed to be — had expanded to fill a life, and drove out everything else.

It wasn't long after the war that Joe's body began to betray him. His back, his neck, were stiff and aching. One knee was always tricky. Then the terrible bone spurs in his feet made every step a shock of pain. In his last couple of years — '50, '51 — the Yankee infielders would sprint halfway out to the fence to take Joe's cutoff throws. By that time, the fabled DiMaggio arm held only one good throw a day. But all the physical woes never diminished *who he was*. Other ballplayers whose skills eroded faded from the public mind — but not he. His fragility, in fact, only made him more treasured — gave poignance to the persona and gravity that raised it to something like literature.

This is the second day now that I do not know the result of the juegos, he thought, Hemingway wrote of his *Old Man and the Sea*. *But I must have confidence and I must be worthy of the Great DiMaggio who does all things perfectly even with the pain of the bone spur in his heel.*

DiMaggio retired and walked away from the game, and from another 35 hundred thousand dollars (an act that cemented his reputation for class). But had he continued to play — it was clear to Joe — he would show himself merely mortal. It was clear to Lefty Gomez, too, who as usual did the talking for them both: "He couldn't be Joe DiMaggio anymore."

To be precise, he couldn't be DiMaggio on the ballfield. For the rest, he was only getting better. Slowly, secretly (and to the vast amusement of the few friends who knew), he was trying to learn new, fancy words to use when forced to public utterance. ("I've just been peregrinating around the block.") He attended the Dale Carnegie Institute. He got his teeth fixed.

A year of postgame shows for Yankee broadcasts turned into misery. Joe had to have everything scripted. He'd be paralyzed and furious if the show began and he couldn't see the first cue card: *HELLO. I'M JOE DIMAGGIO* . . . But he found a more congenial way to be DiMaggio. A company that supplied America's military bases hired Joe to entertain visiting generals. It was easy. He'd take the brass to a ballpark, chat about the game, and present them with a watch inscribed *From Joe DiMaggio*. Then they'd go out to dinner—the greatest night those generals ever had. They'd walk into the place with DiMaggio . . . and people went crazy!

Of course, it happened for Joe every night—anywhere in the country . . . or the world. When he arrived with a team of major leaguers to tour Japan in 1951, he was cheered (*Bonzai DiMaggio!*) by a million fans on the Ginza. It was surely the greatest welcome any ballplayer ever received . . . until 1954, when DiMaggio returned to Tokyo—this time with his new bride, Marilyn Monroe. Then the honeymoon couple couldn't even get out of the airplane.

In the long years afterward, it was fashionable to say they were always ill suited. Joe and Marilyn . . . how could that Old World Italian—so conservative, shy, and inward—get along with a wife who didn't wear underpants? But it didn't look like a mismatch to Joe.

They had dinner together for purpose of publicity (hers): she was still building her fame in '52. By all accounts, dinner didn't go well—mostly, her PR man chattered. After a decent interval, DiMaggio said he had to leave. He'd catch a cab . . . but she offered him a ride. He never got home that night. [40]

By her account, they were terrific in bed. (DiMaggio was no stranger to that playing field—in fact, showgirls, blondes, were his specialty.) She thought his body was perfect—like Michelangelo's David. He thought hers was—well, as he said in one boyish letter to her: "Wow."

If that had been all, they might have come out unscathed. But there was much more. There was the part of Marilyn that thought she wanted to settle down—to have a "real" life (with children, certainly!)—and Joe had such a solid feel, the one man she'd met who wasn't blown about by the Hollywood whirlwinds.

There was his pride in her, when they'd show up around New York . . . At Toots Shor's Christmas party, Joe was grinning like a kid, with the stir they caused. "Hiya Joe! . . . Hey Dago!" the old crowd was calling, and Joe would shrug happily and say, "I'm just with her."

There was the way she tried happily to "fit in" with his family—there she was in the kitchen of the San Francisco rowhouse, earnestly inquiring how to make the spaghetti with sardines. There was the way Joe Jr. took to her: father and son had never learned to be close—now, maybe, there'd be a chance.

And there was everything Big Joe and Marilyn had in common—or rather, one enormous thing. Both of them lived for years alone, inside the vast personages created for them by the hero machine. Marilyn was supposed to be the little orphan girl who grew up to be America's child- [45]

vamp-goddess. And if, in fact, she was neither orphan nor childlike, America did not want to know. Joe was supposed to be the immigrant poor boy who only loved baseball, who learned to hit with a broken oar and grew up to be the American apotheosis of manly grace. If, in fact, he played ball mostly for the money, that was better left unsaid. They'd both been too busy, or too hungry, to feed the person inside the personage. (In Marilyn's rented rooms, there was nothing of her, either.) In their loneliness, they might as well have been brother and sister.

Instead, they married in January 1954 — city hall, San Francisco — and things went sour in a hurry. On that honeymoon trip to Tokyo, Joe felt besieged, assaulted by the frenzy that Marilyn set off in crowds. Then a U.S. general flew in from Korea and invited Marilyn to entertain the troops. Marilyn looked at Joe, Joe looked at Marilyn. He said, "Do what you want. It's your honeymoon." So she went, and Joe stayed in Tokyo, alone.

When they came back to the States, it was worse. Marilyn started working again — in Los Angeles, a town Joe detested. He could stay alone in San Francisco, or fly down to stay at her place — alone. Marilyn had to wake at 5 A.M., get to the studio. She wouldn't be back till 7 or 8 at night. Maybe they'd get some food, watch an hour of TV — that was it. Worse still, he hated the work she was doing, the blond-bombshell roles she got, her skimpy costumes, the breathy suggestive lines . . . the way they promoted her, like a piece of flesh . . . and he hated how hungry she was for more. He'd had his fill of the public's worship. She couldn't get enough.

They fought and screamed. She drank. He hit her. In New York, Walter Winchell made sure Joe was present as Marilyn posed for publicity photographs for *The Seven Year Itch*. It was the famous scene where the wind from the subway grate blew her skirt up, exposing everything below. Joe was enraged as he watched the photographers snapping away, with their lenses pointed at his wife's crotch. That night there was a terrible fight — the beginning of the end. By October — 274 days after the wedding — she filed for divorce in California. Once again, Joe wouldn't fight.

But even while she was Mrs. Arthur Miller, Marilyn (according to her maid) kept a picture of Joe taped inside her closet door. Near the end of her life, as Marilyn was thanking her psychiatrist for helping her (finally!) to attain a real orgasm, she mused in midtherapy: "I'd like to see Joe, now, and give him a real one."

It turned out, of all the men, Joe was the strong one, the one she could   50
lean on. It was he whom she called when she was horrified to find herself locked away in a mental hospital — and they wouldn't let her go. Joe arrived, and demanded at the front desk: "I want my wife." (At that point, they hadn't been married for seven years.) "But Mr. DiMaggio," the hospital staff protested, "we don't have authority to release her to you, or to anyone else!" Joe spoke again, very clearly: "I want my wife. And if you don't give her to me, I will take this place apart, piece of wood by piece of wood." At that point, the staff discovered Miss Monroe was free to go.

They were closest at the end—nicer to each other than they'd ever been in marriage. As Marilyn's world came unglued, Joe was there for her, worrying about her, calling, writing. He took her to spring training at the Yankee camp in Florida. In '62, he told friends that they were going to remarry. Marilyn and Joe—back again! She was ready to give up all that Hollywood sickness. They had it all set. She had her dress and everything. Then she was gone—August '62 . . . they called it suicide.

Joe never said how he thought she died. But he made it apparent whom he blamed: the Kennedy boys (yeah, he knew about that), Sinatra (his former friend!), that snake Peter Lawford and all the rest of the rat-pack scum. He wouldn't let them near her funeral—none of them. Producers, directors, flacks, and stars—all equally unwelcome. The studio brass tried to reason with Joe: *These are very big people! What can we tell them?* "Tell them," said DiMaggio, "if it wasn't for them, she'd still be here."

> What's that you say, Mrs. Robinson?
> Joltin' Joe has left and gone away.

When Paul Simon's song from *The Graduate* echoed around the country, Joe wanted to sue: "What're they talking about?" he complained. "I haven't gone anywhere. I'm employed."

But he had gone away, for years that weren't worth a damn. There was a bit of public-relations work, some golf, near-constant travel, too much drink, a lot of blondes—from the screen stars of the moment down to the strippers who made their living by undressing-up like Marilyn onstage.

Of course, no one heard a word about that—certainly not from him. He wouldn't discuss how he felt, any more than he would rub the spot where it hurt when he was hit with a pitch. When anybody new would meet Joe, the friend who made the introduction would counsel before the first handshake: "Remember! You mention Marilyn, he's gone."

The only one who really understood was his son. They'd clung to one another at her funeral. That was the closest they'd ever been. But after she was gone, it was worse than before. Big Joe bought Junior a big-rig truck, but the kid wrecked it and lost his license. After a while, Junior was drinking—said the only thing he wanted to be was a bum. So Dad helped him with his wish and cut him off. They never spoke. Big Joe spent his time doing autograph deals for millions of dollars—piling up a fortune that he would never leave to his son.

His name still moved a nation—25 years after he stopped playing ball. Joe learned to live with the attention, adulation—he even liked it, at a safe remove. He took a chance in the '70s on TV ads—the Bowery Bank in New York, and Mr. Coffee, nationwide. Joe still wasn't comfy on TV. But the money was good, and these were scripted spots. And the agency men wanted exactly the DiMaggio he preferred to show the

55

world: quiet, dignified, solid . . . a bit aloof even from the commerce that landed him on the screen.

It worked out brilliantly for everyone involved. Joe found out that with TV working for you—over and over, a million screens, a million times—not only can you make your own image (and enforce it) . . . but it *satisfies:* people stop asking about anything else. They want you to be what they know—to validate their time, their attention—they just want you to be *that guy on TV!* . . . Talk about a safe remove!

And when you added that TV power to the dusty history of real achievement—a plaque in Cooperstown . . . and there was Dad, or Grampa, struggling to describe the grace of the Clipper in centerfield . . . and Mom approving, with tears in her eyes, the way that man buried poor Marilyn—and then sent roses every week! . . . well, Joe was bigger than ever—and more distant. It was beyond fame . . . to veneration. And it was everyone—no matter how old, or where they came from. Joe was the same icon of past perfection and present dignity to an aged *paisano* in the Bronx . . . or a child of the '60s from Hootin' Holler, Arkansas.

Just a few years ago, Joe signed on to attend the big blowout for Cal   60
Ripken and his Ironman Streak—on the night Cal was going to break Lou Gehrig's old record. The Orioles only paid expenses for Joe to come . . . but what the hell—everybody wanted to be there. It was the first bit of big-time, wholesome glamour that baseball had mustered in a generation . . . and sure enough, here came Arkansas's Number One Baby Boomer: Bill Clinton was up in the sky-box suites, giving interviews. So The Baltimore Sun's guy on the job was Carl Cannon and he took notes while Clinton discoursed on the importance of Ripken's streak, the value of hard work, the lessons communicated to our youth in a nation troubled by blah blah blah. After about 15 minutes, he put away the notepad, and then it was just him and Clinton watching the game. Of course, the place was packed, and the fans were going mental, waiting for the moment when the game was official, and Ripken was the King.

"It's awesome," Cannon said. "It's amazing."

"Yeah," Clinton said, idly . . . and then he reached over and grabbed Cannon's arm. The president's eyes were alight, as he almost whispered: "You know . . . DiMaggio's here!"

Left and Gone Away: Joe DiMaggio (1914–1999)

PAUL GRAY

Paul Gray, longtime staff writer at Time *magazine, grew up in Chicago and spent many a day at Comiskey Park watching the White Sox play baseball. When the New York Yankees were in town, he got to see Joltin' Joe play in person. As an eleven-year-old in 1951, Gray remembers securing the famous DiMaggio's autograph as he left the hotel to board the team bus for the ballpark. What Gray didn't realize at the time was that 1951 was to be DiMaggio's last year in uniform.*

Forty-eight years later, Gray pays a final tribute to the man who roamed centerfield in Yankee Stadium for thirteen years between 1936 and 1951. "Left and Gone Away" appeared in Time *magazine on March 22, 1999.*

He was idolized by millions who never saw him hit or catch a baseball. During the 13 seasons Joe DiMaggio played center field for the New York Yankees, baseball was still the national pastime, but one that a majority of fans followed from afar. The 16 major league teams were clustered in only 10 cities, with St. Louis as the westernmost outpost. In that pre-television era, sports heroes were made out of words, those spoken over the radio during play-by-play broadcasts and those printed in newspapers the next morning. No wonder legends arose. Most people experienced baseball by reading adventure stories in the daily press or by listening, the way the ancient Greeks did, to the voices of the bards.

Baseball's mythmaking machinery went into overdrive when it encountered DiMaggio. Sportswriters for New York City's nearly a dozen daily papers fell in love with the shy 21-year-old who came up with the Yankees from spring training in 1936. Babe Ruth wasn't around anymore to provide reliably flashy copy, and without him the team lacked charisma. This handsome new kid, the son of a Sicilian immigrant fisherman, looked promising. His awkwardness and reticence with reporters might be portrayed as enigmatic, as might his absolutely deadpan demeanor on the field. And advance word from DiMaggio's minor league exploits with the San Francisco Seals was that he could, in baseball parlance, "do it all": hit, hit for power, run, field, and throw.

Whatever pressure the rookie felt from all these ravenous expectations never showed on the diamond. He not only did it all, he did it with a stylishness that awed sportswriters and spectators alike. DiMaggio was the leading American League vote getter for the 1936 All-Star game. That same summer he appeared on the cover of this magazine. His Yankees cruised to the AL pennant, the team's first since 1932, and beat the rival New York Giants in the World Series. (During DiMaggio's 13 years as the Yankees' star player, the team appeared in 10 Series and won nine.)

His successful rookie season confirmed and enhanced the DiMaggio mystique. The next year, a radio broadcaster called him "the Yankee Clipper," a tribute to the way he sailed so majestically while pursuing fly balls across the green expanses of center field. His batting skill won him the sobriquet "Joltin' Joe." Meanwhile, the young man from Fisherman's Wharf was acquiring a Manhattan polish. He took up tailored suits and the high life at Toots Shor's nightclub, where the habitues treated him like a god who had inexplicably deigned to join their mortal company. He dated beautiful women, including actress Dorothy Arnold, whom he later married and with whom he had a son, Joe Jr.

The defining event of DiMaggio's career occurred in 1941, when he got at least one base hit in 56 consecutive games—a feat of consistency no other player has come close to matching. Evolutionary biologist (and sports buff) Stephen Jay Gould once wrote that "DiMaggio's streak is the most extraordinary thing that ever happened in American sports." 5

DiMaggio retired at the end of the 1951 season, after having been hobbled for several years by painful bone spurs in his right heel. (A few sportswriters did not blush at comparing him to Achilles.) Those who never saw him play and who consult the common statistical benchmarks may wonder at DiMaggio's renown. His lifetime batting average (.325) was good, but not so high as those of his rough contemporaries Stan Musial (.331) and Ted Williams (.344). DiMaggio's career home runs (361) also trailed Musial's (475) and Williams' (521). But Joltin' Joe drove in more runs per game than either man and had far fewer strikeouts than any comparable slugger. [. . .]

Once out of baseball, DiMaggio did the only thing that would attract more attention than his 1941 streak. Long divorced from his first wife, he courted and in 1954 married Marilyn Monroe. This union was passionate but star-crossed. Freed at last from the demands and expectations created by his on-field heroics, he craved privacy and a quiet life; she attracted, wherever she went, a maelstrom of publicity. He believed in punctuality; she was always late. He expected an Old World housewife; she was a New World sex goddess. He wanted her to abandon the movies and settle with him in San Francisco; she was reveling in a fame that outstripped even her teenage fantasies.

Gay Talese was one of the few journalists to gain a measure of DiMaggio's trust in later years, and an article in his 1970 collection Fame and Obscurity called "The Silent Season of a Hero" recounts a telling vignette from the nine-month Monroe-DiMaggio marriage. During their delayed honeymoon in Japan, she was asked by a U.S. Army general to visit the troops in Korea. When she got back, she said, "It was so wonderful, Joe. You never heard such cheering." He replied, "Yes I have."

Being the man who had won and lost Marilyn Monroe added a new dimension to the DiMaggio legend. So did his quiet grief after her death in 1962, when he arranged her funeral—barring the Hollywood types whom he felt had betrayed her—and ordered fresh flowers placed weekly on her grave. The great poker-faced star had a heart after all, and the world could see that it had been broken.

He spent his 48 years after baseball essentially being Joe DiMaggio. 10 The less he said about himself during his dignified public appearances, the more others talked about him. Ernest Hemingway put him into *The Old Man and the Sea* ("I would like to take the great DiMaggio fishing," the old man said. "They say his father was a fisherman.") Paul Simon's song "Mrs. Robinson," written for the movie *The Graduate* (1967), asked, "Where have you gone, Joe DiMaggio? A nation turns its lonely eyes to you," evoking a '60s sense of vanished heroes.

Now that he has really gone—a longtime three-pack-a-day smoker dead last week of lung cancer at age 84—those of us old enough to re-member him in uniform and full glory feel especially bereft. I not only saw the Yankee Clipper play in person; I got his autograph twice. The first time was in the spring of 1951, when I was an 11-year-old fan hang-ing around with my schoolmates outside the entrance to the Del Prado hotel on Chicago's South Side, where visiting AL teams stayed when they played the White Sox. The Yankees were in town, and I was waiting for my hero Joe DiMaggio. At last he emerged to get on the team bus for a night game at Comiskey. He told all of us to line up, and he signed our books.

Several months later, the Yankees were back at the Del Prado, and so were my buddies and I. When DiMaggio came out, I noticed that none of my friends approached him. Maybe it was because they already had his autograph or because he was injured and hadn't been playing much. But I thought it was wrong for DiMaggio to board the bus unpestered by any worshipers, so I turned over a page in my autograph book—to make sure he wouldn't see that I already had him—and asked him to sign it. He did and got on the bus and took what I realized was his regular seat next to the front window on the right side. I looked up at him. He looked down and noticed me and waved. I waved back then, and I do so now for all of us who admired his graceful career and life.

WRITING SUGGESTIONS: MAKING CONNECTIONS

1. Joe DiMaggio is by all accounts one of the true sports legends of the twentieth century. From your reading of the three articles, what do you think is particu-larly heroic or legendary about DiMaggio? To what extent did the media help to create the DiMaggio legend? To what extent do these three articles help to perpetuate it? In an essay, explore the role of the media in creating sports he-roes and legends. Before starting to write, you may find it helpful to review what you wrote in response to the journal prompt on page 446.

2. While reading the three articles about Joe DiMaggio, what verifiable facts did you note? What examples of slanted or charged language are in each? In an essay, explore the ways in which each writer's use of facts and diction help to create a dominant impression of Joe DiMaggio.

3. Using these three portraits of DiMaggio and other research, write your own profile of this baseball legend. Before you start writing, think about the dominant impression you wish to create and what information you will need to do this.

11

Doublespeak, Euphemism, and Jargon

Airline English: Why Flight Attendants Talk Like That

Cullen Murphy

A 1974 graduate of Amherst College, Cullen Murphy has been the managing editor of the Atlantic Monthly *since 1985. He teamed up with William Rathje of the University of Arizona to write* Rubbish! *(1992), an in-depth study of our nation's landfills, and he published his* Harper's *and* Atlantic Monthly *essays in the collection* Just Curious *(1995). For over twenty years Murphy has also written the text for the popular comic strip* Prince Valiant, *which his father draws.*

In the following essay, first published in the online magazine Slate *in August 1996, Murphy humorously explores the robotlike language that airline flight attendants use with passengers.*

Writing to Discover: *Think about your own experiences with airline travel or examples of it in movies or on television. Make a list of everything you can recall flight attendants or pilots saying to passengers. How does their language make passengers feel? Are these feelings the intended response?*

In an opening monologue not long ago, *Late Night* host Jay Leno told his audience that Air Force One had hit a patch of turbulence during a recent trip, forcing President Clinton to return the flight attendant "to her full upright and locked position."

465

What social historians of the future may find most notable about Leno's joke is not what it says about popular perceptions of Bill Clinton's sex life, but what it says about the language of air travel, and how its sui-generis vocabulary ("seat pocket," "ground personnel," "emergency flotation"), its stilted constructions ("We are now ready to pre-board those passengers who . . ."), its sometimes counterintuitive rhythms and emphases ("The captain *has* turned off the seat-belt sign. . . ."), its un-blinking, look-you-in-the-eye reliance on euphemisms ("In the unlikely event of a water landing . . ."), its blasé invocation of an all-enveloping legal regime ("We remind you that it is a federal offense to tamper with, disable, or destroy any lavatory smoke detector. . . ."), and its utter regu-larity across corporate and international boundaries—how all these things have become matters of mass familiarity.

Airline English has, in a way, become the linguistic equivalent of the worldwide nonverbal graphic system that conveys such meanings as "ladies' room," "no parking," "first aid," and "information." It is just as streamlined, just as stylized, often in the same oddly archaic sort of way. The worldwide symbol for "cocktail lounge" is a martini glass with olive, even though martinis themselves are a relatively uncommon sight these days. The symbol for "pharmacy" is a mortar and pestle. Airline language is similarly atavistic. Whenever else does one hear the word "stow" being used, except as part of the command to "stow your belongings in the overhead bins"?

Actually, the other place where "stow" is frequently used is on board boats and ships. One significant element of airline language, including many of its archaisms, derives from the nautical terminology that the pio-neers of air travel appropriated—not unnaturally, given the obvious parallels between the two modes of transportation (fragile means of conveyance, built to negotiate a boundless, often turbulent medium of fluid or gas). An airplane is a "craft," and its "crew," including a "cap-tain," "first officer," and "purser," operates from a "deck" inside a "cabin." The aircraft is segmented by "bulkheads." Its kitchens are "galleys." It carries cargo in "holds."

But the compressed time of air travel gives its language a focused,   5
liturgical quality that oceanic travel has never had (at least for passen-gers), from the initial welcome aboard to the cautionary homily to the ritual meal—on more and more flights, a merely symbolic activity—to the final "Good-bye. Good-bye. Good-bye. Good-bye. Good-bye." The linguistic contours of a typical airline flight are every bit as scripted as those of a religious service. For American carriers, the Nicene Creed of official cabin talk comes in the form of a number of Federal Aviation Ad-ministration regulations, such as No. 121.571 ("Briefing passengers be-fore take-off") and No. 121.573 ("Briefing passengers: extended overwater operations"). The subject matter of these dense passages of text, which in their original versions date back to the early 1960s, con-

cerns everything from seat belts and life jackets to emergency exits and oxygen masks. The regulations are distilled by each airline into detailed scripts which are reviewed by company lawyers and must be approved, finally, by the FAA. The scripts are then circulated to in-flight personnel.

Credal formulations aside, airlines have considerable latitude when it comes to routine announcements; again, though, the language is often fastidiously scripted, down to even the most casual remarks. ("Would you like Coke or Sprite?" appears in a script provided by the Association of Professional Flight Attendants.) Most of the dozen or so airlines contacted were reluctant to furnish actual transcripts of approved language manuals, although one veteran pilot (with United) asserted: "You're gonna hear the same thing, but you'll hear it just a bit differently." Southwest Airlines did provide an example of an unusual rap announcement that some of its ground personnel have used. It reads, in part: "We board in groups of thirty,/ According to your card;/ One thru thirty boards first,/ It's really not that hard." And it goes on, "Federal law prohibits smoking/ On most domestic flights./ No smoking is permitted,/ So don't even try to light." Southwest's corporate culture of officially sanctioned iconoclasm, if there can be such a thing, is far from typical.

From time to time, passengers may notice a crew member reading an announcement from a laminated text—changes do get made and are distributed airline-wide—but for the most part the scripts are committed to memory, and the habits born of rigorous training die hard. Not long ago, one of my sisters discovered that she was to be the only passenger on a commercial flight, and settled in for the journey. As she prepared for the plane to push back, a flight attendant materialized for the safety briefing, and in the one concession to the circumstances, sat down in the seat next to my sister instead of standing in the aisle at the front of the cabin. The dull monotone was the same as ever. "As we prepare for takeoff," the flight attendant said, looking at my sister from six inches away, "please check that your seat belt is fastened"—and here she made the requisite clicking and unclicking movements with the demonstration model—"and *do* take time to look through the safety information in the seat pocket in front of you. Our aircraft is equipped with four emergency exits. . . ."

As you might imagine, my sister, at that point, was ready to use them all.

FOCUSING ON CONTENT

1. What, for Murphy, are the chief features of the language of air travel? What does he think social historians are likely to find interesting about this language? Why?

2. What are some of the similarities that Murphy sees between airline English and the worldwide nonverbal graphic system? What does he mean when he says that "airline language is similarly atavistic" (3)?

3. Why, according to Murphy, did the pioneers of air travel appropriate nautical terminology? In addition to the words Murphy mentions, what other terms are shared by these two modes of transportation?

4. In paragraph 5 Murphy states, "The regulations are distilled by each airline into detailed scripts which are reviewed by company lawyers and must be approved, finally, by the FAA." Why do you think airlines are so careful in crafting these scripts for their in-flight personnel? What does Murphy mean when he says that such language has a "focused, liturgical quality"? How much latitude do airlines have in wording their routine announcements?

FOCUSING ON WRITING

1. How did you react to Jay Leno's play on language in Murphy's opening paragraph? Do you think it was an effective beginning? (Glossary: *Beginnings and Endings*) What were your expectations after reading it?

2. Murphy provides parenthetical examples for each of the distinctive features of airline language listed in paragraph 2. Why do you suppose he felt the need to supply these examples? (Glossary: *Examples*) Do you find them helpful? Explain.

3. Explain how Murphy uses repeated words and references to earlier ideas to make transitions from one paragraph to the next almost seamless. (Glossary: *Transitions*) Which transitions work best for you?

4. Murphy concludes his essay with the example of how his sister was treated by a flight attendant when she was the only passenger on board. How does this culminating example help Murphy make his point about airline English?

5. What is Murphy's tone in this essay? (Glossary: *Tone*) Do you find this tone appropriate for both his subject and purpose? Why or why not?

LANGUAGE IN ACTION

Carefully read the following parody by Tom Kock of a subscription-renewal letter from *Mechanix Illustrated* (*Mad Magazine*, 1973). What features of the language of home craftsmen is the writer poking fun at? Explain.

MECHANIX Illustrated

π R SQUARE
PLUMBER'S WRENCH, N.C.

Dear Fellow Craftsman,

   With your current subscription to *Mechanix Illustrated* due to expire in three months, it's high time you were getting down to your basement shop to start work on a renewal application. A professional-looking job can be done with a minimum of power tools merely by following these step-by-step directions:

1. Detach subscription coupon (A) from this letter (B) along perforated line (C). A linoleum knife or tinsmith shears will do the trick, although any tool sharp enough to cut paper (such as No. 8 household scissors) may also be used.

2. With a strong, dependable marking instrument, such as a pencil (D) or pen (E), fill out subscription coupon (A) as follows: On blank line opposite the printed word "NAME" (F), print your name. Taking care not to smudge, follow similar procedure for inserting your address (G) and zip code (H).

3. Before returning marking instrument to its drawer or holder (I or J), utilize it to make out a check for $8.50 (K). Your local banker (L) probably can show you how to do this.

4. Place completed coupon (A) and signed check (K) *inside* envelope (M) and affix stamp (N) to upper-right-hand corner of *outside* of envelope. Making stamp adhere to envelope can be simplified by first wetting sticky side of stamp with a liquid-base compound, such as household water or spit.

5. Drop completed project in corner mailbox (O) after making sure you have not committed common error of placing stamp *inside* while leaving check and coupon *outside*. Should this mistake occur, it can easily be rectified merely by starting all over.

Anxiously awaiting your handiwork,

Phillips S. Driver
Editorial Putterer

WRITING SUGGESTIONS

1. (*Writing from Experience*) Using Murphy's story of his sister's experience as a model, write an essay in which you recount an experience you've had in which occupational jargon or technical language figured prominently. (Glossary: *Technical Language*) Be sure to show the exact role this language played and to explain how you felt about it.

2. (*Writing from Reading*) Recently, England banished Latin legalisms from its civil courts in an effort to make the language of the law more understandable and less intimidating to the public. In its May 10, 1999, issue, *Newsweek* provided a sample of the queen's new simplified English:

Old	New
subpoena	witness summons
in camera	in private
guardian ad litem	litigation friend
ex parte	without notice
minor	child
interrogatory	request for information

Using examples from Murphy's essay, write a letter to an American airline company or to the FAA in which you propose changes in the language of pilots and flight attendants that would make it more customer-friendly. Be careful to differentiate the language that is required by federal regulations from language that is not. Make your proposal as specific as possible. You might even offer some alternative scripts, such as the rap announcement used by Southwest's ground personnel.

3. (*Writing from Research*) As we eat in various restaurants, we often hear the colorful language of chefs, short-order cooks, waitpersons, and lunch-counter staff. Using materials available in your library or on the Internet as well as personal excursions to eateries and interviews with restaurant staff, write a paper in which you explore some facet of the language of food and restaurants. The following glossary of roadside-diner language may help you get started. It was compiled by Dan Carlinsky for a *New York Times* article entitled "The Traveler's Guide to Hash-House Greek" (September 5, 1971).

Adam and Eve on a raft Two poached eggs on toast.

All the way With a full complement of condiments; e.g., a burger *all the way* has catsup, onions, relish, salt, and pepper. Can also mean well done.

—and Signifies the second half of a ham and eggs; coffee *and*—coffee and donut, etc.

apple Apple pie, as in a slice of *apple*.

black and white Chocolate soda with vanilla ice cream.

blood Cherry flavoring: stretch one, let it *bleed* (or make it *bloody*) — a cherry Coke. Also refers to rare meat; a *bloody* burger—a rare hamburger.

b.l.t. Bacon, lettuce, and tomato sandwich.

bowl Bowl of soup, as in a *bowl* of chicken. In one-soup establishments, a *bowl* is a bowl of the soup du jour.

bowl of red; bowl of fire Bowl of chili.

bridge Four orders of an item. Derives from foursome at bridge game.

bucket of mud Dish of chocolate ice cream.

burn it; burned Well done.

burn one Make a malted milk shake.

c.b. Corned beef.

china Cup of tea. See **spot.**

cow Milk, as in a glass of *cow;* also cream, as in draw one, hold the *cow*—a cup of coffee, no cream. See **grade "a."**

crowd Three orders of an item. Derives from "two's company, three's a crowd."

down Toasted, as in b.l.t. *down;* also used as a noun; as in an order of *down,* smeared—buttered toast.

draw one Pour a cup of coffee. Derives from the motion of drawing the handle of the coffee-urn spigot.

drop Sundae. Derives from the action of dropping a scoop of ice cream into a dish.

eighty-six Unavailability of an item. Also used to signify an undesirable customer, suggesting that for him the restaurant is out of everything. Derives from rhyme with "nix."

g.j. Grapefruit juice.

grade "a" Milk. See **cow.**

hail Ice, as in hold the *hail*—without ice.

handful Five orders of an item. Derives from the number of fingers on a hand.

let it walk The order is to be taken out, to go. See **on wheels.**

nineteen Banana split.

ninety-five A customer who walks out without paying.

o.j. Orange juice.

on the hoof Very rare. Derives from vision of the meat still attached to the rest of the animal.

on wheels To go. See **let it walk.**

over Of an egg, fried on both sides, as in two *over*.

over easy Of an egg, fried on both sides, softly.

patch Strawberry. Derives from strawberry patch.

radio Tuna sandwich on toast. Derives from "tune 'er down."

r.b. Roast beef.

set-up Silverware and paper napkin on the table.

side A side order, which costs extra; e.g., a *side* of french — french-fried potatoes in addition.

smear Butter.

spot Cup of tea. Derives from English expression "spot of tea." Cold *spot* — iced tea.

stack Hot-cakes, as in a *stack* of wheat — wheatcakes; toast, as in a buttered *stack;* ice cream in a dish, as in a *stack* of van — a scoop of vanilla ice cream in a dish.

stretch Coca-Cola. Derives from shoot one and *stretch* it — take a shot of syrup, enough for a small (6-ounce) Coke, and stretch it with extra soda water to make a large (10-ounce) glass. Used as verb (*stretch* a pair) and noun (gimme a crowd of *stretches*).

suds Root beer. Derives from bartenders' term for beer, coming from the foamy head. Sometimes refers to coffee, deriving from joking reference to the taste of dishwater.

thirteen The boss is around — watch out.

twist Slice of lemon; a spot with a *twist* — tea with lemon.

up Of an egg, fried on one side (sunny side up), as in two *up*.

with Used like — and (which see); burger *with* — hamburger with onion (or with french fries), etc.

working The order is being prepared, as in "Hey, cookie — I've got a burger on the hoof all the way *working!*" or, in answer to "Where's my milk shake, please?" — it's *working!*"

wreck 'em Of eggs, scramble them, as in Adam and Eve on a raft, *wreck 'em;* a stack of wheat, smeared; a large g.j., give me hail; a large o.j., hold it; draw two and make one with extra cow.

She's Your Basic L.O.L. in N.A.D.

Perri Klass

Born in Trinidad in 1958, Perri Klass is a pediatrician as well as a writer. She graduated from Harvard Medical School in 1986. Klass's book-length publications include a collection of short stories I Am Having an Adventure *(1986); two novels,* Recombinations *(1985) and* Other Women's Children *(1990); and two autobiographical collections of essays,* A Not Entirely Benign Procedure: Four Years as a Medical Student *(1987) and* Baby Doctor: A Pediatrician's Training *(1992). In addition, Klass's essays appear regularly in the* New York Times, Self, Discover, *and other newspapers and magazines.*

The following essay, which Klass wrote in 1984 while she was in medical school, first appeared as a "Hers" column in the New York Times. *Here she examines the technical language of the medical profession. She finds such language efficient for physicians yet confusing and insensitive for patients.*

WRITING TO DISCOVER: *Have you or someone you know ever felt confused or frightened when talking with medical caregivers? Did you find yourself wanting them to talk with you in plain English? Write about what exactly you found unsettling during such conversations.*

"Mrs. Tolstoy is your basic L.O.L. in N.A.D., admitted for a soft rule-out M.I.," the intern announces. I scribble that on my patient list. In other words Mrs. Tolstoy is a Little Old Lady in No Apparent Distress who is in the hospital to make sure she hasn't had a heart attack (rule out a myocardial infarction). And we think it's unlikely that she has had a heart attack (a *soft* rule-out).

If I learned nothing else during my first three months of working in the hospital as a medical student, I learned endless jargon and abbreviations. I started out in a state of primeval innocence, in which I didn't even know that "s̄ C.P., S.O.B., N/V" meant "without chest pain, shortness of breath, or nausea and vomiting." By the end I took the abbreviations so for granted that I would complain to my mother the English Professor, "And can you believe I had to put down *three* NG tubes last night?"

"You'll have to tell me what an NG tube is if you want me to sympathize properly," my mother said. NG, nasogastric—isn't it obvious?

I picked up not only the specific expressions but also the patterns of speech and the grammatical conventions; for example, you never say that a patient's blood pressure fell or that his cardiac enzymes rose. Instead, the patient is always the subject of the verb: "He dropped his pressure." "He bumped his enzymes." This sort of construction probably reflects that profound irritation of the intern when the nurses come in the middle of the night to say that Mr. Dickinson has disturbingly low blood pressure. "Oh, he's gonna hurt me bad tonight," the intern may say, inevitably angry at Mr. Dickinson for dropping his pressure and creating a problem.

When chemotherapy fails to cure Mrs. Bacon's cancer, what we say is, "Mrs. Bacon failed chemotherapy." 5

"Well, we've already had one hit today, and we're up next, but at least we've got mostly stable players on our team." This means that our team (group of doctors and medical students) has already gotten one new admission today, and it is our turn again, so we'll get whoever is next admitted in emergency, but at least most of the patients we already have are fairly stable, that is, unlikely to drop their pressures or in any other way get suddenly sicker and hurt us bad. Baseball metaphor is pervasive: a no-hitter is a night without any new admissions. A player is always a patient—a nitrate player is a patient on nitrates, a unit player is a patient in the intensive-care unit and so on, until you reach the terminal player.

It is interesting to consider what it means to be winning, or doing well, in this perennial baseball game. When the intern hangs up the phone and announces, "I got a hit," that is not cause for congratulations. The team is not scoring points; rather, it is getting hit, being bombarded with new patients. The object of the game from the point of view of the doctors, considering the players for whom they are already responsible, is to get as few new hits as possible.

These special languages contribute to a sense of closeness and professional spirit among people who are under a great deal of stress. As a medical student, it was exciting for me to discover that I'd finally cracked the code, that I could understand what doctors said and wrote and could use the same formulations myself. Some people seem to become enamored of the jargon for its own sake, perhaps because they are so deeply thrilled with the idea of medicine, with the idea of themselves as doctors.

I knew a medical student who was referred to by the interns on the team as Mr. Eponym because he was so infatuated with eponymous terminology, the more obscure the better. He never said "capillary pulsation" if he could say "Quincke's pulses." He would lovingly tell over the multinamed syndromes—Wolff-Parkinson-White, Lown-Ganong-Levine, Henoch-Schonlein—until the temptation to suggest Schleswig-Holstein or Stevenson-Kefauver or Baskin-Robbins became irresistible to his less reverent colleagues.

And there is the jargon that you don't ever want to hear yourself 10 using. You know that your training is changing you, but there are certain changes you think would be going a little too far.

The resident was describing a man with devastating terminal pancreatic cancer. "Basically he's C.T.D.," the resident concluded. I reminded myself that I had resolved not to be shy about asking when I didn't understand things. "C.T.D.?" I asked timidly.

The resident smirked at me. "Circling The Drain."

The images are vivid and terrible. "What happened to Mrs. Melville?"

"Oh, she boxed last night." To box is to die, of course.

Then there are the more pompous locutions that can make the beginning medical student nervous about the effects of medical training. A friend of mine was told by his resident, "A pregnant woman with sickle-cell represents a failure of genetic counseling."

Mr. Eponym, who tried hard to talk like the doctors, once explained to me, "An infant is basically a brainstem preparation." A brainstem preparation, as used in neurological research, is an animal whose higher brain functions have been destroyed so that only the most primitive reflexes remain, like the sucking reflex, the startle reflex, and the rooting reflex.

The more extreme forms aside, one most important function of medical jargon is to help doctors maintain some distance from their patients. By reformulating a patient's pain and problems into a language that the patient doesn't even speak, I suppose we are in some sense taking those pains and problems under our jurisdiction and also reducing their emotional impact. This linguistic separation between doctors and patients allows conversations to go on at the bedside that are unintelligible to the patient. "Naturally, we're worried about adeno-C.A.," the intern can say to the medical student, and lung cancer need never be mentioned.

I learned a new language this past summer. At times it thrills me to hear myself using it. It enables me to understand my colleagues, to communicate effectively in the hospital. Yet I am uncomfortably aware that I will never again notice the peculiarities and even atrocities of medical language as keenly as I did this summer. There may be specific expressions I manage to avoid, but even as I remark them, promising myself I will never use them, I find that this language is becoming my professional speech. It no longer sounds strange in my ears—or coming from my mouth. And I am afraid that as with any new language, to use it properly you must absorb not only the vocabulary but also the structure, the logic, the attitudes. At first you may notice these new alien assumptions every time you put together a sentence, but with time and increased fluency you stop being aware of them at all. And as you lose that awareness, for better or for worse, you move closer and closer to being a doctor instead of just talking like one.

FOCUSING ON CONTENT

1. According to Klass, what effects — both positive and negative — does medical language seem to have on health-care givers? What did this new language do for her as a medical student?

2. Klass points out that the language of the medical profession is more than vocabulary or specific expressions. As she notes in paragraph 4, it is also "the patterns of speech and the grammatical conventions." In what ways does the baseball metaphor (6–7) illustrate the various characteristics of doctors' language?

3. In paragraph 9, Klass presents the example of Mr. Eponym. What kind of medical jargon is he particularly fond of? Does Klass hint at why he might use such jargon? What is Klass's attitude toward medical students like Mr. Eponym?

4. In paragraph 17, Klass states that the "linguistic separation between doctors and patients allows conversations to go on at the bedside that are unintelligible to the patient." In your opinion, is this always good for the patient's peace of mind? Explain.

FOCUSING ON WRITING

1. Klass opens her essay with a brief example of an intern using medical jargon and abbreviations to describe a woman patient to her. (Glossary: *Technical Language*) For the reader's benefit, she immediately translates what the intern has just told her. What assumptions has Klass made about her audience, and what does she do throughout her essay to accommodate this audience? (Glossary: *Audience*)

2. What do you think Klass's purpose is in writing this essay — to express personal thoughts and feelings, to inform, to argue a point? (Glossary: *Purpose*) What in her essay leads you to this conclusion?

3. How does Klass organize her essay? (Glossary: *Organization*) What do you consider its main sections? In what ways does her organization reflect the changes that she herself underwent during her summer stint in the hospital? Explain.

4. In paragraph 10, Klass refers to jargon that makes her uncomfortable — language that "would be going a little too far." What kinds of examples does she use to support her generalization? (Glossary: *Examples*) Do you find them convincing? Why or why not?

LANGUAGE IN ACTION

Consider the following cartoon from John McPherson's *The Get Well Book* (1998) in light of Klass's discussion of medical jargon. What does the cartoon tell you about the public's attitude toward doctors and their language?

"Joyce, write this down in Mr. Cutler's file:
'thump . . . thump-thump . . . thumpety thump . . .
boink.'"

WRITING SUGGESTIONS

1. (*Writing from Experience*) Using Klass's essay as a model, write an essay that explores the jargon of school, the language of students. Is the language of high school students different from that of college students? How does the language of school allow students to distance themselves from their teachers or parents? Do you agree with Klass that to use a new language properly, "you must absorb not only the vocabulary but also the structure, the logic, and the attitude" (18)?

2. (*Writing from Reading*) Watch episodes from three different television shows featuring doctors. Analyze the professional language used in these shows, paying close attention to the types of language used (technical language, abbreviations, eponyms, metaphors, and so forth) and the similarities among the shows. Then write an essay in which you discuss how accurately television shows present the medical profession as described by Klass. Before starting this essay, you may find it helpful to read "Information Please" by Caryn James (432–34).

3. (*Writing from Research*) Select an occupation that interests you, such as banker, coach, real-estate broker, news reporter, or teacher. Using the resources in your library, on the Internet, or in your community, write an essay about the language of the people in that field. What functions does the occupational jargon serve? What seem to be the main advantages of the jargon? Disadvantages? If possible, try to interview at least one person in the field you chose.

Getting High on Classified Dreams

KATE KLISE

A native of Illinois, Kate Klise now lives in Norwood, Missouri, in the heart of the Ozark Mountains. She is a reporter for People *magazine and has a special interest in country music. Her fascination with this music and with the Ozarks resulted in the book* The Insider's Guide to Branson & the Ozark Mountains *(1995). Klise has also written two books for adolescents—*Letters from Camp *(1999) and* Regarding the Fountain: A Tale, in Letters, of Liars & Leaks *(1998)—as well as scripts for educational films and videos.*

In the following essay, which first appeared in the St. Louis Post-Dispatch's Everyday Magazine *on May 31, 1992, Klise takes a lighthearted look at the language some professionals use in the classified ads of local newspapers.*

WRITING TO DISCOVER: *Write about your experience with the classified section of your local newspaper. Have you ever looked in the classifieds for a job, a relationship, an apartment, a car, or something else? While reading the classifieds for a specific item, did you ever get caught up in reading other ads? Have you ever placed a classified ad? How did you go about writing the ad?*

There's nothing like the face of a kid eating a Hershey Bar. Except maybe that of an adult reading a good classified ad.

It's the same face actually. The very picture of bliss. Serenity. Happiness in the Aristotelian sense.

And while chocolate is widely acknowledged to be an aphrodisiac, few people appreciate the similar properties contained in the humble words "Help Wanted" and "For Sale."

Take real estate, for example. Never mind the mock-Tudor-style homes pictured in full color on the back page. They cost real money. Plus, what fun is there in finding a house this way? It smacks too much of the watch ordered from the back of the Chex box.

More to our hunter/gatherer instinct (the same instinct that has us foraging through a box of stale caramel corn in search of a stick-on tattoo) are those cryptic listings coyly placed in the middle of the "Acreage/Other" section. 5

These clever ads are never accompanied by a photo. And yet they successfully seduce us by conjuring up intoxicating images. "Gracious old mill," they say. "Abandoned farm with old schoolhouse." "Turn-of-the-century carriage House."

The implied message is, of course, that this is a fabled hilltop estate. Our eyes gloss over the "needs tlc" in small type. We're thinking Brideshead. Formal gardens. Mazes. High tea.

This is the kind of place money can't buy. Heavens no. The owners will meet you at the wrought-iron gates and decide that you alone are worthy of carrying on the tradition of Sir Geoffrey. They'll ask you, beseech you, to take the estate, free, with their blessing.

It's a Hershey Bar, pure and simple. Envisioning your new life on the estate is as pleasant as a good sugar high. That is, until you make the unforgiveable decision to pursue the ad. Then, poof! Your mirage dissolves into the reality of a rusty mobile home sitting behind the "Abandoned Farm, 4 Sale" sign.

The same goes for job listings. Certain words — "international," "innovative," "global vision," "Nairobi" — are guaranteed to bring the un- and underemployed to their knees with longing. So too do those ads that use the word "remuneration" in place of "salary" and casually mention free furnished accommodations, pension, education, and travel grants in addition to the "tax-free remuneration in line with comparable international organizations."

Any ad written in a foreign language is also sure to intrigue the classified devotee.

Other job listings are so vague as to be perfectly mesmerizing: "An organization of great size and diversity, we operate within a complex external policy framework that has far-reaching influence over our business . . ." (Here, you begin to lapse into dream sequence.) ". . . Effective board-level strategy formulation therefore depends on expert analysis of external issues, which is carried out within our small, high-powered policy office."

Again, the implied message is only thinly veiled. To men, it reads Armani. James Bond. Indiana Jones. Frank Gifford.

To women, it recalls Donna Karan's new ad featuring the first female president.

The image is clear: Breakfast meetings in Rome. Lunch in Milan. Sangria with clients in Madrid. And armloads, baskets, trunk-loads full of fancy hotel-sized shampoos.

This is the stuff dreams are made of. A great job. Fun colleagues. The image of yourself, sprawled out in your office on a cloud-like sofa, leafing through magazines, sipping a tall one, and effortlessly dictating a witty business letter into a sleek little recorder.

But don't ruin it by foolishly pursuing one of these ads. The disappointment will take one of two tracks: Either you'll be laughed out of the corporate headquarters ("Hey Joe, Come 'ere! You gotta hear this. OK kid, say it again. Where'd you graduate from? (Har Har) When? (Har) In what? (Har Har Har)"). Or "Strategic International Communications Specialist" means telemarketing food dehydrators to Canadians.

Disillusioning? Sure. But no worse than the disappointment of swallowing that last bite of a Hershey Bar. And in an age when good, clean fun is hard to come by, it's comforting to know that the classified ads, like chocolate, instill a cheap, legal, and relatively harmless form of entertainment.

Harmless, that is, provided this little flight of fancy doesn't inspire you to break the lease on your apartment or quit your day job. Or worse, order too many rounds of sangria for imaginary clients.

FOCUSING ON CONTENT

1. In your own words, state Klise's main point in this essay.

2. Which areas of the classifieds does Klise enjoy reading? What does she like about ads that have no accompanying photograph?

3. What kinds of language appeal to the "classified devotee"? How does this language affect these readers? How do they read their own fantasies into the ads? Why do you think their eyes tend to gloss over such phrases as "needs tlc"?

4. In paragraph 9, why does Klise call the decision to pursue an ad "unforgiveable"?

FOCUSING ON WRITING

1. In the opening paragraph, Klise likens the satisfaction derived from eating a Hershey Bar to that of reading a good classified ad. How does she develop this metaphor throughout her essay? (Glossary: *Figures of Speech*) How is the Hershey Bar metaphor related to her main point? Do you think this metaphor is effective, or do you find it a little too gimmicky? Explain.

2. Klise uses two main examples—real estate and employment—to illustrate the pleasures of reading classifieds. Are these two examples enough to convince you? Why or why not?

3. How would you characterize Klise's style in this essay? (Glossary: *Style*) Do you find this style appropriate given her subject matter? Explain.

4. What is Klise's tone in this essay? (Glossary: *Tone*) What specific words or phrases help to create this tone? (Glossary: *Diction*)

LANGUAGE IN ACTION

As Klise suggests, real estate salespeople often use language that is designed to let potential buyers' imaginations run wild. For example, one language analyst notes that in her hometown "adorable" meant "small," "eat-in kitchen" meant "no dining room," "handyman's special" meant "portion of building still standing," "by appointment only" meant "expensive," and "starter home" meant "cheap." In this context, discuss the following 1990 cartoon by Jeff Danziger of the *Los Angeles Times*.

And here's that cozy eat-in kitchen, with that lovely view of the water!

WRITING SUGGESTIONS

1. (*Writing from Experience*) Imagine that you are either an employer or a landlord. Then write a 200-word ad either for a job that you've held or for a place (apartment, dorm room, house) that you've lived in. Ask several peers to read your ad and give you their responses. Revise your ad accordingly.

2. (*Writing from Reading*) With an open mind, read the classified section of your local Sunday newspaper. As Klise suggests, look closely at the ads listed under the headings "Help Wanted," "For Sale," or "Acreage/Other." Do you find any interesting or entertaining items? Write an essay about whether or not you agree with Klise that "it's comforting to know that the classified ads, like chocolate, instill a cheap, legal, and relatively harmless form of entertainment."

3. (*Writing from Research*) Using local newspapers and/or real estate magazines, write an essay in which you analyze the language used in advertisements for single-family homes or commercial properties. How much of the language is technical in nature? Does the language conjure up what Klise calls "intoxicating images"? Do the offerings of one company sound better to you than those of another company? Do any realtors have their own special vocabulary? What general conclusions can you draw about the language of the real estate industry?

Who Said PC Is Passé?

JOHN LEO

Dubbed the "cult columnist of the intelligentia" by Vanity Fair, *John Leo writes a weekly column on the state of our culture that appears in* U.S. News & World Report *and in over 140 newspapers across the country. He has been a reporter for the* New York Times, *covering intellectual trends and religion, and a senior writer for* Time *magazine, specializing in behavior and the social sciences. Leo has two books to his credit,* Two Steps Ahead of the Thought Police *(1994), a collection of his* U.S. News & World Report *columns, and* How the Russians Invented Baseball and Other Essays of Enlightenment *(1989), a book of humor.*

In the following essay, which first appeared in U.S. News & World Report *on May 12, 1997, Leo questions the usefulness of political correctness. Never one to duck an issue, Leo asks his readers to think about a series of humorous—if not always enlightened—examples.*

WRITING TO DISCOVER: *When you hear the term* political correctness *or its abbreviation,* PC, *what comes to mind? Write about your response to this term. Is it positive or negative? To what would you attribute your response?*

Like death and taxes, political correctness is always with us. But at least it's funnier than the other two permanent burdens. Some PC items in the news:

Thank God for magazines like this

Anyone who says, "God bless you," after you sneeze is trying to deprive you of your constitutional rights, according to *Free Inquiry,* a secular humanist magazine. Also on the magazine's list of "people or situations aimed at taking away your liberties and rights guaranteed by the U.S. Constitution" were such stark offenses as: 1) asking anyone, "Did you have a merry Christmas?" 2) inviting folks to a wedding that includes a religious ceremony, and 3) saying grace at a dinner party in your own home.

Mandatory sensitivity

The PC language rumor of the year is that the word "squaw" may come from a French corruption of the Iroquois slang word for "vagina." In

Minnesota, students grew alarmed and complained to the Legislature. So the state passed a law ordering its counties to banish the word "squaw" from the names of all lakes, rivers, or other geographical features. One county responded to the order by officially changing the names of Squaw Creek and Squaw Bay to Politically Correct Creek and Politically Correct Bay. No dice. The state overrode the new names as insensitive. Now it's time for Minnesota to finish the job by banning genital slurs from ice cream cartons—the word "vanilla" also comes from a word for vagina.

Comfortable with censorship

Fans of political correctness remember the fuss over *Naked Maja,* the classic Goya painting accused of harassing a sensitive college instructor at Penn State in 1991. The painting had been hanging there quietly in a classroom for 10 years before it started harassing the teacher. Now *Gwen,* a painting hanging in a Tennessee city hall, has been accused of harassing a female municipal employee and creating a hostile environment.

The problem is that part of one nipple is visible in the painting, a   5
work by artist Maxine Henderson. The city attorney said he "felt more comfortable" siding with the Civil Rights Act's Title VII sexual harassment protections than with First Amendment protections, so the painting was removed. Henderson sued and won a judgment ($1), but the painting stayed down. Museums beware: The triumphant harassee explained that she finds Greek statues offensive and degrading too.

No white writers, please; we're students

California State University–Monterey Bay is the newest and most multicultural school in the California system. Nothing much is being taught there on America's cultural and historic roots, but faculty members say the students already know that stuff from high school. The college does, however, have a "vibrant" requirement, which means that students must "demonstrate knowledge of holistic health and wellness theory, concepts, and content."

Literature students must "compare and contrast the literatures of at least three different cultural groups, two of which are non-Eurocentric." The Eurocentric part might be a bit difficult since a recent visitor to the university bookstore found no literature by white authors. But Qun Wang, a literature instructor, hastened to note that one "Jewish-American" writer was being read (Bernard Malamud) as well as Emily Dickinson, who, although white, presumably made the cut as a female. Wang noted in a letter that he supports the arguments of others that "we should not deify Shakespeare." The guiding spirit and paid adviser of the new college is Eurocentrically pigmented Leon Panetta, former White House chief of staff.

How about adding "vegetarians"?

Identity politics group of the year: At last, men who 1) live in Baltimore, 2) are gay, 3) are into S&M, and 4) suffer hearing loss have a group of their own: the Baltimore Leather Association of the Deaf.

Wimpy anti-president sought

Goddard College in Plainfield, Vt., took out a newspaper ad in the *Chronicle of Higher Education* saying it needed a new college president "who is prepared to lead us through a process that questions the necessity of a president in the first place." Personally, we think it's a stupid, pointless job, so consider us hired.

So that's it!

Penn State art student Christine Enedy produced a campus sculpture 10 of the Virgin Mary emerging from a bloody vagina. Turmoil followed. Asked what she had in mind, exactly, she explained that the bloody Mary demonstrated her view of women's oppression in the church and elsewhere.

Yes, size matters

The Rev. John Papworth, Anglican priest in North London, England, said it is morally justifiable to steal from large supermarkets because these stores are putting smaller ones out of business.

Disney's pro-woman pirates

The pirates at the Pirates of the Caribbean ride in Disneyland are no longer chasing women around in wild abandon, as they have for 30 years. Instead, they are becoming sensitive New Age guys, showing the kind of respect for women that real pirates probably felt deep inside but were afraid to express. Columnist Clarence Page thinks Disney can go further. He thinks that David Crockett should no longer kill a bear at Disneyland— he should gently subdue the magnificent mammal and put it in a petting zoo.

Warning: This item may cause discomfort

Oberlin College's B&D/SM club, devoted to bondage, discipline, sadism, and masochism, generated quite a controversy on campus. Not the B&D/SM itself, of course, but the fact that the club held a campus "slave auction" that offended members of Abusua, the black student union. The S&Mers, in turn, were offended by criticism from people who don't know and respect their culture.

This comes from a year-in-retrospect article in the *Oberlin Review* exploring a year's worth of hurt feelings among campus race and sex groups. Four groups were offended by not being invited to a dinner at the college president's house. It was a mailing-list mistake, but the hurt feelings were all aired at the dinner, and all parties agreed that nobody should be marginalized.

A poster using the words "tribal sex" hurt the feelings of the Third   15
World Co-op, and talks were held "to discuss how to be more sensitive in the future." Some women were "made to feel uncomfortable" by pictures in a campus art journal depicting women in submissive positions, but as the *Review* summed up positively, "Efforts were made by residents to rebuild the community through discussions and house meetings."

Heterophobia — a city's secret shame

A straight couple was thrown out of a gay bar in San Francisco for violating the bar's rules against heterosexual kissing. Morgan Gorrono, manager of the bar, The Café, said he doesn't really mind heterosexual behavior among his customers as long as they don't openly flaunt it. Besides, he said, the two straight kissers were drunk.

Why not just make the slaves white?

A six-part British miniseries due in 1998, *Sacred Hunger,* is based on the prize-winning novel by Barry Unsworth about the African slave trade, including the African slave barons who captured other blacks and sold them to white merchants. An American company offered to help finance the series and show it on U.S. television on one condition — none of the slave traders could be black. No deal. The British producer, Sir Peter Hall, declined to reveal the name of the American company but complained about the "puritanical Stalinism" of political correctness.

New war against Asian-Americans

When the student senate at Tufts University cut $600 from the budget of the Chinese Culture Club, a club spokesman said the cut wasn't "face-to-face racism" but reflected "institutional bias." And since some of the missing funds were intended to pay for containers of Chinese food on Chinese New Year's, the spokesman said the budget cut "questioned the authenticity of takeout food as part of our culture."

Peter Leibert, an art professor at Connecticut College, creates works that play on the word "wok," such as "Board Wok" and "Wok on the Wild Side." But trouble arose when a New London museum displayed

Leibert's "Two Dogs on a Wok," which consisted of two tiny clay dogs in a stoneware wok. An art critic suggested that the work was an ethnic slur implying that Chinese-Americans like to eat dogs. The secretary of the state's Asian-American League quickly agreed. Leibert calls the league's interpretation "nutso."

Hiring the PC way

Alvaro Cardona applied for a $12.43-per-hour job at UCLA tutoring   20
needy students in English. He is a Latino honor student at the university and an experienced tutor, but he didn't get the job. During his job interview, tutoring and English never came up. Instead, he was grilled on whether he supports affirmative action (yes) and whether he sees lots of "institutional racism" on campus (no).

Cardona says the interview was to test his ideological commitment to politically correct race and gender "sensitivity." The supervisor said, no, Cardona was rejected because he would have been the kind of person who stressed learning, which is only 50 percent of the job. The missing 50 percent, she said, was validating the feelings of students.

FOCUSING ON CONTENT

1. What general subjects or issues attract the attention of those interested in political correctness? What do you suppose motivates those who insist on politically correct language?

2. In paragraph 1, Leo states somewhat whimsically that political correctness is funnier than death or taxes. Do you find all of his examples humorous, or do some of them strike you as reasonable? Explain.

3. Why did the Minnesota legislature ban the word *squaw* from all place names or other geographical features in the state? What other reasons can you think of to ban the word *squaw*? What message did the county that came up with the names Politically Correct Creek and Politically Correct Bay send to the legislature?

4. What is Leo's central point, or thesis, about political correctness? (Glossary: *Thesis*) Is it stated directly or implied? In your opinion, which of his many examples best illustrates this point?

FOCUSING ON WRITING

1. What is John Leo's attitude toward political correctness? (Glossary: *Attitude*) What in his diction leads you to this conclusion? (Glossary: *Diction*)

2. Leo uses brief headings for each of his examples. What function(s) do they serve within the essay? Do you find them effective? Why or why not?

3. What is Leo's purpose in this essay? (Glossary: *Purpose*) Do you find his use of examples an appropriate strategy for development, given his thesis and purpose? Explain.

4. Leo provides very little — if any — commentary about his examples. Do you find this technique of letting his examples "speak for themselves" effective? Why or why not? What else could he have done to make his point? Explain.

LANGUAGE IN ACTION

Comment on the following 1999 cartoon by Carlson, which appeared in the *Milwaukee Journal Sentinel*. What, for you, are the connotations of the term *language police?* What is Carlson's attitude toward political correctness? How do you suppose John Leo would respond to this cartoon?

WRITING SUGGESTIONS

1. (*Writing from Experience*) Where does your campus stand in the debate over political correctness? Write an essay about a situation you were involved in, witnessed, or read about in which a person was challenged by another because of the language that he or she used. Briefly recount the incident or event. What did the challenger find offensive? How was the situation resolved, if at all?

2. (*Writing from Reading*) After reading Leo's article and looking at Carlson's cartoon, write an essay in which you argue one of the following positions: that the political correctness movement has taken a good idea and pushed it too far, or that there is an ongoing need to monitor our language. Use examples from Leo's article, Carlson's cartoon, or your own experiences to support your points.

3. (*Writing from Research*) What is the history of the term *politically correct*? When was it first used, by whom, and with what meaning? Has the meaning of the term changed over time? What is the status of the term today? Using research materials found in your library or on the Internet, write a report on the term *politically correct* and the history of its usage in America.

Big Brother Is Listening

ETHAN BRONNER

Ethan Bronner was born in New York City in 1954. A graduate of Wesleyan University and Columbia University's Graduate School of Journalism, he has been the national education correspondent for the New York Times *since the summer of 1997. He writes about trends in both higher education and grades K–12. Before joining the* Times, *Bronner wrote for the* Boston Globe *for twelve years. While serving as the* Globe's *legal affairs and Supreme Court corespondent in Washington, he authored* Battle for Justice: How the Bork Nomination Shook America *(1989).*

In the following selection, which first appeared in the Education Life supplement to the New York Times *on April 4, 1999, Bronner revisits the speech codes that U.S. colleges and universities put into place more than a decade ago in an effort to create a more sensitive climate. Critics of such codes label them the worst form of political correctness, whereas supporters are fearful of a future without them.*

WRITING TO DISCOVER: *Did you ever attend a school or work for a company that had an official speech code, dress code, or some other code governing behavior? In your opinion, what is the purpose of such codes? Write about your attitude toward codes like these. Do you think they should be strictly enforced or eliminated? Does your opinion about them change, depending on the code in question?*

MADISON, WIS.

The issue that gray February day was one of delicate balance: how to assure the freedom to discourse on Hitler's *Mein Kampf,* as one participant put it, but not to use the word "Jew" as a verb, to lecture on sexuality but not to refer to female students as "babes."

The debate—over a faculty speech code—filled the pale blue faculty senate room in Bascom Hall with passion. It was the latest round in a dispute that began on the lakeside campus of the University of Wisconsin nearly two years ago but had been simmering, in some fashion, for generations. A plaque on the building's entrance celebrates freedom of inquiry—the "fearless sifting and winnowing by which alone the truth can be found"—installed after the 1894 exoneration of an economics professor accused of teaching socialism and other "dangerous ideas."

The question on the floor—and it is being mulled on hundreds of campuses across the country, from the University of California to Bowdoin College in Maine—was how to promote such "fearless sifting"

while still creating a welcoming environment for groups that have historically felt slighted at American universities. For while robust intellectual
inquiry is a self-stated goal of every university, so too is creating a diverse
and tolerant nation.

Student and faculty codes punish, sometimes through suspension,
expulsion, or firing, words or deeds that create an environment perceived
as hostile. Backers say codes insure that minorities and other vulnerable
groups will not be mistreated.

"There is a cost to freedom of speech and it is borne unfairly by cer-   5
tain members of the community," asserted Stanlie M. James, a professor
of Afro-American and women's studies. "The harm is immeasurable."

Opponents see codes as the worst form of politically correct paternalism.

"We don't want Big Brother stepping in and telling us what to
think," said Jason Shepard, a student member of the committee examining the Wisconsin faculty code. "They assume that all minority students,
all members of the same group, have the same response to speech. That's
ridiculous."

Alan Charles Kors, a professor at the University of Pennsylvania, and
Harvey A. Silverglate, a Boston lawyer, sought to document the effect of
the codes and similar programs in their 1998 book *The Shadow University.* The university today, they complained, "hands students a moral
agenda upon arrival, subjects them to mandatory political re-education,
sends them to sensitivity training, submerges their individuality in official
group identity, intrudes upon private conscience, treats them with scan-
dalous inequality and, when it chooses, suspends or expels them."

Between 1987 and 1992, about a third of the nation's colleges and
universities enacted codes of conduct that covered offensive speech, said
Jon Gould, a visiting scholar at the University of California, Berkeley,
who wrote his doctoral dissertation on codes.

Typical was the code passed in 1987 at the University of Pennsylva-   10
nia that forbade "any behavior, verbal or physical, that stigmatizes or vic-
timizes individuals on the basis of race, ethnic or national origin . . . and
that has the purpose or effect of interfering with an individual's academic
or work performance; and/or creates an intimidating or offensive academic, living, or work environment."

Most famously, the code was applied against a white Penn student
named Eden Jacobowitz in 1993, when he called a group of noisy black
sorority sisters outside his window "water buffalo." The university's judicial inquiry officer charged him with racial harassment. An Israeli-born
Jew, Mr. Jacobowitz insisted the term—from the Hebrew *behema,* slang
for a rude person but literally water buffalo—has no racial overtones.
After a highly publicized hearing before an administrative board, charges
were dropped. Later, the code was abandoned.

While some codes have been struck down by Federal courts as
patently illegal or amended after coming under attack in the media or by

students, many colleges and universities still have them, though they are rarely invoked.

That, in fact, was the situation with the faculty code at Wisconsin until last year, when First Amendment advocates decided it was time for it to be abolished. This was partly because the code, which had never led to a disciplinary act, had still been the basis of several investigations of faculty members. Its existence, opponents argued, chilled discourse. The Wisconsin student speech code had been struck down by a Federal court in 1991. Now it was the faculty's turn. But efforts to kill the code proved more complex than imagined.

The February debate began with the usual legal disquisitions from the podium — how to interpret the First Amendment in conjunction with Federal harassment regulations — but shifted course when Amelia Rideau from Montclair, N.J., rose to speak.

Ms. Rideau, a 20-year-old junior, recounted how in a recent Chaucer   15
class her professor described a character as "niggardly." Ms. Rideau, a vice president of the Wisconsin Black Student Union, did not know the word, which means stingy and has no racial origins. She was unaware of the controversy in Washington the previous week over the firing (and ultimate rehiring) of a white mayoral aide for using the same word. The only black in the class of 50, Ms. Rideau said she approached the professor afterward and told him of her feelings.

Ms. Rideau thought the teacher had understood and agreed not to use the word again. But at the next class the professor brought in an article about the Washington flap and began a discussion about it.

"He used the word 'niggardly' over and over, five or six times," she said. "I ran out of the class in tears. It was as if he was saying to me, 'Your opinion has no value.'"

When her speech ended to vigorous applause from minority students in the Madison audience, most members of the faculty senate — historians, geneticists, and philosophers in worn sweaters and hiking shoes — sat in silence. There was no doubting the depth of Ms. Rideau's pain. But there was no way any code could be enacted that would bar a professor from using the word "niggardly." And that put the faculty in a quandary.

"Her talk created a sense that there are things here that students of color want that we can't deliver," David Ward, the university chancellor, asserted later.

Two percent of the student body at the University of Wisconsin, one   20
of the nation's premier research institutions, is black. How to increase that representation is very much a concern of administrators.

"In the early 70's, institutions like ours made promises to recruit minority groups, and by the late 1980's it was clear many had failed," said Roger W. Howard, the associate dean of students. "There built up a very significant level of frustration. We had said we wanted to be a different place, a more welcoming place. Yet we kept getting told that this was not a comfortable place for minorities. So we asked ourselves, 'What else can we do?' And that is partly where the speech codes came from."

After much debate in early March, the faculty senate decided, by a vote of 71 to 62, to narrow its speech code but not quite abolish it. Starting with the pledge that the university is "unswervingly committed to freedom of speech," the new language says that "all expression germane to the instructional setting—including but not limited to information, the presentation or advocacy of ideas, assignment of course materials, and teaching techniques—is protected from disciplinary action." This means that even if students are offended, professors cannot be punished if they prove the words were relevant to the lesson.

Wisconsin is not alone in its concerns or its solution. Attracting and retaining minority students is a top goal of every major university in the face of the growing legal and political threat to race-conscious admissions. In fact, the movement to end the codes is often allied with efforts to end those admissions policies. But just as often, the movement is spearheaded by people who believe universities have trampled on sacred free-speech grounds.

Mount Holyoke College in South Hadley, Mass., is reviewing its student and faculty speech code to support free expression more vigorously. At Southern Utah University, a computer-use policy, which bars downloading material that is "racially offensive, threatening, harassing, or otherwise objectionable," has also come under attack and university review.

Yet, despite some people's belief that colleges today are Stalinist outposts where the slightest misstep into apparent intolerance is punished by the political correctness police force (also known as deans of student affairs), campuses report few bias-related incidents. While there are occurrences involving hate E-mails or posters with racial slurs and intimidation of homosexuals, university officials say campuses are not plagued with the problems of a decade ago, when the codes were drafted.

For both faculty and students, it was a difficult time of transition from a mostly homogeneous society to a more mixed culture. Before the 1980's, campuses were mostly white-guy clubs: homosexuality was less accepted, campus culture less accommodating of minority concerns, and far fewer women were found on faculties and in professional schools.

As colleges diversified, speech codes for students and faculty were seen as one buffer. Brown University ejected a student for yelling racial and religious epithets outside the dormitories one night; Sarah Lawrence College brought disciplinary action against a student using an antigay slur and engaging in "inappropriate laughter" seen as mocking a gay student.

The University of Connecticut banned "exhibiting, distributing, posting, or advertising publicly offensive, indecent, or abusive matter" after a 1987 incident in which eight Asian-American students were spat on and taunted by six white students. Paradoxically, it was another Asian-American, Nina Wu, a junior, who challenged the protective policy by hanging a

25

poster listing groups she disliked, including "homos," on her dormitory door. After throwing Ms. Wu out of university housing, the university reinstated her under a judge's order and withdrew the restrictions.

In the mid-80's, when the Massachusetts Institute of Technology was still heavily male (today it is nearly half female), a group of women students complained to the provost about sexual harassment on campus. The provost, John Deutch, asked one of his deputies, Samuel Jay Keyser, to devise a policy against sexual harassment.

Among the rules written by Mr. Keyser's committee was the banning   30
of any sexually explicit film on campus without a film board's approval. The board, a mix of faculty, students, and administrative staff members, was called the Ad Hoc Pornography Screening Committee, and it adopted guidelines that included an insistence that the film "reflect believable reality or normalcy in the relationships and sexuality displayed" and that the film "not unfairly reflect the viewpoint and sexual feelings of men and/or women."

The code was challenged by Adam Dershowitz, a student (and nephew of Alan Dershowitz, the Harvard law professor), who projected the movie *Deep Throat* on the wall of an M.I.T. dormitory common room on registration day, 1987. He was prosecuted by the university under the code, but the charges were dismissed by a faculty-student committee, which found that the film rules were "an excessive restraint on freedom of expression at M.I.T." The code was quietly abandoned several years later.

Conservatives, horrified by what they saw as social engineering, soon joined forces with liberals who were worried about free speech to condemn all such codes. Critics said vigorous, sometimes hurtful debate was the point of a university. As Jonathan Rauch wrote in his 1993 book *Kindly Inquisitors,* "If you insist on an unhostile or nonoffensive environment, then you belong in a monastery, not a university."

Mr. Shepard, the University of Wisconsin student, said such codes do more harm than good by offering false comfort. The better way, he says, is for vulnerable groups to face the discomfort straight on: "Pursuit of knowledge requires us to ask the tough questions," Mr. Shepard, who is gay, said. "And when we do so, people feel uneasy. There is no way around that."

Today, Mr. Keyser, who is retired, agrees. "The codes were a mistake. They were a response to a significant group in our community that was unhappy. But you can't solve the problem with a code. It was an easy solution that didn't work."

That view is not universal. Apart from black, gay, and Hispanic stu-   35
dent groups who say that they suffer from humiliation, a number of women faculty members at Madison recalled the uneasy life before codes. Theresa Duello, a professor of obstetrics and gynecology at Wisconsin's medical school, said that when she joined her department in 1982, she was told by the chairman that he could not believe he had to introduce a

woman who was taller than he and thought he would ask her to begin by discussing her first date.

Carin A. Clauss, a law professor who campaigned to keep the code, said she was especially sensitive to the need for regulations supporting minority groups and women because she went to law school when women made up fewer than one percent of the class.

Professor Clauss's main opponent in Madison was Donald Downs, a political scientist who has come full circle. His first foray into the free-expression issue was in 1978, when he wrote a book on American Nazis seeking to march in Skokie, Ill., home to many Holocaust survivors.

"I really identified with how the survivors felt," Professor Downs recalled. "I argued that targeted racial vilification as a form of assaultive speech crosses the First Amendment line. I hadn't thought hard enough about the special place of free speech in a public forum."

Today, he says, he would favor permitting the Nazis to march in Skokie just as he favors doing away with all speech codes because they sacrifice something too significant. He draws parallels with Prohibition. He also sees an analogy with affirmative action, saying that, like codes, it gives rights to one group by taking rights away from another, something he opposes.

This is a central point made by Professor Kors and Mr. Silverglate in 40
their book *The Shadow University.*

They see the codes as part of a larger liberal orthodoxy imposed by the 60's generation that has taken over college faculties and administrations, especially the offices of student affairs, which promote sensitivity and diversity training during freshman orientation, for dormitory advisers and in classrooms.

They say the main victims of this orthodoxy are those who are not part of it, like Christians who consider homosexuality and abortion unacceptable and find themselves unable to express themselves on campuses.

There are others who say that while they oppose the codes now, they served a role when they were enacted. "There is no question that the codes did, to some unmeasurable extent, influence and help create more appropriate attitudes toward race and gender and sexual orientation," Professor Downs said. "But this was at the cost of instilling fear of intellectual honesty."

Richard Delgado, a law professor at the University of Colorado and an early advocate of codes, says that social scientists increasingly favor what is called the confrontation theory, which holds that the best way to dampen racism is through clear rules that punish offenders because the rules' very existence leads people to conform to their principles. He says this has largely replaced the social-contact theory, which asserts that racism is best overcome by placing people of different creeds in constant contact with one another, and that through such contact they will see the error of racist attitudes.

Despite the codes, despite the changes campuses have made in recent 45
years, the vulnerability felt by minorities remains raw.

Michael S. McPherson, the president of Macalester College in St. Paul, says that in October 1997, a black student found racist slurs written on the note board she had hung outside her dormitory room. The culprit was never found but students held a vigil and public meetings. Even though there has been no similar event on the campus since, black students still tell Mr. McPherson how the incident upset them.

It is that gnawing sense of vulnerability that has made the idea of removing the codes unpalatable to the people they were set up to protect. They recognize the shaky legal ground on which they sit — no student speech code that has been challenged in court has survived — and worry that the codes will be abused if left on the books. But they fear the signal such a change would send to minority groups.

"As we have become more integrated, I have a sense that the sorts of incidents we had 10 years ago we don't really have today," observed Professor Clauss of Wisconsin. "Now, women make up 47 percent of our law school and things are certainly easier. But we are getting Hmong and Muslim students. I am never sure that minority interests are adequately protected. There was a Muslim student in the health program here who raised religious objections to massage therapy and wanted accommodations to respect his belief. Whether we take those things seriously depends on sensitizing people. Who knows what minority will arrive tomorrow?"

FOCUSING ON CONTENT

1. According to Bronner, what is the main argument in favor of speech codes? The main argument against?

2. According to Alan Charles Kors and Harvey A. Silverglate, what has been the effect of speech codes on colleges and universities? What do they believe happens when schools "promote sensitivity and diversity training during freshman orientation" (41)? What is your own school's policy in regard to speech codes?

3. At the University of Wisconsin, Amelia Rideau, an African American student from Montclair, New Jersey, objected to her professor's use of the word *niggardly* in a Chaucer class (14–18). When he used the word again, after she had voiced her objections, Rideau cried foul. In what ways does this example get to the heart of the debate over speech codes? Why do you think it "put [Wisconsin's] faculty in a quandary"?

4. Between 1987 and 1992, approximately one-third of the nation's colleges and universities adopted codes that addressed offensive speech. What has been the fate of these codes in the intervening years? Why do you suppose the codes are "rarely invoked" at those institutions that still have them?

5. According to law professor Richard Delgado, there are differing theories — the confrontation theory and the social-contact theory — about how best to combat racism (44). Explain these two theories in your own words. Has ei-

ther of them been tried on your campus? If so, for how long and with what success?

6. Why did Donald Downs change his stance on free speech (37–39)? What is his attitude toward speech codes today?

FOCUSING ON WRITING

1. In your opinion, what is Bronner's purpose in writing this essay—to express his personal feelings about speech codes, to inform readers of the current status of the speech-code debate, or to argue for or against speech codes? (Glossary: *Purpose*) What in his essay leads you to this conclusion?

2. Bronner uses the speech-code debate that is still occurring at the University of Wisconsin at Madison to anchor his essay. Why do you think he surrounds the Wisconsin debate with examples from campuses across the country? (Glossary: *Examples*) What effect did Bronner's decision to use these other examples have on you as a reader?

3. Bronner uses direct quotations from a variety of people: students, college and university professors, and university administrators. Why do you suppose he decided to use direct quotations instead of simply paraphrasing or summarizing what each person said? (Glossary: *Direct Quotation*) In what ways do these quotations give authority to Bronner's essay?

4. How would you characterize Bronner's tone in this essay? (Glossary: *Tone*) As a writer, does he treat the two sides of the speech-code debate equally? Where do you think Bronner himself stands on this issue? What in the essay makes you think so?

LANGUAGE IN ACTION

The late Mike Royko wrote the following column for the *Chicago Tribune* on April 26, 1994. In it he recounts the story of Jack Draper and his store Crazy Larry's Waterbeds. After reading the column, discuss where, if at all, you think people need to draw the line in pursuing political correctness.

IT CERTAINLY IS CRAZY, BUT IS IT REALLY POLITICALLY INCORRECT?

I have to begin by saying that this story is kind of crazy.

It concerns a man named Jack Draper, who owns a waterbed and bedroom furniture store in Evansville, Ind.

His store is called Crazy Larry's Waterbeds, a name he picked 14 years ago because he had an eager-beaver ad manager named Larry and they thought it was catchy.

Recently, Draper received a stern letter from Rich Allen, the community services director of the Evansville State Hospital, a mental institution.

Allen wrote, in part: "At a time of growing sensitivity to racist and sexist language, no such caution governs the use of the vocabulary associated with mental illness.

"Words such as 'nuts,' 'maniac,' 'psycho,' and 'crazy' are offensive to those with a mental illness. Use of such words tends to perpetuate the stigma associated with the disease. Negative attitudes and misunderstanding continue because of the offhanded portrayals of the mentally ill in movies and in advertising."

When he read the letter, Draper says, "I couldn't believe it. So I called the head of the hospital and he said he approved the letter.

"He thinks the name of my place can offend his patients. I said I'd apologize to anyone I offended. And I asked if it would be better if we called the place, 'Psychologically Imbalanced Larry's Waterbeds.' He didn't think that was funny.

"But I'm not going to change the name of my store. This is the first time I've heard from anyone complaining. And they should look in the dictionary. There is more than one definition of 'crazy.'"

He's right, of course. Besides "affected with madness; insane," there is also "departing from proportion or moderation . . . possessed by enthusiasm or excitement . . . intensely involved or preoccupied . . . foolish or impractical. . . ."

If a young man proposes marriage or some other arrangement to a young woman, and says, "I am crazy about you," should she assume that he is admitting to a severe mental disorder and flee?

But Mr. Allen, who wrote the letter, believes most people don't take mental illness seriously enough, so he keeps a keen eye out for what he considers misuse of the word "crazy."

"You want to know how this whole thing got started?" Allen asked. "There was an article in a newspaper about a new Italian restaurant. You know what it was called? The Crazy Tomato. Can you believe that?"

Yes, I can believe it. And if I walked into that restaurant, I wouldn't be at all concerned that a big, deranged tomato would splat me in the face.

That's the way I feel about crazy quilts, too. If I took a nap under one, I wouldn't expect it to smother me in my sleep.

But Allen feels otherwise. "So I fired off a letter to the owner of the Crazy Tomato. Then I fired off the same letter to Crazy Larry's Waterbeds."

This seems to be another example of political correctness meddling with commonly used and generally accepted language.

If Allen had his way, when a batter hit a game-winning grand-slam home run, it would not be permissible for an announcer to say: "The fans went crazy." Instead, he'd have to say: "The fans were intensely involved and preoccupied and reacted with great enthusiasm and excitement."

But with political correctness now part of the cultural struggle, we're going to have one crazy argument after another. It's enough to drive you nuts.

WRITING SUGGESTIONS

1. (*Writing from Experience*) Many people have had experiences similar to Rideau's at the University of Wisconsin in which another's words have caused emotional pain. Have you or a person you know ever been offended

by another's language? What specifically was said or written, and what feelings did you or the person you know have at the time? What action did you or the other person take? How was the situation resolved? Write an essay in which you recount your experiences and the lessons learned.

2. (*Writing from Reading*) After reading Bronner's article, where do you stand on the issue of speech codes? Historically, what were the stated reasons for instituting speech codes? Do you think they have, in fact, served a worthwhile purpose? Or, as their detractors claim, have speech codes silenced a segment of the American public? At the millennium, do you believe there is still a need to maintain speech codes? Write an essay in which you explain your position on campus speech codes.

3. (*Writing from Research*) In recent years, controversy has swirled about the following question: Which is more harmful to democracy, the expression of racist stereotypes or the measures taken to discourage such expression? Answer this question in an essay by researching the debate in the United States surrounding hate speech and acts, political correctness, or speech codes. You may want to check newspaper archives, congressional records (which are often available online) or judicial records from the Supreme Court.

The World of Doublespeak

WILLIAM LUTZ

Originally from Racine, Wisconsin, William Lutz is a professor of English at Rutgers University, and he edits the Quarterly Review of Doublespeak. *Through his book* Doublespeak: From Revenue Enhancement to Terminal Living *(1980), Lutz first awakened Americans to how people in important positions were manipulating language. As chair of the National Council of Teachers of English's Committee on Public Doublespeak, Lutz has been a watchdog of public officials who use language to "mislead, distort, deceive, inflate, circumvent, and obfuscate." Each year the committee presents the Orwell Awards, recognizing the most outrageous uses of public doublespeak in the worlds of government and business. Lutz's most recent books are* The New Doublespeak: Why No One Knows What Anyone's Saying Anymore *(1997) and* Doublespeak Defined: Cut through the Bull**** and Get the Point *(1999).*

In the following essay, which first appeared in Christopher Ricks and Leonard Michaels's anthology State of the Language *(1990), Lutz examines doublespeak, "language which pretends to communicate but doesn't, language which makes the bad seem good, the negative appear positive, the unpleasant attractive, or at least tolerable." He identifies the various types of doublespeak and cautions us about the possible serious effects that doublespeak can have on our thinking.*

WRITING TO DISCOVER: *Have you ever heard or read language that you thought was deliberately evasive, language that manipulated your perception of reality, or, worse yet, language that communicated nothing? Jot down your thoughts about such language. For example, what kinds of language do people use to talk about death, cancer, mental illness, firing a person, killing someone, or ending a relationship? Do you think evasive or manipulative language is ever justified? Explain.*

Farmers no longer have cows, pigs, chickens, or other animals on their farms; according to the U.S. Department of Agriculture farmers have "grain-consuming animal units" (which, according to the Tax Reform Act of 1986, are kept in "single-purpose agricultural structures," not pig pens and chicken coops). Attentive observers of the English language also learned recently that the multibillion dollar stock market crash of 1987 was simply a "fourth quarter equity retreat"; that airplanes don't crash, they just have "uncontrolled contact with the ground"; that janitors are really "environmental technicians"; that it was a "diagnostic misadventure of a high magnitude" which caused the death of a patient in a Philadelphia hospital, not medical malpractice; and that President Reagan wasn't really unconscious while he underwent minor surgery, he was just in a "non-decision-making form." In other words, doublespeak continues to spread as the official language of public discourse.

Doublespeak is a blanket term for language which pretends to communicate but doesn't, language which makes the bad seem good, the negative appear positive, the unpleasant attractive, or at least tolerable. It is language which avoids, shifts, or denies responsibility, language which is at variance with its real or its purported meaning. It is language which conceals or prevents thought. Basic to doublespeak is incongruity, the incongruity between what is said, or left unsaid, and what really is: between the word and the referent, between seem and be, between the essential function of language, communication, and what doublespeak does—mislead, distort, deceive, inflate, circumvent, obfuscate.

When shopping, we are asked to check our packages at the desk "for our convenience," when it's not for our convenience at all but for the store's "program to reduce inventory shrinkage." We see advertisements for "preowned," "experienced," or "previously distinguished" cars, for "genuine imitation leather," "virgin vinyl," or "real counterfeit diamonds." Television offers not reruns but "encore telecasts." There are no slums or ghettos, just the "inner city" or "substandard housing" where the "disadvantaged," "economically nonaffluent," or "fiscal underachievers" live. Nonprofit organizations don't make a profit, they have "negative deficits" or "revenue excesses." In the world of doublespeak dying is "terminal living."

We know that a toothbrush is still a toothbrush even if the advertisements on television call it a "home plaque removal instrument," and even that "nutritional avoidance therapy" means a diet. But who would guess that a "volume-related production schedule adjustment" means closing an entire factory in the doublespeak of General Motors, or that "advanced downward adjustments" means budget cuts in the doublespeak of Caspar Weinberger, or that "energetic disassembly" means an explosion in a nuclear power plant in the doublespeak of the nuclear power industry?

The euphemism, an inoffensive or positive word or phrase designed   5
to avoid a harsh, unpleasant, or distasteful reality, can at times be doublespeak. But the euphemism can also be a tactful word or phrase; for example, "passed away" functions not just to protect the feelings of another person but also to express our concern for another's grief. This use of the euphemism is not doublespeak but the language of courtesy. A euphemism used to mislead or deceive, however, becomes doublespeak. In

1984, the U.S. State Department announced that in its annual reports on the status of human rights in countries around the world it would no longer use the word "killing." Instead, it would use the phrase "unlawful or arbitrary deprivation of life." Thus the State Department avoids discussing government-sanctioned killings in countries that the United States supports and has certified as respecting human rights.

The Pentagon also avoids unpleasant realities when it refers to bombs and artillery shells which fall on civilian targets as "incontinent ordnance" or killing the enemy as "servicing the target." In 1977 the Pentagon tried to slip funding for the neutron bomb unnoticed into an appropriations bill by calling it an "enhanced radiation device." And in 1971 the CIA gave us that most famous of examples of doublespeak when it used the phrase "eliminate with extreme prejudice" to refer to the execution of a suspected double agent in Vietnam.

Jargon, the specialized language of a trade or profession, allows colleagues to communicate with each other clearly, efficiently, and quickly. Indeed, it is a mark of membership to be able to use and understand the group's jargon. But it can also be doublespeak—pretentious, obscure, and esoteric terminology used to make the simple appear complex, and not to express but impress. In the doublespeak of jargon, smelling something becomes "organoleptic analysis," glass becomes "fused silicate," a crack in a metal support beam becomes a "discontinuity," conservative economic policies become "distributionally conservative notions."

Lawyers and tax accountants speak of an "involuntary conversion" of property when discussing the loss or destruction of property through theft, accident, or condemnation. So if your house burns down, or your car is stolen or destroyed in an accident, you have, in legal jargon, suffered an "involuntary conversion" of your property. This is a legal term with a specific meaning in law and all lawyers can be expected to understand it. But when it is used to communicate with a person outside the group who does not understand such language, it is doublespeak. In 1978 a National Airlines 727 airplane crashed while attempting to land at the Pensacola, Florida, airport, killing three passengers, injuring twenty-one others, and destroying the airplane. Since the insured value of the airplane was greater than its book value, National made an after-tax insurance benefit of $1.7 million on the destroyed airplane, or an extra eighteen cents a share. In its annual report, National reported that this $1.7 million was due to "the involuntary conversion of a 727," thus explaining the profit without even hinting at the crash and the deaths of three passengers.

Gobbledygook or bureaucratese is another kind of doublespeak. Such doublespeak is simply a matter of overwhelming the audience with technical, unfamiliar words. When asked why U.S. forces lacked intelligence information on Grenada before they invaded the island in 1983, Admiral Wesley L. McDonald told reporters that "We were not micromanaging Grenada intelligence-wise until about that time frame."

Some gobbledygook, however impressive it may sound, doesn't even   10
make sense. During the 1988 presidential campaign, vice presidential candidate Senator Dan Quayle explained the need for a strategic defense initiative by saying: "Why wouldn't an enhanced deterrent, a more stable
peace, a better prospect to denying the ones who enter conflict in the first
place to have a reduction of offensive systems and an introduction to defensive capability. I believe this is the route the country will eventually go."

In 1974, Alan Greenspan, then chairman of the President's Council
of Economic Advisors, was testifying before a Senate Committee and was
in the difficult position of trying to explain why President Nixon's economic policies weren't effective in fighting inflation: "It is a tricky problem to find the particular calibration in timing that would be appropriate
to stem the acceleration in risk premiums created by falling incomes without prematurely aborting the decline in the inflation-generated risk premiums." In 1988, when speaking to a meeting of the Economic Club of
New York, Mr. Greenspan, now Federal Reserve chairman, said, "I guess
I should warn you, if I turn out to be particularly clear, you've probably
misunderstood what I've said."

The investigation into the Challenger disaster in 1986 revealed the
gobbledygook and bureaucratese used by many involved in the shuttle
program. When Jesse Moore, NASA's associate administrator, was asked
if the performance of the shuttle program had improved with each launch
or if it had remained the same, he answered, "I think our performance in
terms of the liftoff performance and in terms of the orbital performance,
we knew more about the envelope we were operating under, and we have
been pretty accurately staying in that. And so I would say the performance has not by design drastically improved. I think we have been able
to characterize the performance more as a function of our launch experience as opposed to it improving as a function of time."

A final kind of doublespeak is simply inflated language. Car mechan-
ics may be called "automotive internists," elevator operators "members
of the vertical transportation corps," and grocery store checkout clerks
"career associate scanning professionals," while television sets are proclaimed to have "nonmulticolor capability." When a company "initiates a
career alternative enhancement program" it is really laying off five thousand workers; "negative patient care outcome" means that the patient
died; and "rapid oxidation" means a fire in a nuclear power plant.

The doublespeak of inflated language can have serious consequences.
The U.S. Navy didn't pay $2,043 a piece for steel nuts; it paid all that
money for "hexiform rotatable surface compression units," which, by the
way, "underwent catastrophic stress-related shaft detachment." Not to be
outdone, the U.S. Air Force paid $214 a piece for Emergency Exit
Lights, or flashlights. This doublespeak is in keeping with such military
doublespeak as "preemptive counterattack" for first strike, "engage the
enemy on all sides" for ambush, "tactical redeployment" for retreat, and

"air support" for bombing. In the doublespeak of the military, the 1983 invasion of Grenada was conducted not by the U.S. Army, Navy, Air Force, and Marines but by the "Caribbean Peace Keeping Forces." But then according to the Pentagon it wasn't an invasion, it was a "predawn vertical insertion."

These last examples of doublespeak should make it clear that double- 15 speak is not the product of careless language or sloppy thinking. Indeed, serious doublespeak is the product of clear thinking and is carefully designed and constructed to appear to communicate but in fact to mislead. Thus, it's not a tax increase but "revenue enhancement," "tax base broadening," or "user fees," so how can you complain about higher taxes? It's not acid rain, it's just "poorly buffered precipitation," so don't worry about all those dead trees. That isn't the Mafia in Atlantic City, those are just "members of a career-offender cartel," so don't worry about the influence of organized crime in the city. The Supreme Court Justice wasn't addicted to the painkilling drug he was taking, it's just that the drug had simply "established an interrelationship with the body, such that if the drug is removed precipitously, there is a reaction," so don't worry that his decisions might have been influenced by his drug addition. It's not a Titan II nuclear-armed, intercontinental, ballistic missile 630 times more powerful than the atomic bomb dropped on Hiroshima, it's just a "very large, potentially disruptive reentry system," so don't worry about the threat of nuclear destruction. Serious doublespeak is highly strategic, and it breeds suspicion, cynicism, distrust, and, ultimately, hostility.

In his famous and now-classic essay "Politics and the English Language," which was published in 1946, George Orwell wrote that the "great enemy of clear language is insincerity. When there is a gap between one's real and one's declared aims, one turns as it were instinctively to long words and exhausted idioms, like a cuttlefish squirting out ink." For Orwell, language was an instrument for "expressing and not for concealing or preventing thought." In his most biting comment, Orwell observes that "in our time, political speech and writing are largely the defense of the indefensible. . . . Political language has to consist largely of euphemism, question-begging, and sheer cloudy vagueness. . . . Political language . . . is designed to make lies sound truthful and murder respectable, and to give an appearance of solidity to pure wind."

Orwell understood well the power of language as both a tool and a weapon. In the nightmare world of his novel *1984,* he depicted language as one of the most important tools of the totalitarian state. Newspeak, the official state language in *1984,* was designed not to extend but to *diminish* the range of human thought, to make only "correct" thought possible and all other modes of thought impossible. It was, in short, a language designed to create a reality which the state wanted.

Newspeak had another important function in Orwell's world of *1984.* It provided the means of expression for doublethink, which Orwell described in his novel as "the power of holding two contradictory beliefs in one's mind simultaneously, and accepting both of them." The classic example of doublethink in Orwell's novel is the slogan "War is Peace." And lest you think doublethink is confined only to Orwell's novel, you need only recall the words of Secretary of State Alexander Haig when he testified before a Congressional Committee in 1982 that a continued weapons build-up by the United States is "absolutely essential to our hopes for meaningful arms reduction." Or the words of Senator Orrin Hatch in 1988: "Capital punishment is our society's recognition of the sanctity of human life."

The more sophisticated and powerful uses of doublespeak can at times be difficult to identify. On 27 July 1981, President Ronald Reagan said in a television speech: "I will not stand by and see those of you who are dependent on Social Security deprived of the benefits you've worked so hard to earn. You will continue to receive your checks in the full amount due you." This speech had been billed as President Reagan's position on Social Security, a subject of much debate at the time. After the speech, public opinion polls recorded the great majority of the public as believing that President Reagan had affirmed his support for Social Security and that he would not support cuts in benefits. Five days after the speech, however, White House spokesperson David Gergen was quoted in the press as saying that President Reagan's words had been "carefully chosen." What President Reagan did mean, according to Gergen, was that he was reserving the right to decide who was "dependent" on those benefits, who had "earned" them, and who, therefore, was "due" them.

During the 1982 Congressional election campaign, the Republican National Committee sponsored a television advertisement which pictured an elderly, folksy postman delivering Social Security checks "with the 7.4 percent cost-of-living raise that President Reagan promised." Looking directly at his audience, the postman then adds that Reagan "promised that raise and he kept his promise, in spite of those sticks-in-the-mud who tried to keep him from doing what we elected him to do."

The commercial was deliberately misleading. The cost-of-living increases had been provided automatically by law since 1975, and President Reagan had tried three times to roll them back or delay them but was overruled by congressional opposition. When these discrepancies were pointed out to an official of the Republican National Committee, he called the commercial "inoffensive" and added, "Since when is a commercial supposed to be accurate? Do women really smile when they clean their ovens?"

In 1986, with the Challenger tragedy and subsequent investigation, we discovered that doublespeak seemed to be the official language of NASA, the National Aeronautics and Space Administration, and of the contractors engaged in the space shuttle program. The first thing we learned is that the Challenger tragedy wasn't an accident. As Kay Parker of NASA said, experts were "working in the anomaly investigation." The "anomaly" was the explosion of the Challenger.

When NASA reported that it was having difficulty determining how or exactly when the Challenger astronauts died, Rear Admiral Richard Truly reported that "whether or not a cabin rupture occurred prior to water impact has not yet been determined by a superficial examination of the recovered components." The "recovered components" were the bodies of the astronauts. Admiral Truly also said that "extremely large forces were imposed on the vehicle as evidenced by the immediate breakup into many pieces." He went on to say that "once these forces have been accurately determined, if in fact they can be, the structural analysts will attempt to estimate the effect on the structural and pressure integrity of the crew module." NASA referred to the coffins of the astronauts as "crew transfer containers."

Arnold Aldrich, manager of the national space transportation systems program at Johnson Space Center, said that "the normal process during the countdown is that the countdown proceeds, assuming we are in a go posture, and at various points during the countdown we tag up on the operational loops and face to face in the firing room to ascertain the facts that project elements that are monitoring the data and that are understanding the situation as we proceed are still in the go condition."

In testimony before the commission investigating the Challenger accident, Allen McDonald, an engineer for Morton Thiokol (the maker of the rocket), said he had expressed concern about the possible effect of cold weather on the booster rocker's O-ring seals the night before the launch: "I made the comment that lower temperatures are in the direction of badness for both O-rings, because it slows down the timing function."   25

Larry Mulloy, manager of the space shuttle solid rocket booster program at Marshall Space Flight Center, responded to a question assessing whether problems with the O-rings or with the insulation of the liner of the nozzle posed a greater threat to the shuttle by saying, "The criticality in answering your question, sir, it would be a real foot race as to which one would be considered more critical, depending on the particular time that you looked at your experience with that."

After several executives of Rockwell International, the main contractor to build the shuttle, had testified that Rockwell had been opposed to launching the shuttle because of the danger posed by ice formation on the launch platform, Martin Cioffoletti, vice president for space transportation at Rockwell, said: "I felt that by telling them we did not have a sufficient data base and could not analyze the trajectory of the ice, I felt he understood that Rockwell was not giving a positive indication that we were for the launch."

Officials at Morton Thiokol, when asked why they reversed earlier decisions not to launch the shuttle, said the reversal was "based on the reevaluation of those discussions." The Presidential commission investigating the accident suggested that this statement could be translated to mean there was pressure from NASA.

One of the most chilling uses of doublespeak occurred in 1981 when then Secretary of State Alexander Haig was testifying before congressional committees about the murder of three American nuns and a Catholic lay worker in El Salvador. The four women had been raped and then shot at close range, and there was clear evidence that the crime had been committed by soldiers of the Salvadoran government. Before the House Foreign Affairs Committee, Secretary Haig said, "I'd like to suggest to you that some of the investigations would lead one to believe that perhaps the vehicle the nuns were riding in may have tried to run a roadblock, or may accidentally have been perceived to have been doing so, and there'd been an exchange of fire and then perhaps those who inflicted the casualties sought to cover it up. And this could have been at a very low level of both competence and motivation in the context of the issue itself. But the facts on this are not clear enough for anyone to draw a definitive conclusion."

The next day, before the Senate Foreign Relations Committee, Secretary Haig claimed that press reports on his previous testimony were inaccurate. When Senator Claiborne Pell asked whether Secretary Haig was suggesting the possibility that "the nuns may have run through a roadblock," Secretary Haig replied, "You mean that they tried to violate . . . ? Not at all, no, not at all. My heavens! The dear nuns who raised me in my parochial schooling would forever isolate me from their affections and respect." When Senator Pell asked Secretary Haig, "Did you mean that the nuns were firing at the people, or what did 'an exchange of fire' mean?" Secretary Haig replied, "I haven't met any pistol-packing nuns in my day, Senator. What I meant was that if one fellow starts shooting, then the next thing you know they all panic." Thus did the Secretary of State of the United States explain official government policy on the murder of four American citizens in a foreign land.

The congressional hearings for the Irancontra affair produced more doublespeak. During his second day of testimony before the Select Committee on Secret Military Assistance to Iran and the Nicaraguan Opposition, Oliver North admitted that he had on different occasions lied to the Iranians, his colleague Maj. Gen. Richard Secord, congressional investigators, and the Congress, and that he had destroyed evidence and created false documents. North then asserted to the committee that everything he was about to say would be the truth.

North used the words "residuals" and "diversions" to refer to the millions of dollars which were raised for the contras by overcharging Iran for arms. North also said that he "cleaned" and "fixed" things up, that he was "cleaning up the historical record," and that he "took steps to ensure" that things never "came out"—meaning he lied, destroyed official government documents, and created false documents. Some documents weren't destroyed; they were "non-log" or kept "out of the system so that outside knowledge would not necessarily be derived from having the documents themselves."

North was also careful not to "infect other people with unnecessary knowledge." He explained that the Nicaraguan Humanitarian Assistance Office provided humanitarian aid in "mixed loads," which, according to North, "meant . . . beans and Band-Aids and boots and bullets." For North, people in other countries who helped him were "assets." "Project Democracy" was a "euphemism" he used at the time to refer to the organization that was building an airfield for the contras.

In speaking of a false chronology of events which he helped construct, North said that he "was provided with additional input that was radically different from the truth. I assisted in furthering that version." He mentions "a different version from the facts" and calls the chronology "inaccurate." North also testified that he and William Casey, then head of the C.I.A., together falsified the testimony that Casey was to give to Congress. "Director Casey and I fixed that testimony and removed the offensive portions. We fixed it by omission. We left out—it wasn't made accurate, it wasn't made fulsome, it was fixed by omission." Official lies were "plausible deniability."

While North admitted that he had shredded documents after being   35
informed that officials from the Attorney General's office wanted to inspect some of the documents in his office, he said, "I would prefer to say that I shredded documents that day like I did on all other days, but perhaps with increased intensity."

North also preferred to use the passive to avoid responsibility. When asked "Where are the non-logged documents?" he replied, "I think they were shredded." Again, when asked on what authority he agreed to allow Secord to make a personal profit off the arms sale to Iran, North replied with a long, wordy response filled with such passive constructions as "it was clearly indicated," "it was already known," and "it was recognized." But he never answered the question.

For North, the whole investigation by Congress was just an attempt "to criminalize policy differences between coequal branches of government and the Executive's conduct of foreign affairs." Lying to Congress, shredding official documents, violating laws, conducting unauthorized activities were all just "policy differences" to North. But North was generous with the committee: "I think there's fault to go on both sides. I've said that repeatedly throughout my testimony. And I have accepted the responsibility for my role in it." While North accepts responsibility, he does not accept accountability.

This final statement of North's bears close reading for it reveals the subtlety of his language. North states as fact that Congress was at fault, but at fault for what he doesn't specify. Furthermore, he does not accept responsibility for any specific action, only for his "role," whatever that may have been, in "it." In short, while he may be "responsible" (not guilty) for violating the law, Congress shares in that responsibility for having passed the law.

In Oliver North's doublespeak, then, defying a law is complying with it, noncompliance is compliance. North's doublespeak allowed him to help draft a letter to Congress saying that "we are complying with the letter and spirit" of the Boland Amendment, when what the letter really meant, North later admitted, was that "Boland doesn't apply to us and so we're complying with its letter and spirit."

Contrary to his claim that he was a "stand up guy" who would tell all   40 and take whatever was coming to him, North disclaimed all responsibility for his actions: "I was authorized to do everything that I did." Yet when he was asked who gave him authorization, North replied, "My superiors." When asked which superior, he replied: "Well, who—look who sign—I didn't sign those letters to the—to this body." And North's renowned steel-trap memory went vague or forgetful again.

After North had testified, Admiral John Poindexter, North's superior, testified before the committee. Once again, doublespeak flourished. In the world of Admiral John Poindexter, one does not lie but "misleads" or "withholds information." Likewise, one engages in "secret activities" which are not the same as covert actions. In Poindexter's world, one can "acquiesce" in a shipment of weapons while at the same time not authorize the shipment. One can transfer millions of dollars of government money as a "technical implementation" without making a "substantive decision." One can also send subordinates to lie to congressional committees if one does not "micromanage" them. In Poindexter's world, "outside interference" occurs when Congress attempts to fulfill its constitutional function of passing legislation.

For Poindexter, withholding information was not lying. When asked about Col. North's testimony that he had lied to a congressional committee and that Poindexter had known that North intended to lie, Poindexter replied, "there was a general understanding that he [North] was to withhold information. . . . I . . . did not expect him to lie to the committee. I expected him to be evasive. . . . I'm sure they [North's answers] were very carefully crafted, nuanced. The total impact, I am sure, was one of withholding information from the Congress, but I'm still not convinced . . . that he lied."

Yet Poindexter protested that it is not "fair to say that I have misinformed Congress or other Cabinet officers. I haven't testified to that. I've testified that I withheld information from Congress. And with regard to the Cabinet officers, I didn't withhold anything from them that they didn't want withheld from them." Poindexter did not explain how it is possible to withhold information that a person wants withheld.

The doublespeak of Alexander Haig, Oliver North, and John Poindexter occurred during their testimony before congressional committees. Perhaps their doublespeak was not premeditated but just happened to be the way they spoke, and thought. President Jimmy Carter in 1980 could call the aborted raid to free the American hostages in Tehran an "incomplete success" and really believe that he had made a statement that clearly communicated with the American public. So too could President Ronald Reagan say in 1985 that "ultimately our security and our hopes for success at the arms reduction talks hinge on the determination that we show here to continue our program to rebuild and refortify our defenses" and really believe that greatly increasing the amount of money spent building new weapons will lead to a reduction in the number of weapons in the world. If we really believe that we understand such language and that such language communicates and promotes clear thought, then the world of *1984* with its control of reality through language is upon us.

FOCUSING ON CONTENT

1. What, according to Lutz, is doublespeak? What are its essential characteristics?

2. What is a euphemism? Are all euphemisms examples of doublespeak? Explain.

3. In his discussion of Oliver North's testimony during the Irancontra hearings, Lutz states, "While North accepts responsibility, he does not accept accountability" (37). Explain what Lutz means here. What differences do you draw between responsibility and accountability?

4. Why, according to Lutz, does "doublespeak continue to spread as the official language of public discourse" (1)? In your opinion, is doublespeak as widespread today as it was when Lutz wrote his article? What examples can you provide to back-up your opinion?

5. Why does Lutz believe that we must recognize doublespeak for what it is and voice our dissatisfaction with those who use it?

FOCUSING ON WRITING

1. In paragraph 2, Lutz provides readers with a comprehensive definition of *doublespeak*. What does he achieve as a writer by clearly defining this term early in his essay? (Glossary: *Definition*)

2. What is Lutz's purpose in this essay — to inform, to express thoughts or feelings, to persuade? (Glossary: *Purpose*) What in his essay leads you to this conclusion?

3. Lutz discusses four basic types or categories of doublespeak — euphemism, jargon, gobbledygook, and inflated language. In what ways does this classification serve to clarify not only the concept of doublespeak but also its many uses? (Glossary: *Classification*)

4. Lutz is careful to illustrate each of the basic types of doublespeak with examples. Why is it important to use plenty of examples in an essay like this?

(Glossary: *Examples*) What do his many examples reveal about Lutz's expertise on the subject?

5. How does paragraph 15 function in the context of the entire essay? How are paragraphs 16–44 related to Lutz's statement that "serious doublespeak is highly strategic, and it breeds suspicion, cynicism, distrust, and, ultimately, hostility" (15)?

LANGUAGE IN ACTION

Consider the following 1999 cartoons, Stahler's from the *Cincinnati Post* and Mike Peters's from the *Dayton Daily News*. How does your knowledge of doublespeak inform your understanding of the humor and intent of each cartoon? Discuss.

WRITING SUGGESTIONS

1. (*Writing from Experience*) Think of the ways that you encounter doublespeak everyday, whether in school or at work, or while reading a newspaper or watching television. How does it affect you? What do you suppose the speakers' or writers' motives are in using doublespeak? Using your own experiences and observations, write an essay in which you explore the reasons why people use doublespeak. Before starting to write, you may find it helpful to review your Writing to Discover response for the Lutz essay.

2. (*Writing from Reading*) In his concluding paragraph Lutz states, "If we really believe that we understand [doublespeak] and that such language communicates and promotes clear thought, then the world of *1984* with its control of reality through language is upon us." In an essay, discuss whether or not Lutz is overstating the case and being too pessimistic and whether or not the American public is really unaware of—or apathetic about—how doublespeak manipulates and deceives. Consider also whether or not the American public has reacted to doublespeak with, as Lutz suggests, "suspicion, cynicism, distrust, and, ultimately, hostility."

3. (*Writing from Research*) Using resources in your library or on the Internet, write a paper about the language of funeral directors, stockbrokers, college professors, health-care professionals, or some other occupation of your choice. How pervasive is doublespeak in the occupation you selected? Based on the results of your research, why do you think people with this type of job use such language? Do you find this language troublesome? If so, what can be done to change the situation? If not, why not?

The E Word

CULLEN MURPHY

Cullen Murphy was born in New Rochelle, New York, and grew up in Greenwich, Connecticut. After graduating from Amherst College in 1974, Murphy went to work for both Change, *an education magazine, and the* Wilson Quarterly. *Later he joined the* Atlantic Monthly *and has been the managing editor there since 1985. His books include* Rubbish! *(1992), a study of landfill practices coauthored with William Rathje, and* Just Curious *(1995), a collection of his* Harper's *and* Atlantic Monthly *essays. For over twenty years Murphy has also written the text for the popular comic strip* Prince Valiant, *which his father draws.*

In the following essay, which first appeared in the Atlantic Monthly *in September 1996, Murphy examines Americans' love affair with the euphemism. In fact, euphemisms — pretty or important-sounding names for essentially harsh realities — have become so widespread that Murphy dubs them "the characteristic literary device of our time."*

WRITING TO DISCOVER: *Many Americans believe that nothing is taboo anymore — that anything that can be imagined can be said, filmed, printed, or sent into cyberspace on the World Wide Web. Write down your views on this kind of thinking. Do you think Americans really tell it like it is, or are there subjects that we talk about only in clothed language, if at all?*

> "We are not at war with Egypt. We are in a state of armed conflict."
> —ANTHONY EDEN, *during the Suez Crisis, 1956*

Driving along a highway in southern New Mexico not long ago, I came within the gravitational pull of a truck stop, and was ineluctably drawn in. This was not one of those mom-and-pop "truck stops," so prevalent in the East, where cars outnumber semis and the restaurant has a children's menu. This was the real thing, lit up in the desert darkness like an outpost in Mad Max, visible from six counties. Cars in the parking lot looked like Piper Cubs at O'Hare. It was the kind of place where tough men sit at the counter and call the waitress "doll," which she likes, and order flesh and starch while they smoke, leaning over the counter, a crescent of lower back visible between pants and shirt. Outside, their mounts hungrily lap up petrochemicals.

In a truck stop such as this the aesthetic pinnacle is typically reached in the design of the men's-room condom dispenser, and here I was not disappointed. Taking up nearly one full wall was a kind of Ghent Altarpiece of prophylaxis, each glass panel displaying its own delicately crafted vignette: a yellow sunset through palm trees, a couple strolling lazily along a beach, a herd of galloping white stallions, a flaxen-haired succubus in gauzy silhouette — exquisite examples of late-*novecento* venereal iconography.

Above it hung a sign saying FAMILY PLANNING CENTER.

Robert Burchfield, for many years the editor of *The Oxford English Dictionary*, once observed that "a language without euphemisms would be a defective instrument of communication." By this criterion, at least, contemporary American English cannot be judged defective. All epochs, of course, have employed euphemisms both to downplay and to amplify: to camouflage the forbidden, to dress up the unseemly and the unpleasant, and, like Chaucer's Wife of Bath, to find genteel expression for some earthy fun. Some periods have specialized. The eighteenth century is famous as a time of inventive sexual innuendo and political circumlocution (consult almost any passage in *Gulliver's Travels*). The Victorians were linguistically circumspect not only about sex and the human body but also about money and death. But in the late twentieth century euphemism has achieved what it never achieved before: it has become a fit medium for the expression of just about everything. Putty as it is in the hands of its employer, bereft (unlike irony) of any solid core, euphemism can take on almost any task at all. It is the characteristic literary device of our time — as much a hallmark of the era as were inflated honorifics in fifth-century Rome.

The one thing that all euphemisms have in common is their willingness to show themselves in public — sometimes with audacity. A press release arrived recently from the Fur Information Council of America, and it contained this sentence: "Twice as many animals are killed each year in animal shelters and pounds as are used by the fur industry." The word "partition" was politically unacceptable in the Dayton Agreement, signed by the warring parties in the former Yugoslavia, and so the agreement does not employ it; but what might the term "inter-entity boundary" mean? A spokesperson for the United Nations, asked to explain the routine disappearance of millions of dollars' worth of computers, vehicles, and cash whenever UN forces withdraw from a locale, blamed a phenomenon she called "end-of-mission *tristesse*." 5

Most euphemisms, though, do not call such attention to themselves; we slide right over them. Some weeks ago I decided to spend a day with the euphemism detector set on high, just to see what kinds of things turned up in newspapers and magazines, on radio and television, and in ordinary conversation. Here is part of the harvest: "deer management" for the enlistment of paid sharpshooters; "remedial college skills" for reading; "traffic-calming measures" for speed bumps; "comparative ads" for attack ads; "legacy device" for an obsolete computer; "assistance devices" for hearing aids: "firm," in the parlance of produce merchants, for underripe; "hand-check," in the parlance of basketball players, for shove; "peace enforcement" for combat;

"hard to place" for disturbed; "growth going backwards" for recession (itself a euphemism); "post-verdict response" for riot; "cult favorite" for lowrated; and "gated community" for affluent residential compound with private security. (Imagine a sign outside Windsor Castle 500 years ago: A GATED COMMUNITY.) This is but a modest sample, and I have not included any euphemism ending with "syndrome" or "challenged."

The newest category of euphemism—which takes the idea into unexplored metaphysical territory—is one in which a euphemistic term is invented for a word or idea that actually requires none, the euphemism thereby implicitly back-tainting the original word or idea itself. In its most widespread manifestation this kind of euphemizing takes its form from such locutions for unutterables as "the F word" and, in a racial context, "the N word." Thus, during his race for the presidency against Michael Dukakis, George Bush castigated his opponent for being a liberal by bringing up what he called "the L word." Since then we have had "the O word," referring to orphanages (or, at the other demographic extreme, to old age); "the T word," referring to taxes; "the U word" (unions); "the V word" (vouchers); and "the W word" (welfare). William Safire, who briefly took note of this phenomenon in its infancy, during the 1988 campaign, predicted that it would "probably peter out in a few years, after we go through the alphabet and begin to get confused about what a given letter is supposed to signify." In fact the euphemistic abecedarium is now both complete and several meanings deep, and seems to be evincing considerable staying power. The cheap mass production of E words has apparently proved irresistible.

On balance, are euphemisms bad for us? One school of thought holds that a truly healthy, stable, psychologically mature society would have no need for euphemisms. Those who subscribe to this school would hold further, with George Orwell, that political euphemism "is designed to make lies sound truthful and murder respectable, and to give an appearance of solidity to pure wind." They might add that the emergence of the new genre of faux euphemism is particularly insidious, in that it implies a kind of equivalence among the concepts or terminology represented by letters of the alphabet—as if "the L word" and "the T word" really did belong in the same category as "the N word." There is something to be said for all these points, the last one in particular. I'm surely not alone in observing that the phrase "the N word" has lately come into the mainstream, as the N word itself never could again.

A second school of thought about euphemisms might be called the white-blood-cell school; it holds that yes, an elevated count might well be a sign of mild or serious pathology—but it's also a sign that a natural defense mechanism has kicked in. By and large my sympathies lie with the white-blood-cell school. Although euphemism sets some to spluttering about its deceitfulness, I suspect that few people are really deceived—that, indeed, the transparent motives and awkward semantics only undermine the euphemist's intention. When a nuclear warhead is referred to as "the physics package," when genocide is referred to as "ethnic cleansing," when wife-beating is referred to as "getting physical"—in all these cases the terminology trains a spotlight on the truth.

Philosophers and linguists will argue the matter for years to come. In   10
the meantime, though, it might be useful to begin acquiring a database of euphemisms by monitoring their prevalence in our national life. The model would be the Consumer Price Index.

The Consumer Price Index does not, of course, keep track of inflation by watching trends in the prices of everything. It focuses on a "basket" of major economic goods and services: food, clothing, rent, oil and gas, interest rates, and so on. With euphemisms, too, a handful of big items account for a disproportionate share of all euphemistic activity. Thus we might devise a preliminary formula with a basket of concepts including sex, God, money, politics, social pathology, bodily functions, disease, and death (along with, perhaps, a few minor bellwether indicators such as euphemisms for criminal behavior by juveniles and for lack of achievement in school). Logoplasticians, as those who study euphemisms might be called, would follow the emergence of promising synonyms in all these areas, producing at regular intervals a Semantic Engineering Index, or SEI.

Some might anticipate that in a society like ours the SEI would show gains quarter after quarter. I am not sure that this would happen in the aggregate: a macro-euphemistic view of history shows significant ups and downs over time. But in any event internal shifts would be abundant and revealing. Euphemisms are fragile organisms, surprisingly sensitive to the outside environment. Frequently they come to embody so fully the thing being euphemized that they themselves demand replacement. H. W. Fowler's *Modern English Usage* (Second Edition) shows how "toilet" is but the latest in a series of progressively superseded euphemisms—"water-closet," "latrine," "privy," "jakes"—going back many centuries. (Last year a Methodist singles group, recognizing the danger of euphemistic succession and hoping to stave it off, held a retreat with the theme "Intimacy Is Not a Euphemism for Sex." Good luck.) Some euphemisms eventually attract such knowing derision that their useful life is abbreviated. This was the case, for instance, with the term "revenue enhancement" as a stealthy substitute for "higher taxes." Other euphemisms, such as "custodial engineer" and "sandwich technician," pass from the moment of coinage into a state of ironic suspension without ever experiencing an intermediate condition of utility.

Given the avidity with which professional lexicographers today comb through books and periodicals for evidence of emerging and fading terminology, compiling a Semantic Engineering Index would no doubt be quite simple. And popular acceptance of the idea of "leading euphemistic indicators" would come easily. "The SEI rose three tenths of a point this month, paced by a rise in the T word and public jitters about peace enforcement." I see a cult favorite already.

FOCUSING ON CONTENT

1. According to Murphy, "All epochs . . . have employed euphemisms both to downplay and to amplify: to camouflage the forbidden, to dress up the unseemly and unpleasant, and, like Chaucer's Wife of Bath, to find genteel expression for some earthy fun" (4). Using Murphy's many examples of euphemisms, illustrate each of the functions he mentions. Can you think of any functions that he doesn't mention? Explain.

2. What do you think Murphy means when he says in paragraph 4, "Putty as it is in the hands of its employers, bereft (unlike irony) of any solid core, euphemism can take on almost any task at all." What types of issues tend to attract the use of euphemisms? Why?

3. What is the euphemism in the Fur Information Council of America's statement, "Twice as many animals are killed each year in animal shelters and pounds as are used by the fur industry (5)? Do you think most readers would detect this euphemism? Explain.

4. What, according to Murphy, is "the newest category of euphemism" (7)? How do the euphemisms in this category work? How does the title of Murphy's essay support what he says about such euphemisms?

5. In his discussion of euphemistic succession, Murphy mentions the Methodist singles group that organized a retreat around the theme "Intimacy Is Not a Euphemism for Sex." What are some of the popular euphemisms for *sex?* What do you think the singles group fears if *intimacy* becomes a euphemism for *sex?*

FOCUSING ON WRITING

1. Murphy illustrates his various points about euphemisms with numerous examples, and he takes these examples from a wide range of subject areas. (Glossary: *Examples*) Why do you suppose he uses as many examples as he does? Which ones do you find most effective? Least effective? Explain.

2. In paragraphs 8 and 9, Murphy compares and contrasts the two schools of thought on whether euphemisms are bad for us. What are the key differences between these two views? How does Murphy organize his comparison? (Glossary: *Comparison and Contrast*) What conclusion does he come to?

3. Murphy starts paragraph 8 with a rhetorical question. (Glossary: *Rhetorical Question*) How does this question function in the context of his essay?

4. Murphy introduces the concept of a Semantic Engineering Index in paragraphs 10–13. In your own words, what is the SEI? What is Murphy's tone in these concluding paragraphs? (Glossary: *Tone*) What in his diction leads you to this conclusion?

LANGUAGE IN ACTION

In an article called "Public Doublespeak," Terence Moran presents the following list of recommended language, which school administrators in

Brooklyn gave their elementary school teachers to use when discussing students with their parents.

FOR PARENT INTERVIEWS AND REPORT CARDS

Harsh Expression (Avoid)	Acceptable Expression (Use)
Does all right if pushed	Accomplishes tasks when interest is stimulated.
Too free with fists	Resorts to physical means of winning his point or attracting attention.
Lies (Dishonest)	Shows difficulty in distinguishing between imaginary and factual material.
Cheats	Needs help in learning to adhere to rules and standards of fair play.
Steals	Needs help in learning to respect the property rights of others.
Noisy	Needs to develop quieter habits of communication.
Lazy	Needs ample supervision in order to work well.
Is a bully	Has qualities of leadership but needs help in learning to use them democratically.
Associates with "gangs"	Seems to feel secure only in group situations; needs to develop sense of independence.
Disliked by other children	Needs help in learning to form lasting friendships.

What are your reactions to these recommendations? Why do you suppose the school administrators made up this list? What purpose does such language serve? Do you believe the "acceptable" language belongs in our nation's schools? Why or why not?

WRITING SUGGESTIONS

1. (*Writing from Experience*) In a September 19, 1969, article entitled "The Euphemism: Telling It Like It Isn't" the editors of *Time* say that "despite its swaggering sexual candor, much contemporary speech still hides behind that traditional enemy of plain talk, the euphemism." Do you think this statement is accurate today? Using examples from your own experiences or observations, write an essay in which you agree or disagree with the position taken by the editors of *Time*. Before you start writing, be sure to reread what you wrote in response to the Writing to Discover prompt for this selection.

2. (*Writing from Reading*) Murphy claims in paragraph 9 that "Although euphemism sets some to spluttering about its deceitfulness, I suspect that few people are really deceived—that, indeed, the transparent motives and awkward semantics only undermine the euphemist's intention." Where do you stand on this issue? Are you as optimistic about the minimal influence of euphemisms as Murphy seems to be? Do you and your peers readily pick up on euphemistic usage? If euphemisms haven't worked in the past—haven't changed people's perception of something simply by changing its name—why are they so widespread? Write an essay in which you answer Murphy's question, "On balance, are euphemisms bad for us?" Be sure to consider the following question as well: Do some euphemisms serve worthwhile social purposes?

3. (*Writing from Research*) Select a controversial policy or issue (such as abortion, school choice, welfare, social security, affirmative action, racism, alcohol consumption, fur products, cigarette smoking, war, gun control, school security, or nuclear energy) and study the language used by the various parties in the controversy. Consult resources in your library, on the Internet, and try to do some personal interviews if possible. How much euphemistic usage do you find, and what seems to be its intent? In his book *Crazy Talk, Stupid Talk* (1976), Neil Postman, a professor of media ecology at New York University, boldly says that "Euphemizing is contemptible when a name makes us see something that is not true or diverts our attention from something that is." Is the euphemizing used to discuss the issue you selected contemptible, deceitful, somewhat annoying, or totally harmless? Write an essay in which you discuss and reach some conclusions about the language surrounding your issue.

LANGUAGE IN USE:
Parodies of Jargon and Political Correctness

One of the fascinating aspects of American English is its diversity, and one of the causes of this diversity is the specialized vocabularies of different occupations in the United States. Essayist Russell Baker parodies several varieties of occupational jargon in the first selection, which is taken from his book *Poor Russell's Almanac* (1972). Here Baker provides a report of a conference on Little Miss Muffet, complete with excerpts from the transcript of the experts' discussion.

In the second selection, James Finn Garner provides a contemporary interpretation of the classic "Little Red Riding Hood." This essay is from Garner's 1994 *Politically Correct Bedtime Stories,* a bestselling book that is full of "translations" of stories that make the reader question the benefits of political correctness. Although the success of Garner's book does not necessarily indicate how American society views the issue of political correctness, it certainly points up the large influence political correctness has had on the way we think.

WRITING TO DISCOVER: *What do you think of when you hear the word* parody? *Write your own definition of* parody. *What do you think is an author's purpose in writing a parody? How, if at all, is humor related to parody?*

Little Miss Muffet Conference

RUSSELL BAKER

Born in Virginia in 1925, Russell Baker graduated from Johns Hopkins University in 1947 and began his career as a newspaper reporter with the Baltimore Sun. *He joined the* New York Times *in 1954; after covering national politics for eight years with the* Times' *Washington bureau, he began writing his syndicated "Observer" column, which is now published once a week. In 1979, he was awarded the Pulitzer Prize, journalism's highest award, for his column. Baker's books include* An American in Washington *(1961),* Poor Russell's Almanac *(1972),* So This is Depravity *(1980), and the autobiographical works* Growing Up *(1982), which won a Pulitzer, and* The Good Times *(1989). An anthology entitled* Russell Baker's Book of American Humor *appeared in 1993.*

Little Miss Muffet, as everyone knows, sat on a tuffet eating her curds and whey when along came a spider who sat down beside her and frightened Miss Muffet away. While everyone knows this, the significance of the event had never been analyzed until a conference of thinkers recently brought their special insights to bear upon it. Following are excerpts from the transcript of their discussion:

Sociologist: We are clearly dealing here with a prototypical illustration of a highly tensile social structure's tendency to dis- or perhaps even destructure itself under the pressures created when optimum minimums do not obtain among the disadvantaged. Miss Muffet is nutritionally underprivileged, as evidenced by the subminimal diet of curds and whey upon which she is forced to subsist, while the spider's cultural disadvantage is evidenced by such phenomena as legs exceeding standard norms, odd mating habits, and so forth.

In this instance, spider expectations lead the culturally disadvantaged to assert demands to share the tuffet with the nutritionally underprivileged. Due to a communications failure, Miss Muffet assumes without evidence that the spider will not be satisfied to share her tuffet, but will also insist on eating her curds and perhaps even her whey. Thus, the failure to preestablish selectively optimum norm structures diverts potentially optimal minimums from the expectation levels assumed to . . .

Militarist: Second-strike capability, sir! That's what was lacking. If Miss Muffet had developed a second-strike capability instead of squandering her resources on curds and whey, no spider on earth would have dared launch a first strike capable of carrying him right to the heart of her tuffet. I am confident that Miss Muffet had adequate notice from experts that she could not afford both curds and whey and, at the same time, support an early-spider-warning system. Yet curds alone were not good enough for Miss Muffet. She had to have whey, too. Tuffet security must be the first responsibility of every diner . . .

Book Reviewer: Written on several levels, this searing and sensitive exploration of the arachnid heart illuminates the agony and splendor of Jewish family life with a candor that is at once breathtaking in its simplicity and soul-shattering in its implied ambiguity. Some will doubtless be shocked to see such subjects as tuffets and whey discussed without flinching, but hereafter writers too timid to call a curd a curd will no longer . . .

Editorial Writer: Why has the Government not seen fit to tell the public all it knows about the so-called curds-and-whey affair? It is not enough to suggest that this was merely a random incident involving a lonely spider and a young diner. In today's world, poised as it is on the knife edge of . . .

Psychiatrist: Little Miss Muffet is, of course, neither little nor a miss. These are obviously the self she has created in her own fantasies to escape the reality that she is a gross divorcee whose superego makes it impossible for her to sustain a normal relationship with any man, symbolized by the

5

spider, who, of course, has no existence outside her fantasies. Little Miss Muffet may, in fact, be a man with deeply repressed Oedipal impulses, who sees in the spider the father he would like to kill, and very well may some day unless he admits that what he believes to be a tuffet is, in fact, probably the dining room chandelier, and that the whey he thinks he is eating is, in fact, probably . . .

Flower Child: Like this beautiful kid in on a bad trip, dig? Like . . .

Student Demonstrator: Little Miss Muffet, tuffets, curds, whey, and spiders are what's wrong with education today. They're all irrelevant. Tuffets are irrelevant. Curds are irrelevant. Whey is irrelevant. Meaningful experience! How can you have relevance without meaningful experience? And how can there ever be meaningful experience without understanding? With understanding and meaningfulness and relevance, there can be love and good and deep seriousness and education today will be freed of slavery and Little Miss Muffet, and life will become meaningful and . . .

Child: This is about a little girl who gets scared by a spider.   10

(The child was sent home when the conference broke for lunch. It was agreed that he was too immature to subtract anything from the sum of human understanding.)

Little Red Riding Hood

JAMES FINN GARNER

Writer and performer James Finn Garner grew up in Dearborn, Michigan, and attended an all-boys Catholic high school in Detroit. After receiving his B.A. from the Honors College at the University of Michigan, Garner held a variety of jobs, including baker, warehouse employee, and freelance writer. Politically Correct Bedtime Stories *(1994) arose from a cabaret show Garner hosted in Chicago called Theater of the Bizarre. He credits his performing career with teaching him respect for humor as a medium. As Garner puts it, "Humor is a great way to clean out people's heads; it should scrape your brain like Drano and make you see the world in a new way."*

There once was a young person named Red Riding Hood who lived with her mother on the edge of a large wood. One day her mother asked her to take a basket of fresh fruit and mineral water to her grandmother's house—not because this was womyn's work, mind you, but because the deed was generous and helped engender a feeling of community. Furthermore, her grandmother was *not* sick, but rather was in full physical and mental health and was fully capable of taking care of herself as a mature adult.

So Red Riding Hood set off with her basket through the woods. Many people believed that the forest was a foreboding and dangerous place and never set foot in it. Red Riding Hood, however, was confident enough in her own budding sexuality that such obvious Freudian imagery did not intimidate her.

On the way to Grandma's house, Red Riding Hood was accosted by a wolf, who asked her what was in her basket. She replied, "Some healthful snacks for my grandmother, who is certainly capable of taking care of herself as a mature adult."

The wolf said, "You know, my dear, it isn't safe for a little girl to walk through these woods alone."

Red Riding Hood said, "I find your sexist remark offensive in the extreme, but I will ignore it because of your traditional status as an outcast from society, the stress of which has caused you to develop your own, entirely valid, worldview. Now, if you'll excuse me, I must be on my way." 5

Red Riding Hood walked on along the main path. But, because his status outside society had freed him from slavish adherence to linear, Western-style thought, the wolf knew a quicker route to Grandma's house. He burst into the house and ate Grandma, an entirely valid course of action for a carnivore such as himself. Then, unhampered by rigid, traditionalist notions of what was masculine or feminine, he put on Grandma's nightclothes and crawled into bed.

Red Riding Hood entered the cottage and said, "Grandma, I have brought you some fat-free, sodium-free snacks to salute you in your role of a wise and nurturing matriarch."

From the bed, the wolf said softly, "Come closer, child, so that I might see you."

Red Riding Hood said, "Oh, I forgot you are as optically challenged as a bat. Grandma, what big eyes you have!"

"They have seen much, and forgiven much, my dear." 10

"Grandma, what a big nose you have — only relatively, of course, and certainly attractive in its own way."

"It has smelled much, and forgiven much, my dear."

"Grandma, what big teeth you have!"

The wolf said, "I am happy with *who* I am and *what* I am," and leaped out of bed. He grabbed Red Riding Hood in his claws, intent on devouring her. Red Riding Hood screamed, not out of alarm at the wolf's apparent tendency toward cross-dressing, but because of his willful invasion of her personal space.

Her screams were heard by a passing woodchopper-person (or log- 15 fuel technician, as he preferred to be called). When he burst into the cottage, he saw the melee and tried to intervene. But as he raised his ax, Red Riding Hood and the wolf both stopped.

"And just what do you think you're doing?" asked Red Riding Hood.

The woodchopper-person blinked and tried to answer, but no words came to him.

"Bursting in here like a Neanderthal, trusting your weapon to do your thinking for you!" she exclaimed. "Sexist! Speciesist! How dare you assume that womyn and wolves can't solve their own problems without a man's help!"

When she heard Red Riding Hood's impassioned speech, Grandma jumped out of the wolf's mouth, seized the woodchopper-person's ax, and cut his head off. After this ordeal, Red Riding Hood, Grandma, and the wolf felt a certain commonality of purpose. They decided to set up an alternative household based on mutual respect and cooperation, and they lived together in the woods happily ever after.

WRITING SUGGESTIONS: MAKING CONNECTIONS

1. Specialized vocabularies are often the targets of parodists, who sometimes question the communication value of such language. Write an essay in which you analyze the devices or techniques that Baker and Garner use to parody professional jargon and the language of political correctness.

2. In their parodies of professional jargon and the language of political correctness, Baker and Garner are actually making serious statements about U.S. so-

ciety. What central points about language is each writer making? How does each writer use humor to bolster his views? Write an essay in which you explore the similarities and differences in the main points of each writer. Use examples from Baker's and Garner's essays to support your comparison.

3. Using Baker's and Garner's pieces as models, write your own politically correct version of "Little Miss Muffet" or some other well-known bedtime story. Before beginning to write, think about the points you want to make with your parody and how you will translate these points into the humor of parody.

12

THE LANGUAGE OF PERSUASION: POLITICS AND ADVERTISING

Propaganda: How Not to Be Bamboozled

DONNA WOOLFOLK CROSS

Donna Woolfolk Cross graduated from the University of Pennsylvania in 1969 and went on to receive her M.A. from the University of California, Los Angeles. A professor of English at Onondaga Community College in Syracuse, New York, Cross has written extensively about language that manipulates, including the books Mediaspeak: How Television Makes Up Your Mind *(1981) and* Word Abuse: How the Words We Use Use Us *(1979), which won an award from the National Council of Teachers of English. Her early work as a writer of advertising copy influences her teaching and writing. In an interview she remarked, "I was horrified to discover that first-year college students were completely unaware of—and, therefore, unable to defend themselves against—the most obvious plays of admen and politicians. [. . .] We tend to think of language as something we use; we are much less often aware of the way we are used by language. The only defense is to become wise to the ways of words."*

Although most people are against propaganda in principle, few know exactly what it is and how it works. In the following essay, which first appeared in Speaking of Words: A Language Reader *(1977), Cross takes the mystery out of propaganda. She starts by providing a definition of it, and then she classifies the tricks of the propagandist into thirteen major categories. Cross's essay is chock-full of useful advice on how not to be manipulated by propaganda.*

WRITING TO DISCOVER: *What do you think of when you hear the word* propaganda? *What kinds of people, organizations, or issues do you associate with it? Write about why you think people use propaganda.*

Propaganda. If an opinion poll were taken tomorrow, we can be sure that nearly everyone would be against it because it *sounds* so bad. When we say, "Oh, that's just propaganda," it means, to most people, "That's a pack of lies." But really, propaganda is simply a means of persuasion and so it can be put to work for good causes as well as bad — to persuade people to give to charity, for example, or to love their neighbors, or to stop polluting the environment.

For good or evil, propaganda pervades our daily lives, helping to shape our attitudes on a thousand subjects. Propaganda probably determines the brand of toothpaste you use, the movies you see, the candidates you elect when you get to the polls. Propaganda works by tricking us, by momentarily distracting the eye while the rabbit pops out from beneath the cloth. Propaganda works best with an uncritical audience. Joseph Goebbels, propaganda minister in Nazi Germany, once defined his work as "the conquest of the masses." The masses would not have been conquered, however, if they had known how to challenge and to question, how to make distinctions between propaganda and reasonable argument.

People are bamboozled mainly because they don't recognize propaganda when they see it. They need to be informed about the various devices that can be used to mislead and deceive — about the propagandist's overflowing bag of tricks. The following, then, are some common pitfalls for the unwary.

1. NAME-CALLING

As its title suggests, this device consists of labeling people or ideas with words of bad connotation, literally, "calling them names." Here the propagandist tries to arouse our contempt so we will dismiss the "bad name" person or idea without examining its merits.

Bad names have played a tremendously important role in the history   5
of the world. They have ruined reputations and ended lives, sent people to prison and to war, and just generally made us mad at each other for centuries.

Name-calling can be used against policies, practices, beliefs and ideals, as well as against individuals, groups, races, nations. Name-calling is at work when we hear a candidate for office described as a "foolish idealist" or a "two-faced liar" or when an incumbent's policies are denounced as "reckless," "reactionary," or just plain "stupid." Some of the most effective names a public figure can be called are ones that may not denote anything specific: "Congresswoman Jane Doe is a *bleeding heart!*" (Did she vote for funds to help paraplegics?) or "The senator is a *tool of Washington!*" (Did he happen to agree with the president?) Senator Yakalot uses name-calling when he denounces his opponent's "radical policies" and calls them (and him) "socialist," "pinko," and part of a "heartless plot." He also uses it when he calls cars "puddle-jumpers," "can openers," and "motorized baby buggies."

The point here is that when the propagandist uses name-calling, he doesn't want us to think — merely to react, blindly, unquestioningly. So the best defense against being taken in by name-calling is to stop and ask, "Forgetting the bad name attached to it, what are the merits of the idea itself? What does this name really mean, anyway?"

2. GLITTERING GENERALITIES

Glittering generalities are really name-calling in reverse. Name-calling uses words with bad connotations; glittering generalities are words with good connotations — "virtue words," as the Institute for Propaganda Analysis has called them. The Institute explains that while name-calling tries to get us to *reject* and *condemn* someone or something without examining the evidence, glittering generalities try to get us to *accept* and *agree* without examining the evidence.

We believe in, fight for, live by "virtue words" which we feel deeply about: "justice," "motherhood," "the American way," "our Constitutional rights," "our Christian heritage." These sound good, but when we examine them closely, they turn out to have no specific, definable meaning. They just make us feel good. Senator Yakalot uses glittering generalities when he says, "I stand for all that is good in America, for our American way and our American birthright." But what exactly *is* "good for America"? How can we define our "American birthright"? Just what parts of the American society and culture does "our American way" refer to?

We often make the mistake of assuming we are personally unaffected   10
by glittering generalities. The next time you find yourself assuming that, listen to a political candidate's speech on TV and see how often the use of glittering generalities elicits cheers and applause. That's the danger of propaganda; it *works.* Once again, our defense against it is to ask questions: Forgetting the virtue words attached to it, what are the merits of the idea itself? What does "Americanism" (or "freedom" or "truth") really *mean* here? [. . .]

Both name-calling and glittering generalities work by stirring our emotions in the hope that this will cloud our thinking. Another approach that propaganda uses is to create a distraction, a "red herring," that will make people forget or ignore the real issues. There are several different kinds of "red herrings" that can be used to distract attention.

3. PLAIN-FOLKS APPEAL

"Plain folks" is the device by which a speaker tries to win our confidence and support by appearing to be a person like ourselves—"just one of the plain folks." The plain-folks appeal is at work when candidates go around shaking hands with factory workers, kissing babies in supermarkets, and sampling pasta with Italians, fried chicken with Southerners, bagels and blintzes with Jews. "Now I'm a businessman like yourselves" is a plain-folks appeal, as is "I've been a farm boy all my life." Senator Yakalot tries the plain-folks appeal when he says, "I'm just a small-town boy like you fine people." The use of such expressions once prompted Lyndon Johnson to quip, "Whenever I hear someone say, 'I'm just an old country lawyer,' the first thing I reach for is my wallet to make sure it's still there."

The irrelevancy of the plain-folks appeal is obvious: even if the man *is* "one of us" (which may not be true at all), that doesn't mean that his ideas and programs are sound—or even that he honestly has our best interests at heart. As with glittering generalities, the danger here is that we may mistakenly assume we are immune to this appeal. But propagandists wouldn't use it unless it had been proved to work. You can protect yourself by asking, "Aside from his 'nice guy next door' image, what does this man stand for? Are his ideas and his past record really supportive of my best interests?"

4. *ARGUMENTUM AD POPULUM* (STROKING)

Argumentum ad populum means "argument to the people" or "telling the people what they want to hear." The colloquial term from the Watergate era is "stroking," which conjures up pictures of small animals or children being stroked or soothed with compliments until they come to like the person doing the complimenting—and, by extension, his or her ideas.

We all like to hear nice things about ourselves and the group we be-   15
long to—we like to be liked—so it stands to reason that we will respond warmly to a person who tells us we are "hard-working taxpayers" or "the most generous, free-spirited nation in the world." Politicians tell farmers they are the "backbone of the American economy" and college students that they are the "leaders and policy makers of tomorrow." Commercial advertisers use stroking more insidiously by asking a question which invites a flattering answer: "What kind of a man reads *Playboy?*" (Does he

really drive a Porsche and own $10,000 worth of sound equipment?) Senator Yakalot is stroking his audience when he calls them the "decent law-abiding citizens that are the great pulsing heart and the life blood of this, our beloved country," and when he repeatedly refers to them as "you fine people," "you wonderful folks."

Obviously, the intent here is to sidetrack us from thinking critically about the man and his ideas. Our own good qualities have nothing to do with the issue at hand. Ask yourself, "Apart from the nice things he has to say about me (and my church, my nation, my ethnic group, my neighbors), what does the candidate stand for? Are his or her ideas in my best interests?"

5. *ARGUMENTUM AD HOMINEM*

Argumentum ad hominem means "argument to the man" and that's exactly what it is. When a propagandist uses *argumentum ad hominem*, he wants to distract our attention from the issue under consideration with personal attacks on the people involved. For example, when Lincoln issued the Emancipation Proclamation, some people responded by calling him the "baboon." But Lincoln's long arms and awkward carriage had nothing to do with the merits of the Proclamation or the question of whether or not slavery should be abolished.

Today *argumentum ad hominem* is still widely used and very effective. You may or may not support the Equal Rights Amendment, but you should be sure your judgment is based on the merits of the idea itself, and not the result of someone's denunciation of the people who support the ERA as "fanatics" or "lesbians" or "frustrated old maids." Senator Yakalot is using *argumentum ad hominem* when he dismisses the idea of using smaller automobiles with a reference to the personal appearance of one of its supporters, Congresswoman Doris Schlepp. Refuse to be waylaid by *argumentum ad hominem* and ask, "Do the personal qualities of the person being discussed have anything to do with the issue at hand? Leaving him or her aside, how good is the idea itself?"

6. TRANSFER (GUILT OR GLORY BY ASSOCIATION)

In *argumentum ad hominem*, an attempt is made to associate negative aspects of a person's character or personal appearance with an issue or idea he supports. The transfer device uses this same process of association to make us accept or condemn a given person or idea.

A better name for the transfer device is guilt (or glory) by association. In glory by association, the propagandist tries to transfer the positive feelings of something we love and respect to the group or idea he

20

wants us to accept. "This bill for a new dam is in the best tradition of this country, the land of Lincoln, Jefferson, and Washington," is glory by association at work. Lincoln, Jefferson, and Washington were great leaders that most of us revere and respect, but they have no logical connection to the proposal under consideration—the bill to build a new dam. Senator Yakalot uses glory by association when he says full-sized cars "have always been as American as Mom's apple pie or a Sunday drive in the country."

The process works equally well in reverse, when guilt by association is used to transfer our dislike or disapproval of one idea or group to some other idea or group that the propagandist wants us to reject and condemn. "John Doe says we need to make some changes in the way our government operates; well, that's exactly what the Ku Klux Klan has said, so there's a meeting of great minds!" That's guilt by association for you; there's no logical connection between John Doe and the Ku Klux Klan apart from the one the propagandist is trying to create in our minds. He wants to distract our attention from John Doe and get us thinking (and worrying) about the Ku Klux Klan and its politics of violence. (Of course, there are sometimes legitimate associations between the two things; if John Doe had been a *member* of the Ku Klux Klan, it would be reasonable and fair to draw a connection between the man and his group.) Senator Yakalot tries to trick his audience with guilt by association when he remarks that "the words 'community' and 'communism' look an awful lot alike!" He does it again when he mentions that Mr. Stu Pott "sports a Fidel Castro beard."

How can we learn to spot the transfer device and distinguish between fair and unfair associations? We can teach ourselves to *suspend judgment* until we have answered these questions: "Is there any legitimate connection between the idea under discussion and the thing it is associated with? Leaving the transfer device out of the picture, what are the merits of the idea by itself?"

7. BANDWAGON

Ever hear of the small, ratlike animal called the lemming? Lemmings are arctic rodents with a very odd habit: periodically, for reasons no one entirely knows, they mass together in a large herd and commit suicide by rushing into deep water and drowning themselves. They all run in together, blindly, and not one of them ever seems to stop and ask, "*Why* am I doing this? Is this really what I want to do?" and thus save itself from destruction. Obviously, lemmings are driven to perform their strange mass suicide rites by common instinct. People choose to "follow the herd" for more complex reasons, yet we are still all too often the unwitting victims of the bandwagon appeal.

Essentially, the bandwagon urges us to support an action or an opinion because it is popular—because "everyone else is doing it." This call to "get on the bandwagon" appeals to the strong desire in most of us to be one of the crowd, not to be left out or alone. Advertising makes extensive use of the bandwagon appeal ("join the Pepsi people"), but so do politicians ("Let us join together in this great cause"). Senator Yakalot uses the bandwagon appeal when he says that "More and more citizens are rallying to my cause every day," and asks his audience to "join them—and me—in our fight for America."

One of the ways we can see the bandwagon appeal at work is in the   25
overwhelming success of various fashions and trends which capture the interest (and the money) of thousands of people for a short time, then disappear suddenly and completely. For a year or two in the fifties, every child in North America wanted a coonskin cap so they could be like Davy Crockett; no one wanted to be left out. After that there was the hula-hoop craze that helped to dislocate the hips of thousands of Americans. More recently, what made millions of people rush out to buy their very own "pet rocks"?

The problem here is obvious: just because everyone's doing it doesn't mean that *we* should too. Group approval does not prove that something is true or is worth doing. Large numbers of people have supported actions we now condemn. Just a generation ago, Hitler and Mussolini rose to absolute and catastrophically repressive rule in two of the most sophisticated and cultured countries of Europe. When they came into power they were welled up by massive popular support from millions of people who didn't want to be "left out" at a great historical moment.

Once the mass begins to move—on the bandwagon—it becomes harder and harder to perceive the leader *riding* the bandwagon. So don't be a lemming, rushing blindly on to destruction because "everyone else is doing it." Stop and ask, "Where is this bandwagon headed? Never mind about everybody else, is this what is best for *me?*" [. . .]

As we have seen, propaganda can appeal to us by arousing our emotions or distracting our attention from the real issues at hand. But there's a third way that propaganda can be put to work against us—by the use of faulty logic. This approach is really more insidious than the other two because it gives the appearance of reasonable, fair argument. It is only when we look more closely that the holes in the logical fiber show up. The following are some of the devices that make use of faulty logic to distort and mislead.

8. FAULTY CAUSE AND EFFECT

As the name suggests, this device sets up a cause-and-effect relationship that may not be true. The Latin name for this logical fallacy is *post hoc ergo propter hoc,* which means "after this, therefore because of this." But just because one thing happened after another doesn't mean that one *caused* the other.

An example of false cause-and-effect reasoning is offered by the story   30
(probably invented) of the woman aboard the ship *Titanic*. She woke up

from a nap and, feeling seasick, looked around for a call button to summon the steward to bring her some medication. She finally located a small button on one of the walls of her cabin and pushed it. A split second later, the *Titanic* grazed an iceberg in the terrible crash that was to send the entire ship to its destruction. The woman screamed and said, "Oh, God, what have I done? What have I done?" The humor of that anecdote comes from the absurdity of the woman's assumption that pushing the small red button resulted in the destruction of a ship weighing several hundred tons: "It happened after I pushed it, therefore it must be *because* I pushed it"—*post hoc ergo propter hoc* reasoning. There is, of course, no cause-and-effect relationship there.

The false cause-and-effect fallacy is used very often by political candidates. "After I came to office, the rate of inflation dropped to 6 percent." But did the person do anything to cause the lower rate of inflation or was it the result of other conditions? Would the rate of inflation have dropped anyway, even if he hadn't come to office? Senator Yakalot uses false cause and effect when he says "our forefathers who made this country great never had free hot meal handouts! And look what they did for our country!" He does it again when he concludes that "driving full-sized cars means a better car safety record on our American roads today."

False cause-and-effect reasoning is terribly persuasive because it seems so logical. Its appeal is apparently to experience. We swallowed X product—and the headache went away. We elected Y official and unemployment went down. Many people think, "There *must* be a connection." But causality is an immensely complex phenomenon; you need a good deal of evidence to prove that an event that follows another in time was "therefore" caused by the first event.

Don't be taken in by false cause and effect; be sure to ask, "Is there enough evidence to prove that this cause led to that effect? Could there have been any *other* causes?"

9. FALSE ANALOGY

An analogy is a comparison between two ideas, events, or things. But comparisons can be fairly made only when the things being compared are alike in significant ways. When they are not, false analogy is the result.

A famous example of this is the old proverb "Don't change horses in 35 the middle of a stream," often used as an analogy to convince voters not to change administrations in the middle of a war or other crisis. But the analogy is misleading because there are so many differences between the things compared. In what ways is a war or political crisis like a stream? Is the president or head of state really very much like a horse? And is a nation of millions of people comparable to a man trying to get across a stream? Analogy is false and unfair when it compares two things that have little in common and assumes that they are identical. Senator Yakalot tries to hoodwink his listeners with false analogy when he says, "Trying to take Americans out of the kind of cars they love is as undemocratic as trying to deprive them of the right to vote."

Of course, analogies can be drawn that are reasonable and fair. It would be reasonable, for example, to compare the results of busing in one small Southern city with the possible results in another, *if* the towns have the same kind of history, population, and school policy. We can decide for ourselves whether an analogy is false or fair by asking, "Are the things being compared truly alike in significant ways? Do the differences between them affect the comparison?"

10. BEGGING THE QUESTION

Actually, the name of this device is rather misleading, because it does not appear in the form of a question. Begging the question occurs when, in discussing a questionable or debatable point, a person assumes as already established the very point that he is trying to prove. For example, "No thinking citizen could approve such a completely unacceptable policy as this one." But isn't the question of whether or not the policy *is* acceptable the very point to be established? Senator Yakalot begs the question when he announces that his opponent's plan won't work "because it is unworkable."

We can protect ourselves against this kind of faulty logic by asking, "What is assumed in this statement? Is the assumption reasonable, or does it need more proof?"

11. THE TWO-EXTREMES FALLACY (FALSE DILEMMA)

Linguists have long noted that the English language tends to view reality in sets of two extremes or polar opposites. In English, things are either black or white, tall or short, up or down, front or back, left or right, good or bad, guilty or not guilty. We can ask for a "straightforward yes-or-no answer" to a question, the understanding being that we will not accept or consider anything in between. In fact, reality cannot always be dissected along such strict lines. There may be (usually are) *more* than just two possibilities or extremes to consider. We are often told to "listen to both sides of the argument." But who's to say that every argument has only two sides? Can't there be a third—even a fourth or fifth—point of view?

The two-extremes fallacy is at work in this statement by Lenin, the great Marxist leader: "You cannot eliminate *one* basic assumption, one substantial part of this philosophy of Marxism (it is as if it were a block of steel), without abandoning truth, without falling into the arms of bourgeois- 40 reactionary falsehood." In other words, if we don't agree 100 percent with every premise of Marxism, we must be placed at the opposite end of the political-economic spectrum—for Lenin, "bourgeois-reactionary false-hood." If we are not entirely *with* him, we must be against him; those are the only two possibilities open to us. Of course, this is a logical fallacy; in real life there are any number of political positions one can maintain *between* the two extremes of Marxism and capitalism. Senator Yakalot uses the two-extremes fallacy in the same way as Lenin when he tells his audience that "in this world a man's either for private enterprise or he's for socialism."

One of the most famous examples of the two-extremes fallacy in re-cent history is the slogan, "America: Love it or leave it," with its implicit suggestion that we either accept everything just as it is in America today without complaint—or get out. Again, it should be obvious that there is a whole range of action and belief between those two extremes.

Don't be duped; stop and ask, "Are those really the only two options I can choose from? Are there other alternatives not mentioned that de-serve consideration?"

12. CARD STACKING

Some questions are so multifaceted and complex that no one can make an intelligent decision about them without considering a wide vari-ety of evidence. One selection of facts could make us feel one way and another selection could make us feel just the opposite. Card stacking is a device of propaganda which selects only the facts that support the propa-gandist's point of view, and ignores all the others. For example, a can-didate could be made to look like a legislative dynamo if you say, "Representative McNerd introduced more new bills than any other mem-ber of the Congress," and neglect to mention that most of them were so preposterous that they were laughed off the floor.

Senator Yakalot engages in card stacking when he talks about the proposal to use smaller cars. He talks only about jobs without mention-ing the cost to the taxpayers or the very real—though still denied—threat of depletion of resources. He says he wants to help his countrymen keep their jobs, but doesn't mention that the corporations that offer the jobs will also make large profits. He praises the "American chrome indus-try," overlooking the fact that most chrome is imported. And so on.

The best protection against card stacking is to take the "Yes, but . . ." 45 attitude. This device of propaganda is not untrue, but then again it is not the *whole* truth. So ask yourself, "Is this person leaving something out that I should know about? Is there some other information that should be brought to bear on this question?" [. . .]

So far, we have considered three approaches that the propagandist can use to influence our thinking: appealing to our emotions, distracting our attention, and misleading us with logic that may appear to be reasonable but is in fact faulty and deceiving. But there is a fourth approach that is probably the most common propaganda trick of them all.

13. TESTIMONIAL

The testimonial device consists in having some loved or respected person give a statement of support (testimonial) for a given product or idea. The problem is that the person being quoted may *not* be an expert in the field; in fact, he may know nothing at all about it. Using the name of a man who is skilled and famous in one field to give a testimonial for something in another field is unfair and unreasonable.

Senator Yakalot tries to mislead his audience with testimonial when he tells them that "full-sized cars have been praised by great Americans like John Wayne and Jack Jones, as well as by leading experts on car safety and comfort."

Testimonial is used extensively in TV ads, where it often appears in such bizarre forms as Joe Namath's endorsement of a pantyhose brand. Here, of course, the "authority" giving the testimonial not only is no expert about pantyhose, but obviously stands to gain something (money!) by making the testimonial.

When celebrities endorse a political candidate, they may not be mak-   50
ing money by doing so, but we should still question whether they are in any better position to judge than we ourselves. Too often we are willing to let others we like or respect make our decisions *for us,* while we follow along acquiescently. And this is the purpose of testimonial—to get us to agree and accept *without* stopping to think. Be sure to ask, "Is there any reason to believe that this person (or organization or publication or whatever) has any more knowledge or information than I do on this subject? What does the idea amount to on its own merits, without the benefit of testimonial?"

The cornerstone of democratic society is reliance upon an informed and educated electorate. To be fully effective citizens we need to be able to challenge and to question wisely. A dangerous feeling of indifference toward our political processes exists today. We often abandon our right, our duty, to criticize and evaluate by dismissing *all* politicians as "crooked," *all* new bills and proposals as "just more government bureaucracy." But there are important distinctions to be made, and this kind of apathy can be fatal to democracy.

If we are to be led, let us not be led blindly, but critically, intelligently, with our eyes open. If we are to continue to be a government "by the people," let us become informed about the methods and purposes of propaganda, so we can be the masters, not the slaves of our destiny.

FOCUSING ON CONTENT

1. According to Cross, what is propaganda? Who uses propaganda? Why is it used? (Glossary: *Propaganda*)

2. Why does Cross believe that it is necessary for people in a democratic society to become informed about the methods and practices of propaganda? What is her advice for dealing with propaganda?

3. What is a "red herring," and why do people use this technique?

4. What is "begging the question"? (Glossary: *Logical Fallacies*)

5. What, according to Cross, is the most common propaganda trick? Provide some examples of it from your own experience.

FOCUSING ON WRITING

1. What is Cross's purpose in this essay? (Glossary: *Purpose*)

2. Given her purpose, why is classification an appropriate strategy of development for this essay? (Glossary: *Division and Classification*) In what other kinds of essays might you use this strategy?

3. How does Cross organize the discussion of each propaganda device she includes in her essay? (Glossary: *Organization*)

4. How does Cross use examples in her essay? (Glossary: *Examples*) What do you think of the examples from Senator Yakalot? What, if anything, does this hypothetical senator add to the essay? Which other examples do you find most effective? Least effective? Explain why.

5. In her discussion of the bandwagon appeal (23–28), Cross uses the analogy of the lemmings. How does the analogy work? Why is it not a false analogy? (Glossary: *Analogy*) How do analogies help you, as a writer, explain your subject to readers?

LANGUAGE IN ACTION

At the beginning of her essay, Cross claims that propaganda "can be put to work for good causes as well as bad." Consider the advertisements on pages 537 and 538 for the U.S. Postal Service's breast-cancer-stamp campaign and for the University of Vermont's Direct Service Programs. How would you characterize the appeal of each? What propaganda techniques does each use? Do you ever find appeals such as these objectionable? Why or why not? In what situations do you think it would be acceptable for you to use propaganda devices in your own writing?

WRITING SUGGESTIONS

1. (*Writing from Experience*) Using several of the devices described by Cross, write a piece of propaganda. You may want to persuade your classmates to join a particular campus organization; support a controversial movement or issue; or vote for a particular candidate in an election.

2. (*Writing from Reading*) Cross acknowledges in paragraph 1 that propaganda is "simply a means of persuasion," but she quickly cautions that people need to recognize propaganda and be alert to its potential for misleading or deceiving. Write an essay for your campus newspaper arguing for a "short

Women Helping Battered Women

Summer or Fall Semester

Internships

Join the fight against domestic violence! You will work in a friendly, supportive environment. You will do challenging work for a worthwhile cause. You will have lots of learning opportunities. We need reliable people who are committed to social justice. You will need good communication skills, an open mind, and the ability to work somewhat independently.

We are now accepting Applications.

Internships will be offered in the following programs:

Shelter Services
Hotline Program
Children's Shelter Services
Children's Playgroup Program
Development and Fundraising

Work Study Positions available in all the above programs as well as in the financial and administrative programs.

All interns in Direct Service Programs have to complete the full Volunteer Training. The next trainings will be in May and September 1999. Call now for more information: 658-3131.

---

course" on propaganda recognition at your school. You might want to consider the following questions in your essay: How do propaganda and argumentation differ? Do both always have the same intended effect? What could happen to people who don't recognize or understand propaganda when they encounter it?

3. (*Writing from Research*) Using Cross's list of propaganda devices, write an essay analyzing several newspaper editorials, political speeches, public-service advertising campaigns, or comparable examples of contemporary prose. What did you learn about the people or organizations as a result of your analysis? How were their positions on issues or their purposes expressed? Which propaganda devices did they use? After reading Cross's essay, did you find yourself "buying" the propaganda or recognizing and questioning it? Submit the original editorials, speeches, or advertisements with your essay.

Politics and the English Language

George Orwell

George Orwell (1903–1950), one of the most brilliant social critics of the twentieth century, grew up in England and received a traditional education at Eton. Instead of going on to a university, he joined the civil service and was sent to Burma at the age of nineteen as an assistant superintendent of police. Disillusioned with British imperialism, Orwell resigned in 1929 and began a decade of studying social and political issues firsthand and then writing about them in such works as Down and Out in Paris and London *(1933) and* The Road to Wigan Pier *(1937). His most famous books are* Animal Farm *(1945), a satire of the Russian Revolution, and* 1984 *(1949), a chilling novel set in an imagined totalitarian state of the future.*

In 1984, *the government has imposed on its subjects a simplified language, Newspeak, which is continually revised to give them fewer words with which to express themselves. Words like* terrible, abhorrent, *and* evil, *for example, have been replaced by the single expression* double-plus-ungood. *The way people use language, Orwell maintains, is a result of the way they think as well as an important influence on their thought. This is also the point of his classic essay "Politics and the English Language." Even though it was published in 1946, the essay is as accurate and relevant now as it was more than fifty years ago. Indeed, during the wars in Vietnam, Iraq, and Kosovo, various American officials were still using euphemisms such as* pacification, transfer of population, *and* ethnic cleansing —words and phrases Orwell had exposed as doubletalk. Orwell, however, goes beyond exposé in this essay. He holds up to public view and ridicule some choice examples of political language at its worst, but he also offers a few short and effective rules for those who want to write more clearly.*

WRITING TO DISCOVER: *Have you ever stopped to think about what clichéd phrases like* toe the line, walk the straight and narrow, sharp as a tack, *and* fly off the handle *really mean? Jot down the clichés that you find yourself or hear others using. What images come to mind when you hear them? Are these words and phrases effective expressions, or are they a kind of verbal shorthand that we automatically depend on? Explain.*

Most people who bother with the matter at all would admit that the English language is in a bad way, but it is generally assumed that we cannot by conscious action do anything about it. Our civilization is decadent and our language—so the argument runs—must inevitably share in the general collapse. It follows that any struggle against the abuse of language is a sentimental archaism, like preferring candles to electric light or hansom cabs to aeroplanes. Underneath this lies the half-conscious belief that language is a natural growth and not an instrument which we shape for our own purposes.

Now, it is clear that the decline of a language must ultimately have political and economic causes: it is not due simply to the bad influence of this or that individual writer. But an effect can become a cause, reinforcing the original cause and producing the same effect in an intensified form, and so on indefinitely. A man may take to drink because he feels himself to be a failure, and then fail all the more completely because he drinks. It is rather the same thing that is happening to the English language. It becomes ugly and inaccurate because our thoughts are foolish, but the slovenliness of our language makes it easier for us to have foolish thoughts. The point is that the process is reversible. Modern English, especially written English, is full of bad habits which spread by imitation and which can be avoided if one is willing to take the necessary trouble. If one gets rid of these habits one can think more clearly, and to think clearly is a necessary first step towards political regeneration: so that the fight against bad English is not frivolous and is not the exclusive concern of professional writers. I will come back to this presently, and I hope that by that time the meaning of what I have said here will have become clearer. Meanwhile here are five specimens of the English language as it is now habitually written.

These five passages have not been picked out because they are especially bad—I could have quoted far worse if I had chosen—but because they illustrate various of the mental vices from which we now suffer. They are a little below the average, but are fairly representative samples. I number them so that I can refer back to them when necessary:

(1) I am not, indeed, sure whether it is not true to say that the Milton who once seemed not unlike a seventeenth-century Shelley had not become, out of an experience ever more bitter in each year, more alien [*sic*] to the founder of that Jesuit sect which nothing could induce him to tolerate.
    Professor Harold Laski (Essay in *Freedom of Expression*)

(2) Above all, we cannot play ducks and drakes with a native battery of idioms which prescribes such egregious collocations of vocables as the Basic *put up with* for *tolerate* or *put at a loss* for *bewilder*.
    Professor Lancelot Hogben (*Interglossa*)

(3) On the one side we have the free personality: by definition it is not neurotic, for it has neither conflict nor dream. Its desires, such as they are, are transparent, for they are just what institutional approval keeps in the forefront of consciousness; another institutional pattern would alter their number and intensity; there is little in them that is natural, irre-

ducible, or culturally dangerous. But *on the other side,* the social bond it-self is nothing but the mutual reflection of these self-secure integrities. Recall the definition of love. Is not this the very picture of a small acade-mic? Where is there a place in this hall of mirrors for either personality or fraternity?

Essay on psychology in Politics (New York)

(4) All the "best people" from the gentlemen's clubs, and all the frantic fascist captains, united in common hatred of Socialism and bestial hor-ror of the rising tide of the mass revolutionary movement, have turned to acts of provocation, to foul incendiarism, to medieval legends of poi-soned wells, to legalize their own destruction of proletarian organiza-tions, and rouse the agitated petty-bourgeoisie to chauvinistic fervor on behalf of the fight against the revolutionary way out of the crisis.

Communist pamphlet

(5) If a new spirit *is* to be infused into this old country, there is one thorny and contentious reform which must be tackled, and that is the humanization and galvanization of the B.B.C. Timidity here will be-speak canker and atrophy of the soul. The heart of Britain may be sound and of strong beat, for instance, but the British lion's roar at present is like that of Bottom in Shakespeare's *Midsummer Night's Dream*—as gentle as any sucking dove. A virile new Britain cannot continue indefi-nitely to be traduced in the eyes or rather ears, of the world by the effete languors of Langham Place, brazenly masquerading as "standard En-glish." When the voice of Britain is heard at nine o'clock, better far and infinitely less ludicrous to hear aitches honestly dropped than the pre-sent priggish, inflated, inhibited, school-ma'amish arch braying of blameless bashful mewing maidens!

Letter in Tribune

Each of these passages has faults of its own, but, quite apart from avoidable ugliness, two qualities are common to all of them. The first is staleness of imagery; the other is lack of precision. The writer either has a meaning and cannot express it, or he inadvertently says something else, or he is almost indifferent as to whether his words mean anything or not. This mixture of vagueness and sheer incompetence is the most marked characteristic of modern English prose, and especially of any kind of po-litical writing. As soon as certain topics are raised, the concrete melts into the abstract and no one seems able to think of turns of speech that are not hackneyed: prose consists less and less of *words* chosen for the sake of their meaning, and more and more of *phrases* tacked together like the sections of a prefabricated henhouse. I list below, with notes and ex-amples, various of the tricks by means of which the work of prose-construction is habitually dodged:

DYING METAPHORS. A newly invented metaphor assists thought by   5
evoking a visual image, while on the other hand a metaphor which is technically "dead" (e.g., *iron resolution*) has in effect reverted to being an

ordinary word and can generally be used without loss of vividness. But in between these two classes there is a huge dump of worn-out metaphors which have lost all evocative power and are merely used because they save people the trouble of inventing phrases for themselves. Examples are: *ring the changes on, take up the cudgels for, toe the line, ride roughshod over, stand shoulder to shoulder with, play into the hands of, no axe to grind, grist to the mill, fishing in troubled waters, on the order of the day, Achilles' heel, swan song, hotbed.* Many of these are used without knowledge of their meaning (what is a "rift," for instance?), and incompatible metaphors are frequently mixed, a sure sign that the writer is not interested in what he is saying. Some metaphors now current have been twisted out of their original meaning without those who use them even being aware of the fact. For example, *toe the line* is sometimes written *tow the line*. Another example is the *hammer and the anvil*, now always used with the implication that the anvil gets the worst of it. In real life it is always the anvil that breaks the hammer, never the other way about: a writer who stopped to think what he was saying would be aware of this, and would avoid perverting the original phrase.

OPERATORS OR VERBAL FALSE LIMBS.   These save the trouble of picking out appropriate verbs and nouns, and at the same time pad each sentence with extra syllables which give it an appearance of symmetry. Characteristic phrases are *render inoperative, militate against, make contact with, be subjected to, give rise to, give grounds for, have the effect of, play a leading part (role) in, make itself felt, take effect, exhibit a tendency to, serve the purpose of,* etc., etc. The keynote is the elimination of simple verbs. Instead of being a single word, such as *break, stop, spoil, mend, kill,* a verb becomes a *phrase,* made up of a noun or adjective tacked on to some general-purpose verb such as *prove, serve, form, play, render.* In addition, the passive voice is wherever possible used in preference to the active, and noun constructions are used instead of gerunds (*by examination of* instead of *by examining*). The range of verbs is further cut down by means of the *-ize* and *de-* formations, and the banal statements are given an appearance of profundity by means of the *not un-* formation. Simple conjunctions and prepositions are replaced by such phrases as *with respect to, having regard to, the fact that, by dint of, in view of, in the interests of, on the hypothesis that;* and the ends of sentences are saved from anticlimax by such resounding common-places as *greatly to be desired, cannot be left out of account, a development to be expected in the near future, deserving of serious consideration, brought to a satisfactory conclusion,* and so on and so forth.

PRETENTIOUS DICTION.   Words like *phenomenon, element, individual* (as noun), *objective, categorical, effective, virtual, basic, primary, promote, constitute, exhibit, exploit, utilize, eliminate, liquidate,* are used to dress up simple statements and give an air of scientific impartiality to biased judgments. Adjectives like *epoch-making, epic, historic, unforgettable, triumphant, age-old, inevitable, inexorable, veritable,* are used to dignify the sordid processes of international politics, while writing that aims at glorifying war usually takes on an archaic color, its characteristic words being: *realm, throne, chariot, mailed fist, trident, sword, shield, buckler, banner, jackboot, clarion.* Foreign words and expressions such as *cul de sac, ancien régime, deus ex machina, mutatis mutandis, status quo, gleichschaltung, weltanschauung,* are used to give an air of culture and elegance. Except for the useful abbreviations *i.e., e.g.,* and *etc.,* there is no real need for any of the hundreds of foreign phrases now current in English. Bad writers, and especially scientific, political, and sociological writers, are nearly always haunted by the notion that Latin or Greek words are grander than Saxon ones, and unnecessary words like *expedite, ameliorate, predict, extraneous, deracinated, clandestine, subaqueous* and hundreds of others constantly gain ground from their Anglo-Saxon opposite numbers.[1] The jargon peculiar to Marxist writing (*hyena, hangman, cannibal, petty bourgeois, these gentry, lacquey, flunkey, mad dog, White Guard,* etc.) consists largely of words and phrases translated from Russian, German, or French; but the normal way of coining a new word is to use a Latin or Greek root with the appropriate affix and, where necessary, the *-ize* formation. It is often easier to make up words of this kind (*deregionalize, impermissible, extramarital, non-fragmentary* and so forth) than to think up the English words that will cover one's meaning. The result, in general, is an increase in slovenliness and vagueness.

MEANINGLESS WORDS.   In certain kinds of writing, particularly in art criticism and literary criticism, it is normal to come across long passages which are almost completely lacking in meaning.[2] Words like *romantic, plastic, values, human, dead, sentimental, natural, vitality,* as used in art criticism, are strictly meaningless, in the sense that they not only do not point to any discoverable object, but are hardly ever expected to do so by the reader. When one critic writes, "The outstanding feature of Mr. X's work is its living quality," while another writes, "The

---

1. An interesting illustration of this is the way in which the English flower names which were in use till very recently are being ousted by Greek ones, *snapdragon* becoming *antirrhinum, forget-me-not* becoming *myosotis,* etc. It is hard to see any practical reason for this change of fashion: it is probably due to an instinctive turning-away from the more homely word and a vague feeling that the Greek word is scientific.

2. Example: "Comfort's catholicity of perception and image, strangely Whitmanesque in range, almost the exact opposite in esthetic compulsion, continues to evoke that trembling atmospheric accumulative hinting at a cruel, an inexorably serene timelessness. . . . Wrey Gardiner scores by aiming at simple bull's-eyes with precision. Only they are not so simple, and through this contented sadness runs more than the surface bittersweet of resignation." (*Poetry Quarterly*)

immediately striking thing about Mr. X's work is its peculiar deadness," the reader accepts this as a simple difference of opinion. If words like *black* and *white* were involved, instead of the jargon words *dead* and *living,* he would see at once that language was being used in an improper way. Many political words are similarly abused. The word *Fascism* has now no meaning except in so far as it signifies "something not desirable." The words *democracy, freedom, patriotic, realistic, justice,* have each of them several different meanings which cannot be reconciled with one another. In the case of a word like *democracy,* not only is there no agreed definition, but the attempt to make one is resisted from all sides. It is almost universally felt that when we call a country democratic we are praising it: consequently the defenders of every kind of regime claim that it is a democracy, and fear that they might have to stop using the word if it were tied down to any one meaning. Words of this kind are often used in a consciously dishonest way. That is, the person who uses them has his own private definition, but allows his hearer to think he means something quite different. Statements like, *Marshal Pétain was a true patriot, The Soviet Press is the freest in the world, the Catholic Church is opposed to persecution,* are almost always made with intent to deceive. Other words used in variable meanings, in most cases more or less dishonestly, are: *class, totalitarian, science, progressive, reactionary, bourgeois, equality.*

Now that I have made this catalogue of swindles and perversions, let me give another example of the kind of writing that they lead to. This time it must of its nature be an imaginary one. I am going to translate a passage of good English into modern English of the worst sort. Here is a well-known verse from *Ecclesiastes:*

> I returned and saw under the sun, that the race is not to the swift, nor the battle to the strong, neither yet bread to the wise, nor yet riches to men of understanding, nor yet favour to men of skill; but time and chance happeneth to them all.

Here it is in modern English: 10

> Objective consideration of contemporary phenomena compels the conclusion that success or failure in competitive activities exhibits no tendency to be commensurate with innate capacity, but that a considerable element of the unpredictable must invariably be taken into account.

This is a parody, but a very gross one. Exhibit (3), above, for instance, contains several patches of the same kind of English. It will be seen that I have not made a full translation. The beginning and ending of the sentence follow the original meaning fairly closely, but in the middle the concrete illustrations — race, battle, bread — dissolve into the vague phrase "success or failure in competitive activities." This had to be so, because no modern writer of the kind I am discussing — no one capable of using phrases like "objective consideration of contemporary phenomena"—would ever tabulate his thoughts in that precise and detailed way. The whole tendency of modern prose is away from concreteness. Now analyze these two sentences a little more closely. The first contains forty-nine words but only sixty syllables, and all its words are those of everyday life. The second contains thirty-eight words of ninety syllables: eighteen of its words are from Latin roots, and one from Greek. The first sentence contains six vivid images, and only one phrase ("time and chance") that could be called vague. The second contains not a single fresh, arresting phrase, and in spite of its ninety syllables it gives only a shortened version of the meaning contained in the first. Yet without a doubt it is the second kind of sentence that is gaining ground in modern English. I do not want to exaggerate. This kind of writing is not yet universal, and outcrops of simplicity will occur here and there in the worst-written page. Still, if you or I were told to write a few lines on the uncertainty of human fortunes, we should probably come much nearer to my imaginary sentence than to the one from *Ecclesiastes*.

As I have tried to show, modern writing at its worst does not consist in picking out words for the sake of their meaning and inventing images in order to make the meaning clearer. It consists in gumming together long strips of words which have already been set in order by someone else, and making the results presentable by sheer humbug. The attraction of this way of writing is that it is easy. It is easier—even quicker, once you have the habit—to say *In my opinion it is not an unjustifiable assumption that* than to say *I think*. If you use ready-made phrases, you not only don't have to hunt about for words; you also don't have to bother with the rhythms of your sentences, since these phrases are generally so arranged as to be more or less euphonious. When you are composing in a hurry—when you are dictating to a stenographer, for instance, or making a public speech—it is natural to fall into a pretentious, Latinized style. Tags like *a consideration which we should do well to bear in mind* or *a conclusion to which all of us would readily assent* will save many a sentence from coming down with a bump. By using stale metaphors, similes, and idioms, you save much mental effort, at the cost of leaving your meaning vague, not only for your reader but for yourself. This is the significance of mixed metaphors. The sole aim of a metaphor is to call up a visual image. When these images clash—as in *The Fascist octopus has sung its swan song, the jackboot is thrown into the melting pot*—it can be taken as certain that the writer is not seeing a mental image of the objects he is naming; in other words he is not really thinking. Look again at the examples I gave at the beginning of this essay. Professor Laski (1) uses five negatives in fifty-three words. One of these is superfluous, making nonsense of the whole passage, and in addition there is the slip *alien* for *akin,* making further nonsense, and several avoidable pieces of clumsiness which increase the general vagueness. Professor Hogben (2) plays ducks and drakes with a battery which is able to write prescriptions, and, while disapproving of the everyday phrase *put up with*, is unwilling to look *egregious* up in the dictionary and see what it means; (3), if one takes an uncharitable attitude towards it, is simply meaningless: probably one could work out its intended meaning by reading the whole of the article in which it occurs. In (4), the writer knows more or less what he wants to say, but an accumulation of stale phrases chokes him like tea leaves blocking a sink. In (5), words and meaning have almost parted company. People who write in this manner usually have a general emotional meaning—they dislike one thing and want to express solidarity with another—but they are not interested in the detail of what they are saying. A scrupulous writer, in every sentence that he writes, will ask himself at least four questions, thus: What am I trying to say? What words will express it? What image or idiom will make it clearer? Is this image fresh enough to have an effect? And he will probably ask himself two more: Could I put it more shortly? Have I said anything that is avoidably ugly? But you are not obliged to go to all this trouble. You can shirk it by simply throwing your mind open and letting the ready-made phrases come crowding in. They will construct your sentences for you—even think your thoughts for you, to a certain extent—and at need they will perform the important service of partially concealing your meaning even from yourself. It is at this point that the special connection between politics and the debasement of language becomes clear.

In our time it is broadly true that political writing is bad writing. Where it is not true, it will generally be found that the writer is some kind of rebel, expressing his private opinions and not a "party line." Orthodoxy, of whatever color, seems to demand a lifeless, imitative style. The political dialects to be found in pamphlets, leading articles, manifestos, White Papers, and the speeches of under-secretaries do, of course, vary from party to party, but they are all alike in that one almost never finds in them a fresh, vivid, homemade turn of speech. When one watches some tired hack on the platform mechanically repeating the familiar phrases—*bestial atrocities, iron heel, bloodstained tyranny, free peoples of the world, stand shoulder to shoulder*—one often has a curious feeling that one is not watching a live human being but some kind of dummy: a feeling which suddenly becomes stronger at moments when the light catches the speaker's spectacles and turns them into blank discs which seem to have no eyes behind them. And this is not altogether fanciful. A speaker who uses that kind of phraseology has gone some distance towards turning himself into a machine. The appropriate noises are coming out of his larynx, but his brain is not involved as it would be if he were choosing his words for himself. If the speech he is making is one that he is accustomed to make over and over again, he may be almost unconscious of what he is saying, as one is when one utters the responses in church. And this reduced state of consciousness, if not indispensable, is at any rate favorable to political conformity.

In our time, political speech and writing are largely the defense of the indefensible. Things like the continuance of British rule in India, the Russian purges and deportations, the dropping of the atom bombs on Japan, can indeed be defended, but only by arguments which are too brutal for most people to face, and which do not square with the professed aims of political parties. Thus political language has to consist largely of euphemism, question-begging, and sheer cloudy vagueness. Defenseless villages are bombarded from the air, the inhabitants driven out into the countryside, the cattle machine-gunned, the huts set on fire with incendiary bullets: this is called *pacification*. Millions of peasants are robbed of their farms and sent trudging along the roads with no more than they can carry: this is called *transfer of population* or *rectification of frontiers*. People are imprisoned for years without trial, or shot in the back of the neck or sent to die of scurvy in Arctic lumber camps: this is called *elimination of unreliable elements*. Such phraseology is needed if one wants to name things without calling up mental pictures of them. Consider for instance some comfortable English professor defending Russian totalitarianism. He cannot say outright, "I believe in killing off your opponents when you can get good results by doing so." Probably, therefore, he will say something like this:

> While freely conceding that the Soviet régime exhibits certain features which the humanitarian may be inclined to deplore, we must, I think, agree that a certain curtailment of the right to political opposition is an unavoidable concomitant of transitional periods, and that the rigors which the Russian people have been called upon to undergo have been amply justified in the sphere of concrete achievement.

The inflated style is itself a kind of euphemism. A mass of Latin words falls upon the facts like soft snow, blurring the outlines and covering up all the details. The great enemy of clear language is insincerity. When there is a gap between one's real and one's declared aims, one turns as it were instinctively to long words and exhausted idioms, like a cuttlefish squirting out ink. In our age there is no such thing as "keeping out of politics." All issues are political issues, and politics itself is a mass of lies, evasions, folly, hatred, and schizophrenia. When the general atmosphere is bad, language must suffer. I should expect to find—this is a guess which I have not sufficient knowledge to verify—that the German, Russian, and Italian languages have all deteriorated in the last ten or fifteen years, as a result of dictatorship.

But if thought corrupts language, language can also corrupt thought. A bad usage can spread by tradition and imitation, even among people who should and do know better. The debased language that I have been discussing is in some ways very convenient. Phrases like *a not unjustifiable assumption, leaves much to be desired, would serve no good purpose, a consideration which we should do well to bear in mind,* are a continuous

15

temptation, a packet of aspirins always at one's elbow. Look back through this essay, and for certain you will find that I have again and again committed the very faults I am protesting against. By this morning's post I have received a pamphlet dealing with conditions in Germany. The author tells me that he "felt impelled' to write it. I open it at random, and here is almost the first sentence that I see: "[The Allies] have an opportunity not only of achieving a radical transformation of Germany's social and political structure in such a way as to avoid a nationalistic reaction in Germany itself, but at the same time of laying the foundations of a cooperative and unified Europe." You see, he "feels impelled" to write—feels, presumably, that he has something new to say—and yet his words, like cavalry horses answering the bugle, group themselves automatically into the familiar dreary pattern. The invasion of one's mind by ready-made phrases *(lay the foundations, achieve a radical transformation)* can only be prevented if one is constantly on guard against them, and every such phrase anesthetizes a portion of one's brain.

I said earlier that the decadence of our language is probably curable. Those who deny this would argue, if they produced an argument at all, that language merely reflects existing social conditions, and that we cannot influence its development by any direct tinkering with words and constructions. So far as the general tone or spirit of a language goes, this may be true, but it is not true in detail. Silly words and expressions have often disappeared, not through any evolutionary process but owing to the conscious action of a minority. Two recent examples were *explore every avenue* and *leave no stone unturned,* which were killed by the jeers of a few journalists. There is a long list of fly-blown metaphors which could similarly be got rid of if enough people would interest themselves in the job; and it should also be possible to laugh the *not un-* formation out of existence,[3] to reduce the amount of Latin and Greek in the average sentence, to drive out foreign phrases and strayed scientific words, and, in general, to make pretentiousness unfashionable. But all these are minor points. The defense of the English language implies more than this, and perhaps it is best to start by saying what it does *not* imply.

To begin with, it has nothing to do with archaism, with the salvaging of obsolete words and turns of speech, or with the setting up of a "standard English" which must never be departed from. On the contrary, it is especially concerned with the scrapping of every word or idiom which has outworn its usefulness. It has nothing to do with correct grammar and syntax, which are of no importance so long as one makes one's meaning clear, or with the avoidance of Americanisms, or with having what is called a "good prose style." On the other hand it is not concerned with

3. One can cure oneself of the *not un-* formation by memorizing this sentence: *A not unblack dog was chasing a not unsmall rabbit across a not ungreen field.*

fake simplicity and the attempt to make written English colloquial. Nor does it even imply in every case preferring the Saxon word to the Latin one, though it does imply using the fewest and shortest words that will cover one's meaning. What is above all needed is to let the meaning choose the word, and not the other way about. In prose, the worst thing one can do with words is to surrender to them. When you think of a concrete object, you think wordlessly, and then, if you want to describe the thing you have been visualizing you probably hunt about till you find the exact words that seem to fit it. When you think of something abstract you are more inclined to use words from the start, and unless you make a conscious effort to prevent it, the existing dialect will come rushing in and do the job for you, at the expense of blurring or even changing your meaning. Probably it is better to put off using words as long as possible and get one's meaning as clear as one can through pictures or sensations. Afterwards one can choose—not simply *accept*—the phrases that will best cover the meaning, and then switch round and decide what impression one's words are likely to make on another person. This last effort of the mind cuts out all stale or mixed images, all prefabricated phrases, needless repetitions, and humbug and vagueness generally. But one can often be in doubt about the effect of a word or a phrase, and one needs rules that one can rely on when instinct fails. I think the following rules will cover most cases:

1. Never use a metaphor, simile, or other figure of speech which you are used to seeing in print.
2. Never use a long word where a short one will do.
3. If it is possible to cut a word out, always cut it out.
4. Never use the passive where you can use the active.
5. Never use a foreign phrase, a scientific word, or a jargon word if you can think of an everyday English equivalent.
6. Break any of these rules sooner than say anything outright barbarous.

These rules sound elementary, and so they are, but they demand a deep change of attitude in anyone who has grown used to writing in the style now fashionable. One could keep all of them and still write bad English, but one could not write the kind of stuff that I quoted in those five specimens at the beginning of this article.

I have not here been considering the literary use of language, but merely language as an instrument for expressing and not for concealing or preventing thought. Stuart Chase and others have come near to claiming that all abstract words are meaningless, and have used this as a pretext for advocating a kind of political quietism. Since you don't know what Fascism is, how can you struggle against Fascism? One need not swallow such absurdities as this, but one ought to recognize that the present political chaos is connected with the decay of language, and that one can probably bring about some improvement by starting at the verbal end. If

you simplify your English, you are freed from the worst follies of orthodoxy. You cannot speak any of the necessary dialects, and when you make
a stupid remark its stupidity will be obvious, even to yourself. Political
language — and with variations this is true of all political parties, from
Conservatives to Anarchists — is designed to make lies sound truthful and
murder respectable, and to give an appearance of solidity to pure wind.
One cannot change this all in a moment, but one can at least change
one's own habits, and from time to time one can even, if one jeers loudly
enough, send some worn-out and useless phrase — some *jackboot,*
Achilles' heel, hotbed, melting pot, acid test, veritable inferno or other lump
of verbal refuse — into the dustbin where it belongs.

FOCUSING ON CONTENT

1. In your own words, summarize Orwell's argument in this essay. (Glossary:
   Argument) Do you agree or disagree with him? Explain why.

2. Grammarians and usage experts have long objected to mixed metaphors (for
   example, "Politicians who have their heads in the sand are leading the country over the precipice") because they are inaccurate. For Orwell, a mixed
   metaphor is symptomatic of a greater problem (12). What is that problem?

3. What are dead and dying metaphors (5)? (Glossary: *Figures of Speech*) Why
   do dying metaphors disgust Orwell?

4. According to Orwell, what are four important prewriting questions scrupulous writers ask themselves (12)?

5. Orwell says that one of the evils of political language is question-begging
   (14). What does he mean? Why, according to Orwell, has political language
   deteriorated? Do you agree with him that "the decadence of our language is
   probably curable" (17)? Why or why not?

FOCUSING ON WRITING

1. What is Orwell's thesis, and where is it presented? (Glossary: *Thesis*)

2. How would you describe Orwell's purpose in this essay? (Glossary: *Purpose*)
   What in the essay leads you to this conclusion?

3. For what audience do you think Orwell wrote this essay? (Glossary: *Audience*) What in his diction leads you to this conclusion? (Glossary: *Diction*)

4. Following are some of the metaphors and similes that Orwell uses in his
   essay. (Glossary: *Figures of Speech*) Explain how each one works and comment on its effectiveness.

   a. "Prose consists less and less of *words* chosen for the sake of their meaning,
      and more and more of *phrases* tacked together like the sections of a pre-
      fabricated hen-house" (4).

    b. "But in between these two classes there is a huge dump of worn-out metaphors which have lost all evocative power" (5).

    c. "The writer knows more or less what he wants to say, but an accumulation of stale phrases chokes him like tea leaves blocking a sink" (12).

    d. "A mass of Latin words falls upon the facts like soft snow, blurring the outlines and covering up all the details" (15).

    e. "When there is a gap between one's real and one's declared aims, one turns [. . .] instinctively to long words and exhausted idioms, like a cuttlefish squiring out ink" (15).

    f. "He [. . .] feels, presumably, that he has something new to say—and yet his words, like cavalry horses answering the bugle, group themselves automatically into the familiar dreary pattern" (16).

5. In this essay, Orwell moves from negative arguments (criticisms) to positive ones (proposals). Where does he make the transition from criticisms to proposals? (Glossary: *Transitions*) Do you find the organization of his argument effective? (Glossary: *Organization*) Explain.

LANGUAGE IN ACTION

Read Robert Yoakum's "Everyspeech," a parody that first appeared in the *New York Times* in November 1994. Yoakum was a speechwriter for John F. Kennedy's successful 1960 campaign. As you read, identify the features of political speech that are the butt of Yoakum's humor. Does he point out the same language abuses that Orwell criticizes in his essay? What propaganda devices does Yoakum use (see Cross's essay on pp. 525–35)?

EVERYSPEECH

    Ladies and gentlemen. I am delighted to see so many friends from the Third Congressional District. And what better site for some straight talk than at this greatest of all state fairs, where ribbons reward American individual enterprise, whether for the biggest beets or the best bull?

    Speaking of bull, my opponent has said some mighty dishonest things about me. But what can you expect from a typical politician? I want to address some fundamental issues that set me apart from my opponent and his failed party—the party of gutlessness and gridlock.

    The American people are ready for straight talk, although don't count on the press to report it straight. The press, like my opponent, has no respect for the public.

    This democracy must return to its roots or it will perish, and its roots are you—the honest, hard-working, God-fearing people who made this the greatest nation on earth. Yes, we have problems. But what problems would not be solved if the press and politicians had faith in the people?

    Take crime, for example. Rampant, brutal crime. My rival in this race believes that redemption and rehabilitation are the answer to the lawlessness that is tearing our society apart.

Well, if R and R is what you want for those robbers and rapists, don't vote for me. If pampering the punks is what you want, vote for my opponent.

Do I believe in the death penalty? You bet! Do I believe in three strikes and you're out? No, I believe in *two* strikes and you're out! I believe in three strikes and you're *dead!*

You can count on me to crack down on crime, but I won't ignore the other big C word: character. Character made out nation great. Character, and respect for family values. A belief in children and parents. In brothers and sisters and grandparents.

Oh, sure, that sounds corny. Those cynical inside-the-Beltway journalists will ridicule me tomorrow, but I would rather be guilty of a corny defense of family values than of coddling criminals.

While I'm making myself unpopular with the press and a lot of politicians, I might as well alienate even more Washington wimps by telling you frankly how I feel about taxes. I'm against them! Not just in an election year, like my adversary, but every year!

I'm in favor of slashing wasteful welfare, which is where a lot of your hard-earned tax dollars go. The American people have said "enough!" to welfare, but inside the Beltway they don't give a hoot about the industrious folks I see before me today. They're too busy with their cocktail parties, diplomatic functions, and society balls.

My opponent loves those affairs, but I'd rather be with my good friends here than with those fork-tongued lawyers, cookie-pushing State Department fops, and high-priced lobbyists. I promise that when elected, my main office will be right here in the Third District. My branch office will be in D.C. And I promise you this: I shall serve only two terms and then return to live with the folks I love.

So on Nov. 8, if you want someone with an independent mind and the courage to change — *to change back to good old American values* — if you've had enough and want someone tough, vote for me. Thank you, and God bless America.

WRITING SUGGESTIONS

1. (*Writing from Experience*) Orwell claims that political speech is filled with such words as *patriotism, democracy, freedom, realistic,* and *justice,* words that have "several different meanings which cannot be reconciled with one another" (8). Why is Orwell so uneasy about these words? What do these words mean to you? How do your meanings differ from those of others? For example, someone who has served in the armed forces, been a political prisoner, or served as a juror may attach distinct meanings to the words *patriotism, freedom,* or *justice.* In a brief essay, recount an experience that gave you real insight into the meaning of one of these words or a word similar to them.

2. (*Writing from Reading*) Collect examples of bureaucratic writing on your campus. How would you characterize most of this writing? Who on your campus seems to be more prone to manipulative language — college administrators, student leaders, or faculty? Use information from the Orwell and Cross articles in this chapter and from Birk and Birk's article "Selection,

Slanting, and Charged Language" (pp. 397–405) to analyze the writing you collect. Then write an essay in which you assess the health of the English language at your school.

3. (*Writing from Research*) Psychiatrist Thomas Szasz writes extensively about the language of oppression. In his book *The Second Sin* (1973), Szasz states that "he who first seizes the word imposes reality on the other: he who defines thus dominates and lives; and he who is defined is subjugated and may be killed." This struggle for definition is particularly apparent in the history of Native Americans and Africans. Carefully read the following two texts, the first by Chiksika, elder brother of the Shawnee chief Tecumseh, and the second by Nelson Mandela.

> When a white man kills an Indian in a fair fight it is called honorable, but when an Indian kills a white man in a fair fight it is called murder. When a white army battles Indians and wins it is called a great victory, but if they lose it is called a massacre and bigger armies are raised. If the Indian flees before the advance of such armies, when he tries to return he finds that white men are living where he lived. If he tries to fight off such armies, he is killed and the land is taken anyway. When an Indian is killed it is a great loss which leaves a gap in our people and a sorrow in our heart; when a white is killed, three or four others step up to take his place and there is no end to it. The white man seeks to conquer nature, to bend it to his will, and to use it wastefully until it is all gone and then he simply moves on, leaving the waste behind him and looking for new places to take. The whole white race is a monster who is always hungry and what he eats is land.
>
> —CHIKSIKA, *to Tecumseh, March 19, 1779*

> Our deepest fear is not that we are inadequate. Our deepest fear is that we are powerful beyond measure. It is our light, not our darkness that most frightens us. We ask ourselves: Who am I to be brilliant, gorgeous, talented, and fabulous? Actually, who are you not to be? You are a child of the universe. Your playing small doesn't serve the world. There's nothing enlightened about shrinking so that other people won't feel insecure about you. We were born to make manifest the glory of God that is within us. It is not just in some of us; it is in everyone. And as we let our own light shine, we unconsciously give other people permission to do the same. As we are liberated from our own fear, our presence automatically liberates others.
>
> —NELSON MANDELA

Using one or both of these passages as a starting point, research in your library or on the Internet the ways language has been used to subjugate or oppress people or the ways it can be used to liberate. Then write an essay in which you demonstrate the power of political language to resolve or worsen conflicts among peoples of the world.

LANGUAGE IN USE:
Three Political Texts

Political speech saturates the American media. In daily newspapers and on the evening news we are bombarded with fiery sound bites and seemingly spontaneous one-liners—all presented as though they contained an entire argument or philosophy.

Politicians are savvy about the time constraints on news media, and their speechwriters make sure that long speeches have at least a few headline-grabbing quotes that might win them wide, albeit brief, coverage. Nevertheless, sustained political oratory is hardly a lost art in the United States. As you read the following political texts by three of this country's former presidents, you will discover the oratorical traditions from which contemporary political speech springs. Note how these presidents from very different eras, speaking in widely divergent contexts, rely on similar rhetorical techniques and strategies to give their texts depth and resonance. Thomas Jefferson, writing on behalf of a fledgling nation, uses the measured prose and sound logic of the eighteenth century to make America's case to the world in the Declaration of Independence. Some eighty years later, Abraham Lincoln, in his "Second Inaugural Address," uses tempered, well chosen words as he calls on Americans to "bind up the nation's wounds" and "achieve and cherish a just and lasting peace." Finally, John F. Kennedy, in his "Inaugural Address" in 1961, ushers in a new era when he challenges Americans and the citizens of the world to work together for peace and the freedom of all peoples.

> **WRITING TO DISCOVER:** *What do you think when you hear the terms political speech or political rhetoric? Do these terms have positive or negative connotations for you? Write about how political speeches differ, if at all, from other kinds of speeches you've heard or read. Does anything set political speeches apart from other forms of public address?*

The Declaration of Independence

THOMAS JEFFERSON

President, governor, statesman, lawyer, architect, philosopher, and writer, Thomas Jefferson was one of the most important figures in the early history of the United States. Born in 1743 in Albemarle County, Virginia, Jefferson attended the College of William and Mary and was admitted to law practice in 1767. With political insight, vision, and rhetorical skill, he drafted the Declaration of Independence in 1776, America's justification of its revolution to the world. Although the Declaration was revised by Franklin, Adams, and the Continental Congress, the document retains, in its logical and direct style, the unmistakable qualities of Jefferson's prose. Jefferson retired in 1809, after two terms as president, to Monticello, a home he had designed and helped build. He died on July 4, 1826, the fiftieth anniversary of the signing of the Declaration of Independence.

When in the course of human events, it becomes necessary for one people to dissolve the political bands which have connected them with another, and to assume among the Powers of the earth, the separate and equal station to which the Laws of Nature and of Nature's God entitle them, a decent respect to the opinions of mankind requires that they should declare the causes which impel them to the separation.

We hold these truths to be self-evident, that all men are created equal, that they are endowed by their Creator with certain unalienable Rights, that among these are Life, Liberty and the pursuit of Happiness. That to secure these rights, Governments are instituted among Men deriving their just powers from the consent of the governed. That whenever any Form of Government becomes destructive of these ends, it is the Right of the People to alter or to abolish it, and to institute new Government, laying its foundation on such principles and organizing its powers in such form, as to them shall seem most likely to effect their Safety and Happiness. Prudence, indeed, will dictate that Governments long established should not be changed for light and transient causes; and accordingly all experience hath shown, that mankind are more disposed to suffer, while evils are sufferable, than to right themselves by abolishing the forms to which they are accustomed. But when a long train of abuses and usurpations pursuing invariably the same Object evinces a design to reduce them under absolute Despotism, it is their right, it is their duty, to throw off such government, and to provide new Guards for their future security. Such has been the patient sufferance of these Colonies; and such is now the necessity which constrains them to alter their former Systems of Government. The history of the present King of Great Britain is a history of repeated injuries and usurpations, all having in direct object the establishment of an absolute Tyranny over these States. To prove this, let Facts be submitted to a candid world.

He has refused his Assent to Laws, the most wholesome and necessary for the public good.

He has forbidden his Governors to pass Laws of immediate and pressing importance, unless suspended in their operation till his Assent should be obtained; and when so suspended, he has utterly neglected to attend to them.

He has refused to pass other Laws for the accommodation of large districts of people, unless those people would relinquish the right of

5

Representation in the Legislature, a right inestimable to them and formidable to tyrants only.

He has called together legislative bodies at places unusual, uncomfortable, and distant from the depository of their Public Records, for the sole purpose of fatiguing them into compliance with his measures.

He has dissolved Representative Houses repeatedly, for opposing with manly firmness his invasions on the rights of the people.

He has refused for a long time, after such dissolutions, to cause others to be elected; whereby the Legislative Powers, incapable of Annihilation, have returned to the People at large for their exercise; the State remaining in the mean time exposed to all the dangers of invasion from without, and convulsions within.

He has endeavoured to prevent the population of these States; for that purpose obstructing the Laws of Naturalization of Foreigners; refusing to pass others to encourage their migration hither, and raising the conditions of new Appropriations of Lands.

He has obstructed the Administration of Justice, by refusing his Assent to Laws for establishing Judiciary Powers.   10

He has made Judges dependent on his Will alone, for the tenure of their offices, and the amount and payment of their salaries.

He has erected a multitude of New Offices, and sent hither swarms of Officers to harass our People, and eat out their substance.

He has kept among us, in time of peace, Standing Armies without the Consent of our Legislature.

He has affected to render the Military independent of and superior to the Civil Power.

He has combined with others to subject us to jurisdictions foreign to   15
our constitution, and unacknowledged by our laws; giving his Assent to their acts of pretended Legislation:

For quartering large bodies of armed troops among us:

For protecting them, by a mock Trial, from Punishment for any Murders which they should commit on the Inhabitants of these States:

For cutting off our Trade with all parts of the world:

For imposing Taxes on us without our Consent:

For depriving us in many cases, of the benefits of Trial by Jury: 20

For transporting us beyond Seas to be tried for pretended offenses:

For abolishing the free System of English Laws in a Neighbouring Province, establishing therein an Arbitrary government, and enlarging its boundaries so as to render it at once an example and fit instrument for introducing the same absolute rules into these Colonies:

For taking away our Charters, abolishing our most valuable Laws, and altering fundamentally the Forms of our Governments:

For suspending our own Legislatures, and declaring themselves invested with Power to legislate for us in all cases whatsoever.

He has abdicated Government here, by declaring us out of his Pro-   25
tection and waging War against us.

He has plundered our seas, ravaged our Coasts, burnt our towns and
destroyed the Lives of our people.

He is at this time transporting large Armies of foreign Mercenaries to
compleat works of death, desolation and tyranny, already begun with circumstances of Cruelty & perfidy scarcely paralleled in the most barbarous
ages, and totally unworthy the Head of a civilized nation.

He has constrained our fellow Citizens taken Captive on the high
Seas to bear Arms against their Country, to become the executioners of
their friends and Brethren, or to fall themselves by their Hands.

He has excited domestic insurrections amongst us, and has endeavoured to bring on the inhabitants of our frontiers, the merciless Indian
Savages, whose known rule of warfare, is an undistinguished destruction
of all ages, sexes and conditions.

In every stage of these Oppressions We Have Petitioned for Redress in   30
the most humble terms: Our repeated petitions have been answered only by
repeated injury. A Prince, whose character is thus marked by every act
which may define a Tyrant, is unfit to be the ruler of a free People.

Nor have We been wanting in attention to our British brethren. We
have warned them from time to time of attempts by their legislature to
extend an unwarrantable jurisdiction over us. We have reminded them of
the circumstances of our emigration and settlement here. We have appealed to their native justice and magnanimity and we have conjured
them by the ties of our common kindred to disavow these usurpations,
which would inevitably interrupt our connections and correspondence.
They too have been deaf to the voice of justice and of consanguinity. We
must, therefore acquiesce in the necessity, which denounces our Separation, and hold them, as we hold the rest of mankind, Enemies in War, in
Peace Friends.

We, therefore, the Representatives of the United States of America,
in General Congress, Assembled, appealing to the Supreme Judge of the
world for the rectitude of our intentions, do, in the Name, and by Au-
thority of the good People of these Colonies, solemnly publish and declare, That these United Colonies are, and of Right ought to be Free and
Independent States; that they are Absolved from all Allegiance to the
British Crown, and that all political connection between them and the
State of Great Britain, is and ought to be totally dissolved; and that as
Free and Independent States, they have full power to levy War, conclude
Peace, contract Alliances, establish Commerce, and to do all other Acts
and Things which Independent States may of right do. And for the sup-
port of this Declaration, with a firm reliance on the protection of Divine
Providence, we mutually pledge to each other our lives, our Fortunes and
our sacred Honor.

Second Inaugural Address

ABRAHAM LINCOLN

Born in Kentucky in 1809, Abraham Lincoln grew up in poverty in southwestern Indiana and taught himself to read and write. As a young man, he moved to Springfield, Illinois. While studying the law, he held a variety of jobs, including postmaster, surveyor, and manager of a mill. Lincoln was well loved in his frontier town for his honesty, strength, and sincerity. Elected to the Illinois state legislature in 1834, he served four successive terms, followed later by one term in Congress. As sixteenth president of the United States, Lincoln worked hard to preserve the Union during the Civil War. Having long regarded slavery as an evil injustice, he issued the "Emancipation Proclamation" in 1862. His famous "Gettysburg Address" galvanized support for the Union in 1863. The "Second Inaugural Address" was delivered in February 1865 as the war was drawing to a close. John Wilkes Booth assassinated Lincoln on April 14, 1865.

Fellow Countrymen:

At this second appearing to take the oath of the presidential office there is less occasion for an extended address than there was at the first. Then a statement, somewhat in detail, of a course to be pursued seemed fitting and proper. Now, at the expiration of four years, during which public declarations have been constantly called forth on every point and phase of the great contest which still absorbs the attention and engrosses the energies of the nation, little that is new could be presented. The progress of our arms, upon which all else chiefly depends, is as well known to the public as to myself, and it is, I trust, reasonably satisfactory and encouraging to all. With high hope for the future, no prediction in regard to it is ventured.

On the occasion corresponding to this four years ago all thoughts were anxiously directed to an impending civil war. All dreaded it; all sought to avert it. While the inaugural address was being delivered from this place, devoted altogether to *saving* the Union without war, insurgent agents were in the city seeking to *destroy* it without war—seeking to dissolve the Union and divide effects by negotiation. Both parties deprecated war, but one of them would *make* war rather than let the nation survive, and the other would *accept* war rather than let it perish, and the war came.

One-eighth of the whole population were colored slaves, not distributed generally over the Union, but localized in the southern part of it. These slaves constituted a peculiar and powerful interest. All knew that this interest was somehow the cause of war. To strengthen, perpetuate, and extend this interest was the object for which the insurgents would rend the Union even by war, while the government claimed no right to do more than to restrict the territorial enlargement of it. Neither party expected for the war the magnitude or the duration which it has already attained. Neither anticipated that the *cause* of the conflict might cease with or even before the conflict itself should cease. Each looked for an easier triumph, and a result less fundamental and astounding. Both read the same Bible and pray to the same God, and each invokes his aid against the other. It may seem strange than any men should dare to ask a just God's assistance in wringing their bread from the sweat of other men's faces, but let us judge not, that we be not judged. The prayers of both could not be answered. That of neither has been answered fully. The Almighty has his own purposes. "Woe unto the world because of offenses; for it must needs be that offenses come, but woe to that man by whom the offense cometh." If we shall suppose that American slavery is one of those offenses which, in the providence of God, must needs come, but which, having continued through his appointed time, he now wills to remove, and that he gives to both North and South this terrible war as the woe due to those by whom the offense came, shall we discern therein any departure from those divine attributes which the believers in a living God always ascribe to him? Fondly do we hope, fervently do we pray, that this mighty scourge of war may speedily pass away. Yet, if God wills that it continue until all the wealth piled by the bondsman's two hundred and fifty years of unrequited toil shall be sunk, and until every drop of blood drawn with the lash shall be paid by another drawn with the sword, as was said three thousand years ago, so still it must be said "the judgments of the Lord are true and righteous altogether."

With malice toward none, with charity for all, with firmness in the right as God gives us to see the right, let us strive on to finish the work we are in, to bind up the nation's wounds, to care for him who shall have borne the battle and for his widow and his orphan, to do all which may achieve and cherish a just and lasting peace among ourselves and with all nations. 5

Inaugural Address

John F. Kennedy

*John Fitzgerald Kennedy was born in Boston in 1917 and gradu-
ated from Harvard University in 1940. In that same year, his first
book* Why England Slept, *based on his senior thesis, became a best-
seller. After serving in the Navy during World War II and barely
escaping death, Kennedy was elected to the U.S. House of Representatives and later the Senate by the people of Massachusetts. His book*
Profiles in Courage *(1956) was awarded a Pulitzer Prize. In
1960, the American people elected Kennedy the thirty-fifth president of the United States. The youngest man ever to serve in that
office, Kennedy was known both for the youthful and hopeful image
he brought to the White House and for the eloquence of his speeches.
In his "Inaugural Address," Kennedy uses powerful rhetoric to
urge people to become involved in the work of their country and to
join the fight against the spread of communism. Kennedy was assassinated in Dallas, Texas, on November 22, 1963.*

Vice President Johnson, Mr. Speaker, Mr. Chief Justice, President
Eisenhower, Vice President Nixon, President Truman, Reverend Clergy,
fellow citizens:

We observe today not a victory of party but a celebration of freedom—
symbolizing an end as well as a beginning—signifying renewal as well as
change. For I have sworn before you and Almighty God the same solemn
oath our forbears prescribed nearly a century and three-quarters ago.

The world is very different now. For man holds in his mortal hands the
power to abolish all forms of human poverty and all forms of human life.
And yet the same revolutionary beliefs for which our forebears fought are
still at issue around the globe—the belief that the rights of man come not
from the generosity of the state but from the hand of God.

We dare not forget today that we are the heirs of that first revolution.
Let the word go forth from this time and place, to friend and foe alike,
that the torch has been passed to a new generation of Americans—born
in this century, tempered by war, disciplined by a hard and bitter peace,
proud of our ancient heritage—and unwilling to witness or permit the
slow undoing of those human rights to which this nation has always been
committed, and to which we are committed today at home and around
the world.

Let every nation know, whether it wishes us well or ill, that we shall   5
pay any price, bear any burden, meet any hardship, support any friend,
oppose any foe to assure the survival and the success of liberty.

This much we pledge—and more.

To those old allies whose cultural and spiritual origins we share, we pledge the loyalty of faithful friends. United there is little we cannot do in a host of cooperative ventures. Divided there is little we can do—for we dare not meet a powerful challenge at odds and split asunder.

To those new states whom we welcome to the ranks of the free, we pledge our word that one form of colonial control shall not have passed away merely to be replaced by a far more iron tyranny. We shall not always expect to find them supporting our view. But we shall always hope to find them strongly supporting their own freedom—and to remember that, in the past, those who foolishly sought power by riding the back of the tiger ended up inside.

To those people in the huts and villages of half the globe struggling to break the bonds of mass misery, we pledge our best efforts to help them help themselves, for whatever period is required—not because the communists may be doing it, not because we seek their votes, but because it is right. If a free society cannot help the many who are poor, it cannot save the few who are rich.

To our sister republics south of the border, we offer a special pledge—   10
to convert our good words into good deeds—in a new alliance for progress—to assist free men and free governments in casting off the chains of poverty. But this peaceful revolution of hope cannot become the prey of hostile powers. Let all our neighbors know that we shall join with them to oppose aggression or subversion anywhere in the Americas. And let every other power know that this Hemisphere intends to remain the master of its own house.

To that world assembly of sovereign states, the United Nations, our last best hope in an age where the instruments of war have far outpaced the instruments of peace, we renew our pledge of support—to prevent it from becoming merely a forum for invective—to strengthen its shield of the new and the weak—and to enlarge the area in which its writ may run.

Finally, to those nations who would make themselves our adversary, we offer not a pledge but a request: that both sides begin anew the quest for peace, before the dark powers of destruction unleashed by science engulf all humanity in planned or accidental self-destruction.

We dare not tempt them with weakness. For only when our arms are sufficient beyond doubt can we be certain beyond doubt that they will never be employed.

But neither can two great and powerful groups of nations take comfort from our present course—both sides overburdened by the cost of modern weapons, both rightly alarmed by the steady spread of the deadly atom, yet both racing to alter that uncertain balance of terror that stays the hand of mankind's final war.

So let us begin anew—remembering on both sides that civility is not   15
a sign of weakness, and sincerity is always subject to proof. Let us never negotiate out of fear. But let us never fear to negotiate.

Let both sides explore what problems unite us instead of belaboring those problems which divide us.

Let both sides, for the first time, formulate serious and precise proposals for the inspection and control of arms—and bring the absolute power to destroy other nations under the absolute control of all nations.

Let both sides seek to invoke the wonders of science instead of its terrors. Together let us explore the stars, conquer the deserts, eradicate disease, tap the ocean depths, and encourage the arts and commerce.

Let both sides unite to heed in all corners of the earth the command of Isaiah—to "undo the heavy burdens . . . (and) let the oppressed go free."

And if a beachhead of cooperation may push back the jungle of suspicion, let both sides join in creating a new endeavor, not a new balance of power, but a new world of law, where the strong are just and the weak secure and the peace preserved. 20

All this will not be finished in the first one hundred days. Nor will it be finished in the first one thousand days, nor in the life of this Administration, nor even perhaps in our lifetime on this planet. But let us begin.

In your hands, my fellow citizens, more than mine, will rest the final success or failure of our course. Since this country was founded, each generation of Americans has been summoned to give testimony to its national loyalty. The graves of young Americans who answered the call to service surround the globe.

Now the trumpet summons us again—not as a call to bear arms, though arms we need—not as a call to battle, though embattled we are—but a call to bear the burden of a long twilight struggle, year in and year out, "rejoicing in hope, patient in tribulation"—a struggle against the common enemies of man: tyranny, poverty, disease, and war itself.

Can we forge against these enemies a grand and global alliance, North and South, East and West, that can assure a more fruitful life for all mankind? Will you join in that historic effort?

In the long history of the world, only a few generations have been granted the role of defending freedom in its hour of maximum danger. I do not shrink from this responsibility—I welcome it. I do not believe that any of us would exchange places with any other people or any other generation. The energy, the faith, the devotion which we bring to this endeavor will light our country and all who serve it—and the glow from that fire can truly light the world. 25

And so, my fellow Americans: ask not what your country can do for you—ask what you can do for your country.

My fellow citizens of the world: ask not what America will do for you, but what together we can do for the freedom of man.

Finally, whether you are citizens of America or citizens of the world, ask of us here the same high standards of strength and sacrifice which we ask of you. With a good conscience our only sure reward, with history the final judge of our deeds, let us go forth to lead the land we love, asking His blessing and His help, but knowing that here on earth God's work must truly be our own.

WRITING SUGGESTIONS: MAKING CONNECTIONS

1. Many political texts such as the ones by Jefferson, Lincoln, and Kennedy in this section and those by Martin Luther King Jr. and Sojourner Truth in Chapter 8 (p. 307)—outlast the occasion for which they were written. Why do you think this is so? In an essay, discuss the language and thought in several of these texts. What specific qualities seem to give these texts their power? Consider the writers' diction and figures of speech as well as their appeals to the emotions of their audience.

2. In "Politics and the English Language" (pp. 539–50), George Orwell claims political speech is filled with "meaningless words" such as *patriotism, democracy,* and *freedom.* Why does Orwell consider these words meaningless? Review the speeches by Lincoln, Kennedy, King (pp. 302–06), and Truth (p. 307), looking for words to which Orwell would object. How does each speaker define the words in question? In an essay, discuss any differences you find in the four speakers' use of certain political words and what you think each leader hoped to gain by using these words the way he or she did. Or, assess Orwell's claim in light of the way these speakers use such words.

3. Write an essay in which you support the following claim made by presidential speechwriter Peggy Noonan in her book *What I Saw at the Revolution:* "Speeches are important because they are one of the great constants of our political history. [. . .] They count. They more than count, they shape what happens." To back up your ideas, use examples from at least three of the texts you have read (Jefferson, Lincoln, Kennedy, King, and Truth). You may want to consult more recent political texts as well.

4. With the possible exception of the Declaration of Independence, no document of American history is as famous as Lincoln's speech dedicating the national cemetery at Gettysburg on November 19, 1863. Since then, millions of Americans have memorized the speech, and countless others have quoted it or imitated its rhetoric for their own purposes. Following is the text of Lincoln's speech.

> Four score and seven years ago our fathers brought forth on this continent, a new nation, conceived in Liberty, and dedicated to the proposition that all men are created equal.
>
> Now we are engaged in a great civil war, testing whether that nation or any nation so conceived and so dedicated, can long endure. We are met on a great battlefield of that war. We have come to dedicate a portion of that field, as a final resting place for those who here gave their lives that that nation might live. It is altogether fitting and proper that we should do this.
>
> But, in a larger sense, we can not dedicate—we can not consecrate—we can not hallow—this ground. The brave men, living and dead, who struggled here, have consecrated it, far above our poor power to add or detract. The world will little note, nor long remember what we say here, but it can never forget what they did here. It is for us the living, rather, to be dedicated here to the unfinished work which they who fought here have thus far so nobly advanced. It is rather for us to be here dedicated to the great task remaining before us—that from these

honored dead we take increased devotion to that cause for which they gave the last full measure of devotion—that we here highly resolve that these dead shall not have died in vain—that this nation, under God, shall have a new birth of freedom—and that government of the people, by the people, for the people, shall not perish from the earth.

Write an essay in which you analyze Lincoln's diction in the "Gettysburg Address." Explore how his diction is calculated to achieve a tone appropriate both for his subject and the occasion and to have a certain effect on listeners and readers. You may wish to compare Lincoln's diction and style here to his diction and style in the "Second Inaugural Address" or to other political texts.

The Hard Sell: Advertising in America

BILL BRYSON

Bill Bryson, an American journalist, lives in England and writes for National Geographic. *His work regularly appears in the* New York Times, *the* Washington Post, Esquire, Granta, *and* GQ. *Bryson's interest in language is reflected in his books* Neither Here Nor There *(1992),* The Mother Tongue *(1990), and* A Dictionary of Troublesome Words *(1987).*

The following essay is a chapter in Bryson's Made in America: An Informal History of the English Language in the United States *(1994). In it, he provides a historical perspective on advertising and explores some of the trends that have appeared over the years. It may surprise many people to learn that advertising as we know it is a modern invention, spanning only about a century. During that time, however, the influence of advertisements has grown so much that they now shape the way we see the world.*

WRITING TO DISCOVER: *Reactions to advertising vary, but most people would say that ads are a necessary evil and that they ignore them whenever possible. Yet advertising is a multibillion-dollar industry, which is financed by what we buy and sell. Think about some recent TV shows you've watched or newspapers you've read. Jot down the names of the products you saw advertised. Do you buy any of these products? Write about the influences, if any, advertising seems to have on the way you spend your money.*

In 1885, a young man named George Eastman formed the Eastman Dry Plate and Film Company in Rochester, New York. It was rather a bold thing to do. Aged just thirty-one, Eastman was a junior clerk in a bank on a comfortable but modest salary of $15 a week. He had no background in business. But he was passionately devoted to photography and had become increasingly gripped with the conviction that anyone who could develop a simple, untechnical camera, as opposed to the cumbersome, outsized, fussily complex contrivances then on the market, stood to make a fortune.

Eastman worked tirelessly for three years to perfect his invention, supporting himself in the meantime by making dry plates for commercial photographers, and in June 1888 produced a camera that was positively dazzling in its simplicity: a plain black box just six and a half inches long by three and a quarter inches wide, with a button on the side and a key for advancing the film. Eastman called his device the *Detective Camera*. Detectives were all the thing—Sherlock Holmes was just taking off with American readers—and the name implied that it was so small and simple that it could be used unnoticed, as a detective might.

The camera had no viewfinder and no way of focusing. The *photographer* or *photographist* (it took a while for the first word to become the established one) simply held the camera in front of him, pressed a button on the side, and hoped for the best. Each roll took a hundred pictures. When the roll was fully exposed, the anxious owner sent the entire camera to Rochester for developing. Eventually he received the camera back, freshly loaded with film, and—assuming all had gone well—one hundred small circular pictures, two and a half inches in diameter.

Often all didn't go well. The film Eastman used at first was made of paper, which tore easily and had to be carefully stripped of its emulsion before the exposures could be developed. It wasn't until the invention of celluloid roll film by a sixty-five-year-old Episcopal minister named Hannibal Goodwin in Newark, New Jersey—this truly was the age of the amateur inventor—that amateur photography became a reliable undertaking. Goodwin didn't call his invention *film* but *photographic pellicule,* and, as was usual, spent years fighting costly legal battles with Eastman without ever securing the recognition or financial payoff he deserved—though eventually, years after Goodwin's death, Eastman was ordered to pay $5 million to the company that inherited the patent.

In September 1888, Eastman changed the name of the camera to *Kodak*—an odd choice, since it was meaningless, and in 1888 no one gave meaningless names to products, especially successful products. Since British patent applications at the time demanded a full explanation of trade and brand names, we know how Eastman arrived at his inspired name. He crisply summarized his reasoning in his patent application: "First. It is short. Second. It is not capable of mispronunciation. Third. It does not resemble anything in the art and cannot be associated with anything in the art except the Kodak." Four years later the whole enterprise was renamed the Eastman Kodak Company.

Despite the considerable expense involved—a Kodak camera sold for $25, and each roll of film cost $10, including developing—by 1895, over 100,000 Kodaks had been sold and Eastman was a seriously wealthy man. A lifelong bachelor, he lived with his mother in a thirty-seven-room mansion with twelve bathrooms. Soon people everywhere were talking about snapshots, originally a British shooting term for a hastily executed shot. Its photographic sense was coined by the English astronomer Sir John Herschel, who also gave the world the terms *positive* and *negative* in their photographic senses.

From the outset, Eastman developed three crucial strategies that have been the hallmarks of virtually every successful consumer goods

5

company since. First, he went for the mass market, reasoning that it was better to make a little money each from a lot of people rather than a lot of money from a few. He also showed a tireless, obsessive dedication to making his products better and cheaper. In the 1890s, such an approach was widely perceived as insane. If you had a successful product you milked it for all it was worth. If competitors came along with something better, you bought them out or tried to squash them with lengthy patent fights or other bullying tactics. What you certainly did not do was create new products that made your existing lines obsolescent. Eastman did. Throughout the late 1890s, Kodak introduced a series of increasingly cheaper, niftier cameras—the Bull's Eye model of 1896, which cost just $12, and the famous slimline Folding Pocket Kodak of 1898, before finally in 1900 producing his eureka model: the little box Brownie, priced at just $1 and with film at 15 cents a reel (though with only six exposures per reel).

Above all, what set Eastman apart was the breathtaking lavishness of his advertising. In 1899 alone, he spent $750,000, an unheard-of sum, on advertising. Moreover, it was *good* advertising: crisp, catchy, reassuringly trustworthy. "You press the button—we do the rest" ran the company's first slogan, thus making a virtue of its shortcomings. Never mind that you couldn't load or unload the film yourself. Kodak would do it for you. In 1905, it followed with another classic slogan: "If It Isn't an Eastman, It Isn't a Kodak."

Kodak's success did not escape other businessmen, who also began to see virtue in the idea of steady product refinement and improvement. AT&T and Westinghouse, among others, set up research laboratories with the idea of creating a stream of new products, even at the risk of displacing old ones. Above all, everyone everywhere began to advertise.

Advertising was already a well-established phenomenon by the turn   10 of the twentieth century. Newspapers had begun carrying ads as far back as the early 1700s, and magazines soon followed. (Benjamin Franklin has the distinction of having run the first magazine ad, seeking the whereabouts of a runaway slave, in 1741.) By 1850, the country had its first *advertising agency,* the American Newspaper Advertising Agency, though its function was to buy advertising space rather than come up with creative campaigns. The first advertising agency in the modern sense was N. W. Ayer & Sons of Philadelphia, established in 1869. *To advertise* originally carried the sense of to broadcast or disseminate news. Thus a nineteenth-century newspaper that called itself the *Advertiser* meant that it had lots of news, not lots of ads. By the early 1800s the term had been stretched to accommodate the idea of spreading the news of the availability of certain goods or services. A newspaper notice that read "Jos. Parker, Hatter" was essentially announcing that if anyone was in the market for hats, Jos. Parker had them. In the sense of persuading members of the public to acquire items they might not otherwise think of buying—

items they didn't know they needed—advertising is a phenomenon of the modern age.

By the 1890s, advertising was appearing everywhere—in newspapers and magazines, on *billboards* (an Americanism dating from 1850), on the sides of buildings, on passing streetcars, on paper bags, even on matchbooks, which were invented in 1892 and were being extensively used as an advertising medium within three years.

Very early on, advertisers discovered the importance of a good slogan. Many of our more venerable slogans are older than you might think. Ivory Soap's "99 44/100 percent pure" dates from 1879. Schlitz has been calling itself "the beer that made Milwaukee famous" since 1895, and Heinz's "57 varieties" followed a year later. Morton Salt's "When it rains, it pours" dates from 1911, the American Florist Association's "Say it with flowers" was first used in 1912, and the "good to the last drop" of Maxwell House coffee, named for the Maxwell House Hotel in Nashville, where it was first served, has been with us since 1907. (The slogan is said to have originated with Teddy Roosevelt, who pronounced the coffee "good to the last drop," prompting one wit to ask, "So what's wrong with the last drop?")

Sometimes slogans took a little working on. Coca-Cola described itself as "the drink that makes a pause refreshing" before realizing, in 1929, that "the pause that refreshes" was rather more succinct and memorable. A slogan could make all the difference to a product's success. After advertising its soap as an efficacious way of dealing with "conspicuous nose pores," Woodbury's Facial Soap came up with the slogan "The skin you love to touch" and won the hearts of millions. The great thing about a slogan was that it didn't have to be accurate to be effective. Heinz never actually had exactly "57 varieties" of anything. The catchphrase arose simply because H. J. Heinz, the company's founder, decided he liked the sound of the number. Undeterred by considerations of verity, he had the slogan slapped on every one of the products he produced, already in 1896 far more than fifty-seven. For a time the company tried to arrange its products into fifty-seven arbitrary clusters, but in 1969 it gave up the ruse altogether and abandoned the slogan.

Early in the 1900s, advertisers discovered another perennial feature of marketing—the *giveaway,* as it was called almost from the start. Consumers soon became acquainted with the irresistibly tempting notion that if they bought a particular product they could expect a reward—the chance to receive a prize, a free book (almost always ostensibly dedicated to the general improvement of one's well-being but invariably a thinly disguised plug for the manufacturer's range of products), a free sample, or a rebate in the form of a shiny dime, or be otherwise endowed with some gratifying bagatelle. Typical of the genre was a turn-of-the-century tome called *The Vital Question Cook Book,* which was promoted as an aid to livelier meals, but which proved upon receipt to contain 112 pages of recipes all involving the use of Shredded Wheat. Many of these had a certain air of desperation about them, notably the "Shredded Wheat Biscuit Jellied Apple Sandwich" and the "Creamed Spinach on Shredded Wheat Biscuit Toast." Almost all involved nothing more than spooning some everyday food on a piece of shredded wheat and giving it an inflated name. Nonetheless the company distributed no fewer than four million copies of *The Vital Question Cook Book* to eager consumers.

The great breakthrough in twentieth-century advertising, however, came with the identification and exploitation of the American consumer's Achilles' heel: anxiety. One of the first to master the form was King Gillette, inventor of the first safety razor and one of the most relentless advertisers of the early 1900s. Most of the early ads featured Gillette himself, who with his fussy toothbrush mustache and well-oiled hair looked more like a caricature of a Parisian waiter than a captain of industry. After starting with a few jaunty words about the ease and convenience of the safety razor—"Compact? Rather!"—he plunged the reader into the heart of the matter: "When you use my razor you are exempt from the dangers that men often encounter who allow their faces to come in contact with brush, soap, and barbershop accessories used on other people." 15

Here was an entirely new approach to selling goods. Gillette's ads were in effect telling you that not only did there exist a product that you never previously suspected you needed, but if you *didn't* use it you would very possibly attract a crop of facial diseases you never knew existed. The combination proved irresistible. Though the Gillette razor retailed for a hefty $5—half the average workingman's weekly pay—it sold by the millions, and King Gillette became a very wealthy man. (Though only for a time, alas. Like many others of his era, he grew obsessed with the idea of the perfectibility of mankind and expended so much of his energies writing books of convoluted philosophy with titles like *The Human Drift* that he eventually lost control of his company and most of his fortune.)

By the 1920s, advertisers had so refined the art that a consumer could scarcely pick up a magazine without being bombarded with unsettling questions: "Do You Make These Mistakes in English?"; "Will Your Hair Stand Close Inspection?"; "When Your Guests Are Gone—Are You Sorry You Ever Invited Them?" (because, that is, you lack social polish); "Did Nature fail to put roses in your cheeks?"; "Will There be a Victrola in Your Home This Christmas?"[1] The 1920s truly were the Age of Anxiety. One ad pictured a former golf champion, "now only a wistful onlooker," whose career had gone sour because he had neglected his teeth. Scott Tissues mounted a campaign showing a forlorn-looking businessman sitting on a park bench

---

1. The most famous 1920s ad of them all didn't pose a question, but it did play on the reader's anxiety: "They Laughed When I Sat Down, but When I Started to Play . . . " It was originated by the U.S. School of Music in 1925.

beneath the bold caption "A Serious Business Handicap — These Troubles That Come from Harsh Toilet Tissue." Below the picture the text explained "65% of all men and women over 40 are suffering from some form of rectal trouble, estimates a prominent specialist connected with one of New York's largest hospitals. 'And one of the contributing causes,' he states, 'is inferior toilet tissue.'" There was almost nothing that one couldn't become uneasy about. One ad even asked: "Can You Buy a Radio Safely?" Distressed bowels were the most frequent target. The makers of Sal Hepatica warned: "We rush to meetings, we dash to parties. We are on the go all day long. We exercise too little, and we eat too much. And, in consequence, we impair our bodily functions — often we retain food within us too long. And when that occurs, poisons are set up — *Auto-Intoxication begins.*"

In addition to the dread of auto-intoxication, the American consumer faced a gauntlet of other newly minted maladies — *pyorrhea, halitosis* (coined as a medical term in 1874, but popularized by Listerine beginning in 1922 with the slogan "Even your best friend won't tell you"), *athlete's foot* (a term invented by the makers of Absorbine Jr. in 1928), *dead cuticles, scabby toes, iron-poor blood, vitamin deficiency* (*vitamins* had been coined in 1912, but the word didn't enter the general vocabulary until the 1920s, when advertisers realized it sounded worryingly scientific), *fallen stomach, tobacco breath,* and *psoriasis,* though Americans would have to wait until the next decade for the scientific identification of the gravest of personal disorders — *body odor,* a term invented in 1933 by the makers of Lifebuoy soap and so terrifying in its social consequences that it was soon abbreviated to a whispered *B.O.*

The white-coated technicians of American laboratories had not only identified these new conditions, but — miraculously, it seemed — simultaneously come up with cures for them. Among the products that were invented or rose to greatness in this busy, neurotic decade were *Cutex* (for those deceased cuticles), *Vick's VapoRub, Geritol, Serutan* ("Natures spelled backwards," as the voiceover always said with somewhat bewildering reassurance, as if spelling a product's name backward conferred some medicinal benefit), *Noxema* (for which read: "knocks eczema"), *Preparation H, Murine* eyedrops, and *Dr. Scholl's Foot Aids.*[2] It truly was an age of miracles — one in which you could even cure a smoker's cough by smoking, so long as it was Old Golds you smoked, because, as the slogan proudly if somewhat untruthfully boasted, they contained "Not a cough in a carload." (As late as 1953, L&M cigarettes were advertised as "just what the doctor ordered!")

By 1927, advertising was a $1.5-billion-a-year industry in the United   20
States, and advertising people were held in such awe that they were asked

---

2. And yes there really was a Dr. Scholl. His name was William Scholl, he was a real doctor, genuinely dedicated to the well-being of feet, and they are still very proud of him in his hometown of La Porte, Indiana.

not only to mastermind campaigns but even to name the products. An ad man named Henry N. McKinney, for instance, named *Keds* shoes, *Karo* syrup, *Meadow Gold* butter, and *Uneeda Biscuits.*

Product names tended to cluster around certain sounds. Breakfast cereals often ended in *-ies (Wheaties, Rice Krispies, Frosties);* washing powders and detergents tended to be gravely monosyllabic (*Lux, Fab, Tide, Duz*). It is often possible to tell the era of a product's development by its termination. Thus products dating from the 1920s and early 1930s often ended in *-ex (Pyrex, Cutex, Kleenex, Windex)*, while those ending in *-master (Mixmaster, Toastmaster)* generally betray a late 1930s or early-1940s genesis. The development of *Glo-Coat* floor wax in 1932 also heralded the beginning of American business's strange and long-standing infatuation with illiterate spellings, a trend that continued with *ReaLemon* juice in 1935, *Reddi-Wip* whipped cream in 1947, and many hundreds of others since, from *Tastee-Freez* drive-ins to *Toys 'Я' Us*, along with countless others with a *Kwik, E-Z,* or *U* (as in *While-U-Wait*) embedded in their titles. The late 1940s saw the birth of a brief vogue for endings in *-matic*, so that car manufacturers offered vehicles with *Seat-O-Matic* levers and *Cruise-O-Matic* transmissions, and even fitted sheets came with *Ezy-Matic* corners. Some companies became associated with certain types of names. Du Pont, for instance, had a special fondness for words ending in *-on.* The practice began with *nylon*—a name that was concocted out of thin air and owes nothing to its chemical properties— and was followed with *Rayon, Dacron, Orlon,* and *Teflon,* among many others. In recent years the company has moved on to what might be called its *Star Trek* phase with such compounds as *Tyvek, Kevlar, Sontara, Condura, Nomex,* and *Zemorain.*

Such names have more than passing importance to their owners. If American business has given us a large dose of anxiety in its ceaseless quest for a healthier *bottom line* (a term dating from the 1930s, though not part of mainstream English until the 1970s), we may draw some comfort from the thought that business has suffered a great deal of collective anxiety over protecting the names of its products.

A certain cruel paradox prevails in the matter of preserving brand names. Every business naturally wants to create a product that will dominate its market. But if that product so dominates the market that the brand name becomes indistinguishable in the public mind from the product itself—when people begin to ask for a *thermos* rather than a "Thermos brand vacuum flask"—then the term has become generic and the owner faces the loss of its trademark protection. That is why advertisements and labels so often carry faintly paranoid-sounding lines like "Tabasco is the registered trademark for the brand of pepper sauce made by McIlhenny Co." and why companies like Coca-Cola suffer palpitations when they see a passage like this (from John Steinbeck's *The Wayward Bus*):

"Got any coke?" another character asked.

"No," said the proprietor. "Few bottles of Pepsi-Cola. Haven't had any coke for a month. . . . It's the same stuff. You can't tell them apart."

An understandable measure of confusion exists concerning the distinction between patents and trademarks and between trademarks and trade names. A *patent* protects the name of the product and its method of manufacture for seventeen years. Thus from 1895 to 1912, no one but the Shredded Wheat Company could make shredded wheat. But because patents require manufacturers to divulge the secrets of their products — and thus make them available to rivals to copy when the patent runs out — companies sometimes choose not to seek their protection. *Coca-Cola*, for one, has never been patented. A *trademark* is effectively the name of a product, its *brand name*. A *trade name* is the name of the manufacturer. So *Ford* is a trade name, *Taurus* a trademark. Trademarks apply not just to names, but also to logos, drawings, and other symbols and depictions. The MGM lion, for instance, is a trademark. Unlike patents, trademark protection goes on forever, or at least as long as the manufacturer can protect it.

For a long time, it was felt that this permanence gave the holder an unfair advantage. In consequence, America did not enact its first trademark law until 1870, almost a century after Britain, and then it was declared unconstitutional by the Supreme Court. Lasting trademark protection did not begin for American companies until 1881. Today, more than a million trademarks have been issued in the United States and the number is rising by about thirty thousand a year.   25

A good trademark is almost incalculably valuable. Invincible-seeming brand names do occasionally falter and fade. *Pepsodent, Rinso, Chase & Sanborn, Sal Hepatica, Vitalis, Brylcreem,* and *Burma-Shave* all once stood on the commanding heights of consumer recognition but are now defunct or have sunk to the status of what the trade calls "ghost brands" — products that are still produced but little promoted and largely forgotten. For the most part, however, once a product establishes a dominant position in a market, it is exceedingly difficult to depose it. In nineteen of twenty-two categories, the company that owned the leading American brand in 1925 still has it today — *Nabisco* in cookies, *Kellogg's* in breakfast cereals, *Kodak* in film, *Sherwin Williams* in paint, *Del Monte* in canned fruit, *Wrigleys* in chewing gum, *Singer* in sewing machines, *Ivory* in soap, *Campbell's* in soup, *Gillette* in razors. Few really successful brand names of today were not just as familiar to your grandparents or even great-grandparents, and a well-established brand name has a sort of self-perpetuating power. As *The Economist* has noted: "In the category of food blenders, consumers were still ranking General Electric second twenty years after the company had stopped making them."

An established brand name is so valuable that only about 5 percent of the sixteen thousand or so new products introduced in America each year bear all-new brand names. The others are variants on an existing product — *Tide with Bleach, Tropicana Twister Light Fruit Juices,* and so on. Among some types of product a certain glut is evident. At last count there were 220 types of branded breakfast cereal in America. In 1993, according to an international business survey, the world's most valuable brand was *Marlboro,* with a value estimated at $40 billion, slightly ahead of *Coca-Cola.* Among the other ten brands were *Intel, Kellogg's, Budweiser, Pepsi, Gillette,* and *Pampers. Nescafé* and *Bacardi* were the only foreign brands to make the top ten, underlining American dominance.

Huge amounts of effort go into choosing brand names. General Foods reviewed 2,800 names before deciding on *Dreamwhip.* (To put this in proportion, try to think of just ten names for an artificial whipped cream.) Ford considered more than twenty thousand possible car names before finally settling on *Edsel* (which proves that such care doesn't always pay), and Standard Oil a similar number of names before it opted for *Exxon.* Sometimes, however, the most successful names are the result of a moment's whimsy. *Betty Crocker* came in a flash to an executive of the Washburn Crosby Company (later absorbed by General Mills), who chose *Betty* because he thought it sounded wholesome and sincere and *Crocker* in memory of a beloved fellow executive who had recently died. At first the name was used only to sign letters responding to customers' requests for advice or information, but by the 1950s, Betty Crocker's smiling, confident face was appearing on more than fifty types of food product, and her loyal followers could buy her recipe books and even visit her "kitchen" at the General Foods headquarters.

Great efforts also go into finding out why people buy the brands they do. Advertisers and market researchers bandy about terms like *conjoint analysis technique, personal drive patterns, Gaussian distributions, fractals,* and other such arcana in their quest to winnow out every subliminal quirk in our buying habits. They know, for instance, that 40 percent of all people who move to a new address will also change their brand of toothpaste, that the average supermarket shopper makes fourteen impulse decisions in each visit, that 62 percent of shoppers will pay a premium for mayonnaise even when they think a cheaper brand is just as good, but that only 24 percent will show the same largely irrational loyalty to frozen vegetables.

To preserve a brand name involves a certain fussy attention to linguistic and orthographic details. To begin with, the name is normally expected to be treated not as a noun but as a proper adjective — that is, the name should be followed by an explanation of what it does: *Kleenex facial tissues, Q-Tip cotton swabs, Jell-O brand gelatin dessert, Sanka brand decaffeinated coffee.* Some types of products — notably cars — are granted an exemption, which explains why General Motors does not have to advertise *Cadillac self-propelled automobiles* or the like. In all cases, the name may not explicitly describe the product's function, though it may hint at what it does. Thus *Coppertone* is acceptable; *Coppertan* would not be.

The situation is more than a little bizarre. Having done all they can to make their products household words, manufacturers must then in their advertisements do all in their power to imply that they aren't. Before trademark law was clarified, advertisers positively encouraged the public to treat their products as generics. Kodak invited consumers to "Kodak as you go," turning the brand name into a dangerously ambiguous verb. It would never do that now. The American Thermos Product Company went so far as to boast, "Thermos is a household word," to its considerable cost. Donald F. Duncan, Inc., the original manufacturer of the *Yo-Yo*, lost its trademark protection partly because it was amazingly casual about capitalization in its own promotional literature. "In case you don't know what a yo-yo is . . ." one of its advertisements went, suggesting that in commercial terms Duncan didn't. Duncan also made the elemental error of declaring, "If It Isn't a Duncan, It Isn't a Yo-Yo," which on the face of it would seem a reasonable claim, but was in fact held by the courts to be inviting the reader to consider the product generic. Kodak had long since stopped saying "If it isn't an Eastman, it isn't a Kodak."

Because of the confusion, and occasional lack of fastidiousness on the part of their owners, many dozens of products have lost their trademark protection, among them *aspirin, linoleum, yo-yo, thermos, cellophane, milk of magnesia, mimeograph, lanolin, celluloid, dry ice, escalator, shredded wheat, kerosene,* and *zipper.* All were once proudly capitalized and worth a fortune.

On July 1, 1941, the New York television station WNBT-TV interrupted its normal viewing to show, without comment, a Bulova watch ticking. For sixty seconds the watch ticked away mysteriously, then the picture faded and normal programming resumed. It wasn't much, but it was the first television *commercial.*

Both the word and the idea were already well established. The first commercial—the term was used from the very beginning—had been broadcast by radio station WEAF in New York on August 28, 1922. It lasted for either ten or fifteen minutes, depending on which source you credit. Commercial radio was not an immediate hit. In its first two months, WEAF sold only $550 worth of airtime. But by the mid-1920s, sponsors were not only flocking to buy airtime but naming their programs after their products—*The Lucky Strike Hour, The A&P Gypsies, The Lux Radio Theater,* and so on. Such was the obsequiousness of the radio networks that by the early 1930s, many were allowing the sponsors to take complete artistic and production control of the programs. Many of the most popular shows were actually written by the advertising agencies, and the agencies naturally seldom missed an opportunity to work a favorable mention of the sponsor's products into the scripts.

With the rise of television in the 1950s, the practices of the radio era were effortlessly transferred to the new medium. Advertisers inserted their names into the program title—*Texaco Star Theater, Gillette Cavalcade of Sports, Chesterfield Sound-Off Time, The U.S. Steel Hour, Kraft*   35

Television Theater, The Chevy Show, The Alcoa Hour, The Ford Star Revue, Dick Clark's Beechnut Show, and the arresting hybrid *The Lux-Schlitz Playhouse,* which seemed to suggest a cozy symbiosis between soapflakes and beer. The commercial dominance of program titles reached a kind of hysterical peak with a program officially called *Your Kaiser Dealer Presents Kaiser-Frazer "Adventures in Mystery" Starring Betty Furness in "Byline."* Sponsors didn't write the programs any longer, but they did impose a firm control on the contents, most notoriously during a 1959 *Playhouse 90* broadcast of *Judgment at Nuremberg,* when the sponsor, the American Gas Association, managed to have all references to gas ovens and the gassing of Jews removed from the script.

Where commercial products of the late 1940s had scientific-sounding names, those of the 1950s relied increasingly on secret ingredients. Gleem toothpaste contained a mysterious piece of alchemy called *GL-70.*[3] There was never the slightest hint of what GL-70 was, but it would, according to the advertising, not only rout odor-causing bacteria but "wipe out their enzymes!"

A kind of creeping illiteracy invaded advertising, too, to the dismay of many. When Winston began advertising its cigarettes with the slogan "Winston tastes good like a cigarette should," nationally syndicated columnists like Sydney J. Harris wrote anguished essays on what the world was coming to—every educated person knew it should be "as a cigarette should"—but the die was cast. By 1958, Ford was advertising that you could "travel smooth" in a Thunderbird Sunliner and the maker of Ace Combs was urging buyers to "comb it handsome"—a trend that continues today with "pantihose that fits you real comfortable" and other grammatical manglings too numerous and dispiriting to dwell on.

We may smile at the advertising ruses of the 1920s—frightening people with the threat of "fallen stomach" and "scabby toes"—but in fact such creative manipulation still goes on, albeit at a slightly more sophisticated level. *The New York Times Magazine* reported in 1990 how an advertising copywriter had been told to come up with some impressive labels for a putative hand cream. She invented the arresting and healthful-sounding term *oxygenating moisturizers* and wrote accompanying copy with references to "tiny bubbles of oxygen that release moisture into your skin." This done, the advertising was turned over to the company's research and development department, which was instructed to come up with a product that matched the copy.

If we fall for such commercial manipulation, we have no one to blame but ourselves. When Kentucky Fried Chicken introduced "Extra Crispy" chicken to sell alongside its "Original" chicken, and sold it at the same price, sales were disappointing. But when its advertising agency

---

3. For purposes of research, I wrote to Procter & Gamble, Gleem's manufacturer, asking what GL-70 was, but the public relations department evidently thought it eccentric of me to wonder what I had been putting in my mouth all through childhood and declined to reply.

persuaded it to promote "Extra Crispy" as a premium brand and to put the price up, sales soared. Much the same sort of verbal hypnosis was put to work for the benefit of the fur industry. Dyed muskrat makes a perfectly good fur, for those who enjoy cladding themselves in dead animals, but the name clearly lacks stylishness. The solution was to change the name to *Hudson seal*. Never mind that the material contained not a strand of seal fur. It sounded good, and sales skyrocketed.

Truth has seldom been a particularly visible feature of American advertising. In the early 1970s, Chevrolet ran a series of ads for the Chevelle boasting that the car had "109 advantages to keep it from becoming old before its time." When looked into, it turned out that these 109 vaunted features included such items as rearview mirrors, backup lights, balanced wheels, and many other components that were considered pretty well basic to any car. Never mind; sales soared. At about the same time, Ford, not to be outdone, introduced a "limited edition" Mercury Monarch at $250 below the normal list price. It achieved this, it turned out, by taking $250 worth of equipment off the standard Monarch.

And has all this deviousness led to a tightening of the rules concerning what is allowable in advertising? Hardly. In 1986, as William Lutz relates in *Doublespeak*, the insurance company John Hancock launched an ad campaign in which "real people in real situations" discussed their financial predicaments with remarkable candor. When a journalist asked to speak to these real people, a company spokesman conceded that they were actors and "in that sense they are not real people."

During the 1982 presidential campaign, the Republican National Committee ran a television advertisement praising President Reagan for providing cost-of-living pay increases to federal workers "in spite of those sticks-in-the-mud who tried to keep him from doing what we elected him to do." When it was pointed out that the increases had in fact been mandated by law since 1975 and that Reagan had in any case three times tried to block them, a Republican official responded: "Since when is a commercial supposed to be accurate?" Quite.

In linguistic terms, perhaps the most interesting challenge facing advertisers today is that of selling products in an increasingly multicultural society. Spanish is a particular problem, not just because it is spoken over such a widely scattered area but also because it is spoken in so many different forms. Brown sugar is *azucar negra* in New York, *azucar prieta* in Miami, *azucar morena* in much of Texas, and *azucar pardo* pretty much everywhere else — and that's just one word. Much the same bewildering multiplicity applies to many others. In consequence, embarrassments are all but inevitable.

In mainstream Spanish, *bichos* means *insects*, but in Puerto Rico it means *testicles*, so when a pesticide maker promised to bring death to the *bichos*, Puerto Rican consumers were at least bemused, if not alarmed. Much the same happened when a maker of bread referred to its product as *un bollo de pan* and discovered that to Spanish-speaking Miamians of Cuban extraction that means a woman's private parts. And when Perdue Chickens translated its slogan "It takes a tough man to make a tender chicken" into Spanish, it came out as the slightly less macho "It takes a sexually excited man to make a chick sensual."

Never mind. Sales soared.   45

FOCUSING ON CONTENT

1. How did George Eastman use language to promote his products? Why do many consider Eastman an innovator in the business world? In what ways was he the founder of modern advertising practices?

2. It is important for companies to prevent their trademarks from becoming household words because they could lose their trademark protection. For example, advertisements for Kleenex and Xerox urge people to ask for a *tissue* or say they're going to *copy* a paper. Identify two or three current trademarks that you think could lose their trademark protection in the future, and explain your reasoning for choosing each trademark.

3. Bryson discusses what he calls a "creeping illiteracy" (37) that has invaded advertising. What form does this illiteracy take? In what ways might using poor English benefit advertisers?

4. In talking about the powers of advertising to persuade, Bryson discusses *commercial manipulation* and *verbal hypnosis* (39). What exactly does he mean by each term? How have advertisers used these techniques to sell their products? How do you think you as a consumer can guard against such advertising practices?

5. According to Bryson, what is one of the more interesting linguistic challenges facing today's advertisers?

FOCUSING ON WRITING

1. Why do you think Bryson begins his essay with an extensive passage on George Eastman before even mentioning advertising, the focus of his essay? Why is this background information important to the rest of the essay? (Glossary: *Beginnings and Endings*) What do you need to consider when writing an introduction to an essay?

2. What is Bryson's purpose in this essay—to express personal thoughts and feelings, to inform his audience, or to argue a particular position? (Glossary: *Purpose*) What in his essay leads you to this conclusion?

3. How does Bryson organize his essay? (Glossary: *Organization*) Is this organization appropriate for his subject matter and purpose? Explain.

4. Bryson peppers his essay with examples from the world of business and advertising. (Glossary: *Examples*) These examples serve not only to illustrate the points he makes but also to help establish his authority on the subject. Which examples do you find most effective? Least effective? Explain why.

LANGUAGE IN ACTION

In 1976, the Committee on Public Doublespeak (a committee of the National Council of Teachers of English) gave Professor Hugh Rank of Governors State University its Orwell Award for the Intensify/Downplay schema he developed to help people analyze public persuasion. As Rank explains, "All people *intensify* (commonly by *repetition, association, composition*) and *downplay* (commonly by *omission, diversion, confusion*) as they communicate in words, gestures, numbers, etc. But, 'professional persuaders' have more training, technology, money, and media access than the average citizen. Individuals can better cope with organized persuasion by recognizing the common ways that communication is intensified or downplayed, and by considering who is saying what to whom, with what intent and what result." Look closely at Rank's schema on pages 579 and 580, at the questions you can ask yourself about any type of advertisement.

Use Rank's schema to analyze the drinking-and-driving advertisements on pages 581–83. Find examples of intensifying and downplaying in each.

WRITING SUGGESTIONS

1. (*Writing from Experience*) Think of a product that you have used and been disappointed by, one that has failed to live up to its advertising claims. Write a letter to the manufacturer in which you describe your experience with the product and explain why you believe the company's advertisements have been misleading. Send your letter to the president of the company or to the director of marketing.

2. (*Writing from Reading*) Many product names are chosen because of their connotative or suggestive values. (Glossary: *Connotation/Denotation*) For example, the name *Tide* for a detergent suggests the power of the ocean tides and the rhythmic surge of cleansing waters; the name *Pride* for the wax suggests how the user will feel after using the product; the name *100% Natural* for the cereal suggests that the consumer is getting nothing less than nature's best; and the name *Taurus* for the Ford car suggests the strength and durability of a bull. Test what Bryson has said about brand names by exploring the connotations of the brand names in one of the following categories: cosmetics, deodorants, candy, paint, car batteries, fast-food sandwiches, pain relievers, disposable diapers, or cat food. You may find it helpful to read the articles by J. C. Herz (pp. 230–33) and Alleen Pace Nilsen (pp. 234–40) in this connection. Report your findings in an essay.

3. (*Writing from Research*) In paragraph 12, Bryson reminds us that successful advertisers have always known the importance of good slogans. Some early slogans, such as the American Florist Association's "Say it with flowers," are still in use today even though they were coined years ago. Research five or six current product slogans that Bryson doesn't mention — like Microsoft's "Where do you want to go?" or Just for Men's "So natural no one can tell" — and write an essay in which you discuss the importance of slogans to advertising campaigns. How, for example, do slogans serve to focus, direct, and galvanize advertising campaigns? What do you think makes some slogans work and others fail? What makes a slogan memorable? As you start this project, you may find it helpful to search out materials in your library or on the Internet relating to slogans in general and how they engage people.

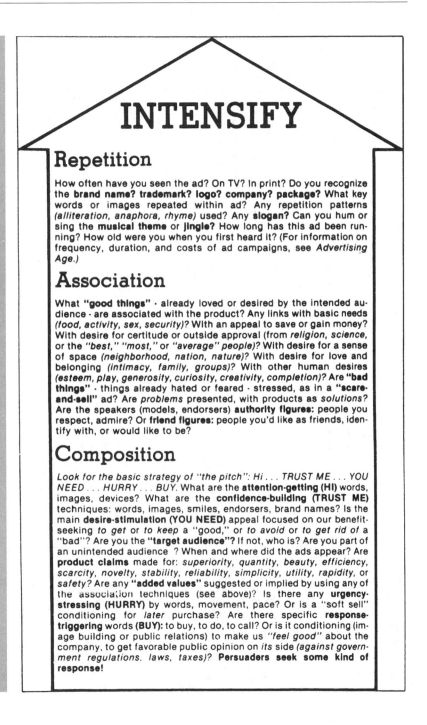

INTENSIFY

Repetition

How often have you seen the ad? On TV? In print? Do you recognize the **brand name? trademark? logo? company? package?** What key words or images repeated within ad? Any repetition patterns *(alliteration, anaphora, rhyme)* used? Any **slogan?** Can you hum or sing the **musical theme** or **jingle?** How long has this ad been running? How old were you when you first heard it? (For information on frequency, duration, and costs of ad campaigns, see *Advertising Age.)*

Association

What **"good things"** · already loved or desired by the intended audience · are associated with the product? Any links with basic needs *(food, activity, sex, security)?* With an appeal to save or gain money? With desire for certitude or outside approval (from *religion, science,* or the *"best," "most,"* or *"average" people)?* With desire for a sense of space *(neighborhood, nation, nature)?* With desire for love and belonging *(intimacy, family, groups)?* With other human desires *(esteem, play, generosity, curiosity, creativity, completion)?* Are **"bad things"** · things already hated or feared · stressed, as in a **"scare-and-sell"** ad? Are *problems* presented, with products as *solutions?* Are the speakers (models, endorsers) **authority figures:** people you respect, admire? Or **friend figures:** people you'd like as friends, identify with, or would like to be?

Composition

Look for the basic strategy of *"the pitch": Hi ... TRUST ME ... YOU NEED ... HURRY ... BUY.* What are the **attention-getting (HI)** words, images, devices? What are the **confidence-building (TRUST ME)** techniques: words, images, smiles, endorsers, brand names? Is the main **desire-stimulation (YOU NEED)** appeal focused on our benefit-seeking *to get* or *to keep* a "good," or *to avoid* or *to get rid of* a "bad"? Are you the **"target audience"?** If not, who is? Are you part of an unintended audience ? When and where did the ads appear? Are **product claims** made for: *superiority, quantity, beauty, efficiency, scarcity, novelty, stability, reliability, simplicity, utility, rapidity,* or *safety?* Are any **"added values"** suggested or implied by using any of the association techniques (see above)? Is there any **urgency-stressing (HURRY)** by words, movement, pace? Or is it a "soft sell" conditioning for *later* purchase? Are there specific **response-triggering** words **(BUY):** to buy, to do, to call? Or is it conditioning (image building or public relations) to make us *"feel good"* about the company, to get favorable public opinion on *its* side *(against government regulations. laws, taxes)?* **Persuaders seek some kind of response!**

Omission

What "bad" aspects, disadvantages, drawbacks, hazards, have been **omitted** from the ad? Are there some unspoken assumptions? An unsaid story? Are some things implied or suggested, but not explicitly stated? Are there concealed problems concerning the **maker,** the **materials, the design, the use,** or the **purpose of the product? Are there any unwanted or harmful side effects:** *unsafe, unhealthy, uneconomical, inefficient, unneeded?* Does any **"disclosure law"** exist (or is needed) requiring public warning about a concealed hazard? In the ad, what gets less time, less attention, smaller print? *(Most ads are true, but incomplete.)*

Diversion

What benefits (low cost, high speed, etc.) get high priority in the ad's claim and promises? Are these **your** priorities? Significant, important to you? Is there any **"bait-and-switch"**? *(Ad stresses* low cost, *but the actual seller switches buyer's priority to* high quality.) Does ad divert focus from **key issues,** important things *(e.g., nutrition, health, safety)*? Does ad focus on **side-issues,** unmeaningful trivia *(common in parity products)*? Does ad divert attention from your other choices, other options: buy something else, use less, use less often, rent, borrow, share, do without? *(Ads need not show other choices, but you should know them.)*

Confusion

Are the words clear or ambiguous? Specific or vague? Are claims and promises absolute, or are there qualifying words *("may help," "some")*? Is the claim measurable? Or is it **"puffery"?** *(Laws permit most* "sellers's talk" *of such general praise and subjective opinions.)* Are the words common, understandable, familiar? Uncommon? Jargon? Any parts difficult to "translate" or explain to others? Are analogies clear? Are comparisons within the same kind? Are examples related? Typical? Adequate? Enough examples? Any contradictions? Inconsistencies? Errors? Are there frequent changes, variations, revisions *(in size, price, options, extras, contents, packaging)*? Is it too complex: too much, too many? Disorganized? Incoherent? Unsorted? Any confusing statistics? Numbers? Do you know exact costs? Benefits? Risks? Are **your own goals,** priorities, and desires clear or vague? Fixed or shifting? Simple or complex? *(Confusion can also exist within us as well as within an ad. If any confusion exists: slow down, take care.)*

DOWNPLAY

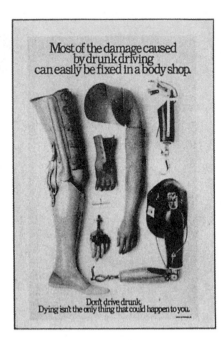

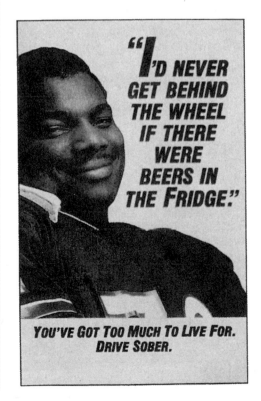

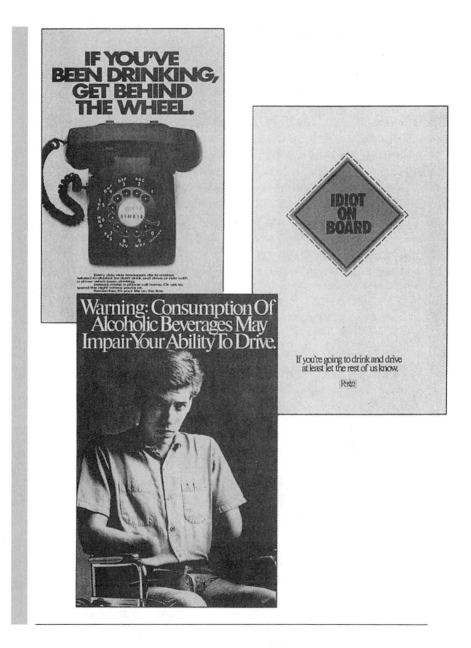

Weasel Words

WILLIAM LUTZ

William Lutz, professor of English at Rutgers University, edits the Quarterly Review of Doublespeak. *Originally from Racine, Wisconsin, Lutz is best known for his important work* Doublespeak: From Revenue Enhancement to Terminal Living *(1980). As chair of the National Council of Teachers of English's Committee on Public Doublespeak, Lutz has been a watchdog of public officials and business leaders who use language to "mislead, distort, deceive, inflate, circumvent, and obfuscate." Each year the committee presents the Orwell Awards, recognizing the most outrageous uses of public doublespeak in the arenas of government and business.*

In the following excerpt from his book Doublespeak, *Lutz reveals some of the ways that advertisers use language to imply great things about products and services without promising anything at all. With considerable skill, advertisers can produce ads that make us believe a certain product is better than it is without actually lying about it. Lutz's word-by-word analysis of advertising claims reveals how misleading—and ridiculous—these slogans and claims can be.*

WRITING TO DISCOVER: *Imagine what it would be like if you were suddenly transported to a world in which there were no advertisements and no one trying to sell you a product. Write about how you would decide what to buy. How would you learn about new products? Would you prefer to live in such a world? Why or why not?*

WEASEL WORDS

One problem advertisers have when they try to convince you that the product they are pushing is really different from other, similar products is that their claims are subject to some laws. Not a lot of laws, but there are some designed to prevent fraudulent or untruthful claims in advertising. Even during the happy years of nonregulation under President Ronald Reagan, the FTC did crack down on the more blatant abuses in advertising claims. Generally speaking, advertisers have to be careful in what they say in their ads, in the claims they make for the products they advertise. Parity claims are safe because they are legal and supported by a number of court decisions. But beyond parity claims there are weasel words.

Advertisers use weasel words to appear to be making a claim for a product when in fact they are making no claim at all. Weasel words get their name from the way weasels eat the eggs they find in the nests of other animals. A weasel will make a small hole in the egg, suck out the insides, then place the egg back in the nest. Only when the egg is examined closely is it found to be hollow. That's the way it is with weasel words in advertising: Examine weasel words closely and you'll find that they're as hollow as any egg sucked by a weasel. Weasel words appear to say one thing when in fact they say the opposite, or nothing at all.

"Help" — The Number One Weasel Word

The biggest weasel word used in advertising doublespeak is "help." Now "help" only means to aid or assist, nothing more. It does not mean to conquer, stop, eliminate, end, solve, heal, cure, or anything else. But once the ad says "help," it can say just about anything after that because "help" qualifies everything coming after it. The trick is that the claim that comes after the weasel word is usually so strong and so dramatic that you forget the word "help" and concentrate only on the dramatic claim. You read into the ad a message that the ad does not contain. More importantly, the advertiser is not responsible for the claim that you read into the ad, even though the advertiser wrote the ad so you would read that claim into it.

The next time you see an ad for a cold medicine that promises that it "helps relieve cold symptoms fast," don't rush out to buy it. Ask yourself what this claim is really saying. Remember, "help" means only that the medicine will aid or assist. What will it aid or assist in doing? Why, "relieve" your cold "symptoms." "Relieve" only means to ease, alleviate, or mitigate, not to stop, end, or cure. Nor does the claim say how much relieving this medicine will do. Nowhere does this ad claim it will cure anything. In fact, the ad doesn't even claim it will *do* anything at all. The ad only claims that it will aid in relieving (not curing) your cold symptoms, which are probably a runny nose, watery eyes, and a headache. In other words, this medicine probably contains a standard decongestant and some aspirin. By the way, what does "fast" mean? Ten minutes, one hour, one day? What is fast to one person can be very slow to another. Fast is another weasel word.

Ad claims using "help" are among the most popular ads. One says, "Helps keep you young looking," but then a lot of things will help keep you young looking, including exercise, rest, good nutrition, and a facelift. More importantly, this ad doesn't say the product will keep you young, only "young *looking*." Someone may look young to one person and old to another.

A toothpaste ad says, "Helps prevent cavities," but it doesn't say it will actually prevent cavities. Brushing your teeth regularly, avoiding sugars in food, and flossing daily will also help prevent cavities. A liquid cleaner ad says, "Helps keep your home germ free," but it doesn't say it actually kills germs, nor does it even specify which germs it might kill.

"Help" is such a useful weasel word that it is often combined with other action-verb weasel words such as "fight" and "control." Consider the claim, "Helps control dandruff symptoms with regular use." What does it really say? It will assist in controlling (not eliminating, stopping, ending, or curing) the *symptoms* of dandruff, not the cause of dandruff nor the dandruff itself. What are the symptoms of dandruff? The ad deliberately leaves that undefined, but assume that the symptoms referred to in the ad are the flaking and itching commonly associated with dandruff. But just shampooing with *any* shampoo will temporarily eliminate these symptoms, so this shampoo isn't any different from any other. Finally, in order to benefit from this product, you must use it regularly. What is "regular use"—daily, weekly, hourly? Using another shampoo "regularly" will have the same effect. Nowhere does this advertising claim say this particular shampoo stops, eliminates, or cures dandruff. In fact, this claim says nothing at all, thanks to all the weasel words.

Look at ads in magazines and newspapers, listen to ads on radio and television, and you'll find the word "help" in ads for all kinds of products. How often do you read or hear such phrases as "helps stop . . . ," "helps overcome . . . ," "helps eliminate . . . ," "helps you feel . . . ," or "helps you look . . ."? If you start looking for this weasel word in advertising, you'll be amazed at how often it occurs. Analyze the claims in the ads using "help," and you will discover that these ads are really saying nothing.

There are plenty of other weasel words used in advertising. In fact, there are so many that to list them all would fill the rest of this book. But, in order to identify the doublespeak of advertising and understand the real meaning of an ad, you have to be aware of the most popular weasel words in advertising today.

Virtually Spotless

One of the most powerful weasel words is "virtually," a word so in-   10
nocent that most people don't pay any attention to it when it is used in an advertising claim. But watch out. "Virtually" is used in advertising claims that appear to make specific, definite promises when there is no promise. After all, what does "virtually" mean? It means "in essence or effect, although not in fact." Look at that definition again. "Virtually" means *not in fact*. It does *not* mean "almost" or "just about the same as," or anything else. And before you dismiss all this concern over such a small word, remember that small words can have big consequences.

In 1971 a federal court rendered its decision on a case brought by a woman who became pregnant while taking birth control pills. She sued the manufacturer, Eli Lilly and Company, for breach of warranty. The woman lost her case. Basing its ruling on a statement in the pamphlet accompanying the pills, which stated that, "When taken as directed, the tablets offer virtually 100% protection," the court ruled that there was no warranty, expressed or implied, that the pills were absolutely effective. In its ruling, the court pointed out that, according to *Webster's Third New International Dictionary,* "virtually" means "almost entirely" and clearly does not mean "absolute" (*Whittington* v. *Eli Lilly and Company,* 333 F. Supp. 98). In other words, the Eli Lilly company was really saying that its birth control pill, even when taken as directed, *did not in fact* provide 100 percent protection against pregnancy. But Eli Lilly didn't want to put it that way because then many women might not have bought Lilly's birth control pills.

The next time you see the ad that says that this dishwasher detergent "leaves dishes virtually spotless," just remember how advertisers twist the meaning of the weasel word "virtually." You can have lots of spots on your dishes after using this detergent and the ad claim will still be true, because what this claim really means is that this detergent does not *in fact* leave your dishes spotless. Whenever you see or hear an ad claim that uses the word "virtually," just translate that claim into its real meaning. So the television set that is "virtually trouble free" becomes the television set that is not in fact trouble free, the "virtually foolproof operation" of any appliance becomes an operation that is in fact not foolproof, and the product that "virtually never needs service" becomes the product that is not in fact service free.

New and Improved

If "new" is the most frequently used word on a product package, "improved" is the second most frequent. In fact, the two words are almost always used together. It seems just about everything sold these days is "new and improved." The next time you're in the supermarket, try counting the number of times you see these words on products. But you'd better do it while you're walking down just one aisle, otherwise you'll need a calculator to keep track of your counting.

Just what do these words mean? The use of the word "new" is restricted by regulations, so an advertiser can't just use the word on a product or in an ad without meeting certain requirements. For example, a product is considered new for about six months during a national advertising campaign. If the product is being advertised only in a limited test market area, the word can be used longer, and in some instances has been used for as long as two years.

What makes a product "new"? Some products have been around for   15
a long time, yet every once in a while you discover that they are being advertised as "new." Well, an advertiser can call a product new if there has been "a material functional change" in the product. What is "a material functional change," you ask? Good question. In fact it's such a good question it's being asked all the time. It's up to the manufacturer to prove that the product has undergone such a change. And if the manufacturer isn't challenged on the claim, then there's no one to stop it.

Moreover, the change does not have to be an improvement in the product. One manufacturer added an artificial lemon scent to a cleaning product and called it "new and improved," even though the product did not clean any better than without the lemon scent. The manufacturer defended the use of the word "new" on the grounds that the artificial scent changed the chemical formula of the product and therefore constituted "a material functional change."

Which brings up the word "improved." When used in advertising, "improved" does not mean "made better." It only means "changed" or "different from before." So, if the detergent maker puts a plastic pour spout on the box of detergent, the product has been "improved," and away we go with a whole new advertising campaign. Or, if the cereal maker adds more fruit or a different kind of fruit to the cereal, there's an improved product. Now you know why manufacturers are constantly making little changes in their products. Whole new advertising campaigns, designed to convince you that the product has been changed for the better, are based on small changes in superficial aspects of a product. The next time you see an ad for an "improved" product, ask yourself what was wrong with the old one. Ask yourself just how "improved" the product is. Finally, you might check to see whether the "improved" version costs more than the unimproved one. After all, someone has to pay for the millions of dollars spent advertising the improved product.

Of course, advertisers really like to run ads that claim a product is "new and improved." While what constitutes a "new" product may be subject to some regulation, "improved" is a subjective judgment. A manufacturer changes the shape of its stick deodorant, but the shape doesn't improve the function of the deodorant. That is, changing the shape doesn't affect the deodorizing ability of the deodorant, so the manufacturer calls it "improved." Another manufacturer adds ammonia to its liquid cleaner and calls it "new and improved." Since adding ammonia does affect the cleaning ability of the product, there has been a "material functional change" in the product, and the manufacturer can now call its cleaner "new," and "improved" as well. Now the weasel words "new and improved" are plastered all over the package and are the basis for a multimillion-dollar ad campaign. But after six months the word "new" will have to go, until someone can dream up another change in the product. Perhaps it will be adding color to the liquid, or changing the shape of the package, or maybe adding a new dripless pour spout, or perhaps a ___. The "improvements" are endless, and so are the new advertising claims and campaigns.

"New" is just too useful and powerful a word in advertising for advertisers to pass it up easily. So they use weasel words that say "new" without really saying it. One of their favorites is "introducing," as in, "Introducing improved Tide," or "Introducing the stain remover." The first is simply saying, here's our improved soap; the second, here's our new advertising campaign for our detergent. Another favorite is "now," as in, "Now there's Sinex," which simply means that Sinex is available. Then there are phrases like "Today's Chevrolet," "Presenting Dristan," and "A fresh way to start the day." The list is really endless because advertisers are always finding new ways to say "new" without really saying it. If there is a second edition of [my] book, I'll just call it the "new and improved" edition. Wouldn't you really rather have a "new and improved" edition of [my] book rather than a "second" edition?

Acts Fast

"Acts" and "works" are two popular weasel words in advertising because they bring action to the product and to the advertising claim. When you see the ad for the cough syrup that "Acts on the cough control center," ask yourself what this cough syrup is claiming to do. Well, it's just claiming to "act," to do something, to perform an action. What is it that the cough syrup does? The ad doesn't say. It only claims to perform an action or do something on your "cough control center." By the way, what and where is your "cough control center"? I don't' remember learning about that part of the body in human biology class.

Ads that use such phrases as "acts fast," "acts against," "acts to prevent," and the like are saying essentially nothing, because "act" is a word empty of any specific meaning. The ads are always careful not to specify exactly what "act" the product performs. Just because a brand of aspirin claims to "act fast" for headache relief doesn't mean this aspirin is any better than any other aspirin. What is the "act" that this aspirin performs? You're never told. Maybe it just dissolves quickly. Since aspirin is a parity product, all aspirin is the same and therefore functions the same. 20

Works Like Anything Else

If you don't find the word "acts" in an ad, you will probably find the weasel word "works." In fact, the two words are almost interchangeable in advertising. Watch out for ads that say a product "works against," "works like," "works for," or "works longer." As with "acts," "works" is the same meaningless verb used to make you think that this product really does something, and maybe even something special or unique. But "works," like "acts," is basically a word empty of any specific meaning.

Like Magic

Whenever advertisers want you to stop thinking about the product and to start thinking about something bigger, better, or more attractive than the product, they use that very popular weasel word "like." The word "like" is the advertiser's equivalent of a magician's use of misdirection. "Like" gets you to ignore the product and concentrate on the claim the advertiser is making about it. "For skin like peaches and cream" claims the ad for a skin cream. What is this ad really claiming? It doesn't say this cream will give you peaches-and-cream skin. There is no verb in this claim, so it doesn't even mention using the product. How is skin ever like "peaches and cream"? Remember, ads must be read literally and exactly, according to the dictionary definition of words. (Remember "virtually" in the Eli Lilly case.) The ad is making absolutely no promise or claim whatsoever for this skin cream. If you think this cream will give you soft, smooth, youthful-looking skin, you are the one who has read that meaning into the ad.

The wine that claims "It's like taking a trip to France" wants you to think about a romantic evening in Paris as you walk along the boulevard after a wonderful meal in an intimate little bistro. Of course, you don't really believe that a wine can take you to France, but the goal of the ad is to get you to think pleasant, romantic thoughts about France and not about how the wine tastes or how expensive it may be. That little word "like" has taken you away from crushed grapes into a world of your own imaginative making. Who knows, maybe the next time you buy wine, you'll think those pleasant thoughts when you see this brand of wine, and you'll buy it. Or, maybe you weren't even thinking about buying wine at all, but now you just might pick up a bottle the next time you're shopping. Ah, the power of "like" in advertising.

How about the most famous "like" claim of all, "Winston tastes good like a cigarette should"? Ignoring the grammatical error here, you might want to know what this claim is saying. Whether a cigarette tastes good or bad is a subjective judgment because what tastes good to one person may well taste horrible to another. Not everyone likes fried snails, even if they are called escargot. (*De gustibus non est disputandum,* which was probably the Roman rule for advertising as well as for defending the games in the Colosseum.) There are many people who say all cigarettes taste terrible, other people who say only some cigarettes taste all right, and still others who say all cigarettes taste good. Who's right? Everyone, because taste is a matter of personal judgment.

Moreover, note the use of the conditional, "should." The complete   25
claim is, "Winston tastes good like a cigarette should taste." But should cigarettes taste good? Again, this is a matter of personal judgment and probably depends most on one's experiences with smoking. So, the Winston ad is simply saying that Winston cigarettes are just like any other cigarette: Some people like them and some people don't. On that statement R. J. Reynolds conducted a very successful multimillion-dollar advertising campaign that helped keep Winston the number-two-selling cigarette in the United States, close behind number one, Marlboro.

CAN IT BE UP TO THE CLAIM?

Analyzing ads for doublespeak requires that you pay attention to every word in the ad and determine what each word really means. Advertisers try to wrap their claims in language that sounds concrete, specific, and objective, when in fact the language of advertising is anything but. Your job is to read carefully and listen critically so that when the announcer says that "Crest can be of significant value . . ." you know immediately that this claim says absolutely nothing. Where is the doublespeak in this ad? Start with the second word.

Once again, you have to look at what words really mean, not what you think they mean or what the advertiser wants you to think they mean. The ad for Crest only says that using Crest "can be" of "significant value." What really throws you off in this ad is the brilliant use of "significant." It draws your attention to the word "value" and makes you forget that the ad only claims that Crest "can be." The ad doesn't say that Crest *is* of value, only that it is "able" or "possible" to be of value, because that's all that "can" means.

It's so easy to miss the importance of those little words, "can be." Almost as easy as missing the importance of the words "up to" in an ad. These words are very popular in sale ads. You know, the ones that say, "Up to 50% Off!" Now, what does that claim mean? Not much, because the store or manufacturer has to reduce the price of only a few items by 50 percent. Everything else can be reduced a lot less, or not even reduced. Moreover, don't you want to know 50 pecent off of what? Is it 50 percent off the "manufacturer's suggested list price," which is the highest possible price? Was the price artificially inflated and then reduced? In other ads, "up to" expresses an ideal situation. The medicine that works "up to ten times faster," the battery that lasts "up to twice as long," and the soap that gets you "up to twice as clean" all are based on ideal situations for using those products, situations in which you can be sure you will never find yourself.

UNFINISHED WORDS

Unfinished words are a kind of "up to" claim in advertising. The claim that a battery lasts "up to twice as long" usually doesn't finish the comparison—twice as long as what? A birthday candle? A tank of gas? A cheap battery made in a country not noted for its technological achievements? The implication is that the battery lasts twice as long as batteries made by other battery makers, or twice as long as earlier model batteries made by the advertiser, but the ad doesn't really make these claims. You read these claims into the ad, aided by the visual images the advertiser so carefully provides.

Unfinished words depend on you to finish them, to provide the   30
words the advertisers so thoughtfully left out of the ad. Pall Mall cigarettes were once advertised as "A longer finer and milder smoke." The question is, longer, finer, and milder than what? The aspirin that claims it contains "Twice as much of the pain reliever doctors recommend most"

doesn't tell you what pain reliever it contains twice as much of. (By the way, it's aspirin. That's right; it just contains twice the amount of aspirin. And how much is twice the amount? Twice of what amount?) Panadol boasts that "nobody reduces fever faster," but, since Panadol is a parity product, this claim simply means that Panadol isn't any better than any other product in its parity class. "You can be sure if it's Westinghouse," you're told, but just exactly what it is you can be sure of is never mentioned. "Magnavox gives you more" doesn't tell you what you get more of. More value? More television? More than they gave you before? It sounds nice, but it means nothing, until you fill in the claim with your own words, the words the advertiser didn't use. Since each of us fills in the claim differently, the ad and the product can become all things to all people, and not promise a single thing.

Unfinished words abound in advertising because they appear to promise so much. More importantly, they can be joined with powerful visual images on television to appear to be making significant promises about a product's effectiveness without really making any promises. In a television ad, the aspirin product that claims fast relief can show a person with a headache taking the product and then, in what appears to be a matter of minutes, claiming complete relief. This visual image is far more powerful than any claim made in unfinished words. Indeed, the visual image completes the unfinished words for you, filling in with pictures what the words leave out. And you thought that ads didn't affect you. What brand of aspirin do you use?

Some years ago, Ford's advertisements proclaimed "Ford LTD— 700% quieter." Now, what do you think Ford was claiming with these unfinished words? What was the Ford LTD quieter than? A Cadillac? A Mercedes Benz? A BMW? Well, when the FTC asked Ford to substantiate this unfinished claim, Ford replied that it meant that the inside of the LTD was 700% quieter than the outside. How did you finish those unfinished words when you first read them? Did you even come close to Ford's meaning?

COMBINING WEASEL WORDS

A lot of ads don't fall neatly into one category or another because they use a variety of different devices and words. Different weasel words are often combined to make an ad claim. The claim, "Coffee-Mate gives coffee more body, more flavor," uses Unfinished Words ("more" than what?) and also uses words that have no specific meaning ("body" and "flavor"). Along with "taste" (remember the Winston ad and its claim to taste good), "body" and "flavor" mean nothing because their meaning is entirely subjective. To you, "body" in coffee might mean thick, black, almost bitter coffee, while I might take it to mean a light brown, delicate coffee. Now, if you think you understood that last sentence, read it again, because it said nothing of objective value; it was filled with weasel words of no specific meaning: "thick," "black," "bitter," "light brown," and "delicate." Each of those words has no specific, objective meaning, because each of us can interpret them differently.

Try this slogan: "Looks, smells, tastes like ground-roast coffee." So, are you now going to buy Taster's Choice instant coffee because of this ad? "Looks," "smells," and "tastes" are all words with no specific meaning and depend on your interpretation of them for any meaning. Then there's that great weasel word "like," which simply suggests a comparison but does not make the actual connection between the product and the quality. Besides, do you know what "ground-roast" coffee is? I don't, but it sure sounds good. So, out of seven words in this ad, four are definite weasel words, two are quite meaningless, and only one has clear meaning.

Remember the Anacin ad — "Twice as much of the pain reliever doctors recommend most"? There's a whole lot of weaseling going on in this ad. First, what's the pain reliever they're talking about in this ad? Aspirin, of course. In fact, any time you see or hear an ad using those words "pain reliever," you can automatically substitute the word "aspirin" for them. (Makers of acetaminophen and ibuprofen pain relievers are careful in their advertising to identify their products as nonaspirin products.) So, now we know that Anacin has aspirin in it. Moreover, we know that Anacin has twice as much aspirin in it, but we don't know twice as much as what. Does it have twice as much aspirin as an ordinary aspirin tablet? If so, what is a ordinary aspirin tablet, and how much aspirin does it contain? Twice as much as Excedrin or Bufferin? Twice as much as a chocolate chip cookie? Remember those Unfinished Words and how they lead you on without saying anything.

Finally, what about those doctors who are doing all that recommending? Who are they? How many of them are there? What kind of doctors are they? What are their qualifications? Who asked them about recommending pain relievers? What other pain relievers did they recommend? And there are a whole lot more questions about this "poll" of doctors to which I'd like to know the answers, but you get the point. Sometimes, when I call my doctor, she tells me to take two aspirin and call her office in the morning. Is that where Anacin got this ad?

FOCUSING ON CONTENT

1. What are weasel words? How, according to Lutz, did they get their name?
2. According to Lutz, why is *help* the biggest weasel word used by advertisers (3–8)? In what ways does it help them present their products without having to make promises about actual performance?

3. Why is *virtually* a particularly effective weasel word (10–12)? Why can advertisers get away with using words that literally mean the opposite of what they want to convey?

4. When advertisers use the word *like,* they often create a simile — "Ajax cleans *like* a white tornado." What, according to Lutz, is the power of similes in advertising (22–24)? Explain by citing several examples of your own.

5. What kinds of claims fit into Lutz's "unfinished words" category (29–32)? Why are they weasels? What makes them so difficult to detect?

6. Which of the various types of weasel words do you find most insidious? Why?

FOCUSING ON WRITING

1. What is Lutz's purpose in writing this essay? (Glossary: *Purpose*)

2. Lutz is careful to illustrate each of the various kinds of weasel words with examples of actual usage. (Glossary: *Examples*) What do these examples add to his essay? Which ones do you find most effective? Explain.

3. For what audience do you think Lutz wrote this essay? (Glossary: *Audience*) Do you consider yourself part of this audience? Do you find Lutz's tone and diction appropriate for his audience? (Glossary: *Tone* and *Diction*) Explain.

4. Lutz uses the strategy of division and classification to develop this essay. (Glossary: *Division and Classification*) Explain how he uses this strategy. Why do you suppose Lutz felt the need to create the "Combining Weasel Words" category? Did the headings in the essay help you follow his discussion? What would be lost had he not included them?

LANGUAGE IN ACTION

Carefully read the text in the advertisement on the opposite page. Jot down any words that Lutz would describe as weasels. How does recognizing such language affect your impression of the product being advertised? What would happen to the text of the ad if the weasels were eliminated?

WRITING SUGGESTIONS

1. (*Writing from Experience*) Choose something that you own and like—a mountain bike, a CD or video collection, luggage, a comfortable sofa, a boombox, or anything else that you are glad you bought. Imagine that you need to sell it to raise some money for a special weekend, and to do so you need to advertise on radio. Write copy for a 30-second advertising spot in which you try to sell your item. Include a slogan or make up a product name and use it in the ad. Then write a short essay about your ad in which you discuss the features of your item you chose to highlight, the language you used to make it sound as appealing as possible, and how your slogan or name makes the advertisement more memorable.

2. (*Writing from Reading*) Pay attention to the ads for companies that offer rival products or services (for example, Apple and IBM, Coca-Cola and Pepsi-Cola, Burger King and McDonald's, Charles Schwab and Smith Barney, and AT&T and MCI). Focusing on a single pair of ads, analyze the different appeals that companies make when comparing their products or services to those of the competition. To what audience does each ad appeal? How many weasel words can you detect? How does each ad use Intensify/Downplay (pp. 579–80) techniques to its product's advantage? Based on your analysis, write an essay about the advertising strategies companies use when in head-to-head competition with the products of other companies.

3. (*Writing from Research*) Look at several issues of one popular women's or men's magazine (such as *Cosmoplitan, Vogue, Elle, Glamour, Sports Illustrated, GQ, Playboy, Car and Driver, Field and Stream*), and analyze the advertisements they contain. What types of products or services are advertised? Which ads caught your eye? Why? Are the ads made up primarily of pictures, or do some have a lot of text? Do you detect any relationship beween the ads and the editorial content of the magazine? Write an essay in which you present the findings of your analysis.

What's Natural about Our Natural Products?

SARAH FEDERMAN

A freelance writer living in San Francisco, Sarah Federman was born in New York City in 1976. She graduated from the University of Pennsylvania in 1998, where she majored in Intellectual History. A strong interest in alternative medicine led her to her current work at the Institute for Health and Healing at California Pacific Medical Center.

Federman wrote the following essay expressly for Language Awareness. *She first became curious about the word* natural *as an undergraduate when she defended its use as a meaningful word on food labels in a debate with one of her professors. Since that time, however, Federman has had a change of heart. As she reports in her essay, the meaning of* natural *is elusive and extremely difficult to pin down.*

WRITING TO DISCOVER: *Jot down your thoughts about "natural" products. Do you think they are better for you than regular products? What natural products do you use? What do you think you're buying when you purchase a product with the word* natural *on its label? Are you willing to pay more for a natural product?*

Whether you're picking up Nature's Energy Supplements, Natrol, Nature's Way, Naturade, Nature's Gate, or Nature's Herbs in the vitamin aisle, attending a lecture on "Natural Sleep Aids," or diving into a bowl of Quaker 100% Natural Granola, you cannot escape the hype. Variations of the words "nature" and "natural" are used for product naming: to distinguish alternative medicine practitioners from their western counterparts and as slogans or names for everything from toothpaste to blue jeans. In a recent issue of *Delicious* magazine, for example, these words were used 85 times in the first 40 pages, with advertisements using them 8 times! Now pet owners can even skim through a copy of *Natural Dog* or *Natural Cat* while waiting at the vet.

Nowhere is the buzzword "natural" more prevalent than at the local grocery store where Fantastic Soups, Enrico's Pizza Sauce, Health Valley Cereals, and Celestial Seasonings tea, among others, brag unabashedly about the "naturalness" of their products. I often find myself seduced by the lure of the "natural" label on goods and services. I throw Tom's Natural Toothpaste, Pop-Secret Natural Flavored Popcorn, and Grape-Nuts Natural Wheat and Barley Cereal into my shopping cart with the utmost confidence that these natural varieties prove far superior to their "unnatural" or "less natural" counterparts. Recently, I took a closer look at the labels of my revered products only to discover the widespread abuse of the word "natural." The word "natural" has become more a marketing ploy than a way to communicate meaningful information about a product.

But this is not news. More than a decade ago the Consumers Union first sounded the alarm about "natural." The report alerted consumers to the fact that their beloved Quaker 100% Natural Cereal contained 24 percent sugar, not to mention the nine grams of fat which, according to the March 1999 *Nutrition Action Health Newsletter,* is the same as a small McDonald's hamburger. But despite the best efforts of the Union, nothing has changed. In fact, things have gotten worse, *especially* in the cereal aisle where 22 varieties, including Froot Loops, proclaim their commitment to "natural" ingredients. Berry Berry Kix, a brightly colored kids' cereal, promises "natural Fruit Flavors." Sure there is some grape juice, right after the sugar, partially hydrogenated oils, and corn syrup, and some strawberry juice, right after the dicalcium and trisodium phosphates. That's it for the fruits, the rest is corn meal and starch.

The Consumer Union's report also pointed out products using "natural" as an "indeterminate modifier," rather than as an adjective to convey some meaningful information about the product. In other words, placing the word "natural" in a slogan or product description without having it refer to anything in particular. For example, most major U.S. supermarkets sell Kraft's Natural Shredded Non-Fat Cheese, Natural Reduced Fat Swiss, and Natural Cheese Cubes. But don't dare to ask the question, What does that mean? Kraft has done nothing special with the cheese itself; "natural" in this case presumably relates to the shredding, reducing, and cubing process. What is natural cubing?

To me, a "natural" product or service suggests any or all of the follow-   5
ing: a healthy alternative, an environmentally friendly product, vegetarian, and or produced without synthetic chemicals. Friends and family have also taken natural to mean wholesome, pure, low-fat, healthy, organic, and, simply, better. The meanings given in one popular dictionary, however, prove less specific: 1) determined by nature, 2) of or relating to nature, 3) having normal or usual character, 4) grown without human care, 5) not artificial, 6) present in or produced by nature. Interestingly, these definitions make no value judgments. There is nothing in the dictionary meaning to suggest, for instance that a natural banana (one grown in the wild) is healthier than one raised by banana farmers. This positive spin we add ourselves.

Unlike using low-fat, organic, and vegetarian, food manufacturers can use "natural" any way they choose. The Nutritional Labeling and Education Act of 1990 (ULEA) restricted the use of the following terms on food labels: low fat, low sodium, low cholesterol, low calorie, lean, extra lean, reduced, good source, less, fewer, light, and more. A calorie-free product, for example, must have fewer than 5 calories per serving, while a cholesterol-free product must have 2 milligrams or less of cholesterol per serving. *Mother Earth News* reports that products labeled "organic" must align themselves with one of the 40 sets of organic standards, most often the California Organic Foods Act of 1990. This leaves "natural" as one of the few unregulated words.

Health-food companies and mainstream producers use the word to create an aura around the product. Actually, they use the word and "we" create the aura, allowing them to get away with higher prices or simply to take up more shelf space at the supermarket. For example, every month thousands of bags of Lays "Naturally Baked" Potato Chips travel through desert and farmland to enable us to "Ohh, ahh" and purchase these natural wonders. When first seeing this name, I had visions of organic farms and rugged, healthy farmers cultivating a much-loved product. Unfortunately, a closer look at the label served to shatter rather than support my countryside fantasy. While the ingredients reveal less fat per serving than the standard chip (1.5 grams versus 9 grams), I found nothing that explained the meaning of "naturally baked." Do you think this means they leave the chips out in the sun to crispen up? Probably not, so why does this natural process cost more per ounce (5.5 ounces for $1.99 versus 7.5 ounces) when it uses less fat?

Motts and Delmonte use "natural" to promote a new line without knocking their standard product. Motts applesauce has three products on the shelf of my local San Francisco market—"Apple Sauce," "Natural Apple Sauce," and "Chunky Apple Sauce." A comparison of the labels reveals that the "natural" version has no corn syrup added. Now, if they just wrote "no corn syrup added" on the label, we consumers would immediately become aware that there is, indeed, sweetener added to their standard version. Delmonte Fruit Cocktail has a two-product line-up with "Fruit Naturals" right next to "Fruit Cocktail." The natural variety costs 6 cents more and actually has *fewer* ingredients, presumably requiring less manufacturing. The natural version has no sugar and preservatives; the standard version has added corn syrup and sugar.

Fantastic, maker of dried soups and instant mixes, uses "natural" to connote something about the food and the type of person who may buy it. Under the heading Instant Black Beans, Fantastic writes "All Natural. Vegetarian." A vegetarian product, we know, means without meat. But what does "all natural" mean? Adding this phrase right before Vegetarian suggested to me that this product should appeal to vegetarians and self-proclaimed naturals. Mildly health-conscious people surely would prefer to ally themselves with natural rather than unnatural foods. Whether or not this product serves as a healthy alternative to other brands is irrelevant because the point is that Fantastic could sell you artery-clogging lard and still use the word.

Next to vitamins, bottled beverages probably use the word more than any other product. Every Snapple bottle promises an "all natural" treat, although the most natural iced tea is quite simply brewed tea with ice. In Snapple's case, you end up paying more for tasty sugar water, but with Hansen's Natural Soda you are outright deceived. Hansen's soda has exactly the same ingredients as Sprite and 7-Up minus the sodium citrate. Blue Sky Natural Soda has fructose sweetener, caramel color, and something called tartaric acid. Doesn't Blue Sky Natural Soda sound refreshing? Too bad your intestines can't distinguish it from Coca-Cola.

At least we have natural bottled water as an alternative. Or do we? The Natural Resources Defense Council, a national environmental group, found dangerous amounts of arsenic in Crystal Geyser's "Natural" Spring water. A four-year study revealed that one-third of the 103 bottled waters tested contained contaminants beyond safe federal limits. Odwalla "Natural" Spring Water, another popular beverage company, especially among health-food lovers, had high bacteria counts in a number of bottles. Hey, bacteria are natural so what's the problem? The problem is that natural or not, some bacteria make us sick. So it seems you cannot win with beverages. "Natural" serves as a meaningless label, a deceptive marketing tool, or means "contains natural critters and natural toxins that may make you sick." Best to just purchase a "Pur" (pronounced "pure") water filter; just don't ask what they mean by pure.

Some products come closer to meeting my expectations. The Hain Food Group, a "natural-food producer" whose projected 1999 annual sales are $300 million, manufactures soup called "Healthy Naturals." Although the split peas are not certified organic, Hain uses no preservatives or MSG. The ingredients are listed as water, split green peas, carrots, celery, onion powder, and spices. This product lives up to my notion of natural. But even Hain veers from their presumed commitment to health food. The 14 product "Hain Kidz" line, introduced early in 1999, includes marshmallow crisp cereal and snack bars, gummybear-like candy, and animal cookies. It appears that as major brands (Krafts, Motts, Quaker) increasingly tout their new-found "naturalness," health-food companies such as Hain have started going toward more "unnatural" products.

So as the line between specialty health-food company and standard food producer becomes more elusive, I begin to wonder why the extra cost? Why do plain peas and carrots cost *more* than highly refined and processed soups? And how did we get to a point where we need a special label to tell us that the product is what it says it is? Before I infuse one more dollar into this industry, I will assuredly read the list of ingredients more carefully and do some research at <http://www.naturalinvestor.com>.

FOCUSING ON CONTENT

1. According to Federman, what is the literal meaning of the word *natural* (5). What connotations do consumers bring to the word? (Glossary: *Denotation and Connotation*)

2. What restrictions does the Nutrition Labeling and Education Act of 1990 place on what manufacturers can say on food labels (6)? How is the word *organic* regulated? What restrictions, if any, are imposed on the use of the term *natural*?

3. What does Federman point to as the two main reasons that companies use the word *natural*? What does she mean when she says companies "use the word and 'we' create the aura" (7)?

4. Why do you think Federman talks about Kraft's Natural Shredded Non-Fat Cheese and Lays "Naturally Baked" Potato Chips? Name some other products whose labels use the words *natural* or *naturally* in an unclear or ambiguous manner.

5. Why do you suppose manufacturers charge more for their "natural" products when, in fact, these products may cost less to produce?

FOCUSING ON WRITING

1. What is Federman's thesis? (Glossary: *Thesis*) Where is it stated?

2. Federman carefully illustrates each of her points with a variety of food products from her local San Francisco grocery store. (Glossary: *Examples*) How do these examples support her thesis? Which examples do you find most interesting and effective? Why?

3. What do you think Federman would like her readers to do as a result of reading her essay? What, in the essay itself, leads you to this conclusion? (Glossary: *Purpose*)

LANGUAGE IN ACTION

Carefully analyze the label on page 602 from a can of Swanson Natural Goodness Chicken Broth. How do you think the manufacturer is using the word *natural?* What other words or phrases on the label suggest that this Swanson product is healthy, wholesome, and good for you?

WRITING SUGGESTIONS

1. (*Writing from Experience*) What, for you, are the connotations of the words *natural* and *fresh?* Do you believe that these words are inherently deceptive? Write an essay in which you argue for or against the regulation of these words in advertising. Before starting to write, you may find it helpful to review your Writing to Discover entry for this selection.

2. (*Writing from Reading*) Federman claims that "*natural* has become more of a marketing ploy than a way to communicate meaningful information about a product" (2). Do you agree? Spend some time at your local supermarket comparing price and ingredients between several natural products and their regular counterparts. Do price differences correlate with ingredient differences? What other factors might affect the prices of natural vs. regular products? In an essay, present your conclusions.

3. (*Writing from Research*) Using the library and the Internet, research the Nutrition Labeling and Education Act of 1990 and food labeling in general. In an essay, address some of the following questions: Why are people so concerned about the language used on our food labels? What issues did the NLEA solve? What food-labeling issues still need to be addressed? What solutions have been proposed for food-labeling problems?

LANGUAGE IN USE:
A Portfolio of Advertisements

Advertising is big business and a very real part of our daily lives. We hear a steady stream of ads on the radio, see them on television, read them in newspapers and magazines, and even wear them on our clothing. Today American businesses spend an estimated $140 billion a year on print ads and television commercials. Appealing to our fantasies of wealth, good looks, power, social acceptance, and happiness, advertising tries to persuade us to purchase particular products or services. Though every business hopes that its ads will be memorable and work effectively, we know that not all of them are successful. What makes one advertisement more effective than another? To answer such a question, we need to become more sensitive to advertising language and the ways advertisers combine images and words.

The following print advertisements present a variety of products and services, each appealing to a particular audience. With specific customers in mind, advertising copywriters carefully weigh the language of each ad and choose images that best compliment the product and the text. As you analyze each of the following ads, identify the audience that you believe the advertiser has in mind and note the language appeals that are made to this audience. What similarities and differences do you find among the advertisements?

WRITING TO DISCOVER: *Jot down your thoughts about print ads and commercials on television. Do you pay attention to ads when you see or hear them? What kinds of ads seem to catch your attention? Which ad campaigns of recent years do you remember? What do you think makes them memorable?*

Zip! Get your tax refund in half the time

Expecting a refund on your federal tax this year? Use IRS *e-file* and get it back in half the usual time. Even faster if you specify Direct Deposit to your bank account!

Click! IRS *e-file* is fast, simple and secure. It's so accurate, there's much less chance you'll get one of those letters from the IRS.

Many professional tax preparers can e-file for you. Or if you do your return on your PC or Mac, take the next step and *file* electronically too.

Even if you owe more tax, you can still e-file your return early and wait until April 15th to pay.

Have any questions? See your tax professional or visit our Web site at **www.irs.ustreas.gov**

IRS *e-file*. It's the fastest way to a tax refund.

CLICK. ZIP.
FAST ROUND TRIP.

The Internal Revenue Service   Working to put service first

Stuart Westland
213 Palisades Drive
Santa Barbara, CA 90432

RE: WESTLAND DIVORCE SETTLEMENT

Stuart:

The following settlement with your ex-wife, Helen, has been reached:

You get: the Palm Springs golf villa; the '89 Bentley; the '57 Mercedes Gull Wing; proceeds from the sale of the Scottsdale, Arizona residence; 2 Mouet paintings; the 80-foot yacht; 3 Afghan Hounds; and the Louis XVI Bowl.

She gets: the Casablanca Cathay ceiling fan from the Scottsdale, Arizona dining room.

Our deepest sympathies,

Albert Drueding

Albert Drueding, ESQ

GELFMAN, DRUEDING, AND O'SHEA / ATTORNEYS-AT-LAW

To learn more about all 256 styles of the world's finest ceiling fan, call 888-227-2178 for your nearest Casablanca dealer or to receive a brochure. Or visit us at www.casablancafanco.com.

Natural Balance

*It's the great awakening.
Shredded Spoonfuls are
nutritious, low in fat,
and completely natural.
It's the most delicious way
to start the day in balance.
No wonder Barbara's
makes the best-selling
natural cereals. So if you're
looking for a really
good cereal, Barbara's is
the natural choice.*

WRITING SUGGESTIONS: MAKING CONNECTIONS

1. Using Hugh Rank's Intensify/Downplay schema (pp. 579–80), analyze one or more of the advertisements in the preceding portfolio (or an ad of your choice, if your instructor wishes). What is being sold in the ad? What audience do you think the ad is aimed at? Is the ad's appeal mainly logical or emotional? What is the relationship between the text of the ad and any visuals? Write up your analysis in an essay.

2. Harvard psychologist Henry A. Miller and advertising and mass-media professor Jib Fowles have developed an inventory of the fifteen human needs that they believe are most susceptible to advertising entreaties. These needs are:

    1. the need for sex
    2. the need for affiliation
    3. the need to nurture
    4. the need for guidance
    5. the need to aggress
    6. the need to achieve
    7. the need to dominate
    8. the need for prominence
    9. the need for attention
    10. the need for autonomy
    11. the need to escape
    12. the need to feel safe
    13. the need for aesthetic sensations
    14. the need to satisfy curiosity
    15. physiological needs: food, drink, sleep, and so forth

    Using Miller and Fowles's list, analyze the advertisements that appear in this portfolio. Identify the needs that each advertiser is appealing to. In an essay, describe your findings and reflect on what these advertisements tell us about American society at the millennium.

3. Use Lutz's discussion of weasel words (pp. 584–93) to help you analyze the advertisements in this portfolio. How many weasels can you identify? What types of weasels predominate? Based on your analysis of these ads — and others of your own choosing, if you wish — write an essay on the use of weasel words in contemporary advertising. Why do you think they are being used — to manipulate and deceive the public, to protect manufacturers, or for some other reasons?

4. Some people believe that advertising performs a useful service to consumers and that most consumers know enough not to be taken in by half-truths and exaggerations. Do you agree? Why or why not? If you agree, what benefits do you think people receive either directly or indirectly from advertising? Does advertising arm consumers with information that in turn leads to informed buying decisions? If you don't believe advertising is useful, do you think it is harmful? Using the advertisements in this portfolio as well as others that you have had experience with, write an essay in which you clearly support your position on this issue.

GLOSSARY OF
RHETORICAL AND
LINGUISTIC TERMS

Abstract   See *Concrete/Abstract*.

Accent   Characteristics of pronunciation that reflect regional or social identity.

Acronym   A word made from the initial letters (in some cases, the first few letters) of a phrase or organization; for example, NATO (North Atlantic Treaty Organization) and scuba (self-contained underwater breathing apparatus).

Allusion   A passing reference to a familiar person, place, or thing drawn from history, the Bible, mythology, or literature. An allusion is an economical way for a writer to capture the essence of an idea, atmosphere, emotion, or historical era, as in "The scandal was his Watergate," "He saw himself as a modern Job," or "Everyone there held those truths to be self-evident."

American Sign Language (ASL, Ameslan)   A system of communication used by deaf people in the United States, consisting of hand symbols that vary in the shape of the hands, the direction of their movement, and their position in relation to the body. It is different from finger spelling, in which words are signed in the order in which they are uttered, thus preserving English structure and syntax.

Analogy   A special form of comparison in which the writer explains something complex or unfamiliar by comparing it to something familiar: "A transmission line is simply a pipeline for electricity. In the case of a water pipeline, more water will flow through the pipe as water pressure increases. The same is true of a transmission line for electricity." When a subject is unobservable or abstract, or when readers may have trouble understanding it, analogy is particularly useful.

Argument   A strategy for developing an essay. To argue is to attempt to convince a reader to agree with a point of view, to make a given decision, or to pursue a particular course of action. Logical argument is based on reasonable explanations and appeals to the reader's intelligence. See also *Persuasion, Logical Fallacies, Deduction,* and *Induction*.

Attitude   A writer's opinion of a subject, which may be very positive, very negative, or somewhere between these two extremes. See also *Tone*.

Audience   The intended readership for a piece of writing. For example, the readers of a national weekly newsmagazine come from all walks of life and have diverse opinions, attitudes, and educational experiences. In contrast, the readership for an organic chemistry journal may be comprised of people with similar scientific interests and educational backgrounds. The essays in this book are intended for general readers, intelligent people who may lack specific information about the subjects being discussed.

Beginnings and Endings   A *beginning* is the sentence, group of sentences, or section that introduces an essay. Good beginnings usually identify the thesis or main idea, attempt to interest the reader, and establish a tone. Some effective ways to begin essays include (1) telling an anecdote that illustrates the thesis, (2) providing a controversial statement or opinion that engages the reader's interest, (3) presenting startling statistics or facts, (4) defining a term that is central to the discussion that follows, (5) asking thought-provoking questions, (6) providing a quotation that illustrates the thesis, (7) referring to a current event that helps to establish the thesis, or (8) showing the significance of the subject or stressing its importance to the reader.

An *ending* is the sentence or group of sentences that brings an essay to closure. Good endings are well planned; they are the natural outgrowths of the essays themselves and give readers a sense of finality or completion. Some of the techniques mentioned above for beginnings may be effective for endings as well.

Biased Language   Language that is used by a dominant group within a culture to maintain its supposed superior position and to disempower others. See also *Racist Language* and *Sexist Language*.

Bidialectalism   The use of two dialects of the same language.

Bilingual Education   Teaching in a child's primary language, which may or may not be the language of the dominant population.

Black English   A vernacular variety of English used by some black people; it may be divided into Standard Black English and Black English Vernacular (BEV). See also *Ebonics*.

Brainstorming   A discovery technique in which writers list everything they know about a topic, freely associating one idea with another. When writers brainstorm, they also make lists of questions about aspects of the topic for which they need information. See also *Clustering* and *Freewriting*.

Cause and Effect Analysis   A strategy for developing an essay. Cause and effect analysis answers the question *why*. It explains the reasons for an occurrence or the consequences of an action. Whenever a question asks *why*, answering it will require discovering a *cause* or series of causes for a particular *effect*; whenever a question asks *what if*, its answer will point out the effect or effects that can result from a particular cause.

Classification   See *Division and Classification*.

Cliché   An expression that has become ineffective through overuse, such as *quick as a flash, dry as dust, jump for joy*, and *slow as molasses*. Writers normally avoid such trite expressions and seek instead to express themselves in fresh and forceful language. See also *Figures of Speech*.

Clustering   A discovery technique in which a writer puts a topic or keyword in a circle at the center of a blank page and then generates main ideas about that topic, circling each idea and connecting it with a line to the topic in the center. Writers often repeat the process in order to add specific examples and details to each main idea. This technique allows writers to generate material and sort it into meaningful clusters at the same time. See also *Brainstorming* and *Freewriting*.

Coherence   A quality of good writing that results when all of the sentences, paragraphs, and longer divisions of an essay are naturally connected. Coherent writing is achieved through (1) a logical sequence of ideas (arranged in chronological order, spatial order, order of importance, or some other appropriate order), (2) the thoughtful repetition of keywords and ideas, (3) a pace suitable for your topic and your reader, and (4) the use of transitional words and expressions. Coherence should not be confused with unity. See also *Unity* and *Transitions*.

Colloquial Expressions   Informal expressions that are typical of a particular language. In English, phrases such as *come up with, be at loose ends,* or *get with the program* are colloquial expressions. Such expressions are acceptable in formal writing only if they are used for a specific purpose.

Comparison and Contrast   A strategy for developing an essay. In comparison and contrast, the writer points out the similarities and differences between two or more subjects in the same class or category. The function of any comparison and contrast is to clarify—to reach some conclusion about the items being compared and contrasted. An effective comparison and contrast does not dwell on obvious similarities or differences; instead, it tells readers something significant that they may not already know.

Conclusions   See *Beginnings and Endings*.

Concrete/Abstract   A *concrete word* names a specific object, person, place, or action that can be directly perceived by the senses: *car, bread, building, book, John F. Kennedy, Chicago,* or *hiking.* An *abstract word,* in contrast, refers to general qualities, conditions, ideas, actions, or relationships that cannot be directly perceived by the senses: *bravery, dedication, excellence, anxiety, friendship, thinking* or *hatred.*

Although writers must use both concrete and abstract language, good writers avoid using too many abstract words. Instead, they rely on concrete words to define and illustrate abstractions. Because concrete words appeal to the senses, they are easily comprehended by a reader.

Connotation/Denotation   Both terms refer to the meanings of words. *Denotation* is the dictionary meaning of a word, its literal meaning. *Connotation,* on the other hand, is a word's implied or suggested meaning. For example, the denotation of *lamb* is a "a young sheep." The connotations of lamb are numerous: *gentle, docile, weak, peaceful, blessed, sacrificial, blood, spring, frisky, pure, innocent,* and so on. Good writers are sensitive to both the denotations and the connotations of words and use these meanings to advantage in their writing.

Deduction   The process of reasoning that moves from stated premises to a conclusion that follows necessarily. This form of reasoning moves from the general to the specific. See also *Syllogism*.

Definition   A strategy for developing an essay. A definition, which states the meaning of a word, may be either brief or extended; it may be part of an essay or an entire essay itself.

Denotation   See *Connotation/Denotation*.

Description   A strategy for developing an essay. Description tells how a person, place, or thing is perceived by the five senses. Objective description reports these sensory qualities factually, whereas subjective description gives the writer's interpretation of them.

Descriptivism A school of linguistic analysis that seeks to describe linguistic facts as they are. See also *Prescriptivism*.

Dialect A variety of language, usually regional or social, that is set off from other varieties of the same language by differences in pronunciation, vocabulary, and grammar.

Diction A writer's choice and use of words. Good diction is precise and appropriate—the words mean exactly what the writer intends, and the words are well suited to the writer's subject, intended audience, and purpose. The word-conscious writer knows, for example, that there are differences among *aged, old,* and *elderly; blue, navy,* and *azure;* and *disturbed, angry,* and *irritated.* Furthermore, this writer knows when to use each word. See also *Connotation/Denotation*.

Direct Quotation A writer's use of the exact words of a source. Direct quotations, which are put in quotation marks, are normally reserved for important ideas stated memorably, for especially clear explanations by authorities, and for proponents' arguments conveyed in their own words. See also *Paraphrase, Summary,* and *Plagiarism*.

Division and Classification A strategy for developing an essay. *Division* involves breaking down a single large unit into smaller subunits, or separating a group of items into discrete categories. *Classification,* on the other hand, involves arranging or sorting people, places, or things into categories according to their differing characteristics, thus making them more manageable for the writer and more understandable for the reader. Division, then, takes apart, while classification groups together. Although the two processes can operate separately, most often they work hand in hand.

Doublespeak According to doublespeak expert William Lutz, "Doublespeak is a blanket term for language which pretends to communicate but doesn't, language which makes the bad seem good, the negative appear positive, the unpleasant attractive, or at least tolerable. It is language which avoids, shifts, or denies responsibility."

Ebonics A term coined in 1973 for African American Vernacular English (AAVE). Public debate centers on whether it is a dialect of English or a separate language with its own grammatical rules and rhythms. See also *Black English*.

Endings See *Beginnings and Endings*.

English-Only Movement The ongoing attempts, which began in the Senate in 1986, to declare English the official language of the United States. Although these attempts have failed thus far at the federal level, a number of states have passed various forms of English-only legislation.

Essay A relatively short piece of nonfiction in which the writer attempts to make one or more closely related points. A good essay is purposeful, informative, and well organized.

Ethnocentricity The belief that one's culture (including language) is at the center of things and that other cultures (and languages) are inferior.

Euphemism A pleasing, vague, or indirect word or phrase that is substituted for one that is considered harsh or offensive. For example, *pacify* is a euphemism for *bomb, pavement deficiency* for *pothole, downsize* or *release from employment* for *fire*.

Evidence   The data on which a judgment or argument is based or by which proof or probability is established. Evidence usually takes the form of statistics, facts, names, examples or illustrations, and opinions of authorities.

Examples   Ways of illustrating, developing, or clarifying an idea. Examples enable writers to show and not simply to tell readers what they mean. The terms *example* and *illustration* are sometimes used interchangeably. An example may be anything from a statistic to a story; it may be stated in a few words or go on for several pages. An example should always be *relevant* to the idea or generalization it is meant to illustrate. An example should also be *representative*. In other words, it should be typical of what the writer is trying to show.

Exemplification   A strategy for developing an essay. In exemplification, the writer uses examples—facts, opinions, anecdotes, or statistics—to make ideas more vivid and understandable. Exemplification is used in all types of essays. See also *Examples.*

Fallacy   See *Logical Fallacies.*

Figures of Speech   Brief, imaginative comparisons that highlight the similarities between things that are basically dissimilar. They make writing vivid and interesting and therefore more memorable. Following are the most common figures of speech:

Simile: An implicit comparison introduced by *like* or *as.* "The fighter's hands were like stone."

Metaphor: An implied comparison that uses one thing as the equivalent of another. "All the world's a stage."

Onomatopoeia: The use of words whose sound suggests the meaning, as in *buzz, hiss,* and *meow.*

Personification: A special kind of simile or metaphor in which human traits are assigned to an inanimate object. "The engine coughed and then stopped."

Freewriting   A discovery technique that involves writing for a brief uninterrupted period of time—ten or fifteen minutes—on anything that comes to mind. Writers use freewriting to discover new topics, new strategies, and other new ideas. See also *Brainstorming* and *Clustering.*

Gobbledygook   The use of technical or unfamiliar words that confuse rather than clarify an issue for an audience.

Grammar   The system of a language including its parts and the methods for combining them.

Idiom   A word or phrase that is used habitually with a particular meaning in a language. The meaning of an idiom is not always readily apparent to nonnative speakers of that language. For example, *catch cold, hold a job, make up your mind,* and *give them a hand* are all idioms in English.

Illustration   See *Examples.*

Indo-European Languages   A group of languages descended from a supposed common ancestor and now widely spoken in Europe, North and South America, Australia, New Zealand, and parts of India.

Induction   A process of reasoning whereby a conclusion about all members of a class is reached by examining only a few members of the class. This form of reasoning moves from a set of specific examples to a general statement or principle. As long as the evidence is accurate, pertinent, complete, and sufficient to represent the assertion, the conclusion of the inductive argument can be regarded as valid; if, however, readers can spot inaccuracies in the evidence or point to contrary evidence, they have good reason to doubt the assertion as it stands. Inductive reasoning is the most common of argumentative structures. See also *Deduction*.

Introductions   See *Beginnings and Endings*.

Irony   The use of words to suggest something different from their literal meaning. A writer can use irony to establish a special relationship with the reader and to add an extra dimension or twist to the meaning.

Jargon   See *Technical Language*.

Language   Words, their pronunciation, and the conventional and systematic methods for combining them as used and understood by a community.

Lexicography   The art of dictionary-making.

Linguistic Relativity Hypothesis   The belief that the structure of a language shapes the way speakers of that language view reality. Also known as the Sapir-Whorf Hypothesis after Edward Sapir and Benjamin Lee Whorf.

Logical Fallacies   Errors in reasoning that render an argument invalid. Some of the more common logical fallacies are listed here:

Oversimplification: The tendency to provide simple solutions to complex problems. "The reason we have inflation today is that OPEC has unreasonably raised the price of oil."

Non sequitur ("It does not follow"): An inference or conclusion that does not follow from established premises or evidence. "It was the best movie I saw this year, and it should get an Academy Award."

Post hoc, ergo propter hoc ("After this, therefore because of this"): Confusing chance or coincidence with causation. Because one event comes after another one, it does not necessarily mean that the first event caused the second. "I won't say I caught cold at the hockey game, but I certainly didn't have it before I went there."

Begging the question: Assuming in a premise that which needs to be proven. "If American autoworkers built a better product, foreign auto sales would not be so high."

False analogy: Making a misleading analogy between logically unconnected ideas. "He was a brilliant basketball player; therefore, there's no question in my mind that he will be a fine coach."

Either/or thinking: The tendency to see an issue as having only two sides. "Used car salesmen are either honest or crooked."

Logical Reasoning   See *Deduction* and *Induction*.

Metaphor   See *Figures of Speech*.

Narration   A strategy for developing an essay. To narrate is to tell a story, to tell what happened. Although narration is most often used in fiction, it is also important in nonfiction, either by itself or in conjunction with other strategies. A good narrative essay has four essential features. The first is *context:* The writer makes clear when the action happened, where it happened, and to whom. The second is *point of view:* The writer establishes and maintains a consistent relationship to the action, either as a participant or as a reporter simply looking on. The third is *selection of detail:* The writer carefully chooses what to include, focusing on those actions and details that are most important to the story while merely mentioning or actually eliminating others. The fourth is *organization:* The writer organizes the events of the narrative into an appropriate sequence, often a strict chronology with a clear beginning, middle, and end.

Objective/Subjective   *Objective writing* is factual and impersonal, whereas *subjective writing*, sometimes called impressionistic, relies heavily on personal interpretation.

Onomastics   The study of the meaning and origins of proper names of persons and places.

Onomatopoeia   See *Figures of Speech*.

Organization   In writing, the thoughtful arrangement and presentation of one's points or ideas. Narration is often organized chronologically, whereas other kinds of essays may be organized point by point or from most familiar to least familiar. Argument may be organized from least important to most important. There is no single correct pattern of organization for a given piece of writing, but good writers are careful to discover an order of presentation suitable for their subject, audience, and purpose.

Paradox   A seemingly contradictory statement that may nonetheless be true. For example, *we little know what we have until we lose it* is a paradoxical statement.

Paragraph   A series of closely related sentences and the single most important unit of thought in an essay. The sentences in a paragraph adequately develop its central idea, which is usually stated in a topic sentence. A well-written paragraph has several distinguishing characteristics: a clearly stated or implied topic sentence, adequate development, unity, coherence, and an appropriate organizational pattern.

Paraphrase   A restatement of the information a writer is borrowing. A paraphrase closely parallels the presentation of the ideas in the original, but it does not use the same words or sentence structure. See also *Direct Quotation, Summary,* and *Plagiarism*.

Personification   See *Figures of Speech*.

Persuasion   An attempt to convince readers to agree with a point of view, to make a given decision, or to pursue a particular course of action. See also *Argument, Induction,* and *Deduction*.

Phonetics   The study of speech sounds.

Phonology   The study of sounds systems in languages.

Plagiarism   The use of someone else's ideas in their original form or in an altered form without proper documentation. Writers avoid plagiarism by (1) putting direct quotations within quotation marks and properly citing them and (2) documenting any idea, explanation, or argument that is borrowed and presented in a summary or paraphrase, making it clear where the borrowed material begins and ends. See also *Direct Quotation, Paraphrase,* and *Summary*.

Point of View   The grammatical person of the speaker in an essay. For example, a first-person point of view uses the pronoun *I* and is commonly found in autobiography and the personal essay; a third-person point of view uses the pronouns *he, she,* or *it* and is commonly found in objective writing.

Prescriptivism   A grammar that seeks to explain linguistic facts as they should be. See also *Descriptivism*.

Process Analysis   A strategy for developing an essay. Process analysis answers the question *how* and explains how something works or gives step-by-step directions for doing something.

Propaganda   Ideas, facts, or rumors purposely spread to further one's cause or to damage the cause of an opponent.

Purpose   What a writer wants to accomplish in a particular piece—his or her reason for writing. The three general purposes of writing are *to express* thoughts and feelings and lessons learned from life experiences, *to inform* readers about something about the world around them, or *to persuade* readers to accept some belief or take some action.

Racist Language   A form of biased language that makes distinctions on the basis of race and deliberately or subconsciously suggests that one race is superior to all others.

Rhetorical Questions   Questions that are asked but require no answer from the reader. "When will nuclear proliferation end?" is such a question. Writers use rhetorical questions to introduce topics they plan to discuss or to emphasize important points.

Sapir-Whorf Hypothesis   See *Linguistic Relativity Hypothesis.*

Semantics   The study of meanings in a language.

Sexist Language   A form of biased language that makes distinctions on the basis of sex and shows preference for one sex over the other.

Signal Phrase   A phrase alerting the reader that borrowed information is to follow. A signal phrase usually consists of the author's name and a verb (for example, "Keesbury argues") and helps to integrate direct quotations, paraphrases, and summaries into the flow of a paper.

Simile   See *Figures of Speech.*

Slang   The unconventional, very informal language of particular subgroups in a culture. Slang words such as *zonk, split, rap, cop,* and *stoned* are acceptable in formal writing only if they are used for a specific purpose. A writer might use slang, for example, to re-create authentic dialogue in a story.

Specific/General   *General words* name groups or classes of objects, qualities, or actions. *Specific words,* on the other hand, name individual objects, qualities, or actions within a class or group. To some extent the terms *general* and *specific* are relative. For example, *dessert* is a class of things. *Pie,* however, is more specific than *dessert* but more general than *pecan pie* or *chocolate cream pie.* Good writing judiciously balances the general with the specific. Writing with too many general words is likely to be dull and lifeless because general words do not create vivid responses in the reader's mind. On the other hand, writing that relies exclusively on specific words may lack focus and direction, which more general statements provide.

Standard English   A variety of English that is used by the government and the media and that is taught in the schools. It is often best expressed in written form.

Style   The individual manner in which a writer expresses his or her ideas. Style is created by the author's particular selection of words, construction of sentences, and arrangement of ideas.

Subjective   See *Objective/Subjective.*

Summary   A condensed form of the essential idea of a passage, article, or entire chapter. A summary is always shorter than the original. See also *Paraphrase, Direct Quotation,* and *Plagiarism.*

Syllogism   An argument that utilizes deductive reasoning and consists of a major premise, a minor premise, and a conclusion. For example,

All trees that lose leaves are deciduous. (major premise)
Maple trees lose their leaves. (minor premise)
Therefore, maple trees are deciduous. (conclusion)
See also *Deduction*.

Symbol   A person, place, or thing that represents something beyond itself. For example, the eagle is a symbol of America, and the bear is a symbol of Russia.

Syntax   The way words are arranged to form phrases, clauses, and sentences. Syntax also refers to the grammatical relationships among the words themselves.

Taboo Language   Language that is avoided in a given society. Almost all societies have language taboos.

Technical Language   The special vocabulary of a trade or profession. Writers who use technical language do so with an awareness of their audiences. If the audience is a group of peers, technical language may be used freely. If the audience is a more general one, technical language should be used sparingly and carefully so as not to sacrifice clarity. Technical language that is used only to impress, hide the truth, or cover insecurities is termed *jargon* and is not condoned. See also *Diction*.

Thesis   A statement of the main idea of an essay, the point the essay is trying to make. A thesis may sometimes be implied rather than stated directly.

Tone   The manner in which a writer relates to an audience, the "tone of voice" used to address readers. Tone may be described as friendly, serious, distant, angry, cheerful, bitter, cynical, enthusiastic, morbid, resentful, warm, playful, and so forth. A particular tone results from a writer's diction, sentence structure, purpose, and attitude toward the subject. See also *Attitude*.

Topic Sentence   The sentence that states the central idea of a paragraph and thus limits and controls the subject of the paragraph. Although the topic sentence normally appears at the beginning of the paragraph, it may appear at any other point, particularly if the writer is trying to create a special effect. See also *Paragraph*.

Transitions   Words or phrases that link the sentences, paragraphs, and larger units of an essay in order to achieve coherence. Transitional devices include parallelism, pronoun references, conjunctions, and the repetition of key ideas, as well as the many transitional expressions such as *moreover, on the other hand, in addition, in contrast,* and *therefore*. See also *Coherence*.

Unity   A quality that is achieved in an essay when all the words, sentences, and paragraphs contribute to its thesis. The elements of a unified essay do not distract the reader. Instead, they all harmoniously support a single idea or purpose.

Usage   The way in which words and phrases are actually used in a language community. See also *Descriptivism* and *Prescriptivism*.

RHETORICAL CONTENTS

The essays in *Language Awareness* are arranged in Chapters 5–12 according to their subjects. The following alternate table of contents, which is certainly not exhaustive, classifies the essays according to the rhetorical strategies they exemplify.

EXAMPLE AND ILLUSTRATION

NARRATION

PROCESS ANALYSIS

INDEX OF AUTHORS AND TITLES